The Transition to Kindergarten

National Center for
Early Development & Learning

A Series from the National Center
for Early Development and Learning

Series Editor: Don Bailey, Ph.D.

This book is part of a series edited by Don Bailey, Ph.D., and developed in conjunction with the National Center for Early Development and Learning (NCEDL). Books in this series are designed to serve as resources for sharing new knowledge to enhance the cognitive, social, and emotional development of children from birth through 8 years of age. For information on other books in this series, please refer to the Brookes web site at www.brookespublishing.com.

The Transition to Kindergarten

edited by

Robert C. Pianta, Ph.D.
University of Virginia, Charlottesville

and

Martha J. Cox, Ph.D.
Frank Porter Graham Child Development Center,
University of North Carolina at Chapel Hill

National Center for
Early Development & Learning

·P A U L·H·
BROOKES
PUBLISHING C⁰

Baltimore • London • Toronto • Sydney

Paul H. Brookes Publishing Co.
Post Office Box 10624
Baltimore, Maryland 21285-0624

www.brookespublishing.com

Typeset by Barton Matheson Willse & Worthington, Baltimore, Maryland.
Manufactured in the United States of America by
Bang Printing, Brainerd, Minnesota.

Library of Congress Cataloging-in-Publication Data

The transition to kindergarten / edited by Robert C. Pianta and Martha
    J. Cox.
        p.   cm.
    "Derived from 'The Transition to Kindergarten: A Synthesis Conference' held
at the University of Virginia at Charlottesville on February 18–20,
1998. The conference was conducted under the auspices of the
National Center for Early Development and Learning (NCEDL), funded
by the Office of Educational Research Improvement, U.S. Dept. of
Education"—Pref.
    Includes bibliographical references and index.
    ISBN 1-55766-399-8 (pbk.)
    1. Kindergarten—United States Congresses.   2. Early childhood
education—United States Congresses.   I. Pianta, Robert C.
II. Cox, Martha J.   III. National Center for Early Development &
Learning (U.S.)
LB1205.T72   1999
372.21'8—dc21   99-28677
                                                                                       CIP

British Library Cataloguing-in-Publication data are available from the British Library.

Contents

About the Editors

Robert C. Pianta, Ph.D., Professor, Curry School of Education, University of Virginia, 405 Emmet Street, 147 Ruffner Hall, Charlottesville, Virginia 22903-2495

Dr. Pianta is Professor of Clinical and School Psychology at the University of Virginia's Curry School of Education. A former special education teacher, he is a developmental, school, and clinical child psychologist who enjoys integrating these multiple perspectives on children in his work. In addition to his work on relationships between teachers and children, Dr. Pianta studies parent–child relationships. He is interested in the role of a range of social contexts in the development of children and particularly the role that social contexts play in the production and reduction of risk for poor development outcomes. Dr. Pianta is a principal investigator on the National Institute of Child Health and Human Development (NICHD) Study of Early Child Care, a senior investigator with the National Center for Early Development and Learning, and an editor of the *Journal of School Psychology*. He teaches courses on intervention with children and the role of social and emotional processes in development. Dr. Pianta is also the father of three children, is a soccer coach, and is learning to play the piano.

Martha J. Cox, Ph.D., Research Professor, Department of Psychology, University of North Carolina at Chapel Hill, CB#8180, 105 Smith Level Road, Chapel Hill, North Carolina 27599-8180

Dr. Cox is Senior Investigator at the Frank Porter Graham Child Development Center and Research Professor of Psychology at the University of North Carolina at Chapel Hill. In her research over the past 15 years, she has focused on the development of competence in young children in family, day care, and early school contexts. Dr. Cox has published in journals her work in developmental psychology, education, clinical psychology, and family process. In addition to this volume, she has co-edited *Conflict and Cohesion in Families: Causes and Consequences* (Lawrence Erlbaum Associates, 1999). She is the past Co-Chair of the National Institute of Mental Health–sponsored Family Research Consortium, a consortium of family scientists that aims to promote intellectual exchange and collaborative research on family risk and resilience processes. She is one of the principal investigators of the National Institute of Child Health and Human Development (NICHD) 10-site collaborative study (Study of Early Child Care), which focuses on children's home, school, and child care environments and the development of adaptive competence. She co-directs a core of researchers on the transition to kindergarten for the National Center for Early Development and Learning and is a faculty member of the Center for Developmental Science at the University of North Carolina at Chapel Hill. She is an action editor for the developmental section of the *Journal of Social and Personal Relationships* and sits on the editorial board of *Developmental Psychology, Journal of Family Psychology,* and *Psychiatry.*

About the Contributors

Karl L. Alexander, Ph.D., John Dewey Professor of Sociology, Johns Hopkins University, 3400 North Charles Street, Baltimore, Maryland 21218

Dr. Alexander's main fields of interest are sociology of education, social stratification, and the sociology and social psychology of individuals over the life course. With Doris R. Entwisle, he is continuing to monitor the life progress of the Beginning School Study (BSS) cohort. Now age 22, the group's participants were just starting first grade when this project commenced. Its history and a list of publications are available on the BSS website: http://bssonline.jhu.edu/hopkids.

Barbara T. Bowman, M.A., President, Erikson Institute for Advanced Study in Child Development, 420 North Wabash Avenue, Suite 600, Chicago, Illinois 60611

Ms. Bowman is one of three faculty members who founded Erikson Institute for Advanced Study in Child Development in 1966. She has teaching experience at both preschool and primary levels and is an authority on early education, cultural diversity, and education of children at risk. At Erikson Institute, Ms. Bowman teaches courses in early childhood education and administration and supervises practice teachers. In addition to teaching, she has directed a wide range of projects, has served on numerous professional boards, and is a frequent speaker at early childhood conferences and at universities in the United States of America and abroad.

Sandra L. Christenson, Ph.D., Professor of Educational Psychology, University of Minnesota, 350 Elliott Hall, 75 East River Road, Minneapolis, Minnesota 55455

Dr. Christenson is Professor of Educational Psychology at the University of Minnesota and Director of the School Psychology Program. Her research is focused on 1) interventions that enhance student engagement with school and learning and 2) identification of contextual factors that facilitate student engagement and increase the probability for student success in school. She is particularly interested in populations that are most alienated from traditional schooling practices and/or at highest risk for nonschool completion. Her recent investigations are aimed at understanding how students make a personal investment in learning and developing ways to promote the role of families in educating students. Dr. Christenson is a principal investigator of a 5-year personnel preparation grant in the area of family–school partnerships and was the 1992 recipient of the Lightner Witmer Award from the American Psychological Association for scholarship and early career contributions to the field of school psychology.

Richard M. Clifford, Ph.D., Senior Investigator, Frank Porter Graham Child Development Center, Co-Director, National Center for Early Development and Learning, University of North Carolina at Chapel Hill, CB#8040, Chapel Hill, North Carolina 27599-8040

Dr. Clifford has been involved in training early childhood personnel for more than 25 years. He is one of the authors of a widely used series of measures for assessing the quality of early childhood learning environments. He also studies public policy issues in early child care and education. From 1996 to 1998, Dr. Clifford served as President of the National Association for the Education of Young Children.

Doris R. Entwisle, Ph.D., Professor, Department of Sociology, Johns Hopkins University, 3400 North Charles Street, Baltimore, Maryland 21218

Dr. Entwisle's major interest is in the sociology of human development. With Karl L. Alexander, she has collaborated since 1982 on the Beginning School Study in Baltimore, which has followed a cohort of African American and Caucasian youth from the fall of their first-grade year up to the present. This study focuses on a broad spectrum of developmental outcomes and on how family, school, neighborhood, and (lately) employment contexts shape life histories of study members.

James J. Gallagher, Ph.D., Kenan Professor of Education, University of North Carolina at Chapel Hill, 137 East Franklin Street, Chapel Hill, North Carolina 27514

Dr. Gallagher has been active in the field of exceptional children for four decades. He has been a professor, an associate commissioner in the United States Office of Education, and a director of the Frank Porter Graham Child Development Center. He has published numerous books, book chapters, and articles and has served in a variety of professional organizations and roles.

Elizabeth Graue, Ph.D., Associate Professor, Department of Curriculum and Instruction, School of Education, University of Wisconsin–Madison, 514-C Teacher Education Building, 225 Mills Street, Madison, Wisconsin 53706-1795

Dr. Graue, a former kindergarten teacher, studies kindergarten policies, practices, and beliefs, with particular attention to issues of readiness. She is the author of *Ready for What? Constructing Meanings of Readiness for Kindergarten* (State University of New York Press, 1998) and, with Daniel Walsh, *Studying Children in Context* (Sage Publications, 1993).

Susan P. Limber, Ph.D., M.L.S., Director, Center for Youth Participation and Human Rights, Institute on Family and Neighborhood Life, Public Service Associate Professor of Psychology, Adjunct Associate Professor of Family and Youth Development, Poole Agricultural Center, Clemson University, Clemson, South Carolina 29634

Dr. Limber is Director of the Center for Youth Participation and Human Rights within the Institute on Family and Neighborhood Life at Clemson University, where she is also Public Service Associate Professor of Psychology. Prior to coming to Clemson, she held positions as Director of School-Based Services and Assistant Director of the Institute for Families in Society at the University of South Carolina. She was the James Marshall Public Policy Fellow for the Society for the Psychological Study of Social Issues, where she worked on a variety of issues related to child and family policy at the American Psychological Association. Her research and writing have focused on legal and psychological issues related to youth violence, child protection, and children's rights. She was the 1997 recipient of the Saleem Shah Award from the American Psychology-Law Society for early career excellence in law and poverty.

John Wills Lloyd, Ph.D., Professor, Curry School of Education, University of Virginia, 405 Emmet Street, Charlottesville, Virginia 22903

After completing doctoral studies in special education at the University of Oregon in 1976, Dr. Lloyd taught at Northern Illinois University for 2 years. In 1978 he joined the faculty of the Curry School of Education at the University of Virginia where he has taught and conducted research on learning and behavior problems experienced by students. Dr. Lloyd's interests in early childhood development center around the contributions of classroom environments to children's acquisition of social and academic competence. He hopes some day to make up for having missed kindergarten in his own early childhood.

Samuel J. Meisels, Ed.D., Professor, University of Michigan, 610 E. University, Room 3210 SEB, Ann Arbor, Michigan 48109-1259

Dr. Meisels is a leading researcher in the area of early childhood assessment. He has developed several assessments that are used extensively in early childhood settings and elementary schools. His research interests span developmental screening, performance assessment, and policy issues regarding testing children at the outset of school.

Gary B. Melton, Ph.D., Director, Institute on Family and Neighborhood Life, Public Service Professor of Psychology, Adjunct Professor of Family and Youth Development, Poole Agricultural Center, Clemson University, Clemson, South Carolina 29634

The author of more than 250 publications, Dr. Melton has written extensively on issues in child and family policy. He was President of the American Psychology-Law Society and the American Psychological Association (APA) Division of Child, Youth, and Family Services. He has received distinguished contribution awards from the APA and two of its divisions, Psi Chi and the National Committee to Prevent Child Abuse. As President of Childwatch International (a global network of child research centers), he has lectured, consulted, and conducted research in 20 countries and territories abroad.

Craig T. Ramey, Ph.D., Director and University Professor of Psychology, Pediatrics, Maternal and Child Health, and Neurobiology, Civitan International Research Center, University of Alabama at Birmingham, 1719 6th Avenue South, Suite 137, Birmingham, Alabama 35294-0021

Dr. Ramey is University Professor of Psychology, Pediatrics, Maternal and Child Health, and Neurobiology and a founding director of the Civitan International Research Center at the University of Alabama at Birmingham. Dr. Ramey specializes in the study of factors affecting the development of intelligence, academic achievement, and social competence in young children. He is author of more than 220 publications, including 5 books, and is a frequent consultant to federal and state governments, private agencies, foundations, and the media. His latest book, written with his wife, Dr. Sharon L. Ramey, *Right From Birth: Building Your Child's Foundation for Life* (Goddard Press, 1999), presents the latest in brain research and its practical implications for parents of young children.

Sharon L. Ramey, Ph.D., Director and Professor of Psychiatry, Psychology, Maternal and Child Health, and Neurobiology, Civitan International Research Center, University of Alabama at Birmingham, 1719 6th Avenue South, Suite 137, Birmingham, Alabama 35294-0021

Dr. Ramey is a founding director of the Civitan International Research Center at the University of Alabama at Birmingham and Professor of Psychiatry, Psychology, Maternal and Child Health, and Neurobiology. She is a developmental psychologist whose professional interests include the study of intellectual and developmental disabilities, early experience and early intervention, the changing American family, and the transition to school. She is the author of more than 150 articles, including 3 books, and is the recipient of numerous citations and awards for her scientific and policy contributions. She and her husband, Dr. Craig T. Ramey, have just completed a congressionally mandated study of more than 11,000 children from kindergarten through third grade and authored *Going to School: How to Help Your Child Succeed: A Handbook for Parents of Children Ages 3–8* (Goddard Press, 1999).

Sara E. Rimm-Kaufman, Ph.D., Research Faculty, National Center for Early Development and Learning, University of Virginia, Post Office Box 9051, Charlottesville, Virginia 22906-9051

Dr. Rimm-Kaufman earned her doctoral degree in developmental psychology with an emphasis on temperament and personality development in early childhood. She currently conducts research on children's transition to school at the National Center for Early Development and Learning at the University of Virginia.

Laura B. Smolkin, Ed.D., Associate Professor, Curriculum, Instruction, and Special Education Department, Curry School of Education, University of Virginia, 405 Emmet Street, 230 Ruffner Hall, Charlottesville, Virginia 22903-2495

Dr. Smolkin is the Language Arts and Children's Literature Professor in the Elementary Education Program at the Curry School of Education. Beginning her teaching career in the early 1970s in Baltimore City's public school system, Dr. Smolkin quickly recognized that students' cultural backgrounds influenced both learning and her approaches to teaching. Since the mid-1980s, Dr. Smolkin has focused her research on preschool children and their family-guided encounters with various genres of texts. She continues her commitment to young children's learning in her present research on early literacy interventions for Pueblo Indian Head Start children.

Donna R. Steinberg, M.Ed., Graduate Student in Clinical Psychology, Curry School of Education, University of Virginia, Post Office Box 9051, Charlottesville, Virginia 22906-9051

Ms. Steinberg has been working with Robert C. Pianta for the past 4 years as a graduate student in clinical psychology at the Curry School of Education at the University of Virginia. Her research interests are in child development, with particular focus on child–parent relationships. She has clinical experience in a variety of settings, including schools, social services agencies, mental health clinics, and psychiatric hospitals. After a year-long internship at Dartmouth, Ms. Steinberg graduates in May 2000.

Terri L. Teague, M.A., Graduate Student/Psychology Intern, Department of Psychology, University of South Carolina, Columbia, South Carolina 29208

Ms. Teague is a doctoral candidate in school psychology at the University of South Carolina. She is currently on internship at the Georgetown University Child Development Center. Ms. Teague's interests are in early childhood, particularly early intervention for children with disabilities.

Mary K. Wilhelm-Chapin, Ms.Ed., Research Specialist, Curry School of Education, University of Virginia, Post Office Box 9051, Charlottesville, Virginia 22906-9051

Ms. Wilhelm-Chapin has 8 years of teaching experience in the elementary classroom. She holds a master's degree in elementary education and a master's degree in supervision and administration. Since 1996 she has been a research staff member for the National Institute of Child Health and Human Development Study of Early Child Care and the National Center for Early Development and Learning Kindergarten Transition Study in the Curry School of Education at the University of Virginia.

Mark Wolery, Ph.D., Investigator, Frank Porter Graham Child Development Center, University of North Carolina at Chapel Hill, CB#8180, Chapel Hill, North Carolina 27599-8180

Dr. Wolery has worked in early intervention and education for young children with disabilities for more than 25 years. He is currently an investigator at the

Frank Porter Graham Child Development Center and Director of Research for the Center's child care program. His research focuses on instructional procedures for young children with disabilities, transfer of stimulus control, individualization within inclusive classrooms, and continuity of caregivers for infants and toddlers in child care.

Nicholas Zill, Ph.D., Vice President and Director, Child and Family Study Area, Westat, 1650 Research Boulevard, Rockville, MD 20850

Dr. Zill is a psychologist and the Director of the Child and Family Study Area at Westat, a survey research firm in the Washington area. He is an expert on the use of surveys and statistics to monitor the education, health, and well-being of children and youth. He is heading a 5-year effort to develop program performance measures for the national Head Start program and is a senior technical adviser for the Early Childhood Longitudinal Study, which Westat is conducting for the U.S. Department of Education. He is a member of the Technical Planning Group on School Readiness for the National Education Goals Panel, and he developed a child health index that the Goals Panel reports annually for each state and the nation as a whole. He recently completed a commissioned paper for the Goals Panel on the feasibility of establishing achievement growth standards for the states.

Foreword

In 1996, a consortium of universities, including the University of North Carolina at Chapel Hill, the University of California at Los Angeles, the University of Virginia at Charlottesville, and the University of Arkansas at Little Rock, was funded to establish the National Center for Early Development and Learning (NCEDL). Funding for an early childhood research center was authorized through a newly reorganized Office of Educational Research and Improvement (OERI) within the U.S. Department of Education (USDE), under the auspices of the National Institute for Early Childhood Development and Education.

Establishment of the institute and the center represented a major shift in thinking by the USDE, which prior to that time had very little in the way of funded research in early childhood. Schooling, and thus research on schooling, began at kindergarten. It has become increasingly obvious, however, that America's public schools have an inherent interest in what happens to children before they enter school. The fact that Congress mandated an early childhood institute within OERI indicates that the traditional view of education as solely a K–12 enterprise is no longer viable. Schools must consider the preparedness of children to enter school. Likewise, they must also consider their own preparedness to receive, accept, and support the tremendous diversity of children and families at the point at which they begin formal schooling.

In developing the NCEDL proposal, we considered a variety of strategies by which the center could play a national leadership role. In examining the literature, we realized that knowledge often develops in a parallel fashion as researchers in separate locations, using a variety of methodologies, address related aspects of a common problem. At some point in the process of knowledge development, it becomes critical for these individuals to come together to discuss research questions, synthesize findings, and generate ideas about future directions. Such a "synthesis conference" can have a powerful effect on a field, defining the state of knowledge in a particular area, and pushing the field forward in new and sometimes unanticipated directions.

We chose the topic of kindergarten transition for one of the first synthesis conferences because of the critical importance of success during the first year of school. Kindergarten is a context in which children make important conclusions about schools as a place where they want to be and about themselves as learners vis-à-vis schools. If no other objectives are accomplished, it is essential that the transition to school occur in such a way that children and families have a positive view of the school and that children have a feeling of perceived competence as learners: "School is okay, and I think that I can make it here." Unfortunately, many children and families reach alternative conclusions about school and about their fit with the school environment during this very first year. Thus the purpose of this conference was to assess what we know about the transition to school and to generate recommendations for future research, policy, practice, and personnel preparation.

Robert C. Pianta and Martha J. Cox deserve a special note of thanks for their efforts in organizing the conference and in preparing this book. They have assembled

a nationally recognized set of scholars who have attempted to reflect our best thinking about these issues of national importance. Hopefully these chapters will serve
as a stimulus for us and for the field to engage in a variety of activities that will help
ensure not only that all children will start school ready to learn, but that they also
experience the beginning of a trajectory toward long-term success in school.

Don Bailey, Ph.D.
Director, Frank Porter Graham Child Development Center
University of North Carolina at Chapel Hill

Preface

It is not surprising that the first National Education Goal is to ensure that all children start school ready to learn by the year 2000. Children's experiences as they enter kindergarten and pass through the early years of school constitute a key life cycle transition both in and outside of school. During these early years children acquire the attitudes and skills that are powerful determinants for later adaptation. Available evidence suggests that by the end of the third grade, most children are on a trajectory of development that they will follow for the remainder of their school years. Although the early years of school appear to play an important role in children's lives, our knowledge of this period of schooling is limited, especially with respect to the ecology of this transition and factors related to transition outcomes.

This book focuses on this early period of schooling and is derived from "The Transition to Kindergarten: A Synthesis Conference" held at the University of Virginia at Charlottesville on February 18–20, 1998. The conference was conducted under the auspices of the National Center for Early Development and Learning (NCEDL), funded by the U.S. Department of Education, Office of Educational Research and Improvement. The overarching purpose of the NCEDL is to generate knowledge about the complex ways in which child, family, program, school, and community variables interact to influence the developing young child. Within this goal, the center focuses specifically on 1) identifying effective practices in the care and education of young children and the policies needed to support those practices, 2) determining the extent to which those practices are being used and why they are not being used, and 3) testing models for improving practices and outcomes for children and families.

The conference focused on integrating our knowledge about the transition to kindergarten. Conference presenters prepared chapters that described the state of knowledge in a given area related to transition, critical issues in the current state of knowledge, and an agenda for the future. Four synthesis groups, each formed from a diverse set of members, including parents, researchers, policy makers, teachers, and trainers, then discussed the presentations in terms of implications for policy, practice, training, and research. This book contains both chapters that formed the bases of the conference presentations as well as chapters that reflect the discussions and deliberations of the synthesis groups.

Our aim in this book is to provide a comprehensive treatment of an area of knowledge that has been neglected for too long and is in need of systematic treatment. It is hoped that the text will be helpful to researchers, policy makers, educators, and practitioners concerned with the education of young children. We want to help organize and frame the debate on critical issues regarding the early primary education of an increasingly diverse group of young children.

We have many people to thank for their contributions to these efforts and their vision of the need to advance knowledge and practice related to the transition to kindergarten. As the Director of the National Institute on Early Childhood Development and Education, Dr. Naomi Karp's support of these efforts has been critical to the creation of this book. Dr. James Griffin, Education Research Analyst for the National Institute on Early Childhood Development and Education, worked with us in planning and executing this conference. We appreciate his efforts and encouragement. Don Bailey, Director of the NCEDL, originated the idea of hosting synthesis conferences and was part of the early discussions that gave rise to the plans for that meeting. In addition, he has been supportive of our efforts on behalf of research on the transition to kindergarten. Marcia Kraft-Sayre, from the University of Virginia staff, was instrumental in organizing the conference, coordinating the multitude of preparations and tasks, and ensuring that the conference ran smoothly. Marcia did a superb job, and we are indebted to her for her efforts. Louise Cruden, also from the University of Virginia staff, provided much-needed assistance in terms of clerical support and operation of the meeting.

Robert C. Pianta, Ph.D.
Professor, Curry School of Education
University of Virginia

Martha J. Cox, Ph.D.
Research Professor
University of North Carolina at
Chapel Hill

The Transition to Kindergarten

National Center for
Early Development & Learning

THE SIGNIFICANCE OF
EARLY SCHOOL TRANSITIONS

Chapter 1

Introduction

An Ecological Approach to Kindergarten Transition

Robert C. Pianta
Sara E. Rimm-Kaufman
Martha J. Cox

Making the transition to formal schooling is of particular importance for children, families, and schools (Love, Logue, Trudeau, & Thayer, 1992). Almost every school in the United States has some program or set of practices related to helping ease this transition, although research indicates that these practices are by and large cursory and not well-suited to families' needs (Love et al., 1992; Pianta, Cox, Early, & Taylor, in press). The National Center for Early Development and Learning (NCEDL) has undertaken a program of research aimed at helping to understand the nature and significance of the transition to school and how to best work with families, schools, and communities to improve outcomes for children during this period. This chapter provides an overview of the conceptual underpinnings of the program, which are reflected in the following chapters and which can provide the impetus for advances in research, policy, teacher training, and practice.

As noted by Meisels, the education of young children, particularly before and while they make the transition to school, is a "matter of context" (1992, p. 1). Thus, it is not surprising that the first National Education Goal—"by the Year 2000 all children will start school ready to learn"—not only emphasizes child-related skills that promote school success but also notes the importance of family, school, and community factors (e.g., access to high-quality preschools) that support the development of children's competencies (National Education Goals Panel, 1995). The slow but consistent progress toward objectives that are agreed upon as indicators of this larger goal (National Education Goals Panel, 1997) is a testament to the complexity of being ready to learn. As practitioners, policy makers, trainers, and researchers approach this national goal, certain tools can help organize the complexity inherent in being sensitive to context (Pianta & Walsh, 1996). One such tool is a conceptual model that can provide a view of the problem in a way that facilitates common understandings and, ultimately, better practice for children.

CONTEXTUALIZING KINDERGARTEN TRANSITION

Consistent with the first National Education Goal, NCEDL has devoted considerable attention to understanding and testing ways to improve the transition to school for children, families, and even schools. An NCEDL conceptual model in which the transition to school is defined and understood in ecological terms has provided the foundation for this effort. The NCEDL ecological model borrows from Bronfenbrenner's work (see Bronfenbrenner & Morris, 1998), which described and mapped the various contexts and levels of context that influence children's development. It also borrows from the work of Ford and Lerner (1992) and Sameroff (1995), who described how general systems theory could be used to derive principles for the functioning of complex developmental systems.

In the NCEDL model, a child's transition to school is understood in terms of the influence of contexts (e.g., family, classroom, community) and the connections among these contexts (e.g., family–school relationships) at any given time and across time. Yet, for the most part, the transition to school has been approached in terms of children's skills and abilities as the key predictors of school success (see Chapter 3; Pianta & McCoy, 1997).

There are two problems with approaching school transition as a function of children's skills and abilities. First, using only children's skills and abilities as predictors of early school success (or failure) does not account for the majority of variability in individual differences in early school adjustment (Laparo & Pianta, 1998; Pianta & McCoy, 1997). Child factors, at best, account for less than 25% of the variance in kindergarten outcomes (Laparo & Pianta, 1998). Thus, understanding child outcomes in kindergarten requires attention to factors other than just the characteristics of children.

Second, the reality of this transition period involves not only how children adjust to kindergarten but also how families and schools interact and cooperate (see Chapter 6; Rimm-Kaufman & Pianta, 1998). In most cases, it is not just the child that makes a transition. That is, transition is a process in which child, family, school, and community interrelate across time.

Pianta and Walsh (1996), in their Contextual Systems Model, emphasized that the transition to kindergarten is fundamentally a matter of establishing a relationship between the home and the school in which the child's development is the key focus or goal. This relationship is influenced by the parents' economic, educational, and personal resources; the school's openness to and communication with families; and community values and culture (see Chapters 6 and 7). Pianta and Walsh (1996) raised the explicit hypothesis that the quality of this relationship is critical for both children and families for whom social or economic resources are strained or for whom there is a large discrepancy in resources or culture between school and home.

Understanding the transition to school in ecological terms is also emphasized in the National Education Goals Panel's focus on "ready schools." For example, the National Education Goals Panel (1998) outlined 10 keys to ready schools. Of the 10 factors outlined, at least 3 relate directly to an ecological perspective. These include the following:

- Ready schools smooth the transition between home and school.
- Ready schools strive for continuity between early care and education programs and elementary schools.
- Ready schools serve children in communities.

In the discussion of smoothing the transition between home and school, the National Education Goals Panel noted that all children can benefit from being supported through the transition to school, even though many children make this adjustment successfully.

> Some districts and schools reach out to local families well before the children reach age five. In written or personal communications, such districts and schools may suggest steps that parents can take . . . to ensure that their children get off to a strong, healthy, start. . . . Many schools have found that home visits by teachers or principals before children enter school can have a substantial impact on kindergartners' adjustment; . . . lively and reassuring orientation sessions for parents and children are also helpful (and) should allow plenty of time for question-and-answer sessions. . . . Parents need to know that they have a standing invitation to visit the school. (1998, pp. 6–7)

The language of the panel clearly reflects the kind of relationship focus that Pianta and Walsh (1996) discussed in that it emphasizes positive connections among home, preschool, and school that are based on personal contacts prior to school entry and coordination of curriculum and orientation activities. Nonetheless, the National Education Goals Panel also noted that "transition activities like these are the exception rather than the rule in our public schools" (1998, p. 7). Love et al. (1992) reported that approximately 20% of the United States' schools have a range of transition activities that meet the needs of both families and students for information and personal contact with the school. An NCEDL national survey of kindergarten teachers suggested that this rate may be lower yet and is significantly lower in African American communities and communities with few economic resources (Pianta et al., in press).

In their discussion of the transition to school, Ramey and Ramey (Chapter 8) list five indicators of a successful transition to kindergarten that also emphasize the importance of an ecological view. Following are some of these indicators:

- Parents and other key adults show positive attitudes toward the school and learning in general and act as partners in their children's learning.
- Teachers and other school personnel recognize and value children's individual and cultural differences and provide developmentally appropriate school experiences.
- Schools, families, and communities are linked in positive and mutually supportive relationships to enhance young children's well-being and education.

The model depicted in Figure 1.1 is a graphic illustration of an ecological perspective on transition. In this model, various contexts and their interrelationships across time are brought to our attention. This model gives rise to practices and policies that facilitate the transition into kindergarten for which there is remarkable concordance (National Education Goals Panel, 1998). For the most part, agreement centers on the following three principles for the actions taken by schools: 1) reach out (link with families and preschools); 2) reach backward in time (establish links before the first day of school); and 3) reach with appropriate intensity (make personal contacts and home visits) (Pianta, Cox, Early, & Taylor, in press). These principles generate a range of possible transition practices that can be implemented in various forms or combinations according to cultural and community needs and resources (Hartford Foundation for Public Giving, 1997).

In short, an ecological perspective generates a rich and varied set of principles for understanding and improving the transition to school for a range of children, families, and schools. Each chapter in this text uses this model to describe, in considerable detail, the state of knowledge with respect to particular aspects of the transition process and implications of this knowledge for the future. The chapters are organized around three core themes:

- Describing early school transitions and their significance
- Describing the ecology of transitions into and through kindergarten
- Influencing transition outcomes for children from diverse families and cultures

DESCRIBING EARLY SCHOOL TRANSITIONS AND THEIR SIGNIFICANCE

Questions such as the following raise issues of stratification in early schooling, readiness for school, and equity in early school environments: How is kindergarten different from preschool? Do the events that occur in children's lives during this period have significance for their later school success? How does the reader know if a child is succeeding in the transition process? Describing early school transitions involves attention to these issues, each of which is addressed by the next three chapters in Section I.

Stratification

In spite of attempts to equalize educational outcomes and processes for children of all ages, particularly children who are just beginning school, considerable evi-

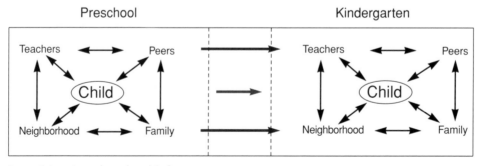

Figure 1.1.   An ecological model of transition.

dence exists that suggests that child outcomes during transition to school replicate the fault lines of culture and society in general (see Chapter 2). African American children, children from low-income families, and children from nondominant cultures are vastly overrepresented in the many forms of "failure" that are present in the first few years of school, including retention, special education, and academic and behavior problems.

It has been noted that children often experience a clash of cultures as they move from home to school. Teachers' expectations about children from minority or impoverished backgrounds can shape interactions between children and teachers in ways that have an impact on achievement. Moreover, educational resources are not evenly distributed across schools or neighborhoods.

In Chapter 2, Entwisle and Alexander present a summary of their work on the relationships between social structure and child outcomes in the early school years and onward. They describe the process of stratification of children's early school success in terms of both neighborhood-level factors that often determine the quality of elementary schools and in terms of the role that time in school plays for children, especially those from low-income or minority families. With respect to the time-in-school issue, Entwisle and Alexander posit that all children, regardless of achievement status at the time of school entry, make similar progress as a function of exposure to the school curriculum during the academic year. However, summer vacation differentially affects children from low-income or minority families and is thus implicated in stratification. Their conclusions have considerable implications for the organization of the school-year schedule and how communities plan for the location and catchment areas of elementary schools.

Readiness

No discussion of the transition to school would be complete without addressing the concept of readiness. Interest in the concept of readiness reflects a broader interest in understanding and describing the children who come to school and their educational needs. This task of characterizing the competencies of the population of children who enter school is fraught with pitfalls and challenges yet remains a critical need if national educational policy is to have an influence on young children. Also, in entering school, children enter a system of evaluation for the first time and are scrutinized in terms of their skills, abilities, and characteristics. Their skills and abilities are compared with performance standards and either meet or fall short of what is expected. Therefore, it is clear why readiness is so often used in discussions of children's skills and abilities in the early school years.

In Chapter 3, Meisels provides a critical discussion of the concept of readiness—how it is defined and assessed and the consequences of these decisions for children. This chapter is critical to an understanding of the transition to school because it carefully "unpacks" this term which is so often invoked at local, state, and national levels to characterize the transition process.

Equity

Addressing the first National Education Goal requires a comprehensive, national-level focus on kindergarten environments, staffing, and programs. The question, "To what do children transition?" directly affects discussions of kindergarten transition. It is critical to have an accurate picture of the environments provided to children in kindergarten in order to advance discussions of policy, practice, and teacher training. One course of action to provide such a picture involves using national survey data. In Chapter 4, Zill uses such data to describe parental satisfaction, the quality of the teaching staff, parental involvement, teacher beliefs and practices, and teachers' views of key outcomes for children as they transition to school. In the context of providing a national-level perspective on these issues, Zill also identifies key features of the school context that vary by income, ethnicity, and region. Thus, these national survey data shed light on issues of equity and access to educational resources in the early school years that in turn relate to the discussions of stratification and readiness in Chapters 2–3.

DESCRIBING THE ECOLOGY OF TRANSITIONS INTO AND THROUGH THE EARLY SCHOOL YEARS

Contexts that surround each child change as he or she makes the transition to kindergarten. The ecology of the kindergarten classroom is different from that of the preschool or home environment. Community and neighborhood, school, family–school interactions, and teacher and parent expectations all change as children move through this transition. Because these interrelated changes occur in such a short period of time, the transition to school for many families and children is itself a somewhat unique ecology. In addition, the transition process is so heavily influenced by community and cultural factors that it in turn is influenced by the ecology in which it occurs. Section II addresses the ecology of transitions into school.

Consider some of the changes that occur in the home–school relationship as children go to school. First, parents may exercise less freedom to choose their child's kindergarten compared with the way in which they may have selected their child's preschool. Furthermore, kindergarten may serve more diverse populations compared with more homogeneous populations often found in preschools. These changes affect the nature of interactions between parents and their children's schools. For example, parental contact with kindergarten teachers and administrators is more formalized and more likely to address learning and/or social problems compared with the kind of interaction that occurs between parents and preschool teachers (Rimm-Kaufman & Pianta, 1999). Parents, too, experience considerable change in the organization and nature of their day-to-day experiences (Pianta & Sayre, in press).

Three central aspects of the ecology of the transition to school are fundamental to any discussion on the subject. Consistent with the model depicted in Figure 1.1 and addressed in Section II, these are kindergarten classroom contexts and practices, relationships between families and schools, and the role that schools play in the context of changing communities and families.

Kindergarten Classroom Contexts and Practices

No area of preschool/early elementary education discourse is as controversial and divisive as that of classroom practices. Understanding the significance of classroom practices for the transition process requires describing the dimensions of classroom practice that often polarize discussion. A critical and integrative view of early school practices is necessary to address forward-looking issues such as standards and personnel preparation.

In Chapter 5, Graue provides a cogent analysis of kindergarten contexts in terms of the actual practices that are conducted with children. This chapter squarely addresses some of the issues that polarize discussions of early childhood education, such as the division between *developmentally appropriate practice* and *direct instruction* as they pertain to the quality of children's experiences in kindergarten. The chapter bridges the discussion of Section I, which focuses in part on policy debates and survey data, with the real-life experiences of children and teachers in schools.

Relationships Between Families and Schools

The most important aspect of the ecology of transition is the family. Evidence suggests that schools have little to no direct or personalized contact with families prior to the time children enter school (Pianta et al., in press). However, it is widely recognized that families play a critical, if not central, role in the success of young children in school. However, it is essential that our understanding of the role of families advance beyond simple notions of "parent involvement" to identify the key process-level roles that families play vis-à-vis the school.

In Chapter 6, Christenson adopts a developmental perspective on the role of home and school contexts in supporting children's learning. This analysis illuminates elements that cut across family and school boundaries to support student learning. Christenson then discusses the roles and responsibilities of families and schools in relation to these common elements. Such a discussion moves beyond simple notions of parent involvement to a larger view of how families and schools operate within a common developmental system to sustain children's progress, growth, and health. This analysis is unique among discussions of home–school relations and has enormous implications for the training of teachers, transition policies, and practices in schools.

Changing Schools to Reflect Changes in the Community

A community-level view of programming and intervention provides an even broader perspective on the ecology of kindergarten transitions. To be sensitive to community-level processes, the discussion of the transition to school must acknowledge the ways in which communities shape families and child development, the mechanisms by which social capital and resources are distributed within and across communities, and how natural supports can be mobilized at the community level to strengthen families.

In Chapter 7, Melton and colleagues draw from their experiences in community support and reform to address the role of communities in the transition to school. This chapter presents a view of schools that is fundamentally different from how most schools are currently organized. In this view, schools and community resources are so closely intertwined that boundaries are blurred and concepts such as transition become less salient. The chapter has implications for how schools, families, and communities work together on behalf of children. Providing culturally sensitive, comprehensive services cannot be accomplished without considering community-level processes.

INFLUENCING TRANSITION OUTCOMES FOR CHILDREN FROM DIVERSE FAMILIES AND CULTURES

The transition to school can be a particularly difficult (and extremely important) period for African American children, children with disabilities, or children from low-income families, when compared with children who do not share these characteristics. Often, the relatively poor outcomes of these children have led to them being characterized as at risk. Along with this characterization is a range of associated concerns about labeling and self-fulfilling expectations. Just as pernicious, the positive outcomes of children from such groups have been designated as a product or indicator of resilience. In both cases, risk and resilience are presented as if they were properties of a child.

Risk and resilience, however, must be thought of as a process involving interactions between the child and context (Resnick, 1994). Risk and resilience are not characteristics of a child, family, or school but are products of a process involving the interactions among them. Unfortunately, children in poverty, African American children, and children with disabilities are among those for whom these interactions most often fail to produce success. Understanding the mechanisms responsible for these outcomes and influencing them to the extent that they produce success is arguably the single largest task facing education in the United States at the start of the 21st century. Section III focuses on issues of diversity in relation to the transition to school.

Children at Risk Due to Poverty

Decades of experience in designing and evaluating early childhood interventions for children and families in poverty has given rise to a model for influencing kindergarten transition processes in these populations. No investigators have contributed more to this endeavor than Ramey and Ramey, the authors of Chapter 8. In this chapter, the Rameys present a model for understanding and influencing the transition to school for children in poverty. This model draws upon experience with the Abecedarian early intervention project and with influencing transition outcomes for children enrolled in Head Start. In particular, the model addresses the nature, timing, and intensity of interventions, among other issues.

Children with Disabilities

A great deal can be learned about the transition to school from the years of experience with special education legislation, policy, and practice. Transition issues for the significant population of children with disabilities, as well as for other risk and nonrisk populations, are quite similar. Also, transition practices have long been mandated by special education law; thus an analysis of the special education literature can provide a unique and informative window on discussions of transition for the general population. In Chapter 9, Wolery uses the past 10 years of experience with special education for preschool children to inform the debate on transition issues.

Evidence from this literature addresses transition issues such as curriculum, assessment, and parent–school collaboration. Most important, this discussion is based on actual data aggregated from systematic attempts to influence transition policies and practices. The chapter has substantial implications for personnel preparation, policy, and practice that affect a range of children.

Children from Low-Income Families and Diverse Cultures

Significant levels of early educational failure exist in children from minority cultures in the United States. This serious national dilemma has received much attention in a variety of contexts, and how classroom practices affect the outcomes of these children is of paramount importance. In Chapter 10, Bowman presents an analysis of kindergarten classroom practices with respect to children from diverse minority cultures and explains how these practices exacerbate or ameliorate the difficulties that these children encounter as they enter school.

Factors related to school success for children from cultural and ethnic minorities are particularly important as a focus for discussion on transition. Such discussions raise serious challenges to teacher training programs, funding and staffing policies, and discussions of curriculum in the early grades. The chapter continues themes raised in previous chapters regarding the need for a better trained work force, increased sensitivity to families, and differential distribution of resources.

IMPLICATIONS FOR RESEARCH, POLICY, PRACTICE, AND PERSONNEL PREPARATION

A central organizing theme for this book was the need to synthesize knowledge from diverse areas to derive implications for four fundamental activities related to early childhood education: research, policy making, practice, and the preparation of teachers and other personnel. Section IV presents summaries of discussions held by four synthesis groups, one for each of the activities noted previously. These groups, composed of parents, researchers, policy makers, program directors, and teachers, held discussions that were in turn compiled and integrated into the four chapters that comprise Section IV.

Finally, in Chapter 15, the editors identify four key trends that will affect research, policy, practice, and training in relation to the transition to school. These four trends—the use of an ecological/developmental model in conceptualizing educational processes, the increasing diversity of American children, the proliferation of public school prekindergarten programs, and the movement toward accountability—will each shape how the nation approaches public education for young children during the first decade of the 21st century. In this chapter, the effects that each of these trends have on approaches to kindergarten transition are discussed.

CONCLUSION

An ecological perspective on the transition to kindergarten provides researchers, policy makers, and educators with a powerful tool for analysis and synthesis of an issue that is of national significance. Although this perspective is more complex than a child-centered perspective that views the transition to kindergarten simply in terms of the abilities and skills that children bring with them on their first day of school, it has advantages for advancing theory and practice in an area that, by definition, must address the interaction of families, children, schools, and communities. The following chapters provide strong support for the ecological model and, more important, delineate the particular contributions of the model to a broad set of national issues related to the education of young children.

REFERENCES

Bronfenbrenner, U., & Morris, P.A. (1998). The ecology of developmental processes. In W. Damon & R.M. Lerner (Eds.), *Handbook of child psychology: Theoretical models of human development* (5th ed., Vol. 1, pp. 993–1029). New York: John Wiley & Sons.

Ford, D.H., & Lerner, R.M. (1992). *Developmental systems theory: An integrative approach.* Thousand Oaks, CA: Sage Publications.

Hartford Foundation for Public Giving. (1997). *Brighter futures initiative.* Hartford, CT: Author.

Laparo, K., & Pianta, R.C. (1998). *Predicting adjustment in the early school years from childrens' competencies: A meta-analysis.* Manuscript in preparation, University of Virginia, Charlottesville.

Love, J.M., Logue, M.E., Trudeau, J.V., & Thayer, K. (1992). *Transitions to kindergarten in American schools.* (Contract no. LC 88089001). Portsmouth, NH: U.S. Department of Education.

Meisels, S.J. (1992). Early intervention: A matter of context. *ZERO TO THREE Bulletin, 3,* 1–6.

National Education Goals Panel. (1995). *National Education Goals report executive summary: Improving education through family–school–community partnerships.* Washington, DC: Author.

National Education Goals Panel. (1997). *The National Education Goals report: Building a nation of learners.* Washington, DC: Author.

National Education Goals Panel. (1998). *Ready schools.* Washington, DC: Author.

Pianta, R.C., Cox, M.J., Early, D., & Taylor, L. (in press). Kindergarten teachers' practices related to the transition to school: Results of a national survey. *The Elementary School Journal.*

Pianta, R.C., & McCoy, S. (1997). The first day of school: The predictive utility of an early school screening program. *Journal of Applied Developmental Psychology, 18,* 1–22.

Pianta, R.C., & Sayre, M. (in press). Parents' observations about their children's transition to kindergarten. *Young Children.*

Pianta, R.C., & Walsh, D.J. (1996). *High risk children in the schools: Creating sustaining relationships.* New York: Routledge.

Resnick, L.B. (1994). Situated rationalism: Biological and social preparation for learning. In L. Hirschfield & S. Gelman (Eds.), *Mapping the mind: Domain specificity in cognition and culture* (pp. 1–20). Washington, DC: American Psychological Association.

Rimm-Kaufman, S.E., & Pianta, R.C. (1998, July). *Differences in family involvement between kindergarten and preschool.* Poster session presented at Head Start's fourth national research conference, Washington, DC.

Rimm-Kaufman, S.E., & Pianta, R.C. (1999). Patterns of family involvement in preschool and kindergarten. Manuscript submitted for publication.

Sameroff, A.J. (1995). General systems theories and developmental psychopathology. In D. Cicchetti & D. Cohen (Eds.), *Developmental psychopathology: Theory and methods* (pp. 659–695). New York: John Wiley & Sons.

Chapter 2

Early Schooling and Social Stratification

Doris R. Entwisle
Karl L. Alexander

This chapter discusses children's early schooling and social stratification in order to shed light on how early schooling of children in the United States shapes the social patterns of both the community and the nation. The major question this chapter seeks to answer is, How can early schooling provide advantages for some children and disadvantages for others that then reinforce the sorting of individuals into the hierarchical layers that are characteristic of the United States and all other human societies?

The intellectual legacies undergirding this chapter draw from three main traditions. The first, "mainstream child development," is probably the most familiar. It begins where projects such as the Collaborative Perinatal Study (Broman, Nicholls, & Kennedy, 1985) leave off when they conclude that social factors outweigh biological or medical factors in explaining children's success in school. The second, a subfield of the study of status attainment in sociology, focuses on how social resources of families, schools, and communities support schooling and thereby eventually influence children's occupational attainment as adults. The third tradition is life course research that emphasizes the means by which children's early schooling can produce social inequality at later points in the life cycle.

Regarding the first legacy, child developmentalists belatedly came to realize that long-term, large-scale research in natural environments is needed to fully understand children's development. For example, in the mid-1950s, the National Collaborative Perinatal Study (Broman et al., 1985) began to monitor children

We are grateful to several government agencies and private foundations without whose support the study featured in this chapter could not have been conducted. We especially thank the W.T. Grant Foundation (Grant Nos. 83079682, 82079600, and 95-164195).

born into 50,000 families in 14 sites scattered across the United States to see how specific perinatal medical events affected their development over the long term. The hypothesis stated that connections between medical events surrounding the birth and children's developmental disorders would exist. However, by the time the children in the study were 4 years old, their intellectual status was far better explained by 8 variables related to their social status than by any of the 161 biomedical variables that assessed the condition of both mothers and children during the first year after birth (Broman, Nicholls, & Kennedy, 1975). Using a later assessment of the same children at age 7, Sameroff summarized the findings as follows: The "primary causal factors [of poor performance] reside not in the child's biomedical history but in . . . the social context of development; . . . lower socioeconomic status (SES), less maternal education, higher birth order and larger family size related to higher rates of academic failure" (1985, p. ix). For purposes of this chapter, the importance of the perinatal study is its conclusion that poor performance early in school is prompted by social disadvantage. This conclusion lays the groundwork for explaining how that disadvantage can be handed down from one generation to the next.

The second intellectual legacy comes from the field of sociology and stems directly from concerns about social inequity. At about the same time that mainstream child developmentalists were becoming convinced that children's social environments strongly affected their development, sociologists began to seriously study how one generation confers social status upon the next (Blau & Duncan, 1967). In every society, individuals sort themselves into occupations of varying prestige, and these prestige orderings are almost perfectly matched from one society to the next. In the United States, educational credentials govern much of this sorting, and sociologists found that they could account for more of the variance in educational attainment than in occupational attainment. As a result, a minor industry developed with the aim of modeling the process of educational attainment.

Models of educational attainment were confined mainly to the secondary school years because these years are closer to when status attainment occurs. Even though children's school performance in secondary school was predicted by performance in elementary school, the early grades of elementary school were neglected, in part because of difficulties in administering surveys to primary-age children. Because these early years set the stage for all that follows, neglecting research on schooling in the earliest grades has seriously undercut the general understanding of how social inequality is created and maintained. In reality, stratification in early schooling forecasts stratification in later schooling. Several studies link first-grade marks or preschool attendance to a broad range of outcomes in adulthood.

A third intellectual legacy, and the most fundamental to this chapter, is research that takes a life course approach, beginning with Elder's (1974) *Children of the Great Depression*. Life course studies testify to the crucible nature of the social context in which children's early development occurs and to how this early development places children on the various pathways that take them to their adult social positions. When Elder (1974) traced the connections between family income loss in the Great Depression and children's life chances, he found that, in families with equally severe economic deprivation, daughters in working-class families had less chance for higher education than daughters of middle-class families. In other words, social class background mediated the schooling decisions that various depression-era families made. Similar studies inquired how a mother's being on welfare affects an adolescent's psychological well-being (Furstenberg, Frank, Brooks-Gunn, & Morgan, 1987) or how the social and economic resources in neighborhoods affect children's cognitive development (Entwisle, Alexander, & Olson, 1994). In both these instances, the social context (family and neighborhood, respectively) strongly impinges on children's development. A life course approach thus focuses attention on the social processes that explain why family SES can predict children's ability to profit from school, as found in the perinatal study. This approach also focuses on how the family's economic level affects children's educational attainment, as found in status attainment research. While all three traditions contribute to explaining variations in human development that are linked to social stratification, the life course approach places more emphasis on explaining how social stratification relates to young children's schooling than do the other two traditions.

TRANSITION ISSUES

Curiously, there is no generally accepted term for the transition that occurs when children begin their formal schooling, and its critical nature for early development has been largely overlooked by the public and policy makers alike. Its significance as a life transition has attracted almost no attention from social science researchers. Yet, in first grade, children assume the *full* role of student, with a new set of supervisors (teachers, principals, other school personnel), a new set of peers (fellow students), and a new set of role obligations. This new role is one that children will occupy for many years, and their early performance in this role determines much of the later sorting of adults into occupational categories. Starting first grade forces children to expand and refine their concepts of themselves and to monitor their relations with other people more carefully. It thus engenders the child's reorientation from "home child" to "school child" by fostering development of new interpersonal relations.

The organization of elementary schools closely parallels the social fault lines in the larger society; therefore, children who are well off are schooled together, as are those who are not so well off. Yet this organization of elementary schools in terms of the social parameters of the larger society is virtually ignored.

Basis of Rewards

Perhaps the most critical feature of the early school transition is that the basis of rewards changes. Once children leave the protective circle of the family and enter school, they are rated according to how well they do compared with other children, whereas they were previously evaluated mainly in terms of how well they did with respect to their own past record. For this reason, they were always rated positively—as 4-year-olds they were naturally bigger and more capable than when they were 3-year-olds. Furthermore, success in school supposedly depends on academic performance, but children soon discover that they are rated on their ability to please the teacher, to impress peers, and to forecast others' reactions, as well as on their ability to read and perform arithmetic. Feedback comes from many sources—teachers, principals, and classmates—and much of it is evaluative. To be successful, children must learn to differentiate carefully among evaluators according to age and social status. Approval from some classmates does not carry the same cachet as approval from others.

Children quickly learn that they are being evaluated but are often confused about what it is that matters (Dornbusch & Scott, 1975). As Finn noted,

> In school [the child] first discovers that not all students receive the same reactions from the teacher, the principal or from others. At this age, the reactions to him [or her] are not colored by his [or her] achievement record so much perhaps, as by his [or her] sex, color, physical appearance, or his [or her] exhibiting proper—that is, docile—behavior. (1972, p. 395)

Children may be placed in the lowest reading group because they did not take a readiness test or because of the unreliability of the screening test used. Their marks may even depend on what an older sibling has done (Seaver, 1973). The possibility that their physical appearance or linguistic style will differ from that of their classmates is outside children's control because it depends on who their classmates happen to be. However, it makes a considerable difference in how some children are treated. In some schools with large enrollments of children who are poor, a child who gets a B in reading may be placed at the head of the class, but in other schools a B may be an undesirable mark.

Decelerating Growth Curves

Relatively small differences among children's performance levels and adjustment to school during the first-grade transition not only persist but become more pronounced over time. Children's gains on standardized tests over elementary school vary directly with their families' economic resources (see Entwisle, Alexander, & Olson, 1997). Children whose families have more resources start school with higher test scores, so relatively small differences among children of various SES exist from the start. However, the longer children stay in school, the wider these gaps become.

It is also important to note that, as children grow older, the number of points they gain on standardized tests diminishes each year (Entwisle & Alexander, 1996; Schneider 1980). Because increments in test scores are much greater in the lower grades than in the higher grades, effects of social inequality on development will be greatest in the early grades. The deceleration in children's cognitive growth during the grade-school years is not a new phenomenon (see 1916 data on speed of silent reading or the 1944 Stanford Achievement Test scores in Stephens [1956]), but its implications for schooling are generally overlooked. As one obvious corollary, the short-term pay-offs for interventions designed to help children in the early years are likely to be greater than later interventions. Another corollary is that, even though yearly gains on test scores diminish, the variance across test scores inevitably grows larger. A larger variance across test scores in the higher elementary school grades increases the ability of first-grade scores to predict fifth- or sixth-grade scores as compared with the ability of scores from first grade to predict second- or third-grade scores. In other words, test scores in first grade are better predictors of later than earlier scores.

Social development is rapid from ages 6 to 8 in part because cognitive development is also rapid. For example, 6- and 7-year-olds are becoming independent from their families. They learn how to find their way around their neighborhoods, monitor their own activities in a limited way, and operate separately from their families during the school day. Unlike parents, teachers, who are the "significant adult other" during the school day, respond to children's social class and ethnicity. They constantly compare children with one another, if not always in terms of physical coordination or physical attractiveness, certainly in terms of mental quickness, cooperativeness, and savoir faire. Children who slip easily into the student role enhance their own development. A child who has the temperament and inclination to fit in well gets better marks and gains more on standardized tests in the early grades than a child who does not (Alexander & Entwisle, 1988).

But "fitting in" is a two-way street. Teachers' own social origins influence how they react to students. Other things being equal, higher-status teachers tend to rate children from low-income or minority families lower than they rate other children in terms of maturity and classroom behavior, and they also tend to hold lower expectations for these children. Not surprisingly, children's gains on standardized tests and marks in first grade are depressed by such teacher disaffection (Alexander, Entwisle, & Thompson, 1987). In short, because social distance between teachers and their first-grade students can lead students to achieve less, it generates inequality of outcomes.

Administrative Practices

Early administrative placement of children, which reflects social structure in the larger society, has serious long-term consequences. Compared with other children, and all else being equal, males, minority group members, and/or children of low SES more often fail a grade or enter special education classes in elementary school (Alexander, Entwisle, & Dauber, 1994; Bianchi, 1984; Entwisle & Alexander, 1988). Once placed in special education programs or retained in a grade, children seldom rejoin the classmates with whom they began school. Later, these same children are more likely to drop out of high school (Consortium of Longitudinal Studies, 1983). Thus, the early grades are critical because whether children meet challenges at this time has serious, long-lasting consequences (e.g., Alexander et al., 1994; Ensminger & Slusarcick, 1992; Entwisle & Hayduk, 1988; Kerckhoff, 1993; Pedersen, Faucher, & Eaton, 1978).

Although the cumulativeness of school performance has never been in doubt, the actual data to support this link are only now beginning to emerge. By the end of third grade, achievement test scores are fairly stable and the quality of children's performance by then is usually a good indicator of future school performance. In the standardization sample for the California Achievement Test (CAT; 1979) battery, third-grade reading scores obtained in the fall of the school year correlate highly (.87) with the scores the following spring. The similar correlation for the mathematics scores is .84. These correlations are close to the reliability of the test, so they are at a practical ceiling. Husén's (1969) large cross-national study also showed that both intelligence scores and teachers' ratings in third grade are strong predictors of children's long-term educational careers. Kraus (1973), who followed children in New York City for more than 20 years, found that the most significant predictor of adult status was the score obtained on third-grade reading achievement tests. Weller, Schnittjer, and Tuten (1992) likewise reported a correlation of .57 between a reading readiness test given at the start of first-grade and tenth-grade reading and math tests (see also Butler, Marsh, Sheppard, & Sheppard, 1985).

Children's marks in first grade strongly forecast marks throughout elementary school and, in some ways, are an even more reliable predictor of future performance than test scores because they are sensitive to the child's gender, ethnicity, and economic background. For instance, a random sample of African

American first-graders in Baltimore in 1982 (Entwisle & Alexander, 1988) received marks that were approximately one fifth of a grade lower than their Caucasian classmates. These children were statistically equated across a range of other characteristics, including their standardized test scores when they began first grade and their socioeconomic backgrounds (Entwisle & Alexander, 1988).

The cumulative nature of schooling and the persistence of early rankings make it essential to determine how social inequality affects children's transition into full-time schooling because inequities at that point translate into disadvantage all along the line. Long before secondary school, the effects of social inequality on schooling must already have taken hold. From this vantage point, it is ironic that studies of social inequality in education have focused mainly on high school when the time for counteracting these inequities has mostly passed.

Beginning School Study

This chapter draws heavily on the Beginning School Study (BSS), using data from the study throughout the chapter to help fill gaps in the literature or to provide specific examples. A word of caution is therefore in order. This chapter is not meant to be a balanced or encyclopedic treatment of schooling. Instead, it is a highly selective discussion of some aspects of elementary schooling that are linked to social inequality and that 1) have effects on young children that are either currently underestimated or misunderstood, and 2) make reference to fairly new and sometimes counter-zeitgeist ideas.

Space does not permit a full description of the study in this chapter (see Alexander & Entwisle, 1988; Entwisle et al., 1997). The BSS began in 1982, when it recruited a two-stage random sample of approximately 800 Baltimore youth. It has since followed them from the time they began first grade to the present (1999). Most of the BSS examples in this chapter are from the elementary school years, but the availability of data on the middle and high school performance of these same individuals permits examination of some longer-term outcomes. Approximately one half of the children were African American and one half were Caucasian. The range in family economic resources across both ethnic groups was considerable, with some parents in both groups having attended college (21% Caucasian, 30% African American). Sixty-seven percent of students were eligible for meal subsidy (54% Caucasian, 77% African American).

Strictly speaking, this study's findings can be generalized only to Baltimore and only to the mid-1980s. However, Baltimore typifies large eastern U.S. cities with large minority populations and high poverty rates. Caution is still necessary because, unlike other eastern cities, in Baltimore, African Americans comprised the majority of the population, and other minority populations combined accounted for only 1.3% at that time.

SOCIAL STRATIFICATION AND SCHOOLING

Rigid social stratification is in place when children begin their formal schooling or even before, yet much of the social sorting at this point in life is overlooked. For one reason, there are still few national data on children's schooling prior to kindergarten. Also, as mentioned, sociologists have been preoccupied with how socioeconomic stratification affects secondary schooling rather than elementary schooling. Research with secondary students says little about schooling for younger students because of differences in the capabilities and developmental needs of children in middle childhood as compared with those in adolescence and, even more, because the organizational patterns of elementary schools are quite different from those of secondary schools. Having said that, it must also be stated that the larger demographic trends that undercut children's performance in secondary school certainly have negative consequences for younger children's schooling as well.

The ways that children's SES, their family structure, and the organization of their elementary schools affect their development over the first few years of school represent a key means by which social inequality impinges on young children's development. At the elementary level, the boundaries of school catchment areas follow the contours of neighborhoods. Where children live dictates the schools they attend. For these reasons, elementary schools are the logical place to look for evidence about how inequity maps onto schooling. In fact, social disadvantage maps onto social inequities in schooling most noticeably at the start, and children's relative standing when they begin school is replicated when they finish. To wait until high school to determine how social disadvantage affects a youth's schooling, or how to counter it, is to wait too long.

A major source of social inequity is that elementary schools are exceedingly homogeneous in terms of their students' socioeconomic background. The boundaries of U.S. neighborhoods faithfully mirror the fault lines in the larger society, and elementary schools function along lines dictated by the socioeconomic characteristics of the neighborhoods in which they are located rather than along lines determined by the school's own educational goals. Children who live in good neighborhoods effectively land on a fast academic track because their parents and teachers perceive them and treat them as "high-ability" children, whereas children who live in poor neighborhoods land on a slow academic track because they are perceived and treated as "low-ability" children. The myth that elementary schools share the same curriculum is false. Even when all schools use the same lesson plans and textbooks, as in Baltimore City, the SES of the neighborhood determines the way instruction proceeds and the quality of life children experience in their classrooms. The remainder of this section discusses how these inequities arise.

The Faucet Theory

In the United States, schools are organized around the calendar. They are in session during the fall, winter, and spring (about 9 months) but closed in the summer (about 3 months). The episodic nature of schooling creates a strategic advantage for studying the process of children's cognitive growth because the opening and closing of schools produces a "natural experiment." When schools are in session, they turn on the "resource faucet." Schools thus provide resources to promote children's cognitive development during the school year but not during the summer, and the intermittent character of schooling clarifies how the resources provided by homes, neighborhoods, and schools dovetail in support of cognitive growth.

The Coleman report (Coleman et al., 1966) and many subsequent large-scale studies concluded that home influences were far more important than school influences for determining differences in children's achievement. Although this conclusion is absolutely true, when students are evaluated on tests given only once per year, the exact role of home resources in producing differences in children's learning is hard to see. During the school year, both schools and families can foster children's academic development. During the summer, however, schools are closed, and only home and neighborhood resources are available to support children's development.

Children who are poor in the BSS, on average, do as well as or better than their better-off classmates when schools are open in the winter (Entwisle et al., 1997). Only in summer do children who are poor fall behind. Because children of all family backgrounds gain equally on achievement tests in elementary schools over the periods when school is in session, strong evidence exists to support the idea that home resources do not reinforce school resources but instead supplant them.

SES is strongly correlated with how much children learn in total, but it does not affect how much children learn while they are in school, judging from data in the BSS (see Entwisle et al., 1997). When elementary schools are in session, children of all SES levels move ahead at the same average pace on standardized tests of reading and math. Only when schools are not in session do children whose families are better off move ahead of children whose families are poor (see Table 2.1). The small differences in achievement levels that correlate with family SES when BSS children started first grade provide an initial advantage to higher-SES children. These small differences are present because until the time when children start school, their development depends mainly on family resources, and some families are able to provide more resources than others. After formal schooling begins, these initial differences increase, because even though the children who are poor keep pace in winter, the better-off children pull farther ahead of the children who are poor each summer. Better-off children have the resources to continue

Table 2.1. Seasonal test score gains in reading and math for Years 1 through 5 by average meal subsidy of school* (Baltimore Beginning School Study)

	Winter gains			Summer gains		
	Low-SES[a] schools	t-test	High-SES schools	Low-SES schools	t-test	High-SES schools
Reading						
Year 1	59.9		61.7	−7.3	b	12.0
Year 2	50.6	b	38.8	−5.5	b	8.7
Year 3	33.8		31.3	−0.5	b	11.4
Year 4	36.5		32.2	4.4		5.4
Year 5	25.5		25.7	0.4		−1.5
Average	41.3		37.9	−1.7		7.2
Math						
Year 1	50.4		47.1	−7.7	b	5.3
Year 2	43.6		41.6	−6.1	b	3.1
Year 3	35.2		36.9	1.0		−.5
Year 4	32.0		36.3	5.6		4.0
Year 5	25.0		29.4	−0.4		3.0
Average	37.2		38.3	−1.5		3.0

*Percent of children on meal subsidy used to define SES level of school.
[a]SES, socioeconomic status.
[b]$p \leq .05$.

learning outside school during the summer, whereas children who are poor do not. By the end of elementary school, the BSS found that the average achievement gaps between children who were better off and children who were poor increased noticeably as a result of the differential gains during the summers, despite the fact that all children learned equivalent amounts when schools were in session. Economic disability in the parents' generation thereby leads to educational disability in the children's generation via unequal achievement growth during the summer (and before school starts).

To show how children's test score gains relate to the calendar, the 20 BSS schools are grouped according to the percentage of children in each school on meal subsidy. The 10 "low-SES" schools and 10 "high-SES" schools are then identified. When their gains on standardized tests of reading comprehension are tallied separately over winters and summers, the BSS children, on average, gained the same amounts on standardized tests during the school year regardless of whether they attended high- or low-SES schools (see Table 2.1). For example, in the first winter, children attending low-SES schools gained approximately 60 points in reading comprehension and those in high-SES schools gained approximately 62 points. These averages do not differ significantly. In the summer after first grade, however, children in high-SES schools gained 12 points, whereas those in low-SES schools lost 7 points. Despite the equal gains that low- and high-SES children made during the school years, children in low-SES schools (who had started school a little behind on these tests) were treated as though they had "low ability."

Table 2.2 shows that the children in the low-SES schools were given lower marks, held back more often, and in other ways rated less favorably by teachers than were the high-SES children. In other words, even though the low-SES children, on average, gained as many points on standardized reading comprehension tests during the first-grade school year as the high-SES children, children in low-

Table 2.2.   Ratings of children's first-grade performance by socioeconomic status (SES) level of school (Baltimore Beginning School Study)

| | SES level of school, Fall 1982 (% meal subsidy)[a] | | | |
| | Low SES[b] | | High SES[b] | |
	Mean	SD	Mean	SD
Reading mark, quarter 1	1.64	.58	2.15	.74
Reading mark, quarter 4	1.94	.73	2.65	.95
Math mark, quarter 1	1.99	.75	2.52	.85
Math mark, quarter 4	2.26	.86	2.88	.90
Proportion retained, year 1	.22	.42	.11	.31
Reading instruction level, quarter 1[c]	1.93	.51	2.21	.80
Reading instruction level, quarter 4[c]	3.69	1.12	4.29	.96

[a]Percent of children on meal subsidy in each school used to define SES level of school. The 20 schools are divided into "low SES" (10 schools with highest meal subsidy rate) and "high SES" (10 schools with lowest meal subsidy rate).

[b]For low-SES schools, sample sizes range from 355 to 405; for high-SES schools, sample sizes range from 332 to 349.

[c]1 = readiness, 2 = preprimer, 3 = primer, 4 = level 1, 5 = level 2, 6 = level 3.

SES schools did not experience the same rewards as children in high-SES schools. They were treated in terms of their scores when they began first grade rather than in terms of the progress they made. They gained as much or more than high-SES children once they started first grade, but because their home background was of a relatively low SES and their initial scores were a little lower to begin with, they were treated as less capable than other children. It is hard to imagine a clearer case of social inequity.

Not only was their actual school progress ignored, but also the children who were poor attended schools in neighborhoods where facilities were inferior to those in better neighborhoods. In Baltimore, even brand-new elementary schools that enroll mainly children who are poor are set in the midst of old rowhouses and tenements surviving from the 19th century, with bars and liquor stores in close proximity. The schools that enroll children who are economically advantaged are set on expanses of grass, among single-family houses with well-kept lawns and shrubbery, generally removed from commercial activity. Even when they share the same school district, as in Baltimore City, elementary schools in the disadvantaged inner city are far different social institutions from schools in well-to-do neighborhoods. These differences among elementary schools lead to a quality of life within schools that is distinctive, and this stratification across schools undermines their effectiveness as social equalizers. Schools are remarkably successful at promoting all children's cognitive growth when in session, but from the earliest days of first grade this is overlooked.

Thus, the first-grade transition, a key life stage for understanding schooling, has to be a bumpy ride for children at the low end of the socioeconomic scale. Society confuses their uneven growth trajectories—advancing rapidly when school is in session but then growing little during the summer—with a reduced ability to grow. Even though BSS children of all socioeconomic levels advanced at the same rate when school was in session, parents and teachers of children in low-SES schools had lower expectations for those children, and those children received much lower marks than their counterparts in higher-SES schools. In addition, many more of the lower-SES children were held back.

The Process of Schooling

Despite the data summarized in the previous section that show family SES does not affect how much children learn while school is in session, most educational research conceptualizes family resources as potentiating school resources. For example, parents' school involvement supposedly helps students to do better in school because involved parents are more likely to check homework or consult teachers when problems arise. The assumption has been that family resources act year round to help students do well—in the winter when school is in session as well as in the summer when school is closed. But the BSS data show that family resources matter for young children mainly—or only—when schools are closed. Family resources do not interact with or add to school resources in underwriting young children's achievements during the school year because, as has been seen, children from all kinds of family backgrounds tend to profit from schooling to the same extent when schools are open. Rather, in the summer, family resources promote cognitive growth that supplements the growth children make during the school year.

Prior research on neighborhoods likewise assumes that they affect children's school performance on a continuous basis. Whether neighborhood influences interact with or add to school influences in the winter is an issue yet to be settled, but so far BSS research suggests that neighborhood resources, similar to home resources, matter mainly in the summer (see Entwisle et al., 1997). That is, family resources and neighborhood resources appear to be redundant with school resources when schools are in session.[1] Neighborhood resources added to home resources in summer periods for BSS children because neighborhoods affected the gains children made during the summer after allowing for family background effects. This issue needs much further study, but observing a seasonal action of neighborhood resources coupled with a seasonal action of family resources on children's school performance suggests that school effects are relatively independent of other contextual effects.

Missing Variables

Another pitfall in understanding the process of schooling over the first-grade transition is that many of the large-scale studies of schooling at later ages omit key variables. Parents' economic standing undergirds schooling in part because, compared with parents who are not as well off, parents who are more affluent tend to place higher value on education, have higher expectations for their children's school performance, have more knowledge of how the educational system works, and have the time and resources to interact with their children in developmentally sensitive ways. All of these psychological resources can support children's development when schools close for the summer. The potency of parents' expectations for shaping young children's school performance has been demonstrated repeatedly, especially for children in the early grades (see Entwisle et al., 1997).

Parent involvement, the topic of a flurry of research (e.g., Booth & Dunn, 1996), may, in fact, be a proxy for parents' expectations. Parents who expect their children to do well will try to help them in every way possible, including being involved in school affairs. The positive consequences currently being attributed to parents' school involvement could instead be the consequences of parents' expectations.

A major contribution of the BSS is finding that parents' psychological resources, which are higher or more plentiful in families of higher SES, bear fruit mainly in the summer when school is closed. The *psychological capital* of the family, which can be independent of its social or financial capital, is a key parental resource for children's achievement. Most succinctly, it is the ability of parents to interact with their children in ways that prompt cognitive growth.

Poverty

Debate on the means by which poverty affects children's schooling has focused mainly on two themes: parents' altered norms and "tastes" for non-normative behavior (e.g., welfare dependence, chronic joblessness) or social structural factors, by which some parents suffer continuing social and economic disadvantage (see Tienda, 1991). This dichotomy is somewhat fictional. If the faucet theory is taken seriously, the resources furnished by schools are sufficient to prompt growth in young children of all SES levels when schools are in session. Still, as has been illustrated, parents and teachers treat children in terms of their social origins—where they start school—rather than in terms of their actual performance. In other

---

[1]The observation that in low-income countries the effects of schools on achievement in primary school are comparatively greater than in high-income countries is also consistent with the authors' ideas about home versus school learning (Heyneman & Loxley, 1983).

words, parents' joblessness and so on lead to norms—ways of viewing children—that do not boost their children's achievement when schools are closed.

The BSS archive suggests that differences in children's achievement levels develop before first grade or during the summers, the times when children must depend entirely on resources furnished by neighborhoods and families. These out-of-school resources appear to be partly the psychological resources that reflect parents' economic resources. For example, if household income is relatively high, parents tend to hold higher expectations for their children's school performance than parents whose income is below poverty level. However, to a considerable degree, parents' psychological resources add to economic resources, especially for young children (see Entwisle & Alexander, 1996). Certainly, the social stratification of families imposed by neighborhood boundaries is a key element in school inequity—the larger social structure does matter—but no doubt much of the impact of this stratification on primary age children is mediated by parents' psychological capital.

ELEMENTARY SCHOOLS AS SOCIAL INSTITUTIONS

Up to this point, the focus of this chapter has been mainly on the home resources of young children and, particularly, on how such resources produce seasonal differences in achievement growth. This focus, although important, is incomplete because schools are institutions that embody the social-structural dimensions of the larger society. Developmental theorists have focused much more intently on what explains changes within the child rather than on how changes in the child's surroundings help or hinder development. Research on schooling helps redress this imbalance because children's achievements do not occur in a social vacuum. Children from minority groups often attend schools where most of the other students are from families who are economically disadvantaged. Household moves often force children who are poor to make "extra" school transitions. Because the family that is poor more often moves its household than the better-off family, the child who is poor more often moves among schools. That is, because school climate reflects the neighborhood's wealth, the nature of the student body and the school context is mainly determined by conditions outside the school. Powerful social forces thus envelop children irrespective of their own characteristics or those of their immediate family.

Socioeconomic Status and Tracking

Elementary schools appear to have the same organizational structure because the topics covered in their curriculum look much the same across grades and schools. With the exception of grouping within classes, society perceives these schools as *untracked*—one program fits all. This perception is wrong: Elementary schools are *not* the same; they are rigidly tracked by family SES level and by administrative fiat. Their tracks are not labeled as such, perhaps because society prefers to repress them from view.

Variability Among Schools

The small size of elementary schools, plus their 3Rs curriculum, helps to support the myth that all elementary schools have the same structure and that not until middle school does tracking begin. Quite the opposite is true, however, because the variation in socioeconomic level among elementary schools outstrips that among secondary schools. During the 1990/1991 school year, for example, the proportion of Baltimore children participating in the subsidized meal program varied across elementary schools on average from 5% to 100% but varied only from 8% to 65% across high schools (Baltimore City Public Schools, 1991). (During the 1990/1991 school year, mean enrollment in Baltimore City public elementary schools was 529; in middle schools, 888; and in high schools, 1,078.) This greater socioeconomic variation across elementary schools is mainly a consequence of their small catchment areas, which differ sharply by family income level. Neighborhoods, in other words, vary in terms of the SES of the families that inhabit them and, therefore, so do their elementary schools. To illustrate this correspondence, the rank-order correlations were calculated between Baltimore schools' meal subsidy levels and three U.S. Census indicators of neighborhood quality: median household income, percentage of families below the poverty level, and the percentage of workers with professional or managerial jobs. These correlations are as follows: .86 (median household income), .66 (percentage of workers with high-status jobs), and .83 (family poverty level). The ranking of the meal subsidy levels of schools thus corresponds closely to all three measures of neighborhood SES.

Differences in Student Characteristics by Neighborhood[2]

Other important correspondences link the school context and students' characteristics. BSS students who lived in the better-off Baltimore neighborhoods began school with higher test scores than students who lived in the poorer neighborhoods. For instance, of the 20 schools that were randomly selected to participate in the study, the school with only 11% of students on subsidized meals enrolled children at the beginning of first grade whose average CAT scores in reading comprehension were 302 and in math concepts were 316. However, in the school with 90% of students on subsidized meals, reading scores averaged 265 (37 points lower, about .9 standard deviation [SD]) and math scores averaged 273 (43 points lower, about 1.3 SDs). The rank-order correlations between the percentage of first-grade students on meal subsidy in a school and students' average reading and math CAT scores when they began first grade are .65 in reading and .72 in math.

The achievement test differences across BSS schools increased as the BSS children progressed through the grades. As stated previously, this increase was because of the summer drop-off for children who were poorer. By the end of year 5, the average difference in standardized test scores between BSS children in the highest and lowest SES schools was almost a full SD (.89 SD in reading and .79 SD in math).

As would be anticipated, the figures for all Baltimore City elementary schools show the same patterns as those in the 20 BSS schools. The gradient in children's

---

[2]The example of the variation among schools in Baltimore City is a "minimal" picture because all these schools are in one of the poorest school districts in Maryland. If schools were contrasted among districts as well, the variation across elementary schools would be much greater. During the 1991/1992 school year, the average expenditure per pupil in Baltimore was $4,947, which was about 85% of the state average ($5,815) at the time, but only 65% of the average ($7,591) for Montgomery County, the wealthiest district. Furthermore, in Baltimore, 67% of children received meal subsidies compared with 17% in Montgomery County (Maryland State Department of Education, 1992). Baltimore City children were thus allotted only two thirds as much money for education as were children in a nearby school district where families were much better off.

reading achievement across schools follows their meal subsidy gradients. In schools with 50% or fewer of students on meal subsidy, children were reading at grade level 3.19 by the end of second grade and more than 1 year above grade level (7.15) by the end of fifth grade (first column, Table 2.3). In schools in which 89% or more of students were on subsidy (last column, Table 2.3), children were reading at half a year below grade level at the end of second grade and slightly below grade level at the end of fifth grade. The gap in reading achievement between the highest and lowest SES schools in Baltimore thus increased between the end of second and fifth grades from about ⅔ of a grade level to 1⅓ grade levels 3 years later.

Other studies also reveal strong patterns of socioeconomic stratification across elementary schools (e.g., Rosenberg, 1979). Although it tends to be overlooked, the Coleman report (Coleman et al., 1966) clearly showed this stratification. In a nationwide sample of more than 400,000 children, this report found greater school-to-school variability in standardized test scores for children in their elementary years (grades 1, 3, and 6) than for children in their secondary years (grades 9 and 12), with variation in reading scores almost 60% greater at grade 3 than at grade 12, and in math scores more than 100% greater at grade 3 than at grade 12. Similar stratification by SES characterizes schools in Great Britain where, as in the United States, primary schools are much smaller than secondary schools. Teachers' salaries, the proportion of oversize classes, expenditures for fuel, and so forth, all vary more among primary schools in Great Britain than do the equivalent indices among secondary schools (Central Advisory Council for Education, 1967). The point of these examples is that elementary schools are typically organized tightly along lines of family and neighborhood SES, with the consequence that SES of elementary children differs markedly among schools.

Despite the variations in their standardized test scores by SES when they started first grade, BSS children of different SES levels progressed at the same rate during first grade, as is illustrated previously. In the winter when schools were in session, the yearly gains of the children in the high- and low-SES groups were

Table 2.3.   Mean grade equivalent for reading and math California Achievement Test (CAT) scores, Baltimore City elementary schools (N = 122) 1987, by percent of students on meal subsidy

	Percent of students on meal subsidy in school			
	11%–50% (N = 31)	51%–73% (N = 30)	74%–88% (N = 31)	89%–100% (N = 30)
Mean	33.4	61.0	81.0	92.4
CAT reading comprehension score				
End of Grade 2	3.19	2.86	2.81	2.53
End of Grade 3	4.29	3.71	3.67	3.41
End of Grade 5	7.15	6.30	5.92	5.85
CAT total math score				
End of Grade 2	3.33	3.13	3.08	2.93
End of Grade 3	4.48	4.09	4.01	3.83
End of Grade 5	7.30	6.82	6.58	6.46

From Baltimore City Public Schools, Office of the Superintendent of Public Instruction. (1988, February). *School profiles: School year 1987–88.* Baltimore: Author; reprinted by permission.

equivalent (within limits of sampling variability). These data lend strong support to the conclusion that students' gains in achievement when school is open are equivalent irrespective of family economic status.

Socioeconomic Stratification and School Contexts

For a long time, it has been known that secondary students' track placement is not simply a consequence of prior achievement or ability (Kilgore, 1991) and often follows social class lines (Alexander, Cook, & McDill, 1978; Heyns, 1978; Jencks et al., 1972). The perceived single curriculum of the elementary school, however, has tended to conceal the extreme tracking by family SES among elementary schools described previously. This variation by SES leads to differences in how elementary schools function. Parents, aware of these school differences, use many strategies, including illegal ones, to get their children into high-SES schools. Mainly they try to locate their households in the most exclusive residential areas they can possibly afford. Others use private schools, and some even pretend the child is living at one address while actually living at another.

Parental concern is justified because the marks teachers give children follow the SES gradient of the neighborhood (Table 2.2). In BSS schools with 30% or fewer children on meal subsidy, the first reading marks that children see are generally 2.0 (C) or better. In schools where more than 30% of children are on subsidy, these first reading marks are in the 1.0-to-2.0 range; in the majority of these schools, no one received a mark higher than a C. (Those who get 1.0s are failing.) In the school with 88% of children on subsidy, all BSS students received a failing mark in the first quarter of first grade. Of the 11 schools with 50% or more children on subsidy, children's average marks in reading were better than 2.0 (C) in only two schools. Nevertheless, children in the low-SES schools made test score gains over first grade when school was in session just as large as those made by children who attended high-SES schools.

Children in low-SES schools were thus perceived differently and treated differently from children in high-SES schools, even though they were doing equally well. The school climates linked to SES are not a consequence of children's actual progress because, when school was in session, children in schools of all SES levels gained equal amounts on standardized tests of achievement in both reading and math. That is, differences by SES in marks and expectations are *not* triggered by differences in the children's actual progress in school. Children are being marked in terms of where they live, or in terms of their scores when they started school, rather than in terms of how they performed in the first-grade classroom.

These same patterns characterize teachers' expectations. At the end of first grade, teachers were asked to predict their students' performance in second grade. First-grade teachers in the 10 high-SES schools generally expected their pupils to get more As and Bs than Cs or lower in reading during the next school year, whereas teachers' expectations in the 10 low-SES schools were for almost all children to get Cs or lower in the next school year.

Parents' perceptions of their children's performance also differed according to the SES of the school. Parents' expectations for their children's first marks in reading, which were ascertained either shortly before or just after school began in September 1982, before any report cards were issued, show a gradient by meal subsidy level of the school. Parents' average expectations in the high-SES schools were for their children to score 2.74 in reading, whereas parents in the low-SES schools expected their children to score 2.59 on average.

Teachers' treatment of children reinforced these differential parental expectations. In the 10 high-SES schools, children's first reading marks averaged 2.15 (a little better than a C). In the bottom 10 low-SES schools, first reading marks averaged only 1.64 (about 40% of the children were failing). Similarly, in the top 10 schools, the average math mark (2.52) was halfway between a C and a B, but in the lower 10 schools it was a C (1.99).

BSS teachers' ratings of children's classroom behavior likewise corresponded to the socioeconomic level of the school. When first-grade teachers rated their students in terms of interest and participation in class, teachers in the school where only 11% of children were on meal subsidy rated their pupils approximately one *SD* higher in interest/participation than did teachers in the school where 90% of children were on subsidy. The rank-order correlation between the school's meal subsidy level and teachers' average interest/participation rating of their first-grade students is .71. Furthermore, in the schools with high percentages of children on subsidy, some children were literally rated "off the scale" (i.e., they were rated at 3 *SDs* less than their school's mean on interest and participation). No student was rated off the scale in the more affluent schools.

The picture becomes more disturbing the longer children are in school. Only 47% of children in the BSS who started first grade in a school where more than 90% of students were on subsidy had reached fifth grade 5 years later because 53% had either been retained or placed in special education. In contrast, 77% of those who started first grade in schools where 50% or less of the children were on subsidy were in fifth grade 5 years later.

Clearly, where children start elementary school effectively places them on a track. Children of high SES have relatively high test scores as they begin first grade and are grouped together. Children of low SES levels have relatively low scores when they begin first grade and are thus grouped together. These same schools report the highest and lowest scores at the end of elementary school, despite the fact that when schools were in session, children of all socioeconomic levels progressed at the same rate. That is, children gained the same amounts on standardized tests over the school year irrespective of socioeconomic level and initial test scores in their school. Their SES did not affect the rate at which they progressed while in school, but out-of-school, either before first grade or in summer when school was closed, their SES level did affect their rate of progress.

For BSS children, correlations are .41 and .55, respectively, between initial CAT scores in reading and math in the fall of first grade and scores on higher levels of the same tests at the end of elementary school. The stratified outcomes later in the educational pipeline can be forecast surprisingly well from the stratification patterns visible in first grade (see also Alexander & Entwisle, 1996; Kerckhoff, 1993). BSS children who had the highest test scores at the end of elementary school took algebra and a foreign language in middle school and thus ended up with the needed prerequisites (algebra and language skills) to move into the college preparatory program in high school. In contrast, students with low scores at the end of elementary school did not take these high-level courses (Dauber, Alexander, & Entwisle, 1996). For example, 62% of children who were placed in the lowest reading group in their first-grade classroom took low-level English in sixth grade. Likewise, 51% of the children who had been retained in first grade were in low-level math in sixth grade.

Socioeconomic differentials across schools match the fault lines in the larger society. Schools in high- and low-SES neighborhoods have different marking standards and treat students differently at a time in life when rates of cognitive growth are extremely rapid. The equivalence in children's progress when schools are in session is completely obscured.

Long-Term Effects

Evidence is mounting that social stratification in the larger society is affected strongly by the nature of children's elementary schooling, especially by events and experiences in first grade or just before. All else being equal, repeating a grade or getting poor marks in elementary school increases the likelihood that students will drop out (see Alexander et al., 1994; Entwisle et al., 1997). The other side of the coin is that attending preschool or kindergarten can improve reading and math achievement in elementary school (Barnett, 1996; Entwisle, Alexander, Pallas, & Cadigan, 1987; Lazar & Darlington, 1982) and long-term follow-ups of attending preschool show that positive preschool effects apparently persist or at least predict better outcomes in adulthood (Barnett, 1996; Consortium of Longitudinal Studies, 1983).

The Baltimore BSS enriches this picture by showing more specifically how and when long-term effects are transmitted (Table 2.4). For example, the amount of BSS children's kindergarten experience (full day versus half day) by itself improved children's chances of avoiding retention in first grade by almost 2 to 1 (with initial test scores and other key variables controlled). Also, children living in single-parent families that included a grandmother in the preschool period had better work habits at the beginning of first grade than children of single parents whose family members did not include a grandmother. Superior work habits helped children avoid retention in first grade (Entwisle et al., 1997). For example, if BSS children's very first marks were high, those marks could pump up test scores over the first-grade year by as much as half a SD, all else being equal (Alexander & Entwisle, 1988). The first-grade teachers' opinion of the child's classroom adjustment provided still another avenue of influence: Children whom teachers perceived as interested or attentive in the classroom gained significantly more on standardized tests in reading and math than other children, all else being equal, including initial test scores. These teachers' perceptions forecast children's year-end test scores even better than children's initial test scores. Both test scores and marks persisted strongly from first grade on; for example, BSS children's CAT scores at the end of the first year correlate .58 and .66 with scores at the end of Year 5 in reading comprehension and math concepts, respectively (see also Alexander et al., 1994).

Studies by other investigators that trace long-term effects of schooling before first grade and in the first few grades also show that effects persist long after elementary school. Studies in both the United States and the United Kingdom (Table 2.5) that used randomized designs link attending preschool to better verbal and reading skills in elementary and secondary school, to lower rates of retention and/or less special education placement, and even to superior adjustment in early adulthood. Drop-out studies show that absences, retention, low reading levels, low marks in the early grades, or early behavior problems in school increase the likelihood that students will drop out before graduation.

POLICY IMPLICATIONS

Most research on school transitions deals with the move from elementary to middle school or junior high school (see Eccles, Midgley, & Adler 1984; Entwisle, 1990). Research on the junior high transition examines socioemotional or affective

Table 2.4.   Long-term effects of first-grade transition (Baltimore Beginning School Study)

Citation	Early school measure	Outcome
Entwisle, Alexander, Cadigan, & Pallas, 1987	Amount of kindergarten	First-grade absence Beginning CAT scores Beginning marks in reading, math
Dauber, Alexander, & Entwisle, 1993	Beginning marks Grade 1 math CAT score	Retention in Years 1–4
Alexander, Entwisle, & Dauber, 1993	Teacher behavioral ratings in Grade 1	School performance in Year 4: Reading, math marks Reading, math CAT scores
Alexander, Entwisle, & Dauber, 1994	Grade 1 retention	Academic self-image, Year 8 Student mark expectations, Year 8 Reading, math marks, Grades 6 and 7 CAT reading, math, Grades 6 and 7
Pallas, Entwisle, Alexander, & Stluka, 1994	Grade 1 reading group assignment	Year 4 CAT scores, reading marks, parent and teacher expectations
Alexander & Entwisle, 1996	Grade 1 reading groups; Grade 1 tracking (reading groups, special education, retention)	Retention in elementary school Grade 6 course placements
Alexander, Entwisle, & Horsey, 1997	Grade 1 CAT reading and math scores; Grade 1 reading and math marks; Grade 1 retention	High school dropout
Unpublished	Grade 1 parent education expectation for student; Grade 1 marks in reading and math	Middle school placement in advanced course tracks
Unpublished	Amount of kindergarten	Retention in Year 1
Unpublished	Work habits Grade 1; Number of school moves	Retention in Year 1 Test scores in Year 5

outcomes, along with cognitive outcomes, because adolescence is when students' developing sense of identity and self-worth occupy center stage. Generally, a decrease in self-image accompanies the junior high transition, but susceptibility to that decline depends on each youth's personal characteristics (Simmons & Blyth, 1987); family characteristics (Rosenberg & Simmons, 1971); social-structural characteristics of schools, such as peer group membership (Eccles et al., 1984); and the interactions among these variables.

In light of the remarkable pay-offs from research on the junior high transition, the dearth of research on the first-grade transition is both worrisome and surprising. Except for Reynolds (1992), who focused on African American youth who are disadvantaged, the BSS is the first relatively large-scale attempt to examine chil-

Table 2.5.   Long-term effects: Other investigators' research

Study	Early schooling	Lasting effect
Bloom, 1964	By Grade 3	At least 50% of the general achievement pattern at age 18 has been developed
Husén, 1969 (N = 1,116; Sweden)	Grade 3 marks (GPA) Teacher ability rating in Grade 3	Attendance at secondary school Future education success (completion of post-secondary study)
Fitzsimmons, Cheever, Leonard, & Macunovich, 1969 (N = 270)	Achievement test scores in reading and math, Grades 1–3	Performance in high school
Stroup & Robins, 1972 (N = 223; African American urban males)	Absences and grade repetition in elementary school	High school dropout
Kraus, 1973 (N = 274)	Grade 3 reading achievement tests	Reading and math marks General academic performance in high school
Lloyd, 1978 (N = 1,562)	Grade 3 marks and CAT reading score	High school graduation
Pedersen, Faucher, & Eaton, 1978 (N = 59; urban disadvantaged)	Exceptional first-grade teacher	Achievement of high adult status Completion of at least 10 years of school
Pope, Lehrer, & Stevens, 1980 (N = 545)	Kindergarten achievement (Wide Range Achievement Test)	Reading achievement
Lazar & Darlington, 1982 (N = 2,008)	Participation in Head Start preschool programs	Reading achievement (Grade 3), math achievement (Grades 3–5) Lower rates of retention and special education
Richman, Stevenson, & Graham, 1982 (N = 705; United Kingdom)	Preschool attendance	Higher IQ-adjusted reading at age 8
Palmer, 1983 (N = 240)	One-to-one preschool instruction at ages 2–3 for 8 months	Higher reading and math achievement at Grades 5 and 7 Lower rates of retention
Royce, Darlington, & Murray, 1983 (N = 1,104)	Preschool attendance	Achievement in reading (Grade 3) and math (Grade 5) Lower rates of special education and retention High school graduation
Schweinhart & Weikart, 1983 (N = 123)	Preschool attendance (Perry Preschool)	Higher CAT scores at ages 7–14 Lower rates of special education placement and delinquent behavior

(continued)

Table 2.5.   (continued)

Study	Early schooling	Lasting effect
Meyer, 1984 (N = 165; economically disadvantaged)	Kindergarten–Grade 3 participation in Distar curriculum with increased allocation of time to basic skills	Higher Grade 9 CAT reading achievement Lower retention rates Higher rates of high school graduation, application and acceptance to college
Berrueta-Clement, Schweinhart, Barnett, Epstein, & Weikart, 1984 (N = 123)	High-quality preschool program (Perry Preschool)	Higher GPA in high school Lower rates of special education Positive outcomes at age 19; High school graduates Postsecondary education Employed Lower rates of crime, delinquency Lower rates of pregnancy
Hess, Holloway, Dickson, & Price, 1984 (N = 47) Butler, Marsh, Sheppard, & Sheppard, 1985 (N = 286)	Maternal expectations for achievement in preschool Battery of tests in kindergarten Grade 1 reading achievement	Grade 6 Iowa Test of Basic Skills (ITBS) scores, vocabulary and math Reading achievement tests in Grade 6
Stevenson & Newman, 1986 (N = 105)	Prekindergarten cognitive measures Elementary achievement Mothers' and teachers' ratings in Grades 2–5	Grade 10 test scores in reading and math Grade 10 self-concept and expectancy for success in reading
Wadsworth, 1986 (N = 1,675; United Kingdom)	Preschool attendance	Higher verbal skills at age 8
Entwisle & Hayduk, 1988 (N = 654)	Parents' estimate of child's ability in Grade 3 Teachers' mark expectations in Grades 1 and 2	English and math achievement tests 4–9 years later, current ability level controlled
Cairns, Cairns, & Neckerman, 1989 (N = 475)	Elementary school retention	High school dropout
Barrington & Hendricks, 1989 (N = 214)	Grade 3 ITBS achievement test scores	High school dropout
Morris, Ehren, & Lenz, 1991 (N = 785)	Grade 4 reading achievement scores	High school dropout
Simner & Barnes, 1991 (N = 193)	Grade 1 reading and math marks	High school dropout
Ensminger & Slusarcick, 1992 (N = 917; African American, urban)	Grade 1 math mark Grade 1 aggressive behavior (especially for males)	High school dropout

Table 2.5.   (continued)

Study	Early schooling	Lasting effect
Weller, Schnittjer, & Tuten, 1992 (N = 415)	Metropolitan Reading Readiness, beginning of Grade 1 Received remediation (Chapter 1) in Grade 3	Comprehensive Test of Basic Skills (CTBS) reading and math scores, Grade 10 (r = .57) CTBS reading and math scores, Year 10 (r = .56)
Brooks-Gunn, Guo, Furstenberg, & Frank, 1993 (N = 254; African American)	Preschool attendance Preschool cognitive ability No elementary grade retention	High school graduation Postsecondary education
Roderick, 1993 (N = 757)	Grade 4 academic marks Grade retention, K–Grade 3	High school dropout
Reynolds, 1994 (N = 1,106; African American, low income)	Follow-on intervention in Grades 1–3 (school-based comprehensive service program providing instructional support and parental involvement)	ITBS reading and math, Grade 5 Cumulative grade retention, Grade 5

dren's transition into full-time schooling in relation to their long-term achievement trajectories. BSS data show convincingly that children's relative standing when they start first grade forecasts where they will be at much later points in their school careers. School helps all children gain the same amounts on achievement tests, as shown in Table 2.1, so those who start ahead tend to stay ahead. However, those who start school behind gain just as much when school is in session as do their more fortunate classmates. This and the importance of early schooling for defining children's long-term educational trajectories make it imperative to focus more research on the pre- and primary school periods.

A major way to improve the school climate in poor neighborhoods would be to correct the mistaken public perception that elementary schools are falling down on the job. Children's families and the public at large need to be made aware that the deficits in school performance of children who are poor are not linked to school attendance. Elementary schools are promoting just as much growth in achievement of children who are poor as in children who are better off. Schools are doing a much better job than they have been credited with. The importance of the success of schools in fostering development of young children irrespective of their home backgrounds is hard to overstate. Schools have undeservedly become the target to blame for most of society's intractable problems.

Retention

A thorny issue for policy is grade retention in elementary school (see Alexander et al., 1994). Many people are negatively disposed toward retention because they blame children's problems on retention itself. They do not fully understand that children who are held back have serious problems long before they are retained and that retention signals rather than creates these pre-existing problems. Therefore, abolishing retention will not erase the problems that lead schools to practice it.

Repeating part of a grade or even just one subject area could be one way to help children who experience a shaky start get back on track. However, the best way to reduce retention would be to get all children up to speed at or before the beginning of first grade. BSS research points to improving children's work habits and to providing more preschool for children who are economically disadvantaged, especially boys, as possible ways to reduce retention rates. This latter method was the goal of the Head Start programs in the 1960s. The Consortium of Longitudinal Studies' (1983) central finding—that attending preschool led to a reduction in retention rates—has been replicated many times (Barnett, 1996).

Social Equity

This chapter begins by discussing three intellectual traditions: ecological studies in mainstream child development, status attainment research in sociology, and a growing body of findings from investigators who take a life course perspective. The mainstream studies established that social variables far outweigh biological or medical variables in explaining young children's learning problems and school deficits. In particular, they identified family economic status and parent configuration as key variables for understanding young children's progress in school. Status attainment research contributed ideas about the structure of models to explain schooling and thereby led to the discovery of the strong seasonal variations in elementary school achievement. The life course approach suggested focusing intensively on the early grades and on the overlapping social contexts in which children develop. A life course approach, moreover, joins the mainstream child development and status attainment traditions and thus helps establish links between early schooling and social stratification.

A fascination with inequality in society is part of the human condition. Along with it goes a fascination for how social inequality is perpetuated (Kerckhoff, 1993). The imagery that a set of occupational slots at the top of the school ladder is ready for the new generation to move into is strong. To us, the authors, this image of society as a set of occupational pigeonholes seems to be upside down. High schools do reflect the stratification patterns in the larger society, but the critical sorting processes occur at the beginning rather than near the end of children's school careers. A focus on the first-grade transition reveals that elementary schools are already layered according to the population's economic resources, and this layering stems from stratification among neighborhoods. Families sort themselves by SES into neighborhoods that then determine the kind and amount of early schooling their children receive. This early sorting is a kind of "sponsoring," but not in terms of demands of the larger society (i.e., that certain slots must be filled by certain types of people). Rather sponsoring is in terms of parents' power to enhance the development of their own children. Parents' choice of a neighborhood is far more important than their choice of a school, and most of what defines a neighborhood are the economic differences that separate it from other neighborhoods.

Organizational theorists from different camps visualize the internal structure of schools as vertical or horizontal because they assume that an organization's needs determine its structure. This approach, which may be rational for organizations such as banks or factories, does not work for schools because the internal structure of schools, or of school systems, depends on the structure of the society in which they exist rather than on their own production goals. Elementary schools became common at the beginning of the 19th century because they fulfilled the need to prepare youth (mainly boys) to function as citizens in a participatory democracy, but also because they occupied children's time in winter months when farms lay dormant. Later in the 19th century, when the steady flow of immigrants from abroad led to an oversupply of labor, enrolling children in schools kept them from competing for jobs in factories. Thus, social forces largely unrelated to children or their needs dictated both when schools became universal and the length and temporal patterns of the school year.

Even now, the internal organizational structures of schools are being driven by economic and social pressures. Parents try to maximize their own and their family's social status, which leads them to place their children on what they perceive to be the most effective paths to compete successfully in the labor markets of the 21st century. They struggle to send their children to Ivy League schools, or even to preschools that lead up to the ivy, not so much because they are deeply committed to their children's intellectual development or to what their children might learn, but because they perceive that once school is over, adult success depends mainly on social capital rather than on human capital. Also, they themselves draw prestige from the quality of the child's college or preparatory school. Schools as institutions serve to perpetuate the social status quo, but the engine that drives the overall system is located mainly in the individual family and in its elementary schools, not in its secondary schools.

Elementary schools tend to maximize the social homogeneity of their student bodies because the social status of neighborhoods determines the social status of students in the elementary school. This distribution does not serve children or society well. As has been stated before, schools are not the problem. The distribution of resources across families and neighborhoods is the problem. Problems in families and neighborhoods cannot be solved only by tinkering with schools.

At the same time, the lack of good preschools for impoverished 3- and 4-year-olds is an important means by which social inequality undercuts schooling. At present, parents who are high school dropouts and/or teenagers are the least likely to enroll their children in center-based programs (NCES, 1994). The lack of facilities for schooling of children who are disadvantaged prior to kindergarten, plus the tendency of these children not to take full advantage of the public kindergartens and preschools already available, is a major way that differential tracking by income levels takes an early hold on children. A few extra test points conferred by preschool or kindergarten attendance could be enough to protect children at an economic disadvantage from low placements or retention in the first few grades (see Entwisle, 1995). In other words, the cognitive boost children get from preschool and kindergarten can ease the first-grade transition. A giant step would be taken if children whose backgrounds are problematic improved their skills before they began first grade. With kindergartens so widely available, the means are there. Kindergarten attendance is discretionary in Baltimore and other localities. Most BSS children attended only half a day and about 10% did not attend at all. All children must be encouraged and/or required to attend full-day kindergartens, preferably in the same schools where they will start first grade.

REFERENCES

Alexander, K.L., Cook, M.A., & McDill, E.L. (1978). Curriculum tracking and educational stratification. *American Sociological Review, 43,* 47–66.

Alexander, K.L., & Entwisle, D.R. (1988). Achievement in the first two years of school: Patterns and processes. *Monographs of the Society for Research in Child Development, 53*(2, Serial No. 218).

Alexander, K.L., & Entwisle, D.R. (1996). Educational tracking in the early years: First grade placements and middle school constraints. In A.C. Kerckhoff (Ed.), *Generating social stratification: Toward a new research agenda* (pp. 83–113). New York: Westview Press.

Alexander, K.L., Entwisle, D.R., & Dauber, S.L. (1993). First grade classroom behavior: Its short- and long-term consequences for school performance. *Child Development, 64,* 801–814.

Alexander, K.L., Entwisle, D.R., & Dauber, S.L. (1994). *On the success of failure: A reassessment of the effects of retention in the primary grades.* New York: Cambridge University Press.

Alexander, K.L., Entwisle, D.R., & Horsey, C.S. (1997). From first grade forward: Early foundations of high school dropout. *Sociology of Education, 70,* 87–107.

Alexander, K.L., Entwisle, D.R., & Thompson, M.S. (1987). School performance, status relations and the structure of sentiment: Bringing the teacher back in. *American Sociological Review, 52,* 665–682.

Baltimore City Public Schools, Office of the Superintendent of Public Instruction. (1988, February). *School profiles: School year 1987–88.* Baltimore: Author.

Baltimore City Public Schools. (1991). *Maryland school performance program report, 1991: School system and schools—Baltimore City.* Baltimore: Author.

Barnett, W.S. (1996). Long-term effects of early childhood care and education on disadvantaged children's cognitive development and school success. *The Future of Children, 5*(3), 25–50.

Barrington, B.L., & Hendricks, B. (1989). Differentiating characteristics of high school graduates, dropouts, and nongraduates. *Journal of Educational Research, 82*(6), 309–319.

Berrueta-Clement, J.R., Schweinhart, L.J., Barnett, W.S., Epstein, A.S., & Weikart, D.P. (1984). *Changed lives: The effect of the Perry Preschool Program on youths through age 19.* (Monograph of the High/Scope Educational Research Foundation). Ypsilanti, MI: High Scope Press.

Bianchi, S.M. (1984). Children's progress through school: A research note. *Sociology of Education, 57,* 184–192.

Blau, P.M., & Duncan, O.D. (1967). *The American occupational structure.* New York: John Wiley & Sons.

Bloom, B.B. (1964). *Stability and change in human characteristics.* New York: John Wiley & Sons.

Booth, A., & Dunn, J.F. (1996). *Family–school links: How do they affect educational outcomes?* Mahwah, NJ: Lawrence Erlbaum Associates.

Broman, S.H., Nicholls, P.L., & Kennedy, W. (1985). *Preschool IQ: Prenatal and early developmental correlates.* Mahwah, NJ: Lawrence Erlbaum Associates.

Brooks-Gunn, J., Guo, G., Furstenberg, J., & Frank, F. (1993). Who drops out and who continues beyond high school? A 20-year follow-up of black urban youth. *Journal of Research on Adolescence, 3*(3), 271–294.

Butler, S.R., Marsh, H.W., Sheppard, M.J., & Sheppard, J.L. (1985). Seven year longitudinal study of the early prediction of reading achievement. *Journal of Educational Psychology, 77,* 349–361.

Cairns, R.B., Cairns, B.D., & Neckerman, H.J. (1989). Early school dropout: Configurations and determinants. *Child Development, 60,* 1437–1452.

California Achievement Test (CAT). (1979). *Technical bulletin 1, Forms C and D, levels 10–19.* New York: McGraw-Hill.

Central Advisory Council for Education. (1967). *Children and their primary schools.* London: Her Majesty's Stationery Office.

Coleman, J.S., Campbell, E.Q., Hobson, C.J., McPartland, J., Mood, A., Weinfeld, F.D., & York, R.L. (1966). *Equality of educational opportunity.* Washington, DC: U.S. Government Printing Office.

Consortium of Longitudinal Studies. (1983). *As the twig is bent: Lasting effect of preschool programs.* Mahwah, NJ: Lawrence Erlbaum Associates.

Dauber, S.L., Alexander, K.L., & Entwisle, D.R. (1993). Characteristics of retainees and early precursors of retention in grade: Who is held back? *Merrill-Palmer Quarterly, 39,* 326–343.

Dauber, S.L., Alexander, K.L., & Entwisle, D.R. (1996). Tracking and transitions through the middle grades: Channeling educational trajectories. *Sociology of Education, 69,* 290–307.

Dornbusch, S.M., & Scott, W.R. (1975). *Evaluation and the exercise of authority.* San Francisco: Jossey-Bass.

Eccles, J.S., Midgley, C., & Adler, T. (1984). Grade-related changes in the school environment: Effects on achievement motivation. In J. G. Nicholls (Ed.), *The development of achievement motivation* (pp. 283–331). Greenwich, CT: JAI Press.

Elder, G.H., Jr. (1974). *Children of the Great Depression: Social change in life experience.* Chicago: University of Chicago Press.

Ensminger, M.E., & Slusarcick, A.L. (1992). Paths to high school graduation or dropout: A longitudinal study of a first-grade cohort. *Sociology of Education, 65,* 95–113.

Entwisle, D.R. (1990). Schools and the adolescent. In S.S. Feldman & G.R. Elliott (Eds.), *At the threshold: The developing adolescent* (pp. 197–224). Cambridge, MA: Harvard University Press.

Entwisle, D.R. (1995). The role of schools in sustaining benefits of early childhood programs. *The Future of Children, 5*(3), 133–144.

Entwisle, D.R., & Alexander, K.L. (1988). Factors affecting achievement test scores and marks received by black and white first graders. *The Elementary School Journal, 88,* 449–471.

Entwisle, D.R., & Alexander, K.L. (1996). Family type and children's growth in reading and math over the primary grades. *Journal of Marriage and the Family, 58,* 341–355.

Entwisle, D.R., Alexander, K.L., Cadigan, D., & Pallas, A.M. (1987). Kindergarten experience: Cognitive effects or socialization? *American Educational Research Journal, 24,* 337–364.

Entwisle, D.R., Alexander, K.L., & Olson, L.S. (1994). The gender gap in math: Its possible origins in neighborhood effects. *American Sociological Review, 59,* 822–838.

Entwisle, D.R., Alexander, K.L., & Olson, L.S. (1997). *Children, schools and inequality.* New York: Westview Press.

Entwisle, D.R., Alexander, K.L., Pallas, A.M., & Cadigan, D. (1987). The emergent academic self-image of first graders: Its response to social structure. *Child Development, 58,* 1190–1206.

Entwisle, D.R., & Hayduk, L.A. (1988). Lasting effects of elementary school. *Sociology of Education, 61,* 147–159.

Finn, J.D. (1972). Expectations and the educational environment. *Review of Educational Research, 42,* 387–409.

Fitzsimmons, S.J., Cheever, J., Leonard, E., & Macunovich, D. (1969). School failures: Now and tomorrow. *Developmental Psychology, 1*(2), 134–146.

Furstenberg, F.F., Frank, F., Brooks-Gunn, J., & Morgan, S.P. (1987). *Adolescent mothers in later life.* New York: Cambridge University Press.

Hess, R.D., Holloway, S.D., Dickson, W.P., & Price, G.G. (1984). Maternal variables as predictors of children's school readiness and later achievement in vocabulary and mathematics in sixth grade. *Child Development, 55,* 1902–1912.

Heyneman, S.P., & Loxley, W.A. (1983). The effect of primary-school quality on academic achievement across twenty-nine high- and low-income countries. *American Journal of Sociology, 88*(6), 1162–1194.

Heyns, B. (1978). *Summer learning and the effects of schooling.* San Diego: Academic Press.

Husén, T. (1969). *Talent, opportunity and career.* Stockholm: Almqvist and Wiksell.

Jencks, C., Smith, M., Ackland, H., Bane, M.J., Cohen, D., Gintis, H., Heyns, B., & Michelson, S. (1972). *Inequality: A reassessment of the effect of failure and schooling in America.* New York: Basic Books.

Kerckhoff, A.C. (1993). *Diverging pathways: Social structure and career deflections.* New York: Cambridge University Press.

Kilgore, S.B. (1991). The organizational context of tracking in schools. *American Sociological Review, 56,* 189–203.

Kraus, P.E. (1973). *Yesterday's children.* New York: John Wiley & Sons.

Lazar, I., & Darlington, R. (1982). Lasting effects of early education: A report from the Consortium for Longitudinal Studies. *Monographs of the Society for Research in Child Development, 47*(2–3).

Lloyd, D.N. (1978). Prediction of school failure from third-grade data. *Educational and Psychological Measurement, 38,* 1193–1200.

Maryland State Department of Education. (1992). *Maryland school performance report, 1992: State and school systems.* Baltimore: Author.

Meyer, L.A. (1984). Long-term academic effects of the direct instruction project follow through. *The Elementary School Journal, 84*(4), 380–394.

Morris, J.D., Ehren, B.J., & Lenz, B.K. (1991). Building a model to predict which fourth through eighth graders will drop out in high school. *Journal of Experimental Education, 59,* 286–293.

38 Entwisle and Alexander

National Center for Education Statistics (NCES). (1994). *The Condition of Education*. NCES 94-104. Washington, DC: U.S. Department of Education.

Pallas, A.M., Entwisle, D.R., Alexander, K.L., & Stluka, M.F. (1994). Ability-group effects: Instructional, social or institutional? *Sociology of Education, 67*, 27–46.

Palmer, F.H. (1983). The Harlem study: Effects by type of training, age of training, and social class. In The Consortium for Longitudinal Studies (Ed.), *As the twig is bent: Lasting effects of preschool programs* (pp. 201–236). Mahwah, NJ: Lawrence Erlbaum Associates.

Pedersen, E., Faucher, T.A., & Eaton, W.W. (1978). A new perspective on the effects of first-grade teachers on children's subsequent adult status. *Harvard Educational Review, 48*, 1–31.

Pope, J., Lehrer, B., & Stevens, J. (1980). A multiphasic reading screening procedure. *Journal of Learning Disabilities, 13*, 98–102.

Reynolds, A.J. (1992). Grade retention and school adjustment: An explanatory analysis. *Educational Evaluation and Policy Analysis, 14*, 101–121.

Reynolds, A.J. (1994). Effects of a preschool plus follow-on intervention for children at risk. *Developmental Psychology, 30*, 787–804.

Richman, N., Stevenson, J., & Graham, P.J. (1982). *Pre-school to school: A behavioral study*. New York: Academic Press.

Roderick, M. (1993). *The path to dropping out: Evidence for intervention*. Westport, CT: Auburn House.

Rosenberg, M. (1979). *Conceiving the self*. New York: Basic Books.

Rosenberg, M., & Simmons, R.G. (1971). *Black and white self-esteem: The urban school child*. (Arnold M. and Caroline Rose Monograph Series). Washington, DC: American Sociological Association.

Sameroff, A. (1985). Foreword. In S. Broman, E. Bien, & P. Shaughnessy (Eds.), *Low achieving children* (pp. vii–xi). Mahwah, NJ: Lawrence Erlbaum Associates.

Schneider, B.L. (1980). *Production analysis of gains in achievement*. Paper presented at the annual meeting of the American Educational Research Association, Boston.

Schweinhart, L.J., & Weikart, D. (1983). The effects of the Perry Preschool Program on youths through age 15—A summary. In The Consortium for Longitudinal Studies (Ed.), *As the twig is bent: Lasting effects of preschool programs*. Mahwah, NJ: Lawrence Erlbaum Associates.

Seaver, W.B. (1973). Effects of naturally-induced teacher expectancies. *Journal of Personality and Social Psychology, 28*, 333–342.

Simmons, R.G., & Blyth, D.A. (1987). *Moving into adolescence: The impact of pubertal change and school context*. Hawthorn, NY: Aldine de Gruyter.

Simner, M.L., & Barnes, M.J. (1991). Relationship between first-grade marks and the high school dropout problem. *The Journal of School Psychology, 29*, 331–335.

Stephens, J.M. (1956). *Educational psychology*. Austin, TX: Holt, Rinehart & Winston.

Stevenson, H.W., & Newman, R.S. (1986). Long-term prediction of achievement and attitudes in mathematics and reading. *Child Development, 57*, 646–659.

Stroup, A.L., & Robins, L.N. (1972). Elementary school predictors of high school dropout among black males. *Sociology of Education, 45*, 212–222.

Tienda, M. (1991). Poor people and poor places: Deciphering neighborhood effects on poverty outcomes. In J. Huber (Ed.), *Macro-micro linkages in sociology* (pp. 244–262). Thousand Oaks, CA: Sage Publications.

Wadsworth, M.E. (1986). Effects of parenting style and preschool experience on children's verbal attainment: Results of a British longitudinal study. *Early Childhood Research Quarterly, 1*, 237–238.

Weller, L.D., Schnittjer, C.J., & Tuten, B.A. (1992). Predicting achievement in grades three through ten using the Metropolitan Readiness Test. *Journal of Research in Childhood Education, 6*(2), 121–129.

Chapter 3

Assessing Readiness

Samuel J. Meisels

In the fall of 1989, President George Bush and the governors of the 50 United States met in Charlottesville, Virginia, for the first Education Summit held since nearly the beginning of the 20th century. Out of this meeting came a renewed federal commitment to improving educational achievement and increasing the United States' commitment to students, teachers, and schools. It was also the occasion for establishing six National Education Goals. First among these goals was the following: "All children in America will start school ready to learn" (National Education Goals Panel, 1991).

In subsequent years and through a new presidential administration, the language of this goal was changed slightly but the message remained constant. The way in which young children begin school is a major national issue. Specifically, it is an objective of the United States that young children are ready to learn when they begin school.

Since the late 1980s, this simple declarative sentence—all children will start school ready to learn—has been the source of numerous meetings, conferences, papers, dissertations, studies, and policies. The National Education Goals Panel appointed a Resource Group and two Technical Review Panels to clarify the meaning of this deceptively simple sounding statement. Many states held "Goal 1 Conferences" to report on their progress in meeting the goal and to garner support for activities intended to improve young children's school readiness. Papers and dissertations concerning various aspects of readiness were written (Browning, 1997; Graue, 1992, 1993; Kagan, 1990; Lopez & Hochberg, 1993; Meisels,

The preparation of this chapter was supported in part by a contract among the U.S. Department of Education, the Office of Educational Research and Improvement (OERI), and the Center for the Improvement of Early Reading Achievement (CIERA) at the University of Michigan.

1992a; Nelson, 1997; Phillips, 1992; Willer & Bredekamp, 1990). The "Readiness Goal," as it came to be known, was even credited with providing an overall framework and incentive to the National Center for Education Statistics (NCES) as it began planning an Early Childhood Longitudinal Study. This study, begun in the fall of 1998, is following more than 23,000 children from kindergarten through fifth grade.

Ernest Boyer, the former president of the Carnegie Foundation for the Advancement of Teaching and the first chair of the Goal 1 Resource Group, described the improvement of the United States' children's readiness as an "epochal task" (Boyer, 1991, p. 125). He claimed that readiness was

> A cause around which everyone can rally. For the first time in our history the President and governors from all fifty states have defined a goal of transcendent national importance, one concerned not just with the equality of schools but, in the larger sense, with the future of the nation. (p. 125)

This chapter addresses several key issues regarding transition to kindergarten and readiness for school. It begins with a discussion of the Readiness Goal to try to clarify why Boyer and other researchers would associate such high stakes with its realization. Next, the chapter turns to the task of defining readiness. Since the Charlottesville Summit, researchers, practitioners, and policy makers have stumbled over the definition of this term. Four competing definitions of readiness are presented, followed by four approaches to assessing readiness that are consistent with these definitions. Finally, the chapter closes by suggesting three aphorisms that have the potential for clarifying the task of assessing readiness in early childhood.

THE READINESS GOAL

In the 4 or 5 years leading up to the Charlottesville Summit, attention was increasingly focused on young children's early school experiences. In particular, concern among professionals was rising about the use of readiness tests and other assessments to label, track, and sometimes retain children in kindergarten before they reached first grade. Following the release of *A Nation at Risk* in 1983 (National Commission on Excellence in Education, 1983), efforts to raise standards and to make school curricula more challenging swept the United States. One unintended outcome of this activity was an escalation of academic demands at the outset of schooling. Described as *academic trickle down* or as the *push down curriculum* (Bredekamp & Shepard, 1989; Shepard & Smith, 1986), the expectations and even the curricular materials of the later grades began to infiltrate kindergartens. Some observers described the kindergartens that were affected by these changes as "boot camps" in which "students are inducted and instructed in a narrow academic curriculum to prepare them for the demands of first grade and future schooling" (Ellwein, Walsh, Eads, & Miller, 1991, p. 159). Many local school districts and state departments of education decided that children should be tested upon entry to kindergarten to determine their readiness for school (Meisels, 1987, 1989). Large numbers of children who failed these tests were placed in extra-year prekindergarten programs, retained in kindergarten for another year, or asked to stay home from school until they were a year older and more mature.

Before long, early childhood professionals began to become alarmed about these practices. Condemnatory reports were issued by the National Association for the Education of Young Children (NAEYC; 1988, 1990), the National Association of Elementary School Principals (1990), the National Association of Early Childhood Specialists in State Departments of Education (1987), the National Association of State Boards of Education (1988, 1991), and the National Commission on Children (1992). The principal message of these reports was that the methods, materials, and logic of educating older students should not be imposed on young children. The following were criticized: policies that increased attention to academic outcomes at the expense of children's exploration, discovery, and play; methods that focused on large-group activities and completion of one-dimensional worksheets and workbooks in place of actual engagement with concrete objects and naturally occurring experiences of the world; and directives that emphasized the use of group-administered, computer-scored, multiple-choice achievement tests to determine a child's starting place in school rather than assessments that rely on active child engagement, teacher judgment, and clinical opinion. By 1989, when the first Education Summit was held, the early childhood community was poised to take steps to clarify how young children should be treated when they begin school by respecting the dynamics of children's development.

Unfortunately, as beginning school policies became increasingly politicized, instead of clarity, confusion and mistrust arose. Politicians sitting on the National Education Goals Panel asked the Resource Panel and Technical Planning Group members why they could not just define *readiness* in simple terms that they and their constituents could understand. It did not seem to be a very difficult task. But for many researchers in the field, defining readiness was and remains a problem. Pianta and Walsh, noting the wide variability among different children's abilities, stated that the concept of readiness is "useless" (1996, p. 33). The Goal 1 Technical Planning Group members did not go this far, but in a report that focused on early childhood development and learning, subtitled "Toward Common Views and Vocabulary," they noted that their report would assiduously avoid use of the term readiness:

> A word that often implies a single dimension and single standard of development and learning. To the contrary, because individual child performance is multidimensional, highly variable across the dimensions, episodic, and culturally and contextually influenced, the establishment of any single "readiness" threshold is misleading and dangerous. (Kagan, Moore, & Bredekamp, 1995, p. 6)

Not all aspects of the Readiness Goal were controversial. Three objectives were attached to Goal 1, and little dispute surfaced around them. They are as follows:

1. All disadvantaged and disabled children will have access to high quality and developmentally appropriate preschool programs to help them prepare for school.
2. Every parent in America will be a child's first teacher and will devote time each day to helping his or her preschool child learn; parents will have access to the training and support they need to accomplish this.

3. Children will receive the nutrition and health care needed to arrive at school with healthy minds and bodies, and the number of low birthweight babies will be significantly reduced through enhanced prenatal health systems. (U.S. Department of Education, 1991, p. 61)

Uncontroversial as these statements are, relatively few new federal resources have been earmarked for programs intended to achieve these critical objectives. Also unclear is the relationship between these objectives and the overall school readiness goal. If these objectives were achieved, would all children enter school ready to learn? Are these objectives correlates of readiness? Are they precursors? In some respects, these objectives may hold the key to ensuring a successful transition to school for many children, but they were never the subject of any explicit focus or program activity.

The main activity surrounded the goal statement itself, not the subsidiary objectives. Goal 1 seemed to arouse fears among many individuals who were close to policy and practice in early childhood. Some individuals pointed out that all children are ready to learn from birth and that they do not need to wait until they are 5 years of age to be ready to learn (Meisels, 1995). Other researchers stated that the goal ignores individual differences in learning and that it will never be the case that all children will attain the same level of performance at a single culturally defined point in time. Individual differences and variations in development associated with both endogenous and exogenous factors make a mockery of chronological benchmarks when they are applied across the board to all children (Pianta & Walsh, 1996). Moreover, the term "readiness" is conceptually confusing. Is "readiness" something that we wait for? Is it something that people impose? Is it a within-the-child phenomenon or something outside the child (Meisels, 1996)? Finally, the simplistic or mechanistic interpretation of readiness that can be derived from the goal contains the potential for encouraging harmful policies for young children. In an educational world that is oriented toward efficiency and accountability, it is easy to imagine that someone will be penalized if the year 2000 is reached and some children are not ready for school. Often, the people who are least advantaged in U.S. society are blamed when public policies intended to assist them go wrong.

Schorr (1997) encapsulated many of these concerns about readiness in a series of questions that focus on one of the main issues provoked by the first goal—how will readiness be assessed? She asked the following:

• Can children's school readiness be assessed without doing them harm?

• Can readiness assessment avoid labeling or stigmatizing children?

• Will preschool programs become distorted if they "teach to the test"?

• Is it possible for readiness testing to recognize the unique character of early development and learning?

• If large numbers of children are not ready for school, will this be viewed as a problem in the child or within the community?

These questions are extremely important. Not only do they raise issues that are central to implementing the Readiness Goal, but they also remind us of the inappropriate testing of young children that was prevalent in the years prior to the Education Summit. Remembering Skinner's axiom that "what is taught often tends to be simply what can be measured by tests and examinations" (1968, p. 235), many early childhood observers feared that a focus on assessing readiness would influence the structure of early childhood programs devised to implement the goal.

The balance of this chapter addresses these fears and these questions. First, competing definitions of readiness are presented. Then, the assessment implications of these definitions are explored. These implications are followed by a discussion and conclusions.

DEFINITIONS OF READINESS

Readiness has a substantial history in modern education. Cuban (1992) reported that teachers in progressive schools in the early 20th century saw the acquisition of information about a child's readiness as very important to their practice. Much like today, they viewed testing as a means of determining a child's preparedness for school and as a way to stratify children into various ability groupings. Cuban stated,

> By 1919, for just kindergarten and primary grades, there were already 84 standardized tests. Intelligence testing in kindergarten for placement in groups there and in the first grade was enhanced by the invention of readiness tests that aimed at sorting those five-year-olds that could make the transition to the first grade from those who could not. The creation of subprimary classes . . . became common ways that Progressive educators managed those five-year-olds who were unready for the first grade. By the end of the 1920s, any elementary school that considered itself modern invested staff time and money in testing and ability grouping in kindergarten and first grade. (1992, p. 188)

Over time, views of testing and readiness waxed and waned, but the idea that assessment data could be used to help teachers be more effective remained relatively constant. As educational psychology became more dominant in the 1950s and 1960s, more emphasis was placed on the hierarchical structure of knowledge. Tyler noted that readiness to learn is derived from analyzing the knowledge and skills required by new cognitive activities: "Once these components are known, they can be arranged in a hierarchy that proceeds from lower to higher levels of knowledge" (1964, p. 238). Bruner's view was similar, though with a twist. He pointed out that the idea of readiness is a "mischievous half-truth . . . largely because it turns out that one *teaches* readiness or provides opportunities for its nurture, one does not simply wait for it" (1966, p. 29). In other words, a child who is ready to learn will not learn unless he or she is taught or unless the conditions are propitious for the child to learn on his or her own. Readiness is not an end in itself; it is the beginning of an active teaching and learning engagement. Waiting for children to demonstrate their readiness by learning something spontaneously without some intervention or preparation of the environment is, in Bruner's view, fruitless.

Bruner's (1966) perspective casts light on the fundamental relativity that is inherent in readiness. If readiness consists of a mastery of simpler skills that permit a person to reach higher or more complex skills, one child's readiness may be another child's long-ago accomplishment or another child's yet-to-be-achieved success. Whenever readiness is defined in terms of a specific level of accomplishment, children who have not had similar life experiences or opportunities for learning are being omitted from this definition. This relativity has posed major difficulties in reaching consensus on a definition of readiness.

Teachers' Definitions

Early in the goals process, the Carnegie Foundation for the Advancement of Teaching surveyed more than 20,000 teachers in all 50 states regarding their perspectives about the readiness of the United States' children. This survey, which was distributed in August 1991, was completed by fewer than 35% of the potential respondents ($N = 7,141$). Because of this low rate of response, its findings are highly questionable. One of the central findings, which Boyer called "troubling, ominous really" (1991, p. 7), is that the respondents claimed that 35% of the United States' children are not ready for school. Forty-two percent of the teachers said that the situation is getting worse compared with 5 years ago; only 25% said that the situation was improving.

Methodologically, not only did the return rate of this major policy-making study threaten its validity, but also the way in which the survey questions were phrased raised significant concerns. Specifically, the survey did not recognize the fundamental relativity that is at the heart of readiness. Teachers were asked to give the percentage of students who were not ready to participate successfully in kindergarten. But no definition of *participate successfully* was provided, and no way of knowing the differences among kindergartens across the United States was available. Similarly, teachers were asked to respond to questions, such as "How serious a problem was language richness [or emotional maturity, or general knowledge, or social confidence, or moral awareness, or physical well-being] for those students who entered school not ready to learn?" These items beg the question of the meaning of "ready to learn" and also assume a common perspective about emotional maturity, social confidence, moral awareness, and so forth. Such data add little to our knowledge about school readiness.

In an attempt to obtain a better understanding of teachers' views about readiness, the Goal 1 Technical Planning Group designed a survey that was administered by the NCES (1993a). The survey, known as a fast response survey, was sent to 1,448 kindergarten teachers. The sample was selected from NCES's Common Core Data School Universe file, which contains information on 85,000 public schools, approximately half of which have kindergarten classes. The schools were selected based on school size, percentage of students eligible for free and reduced lunch, and percentage of minority students. Data collection was completed by April 1993, with a return rate of 95%. The principal subscales included in this brief survey were public school kindergarten teachers' judgments and beliefs about school readiness ($\alpha = .632$), teachers' judgments about the qualities of school readiness ($\alpha = .883$), and information about teachers' practices in kindergarten ($\alpha = .524$). In addition, background characteristics of the teachers were also surveyed.

Rather than asking teachers to assume a common definition of readiness, this survey sought to construct the teachers' views of readiness from a series of questions that explored their opinions about early childhood education. For example, when asked to state how important each of 15 qualities was for a child to be ready for kindergarten, teachers indicated that the following characteristics were essential: A child should be physically healthy, rested, and well-nourished; able to communicate needs, wants, and thoughts verbally; and enthusiastic and curious in approaching new activities (NCES, 1993a). Figure 3.1 displays the ranked percentages of teachers' ratings of these qualities.

The characteristics considered least important by the respondents were good problem-solving skills (only 24% selected this as most important), ability to identify primary colors and basic shapes (24%), ability to use pencils and paint brushes (21%), knowledge of the alphabet (10%), and ability to count to 20 (7%) (NCES, 1993). Strikingly, these responses run counter to conventional opinions of typical readiness characteristics. For example, Powell reported that readiness for school typically embraces "a specific and often narrow set of cognitive and language skills, usually assessed by determining whether children can master such tasks as identifying four colors by name, copying a square, and repeating a series of four or five numbers without assistance" (1995, p. 15). But the teachers in this sample did not value these indicators as highly as the more social characteristics noted in Figure 3.1.

Other items in the survey showed a similar lack of emphasis on conventional markers of readiness. Table 3.1 contains eight statements that had the highest and lowest agreement of the respondents with various views of readiness. Using a five-point scale ranging from *strongly disagree* (1) to *strongly agree* (5), teachers were

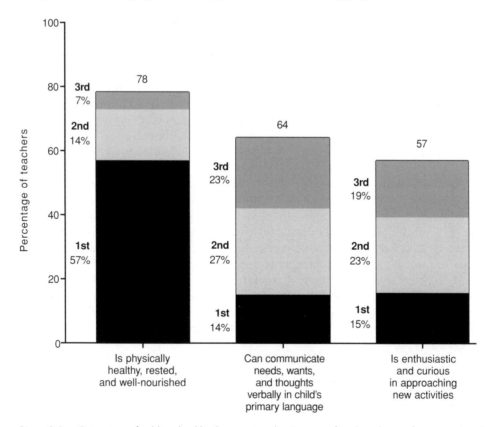

Figure 3.1.   Percentage of public school kindergarten teachers' ratings of qualities that are first, second, and third most important for a child to be ready for school. (Source: National Center for Education Statistics [NCES], 1993.)

Table 3.1.   Means of high and low items on Teachers' Views of Readiness scale

Item	Mean	SD
Parents should read to their children and play counting games at home regularly.	4.9	.4
One of the best ways to help children learn to read is by reading to them.	4.8	.5
I can enhance children's readiness by providing experiences they need to build important skills.	4.6	.7
Readiness comes as children grow and mature; you can't push it.	4.4	.9
I assume that by the end of the kindergarten year all children will be ready for first grade.	2.5	1.2
Most children should learn to read in kindergarten.	2.3	1.1
The best way to learn how to read is to practice matching letters and sounds repeatedly.	2.1	1.1
Homework should be given in kindergarten almost every day.	2.1	1.3

SD, standard deviation.
Sources: National Center for Education Statistics (NCES) (1993a) and Nelson (1997).

asked to indicate their concordance with a list of 17 statements. The means for these statements (see Nelson, 1997, for calculations of means) show a high value on interaction with children and a low emphasis on more typically academic concerns (i.e., homework, matching letters and sounds, drill and practice). However, the statements with the highest agreements also reveal a significant ambiguity among the teachers who were included in this sample. They embraced both an active learning position ("I can enhance children's readiness by providing experiences they need to build important skills") and a more passive approach ("Readiness comes as children grow and mature; you can't push it"). These contradictory outlooks or ideologies about teaching and learning may relate to whether the referent of the item is academic or social. For example, most teachers expressed a greater concern with a child's ability to take turns and share (64% indicated that this was a strong emphasis) than with teaching children to read (44% agreed with the statement that kindergarten children should not be given reading instruction unless they show an interest). In short, readiness among these teachers seemed to relate more to social indicators than to academic concerns, although among schools with high levels of poverty and with teachers who are African American there was a higher value on academic outcomes and marginally lower emphasis on social indicators. Nevertheless, only approximately one quarter of the teachers (27%) believed that by the end of the kindergarten year all children would be ready to advance to first grade. Given this conclusion, it is critical to arrive at a clear conception of what readiness is and how to assess it so that children who need early intervention receive it and so that all children have better opportunities for success.

CONCEPTIONS OF READINESS

Despite the high return rate and the excellent quality of the NCES survey, a common definition of readiness remains elusive. Indeed, four conceptions of readiness have been advanced in the literature: idealist/nativist, empiricist/environmental, social constructivist, and interactionist. A discussion of these varied approaches may bring some clarity to the issues surrounding readiness.

Idealist/Nativist

One common view of readiness holds that children are ready to start school when they reach a level of maturity that enables them to sit quietly, focus on work, engage with their peers in socially acceptable ways, and accept direction from adults. Development is only marginally influenced by external forces; endogenous factors control behavior and learning, which are closely linked. This view is often ascribed to adherents of Arnold Gesell's maturational philosophy (see Ilg & Ames, 1972) and can be characterized in a number of different ways. It is an idealist philosophy in the sense that it conceptualizes development in highly abstract terms; it is almost Platonic in its view of how growth occurs. Rather than focus on the impact of such external elements as parental nurture, the economic environment, educational inputs, or other social factors, this perspective privileges the internal dynamics of the child and consigns exogenous factors to the background. This view does not deny the power of the environment to alter a child's life, but it asserts the primacy of the ideal aspects of development over all other elements, making the latter subject to the control of the former. The true meaning of development, therefore, lies in the ideal sphere of inner development rather than in the phenomenal areas of external activity.

Described as a romantic view by Kohlberg and Mayer (1972), this perspective posits an internal clock within the child that continues to advance despite the activity that surrounds it. Educators' roles are to nurture the child's natural unfolding, much as Plato metaphorically described the task of the educator to be that of tending a garden in order to bring to fruition the seeds that are planted there. Smith and Shepard's (1988) term for this approach to early learning and development is *nativism*. They noted that nativism holds that "nearly all functions of the organism, including the mental ones such as perception, are innate rather than acquired through the senses" (1988, p. 332). School readiness can thus be defined as the task of allowing the psychological forces underlying learning to unfold so that physiological and constitutional structures can eventually emerge.

In short, the idealist/nativist perspective on readiness holds that children are ready to learn when they are ready. There is little that can be done to accelerate this process. Rather, as a result of an internal, organismic process that is independent of environmental manipulation, children will eventually be able to concentrate in school, focus on activities that are novel, relate appropriately to adults and peers, and gain satisfaction from being part of a community of students.

Empiricist/Environmental

In contrast to the idealist/nativist view, an empiricist/environmental conception defines readiness entirely in terms of the practical characteristics of the child's behaviors. Instead of a "mentalist" perspective of an unfolding, endogenous learner, the empiricist or materialist view focuses on the external evidence of learning. In this Lockean picture, readiness is commensurate with knowing colors, shapes, one's address, and how to spell one's name; with identifying one object which is similar to another that is embedded in an array of dissimilar objects; and with counting to 10, saying the letters of the alphabet, and behaving in a polite and socially expected manner. Instead of focusing on the mental structure of the child, this approach concentrates on what the child can do and how the child behaves.

Also known as a *cultural transmission* (Kohlberg & Mayer, 1972) or *environmentalist* model (Smith & Shepard, 1988), this view reflects an externally driven approach to development. In it, the child's development is assumed to be controlled almost totally by events and conditions that dominate his or her social and cultural world. School readiness is characterized by a cumulative skills model that posits a hierarchy of tasks that culminate in a final task, and in which intermediate tasks cannot be mastered before earlier goals are achieved (Gagné, 1970).

Kagan (1990) called this approach *readiness for school* as contrasted to *readiness for learning*. She pointed out that this view emphasizes specific skills or experiences that are valued as the precursors to successful school experience, rather than as ends in themselves. Children acquire these skills and information through external guidance or teaching. Those who cannot demonstrate these skills are not ready for school and may need special assistance or enrollment in such extra-year programs as "Developmental Kindergartens" or "Young 5s" programs (this is also the solution of choice for children who are not ready in the idealist/nativist perspective). Fundamental to this view is the belief that readiness is an absolute state of affairs (see Meisels, 1996)—an end point that children and teachers can strive for—and that the criteria for readiness are stable and universal.

Social Constructivist

A different approach emerges from the perspective that takes seriously the basic relativity that characterizes readiness among young children. This view rejects the notion that readiness is something within the child (idealism) or something absolute and external to the child against which the child must be evaluated (empiricism). Rather, this perspective sees readiness in social and cultural terms. Readiness is

> A set of ideas or meanings constructed by people in communities, families, and schools as they participate in the kindergarten experience. These ideas come out of community values and expectations and are related to individual children in terms of attributes like their age, sex, and preschool experience. (Graue, 1992, p. 226)

This view shifts the focus of assessment away from the child and toward the community in which the child is living. Specifically, perceptions of teachers, parents, and others regarding a child's readiness become the foreground for this discussion. Love noted,

> Developmental status by itself does not determine readiness because the skills and abilities necessary for school success may vary substantially from one school to another, or even from one classroom to another within a school. For a given set of school expectations, there can even be considerable variation in the *specific* skills and abilities that lead to successful school performance. (1995, p. 1)

Because of these factors, the typical definition of readiness provides little or no guidance on how to resolve differences that are found among communities, schools, or even classrooms.

In a study of three teachers in three quite different schools, Graue (1993) found that readiness was most accurately defined in terms of community and contextual demands, rather than absolute characteristics of children. Smith and Shepard (1988) also found a range of opinions about readiness without having to leave a single school district. In their study of six schools located in the same school district, they discovered that teachers' beliefs about readiness varied substantially and could be described and ordered along a dimension of nativism. These opinions were influenced by local views of school readiness that sprung from the particular values, expectations, and socioeconomic mix of the school, as well as teachers' prior dispositions, training, and personal experiences.

In other words, a social constructivist perspective on readiness abjures absolute definitions and looks to the setting for its definition of readiness. A child who may be ready in one community or even in one school in the same community may not be ready in another school or community. Readiness is in the eye of the beholder.

Interactionist

The final perspective on readiness can be described as interactionist. It incorporates information about the child as well as information about the milieu in which the child is reared and is taught. In this view, readiness is a *bidirectional* concept. It focuses on children's learning and on schools' capacities to meet the individual needs of their students. Stated formally,

> Readiness and early school achievement are bi-directional concepts that focus both on children's current skills, knowledge, and abilities and on the conditions of the environment in which children are reared and taught. Because different children are prepared for different experiences, and different children respond differentially to apparently similar environmental inputs, readiness is a relative term. Although it can be applied to individual children, it is not something in the child, and it is not something in the curriculum. It is a product of the interaction between children's prior experiences, their genetic endowment, their maturational status, and the whole range of environmental and cultural experiences that they encounter. (Meisels, 1996, p. 410)

This is a comprehensive view of readiness. With a dual focus on the child and the environment in which the child is being taught, it integrates an emphasis on child development with a recognition that the perceptions of the individuals in the child's environment shape the content of what is taught, learned, and valued. In this view, the interaction relates to how the child's activity alters the expectations of the environment even as the environment modifies what the child is able to accomplish. Stated differently, this perspective addresses both the child's contributions to schooling and the school's contribution to the child. It is directed toward future possibilities rather than past deficiencies. It is based on a commitment to helping all children become learners, and it suggests that educational success will depend on the emergence of a reciprocal relationship between school and child, this relationship to be mentored by the child's teacher.

The interactional view of readiness reformulates apparent opposites so that they coexist instead of conflict. For example, children's skills are not considered to be solely inborn or primarily externally contingent; rather, they reflect joint contributions of inheritance and experience. Similarly, educational interventions are not viewed as strictly individualistic (created in response to a child's unique set of skills, experiences, accomplishments, or needs) or as "one size fits all." Instead, the interactionist view assumes a set of clear and explicit standards that admit a range of continua in their realization. Teachers apply these standards through documenting children's performance in school, evaluating that performance in relationship to external standards, formulating plans for working with children based on this information, and then repeating the process of documentation and evaluation over time, based on cumulative experiences. In this manner, the central axes in the readiness equation—the child and the educational environment—are mutually altered and transformed.

Summary

These four characterizations of the readiness construct are essential for understanding what is meant by readiness. Similarly, a definition of the readiness construct is necessary in order to take the next step of determining how to assess young children's readiness—that is, how to evaluate their status at the outset of school. Conventionally, readiness has been assessed by tests that are variations of achievement tests. The principal difference between readiness tests and achievement tests is temporal: Readiness tests are administered at the outset of the school year; achievement tests are usually given at the end. The content of the two types of tests is related in that readiness tests more or less reflect earlier versions of skills that are assessed later by achievement tests at more advanced levels. Fundamentally, readiness tests depict a child's relative preparedness to take advantage of a specific program or curriculum by describing the child's current level of skill achievement or preacademic preparedness.

MODELS OF ASSESSSMENT

After the 1989 Education Summit, the problem of determining how to assess readiness moved to center stage among policy makers. If the United States was indeed to have confidence that all children will enter school ready to learn, some form of readiness assessment must be possible for purposes of accountability. Different constructs of readiness call for different approaches to assessment. Four different models of assessment are discussed in this section, corresponding to the four definitions presented previously.

Idealist/Nativist

The idealist/nativist theoretical conception sees readiness as a within-the-child phenomenon. Whether a child is ready for school is a function of maturational processes inherent in the child that eventually enable the child to perform adequately in school. The chief exponent of this view is Arnold Gesell and his followers (see Gesell & Amatruda, 1941; Ilg & Ames, 1972), although this view is also part of the widely held "common wisdom" about childhood development on which many parents, professionals, and policy makers rely (see Barth & Mitchell, 1992). The Gesell perspective views development as occurring in predictable stages that are regulated by forces internal to the child. Environmental inputs have little impact on this natural unfolding. However, because development takes place according to prescribed stages, it is possible to measure relative progress of children as they move through these stages by means of specialized assessments.

The use of the Gesell School Readiness Test (Haines, Ames, & Gillespie, 1980) to determine whether a child should enter kindergarten, stay at home (thus enjoying a "gift of time"), or be placed in an extra-year program ("developmental kindergarten") became a *cause célèbre* among early childhood educators in the late 1980s and early 1990s. Estimates of the frequency of use of the Gesell in early childhood programs were very high (see Graue & Shepard, 1989), and growing numbers of children were held back at the outset of school because of their performance on this test (see Meisels, 1987, 1989, 1992a). The situation became so charged that some states began to raise the required minimum age of entry for kindergarten to account for the "unreadiness" that was being uncovered among their state's population (Meisels, 1992a). National talk shows and network news magazines began to feature programs in which children and parents testified about the negative impact of testing children at the outset of school. In some states, such as Michigan, the Attorney General was even called on to affirm that children be allowed to enroll in kindergarten "despite the recommendation of school district personnel that [they] attend an alternative 'Early 5' or 'Developmental Kindergarten' program" (State of Michigan, 1987, p. 1).

At issue were both the construct being assessed and the assessment itself. Maturational theory was an outgrowth of the 1920s and 1930s, when the study of child development was truly in its infancy. The assessment that began to enjoy great popularity in the mid-1980s was derived from work that Gesell had done more than one half of a century before, although little cumulative empirical research was available to establish its accuracy or stability. Over the years, maturational theory was surpassed by more complex and better researched theories that were at odds with both the premises and conclusions of this view (Fischer & Silvern, 1985; White, 1996).

Many scholars began to report studies demonstrating the problems of misclassification attributable to the Gesell. (See Graue and Shepard, 1989, and Meisels, 1989, for reviews of these studies.) An example of the kind of problems encountered in the research literature can be seen in a study intended to defend the validity of the Gesell (Walker, 1992). This investigation used a multitrait, multimethod approach to show the relationship between 4- and 6-year-old children's scores on the Gesell Developmental Assessment (GDA; a version of the Gesell School Readiness Test) and a variety of outcome measures at age 8½ years. However, the study showed that children's average performance on the GDA fell below chronological age expectations. The discrepancy ranged from 2 months at age 4 to nearly 7 months by age 6.

Findings of such magnitude and consistency would normally suggest that the GDA is in need of recalibration, because in a representative sample it is unlikely that so many children would be delayed (see Meisels, 1992b, from which this argument is derived). However, Walker (1992) concluded that the problem lies within the children rather than within the test. Lichtenstein (1990) reported similar findings for the full Gesell School Readiness Screening Test (GSRST), of which the GDA is a prominent element. But unlike Walker, he interpreted the greater than 50% discrepancy between "developmental" and chronological age as evidence of the GSRST's miscalibration.

In Walker's (1992) study, it could be objected that the GDA's unexpected relationship to chronological age is vindicated by its correlations with follow-up assessments. Such correlations, if high enough, would indeed place the onus on the children rather than on the assessment. But before this conclusion can be drawn, two others must be established. First, it must be shown that the correlations that were obtained were not influenced by teachers' prior knowledge or exposure. Lichtenstein (1990) demonstrated that teachers' "tendency to perceive children as unready is directly proportional to the extent of Gesell Institute training received" (p. 371). In other words, low scores on the GDA may have set up an expectancy among the children's teachers concerning the children's performance. Only a completely "blind" trial, in which the Gesell findings were concealed from the preschool and follow-up teachers and/or examiners and these examiners were uninformed about Gesell teachings and practice, could eliminate this powerful source of potential bias. However, the examiners in Walker's study were not all blind to the children's previous results, and they were all trained in Gesell ideology and practice.

Second, given that bias is controlled, it must be demonstrated that the preschool indicator, the GDA, is highly predictive of the classifications obtained on the 8-year-old measures. Walker's (1992) study showed that, in the vast majority of cases, children changed classifications in the follow-up assessment. Indeed, on three of the four outcome measures, the preschool ratings were lower than the average performance across all quartiles (in one area, reading, the prediction was identical to the outcome). Thus, it appears that the GDA's underestimation of children's abilities—actually, a reverse "Lake Wobegon effect" (Koretz, 1988)—is highlighted by these comparisons. These data, similar to so many other independent studies of the Gesell, do not support its use for assessing readiness. Ironically, through its consistent finding of developmental ratings below chronological age expectancies, the study asks us to believe in the test rather than in the child—a peculiar position indeed for advocates of developmentally appropriate practice.

Empiricist/Environmental

The empiricist/environmental perspective holds that readiness is something that lies outside the child. It consists of several modal skills, behaviors, and personality traits that can be evaluated empirically and that are considered basic precursors to successful school performance in young children. Assessment of such skills has a long history that can be traced to the reading readiness tests of the 1930s and is still alive today. Stallman and Pearson (1990) pointed out that these tests were intended to measure traits and achievements that were correlated with readiness for first-grade instruction. Over the years, the major tests of early school achievement—consisting of the Iowa Tests of Basic Skills, the Comprehensive Tests of Basic Skills, the California Achievement Test, and the Stanford Early School Achievement Test—have not differed significantly from one another in form ("fill in the bubbles and ovals"), psychometrics (they are often validated in a self-referential manner against one another), construct (skills are reduced to decontextualized subparts), and content (primarily low-level preliteracy and literacy items). Table 3.2 shows the subtests of these tests. Not only do the tests resemble one another, but they are also similar to the original reading readiness tests that were formulated more than half a century ago. Stallman and Pearson found that these tests assess children "on isolated skills in decontexturalized settings rather than on reading tasks in situations in which they are asked to behave like readers" (1990, p. 38). These tests also focus on recognition skills, not production or even identification. This omits any view of reading as a process of active cognitive construction.

Table 3.2.   Subtests of kindergarten achievement tests

ITBS[a]	CTBS[b]	CAT[c]	MAT[d]	SESAT[e]
Word analysis	Sound recognition	Word analysis	Reading	Sound recognition
Vocabulary	Vocabulary	Vocabulary	Language	Words
Language	Comprehension	Comprehension	Science	Reading
Listening	Visual recognition	Language expression	Social studies	Letters
Math	Math	Math	Math	Math
				Environment
				Listening

From Meisels, S.J. (1996). Performance in context: Assessing children's achievement at the outset of school. In A.J. Sameroff & M.M. Haith (Eds.), *The five to seven year shift: The age of reason and responsibility* (pp. 410–431). Chicago: University of Chicago Press; reprinted by permission.

[a]ITBS, Iowa Tests of Basic Skills.
[b]CTBS, Comprehensive Tests of Basic Skills.
[c]CAT, California Achievement Test.
[d]MAT, Metropolitan Achievement Test.
[e]SESAT, Stanford Early School Achievement Test.

In addition to these early school achievement tests, another exemplar of the empiricist model in assessment is found in conventional readiness tests, a large number of which are available. Although tests of early school achievement may be narrow in terms of the domains they cover and the methods they use to obtain information from children (i.e., they are primarily group-administered tests that rely exclusively on pencil-and-paper methods), readiness tests are often individually administered and may sometimes include a variety of responses (e.g., building with blocks, gross motor tasks, drawing). In this respect, some readiness tests resemble developmental screening tests, which are administered to individual children and include diverse response formats. However, the similarity ends there because the content of these two types of tests is dissimilar, and the use that can be made of the data obtained from the tests is quite discrepant. The purpose of developmental screening for 3-, 4-, and 5-year-olds is to assess children briefly to identify those who may be at risk for school failure. Criteria for developmental screening instruments are that they be brief, efficient, inexpensive, objectively scored, reliable, valid, culture- and language-fair, and broadly developmental in focus (Meisels, with Atkins-Burnett, 1994). In contrast, most readiness tests are criterion-referenced, unstandardized, and lack data concerning reliability and validity. Developmental screening instruments serve a critical purpose in early childhood by identifying children who may need special services so that intervention can begin early. (See Meisels, Marsden, Wiske, & Henderson, 1997, for an example of a well-standardized screening instrument, or Meisels, with Atkins-Burnett, 1994, and Meisels & Provence, 1989, for reviews of a variety of screening instruments.)

Perhaps the greatest problem with readiness tests is their lack of validity. This problem creates substantial danger of misclassification. One study of four readiness tests found that children who were poor, male, African American, and young in relation to their peers were much more likely to be classified by these tests as unready or at risk. "When kindergarten screening tests are used for placement decisions, one may witness disproportionate placement of such children in special programs. . . . We are concerned that uncritical acceptance and use of these scores may reinforce, if not exacerbate, tendencies to create 'ghetto' junior kindergartens" (Ellwein et al., 1991, p. 170). One of the readiness tests used in this study was the Brigance K and 1 Screen (Brigance, 1982). This widely used test is a brief assessment of young children's language development, motor abilities, number skills, body and social awareness, and auditory and visual discrimination. In the Ellwein et al. (1991) study, this test accounted for only one fifth of the variance in the quantitative outcome and 15% of the variation in the prereading subtest of the Metropolitan Readiness Test in first grade; on an assessment of cognitive development, it accounted for less than one fourth of the variance.

Previous research about the Brigance K and 1 Screen demonstrated similar results, with one review summarizing its findings by saying that "any school system that uses the Brigance inventories without going through a local validation effort is placing itself at risk legally" (Robinson & Kovacevich, 1984, p. 98). However, a new technical report has been published for the Brigance Screenings (Glascoe, 1997). Unfortunately, these new data do not provide conclusive evidence concerning the validity of the instrument. The kindergarten sample for this standardization consisted of only 74 children. The criterion measures for the screening were a combination of parent report scales (themselves of questionable validity) and standardized achievement tests. The most critical information for deciding whether a test can be used for classification is the proportion of children correctly identified with a placement instrument (i.e., sensitivity) and the proportion of children without the condition in question who are correctly not identified (i.e., specificity). The technical manual produced by the Brigance publisher shows that 25% of the children not at risk academically on the follow-up examinations would be considered to be at risk, and 23% of those who were at risk would be missed altogether (Glascoe, 1997). This "hit rate" is not sufficient to justify the use of the Brigance as a test to classify children or to determine their readiness for school.

It is important to know the accuracy of developmental screening and readiness tests because both contain an implicit prediction. That is, they imply that failure on either instrument will lead to difficulties in school. However, no readiness tests have yet been developed that have acceptable predictive validity. (In contrast, see Meisels et al., 1997, and Meisels, Henderson, Liaw, Browning, & Ten Have, 1993, for an example of high predictive validity of a developmental screening instrument.) Without a reasonable level of accuracy (i.e., sensitivity and specificity at or above .80), the probability is high that there will be false identifications, mistaken placements, and inappropriate classifications. Of all the reasons that explain the lack of long-term accuracy of school readiness tests, none is more compelling than the basic rationale presented previously. Readiness tests are concerned with determining whether a child has acquired a cluster of curriculum-related skills. Not only do children, especially young children, acquire skills at different rates and in different ways, but they are also exquisitely sensitive to the opportunity to learn. If a child has not been taught his or her colors or shapes or has not been exposed to opportunities to acquire these skills, then that information will not be available to the child. Frisbie and Andrews noted that, because of the limited scope of skills that readiness tests and batteries are able to assess,

> The scores should not be expected to make major contributions to many of the decisions educators might want to make about kindergarten pupils. For example,

the scores are not valid as indicators of who is or is not ready for kindergarten. The deficiencies represented by low readiness scores may be "treated" in relatively short order through instruction. (1990, p. 447)

Children arrive at school with a plethora of diverse previous experiences. Readiness tests and the empiricist/environmental rationale that support them assume a common core of learning before school; but this is unjustified. Children who do poorly on readiness tests often do well on similar assessments by the end of their kindergarten year, whereas those who begin at a high level may plateau or even drop in skill achievement as expectations rise (Meisels, 1987). Such variability again shows that the problem is not with the children but with the tests. The evidence does not support this perspective on assessing children's readiness.

Social Constructivist

The social constructivist approach assumes that readiness is situationally specific, locally generated, and highly relative (Graue, 1992, 1993). Readiness "cannot be defined without reference to how children's behavior and development are supported and what the children should be ready for" (Love, Aber, & Brooks-Gunn, 1994, p. 2). The social constructivist view recognizes that local communities hold different values, expectations, and norms for their children. Differences in parental wealth, ethnicity, education, and background account for some of these differences. However, differences also flow from variations in many other sources (e.g., teaching staff, school principals, policy makers). In short, this perspective holds that to understand and assess a child's readiness, it is essential to take into account the context in which the child is reared and the setting in which the child will be educated.

How is readiness assessed under these conditions? Love et al. (1994) suggested establishing a methodology at a community level to provide information about the collective status of children entering kindergarten. Their proposal is not intended for assessing individual children but for producing community aggregate measures. Their community assessment strategy includes nine requirements, which are shown in Table 3.3 and are described as follows.

The first requirement calls for all key dimensions of the First National Goal to be assessed. These dimensions, which were proposed by the Technical Review Group and ratified by the National Education Goals Panel, include the following domains: 1) physical well-being and motor development, 2) social and emotional development, 3) approaches toward learning, 4) language usage, and 5) cognition and general knowledge (Kagan et al., 1995). Love et al. (1994) suggested 18 indicators of these dimensions that can be used to show the strengths and weaknesses of child development–related outcomes in the community. Second, they suggested a focus on the collective status of all entering kindergartners. Their purpose is to develop a community profile of the status of children and institutions. Therefore, only aggregate measures are to be used, and a matrix sampling design will be employed whereby children in the community will not all receive every assessment. Only a sample will participate, and each member of the sample will be administered a portion of the entire assessment from which generalizations can be drawn.

Third, Love and colleagues (1994) suggested that the community assessment rely on existing instruments. To respond to children's and communities' needs as quickly as possible, they chose 22 indicators from several reliable and valid in-

Table 3.3.   Requirements for a community readiness assessment strategy

1.   Assess all key dimensions relevant to the Readiness Goal.
2.   Focus on the collective status of entering kindergartners.
3.   Rely primarily on existing instruments.
4.   Incorporate multiple modes of assessment.
5.   Incorporate multiple perspectives in the assessment.
6.   Be adaptable to local circumstances.
7.   Be appropriate for diverse cultural and racial/ethnic groups.
8.   Balance positive and negative indicators of the readiness dimensions.
9.   Be ready for implementation.

From Love, J.M., Aber, J.A., & Brooks-Gunn, J. (1994). *Strategies for assessing community progress toward achieving the first national educational goal.* Princeton, NJ: Mathematica Policy Research; reprinted by permission.

struments. Their fourth and fifth suggestions are closely related: They encourage the use of multiple modes of assessment and multiple perspectives in assessment. Specifically, they recommend that direct assessments of children's development be supplemented with indirect reports from teachers and parents, observations of children in groups, and surveys of adults in the child's world. Thus, this strategy incorporates the perspectives of a range of individuals commenting on a large number of indicators of importance in the life of children and the community.

Sixth, Love et al. (1994) cautioned educators to be adaptable to local circumstances. Some communities may focus on bilingualism, enhanced cognition, or socially adaptative strategies. The key is that the battery of assessments that is finally selected should reflect the values of a particular community. The seventh recommendation is a correlate of the sixth: Assessments should be appropriate for diverse cultural and racial/ethnic groups. As an example, they pointed out that, in some communities, neighborhood violence occurs so infrequently that "it makes little sense to track it over time to assess within-community change. For other communities, however, the incidence of violence may be relatively high, and its reduction may be key to improving children's school readiness" (Love et al., 1994, p. 10).

Their final two suggestions are to balance positive and negative indicators of the readiness dimensions and to be ready for implementation. Balance reminds us to focus not only on the problems of a community but also on the available strengths and resources. One of these strengths is a community's will to engage in this assessment process as soon as possible, using the existing measures that are suggested, to help all children become ready for successful school experiences.

As Love et al. (1994) suggested, the limitations of this overall strategy arise from its strengths. Collected here are a range of indicators that provide a profile or general index of the readiness of children in a community. Because the focus is on the readiness of a community's children, specific information needed for parents, educators, or policy makers regarding individual children is absent. Another problem in this approach is its complexity and potential cost. Not only are large numbers of measures employed in this strategy, but they must also be coordinated during their administration and interpreted after their aggregation. This costs money and requires expertise that may not be available in many communities. Nevertheless, the approach described here is an excellent design for beginning to understand the forces that result in different communities adopting different pro-files about readiness. This methodology answers the question, "Ready for what?"

Interactionist

The interactionist view holds that readiness is a relational, interactional construct that reflects a joint focus on the child's status and the characteristics of the edu-cational setting. Readiness is not something for which people wait, and it is not something that is imposed. It is not a within-the-child phenomenon or something specifically outside the child. Rather, it is the product of a set of educational deci-sions that are differentially shaped by the skills, experiences, and learning oppor-tunities that the child has had and by the perspectives and goals of the commu-nity, classroom, and teacher.

When readiness is defined as an interaction, two conditions are critical for its assessment. First, there must be sustained opportunities for teacher–child interac-tions to occur. Second, these interactions must occur over time, rather than on a single occasion. These two conditions are at once obvious but also represent a dra-matic departure from conventional paradigms and from all three models pre-sented previously. The difference from other conceptions of readiness lies in the joint focus on the child and educational environment and in the recognition of a temporal dimension to readiness assessment. This view does not hold that all the kindergarten children in a community can be "rounded up" on a given day and tested to determine their readiness. Rather, it suggests that readiness can only be assessed over time and in context. Perhaps this is what Bruner (1966) really meant when he said that readiness is a "half truth."

Currently, a methodology exists that can provide the type of readiness as-sessment that occurs over time and in interaction. Specifically, curriculum-embedded performance assessments can be viewed as means for helping teachers and children reach their potential in early childhood and early elementary class-rooms. Performance assessments are founded on the notion that learning and de-velopment can only be assessed over time and in interaction with materials, peers, and other people. Classrooms in which curriculum-embedded performance as-sessments (also known as "authentic performance assessments" [see Wiggins, 1989]) take place not only contain a joint focus on the child's status and the char-acteristics of the child's educational setting, but they also encourage individual planning, programming, and evaluation. These characteristics can be incorpo-rated into the components of a curriculum-embedded performance assessment, similar to those described for older students by Darling-Hammond and Ancess (1996) and Wolf and Reardon (1996) or for children from preschool through grade 5 in the Work Sampling System (Meisels, 1997; Meisels, Jablon, Marsden, Dichtel-miller, & Dorfman, 1994). This latter approach offers an empirical test of the in-teractional definition of readiness. Relying on developmental guidelines and checklists, portfolios, and summary reports, the Work Sampling System is based on using teachers' perceptions of their students in actual classroom situations while informing, expanding, and structuring those perceptions. It involves stu-dents and parents in the learning and assessment process, instead of relying on measures that are external to the community, classroom, and family context, and it makes possible a systematic documentation of what children are learning and how teachers are teaching. In short, the Work Sampling System draws attention to what the child brings to the learning situation and vice versa. As active constructors of knowledge, children should be expected to analyze, synthesize, evaluate, and interpret facts and ideas. This approach to performance assessment provides teachers with the opportunity to learn about these processes by documenting children's interactions with materials, adults, and peers in the classroom environment and using this documentation to evaluate children's achievements and plan future education interventions. Evidence of the reliability and validity of the Work Sampling System with kindergarten children is available (Meisels, Bickel, Nicholson, Xue, & Atkins-Burnett, 1998; Meisels, Liaw, Dorfman, & Nelson, 1995).

For this proposal to be successful, it must be implemented cautiously. Only performance assessments that meet several critical criteria will actually help educators to reach their goals of assessing readiness interactionally. Following the suggestions of Calfee (1992), these criteria include the following. First, such assessments should be *integrative*, bringing together various skills into visible displays and demonstrations of behavior that occur during the context of instruction. In this paradigm, children are expected to construct models, solve problems, and prepare reports that call upon a range of skills, experiences, and knowledge. Second, these assessments should *emphasize top-level competence*. Unlike conventional group-administered norm-referenced tests, performance assessments ask children to show what they can do, and teachers are expected to work with their students to help them achieve their best possible work—work that reflects their special talents or interests.

Third, performance assessments should *encourage metacognition* and the capacity to articulate as well as reflect on performance. Through performance assessments, children are engaged in the learning process. They evaluate their own work and reflect on their own progress, rather than being passive recipients of instruction or compliant occupants of the classroom. Finally, performance assessments are guided by *developmental standards*. These standards are embedded in the longitudinal character of children's work that is captured by the continuous progress format of curriculum-embedded performance assessments. These standards also emphasize the continuity of curricular development between children at different ages, grades, and levels of functioning.

This view represents a significant change in the expectations for readiness assessment. No longer can it be determined whether a child should be enrolled in general kindergarten based on a brief evaluation of core skills that should be achieved by all children, or as a result of maturation. Rather, readiness is something to be demonstrated by children in situ, over time, and differentially when teachers are systematically prepared to observe, document, and evaluate it and to apply community-based standards established in relation to a nationally validated understanding of curriculum domains, as exemplified by the Work Sampling System (Meisels, 1996). Readiness, it turns out, cannot be assessed easily, quickly, or efficiently.

The type of performance assessment described in this chapter as a readiness assessment is not adopted easily or without expense. It requires extensive professional development for teachers; changes in orientation regarding testing, grading, and student classification by educational policy makers; and alteration in expectations by parents and the community. Such changes entail financial burdens; the need for centralized coordination and program evaluation; and long-term commitment from teachers, parents, and the community—all of which are potential obstacles to implementation.

Although these obstacles exist, this perspective is consistent with the most recent call to the field from the Goal 1 Technical Planning Group regarding the status of readiness testing:

> The Technical Planning Group, while understanding the complexity of the technical challenges associated with defining and assessing early development and learning . . . is convinced that new assessments are doomed to repeat past problems unless such efforts are permeated by a conceptual orientation that accommodates cultural and contextual variability in *what* is being measured and in *how* measurements are constructed. Within the broad parameters of standardization, then, flexibility and inventiveness must be brought to bear on the content and the process of assessment. (Kagan et al., 1995, p. 42)

The approach to assessing readiness from an interactional perspective using curriculum-embedded performance assessment meets this challenge.

CONCLUSION: THREE APHORISMS
CONCERNING THE ASSESSMENT OF READINESS

The readiness issue is thick with dilemmas. It calls for achievement testing before children reach school, even though it is known that common assumptions about conditions of learning before formal education begins cannot be made. It implies an assumption of homogeneity and equity in opportunities before kindergarten, but it is clear that children come from heterogeneous backgrounds and are raised in dramatically different ways with access to a variety of personal and material resources. It also suggests that all children are being prepared for a similar educational program when the field of early education is marked by lack of uniformity and by vast differences in curriculum and methods.

The solution offered in this chapter cuts through these dilemmas by recognizing the heterogeneity in preparation, life experiences, and educational environments that children will have encountered by the time they enter school. The assessment methodology suggested previously represents a common denominator of standards and methods to determine if and at what levels of accomplishment children have achieved these standards. Despite substantial use of this approach (see Meisels, 1997), the task of implementation is at least as challenging as the responsibility to use assessments fairly and appropriately with young children. Three aphorisms can be advanced in light of this chapter's discussions to summarize views on the issues facing readiness assessments and on how Goal 1 should be construed:

- Testing is not a monolith.
- High-stakes testing does not promote early childhood learning.
- Readiness assessment calls for a comprehensive view of learning and development.

Testing Is Not a Monolith

There are many different types of assessments and assessment purposes. No single assessment will satisfy all our educational needs or solve all our educational problems. One way that resources are squandered and children are placed at risk is by using assessments as blunt instruments, in which one type of assessment is expected to perform the functions of others. The Committee on School Health and Committee on Early Childhood of the American Academy of Pediatrics made clear the dangers inherent in the inappropriate use of school readiness tests:

> When instruments and procedures designed for screening are used for diagnostic purposes, or when tests are administered by individuals who have a limited perspective on the variations of normal development, or when staff with little formal training in test administration perform the screening, children can be wrongly identified and their education jeopardized. (1995, p. 437)

Thus, assessments must be used carefully and appropriately to resolve educational problems, rather than to create such problems.

This maxim cautions us to use assessments in the way that they were designed and intended. A range of assessment purposes that are appropriate for young children can be described (see Meisels, 1994). Because a variety of assessment purposes may need to be fulfilled, it is unjustified to assume that these purposes can be satisfied by one or two types of assessment instruments. However, not all purposes are appropriate for young children or are consistent with the interactional purposes described previously. For example, Kagan, Rosenkoetter, and Cohen suggested that assessment for accountability (that is, measurement for the purpose of "informing the public about the collective status of children") is also suitable for young children (1997, p. 7). This can be disputed.

High-Stakes Testing Does Not Promote Early Childhood Learning

Accountability issues nearly always raise the stakes of assessment so that poor scores on such examinations result in negative sanctions. *High-stakes testing* refers to the use of assessment data to make decisions about enrollment, retention, promotion, incentives for children or teachers, or other tangible rewards or punishments (Madaus, 1988; Meisels, 1989). The evidence about the negative impact of these assessments on young children is strong. In a study of 12 elementary schools in New York State during a period of increased use of high-stakes assessment accountability (1978–1989), Allington and McGill-Franzen (1992) found that retention and special education placements increased in the primary grades in step with an increase in accountability pressures. Studying elementary schools in Arizona, Smith found other negative effects of testing on teachers:

> Testing programs substantially reduce the time available for instruction, narrow curricular offerings and modes of instruction, and potentially reduce the capacities of teachers to teach content and to use methods and materials that are incompatible with standardized testing formats. (1991, p. 8)

As accountability pressures increase, not only do teachers and other educators react by resorting to retention and special education placements more frequently, but parents also begin to take matters into their own hands. Recognizing the escalation of academic and accountability demands in kindergarten as a perversion of the historic view of kindergartens as "gardens of children," an increasing number of parents try to protect their children from these demands by holding them out of school until they are a year older than the standard entry age. *Holding out* refers to the practice whereby parents choose to delay their child's entry to kindergarten to give their child more time to "get ready" for the more highly charged educational setting in which he or she will be enrolled. Data about the prevalence of holding out are difficult to obtain, but the Fast Response Survey of kindergarten teacher attitudes toward readiness (NCES, 1993a) showed that 13% of the children in the classes taught by the respondents were 6 years of age or older in October of their kindergarten year. This may have included some children who were retained in grade, but included here as well were certainly children whose parents decided to "red shirt" them, or hold them out for a year before kindergarten. Some researchers suggest that holding out reflects an assumption that students must be ready before they attend school. Bellisimo, Sacks, and Mergendoller noted that "as expectations increase for what students must do to prove readiness, more children are deemed by their parents to be *not ready* for the demands of kindergarten" (1995, p. 205). But the "bet" parents make about holding their children out of school for a year is not a good wager. Research shows that chronological age is not nearly as powerful an influence on the developmental progress of children as schooling. Some studies have shown that the independent effects of schooling are four times greater than those of age (Bentin, Hammer, & Cahan, 1991) and that any advantage conferred by chronological age at entrance to first grade is lost within a few years (Bickel, Zigmond, & Strahorn, 1991).

Of great importance, data suggest that there are negative effects of a child being old for his or her grade that may be associated with patterns of parental holding out. In two studies, Byrd and his colleagues described increased behavior problems that they attributed to delayed school entry and delayed school progress. Byrd, Weitzman, and Doniger's (1996) first study showed that students who were older than their same-grade peers were at increased risk of drug use when studied in adolescence, even when old-for-grade status was determined by third grade. This study did not distinguish between students who were retained in grade and those who were held out. However, in their second study, Byrd, Weitzman, and Auinger (1997) sought to determine whether higher rates of reported behavior problems were independent of retention in grade. Using data from 9,079 children ages 7–17 years who participated in the Child Health Supplement to the 1988 National Health Interview Study, they found that both grade retention and simply being old for grade were associated with increased rates of problematic behaviors, especially among adolescents. In disentangling delayed entry to school and retention, they found what may be considered a latent adverse behavioral outcome resulting from delaying children's school entry. (For a contrasting view based on a different methodology and a sample followed for a shorter period of time, see Zill & West, 1997.) Byrd et al. (1997) concluded that the question, "At what age should children start first grade?" may have a lifelong impact on a child. The accountability culture created in our schools is a major contributor to the initiation of unnecessary risks that may be extremely persistent.

Readiness Assessment Calls for a
Comprehensive View of Learning and Development

One of the key issues in the readiness debate concerns where the burden of proof should lie. Should children be expected to be ready for schools, or should schools be expected to be ready for children? This way of formulating the problem is not very felicitous because it adopts a deficit orientation that is at odds with the entire enterprise of welcoming children into their first formal school experience. The California School Readiness Task Force issued a report entitled, *Here They Come: Ready or Not!* (California State Department of Education, 1988), that stated their view of the inevitability of children entering school whether the schools or the children were well prepared. This view still rings true today.

Many informal conversations surrounding the first national goal seem to imply that lack of readiness is a problem to be eradicated. However, readiness is a process that occurs over time and is not complete by the first day of kinder-garten. Thinking about eliminating it as a problem is simply not helpful. One of the themes debated among those who first met as part of the Goal 1 Resource Panel was whether readiness should be considered something that is demon-strated by kindergarten or by first grade. Like many others, this author advocated for kindergarten and was wrong. If readiness is a process and schools are by ne-cessity a major contributor to this process, then a period of common schooling needs to occur in which this process can take place.

Readiness must be thought of as much more than knowledge of a few skills that are seen in the first few weeks of kindergarten or behavior patterns that are consistent with those of compliant children who have prodigiously long attention spans. Pianta and Walsh, adopting what can be called an "input" view of readi-ness, said that children are ready for school when,

> For a period of several years, they have been exposed to consistent, stable adults who are emotionally invested in them; to a physical environment that is safe and predictable; to regular routines and rhythms of activity; to competent peers; and to materials that stimulate their exploration and enjoyment of the object world and from which they derive a sense of mastery. (1996, p. 34)

This list of readiness precursors can be expanded and refined. In their mono-graph entitled, *Heart Start: The Emotional Foundations of School Readiness*, ZERO TO THREE: National Center for Infants, Toddlers, and Families (1992) discussed the characteristics that equip children to come to school with a knowledge of how to learn. These characteristics include confidence, curiosity, intentionality, self-control, relatedness, capacity to communicate, and cooperativeness. Some of these charac-teristics are incorporated into the dimension of "approaches to learning" that is part of the proposed readiness assessment suggested by the Goals Panel. Beyond this, these qualities suggest a way of raising and caring for children throughout their first years of life that does not reflect a sole preoccupation with establishing a fund of general knowledge; an ability to read or recite the alphabet; familiarity with numbers or colors; or skills of hopping, balancing, or skipping. Fundamen-tal to the attainment of these skills is a sense of self that can only be developed over time and in interaction with trustworthy and caring adults.

Modifying the readiness goal to accommodate these ideas is not difficult. Readiness must be conceptualized as a broad construct that incorporates all aspects of a child's life that contribute directly to that child's ability to learn. Def-initions of readiness must take into account the environment, context, and con-ditions under which the child acquires skills and is encouraged to learn. Assessments of readiness must, in consequence, incorporate data collected over time from the child, teacher, parents, and community. In short, these thoughts help us restate the first national goal as follows: *By the year 2000 all children will have an opportunity to enhance their skills, knowledge, and abilities by participating in classrooms that are sensitive to community values, recognize individual differences, reinforce and extend children's strengths, and assist them in overcoming their difficulties.*

Readiness need no longer be a mystery or a set of confusing constructs. Now that systematic models of performance assessment have been developed, assessing readiness also does not need to be a source of frustration. In perceiving the basic relativity inherent in children's preparation for school and in recognizing the remarkable power to build from children's strengths in addressing their areas of difficulty, this restatement of Goal 1 captures the spirit of what we desire for all children at the outset of school—an opportunity to take the first steps toward school success.

REFERENCES

Allington, R.L., & McGill-Franzen, A. (1992). Unintended effects of educational reform in New York. *Educational Policy, 6,* 397–414.

Barth, P., & Mitchell, R. (1992). *Smart start: Elementary education for the 21st century.* Golden, CO: North American Press.

Bellisimo, Y., Sacks, C.H., & Mergendoller, J.R. (1995). Changes over time in kindergarten holding out: Parent and school contexts. *Early Childhood Research Quarterly, 10,* 205–222.

Bentin, S., Hammer, R., & Cahan, S. (1991). The effects of aging and first grade schooling on the development of phonological awareness. *Psychological Science, 2,* 271–274.

Bickel, D.D., Zigmond, N., & Strahorn, J. (1991). Chronological age at entrance to first grade: Effects on elementary school success. *Early Childhood Research Quarterly, 6,* 105–117.

Boyer, E.L. (1991). *Ready to learn: A mandate for the nation.* Princeton, NJ: The Carnegie Foundation for the Advancement of Teaching.

Bredekamp, S., & Shepard, L.A. (1989). How best to protect children from inappropriate school expectations, practices, and policies. *Young Children, 44,* 14–24.

Brigance, A.H. (1982). *Brigance K and 1 Screen for Kindergarten and First Grade.* North Billerica, MA: Curriculum Associates.

Browning, K. (1997). *Michigan public preschool teachers' views on risk status and readiness for kindergarten.* Unpublished doctoral dissertation, University of Michigan, Ann Arbor.

Bruner, J.S. (1966). *Towards a theory of instruction.* Cambridge, MA: Harvard University Press.

Byrd, R.S., Weitzman, M., & Auinger, P. (1997). Increased behavior problems associated with delayed school entry and delayed school progress. *Pediatrics, 100,* 654–661.

Byrd, R.S., Weitzman, M., & Doniger, A.S. (1996). Increased drug use among old-for-grade adolescents. *Archives of Pediatrics & Adolescent Medicine, 150,* 470–476.

Calfee, R. (1992). Authentic assessment of reading and writing in the elementary classroom. In M.J. Dreher & W.H. Slater (Eds.), *Elementary school literacy: Critical issues* (pp. 211–226). Norwood, MA: Christopher-Gordon.

California State Department of Education. (1988). *Here they come: Ready or not!* (Report of the School Readiness Task Force). Sacramento, CA: Author.

Committee on School Health and Committee on Early Childhood of the American Academy of Pediatrics. (1995). The inappropriate use of school "readiness" tests. *Pediatrics, 95,* 437–438.

Cuban, L. (1992). Why some reforms last: The case of the kindergarten. *American Journal of Education, 100,* 166–194.

Darling-Hammond, L., & Ancess, J. (1996). Authentic assessment and school development. In J.B. Baron & D.P. Wolf (Eds.), *Performance-based student assessment: Challenges and possibilities. Ninety-fifth yearbook of the National Society for the Study of Education, Part 1* (pp. 52–83). Chicago: University of Chicago Press.

Ellwein, M.C., Walsh, D.J., Eads, G.M., & Miller, A., (1991). Using readiness tests to route kindergarten students: The snarled intersection of psychometrics, policy, and practice. *Educational Evaluation and Policy Analysis, 13,* 159–175.

Fischer, K.W., & Silvern, L. (1985). Stages and individual differences in cognitive development. In M.R. Rosenzweig & L.W. Porter (Eds.), *Annual review of psychology* (Vol. 36, pp. 613–648). Palo Alto, CA: Annual Reviews.

Frisbie, D.A., & Andrews, K. (1990). Kindergarten pupil and teacher behavior during standardized achievement testing. *The Elementary School Journal, 90,* 435–448.

Gagné, R.M. (1970). *The conditions of learning* (2nd ed.). Austin, TX: Holt, Rinehart, & Winston.

Gesell, A., & Amatruda, C.S. (1941). *Developmental diagnosis.* New York: Hoeber.

Glascoe, F.P. (1997). *Technical report for the Brigance screens.* Billerica, MA: Curriculum Associates.

Graue, M.E. (1992). Social interpretations of readiness for kindergarten. *Early Childhood Research Quarterly, 7,* 225–243.

Graue, M.E. (1993). *Ready for what? Constructing meanings of readiness for kindergarten.* Albany: State University of New York Press.

Graue, M.E., & Shepard, L.A. (1989). Predictive validity of the Gesell School Readiness Tests. *Early Childhood Research Quarterly, 4,* 303–315.

Haines, J., Ames, L.B., & Gillespie, C. (1980). *The Gesell Preschool Test manual.* Lumberville, PA: Modern Learning Press.

Ilg, F., & Ames, L.B. (1972). *School readiness.* New York: HarperCollins.

Kagan, S.L. (1990). Readiness 2000: Rethinking rhetoric and responsibility. *Phi Delta Kappan, 72,* 272–279.

Kagan, S.L., Moore, E., & Bredekamp, S. (1995). *Reconsidering children's early development and learning: Toward common views and vocabulary.* Washington, DC: National Education Goals Panel.

Kagan, S.L., Rosenkoetter, S., & Cohen, N.E. (1997). *Considering child-based results for young children: Definitions, desirability, feasibility, and next steps.* New Haven, CT: Yale Bush Center in Child Development and Social Policy.

Kohlberg, L., & Mayer, R. (1972). Development as the aim of education. *Harvard Educational Review, 42,* 429–496.

Koretz, D. (1988). Arriving in Lake Wobegon: Are standardized tests exaggerating achievement and distorting instruction? *American Educator, 12,* 8–15, 46–52.

Lichtenstein, R. (1990). Psychometric characteristics and appropriate use of the Gesell School Readiness Screening Test. *Early Childhood Research Quarterly, 5,* 359–378.

Lopez, M.E., & Hochberg, M.R. (1993). *Paths to school readiness: An in-depth look at three early childhood programs.* Cambridge, MA: Harvard Family Research Project.

Love, J.M. (1995). *Conception of readiness for ECLS and HSLS.* Unpublished memorandum, Mathematica Policy Research, Princeton, NJ.

Love, J.M. , Aber, J.A., & Brooks-Gunn, J. (1994). *Strategies for assessing community progress toward achieving the first national educational goal.* Princeton, NJ: Mathematica Policy Research.

Madaus, G.F. (1988). The influence of testing on the curriculum. In L.N. Tanner (Ed.), *Critical issues in curriculum: Eighty-seventh yearbook of the National Society for the Study of Education* (pp. 83–121). Chicago: University of Chicago Press.

Meisels, S.J. (1987). Uses and abuses of developmental screening and school readiness testing. *Young Children, 42,* 4–6, 68–73.

Meisels, S.J. (1989). High stakes testing in kindergarten. *Educational Leadership, 46,* 16–22.

Meisels, S.J. (1992a). Doing harm by doing good: Iatrogenic effects of early childhood enrollment and promotion policies. *Early Childhood Research Quarterly, 7,* 155–174.

Meisels, S.J. (1992b). The Lake Wobegon effect reversed: Commentary on "The Gesell assessment: Psychometric properties." *Early Childhood Research Quarterly, 7,* 45–46.

Meisels, S.J. (1994). Designing meaningful measurements for early childhood. In B.L. Mallory & R.S. New (Eds.), *Diversity in early childhood education: A call for more inclusive theory, practice, and policy* (pp. 205–225). New York: Teachers College Press.

Meisels, S.J. (1995). Out of the readiness maze. *Momentum, 26,* 18–22.

Meisels, S.J. (1996). Performance in context: Assessing children's achievement at the outset of school. In A.J. Sameroff & M.M. Haith (Eds.), *The five to seven year shift: The age of reason and responsibility* (pp. 410–431). Chicago: University of Chicago Press.

Meisels, S.J. (1997). Using Work Sampling in authentic performance assessments. *Educational Leadership, 54,* 60–65.

Meisels, S.J., with Atkins-Burnett, S. (1994). *Developmental screening in early childhood: A guide* (4th ed.). Washington, DC: National Association for the Education of Young Children.

Meisels, S.J., Bickel, D.D., Nicholson, J., Xue, Y., & Atkins-Burnett, S. (1998). *Pittsburgh Work Sampling Achievement Validation Study: Technical Report.* Ann Arbor: University of Michigan.

Meisels, S.J., Henderson, L.W., Liaw, F., Browning, K., & Ten Have, T. (1993). New evidence for the effectiveness of the Early Screening Inventory. *Early Childhood Research Quarterly, 8,* 327–346.

Meisels, S.J., Jablon, J.R., Marsden, D.B., Dichtelmiller, M.L., & Dorfman, A.B. (1994). *The Work Sampling System.* Ann Arbor, MI: Rebus.

Meisels, S.J., Liaw, F.-R., Dorfman, A.B., & Nelson, R. (1995). The Work Sampling System: Reliability and validity of a performance assessment for young children. *Early Childhood Research Quarterly, 10(3),* 277–296.

Meisels, S.J., Marsden, D.B., Wiske, M.S., & Henderson, L.W. (1997). *The Early Screening Inventory·Revised (ESI·R).* Ann Arbor, MI: Rebus.

Meisels, S.J., & Provence, S. (1989). *Screening and assessment: Guidelines for identifying young disabled and developmentally vulnerable children and their families.* Washington, DC: National Center for Clinical Infant Programs.

National Association for the Education of Young Children (NAEYC). (1988). NAEYC position statement on standardized testing of young children 3 through 8 years of age. *Young Children, 43,* 42–47.

National Association for the Education of Young Children (NAEYC). (1990). NAEYC position statement on school readiness. *Young Children, 46,* 21–23.

National Association of Early Childhood Specialists in State Departments of Education. (1987). *Unacceptable trends in kindergarten entry and placement.* Springfield, IL: Author.

National Association of Elementary School Principals. (1990). *Early childhood education: Standards for quality programs for young children.* Alexandria, VA: Author.

National Association of State Boards of Education (NASBE). (1988). *Right from the start.* Report of the National Task Force on School Readiness. Alexandria, VA: Author.

National Association of State Boards of Education (NASBE). (1991). *Caring communities: Supporting young children and families.* Report of the NASBE Task Force on Early Childhood Education. Alexandria, VA: Author.

National Center for Education Statistics (NCES). (1993). *Fast response survey system, kindergarten teacher survey on student readiness.* Washington, DC: U.S. Department of Education.

National Center for Education Statistics (NCES). (1993). *Public school kindergarten teachers' views on children's readiness for school.* Washington, DC: U.S. Department of Education, Office of Educational Research and Improvement.

National Commission on Children. (1992). *Beyond rhetoric: A new American agenda for children and families.* Washington, DC: Author.

National Commission on Excellence in Education. (1983). *A nation at risk.* Washington, DC: U.S. Department of Education.

National Education Goals Panel. (1991). *The National Education Goals report.* Washington, DC: Author.

Nelson, R.F. (1997). *Kindergarten teachers' beliefs about school readiness.* Unpublished doctoral dissertation, University of Michigan, Ann Arbor.

Phillips, N.H. (1992). Two-tiered kindergarten: Effective for at-risk 5-year-olds? *Early Childhood Research Quarterly, 7,* 205–224.

Pianta, R.C., & Walsh, D.J. (1996). *High-risk children in schools: Constructing sustaining relationships.* New York: Routledge.

Powell, D.R. (1995). *Enabling young children to succeed in school.* Washington, DC: American Educational Research Association.

Robinson, J.H., & Kovacevich, D.A. (1984). The Brigance inventories. In D.J. Keyser & R.C. Sweetland (Eds.), *Test critiques* (Vol. 1). Kansas City, MO: Test Corporation of America.

Schorr, L.B. (1997). Judging interventions by their results. In S.L. Kagan, S. Rosenkoetter, & N.E. Cohen (Eds.), *Considering child-based results for young children: Definitions, desirability, feasibility, and next steps* (pp. 36–47). New Haven, CT: Yale Bush Center in Child Development and Social Policy.

Shepard, L.A., & Smith, M.L. (1986). Synthesis of research on school readiness and kindergarten retention. *Educational Leadership, 44,* 78–86.

Skinner, B.F. (1968). *The technology of teaching.* Stamford, CT: Appleton-Century-Crofts.

Smith, M.L. (1991). Put to the test: The effects of external testing on teachers. *Educational Researcher, 20,* 8–11.

Smith, M.L., & Shepard, L.A. (1988). Kindergarten readiness and retention: A qualitative study of teachers' beliefs and practices. *American Educational Research Journal, 25,* 307–333.

Stallman, A.C., & Pearson, P.D. (1990). Formal measures of early literacy. In L.M. Morrow & J.K. Smith (Eds.), *Assessment for instruction in early literacy* (pp. 7–44). Upper Saddle River, NJ: Prentice-Hall.

State of Michigan. (1987). *Attorney General Opinion No. 6467: Right of child to attend kindergarten.* Lansing: Author.

Tyler, F. (1964). Issues related to readiness to learn. In E. Hilgard (Ed.), *Theories of learning and instruction: The sixty-third yearbook of the National Society for the Study of Education, Part 1* (pp. 210–239). Chicago: University of Chicago Press.

U.S. Department of Education. (1991). *America 2000: An education strategy.* Washington, DC: Author.

Walker, R.N. (1992). The Gesell Assessment: Psychometric properties. *Early Childhood Research Quarterly, 7,* 21–43.

White, S.H. (1996). The child's entry into the "Age of reason." In A.J. Sameroff & M.M. Haith (Eds.), *The five to seven year shift: The age of reason and responsibility* (pp. 17–32). Chicago: University of Chicago Press.

Wiggins, G. (1989). A true test: Toward more authentic and equitable assessment. *Phi Delta Kappan, 70,* 703–713.

Willer, B., & Bredekamp, S. (1990). Redefining readiness: An essential requisite for educational reform. *Young Children, 45,* 22–24.

Wolf, D.P., & Reardon, S. (1996). Access to excellence through new forms of student assessment. In J.B. Baron & D.P. Wolf (Eds.), *Performance-based student assessment: Challenges and possibilities. Ninety-fifth yearbook of the National Society for the Study of Education, Part 1* (pp. 1–31). Chicago: University of Chicago Press.

ZERO TO THREE: National Center for Infants, Toddlers, and Families. (1992). *Heart Start: The emotional foundations of school readiness.* Washington, DC: Author.

Zill, N., & West, J. (1997). *The elementary school performance and adjustment of children who enter kindergarten late or repeat kindergarten: Findings from national surveys.* Washington, DC: National Center for Education Statistics.

Chapter 4

Promoting Educational Equity and Excellence in Kindergarten

Nicholas Zill

Most parents in the United States now subscribe to the notion that going far and doing well in school is critical to the careers of their children in the job market and in life in general. Surveys show that virtually all parents want their children to attend college, and most expect their children to graduate from college (Zill & Nord, 1994). The reality is, of course, that although average educational attainment has been increasing, only about one quarter of all young people complete college. Furthermore, there are still large differences among children from different socioeconomic, racial, and ethnic groups in average educational attainment and tested achievement (Snyder, Hoffman, & Geddes, 1998). These differences have profound consequences for the employment and earnings patterns of adults from these groups.

There has been a decades-long movement in the United States to try to reduce these disparities and increase educational equity (Jencks et al., 1972). There has also been a movement to raise educational standards across the board and ensure that young people who graduate from high school and college have substantial knowledge and strong skills (National Commission on Excellence in Education, 1983). Efforts to increase equity and efforts to promote excellence are sometimes at odds with one another, but both movements have paid more attention in recent years to what happens to children before they enter school and in the early years of their formal schooling. There has been a growing realization among educators, policy makers, parents, and researchers that what happens to children prior to elementary school, and in the early years of elementary school, may have a profound influence on their later achievement and attainment. The early years are important because they are the years in which basic skills are acquired that serve as the foundation for later learning. They are the time when parents' beliefs about their children's abilities are shaped and children's own academic self-concepts start to be formed. These years are also the time when children begin to acquire reputations among teachers, school administrators, and peers, as well as written records concerning their accomplishments and conduct that will follow them through the elementary grades and beyond (Alexander & Entwisle, 1988; Early, Pianta, & Cox, 1999). Because educators now see school entry as a pivotal time in children's development, they are placing more emphasis on children being as prepared as possible for their initial encounters with formal schooling and on schools being ready for young children in all their variety.

Although law in most states does not require attendance,[1] kindergarten is now a nearly universal experience for American children. National survey data show that among recent cohorts of first and second graders in the United States, 98% attended kindergarten prior to entering first grade (West, Hausken, Chandler, & Collins, 1992). In many systems, assessments are made of young children at kindergarten entry or during kindergarten that could well influence their entire school careers. For these reasons, kindergarten could justifiably be described as the start of formal schooling for today's children.

However, although kindergarten is a nearly universal experience for young children, it is by no means a uniform one. The kindergarten experiences of different groups of children are quite diverse. For example, whereas some attend kindergarten in the same public school systems in which they will get their elementary school educations, a substantial minority of students attend kindergarten in various kinds of private programs and then shift to public school in the first grade. Some go to full-day kindergartens, whereas others go to half-day programs. Children also differ in the educational backgrounds and degrees of preparation they bring to kindergarten. For some children, kindergarten is their first experience with group care, whereas many others are already seasoned veterans of a succession of center-based child care or early education programs. Likewise, some children enter kindergarten unable to identify a single letter of the alphabet, whereas others are reading simple sentences and stories on their own. The extent of diversity in entering pupils' backgrounds and experiences has been magnified by the high rates of immigration from non–English-speaking countries and the rapid pace of change in family living arrangements that the United States has experienced.

Given the variety of kindergarten program types and the heterogeneity in the experiences and capabilities of entering kindergarten students, it is natural to ask the following: How successful are kindergartens at smoothing the transition into formal schooling and launching children on their academic careers? Are they helping children who may have lacked the advantages of stimulating family environments and extensive preschool preparation to make up for these deficiencies? In so doing, are they requiring children who are relatively advanced to go over familiar material, mark time, and be thoroughly bored during their first year of schooling? Do kindergartens have sufficiently ample instructional resources and sufficiently small group sizes to allow children with different developmental

---

[1] As of 1995, kindergarten attendance was required of 5-year-old children in 12 states and the District of Columbia. Most of these states required only half-day attendance (Snyder, Hoffman, & Geddes, 1998).

needs to be served adequately? This question becomes particularly germane given the current ideological abhorrence of any sort of achievement-related tracking or grouping of pupils.

What are kindergarten programs like today? How large are kindergarten classes? What qualifications do kindergarten teachers have? In what activities do children engage in class? How involved are parents? Are there indications that substantial numbers of pupils have difficulties adjusting to the classroom environment and curricular demands of kindergarten? Are children from low-income families and families with other social or demographic risk factors more likely to experience these difficulties? Are the difficulties lessened when children have been exposed to preschool programs such as Head Start or publicly funded pre-kindergarten? Some have criticized modern kindergarten programs for becoming too didactic and academic, whereas others have criticized them for not being didactic enough and neglecting the teaching of basic skills. Does the evidence support either of these lines of criticism?

In truth, thorough-going answers to these questions do not exist because there is still a relative paucity of information about kindergarten pupils, teachers, and programs, especially information based on representative national samples. In the past, large-scale statistical studies of public and private education have tended to focus on the secondary school years and ignore the elementary years, especially the earliest years. This imbalance is being remedied, notably by the Early Childhood Longitudinal Study of a kindergarten cohort (ECLS-K), which was launched in 1998 by the National Center for Education Statistics (NCES) of the U.S. Department of Education. Although much remains to be learned, our knowledge has improved during the 1990s, thanks to several surveys of parents of young children and of kindergarten teachers, most of them conducted by NCES.[2] This chapter provides a descriptive overview of the kindergarten and postkindergarten experiences of American children based on these data.

In particular, the chapter focuses on two groups of children and their kindergarten experiences. The first group would be expected to have more difficulty in school based on previous research—namely, children from families whose incomes are below the official poverty line. The second group would be expected to have greater success as a result of attending private school programs—namely, children who are advantaged in socioeconomic terms and who have parents who seek educational excellence.

In addition to the questions posed previously, the chapter seeks to answer the following research questions: How different are the early educational experiences of children from low-income families and those from families with more adequate financial resources? How different are the experiences of children who attend private kindergarten programs as compared with those of children who go to kindergarten in their local public schools? Is there evidence that the public kindergarten programs attended by children from low-income families are notably inferior to

---

[2]The surveys are the National Household Education Surveys (NHESs) of 1993, 1995, and 1996 (Brick et al., 1994; Collins et al., 1997; Zill et al., 1997), the Fast Response Survey System Survey of Public School Kindergarten Teachers (Heaviside & Farris, 1993), the NCEDL Transition Practices Survey (Pianta et al., 1998), and special tabulations from the 1993–1994 Schools and Staffing Survey (Henke, Choy, Geis, & Broughman, 1996) prepared for the National Center for Early Development and Learning (Early et al., 1999). The sample sizes, response rates, and other technical characteristics of these surveys are given in the cited references.

those attended by children from middle- to high-income families? Are children from low-income families more likely to be retained in kindergarten, and, if so, what are the implications of such retention for later performance and adjustment in the elementary grades? What do the survey findings suggest about what kindergartens and elementary schools could be doing better to promote equity and excellence in education during the early grades?

The chapter begins by describing *demographic trends* affecting the composition, performance, and behavior of contemporary kindergarten classes, showing the challenges that educators face because of the rapidly changing characteristics of the child population. Next is an examination of the *preparation children receive for kindergarten* in their families and through participation in preschool programs, followed by a description of differences in the *developmental status of different groups of children* when they reach kindergarten. This is followed by a brief description of the *types of kindergarten programs* that U.S. children attend, looking at such things as the proportion of children who attend private versus public kindergarten programs and full-day versus part-day programs. The chapter then examines *characteristics of kindergarten programs,* including class size, teacher qualifications and beliefs, and classroom activities.

The chapter looks at parent participation in school-related activities and at parents' satisfaction with the kindergarten programs their children attend, focusing especially on communication between school and home, encouragement of parental participation, and parental involvement in school decision making. This brings us to children's experiences in kindergarten, including teacher judgments of the success of the transition to school and parent reports about the feedback from kindergarten teachers that they receive concerning the learning and classroom behavior of their children. Following this, the chapter examines what happens to children after kindergarten, both with respect to promotion into first grade and with respect to performance and adjustment in the early grades of elementary school. Throughout, contrasts are made between the experiences of children from low-income and middle- to high-income families, and between those in private, as opposed to public, kindergarten programs.

DEMOGRAPHIC TRENDS AFFECTING THE COMPOSITION AND PERFORMANCE OF CONTEMPORARY KINDERGARTEN CLASSES

A demographic profile of today's kindergartners shows some of the challenges that educators face in trying to meet the dual goals of equity and excellence in schooling. Large numbers of young children come from family backgrounds that have traditionally had problems with achievement or classroom conduct, either because of receiving inadequate intellectual stimulation at home or experiencing high levels of family stress and turmoil, among other reasons. One in every four kindergartners comes from a family whose annual income is below the official poverty line. Due to high recent rates of immigration, especially from Mexico and Central America, higher proportions of today's young children come from families in which a language other than English is spoken in the home. Today's children are more likely to be growing up in single-parent families or families disrupted by marital separation or divorce. Research has shown that as they progress through school, these children are at greater risk of academic failure, grade repetition, suspension or expulsion, and other school-related difficulties (Zill, 1996a).

It is important not to overlook the fact that there have been important positive developments in the demography of early childhood. Today's families are smaller, which means that children are less likely to have to compete with numbers of young siblings for their parents' attention (Zill & Rogers, 1988). Also, because of rising educational attainment among American adults, average parent educational levels are considerably higher than they were in the past. It is still the case, however, that more than one child in eight is reared by a mother who has not completed high school (Zill, 1996b). Indeed, the potential positive effects of rising adult education levels have been attenuated by the recent influx of immigrant families from Latin America and other less-developed Asian and Middle Eastern countries. Parents from these countries often have very low levels of education because of the limited schooling opportunities in their native nations (Nord & Griffin, 1998).

Age Distribution

As of the 1995/1996 school year, there were 3.9 million children in kindergarten classes across the United States (see Figure 4.1). More than two thirds (68%) of these kindergarten children were 5 years old as of the end of the calendar year (December 31, 1995). Twenty-eight percent were 6 years old or older as of the same date, and four percent were 4 years old or younger (National Household Education Survey [NHES], 1996). Starting school with first grade at age 6 used to be the norm in the United States, whereas now most children go to kindergarten at age 5 (West et al., 1992). But the 5-year-olds in today's kindergarten classes are older than the kindergartners of the past. Whereas it had been standard practice to require kindergartners entering school in September to be 5 years of age by the following December or January, changes in state age eligibility laws have made it increasingly common for schools to require children to be 5 years of age by September or October, or even earlier (Zill, Loomis, & West, 1997).

The age distribution of kindergartners has also been affected by the practice of delayed entry: Some parents choose to delay their children's enrollment in kindergarten by a year (Cameron & Wilson, 1990; Shepard & Smith, 1988). In 1995, 9% of first and second graders in the United States had experienced delayed entry into kindergarten, as reported by parents (Zill et al., 1997). The rationale is usually that the additional year will give children who have late birthdays, or are somewhat behind their agemates in social, motor, or academic skills, extra time to mature. In other instances, the parents' motivation for delaying school entry is frankly competitive. Even though the child may be capable of handling the demands of kindergarten, the parents want to give him or her an edge over other pupils, both in kindergarten and in later grades. A number of critics have deplored the possible effects this practice may be having on the kindergarten curriculum and on teacher judgments regarding children who enter kindergarten "on time" (Bredekamp & Shepard, 1989; Zill et al., 1997).

Racial and Ethnic Composition

The racial and ethnic make-up of today's kindergarten classes reflect the changing demography of the United States and foreshadow the composition of the overall population in the 21st century. The Caucasian majority is smaller and the Hispanic minority considerably larger than in today's adult population. There are nearly as

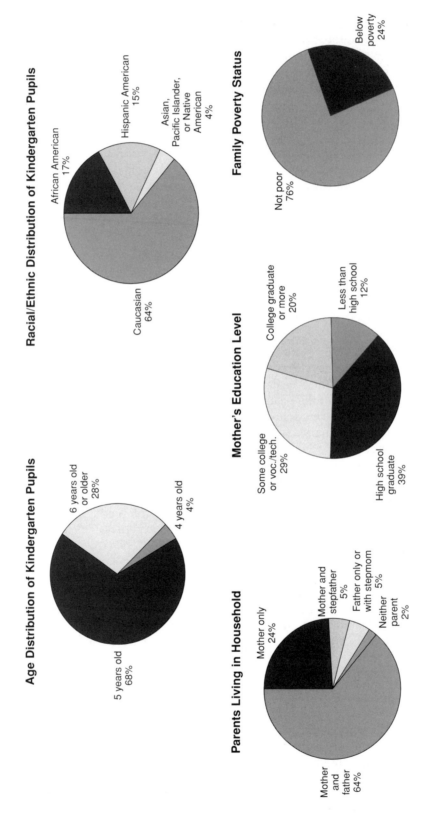

Figure 4.1. Demographic profile of the kindergarten class of 1996. (Source: National Household Education Survey, 1996.)

many Hispanic students as there are African American students. This reflects both high rates of immigration and higher birth rates among Hispanics (see Table 4.1).

Minority Language Status

In 1993, 8% of kindergartners had parents one or both of whom spoke a language other than English at home most of the time (NHES, 1993). According to data from the Census Bureau's Current Population Survey, the proportion of all school-age children who spoke a language other than English at home increased from 9% in 1979 to 14% in 1995. The number of school-age children who spoke a language other than English at home *and* had difficulty speaking English almost doubled during this period, going from 1.25 million to 2.44 million, whereas the proportion increased from 3% to 5%. Thirty-one percent of Hispanic children had difficulty speaking English in 1995, and 74% of these children spoke Spanish at home. Likewise, 14% of children of "other" races (including Asians) had difficulty speaking English, whereas 46% of these children spoke a language other than English at home (Federal Interagency Forum on Child and Family Statistics, 1997).

Kindergartners from families with incomes below the poverty level are twice as likely to have parents who speak Spanish or another language other than English at home. In 1993, 14% of kindergartners who were poor had parents one or both of whom mostly spoke Spanish or another minority language at home. The same was true of 6% of kindergartners who were not poor (NHES, 1993). Public and private school kindergartners did not differ greatly in the proportion with parents who spoke a minority language: 8% of public school pupils versus 6% of private school kindergartners had such parents (NHES, 1993).

Family Composition

The families in which today's kindergarten students live show the effects of the high rates of separation, divorce, and single parenting that the U.S. population has displayed since the mid-1970s. In 1996, 64% of kindergarten students were reported to have both birth parents or two adoptive parents living at home with them. Nearly one quarter (24%) were living with their mothers only. Six percent were living with one birth parent and one stepparent, whereas three percent were living with their fathers only. Two percent had neither birth parent present; they were living with grandparents or other relatives, or foster parents or guardians (NHES, 1996).

Table 4.1.   Changing racial and ethnic composition of U.S. kindergarten pupils

Race/Ethnicity	Year		
	1980	1995	2010 (projected)
Caucasian	72%	64%	59%
African American	15%	17%	16%
Hispanic American	10%	15%	19%
Asian, Pacific Islander, or Native American	3%	4%	7%
Total	100%	100%	101%

Sources: The National Household Education Survey (1996) and U.S. Bureau of the Census (1982, 1983, 1997).

By comparison, 85% of all U.S. children younger than 18 years of age lived with two parents in 1970, and 77% did so in 1980 (these figures include children who lived with a birth parent and a stepparent). The proportion living with their mothers only was 11% in 1970 and 18% in 1980 (Federal Interagency Forum on Child and Family Statistics, 1997).

Parent Education

The parents of today's kindergartners have higher levels of educational attainment, on average, than previous generations of parents. Looking at the education level of the parent with more education, 92% of kindergarten students in 1993 had parents with at least a high school education. In contrast, in 1970, 62% of U.S. children of elementary school age had parents who had completed high school or more, whereas in 1985 the proportion was 78% (Zill & Rogers, 1988). Nearly one quarter of the 1993 kindergartners had parents who were college graduates or more, and 58% had parents who had at least some college or other post–high school training (NHES, 1993).

There have been dramatic gains in the educational attainment of African American parents since the early 1970s, and more modest gains in the attainment of Hispanic American parents (Select Committee on Children, Youth, and Families, U.S. House of Representatives, 1989). Nevertheless, children from these minority groups still tend to have parents with lower educational attainments, on average, than children from the Caucasian majority. In 1996, for example, among children of elementary school age, 50% of Hispanic children had parents who were high school graduates or more, as did 78% of African American children, compared with 91% of Caucasian children (U.S. Bureau of the Census, 1998).

Poverty Levels

A substantial minority of kindergarten students live in families whose household incomes are below the official poverty level. This was true of nearly 25% of all kindergarten students in 1996. By comparison, in 1969, 14% of all U.S. children were in families with incomes below the poverty level (Zill & Rogers, 1988).

The relatively high poverty rate for today's kindergartners is partly attributable to the considerable fraction of their families that are single-parent families or from minority racial or ethnic backgrounds, as noted previously. The proportion of elementary school age children living below the poverty level during 1995 was 10% among those living with both parents, as opposed to 49% among those living with their mothers only and 18% among those living with their fathers only. Among children living with never married mothers, the poverty rate was 63%. In the same year, the poverty rate among elementary school age children of Caucasian background was 12%, whereas it was 40% among those of African American or Hispanic background (U.S. Bureau of the Census, 1998).

In addition to family structure and economic opportunity factors, parents of kindergartners tend to be relatively young adults, whose work experience and earnings are generally more limited than those of parents of students in the upper-elementary or secondary grades or other older adults.

Welfare Receipt

Consistent with their elevated poverty levels, families of kindergarten students also show relatively high rates of receiving welfare and other income-related benefits. In 1996, for example, 20% of kindergartners' families were receiving food stamps, and 14% had participated in the Supplemental Nutrition Program for Women, Infants, and Children (WIC). The same percentage—14%—was receiving welfare cash assistance under a program formerly called Aid to Families with Dependent Children (AFDC), now called Temporary Assistance to Needy Families (TANF).

Maternal Employment

Two thirds of today's kindergarten children have mothers who are employed outside the home. In 1993, 27% of kindergarten students had mothers who worked full time throughout the previous year, and 40% had mothers who worked part time or for part of the year only (NHES, 1993). Employment by mothers whose children are just beginning school has risen dramatically since the early 1970s. Among married mothers of 5-year-olds, the proportion who were in the labor force rose from 37% in 1970 to 52% in 1980, and to 64% by 1986 (Select Committee on Children, Youth, and Families, U.S. House of Representatives, 1989).

Kindergartners from families with incomes below the poverty level are less likely to have a mother who is employed outside the home. (Of course, one could also say that kindergartners whose mothers are not employed are more likely to be growing up in poverty.) In 1993, only 12% of kindergarten pupils from poor families had a mother who worked full time throughout the previous year, whereas the same was true of 33% of kindergartners from middle- to high-income families. Nearly one half of poor kindergartners (48%) had mothers who did not work at all during the year, compared with 27% of kindergartners from middle- to high-income families (NHES, 1993).

Children in private kindergarten programs are more likely to have mothers who were employed than are public school kindergartners. In 1993, 75% of private school kindergartners had employed mothers, compared with 66% of the public school pupils. In addition, 34% of the private school kindergartners had mothers who worked full time, year round, compared with 26% of the public school pupils (NHES, 1993).

Number of Siblings

The majority of today's children of elementary school age (54%) have only one brother or sister living with them at home or none at all (U.S. Bureau of the Census, 1998). Twenty-eight percent have two brothers or sisters, whereas only eighteen percent have three or more siblings. The average number of brothers or sisters an American child of elementary school age had in 1996 was less than two (1.61). A majority of Hispanic schoolchildren (59%) and just more than one half of African American schoolchildren (52%) had two or more siblings living with them, whereas a majority of Caucasian schoolchildren (58%) had one sibling or no siblings. The mean number of siblings per child was 1.92 for Hispanic children from ages 6 to 11; 1.75 for African American children of the same ages; and 1.51 for Caucasian children (U.S. Bureau of the Census, 1998).

Although average family sizes in the United States have been somewhat larger in the 1990s than they were in the late 1970s and 1980s, they are still considerably smaller than they were in the 1960s and 1970s. The average number of children born per woman (the total fertility rate) fell from 3.65 in 1960 and 2.48 in 1970 to 2.03 in 1996 (Ventura, Martin, Curtin, & Mathews, 1998; Select Committee on Children, Youth, and Families, U.S. House of Representatives, 1989). Among African American women, the average number of children born per woman fell from 4.54 in 1960 to 2.14 in 1996. Among Hispanic women, the average number of children born per woman was 3.05 in 1996, whereas among Caucasian women it was 1.80 (Ventura et al., 1998). Trend data are not available as far back for Hispanic women because birth certificates in many states did not include Hispanic origin until relatively recently. There is also considerable variation in family size across the major Hispanic subgroups. In 1996, for example, women of Mexican origin had an average family size of 3.35 children per woman, compared with 2.16 for those of Puerto Rican origin, 1.77 for those of Cuban origin, and 2.76 for those of other Hispanic origin.

Multiple Risk Factors

Some theorists believe that the presence of a single sociodemographic risk factor such as poverty or low parent education is less significant for a child's chances of academic success than the presence of multiple risk factors (Meisels & Wasik, 1990). In a study that examined the relationship between risk factors and children's developmental accomplishments and difficulties at age 4, five specific risk factors were considered: poverty, low parent education, minority language status, single-parent status, and being born to an unmarried mother. Fifty-one percent of all 4-year-olds in the United States who had not yet entered kindergarten were found to have at least one of these risk factors. The proportions who had more than one were considerably smaller, although hardly insignificant: 31% of the children had two or more risk factors, and 15% had three or more (Zill, Collins, West, & Germino Hausken, 1995). As described in the next section, children with multiple risk factors had fewer early academic accomplishments and more developmental difficulties than those with no risk factors or only one.

PREPARATION FOR KINDERGARTEN AND ELEMENTARY SCHOOL

A child's developmental status at kindergarten entry is positively influenced by the amount and type of educational activities in which parents and other family members engage with the child prior to formal schooling as well as by the child's participation in center-based preschool programs such as Head Start, nursery school, or prekindergarten. Two positive trends affecting young children that are not sufficiently appreciated by social commentators are a growing awareness among parents of all social classes of the importance of the stimulation they provide at home and increases in the proportion of children who attend preschool programs prior to kindergarten. Unfortunately, despite this progress, there are still sizable inequalities in the provision of these early educational experiences to children in different socioeconomic groups.

Educational Activities that Parents Do at Home with Their Children

Much of the early knowledge that young children acquire is learned before they ever set foot in a classroom. Parents play a key role in teaching their children basic words, numbers, facts, concepts, and skills. In addition, parents usually encourage their children to explore the environment and learn by doing, while also supervising them to ensure that their explorations do not put them in danger. Recognizing the importance of the intellectual guidance that parents provide, the National Education Goals Panel sought to ensure that all mothers and fathers would provide such stimulation to their young children. One of the key objectives under Goal 1 of the National Education Goals, the so-called "school readiness" goal, is that parents should be their children's first teachers, devoting time each day to helping their preschool children learn (National Education Goals Panel, 1996).

The NHES and other surveys found that most American parents, in fact, regularly perform activities with their preschool-age children, such as reading to them, providing basic instruction in preacademic skills, playing games that have a strong teaching component, and arranging opportunities for exploration and skill building. In 1996, for example, more than 90% of U.S. children ages 3 through 5 had parents who reported teaching their preschoolers letters, words, or numbers in the past week; most said they had done such teaching three or more times during the week (NHES, 1996). Large majorities of preschoolers also had parents who reported teaching the child songs or music, working on arts and crafts together, playing a game or sport together, taking the child along on errands, and involving him or her in household chores (National Education Goals Panel, 1995). Eighty-three percent had parents who reported reading stories to the child three or more times in the past week. Fifty-six percent had parents who said they read to the child every day (Snyder et al., 1998).

Because there are no comparable survey measurements from the 1960s and 1970s, it cannot be said for certain that today's parents do more with their children than earlier generations of parents did. But it seems likely that this is the case. The higher education levels of today's parents and greater public awareness of the importance of educational activities in early childhood seem to have more than offset any possible diminution in parent–child activities that may have resulted from increased family disruption, single parenthood, or maternal employment. Even in the 1990s, there have been significant increases in the reported frequency with which parents read to their preschool children and carry out other educational activities with them (National Education Goals Panel, 1997; Snyder et al., 1998).

Much of the data that exists on parent activities is self-reported, and parents may say they regularly partake in educational activities with their children because they feel that they ought to be carrying out such activities, rather than because they actually did these things. However, even the possibility that parents might be motivated to exaggerate in this way indicates that the importance of early parental stimulation has been communicated to a very broad spectrum of American parents.

Despite the generally high level of parent activities with their young children and the evidence of increases in the frequency of these activities, there remain significant group differences in the regularity with which parents engage in these activities (Zill, Moore, Smith, Stief, & Coiro, 1995). As usual, these differences tend to work in favor of those children who are already more advantaged in terms of family resources. During 1995, for example, 74% of preschoolers with parents who were college graduates were read to on a daily basis, compared with 52% of preschoolers with parents who were high school graduates only, and 37% of preschoolers whose parents had less than a high school education (National Education Goals Panel, 1995). In 1996, 46% of preschoolers whose families had incomes below the poverty level were read to every day, compared with 60% of preschoolers whose families were above the poverty level. Twenty-seven percent of preschoolers from families with incomes below the poverty line were taken to a library by their parents during the previous month, compared with 41% of the latter group (NHES, 1996).

Participation in Early Childhood Education Programs

Today's kindergartners are more likely than earlier generations of young children to have participated in preschool and early childhood education programs. According to data from the Census Bureau's Current Population Survey, the percentage of 3- and 4-year-old children who were attending preschool in October rose from 30% in 1980 to 45% in 1996 (Federal Interagency Forum on Child and Family Statistics, 1998). When participation in a broader group of early childhood programs is examined, including day care centers, nursery schools, Head Start programs, and prekindergarten classes, more than half (53%) of 3- and 4-year-olds not yet in kindergarten were attending such programs in the late winter and early spring of 1996 (NHES, 1996).

Participation in center-based programs varies considerably across social groups, with children whose parents have lower income and education levels being less likely to attend than children from more advantaged families (Hofferth, West, Henke, & Kaufman, 1994). For example, among 3- and 4-year-olds whose families had incomes below the official poverty line, 41% were attending center-based programs in 1996 compared with 58% of children whose families were above the poverty line (Federal Interagency Forum on Child and Family Statistics, 1998). Likewise, 37% of preschoolers whose mothers had less than a high school education were attending center-based programs in the same year, compared with 71% of children whose mothers had completed college.

Rates of preschool participation also vary across racial and ethnic groups, and the variations are not simply a function of average parental education and income levels of the different groups. Specifically, African American children are somewhat more likely to attend center-based programs than Caucasian children, whereas Hispanic children have relatively low rates of preschool participation. In 1996, 63% of African American 3- and 4-year-olds were attending center-based early childhood programs, compared with 54% of Caucasian children and 37% of Hispanic children of the same ages (Federal Interagency Forum on Child and Family Statistics, 1998).

CHILDREN'S DEVELOPMENTAL STATUS AT KINDERGARTEN ENTRY

Some education theorists hold that young children from different social classes begin formal schooling on a more or less equal footing in terms of their developmental accomplishments and difficulties. These theorists contend that schools create or greatly magnify inequality in pupil achievement across social groups, presumably because of gross inequities among school systems in educational resources and average teacher and administrator quality (Kozol, 1991). However, there is substantial evidence that there already are sizable differences in the developmental status of children from different social groups before they enter kindergarten. These differences are believed to relate to differences in the amounts and types of intellectual stimulation and emotional support that children from different groups receive at home, to differences in access to high-quality child care and preschool programs, to differences in environmental stress and family turmoil, to health and nutritional influences, and perhaps to genetic factors (the latter is, of course, controversial) (Jencks et al., 1972; Mayer, 1997; Rowe, 1994; Rutter & Rutter, 1993).

Not only poverty but also other sociodemographic risk factors, such as having parents who have not completed high school, being born to a mother who was unmarried at the time of the child's birth, living in a single-parent family, and having parents who speak a language other than English at home, have been associated with fewer signs of early achievement and more developmental difficulties at school entry. In general, the more risk factors to which a child is subject, the lower the number of accomplishments and the higher the number of difficulties he or she is likely to experience. Researchers have found a linear relationship between a cumulative risk score and measures of verbal IQ and social adjustment in 4-year-old children (Sameroff, Seifer, Barocas, Zax, & Greenspan, 1987); vocabulary and math test scores in 4- and 5-year-olds (Nord, Zill, Prince, Clarke, & Ventura, 1994); and parent reports of emerging literacy, motor skills, and developmental difficulties in 4-year-old preschoolers (Zill et al., 1995).

In Zill et al. (1995), for example, preschoolers from families with three or more risk factors were five times as likely to be in less than optimal health compared with children from families with none of five sociodemographic risk factors. They were three times as likely to have speech difficulties and twice as likely to display hyperactive behavior. On average, the high-risk preschoolers displayed one and a half fewer signs of emerging literacy (out of five) than preschoolers with no risk factors. Differences linked to poverty and other sociodemographic factors remained significant after controlling for other factors, such as the child's month of birth, sex, race and ethnicity, and number of young siblings in the family (Zill, Collins, et al., 1995; Zill & Davies, 1994).

Effects of Preschool Participation and Home Environment on School Readiness

There is considerable evidence that children who have attended Head Start, prekindergarten, or other center-based preschool programs come to kindergarten with more accomplishments than children who have not attended such programs. Earlier studies typically showed that children who attended preschool did better on standardized IQ or achievement tests than those who did not attend, although the nonattendees usually caught up by the end of first grade (Jencks et al., 1972). Longitudinal (albeit relatively small-scale) studies of high-quality early childhood programs, such as the Perry Preschool Program or the Abecedarian Project, found that these programs had long-term positive effects on the school completion rates of low-income minority children (Barnett, 1992).

The national study of the developmental accomplishments and difficulties of 4-year-old preschoolers cited previously found that preschool participation is associated with higher emerging literacy scores amounting to an average of nearly one full accomplishment out of five. The difference remained significant when other child and family characteristics were controlled (Zill, Collins, et al., 1995; Zill & Davies, 1994). The benefit accrued to children from both high- and low-risk family backgrounds. Thus, although preschool programs bolster the emerging literacy of low-income children, they do not close the gap between these children and those from middle- to high-income families (Jencks et al., 1972).

In addition to the effects of preschool program attendance, research has shown that the educational quality of the home environment makes a difference with respect to the cognitive aspects of school readiness. Young children from low-income families whose parents read to them frequently, tell stories, sing songs, and play informal learning games come to kindergarten with more advanced cognitive skills and more signs of emerging literacy than children from similar families whose parents do not provide such frequent intellectual stimulation (Bradley & Caldwell, 1981; Moore & Snyder, 1991; Zill & Davies, 1994).

Preschool attendance is not found to be associated with fewer behavioral or speech difficulties, or with better health status in preschoolers (Zill, Collins, et al., 1995). However, the national study that examined the relationship of preschool attendance to these aspects of school readiness had no measure of the quality of the preschool programs attended and could not determine whether high-quality programs might have made some difference in these areas. Program directors and teachers in Head Start and other preschool programs serving children from low-income families have been less focused on raising children's test scores and more concerned with providing supportive, unstructured socialization programs (Jencks et al., 1972). Presumably, these programs should have some measurable effect on the social skills that children bring to kindergarten. There is evidence that this is the case (Administration on Children, Youth, and Families, Research, Demonstration, and Evaluation Branch, 1998), but more research is needed on this question.

KINDERGARTEN PROGRAMS ATTENDED BY AMERICAN CHILDREN

There is considerable diversity in the kinds of kindergarten programs that children attend today. About 16% of all kindergarten students in the United States are enrolled in private schools (including religion-affiliated programs) rather than public school programs. The student body and program characteristics of private kindergartens differ considerably from those of public kindergartens, as detailed in this section.

Fifty-five percent of kindergarten children attend part-day programs (i.e., those that have classes only in the morning or only in the afternoon). Forty-five percent attend "full-day" programs. (*Full-day* generally means 9 A.M. to 3 P.M., and *half-day* means 8:30 A.M. to 11:30 A.M., or noon to 3 P.M.) Children in private kindergartens are more likely to be in full-day programs: 56% versus 43% of children who attend public school kindergarten.

Types of Programs Attended by Children from Low-Income Families

Children from families whose incomes are below the official poverty line are less than half as likely to attend private kindergarten programs as are children from families with incomes above the poverty line. In 1993, for example, 8% of kindergarten students from low-income families were enrolled in private kindergartens, compared with nearly 19% of those from middle- to high-income families (NHES, 1993).

However, children from low-income families are more likely than those from middle- to high-income families to be enrolled in full-day, as opposed to half-day, kindergarten programs. Overall, 45% of U.S. kindergarten students were enrolled in full-day kindergarten programs in 1993. But nearly 49% of public school kindergarten students from low-income families were attending full-day programs, whereas the same was true of only 40% of public school kindergarten students from middle- to high-income families (NHES, 1993). This difference is partly a regional one: A disproportionate share of low-income families with young children are from the South, and Southern states and school districts tended to introduce public kindergarten later than those in other regions of the United States. When public kindergartens were introduced in the South, however, they tended to be full-day programs.

It may also be that, where they have a choice, low-income families prefer to send their children to full-day kindergartens because they are less able to afford the additional child care that is required if parents are employed and the child is enrolled in a part-day kindergarten program. Of course, even so-called "full-day" kindergartens do not extend for the entire working day. Therefore, some form of additional care arrangement or "wraparound" care at the school is usually needed. As noted previously, low-income families were less than half as likely as middle- to high-income families to contain mothers who were employed on a full-time, year-round basis, and almost twice as likely to contain mothers who were not employed at all during the previous year.

The kindergarten programs attended by children from low-income families are more likely than the programs attended by children from middle- to high-income families to be racially and ethnically integrated. In 1996, 44% of kindergartners from families with incomes below the poverty line were said to be going to classes that had a substantial mix of racial and ethnic groups (between 25% and 75% of the other students were of the same race and ethnic group as the child), whereas the same was true of only 34% of kindergartners from middle- to high-income families (NHES, 1996). Of course, U.S. kindergartners from low-income families are themselves more likely to come from a variety of racial and ethnic groups, whereas children from middle- to high-income families are predominantly Caucasian and non-Hispanic (72% of kindergartners from middle- to high-income families were Caucasians in 1976, compared with 36% of kindergartners from low-income families).

About as many low-income families with kindergartners (47%) as middle- to high-income families (48%) report that their choice of where to live was influenced by where their child would go to school (NHES, 1993).

Family Characteristics of Private and Public School Kindergarten Pupils

Children who attend private kindergartens tend to come from families that are relatively advantaged socioeconomically. In 1996, only 5% of pupils in private kindergartens were from families with incomes below the poverty line, compared with 28% of pupils in public kindergarten.[3] Six percent of the private kindergarten pupils were in families that received food stamps, compared with 21% of the pupils in public kindergartens. More than 75% of the pupils in private kindergartens lived with both of their parents (biological or adoptive), whereas the same was true of 62% of pupils in public kindergartens. Nearly one half of the kindergartners in private school (49%) had at least one parent who was a college graduate, whereas the same was true of 23% of kindergartners in public school (NHES, 1996).

Private kindergarten pupils are more likely to be living in a home that their parents own and are less likely to have changed residences or neighborhoods dur-

---

[3]Estimates from the 1996 and 1993 NHES are discrepant in terms of the proportion of private kindergartners from poverty-level families. The 1993 survey found 14% of the private pupils and 31% of the public pupils to be from families below the poverty line. The inconsistency is probably due to the small number of cases on which the estimates are based. The two surveys agree in finding the proportion of pupils from low-income families to be substantially lower in private kindergartens.

ing their young lives. In 1993, 71% of the children in private kindergartens had parents who owned their own homes, compared with 52% of the children in public kindergartens. Also, 43% of the private kindergarten pupils had lived at the same address since birth, compared with 30% of the public kindergarten pupils. Conversely, the families of 18% of the students in private kindergartens had moved three or more times since the child's birth, compared with 28% of the students in public kindergartens (NHES, 1993).

Private kindergartners are more likely to be drawn from the Caucasian majority of the U.S. population, and the schools and classes they attend tend to reflect that fact. In 1996, nearly three quarters of children in private kindergartens (74%) were from Caucasian families, compared with 61% of children in public kindergartens. Only 27% of the children in private kindergartens attended classes that had a substantial mix of racial and ethnic groups (between 25% and 75% of the other students were of the same race and ethnic group as the child), compared with 38% of pupils in public kindergartens (NHES, 1996).

Private and public programs do not differ significantly in the proportion of pupils who have one or both parents who were born in a country other than the United States. In 1996, this was true of 17% of children in private kindergartens and 15% of children in public kindergartens (NHES, 1996). In 1993, 6% of children in private kindergartens had parents whose primary language was something other than English, whereas the same was true of 8% of children in public kindergartens (NHES, 1993).

Interestingly, there also seems to be a difference in the age and sex composition of private and public kindergartens. In 1996, a majority of private kindergarten pupils were females (55%), whereas a slight majority of public kindergarten pupils were males (51%). A larger minority of the pupils in private kindergartens were less than 5 years old as of the end of the previous calendar year (1995): 12%, compared with only 3% of public kindergarten students. The first difference may reflect a desire of parents to be more protective of their young girl children, if they have the wherewithal to send them to private school. The second difference may occur because private kindergarten programs are more flexible about admission-age cutoffs than public programs.

The abundance of material and intangible resources that children from private school families have available to them would lead one to expect that the educational task facing teachers and administrators in private kindergartens should be considerably easier than that confronting teachers and administrators in public school programs. Whether these advantages translate into easier pupil adjustment to private kindergarten classes or greater parent satisfaction with the educational programs that private kindergartens provide is yet to be seen.

CHARACTERISTICS OF KINDERGARTEN PROGRAMS

What are the kindergarten classes like that today's 5-year-olds attend? Given the diversity in the skills, knowledge, and reaction patterns that young children bring to the programs, are class sizes small enough for teachers to devote significant time to small groups or individuals within the class, catering to their particular instructional needs? Are most kindergarten teachers well qualified to teach young children? In what kinds of activities do children engage in kindergarten classes? Does there seem to be justification for the criticism that kindergarten has become "too academic" in its orientation and that many of the activities that go on there are not "developmentally appropriate"? Or do kindergarten teachers devote too *little* time and effort to nurturing early academic skills, as other critics contend?

Class Size and Child-to-Adult Ratio

American kindergarten pupils vary widely in the knowledge and skills they bring with them to school, and significant fractions exhibit developmental delays or difficulties (Zill, Collins, et al., 1995). There can be and often is substantial variation in children's developmental levels within a given school and classroom. Thus, schools must be prepared to offer a broad array of activities and materials to their kindergarten students. Otherwise, they risk having some children be unchallenged and bored, while others are struggling to keep up with the class. It is certainly possible to conduct a diverse set of learning activities, even within a single classroom, provided the group size and the child–staff ratio are not too large. The main teacher must also be skilled and energetic enough to manage a class in which many different things are happening at once.

Unfortunately, the size of the average kindergarten class in the United States is such that most teachers would find it quite challenging to devote a lot of individual attention to children without considerable help from assistant teachers or volunteer aides. In the 1992/1993 school year, for example, public school teachers reported an average kindergarten class size of 21 students in full-day kindergarten classes and 22 students in half-day classes (Heaviside & Farris, 1993). One quarter had class sizes of 26 or more. Other teacher surveys have produced similar results, with an average kindergarten class size of more than 23 students being found in the NCES 1993–1994 Schools and Staffing Survey (NCES, 1996) and an average size of 22 students being found in the National Center for Early Development and Learning 1996 Transition Practices Survey (Pianta et al., 1998).

Average class sizes tend to be somewhat smaller in rural areas (mean of 18 students in 1992/1993) than in urban or suburban areas (Heaviside & Farris, 1993). Schools with more minority students have larger class sizes than those with fewer minority students, but class size does not vary with district poverty levels (Pianta et al., 1998). Class size remains fairly constant across other school characteristics.

During the 1992/1993 school year, 61% of kindergarten teachers had the help of paid adult assistants (including co-teachers or team teachers) in their classes. On average, those teachers with paid assistants had one such assistant for 64% of the time that the class met, or an average of 13.5 hours per week. Nearly one half of kindergarten teachers (49%) reported getting help from at least one adult volunteer during a typical week. Of teachers who had such volunteer help, the average number of volunteers was three, each of whom contributed an average of 3 hours per week. Counting paid assistants or team teachers, the average student-to-staff ratio for kindergarten classes was 15 to 1 during the 1992/1993 school year, based on full-time equivalents. With adult volunteers factored in, the student-to-adult ratio was 14 to 1 (again, based on full-time equivalents) (Heaviside & Farris, 1993). The 1996 Transition Practices Survey found similar results (Pianta et al., 1998).

Guidelines put forth by the National Association for the Education of Young Children (NAEYC) call for kindergartners to be in classes of no more than 20 children with 2 adults, implying a student-to-staff ratio of only 10 to 1 (Bredekamp, 1987). In addition to the actual average ratio being considerably higher than this, in 39% of public kindergarten classes the teacher did not have a paid assistant to help with the students. Clearly, many American kindergarten classes fail to meet NAEYC guidelines. Teachers in these classes are likely to have a hard time providing suitable activities for pupils with widely varying accomplishments or coping with multiple students with developmental difficulties (Zill, Collins, et al., 1995).

Teacher Demographics

Almost all (98%) public kindergarten teachers in the United States are women. About 85% are Caucasian, 8% or 9% African American, and 5% Hispanic (Heaviside & Farris, 1993; NCES, 1996). Teachers in central city districts are more likely to be African American or Hispanic, as are those in high-poverty districts and in schools with high minority enrollments (Pianta et al., 1998).

Teacher Qualifications

Virtually all kindergarten teachers have bachelor's degrees, and 40% have master's or other advanced degrees (Henke, Choy, Geis, & Broughman, 1996). Fewer teachers in rural areas than in central city or suburban areas hold advanced degrees, but educational attainment does not differ significantly among central city and suburban areas, nor does it vary with district poverty levels or the percentage of minority students in the school (Pianta et al., 1998). More than one half of kindergarten teachers (54%) majored in early childhood education at either the undergraduate or graduate level. Almost all (93%) have completed course work in early childhood education, with nine courses being the average number of early childhood courses taken across all teachers (Heaviside & Farris, 1993).

The average kindergarten teacher has at least one state-level certification in elementary or early childhood education. In 1996, more than three quarters of U.S. kindergarten teachers had an elementary education certification that included kindergarten, one half held a certification specific to kindergarten or the primary grades, and 14% held a "preschool" certification. Other common certifications were in special education (6%), reading (6%), and bilingual education or English as a Second Language (5%) (Pianta et al., 1998).

On average, public school kindergarten teachers have been teaching for about 14 years (Henke et al., 1996), with about 9 years of experience at the kindergarten level (Heaviside & Farris, 1993). Teachers in low-level poverty districts tend to have more kindergarten teaching experience than those in middle-level poverty districts, but average experience does not vary significantly with minority student enrollment or metro status (Pianta et al., 1998).

Training and Information on Transitions to Kindergarten

Less than one quarter of kindergarten teachers report that they have received any specialized training on how to enhance or facilitate children's transition into kindergarten. Even those reporting that they had some such training seem to be mostly referring to general early childhood training, rather than training specific to the transition process. Even fewer teachers (23%) report that they receive information about strategies for enhancing transitions. The most frequent sources of this information are workshops (70%), magazines and journals for teachers (67%), discussions with other teachers (49%), and school officials (37%) (Pianta et al., 1998).

Classroom Activities

Some education researchers contend that U.S. kindergarten programs have moved away from the "whole child," developmental approach that originally characterized kindergarten and toward a more structured, academic curriculum that is inappropriate for many of the children who are enrolled in kindergarten classes (Freeman & Hatch, 1989; Shepard & Smith, 1988; Walsh, 1989). But evidence from surveys of kindergarten teachers does not seem to support this line of criticism. At least as described by the teachers, most kindergarten pupils spend a good deal of class time in free choice and self-discovery activities of the sort that developmentalists endorse and relatively little in preacademic drill work. The beliefs of kindergarten teachers also seem to favor self-directed activities and oppose the use of preacademic drill work. However, parents' reports on the feedback they get from teachers suggest that there may be more of an academic flavor to kindergarten classes than one would conclude from listening to teachers only.

Most public school kindergarten classes meet 5 days per week, with full-day kindergartens meeting an average of 31 hours per week, and half-day kindergartens meeting either 16 hours (when two half-day sessions are taught) or 14 hours (when only one session is taught) (Heaviside & Farris, 1993). According to teachers' estimates, approximately equal amounts of class time are spent in teacher-directed group instruction in reading, numbers, or the alphabet (31%) and individual or small-group projects in which children select the activities (30%). No significant variation in this balance is found across different types of schools or teachers (Heaviside & Farris, 1993).

The vast majority of public school kindergartens (97%) have activity centers, that is, "clearly delineated, organized, thematic work and play areas where children interact with materials and other children without the teacher's constant presence or direction (such as a language arts area, a block area, a dramatic play area)" (Heaviside & Farris, 1993, p. 113). Only 19% of kindergarten classes are set up with a desk for each child, and virtually all of these (18% out of 19%) have activity centers as well. The use of activity centers is believed to reflect a child-centered approach to early education that is more conducive to active, hands-on learning (Heaviside & Farris, 1993).

When public school kindergarten teachers are asked to report how many days per week their pupils engage in various kinds of activities, the most frequently reported activity is listening to stories read aloud. Ninety percent of teachers say they read stories to their students 5 days per week; another 9% say they read to their students 3 or 4 days per week. Also frequent are creative activities such as dramatic play, arts and crafts, music, free play, and choosing from a set of options such as building blocks, manipulatives, or books. About 90% of teachers report that their pupils engage in creative activities, free play, and choosing from options at least 3 or 4 days per week. Running, climbing, jumping, and other gross motor activities are also common, with about 80% of teachers reporting their pupils engage in these activities at least 3 or 4 days per week (Heaviside & Farris, 1993).

Much less common is the use of worksheets for the development of literacy skills or for learning math or science. The majority of kindergarten teachers report using worksheets only 1 or 2 days per week or less, and 20% say they never use them. Only about one fifth of teachers report using worksheets on a daily basis. More frequent is the reported use of manipulatives for teaching math or science. Nearly one half of kindergarten teachers say their pupils do this on a daily basis, and 87% report their pupils do this at least 3 or 4 days per week.

Kindergarten teachers in schools where 50% or more of the students are eligible for free lunches or in classes where 50% or more of the pupils are from racial or ethnic minorities are more likely to use worksheets and manipulatives for math or science than are teachers with fewer children from low-income families or from racial and ethnic minority groups. A 57% majority of these teachers report using manipulatives for math or science on a daily basis, and about a quarter say they make daily use of worksheets for building literacy skills in their pupils (Heaviside & Farris, 1993).

Teacher Beliefs

Most kindergarten teachers espouse beliefs about early childhood education that could be characterized as "developmental" rather than "didactic." They do not view kindergarten as a setting for preacademic instruction and drill work but rather as an opportunity for children to engage in learning through play and self-directed activities. For example, a 62% majority of public school kindergarten teachers do not believe that "Most children should learn to read in kindergarten," and 72% disagree with the statement, "Homework should be given in kindergarten almost every day" (Heaviside & Farris, 1993). Most teachers are opposed to phonics instruction, with two thirds disagreeing with the statement, "The best way to learn how to read is to practice matching letters and sounds over and over."

However, most teachers believe in the value of activities such as reading aloud to children and playing number games with them. Ninety-seven percent of public school kindergarten teachers agree that "One of the best ways to help children learn to read is by reading to them," and 99% believe that "Parents should read to their children and play counting games at home regularly" (Heaviside & Farris, 1993). Teachers are divided about the general appropriateness of formal reading and math instruction in the preschool years. For example, when asked whether they agree with the statement, "Children who begin formal reading and math instruction in preschool will do better in elementary school," more disagree (46%) than agree (31%), but nearly one quarter are neutral or undecided. Also, nearly one half agree with the statement, "Parents should set aside time every day for their kindergarten children to practice schoolwork" (Heaviside & Farris, 1993).

Minority teachers and teachers in high poverty schools are more likely to advocate phonics and a more didactic approach to the kindergarten curriculum. For example, 45% of African American teachers, as opposed to 12% of Caucasian teachers, hold that matching letters and sounds repeatedly is the best way to learn how to read. Furthermore, 21% of teachers in high poverty schools, versus 8% of those in low poverty schools, believe in the importance of matching letters and sounds. Also, whereas only 19% of all public school kindergarten teachers believe it is appropriate to give kindergartners homework every day, 41% of African American teachers believe this, as do 33% of teachers in large schools, 29% of those in high poverty schools, and 34% of those with high minority enrollment classes (Heaviside & Farris, 1993).

Qualities Important for School Readiness

Kindergarten teachers express divided and somewhat contradictory views on whether school readiness is primarily a matter of individual maturation or a matter of adequate preparation. The vast majority of teachers endorse a "maturational readiness" approach to children's developmental status. When asked whether they agree or disagree with the statement, "Readiness comes as children grow and mature; you can't push it," 88% of teachers agree. At the same time, 94% agree with the apparently contrasting statement, "I can enhance children's readiness by providing experiences they need to build important skills." Fifty-five percent of kindergarten teachers suggest that children with readiness problems wait a year before enrolling in kindergarten. But 56% would enroll children as soon as they are eligible, even if they seem unready, "so they can be exposed to the things they need" (Heaviside & Farris, 1993).

When asked how important various pupil characteristics are for a child to be ready for kindergarten, most kindergarten teachers put more of an emphasis on physical well-being, self-expression, social development, and curiosity than on mastery of basic cognitive skills. Almost all teachers believe that being physically healthy, rested, and well nourished is an essential or important quality for school readiness. More than three fourths hold that children should be able to communicate their needs, wants, and thoughts in their primary language and should be enthusiastic and curious when approaching new activities. More than one half believe that being sensitive to other children's feelings and able to take turns and share are essential or very important for kindergarten readiness (Heaviside & Farris, 1993).

However, less than one quarter of public school kindergarten teachers think it is very important that children have good problem-solving skills, be able to identify primary colors and basic shapes, be able to use pencils, know the alphabet, or count to 20. A majority of the teachers rated knowing the alphabet or counting as not very important or not at all important to be ready for kindergarten, perhaps believing these were things that they could teach children to do in kindergarten. Parents are much more likely to view these early cognitive skills as being important for school readiness (West, Germino Hausken, & Collins, 1993).

Teachers are more divided about the importance of behavioral characteristics such as following directions, not being disruptive of the class, and sitting still and paying attention for school readiness. Sixty percent rate it very important or essential for the child to be able to follow directions and not be disruptive of the class, and 42% say the same for being able to sit still and pay attention. But 40%–60% rate these behavioral qualities as only somewhat important or not important. The same is true of knowing the English language, which 41% of teachers describe as a very important or essential quality for school readiness (Heaviside & Farris, 1993).

Interestingly, longitudinal studies of child characteristics predictive of academic performance and school adjustment have found that the child's general level of cognitive development is a significant predictor of whether a child will be successful or have difficulties in elementary school (Horn & Packard, 1985; Pianta & McCoy, 1997). In addition, early behavior problems, such as having a limited attention span or being hyperactive or aggressive, are also significant predictors. Also, as detailed in the following section, parents of kindergartners frequently report that they receive negative feedback from their children's teachers concerning the child's difficulties paying attention and sitting still or his or her disruptive behavior.

KINDERGARTEN PARENTS' INVOLVEMENT IN SCHOOL-RELATED ACTIVITIES

How involved are kindergarten parents in school-related activities? How satisfied are they with the practices of kindergarten programs, especially with respect to how well the teachers and administrators communicate with parents and provide parents with opportunities for meaningful involvement in school decision making? How do parent involvement and parent satisfaction vary across income groups and between public and private programs? Before examining survey findings about children's experiences in kindergarten, we examine survey findings on parent participation in, and parent perceptions about, the kindergarten classes their children attend.

In 1996, a large majority of U.S. kindergarten parents (80%) reported that they had attended a general school meeting, such as an open house, a back-to-school night, or a meeting of a parent–teacher organization. Sixty-three percent said they had been to a class or school event, such as a play or sports event, and 50% said they had acted as a volunteer aide or served on a school committee (NHES, 1996). Based on criteria used in a parent involvement scale developed for the NHES, 35% of U.S. kindergarten students have parents who exhibit a high level of involvement in school-related activities; 32% have parents who are moderately involved; and 33% have parents who display only a low level of involvement in their kindergarten programs.[4] Summing the "moderate" and "high"category percentages, 67% of kindergarten children have parents who are at least moderately involved in their kindergarten programs.

The level of parent involvement in 1996 shown by kindergarten families is lower than the parent involvement of elementary school children (first through fifth grades). Seventy-three percent of parents of elementary school children show at least a moderate level of involvement in school-related activities, whereas 27% show low involvement (Nord, Brimhall, & West, 1997). However, the lower involvement scores for kindergarten parents may be due to the involvement questions being less applicable to kindergarten activities than they are for the higher elementary grades. Specifically, kindergarten programs are probably not as likely to have class plays or sports events for parents to attend.

As in the higher grades, mothers of children in kindergarten are far more likely to be actively involved in school-related activities than are fathers. Sixty percent of kindergarten mothers show moderate-to-high levels of involvement, compared with only 24% of kindergarten fathers. (The fathers' percentage is based only on households containing a resident father or stepfather.)

Involvement of Low-Income Families in Kindergarten Activities

Kindergarten parents with household income levels below the poverty level are less likely to be actively involved in their children's kindergarten programs than are parents from middle- to high-income families. Among parents whose children are enrolled in public kindergartens, less than one half of low-income parents (47%) are at least moderately involved in school activities, compared with 70% of middle- to high-income parents. Only 17% of low-income parents are highly in-

---

[4]Parents who had done none of the three things, or only one of them, were categorized as displaying a *low* level of involvement in school-related activities. Those who answered affirmatively to two of the questions were classified as having a *moderate* level of involvement, whereas those who had done all three were said to have a *high* level of involvement. This was the same scale previously applied to data from the 1993 NHES and presented in the report *Running in Place: How American Families Are Faring in a Changing Economy and an Individualistic Society* (Zill & Nord, 1994). However, data on kindergarten parents were not collected in 1993.

volved in their children's kindergarten programs, whereas the same is true of twice as many middle- to high-income parents (38%). A majority of low-income parents of kindergartners have been to a general school meeting since the start of the school year, but the majority is smaller than that for middle- to high-income parents: 71% versus 82%. Less than half of low-income parents (47%) have attended a class or school event, such as a play, compared with two thirds (65%) of middle- to high-income parents. Only 30% of low-income parents have acted as volunteer aides or served on school committees, whereas 53% of middle- to high-income parents have done this (NHES, 1996).

These differences occur despite the fact that, as noted previously, most low-income parents say their schools do a good job of communicating with parents and telling them about opportunities to participate at school. These differences occur also despite the fact that low-income mothers would appear to have more opportunity to perform volunteer activities at school, inasmuch as they are less likely than middle- to high-income mothers to be employed outside the home.

Multivariate analysis of school participation data shows that it is not just the meager incomes of poor parents that are associated with their lower involvement levels. Factors that are often present in today's low-income families, especially lower parent education levels and not having both parents present in the household, show stronger negative associations with parent involvement than poverty status as such (Zill & Nord, 1994). The lower participation levels of low-income families do not bode well for their children's later achievement. Previous studies have shown the importance for children's school success of parents getting and remaining actively involved in school-related activities (Brick et al., 1994; Henderson, 1987; Henderson & Berla, 1994; Nord et al., 1997; Zill, 1996a; Zill & Nord, 1994).

Involvement of Parents of Children in Private Kindergarten

As in the higher grades of school, parents with children in private kindergarten are more likely to be actively involved in school-related activities than are parents of children in public kindergarten. In 1996, 85% of parents of children in private kindergarten were at least moderately involved in school-related activities, compared with 64% of all parents of children in public kindergarten. A 55% majority of parents of children in private kindergarten were highly involved in their children's kindergarten programs, compared with 32% of parents of children in public kindergarten (NHES, 1996). The participation gap between parents of children in private kindergarten and those of children in public kindergarten was particularly large with respect to volunteering at school or serving on committees: 70% of parents of children in private kindergarten reported this kind of participation in the current school year, compared with 46% of parents of children in public kindergartens.

The higher participation rates of parents of children in private kindergarten is partly attributable to their higher education and income levels and their having a higher prevalence of intact two-parent families. But even when these factors are statistically controlled, having children in private school is associated with significantly higher levels of parent participation in school-related activities (Zill & Nord, 1994). In another respect, the high involvement rate of parents of children in private kindergarten is especially impressive because, as noted previously, mothers of children in private kindergarten programs are more likely than mothers of children in public kindergarten to be working in full-time, year-round jobs.

VIEWS OF PARENTS OF CHILDREN IN
KINDERGARTEN ABOUT SCHOOL PRACTICES

Most parents in the United States with children in kindergarten believe the schools that their children attend are doing a reasonably good job of communicating with parents and providing opportunities for parental involvement in school. In 1996, for example, when parents of children in kindergarten were asked how well their child's kindergarten lets parents know how their child is doing in school, more than two thirds of kindergarten parents said the school "does this very well" (NHES, 1996). Smaller majorities of parents said the kindergarten does very well at providing "workshops, materials, or advice about how to help child learn at home" and at helping them "understand what children of child's age are like" (NHES, 1996) (see Figure 4.2).

Communication between school and home: Most kindergarten parents report being contacted by the child's teacher or school without having contacted them first. Ninety-six percent report receiving newsletters, memos, or notices addressed to all parents. Fifty-three percent report that the school sent them personal notes, and 43% say the teacher or school called them on the telephone at least once or twice during the current school year (NHES, 1996).

Involvement in school decision making: A substantial majority of kindergarten parents believe that they have some say in school decision making. Three quarters of parents report that their schools put parents on committees that make decisions about school policies. A smaller but still substantial majority (69%) believe that "parents have a real say in school policy decisions." However, only 32% of all parents of children in kindergarten report that their school has a written parent involvement agreement or "learning compact" that says "how parents and the school will share responsibility for their children's education" (NHES, 1996).

Satisfaction of Low-Income Families with School Practices

Somewhat surprisingly, low-income families with children in kindergarten are more, not less, likely to report that their schools do a good job of communicating with parents. For example, 73% of low-income parents, versus 63% of middle- to high-income parents, say the school "does very well" at letting them know how the child is doing in school.

These results would lead one to believe that public kindergarten programs that serve low-income families are doing a reasonable job of trying to involve parents and assist them to be better nurturers of their children. An alternative and less charitable explanation of the findings is that low-income parents are less demanding of the schools and less likely to be "quality connoisseurs" of teacher and school administrator performance than middle- to high-income parents. As just reported, it is relatively rare for low-income parents to act as volunteers at school or serve on school committees. Thus, they may be less knowledgeable about what actually goes on in school. Nonetheless, the survey findings do not support the view that the learning problems of low-income children are largely attributable to the dismal quality of the schools they attend.

Satisfaction of Parents of Children in Private Kindergarten with School Practices

Although low-income parents of children in public kindergarten describe their school's communication efforts in more positive terms than do middle- to high-

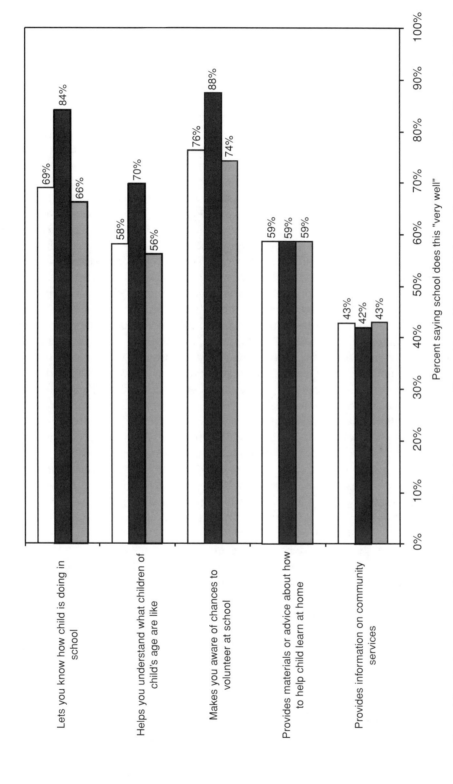

Figure 4.2. Kindergarten parents' views on how well school communicates. (Source: National Household Education Survey, 1996.) (Key: □, Total; ■, Private; ▨, Public.)

income parents of children in public kindergarten, parents who have their children in private kindergarten are more positive than both public kindergarten groups (see Figure 4.2). It is not surprising that private schools, which are typically reliant on parental assistance, would be active in making parents aware of chances to volunteer. It is more noteworthy that more parents of children in private kindergarten are pleased with their schools' efforts in letting parents know how their children are doing in school and in helping the family understand what children are like at this age.

More frequent communication between school and home: Parents of children in private kindergarten report more frequent communication between the school and the home. Parents in both groups do not differ with respect to saying that the school "provided newsletters, memos, or notices addressed to all parents" during the current school year. But more parents of children in private kindergarten say they have been sent a personal note by the child's teacher (58% versus 52% of parents of children in public kindergarten) and that they have been called on the telephone by the teacher or someone else from the school (52% compared with 42% of parents of children in public kindergarten).

Similar involvement in school decision making: Parents of children in private kindergarten are less likely than parents of children in public kindergarten to report that their "school includes parents on committees . . . that make decisions about school policies having to do with the school budget, what will be taught, discipline, or other policies." Sixty-seven percent of the parents of children in private kindergarten say yes to this question, compared with 76% of parents of children in public kindergarten. But some of the parent representation on public school governing bodies seems to be merely token: Private and public kindergarten parents are about equally likely to think that "parents have a real say in school policy decisions." Sixty-seven percent of parents of children in private kindergarten say this, compared with 70% of parents of children in public kindergarten.

Unlike the survey findings about low-income parents, the findings about parents of children in private kindergarten are consistent with the view that public kindergartens could be doing better at communicating with parents and involving them in school activities. Although most parents of children in public kindergarten appear to be satisfied with their schools' performance in these areas, parents of children in private kindergarten are more satisfied. The positive views of parents of children in private kindergarten are particularly impressive, given that their relatively high education levels and their high rates of involvement in school activities are likely to make them both quality conscious and knowledgeable about school practices. Of course, skeptics will say that parents of children in private kindergarten have positive views to reduce their cognitive dissonance about the money they are spending to send their children to kindergarten. Although there may be some truth to such an interpretation, the differences in parent perceptions also seem to reflect real differences in school practices.

JUDGMENTS OF CHILDREN'S EXPERIENCES IN KINDERGARTEN

According to kindergarten teachers, almost one half of all their pupils enter kindergarten with some or many problems. However, only one pupil in six has serious difficulty making the transition to formal schooling. The types of problems that are fairly widespread in kindergarten classrooms are difficulty following directions, lack of academic skills, family disorganization, and difficulty working independently. Problems are more common in communities with high concentrations of poverty, in urban and rural communities as opposed to suburban communities, and in schools with high concentrations of minority pupils.

Parents of kindergarten children are more sanguine than teachers about pupil adjustment and performance in the first year of school. According to parents, the majority of U.S. kindergartners adjust to the beginning of their formal schooling in positive ways, without major difficulties. However, a sizable minority of children experience at least some transitory adjustment problems at the start of kindergarten. These initial difficulties seem about equally common among pupils from low-income families as among those from middle- and high-income families and among children in public kindergartens as among those in private ones. Most parents also say that they hear good things about their children from kindergarten teachers. But parents of the average kindergartner report receiving some negative feedback from teachers concerning their children's learning or behavior. Parents in low-income families receive considerably more negative teacher feedback about their children than do parents from middle- and high-income families.

Teacher Judgments of Success in the Transition to Kindergarten

According to kindergarten teachers, just more than one half of all children entering kindergarten (52%) have a "very successful entry, with virtually no problems." About another one third (32%) have a "moderately successful entry," with "some problems, mostly minor." About one child in six (16%) has a "difficult or very difficult entry," with many problems or the teacher having "serious concerns" about the child's academic progress or adjustment to school (Pianta et al., 1998). According to teachers, the most common problems exhibited by large numbers of entering kindergarten pupils ("about one half the class or more") are difficulty following directions (46% of teachers report this as a common problem), lack of academic skills (36%), difficulty working independently (34%), and difficulty working as part of a group (30%). Teachers also perceive aspects of the child's family environment or preschool experience as creating problems at school entry. The most frequent are a disorganized home environment (35% of teachers see this as a problem for one half of the class or more) and a lack of any formal preschool experience (31%).

The prevalence and types of transition problems that children experience relate to the poverty level and metropolitan status of the community and the minority composition of the school. Lower levels of successful school entry are found in communities with poverty rates of more than 15%. Transition problems are more frequent in central city communities than in rural areas and are least frequent in suburban communities. The prevalence of transition problems also rises as the minority composition of the school increases. As levels of poverty increase, teachers are more likely to report that majorities of their pupils lack social skills and have problems following directions, working independently, and working as part of a group. In rural areas, teachers are more likely to report that the majority of their pupils come from disorganized home environments. In schools with high concentrations of minority pupils, teachers are likely to report that large numbers of their pupils have a variety of adjustment difficulties: academic, social, cultural, developmental, and communication (Pianta et al., 1998).

Nonminority teachers in schools with high concentrations of minority pupils are more likely to report that majorities of their pupils have difficulty following directions, problems with social skills, and immaturity than are nonminority teachers in schools with moderate or low concentrations of minority pupils. Similar differences are not found in the reports of minority teachers. This may reflect cultural differences in norms about acceptable behavior at school. More experienced kindergarten teachers are found to report fewer transition problems. This may stem from the experienced teachers being more pragmatic in their expectations based on their previous experience with classroom misbehavior (Pianta et al., 1998).

Parent Reports on Teacher Feedback About Children's Learning and Behavior in Kindergarten

Most parents say that they hear good things about their children from kindergarten teachers. For example, 90% report that the teacher said their child "gets along with other children or works well in a group." Eighty-eight percent claim that the teacher said the child "has been doing really well in school," and 85% say that they have heard that their child "is very enthusiastic and interested in a lot of different things" (NHES, 1993). But the parents of the average kindergarten student in the United States also report receiving some negative feedback from teachers concerning their children's learning or classroom behavior.

Of nine specific learning and conduct problems covered in the national survey data, the most frequently reported teacher complaint concerns the child's attention span and ability to focus on schoolwork. Nearly one kindergarten pupil in every four (23%) was described as "doesn't concentrate, doesn't pay attention for long." A related problem behavior, being overly active ("has been very restless, fidgets all the time, or doesn't sit still"), was reported as a teacher complaint by the parents of one in seven kindergarten children (14%). Also quite common is the charge that the child "has been acting up in school or disrupting the class." This was reported for almost one child in every five (18%) (NHES, 1993). Other relatively common items of negative feedback are shown in Figure 4.3.

It is interesting that these items of negative teacher feedback were so common. When public kindergarten teachers are surveyed about the importance of various child characteristics "for a child to be ready for kindergarten," less than one half say it is "essential" or "very important" that the child "sits still and pays attention" (Heaviside & Farris, 1993). Yet parents apparently hear it from teachers when their child does not show such behavioral control in the classroom.

Although the individual negative feedback items are each reported for only a minority of children, it is common for a parent to say he or she received at least one or two such teacher comments about his or her child. Indeed, of the eight most common negative feedback items shown in Figure 4.3, the mean number received was 1.74 (Zill & Davies, 1994).

Family and Child Characteristics Associated with Receipt of Negative Teacher Feedback

Although many families get some negative feedback from teachers about the learning or conduct of their kindergarten child, some types of children and families tend to receive more of these critical comments. Children whose parents have less than a high school education or income levels near or below the poverty line

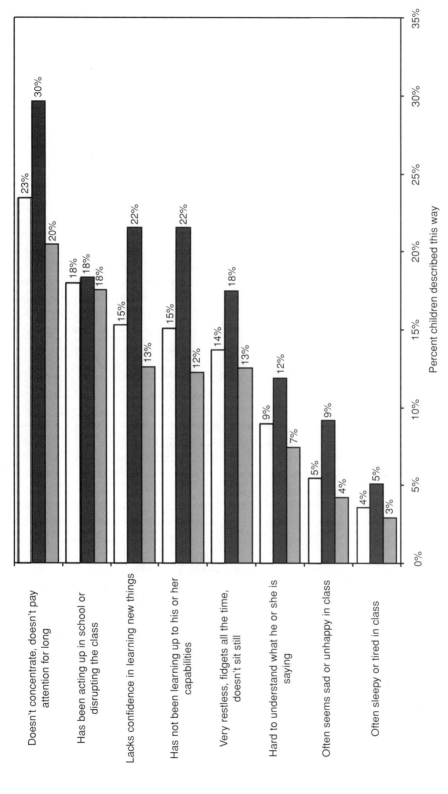

Figure 4.3. Negative teacher feedback received by parents of kindergarten children. (Source: National Household Education Survey, 1993.) (Key: □, Total; ■, Low-income ■, Middle- to High-Income.)

get more negative comments than those whose parents have more education and higher income levels. The same is true of families that have been disrupted by marital separation or divorce and those in which the parents have not married. Children from families in which only the mother is present in the household, or only the father, or the mother and a stepfather, or neither birth parent all get more negative reports from their kindergarten teachers than children from families in which both birth parents are present in the household.

Boys are more likely than girls to be described as having learning or behavior problems in kindergarten. Children with larger numbers of young siblings in the household (who would presumably have to compete with these siblings for attention from their parents) have more such problems as well. Children whose mothers work full time, year round (but not those whose mothers work part time or part of the year) get more negative reports from kindergarten teachers than those whose mothers are homemakers. The more of these characteristics the family and/or child have, the more negative feedback the parent is likely to receive.

Teacher feedback is also related to parent educational activities at home with the child. Children whose parents reported that they read stories to the child infrequently, or not at all, during the previous week received more negative comments from teachers than children who were read to more often. Activity-related differences were found even after controlling for factors such as parent education level and family income.

Low-Income Parents More Likely to Receive Negative Feedback

As mentioned in the previous sections, kindergarten parents whose family incomes are below the poverty line are more likely to report that they have received negative feedback from teachers concerning their children's learning or behavior than parents whose family incomes are above the poverty level. Over the seven most common negative feedback items, the mean number reported for children in low-income families was 1.91, whereas for children in middle- to high-income families, it was 1.68 (Zill & Davies, 1994).

Kindergartners from low-income families are more likely to be described as hyperactive. Among kindergartners in public programs, 30% of those from low-income families were described as not paying attention in class, compared with 20% of pupils from middle- to high-income families. Eighteen percent of the children from low-income families were reported to be "very restless, fidgets all the time," compared with 13% of the children whose family incomes were above the poverty line. Children from low-income families tend to have more problems with learning new skills and concepts. Twenty-two percent of the low-income students were said to be "not learning up to capabilities" and to "lack confidence in learning new things," whereas the same comments were applied to about 13% of children from middle- to high-income families (NHES, 1993).

Children from low-income families have more problems communicating their wants, needs, and thoughts to teachers. Teachers noted that it was "hard to understand what child is saying" for 12% of the children from low-income families, versus 7% of children from middle- to high-income families. Although the comment is applied to fewer than 1 child in 10, children from low-income families are twice as likely to appear depressed in school: 9% of children from low-income families were said to be "often sad or unhappy in class," compared with 4% of children from middle- to high-income families.

Unexpectedly, given stereotypes about the behavior of children from low-income family backgrounds, parents from low-income families were not more likely than parents from middle- to high-income families to report that teachers described their children as "acting up in school or disrupting the class." It may be that low-income parents are more reluctant to acknowledge this type of conduct on the part of their young children. Alternatively, it could be that low-income children are less likely to be disruptive because they find the kindergarten classroom environment to be relatively interesting and stimulating, compared with their home environments.

When the receipt of negative feedback from kindergarten teachers was analyzed in multivariate models, low family income did not prove to be as potent a predictor of the total number of child learning or behavior problems reported as it was in bivariate analyses. Other factors associated with poverty, especially lower parent education levels, family disruption, and a larger number of young siblings in the household, were more closely linked with the number of negative comments received than was poverty per se (Zill & Davies, 1994).

Private Kindergarten Parents Just as Likely to Receive Negative Feedback

Parents with children in private kindergarten programs report receiving negative feedback from their children's teachers with about the same frequency as parents with children in public kindergartens. This held true across all the individual items discussed previously (NHES, 1993). It is, of course, possible that the children in private kindergarten had fewer learning and behavior problems but that their parents were more likely to receive feedback from teachers (both positive and negative) and that the two differences balanced out. Private kindergarten parents do report more frequent communication between the school and the home, as noted here. It is also possible that private school kindergarten teachers used more stringent (or at least different) criteria in judging the learning and behavior of their pupils. There is no way of ascertaining from the survey data whether this was true. The sample of children from low-income families in private kindergartens was too small to detect reliable differences in their relative adjustment and behavior in private as opposed to public kindergarten programs.

Children Who Attended Preschool Programs Receive More Negative Feedback

Most of the associations described previously are congruent with previous research findings based on direct assessments of children as well as on parent and teacher reports of learning accomplishments or behavior problems in young children (Coiro, Zill, & Bloom, 1994; Mayer, 1997; Zill, 1996a; Zill, Collins, et al., 1995). (One exception is the correlation between full-time maternal employment and child learning or behavior problems. Such an association is usually not found in the child development literature.) The observed correlations are also mostly consistent with generally accepted theories about individual and family factors that are significant for early learning or children's emotional well-being (Rutter & Rutter, 1993). However, one of the child background factors that is significantly associated with negative teacher feedback in the multivariate model is puzzling. This is that children who had attended a center-based preschool program prior to kindergarten, whether it was Head Start, a private preschool program, or a public prekindergarten program, are more, not less, likely to get critical reports from their teachers with regard to their learning or classroom behavior.

This finding is especially paradoxical, given that similar multivariate analyses with direct assessment measures or parent-reported data on developmental accomplishments of preschool children show a positive correlation between preschool program attendance and emerging literacy (Zill, Collins, et al., 1995). Although the finding is puzzling, it is not without precedent. There have been informal reports for years that some kindergarten teachers report more classroom problems with children from Head Start (E. Zigler, personal communication, March 22, 1995), and Mott and Quinlan (1992) found some evidence of increased problem behavior (as reported by parents) in Head Start graduates in data from the National Longitudinal Survey of Youth, Mother and Child Supplement.

CHILDREN WHO ARE RETAINED IN KINDERGARTEN

One indication that children have had a problematic time in kindergarten is when the school believes that the child should repeat kindergarten or attend a transitional class, rather than being promoted to a general first-grade class along with most other kindergartners. The difficulty in using retention in kindergarten as an indicator is that schools and school systems vary in the extent to which they employ kindergarten retention, if they employ it at all, and many schools have changed their policies regarding its use in recent years. There has been a great deal of contentious debate about retention in the early grades but little representative data on the actual extent and circumstances of its use. Employing data from both the 1993 and 1995 NHESs, Zill et al. (1997) examined the proportion of U.S. first and second graders who were retained in kindergarten, the characteristics of these children, and the implications of kindergarten retention for the school performance and adjustment of children in the early elementary grades. Although there have been a number of smaller-scale studies of kindergarten retention, the NHES study provides estimates based on large-scale, nationally representative samples.

Repetition of Kindergarten

Five percent of first and second graders in 1995 and six percent in 1993 had to repeat kindergarten or attend a transitional class before first grade. These proportions projected to almost 383,000 children who had repeated kindergarten in 1995. The number of children who repeat kindergarten is several times smaller than the number who are reported to experience significant learning or behavior problems in kindergarten.

Child characteristics that are consistently overrepresented among children who have been required to repeat kindergarten are being male and having had a marked delay in growth or development earlier in life. In 1995, 63% of kindergarten repeaters were boys, compared with 51% of the general population of elementary students. Also, 18% of the repeaters had had developmental delays, compared with 5% of all first and second graders.

The study found a link between low-income status and grade repetition, but it was not consistent across surveys. In 1993, children from low-income families were at significantly greater risk of repeating kindergarten, and this association held up when other factors were controlled. However, in the 1995 survey, in a multivariate analysis, poverty status was actually associated with a lower risk of kindergarten repetition. Overall, African American children were found to repeat kindergarten at greater rates. Also, children who attended Head Start, prekindergarten, or other center-based preschool programs were at significantly lower risk of having had to repeat kindergarten in the multivariate analysis. Neither of the latter two relationships was significant in the 1993 analysis.

Despite the inconsistencies from survey to survey, the overall pattern of results indicates that children who are required to repeat kindergarten are a comparatively disadvantaged group in ethnic, developmental, and socioeconomic terms. There is a particular contrast that the study found with children whose parents had delayed their entry into kindergarten. These children also tended to be boys, and they were children whose birthdays tended to fall in the latter half of the year. In other respects, however, they were a comparatively advantaged group.

African American children were underrepresented among delayed entry children, and, in 1993 at least, there was a significant association between having college-educated parents and starting kindergarten later. At the same time, it is clear that socioeconomic differences in kindergarten repetition and delayed entry are not as pronounced as has been sometimes suggested in earlier research and commentary on these issues. Both groups contain children drawn from nearly all segments of U.S. society.

It is not clear whether the disparities between the findings of the two surveys were simply a product of sampling fluctuation and measurement error or reflected actual changes in the practices of schools with respect to the numbers and kinds of pupils who were being retained in kindergarten. It is possible that school policy changes restricting the use of retention among children from low-income families or racial minorities may have been a factor in the modest socioeconomic differences found, especially in 1995. These issues are worth examination in future research.

STUDENT PERFORMANCE AND BEHAVIOR AFTER KINDERGARTEN

Parent reports about student performance and adjustment after kindergarten, in the early grades of elementary school, show patterns similar to those noted previously with respect to kindergarten. Nearly one half of all first and second graders were reported to exhibit some significant learning or behavior problems in school. Thirty percent had trouble concentrating or paying attention in class. Between one in five and one in four were having schoolwork problems or not learning up to his or her capabilities. One in five was said to engage in troublesome behavior or disrupt the class. One in twenty had to repeat first or second grade (Zill et al., 1997).

The same child and family factors that were associated with difficulties in kindergarten, or with having to repeat kindergarten, were associated with learning or behavior problems in the early elementary grades. More boys than girls had problems, and children who had experienced developmental delays early in childhood were more likely to be encountering difficulties. Children with birthdays that were late in the year were also more likely to be having problems, although this was only found in the 1993 survey.

Lower parent education levels, family disruption or single parenthood, and family poverty were all associated with higher frequencies of school adjustment problems. As before, poverty itself was not as potent a predictor of classroom difficulties as were factors associated with poverty, such as low parent education and single parenthood. Minority racial status was also associated with a higher frequency of problems, even after education, income, and family structure were controlled. This was not the case in the kindergarten analyses, where race and ethnicity were not independently predictive of child learning or behavior problems, apart from their association with socioeconomic disadvantages (Zill et al., 1997).

As was the case in kindergarten, attendance at a center-based preschool program was associated with a significantly greater likelihood of negative teacher feedback, even after other factors were controlled. This was only found in the 1993 survey. In the 1995 data, preschool program attendance neither increased nor decreased the likelihood of school performance problems.

Implications of Kindergarten Retention for Performance in Elementary School

Children who were required to stay in kindergarten for a second year were reported by their parents to be doing worse than their classmates on most of the school performance indicators that were available in the two surveys. In 1993, two thirds of the retained pupils had received some negative feedback from their elementary school teachers, whereas the same was true of less than one half of nonretained pupils. Forty to fifty percent higher proportions of retained than nonretained pupils were described as having problems concentrating, as not learning up to capabilities, or as acting up and disrupting the class. Twice as many of the retained pupils were said to have trouble taking turns and sharing with others (Zill et al., 1997).

In the 1995 survey, 60% of retained pupils were reported to have at least one significant school performance problem, compared with 47% of nonretained pupils. When comparisons between retained and nonretained pupils were controlled by multiple logistic regression, the retained children in 1993 continued to receive more negative feedback than their classmates. In the 1995 analysis, however, the differences between retained and nonretained children were wholly accounted for by other factors in the model (Zill et al., 1997).

The contrast between the performance of retained students with the later performance of children who had experienced delayed entry into kindergarten was particularly striking. These children were doing better on the performance indicators and continued to have fewer problems, according to the 1993 analysis, after other related factors were controlled. In the 1995 analysis, controlling for other factors reduced the positive difference for delayed entries to nonsignificance.

Despite the somewhat disparate results, the best that could be said about the school performance of retained pupils was that they were doing less well than most other first and second graders but no worse than would be expected, given their other background and developmental characteristics. There was no indication in the findings of either survey that requiring the children to repeat kindergarten or attend a transitional class had had a beneficial effect on their school performance. One might, indeed, argue that kindergarten repetition had made matters worse. However, another interpretation of the results is that in requiring some pupils to repeat kindergarten, the schools merely identified pupils who were slated to have further achievement or adjustment problems anyway. According to this argument, the fact of kindergarten repetition does not create the later problems, it is only an indicator of other, underlying disorders in the child's constitution or home environment.

SUMMARY AND IMPLICATIONS

The survey findings summarized in this chapter contain a lot of positive information about the state of American kindergarten programs and the experiences of young children in those programs. Most kindergarten teachers seem well qualified to work with young children and confident that they can make a meaningful difference in the lives and academic careers of their pupils. Most kindergarten parents are at least moderately involved in school-related activities and reasonably content with the school's efforts to keep them informed about how their children are progressing and to involve them in school activities. Kindergarten programs appear to offer a balance between free play and self-discovery activities and more structured academic activities, although many teachers seem to shun the use of worksheets and explicit drills in phonics. According to their parents, most kindergarten pupils have predominantly positive experiences in kindergarten, and 95% are promoted to first grade.

There do not appear to be gross disparities between the program quality of the public kindergarten classes that low-income children attend and the quality of public classes attended by children from families with greater financial resources. Indeed, in some ways low-income parents are more satisfied with the efforts of their schools than are public school parents with more resources. However, neither group of public school parents describe the communication and outreach efforts of their schools in as positive terms as do parents with children in private kindergarten programs.

Despite the preponderance of good news, there are clearly survey results that lend support to the central thesis of this volume, namely, that school administrators, teachers, and parents need to explore ways of ensuring a better fit between the demands of the kindergarten classroom and the diverse capabilities and behavior patterns of U.S. 5-year-olds. Many kindergarten classes appear to be too large, and to have too few assistant teachers or aides, to provide individual or small-group attention to children who are at widely different places in the developmental trajectory. Although there was not explicit survey evidence to this effect, it is almost inevitable that the instructional or emotional needs of some students are short-changed in classes of 26 students or more with minimal help from aides or assistant teachers. Although the children who get neglected may be those who are somewhat behind in their development, it may also be those who are more advanced, whose potential for excellence does not get encouraged.

Both teachers and parents report that around one half of all pupils exhibit some behavior, learning, or social difficulties in the kindergarten classroom, and one in five or six experiences serious adjustment problems. These problems are more common among boys and among children from low-income families and families with other sociodemographic risk factors, such as low parent education levels, single parenthood, numerous young siblings, or minority language backgrounds. Transition problems are more prevalent in schools in high poverty areas, in central city and rural as opposed to suburban communities, and in schools with high concentrations of minority pupils. It is interesting, however, that parent reports of negative teacher feedback about child learning or conduct problems were as common in private as in public kindergarten programs.

It is also noteworthy that some of the more common negative feedback items were in nonacademic areas that a majority of kindergarten teachers believe to be very important for school readiness and success in kindergarten. This suggests that families and preschool programs may not be doing all they can to nurture social and communication skills that will enable children to function more effectively in the larger and more structured environment of the kindergarten classroom.

A disquieting finding is the disconnection between teacher opinion regarding attributes needed for school readiness (which downplays the importance of paying attention and sitting still) and the kind of negative feedback that kindergarten teachers most frequently give to parents (which focuses on the child's inability to pay attention and sit still). It is hardly surprising, of course, that young children should have some difficulties focusing their attention or restraining their natural animation for extended periods of time. One might think that kindergarten teachers who endorse developmentally appropriate practices would not make great demands on their pupils in this regard. Yet many teachers apparently do make demands to which a substantial minority of students cannot live up. One explanation for this may be that the large sizes of many kindergarten classes require a certain amount of pupil restraint merely for reasons of "crowd control." Whatever the reasons, the area of behavioral control requirements is clearly one that deserves attention from educational researchers and policy makers who want to make the transition to kindergarten a smooth and successful one for all children.

Another troubling result is the finding that children who have attended center-based preschool programs, despite showing greater emerging literacy and numeracy skills than children who have not attended such programs, are more likely to receive negative teacher feedback. One may speculate as to the possible reasons that children with preschool experience may receive negative reactions from their kindergarten teachers. One possible interpretation is that children who attended preschool are apt to be more advanced than other children in their kindergarten classes. This in turn may lead to them being bored and restless in class. Another possible interpretation is that the rules for appropriate conduct in class change between preschool and kindergarten, with children having more leeway for free play and gross motor activities in preschool than in kindergarten. Children with center-based preschool experience may have more difficulty adapting to the new rules than those without such experience. It is also possible that at least some preschool veterans have learned aggressive or mischievous behavior patterns from their preschool classmates. Further research is needed to better understand the reasons behind the negative teacher reactions and their implications for young children's academic careers.

Although the public kindergarten programs that children from low-income families attend are not notably inferior in terms of teacher qualifications, classroom activities, or communication and outreach to parents, it is apparent that these programs have to contend with a greater prevalence of family risk factors than public programs serving predominantly middle-class children or private kindergarten programs. It is discouraging to see that low-income kindergarten parents tend to be less involved in school-related activities and do less with their children at home in the way of informal educational activities. Both parent involvement and parent reading to children relate to better achievement and fewer disciplinary problems in the later years of elementary school and secondary school. Although kindergarten programs seem to be doing things to encourage parent involvement and parent teaching activities, they may need to do more along these lines.

Survey findings do not show notably higher rates of kindergarten retention among children from low-income families, although earlier surveys did find a greater risk of retention among these children. However, surveys do show that children from low-income families have more academic and behavioral difficulties in first and second grades than do children from middle- and high-income families, whether they have been retained or not. Pupils from low-income families are more likely to be described as below the middle of their class, to have to repeat first or second grade, and to be getting special help for reading difficulties. Whereas preschool education programs are bolstering the early literacy, numeracy, and social skills of children from poor families, these programs have not succeeded in closing the gap between children from low-income families and those from middle- to high-income ones. Survey findings also indicate that more attention should be paid to behavioral and conduct issues that preschool programs are currently not addressing, or at least not addressing with any notable success. By developing innovative approaches and making greater efforts to tackle these issues in kindergarten, kindergarten programs will not only do a better job of smoothing children's transition to formal schooling but will also increase the chances that children will have fewer problems and more success in the later years of elementary school and beyond.

REFERENCES

Administration on Children, Youth, and Families, Research, Demonstration, and Evaluation Branch. (1998). *Second Head Start program performance measures report.* Washington, DC: U.S. Department of Health and Human Services.

Alexander, K.L., & Entwisle, D.R. (1988). Achievement in the first 2 years of school: Patterns and processes. *Monographs of the Society for Research in Child Development, 53*(2, Serial No. 218).

Barnett, S.W. (1992). Benefits of compensatory preschool education. *Journal of Human Resources, 27,* 279–312.

Bradley, R.H., & Caldwell, B.M. (1981). The HOME inventory: A validation of the preschool scale for black children. *Child Development, 52,* 708–710.

Bredekamp, S. (Ed.). (1987). *Developmentally appropriate practice in early childhood programs serving children from birth through age 8.* (Expanded edition.) Washington, DC: National Association for the Education of Young Children.

Bredekamp, S., & Shepard, L. (1989). How best to protect children from inappropriate school expectations, practices, and policies. *Young Children, 44*(3), 14–24.

Brick, J.M., Collins, M.A., Nolin, M.J., Ha, P.C., Levinsohn, M., & Chandler, K. (1994). *National Household Education Survey of 1993: School readiness data file user's manual* (NCES 94-193). Washington, DC: U.S. Department of Education, National Center for Education Statistics.

Cameron, M.B., & Wilson, B.J. (1990). The effects of chronological age, gender, and delay of entry on academic achievement and retention: Implications for academic red-shirting. *Psychology in the Schools, 27,* 260–263.

Coiro, M.J., Zill, N., & Bloom, B. (1994). Health of our nation's children. *Vital and Health Statistics, 10*(191). Washington, DC: U.S. Government Printing Office.

Collins, M.A., Brick, J.M., Nolin, M.J., Vaden-Kiernan, N., Gilmore, S., Chandler, K., & Chapman, C. (1997). *National Household Education Survey of 1996: Data file user's manual* (Vol. 1) (NCES 97-425). Washington, DC: U.S. Department of Education, National Center for Education Statistics.

Early, D.M., Pianta, R.C., & Cox, M.J. (1999). Kindergarten teachers and classrooms: A transition context. *Early Education and Development, 10,* 25–46.

Federal Interagency Forum on Child and Family Statistics. (1997). *America's children: Key national indicators of well-being, 1997.* Washington, DC: U.S. Government Printing Office.

Federal Interagency Forum on Child and Family Statistics. (1998). *America's children: Key national indicators of well-being, 1998.* Washington, DC: U.S. Government Printing Office.

Freeman, E.B., & Hatch, J.A. (1989). What schools expect young children to know and do: An analysis of kindergarten report cards. *The Elementary School Journal, 89,* 595–605.

Heaviside, S., & Farris, E. (1993). *Public school kindergarten teachers' views on children's readiness for school* (NCES 93-410). Washington, DC: U.S. Department of Education, National Center for Education Statistics.

Henderson, A.T. (1987). *The evidence continues to grow: Parent involvement improves student achievement*. Columbia, MD: National Committee for Citizens in Education.

Henderson, A.T., & Berla, N. (1994). *A new generation of evidence: The family is critical to student achievement*. Washington, DC: National Committee for Citizens in Education.

Henke, R.R., Choy, S.P., Geis, S., & Broughman, S.P. (1996). *Schools and staffing in the United States: A statistical profile, 1993–94* (NCES 96-124). Washington, DC: U.S. Department of Education, National Center for Education Statistics.

Hofferth, S.L., West, J., Henke, R., & Kaufman, P. (1994). *Access to early childhood programs for children at risk*. (NCES 93-372). Washington, DC: U.S. Department of Education, National Center for Education Statistics.

Horn, W.F., & Packard, T. (1985). Early identification of learning problems: A meta-analysis. *Journal of Educational Psychology, 77*, 597–607.

Jencks, C., Smith, M., Acland, H., Bane, M.J., Cohen, D., Gintis, H., Heyns, B., & Michelson, S. (1972). *Inequality: A reassessment of the effect of family and schooling in America*. New York: Basic Books.

Kozol, J. (1991). *Savage inequalities: Children in America's schools*. New York: Crown.

Mayer, S.E. (1997). *What money can't buy: Family income and children's life chances*. Cambridge, MA: Harvard University Press.

Meisels, S.J., & Wasik, B.A. (1990). Who should be served? Identifying children in need of early intervention. In S.J. Meisels & J.P. Shonkoff (Eds.), *Handbook of early childhood intervention* (pp. 605–632). New York: Cambridge University Press.

Moore, K.A., & Snyder, N.O. (1991). Cognitive attainment among firstborn children of adolescent mothers. *American Sociological Review, 56*, 612–624.

Mott, F.L., & Quinlan, S.V. (1992). *Participation in Project Head Start: Determinants and possible short-term consequences*. Columbus, OH: Center for Human Resource Research, The Ohio State University.

National Commission on Excellence in Education. (1983). *A nation at risk: The imperative for educational reform*. Washington, DC: U.S. Government Printing Office.

National Education Goals Panel. (1995). *Data for the National Education Goals report, 1995. Volume one: National data*. Washington, DC: U.S. Government Printing Office.

National Education Goals Panel. (1996). *The National Education Goals report: Building a nation of learners, 1996*. Washington, DC: U.S. Government Printing Office.

National Education Goals Panel. (1997). *The National Education Goals report: Building a nation of learners, 1997*. Washington, DC: U.S. Government Printing Office.

National Household Education Survey (NHES). (1993). *Analyses of public use data file carried out by Nicholas Zill, Christine Winquist Nord, and Laura Loomis*. Rockville, MD: Westat.

National Household Education Survey (NHES). (1996). *Analyses of public use data file carried out by Nicholas Zill and Christine Winquist Nord*. Rockville, MD: Westat.

Nord, C.W., Brimhall, D., & West, J. (1997). *Fathers' involvement in their children's schools*. (NCES 98-09). Washington, DC: U.S. Department of Education, National Center for Education Statistics.

Nord, C.W., & Griffin, J. (1998). Educational profile of 3 to 8 year old children of immigrants. In D.J. Hernandez (Ed.), *Children of immigrants: Health adjustment, and public assistance*. (Report prepared for Committee on the Health and Adjustment of Immigrant Children and Families, Board on Children, Youth, and Families.) Washington, DC: National Academy Press.

Nord, C.W., Zill, N., Prince, C., Clarke, S., & Ventura, S. (1994). Developing an index of educational risk from health and social characteristics known at birth. *Bulletin of the New York Academy of Medicine, 71*(2), 167–187.

Pianta, R.C., Cox, M.J., Early, D.M., Rimm-Kaufman, S., Laparo, K., & Taylor, L. (1998). *A national perspective of entry to school: The NCEDL's Transition Practices Survey*. Symposium presentation at the annual meeting of the American Educational Research Association, San Diego.

Pianta, R.C., & McCoy, S.J. (1997). The first day of school: The predictive validity of early school screening. *Journal of Applied Developmental Psychology, 18*, 1–22.

Rowe, D.C. (1994). *The limits of family influence: Genes, experience, and behavior*. New York: The Guilford Press.

Rutter, M., & Rutter, M. (1993). *Developing minds: Challenge and continuity across the life span*. New York: Basic Books.

Sameroff, A., Seifer, R., Barocas, R., Zax, M., & Greenspan, S. (1987). Intelligence quotient scores of 4-year-old children: Socio-environmental risk factors. *Pediatrics, 79,* 343–350.

Select Committee on Children, Youth, and Families, U.S. House of Representatives. (1989). *U.S. children and their families: Current conditions and recent trends, 1989.* Washington, DC: U.S. Government Printing Office.

Shepard, L.A., & Smith, M.L. (1988). Escalating academic demand in kindergarten: Counterproductive policies. *The Elementary School Journal, 89*(2), 135–145.

Snyder, T.D., Hoffman, C.M., & Geddes, C.M. (1998). *Digest of education statistics, 1997.* (NCES 98-015). Washington, DC: U.S. Department of Education, National Center for Education Statistics.

U.S. Bureau of the Census. (1982). *Current population reports, Series P-25, No. 917, Preliminary estimates of the population of the United States, by age, sex, and race: 1970 to 1981.* Washington, DC: U.S. Government Printing Office.

U.S. Bureau of the Census. (1983, May). *1980 census of population. Volume 1. Characteristics of the population. Chapter B. General population characteristics. Part 1. United States summary.* (PC80-1-B1). Washington, DC: U.S. Government Printing Office.

U.S. Bureau of the Census. (1997). *Statistical abstract of the United States: 1997* (117th ed.). Washington, DC: U.S. Government Printing Office.

U.S. Bureau of the Census. (1998). *Marital status and family living arrangements: March 1996.* Washington, DC: U.S. Government Printing Office.

Ventura, S.J., Martin, J.A., Curtin, S.C., & Mathews, T.J. (1998). *Report of final natality statistics, 1996. Monthly vital statistics report* (Vol. 46, No. 11 supp.). Hyattsville, MD: National Center for Health Statistics.

Walsh, D.J. (1989). Changes in kindergarten: Why here? Why now? *Early Childhood Research Quarterly, 4,* 377–391.

West, J., Germino Hausken, E., & Collins, M. (1993). *Readiness for kindergarten: Parent and teacher beliefs.* Washington, DC: U.S. Department of Education, National Center for Education Statistics.

West, J., Hausken, E.G., Chandler, K., & Collins, M. (1992). *Experiences in childcare and early childhood programs of first- and second-graders. Statistics in brief.* (NCES 92-005). Washington, DC: U.S. Department of Education, National Center for Education Statistics.

Zill, N. (1996a). Family change and student achievement: What we have learned, what it means for schools. In A. Booth & J.F. Dunn (Eds.), *Family-school links: How do they affect educational outcomes?* (pp. 139–174). Mahwah, NJ: Lawrence Erlbaum Associates.

Zill, N. (1996b). Parental schooling and children's health. *Public Health Reports, 111,* 34–43.

Zill, N., & Davies, E. (1994). *Public television children's programs: Are they helping young children get ready for school?* Report prepared for the Corporation for Public Broadcasting. Rockville, MD: Westat.

Zill, N., Collins, M., West, J., & Germino Hausken, E. (1995). *Approaching kindergarten: A look at preschoolers in the United States.* (NCES 95-280). Washington, DC: U.S. Department of Education, National Center for Education Statistics.

Zill, N., Loomis, L.S., & West, J. (1997). *The elementary school performance and adjustment of children who enter kindergarten late or repeat kindergarten: Findings from national surveys.* (NCES 98-097). Washington, DC: U.S. Department of Education, National Center for Education Statistics.

Zill, N., Moore, K.A., Smith, E.W., Stief, T., & Coiro, M.J. (1995). The life circumstances and development of children in welfare families: A profile based on national survey data. In P.L. Chase-Lansdale & J. Brooks-Gunn (Eds.), *Escape from poverty: What makes a difference for children?* (pp. 38–59). New York: Cambridge University Press.

Zill, N., & Nord, C.W. (1994). *Running in place: How American families are faring in a changing economy and an individualistic society.* Washington, DC: Child Trends.

Zill, N., & Rogers, C.C. (1988). Recent trends in the well-being of children in the United States and their implications for public policy. In A.J. Cherlin (Ed.), *The changing American family and public policy* (pp. 31–115). Washington, DC: Urban Institute Press.

THE ECOLOGY OF
TRANSITIONS INTO
AND THROUGH KINDERGARTEN

Chapter 5

Diverse Perspectives on Kindergarten Contexts and Practices

Elizabeth Graue

The transition to kindergarten is educationally important. It is a shift from more family-controlled settings to contexts that are specifically designed for the education of young children. But that transition is also symbolically important because it represents a movement into the broader community context. In this context, children have access to more resources and people; however, the demands are also more complex. For many children, it is considered to be the beginning of *real* school, where the foundation is set for later success. Whether this transition is easy depends on the match between the characteristics and experiences of individual children and the resources and expectations of school personnel responsible for their success. This match is not solely a matter of making sure that children are "ready" to meet the demands of school. It also involves ensuring that schools are ready to adapt to the diverse and changing needs of real children whose lives depend on our willingness to extend ourselves to them.

Negotiating this transition—that is, fine-tuning this match between child and context—is the focus of this book. This chapter focuses particularly on the knowledge base related to kindergarten contexts and practices. It examines what is known about this special time in a child's educational life—about how we organize for instruction, how we choose what to teach, and what implications these choices have for the success of our students.

This discussion is organized around three questions. The first, *Who can we teach?* addresses the idea that teachers do not instruct generic students. Instead, they are working with both their ideas of who can benefit from instruction and real children. The answer to this question shapes decisions regarding which children enter kindergarten, when they will begin, and how they will be grouped for instruction. The second question, *How can we teach?* is related to decisions about how the instructional day is scheduled and which philosophical orientations are used to shape instruction. It is concerned with the images of appropriate kindergarten practice and what we use as the catalyst and methods for instruction. The third question, *What can we teach?* explores the content of instruction in kindergarten. Answers to this particular question relate to our notions of the intellectual substance of our work with children (i.e., what is worth knowing for 5-year-olds). All three questions are interrelated but are presented thematically as a way to organize the tangled literature on teaching and learning in kindergarten.

WHO CAN WE TEACH?

The first question that needs to be addressed when examining practices in early education is how the parameters of the teaching practice are defined. The question, *Who can we teach?* is a question that defines a successful transition, one that is the foundation for curriculum and that shapes standards for children, teachers, and programs. In an ideal world, programs would be open to all children and would be able to meet all their needs. But as the world is constructed, there are parameters on expectations and practices that are historical, ideological, philosophical, and pedagogical.

Readiness

Although other authors address issues of readiness (see Chapters 3 and 4), it is impossible to discuss classroom practices in the early years without addressing conceptions of, and practices and policies connected to, readiness. It is the quintessential early childhood construct, part science, part theory, part myth, part perception, and part passion; it sets the stage for particular exceptions and tasks for children when they enter school (Graue, 1993b). Because of its centrality in decision making for young children, in this chapter I discuss readiness policies and practices that set parameters for who is taught and, therefore, what and how it is taught.

Entrance Age   When an entrance cutoff date is set, a statement is made about the lower bounds of typical development that can be accommodated in instructional practices. In addition, we are establishing what many believe is the most equitable entry gate—a concrete entrance date is information that is accessible to most families and that requires minimal decision making. However, setting that date is a nontrivial task. Since the late 1960s, the modal kindergarten entrance date has shifted from December to September, a move that has made kindergartners older. The rationale for moving the date back is related to concerns about readiness, a theme that comes up repeatedly in discussions about education and young children.

The key item of contention is that, by changing the entrance date, policy makers are addressing the issue of who can be taught. The assumption is that older kindergartners are better able to meet the demands of formal schooling. This trend occurs as increasing numbers of children are receiving out-of-home care and as educational experiences and broadened interventions are being offered for young children considered at risk.

Policy makers and practitioners search for the perfect entrance date in the hope of increasing readiness. But available research indicates that there is not a magic date by which all children will be ensured success. By now this topic should be a nonissue, but it has resurfaced again because the state of California has contemplated changing its entrance date to an earlier one. Research does not need to go into comparisons of children in the oldest and youngest quartiles of age distribution. It has already been found that the differences are small and are diminished for the most part by third grade (Shepard & Smith, 1986). More attention needs to be paid to the mechanics that drive these differences, examining the duration of age-related differences and how changing the date provides differential advantage for subgroups of children.

Interventions   There are a variety of interventions related to concerns about readiness. These interventions include official and unofficial practices that change the school careers of students by adding a year to the time it takes them to move through elementary school. Delaying kindergarten entry (also known as academic red-shirting), transitional programs prior to kindergarten or first grade, or early school retention are all strategies promoted to ease the movement of students considered not ready for the rigors of existing curriculum. Typically, red-shirting is chosen informally by parents (although often at the suggestion of school personnel) so that their children can avoid potential failure in elementary school. Transitional programs and retention are school-sanctioned programs chosen for children who are not measuring up to school expectations. The first two are undertaken for developmental reasons, attempting to match child level to curriculum in ways that are kinder and gentler. Transitional programs are specially designed programs with smaller class sizes and more child-centered curricula, whereas retention requires a child to repeat a grade.

What is interesting about all three of these interventions is that none has adequate empirical support. For example, retention increases the probability of children dropping out of school, fails to increase student achievement, is disproportionately used with children of color or from low-income families, and has serious emotional fallout for those who experience it (Byrnes, 1989; Grissom & Shepard, 1989; Shepard, 1989; Shepard & Smith, 1989; Zill, Loomis, & West, 1997). Furthermore, transitional programs fail to improve achievement (Gredler, 1984; Shepard, 1989). Children who have delayed school entry do not academically outperform their grade peers or even children who are typically considered at risk for readiness problems (i.e., children who are young relative to the entrance cutoff but who enroll in school on time; Cameron & Wilson, 1990; Graue, DiPerna, & Dixson, 1998; Morrison, Griffith, & Alberts, 1997). Teacher ratings of the social and emotional development of children who have delayed entry do not differ from comparison groups, and red-shirts appear to have greater social problems later in their school careers as well as higher participation in special education programs (Byrd, Weitzman, & Auinger, 1997; Graue et al., 1998; Zill et al., 1997). Comparisons of retainees and red-shirts favor red-shirts, who have higher levels of achievement and lower levels of negative feedback from teachers, but who also come from more advantaged backgrounds (Graue et al., 1998; Zill et al., 1997).

Concern about results showing no difference is arguable. The growing literature indicates that intervention has a potentially negative impact on the school careers of children. This should be a cause for alarm. Choices that lessen the likelihood of a child's success must be closely scrutinized and halted. Furthermore, readiness-based interventions appear to have systemic effects on classroom practice that shape the opportunities available to others. When children are red-shirted, placed in transitional programs, or retained, a lower bound is moved in the ecology of the classroom (Graue, 1993b; Shepard & Smith, 1986). Children who challenge teachers' expectations of who they can teach are shifted to another group and their needs no longer have to be accommodated. Early kindergarten activities, such as learning to be part of a large group or learning about colors, can be removed from the kindergarten curriculum because the children who could really benefit from that content are no longer there. Such activities are removed without the attending responsibility to educational practice. Development or maturation, rather than expectations and inclusiveness of curriculum, becomes the causal element. This allows the bar to be set a little higher without anyone having to do the work. This is not, however, working to high standards. Frankly, this is the lazy way out. This approach blames the child for being outside the narrow ideas of who can benefit from our efforts. When evidence exists that the most productive approach is to keep children with their age cohorts and to provide tailored support for their challenges (Leinhardt, 1980), the increasing social pressure to reinstate retention policies (Lawton, 1997) and the continued faith in red-shirting is particularly troubling.

In the 1980s, a clear body of research developed that provided evidence, both qualitative and quantitative, that argued against the use of retention as an educational strategy. Nothing empirically credible has been presented since then that should bring up questions about student promotion policies. However, public and political concern has arisen about what people see as the failure of social promotion—passing children from grade to grade without assurance that students have achieved the goals set for the curriculum. Unfortunately, presenting the issue as a dichotomous choice between social promotion and retention misses the alternatives between these two options. Further work at the policy level needs to focus on developing options for children who fall between grade levels (i.e., programs that attend to the deficits identified by school personnel, while also keeping students in the appropriate grade cohort). Another challenge is the development of teacher education content related to readiness interventions. Ideas about readiness are common cultural ideas that are strongly held and kept alive through storytelling about the success stories of retention or red-shirting. The stigma related to experiencing these interventions often closes off discussion of their potential problems if it is not consciously brought up in courses and professional development. Although the worth of research-based versus experience-based knowledge of teaching practice could be argued, in the case of retention it seems important that at the least, teacher education programs should present both sides of the retention debate to assure that the empirical knowledge on the subject is discussed.

One of the main holes in our knowledge is related to red-shirting. Parents and educators are passionate about this issue and focus attention on two aspects of effect—the social and the academic. A broad study that explores both long- and short-term effects of delayed kindergarten entry on students' academic achievement and their social status (teacher ratings of behavior, observations of interactions, and measures of peer status) needs to be conducted. Furthermore, a clear idea of how the choices of some affect the opportunities of others is necessary. Although inferential and interpretive knowledge of these ripple effects exists (e.g., teachers stating that they can now escalate their program because the children who typically would have needed attention to things such as colors and shapes are elsewhere), judgments about children as being not ready merely because they are the youngest in a kindergarten setting, or timing conception of a child so that he or she does not have a summer birthday, could be avoided (Graue, 1993a, 1993b).

It is necessary for researchers to explore how systems of expectations and probabilities for success are set for children because of readiness interventions and to examine how these interventions could be differentially effective for subgroups of children. In other words, who benefits from red-shirting and who is harmed? Some researchers have suggested that the presence of older children who are more advantaged reduces the probability that typical younger children will be put at risk by a shift in school standards (Shepard, 1990). The tradeoffs for promoting increased achievement for certain children must be assessed against the contexts they establish for peers. Finally, a campaign is needed to help the public understand the complex issues in a way that is bound to real educational policy.

Groupings

Groupings are related to the question, *Who can we teach?* because they operationalize ideas about forming instructional contexts. Teachers regularly attempt to manage student variability through grouping. The basis for forming these groups is related to how teachers think about the needs of students. Grouping for sameness implies a different view of how children learn and how teachers instruct than does grouping for heterogeneity. Students can be grouped by age or mixed, and groupings can be developed within or across classes to form subgroups by interest, skill, perceived ability, and so on. In the next section, practices that put children into groups that illustrate particular ways of thinking about learning are examined. I also discuss the research literature about groupings by age or perceived ability, length of student–teacher relationships, and group size.

Age Groupings   Early childhood classrooms are likely to be organized according to age levels, with year-long age spans. This school organization strategy evolved from the efficiency movements of the 19th century and is likely to be closely related to developmental approaches to teaching that assume that children's growth and learning are patterned and highly correlated with age. From this perspective, teachers are more likely to develop appropriate activities for children of the same age because their needs and interests are apt to be similar. For advocates of age-structured programming, the developmental needs of children dictate homogeneous groups, with age being the selection criterion. In addition, mapping curricula has been most efficiently performed through age grading, which allows various stakeholders to anticipate and be responsible for content at various levels. This can be most visibly seen in current standards movements in education, which set out benchmarks at pivotal points in educational careers.

Age-structured programming is only one option for setting up classrooms. Other strategies include multigrade organizations in which students from more than one grade level receive instruction from one teacher in a classroom simultaneously. Students retain grade-level assignments and curricula, and the organization is typically chosen for administrative reasons (e.g., when there are not enough students for separate sections of kindergarten and first grade). In contrast, some schools, using multi-age philosophy, mix ages for expressed educational purposes. In these schools, teachers value heterogeneity in groups over homogeneity for the additional resources breadth of skills can provide in instructional groups (Katz, 1992). Multi-aging is done for pedagogical reasons and requires generation of curriculum *across* ages (Veenman, 1995). The focus is on teachers addressing the developmental needs of the children in their care at one moment in time rather than on a modal notion of what a 5-year-old needs.

Another dimension, although not a fixed one, is lengthening relationships among teachers and students. In multi-age programs, lengthening is achieved by having students stay with teachers for more than the typical 1-year time period (typically 2–3 years). Another variant is known as *looping*, in which teachers follow single age groups from one grade to another. The promise of multiyear teacher–student relationships is related to capitalizing on the knowledge accrued by teachers and students, which must then be re-created each time students move to another teacher.

Assessing the efficacy of these organizational structures is quite difficult. The distinction between multi-age and multigrade is philosophically and pedagogically pivotal, but the labels are murky for many. Furthermore, it is difficult to discern the treatment in most studies (mixing ages is but one component of the treatment). The issues addressed in early childhood studies (preschool) and in elementary research are quite different. In early childhood studies, researchers explore the interactions among children, assessing complexity of language and play in same-age and mixed-age groups. These studies find that children adapt their interactions to their context—with younger peers, strategies become less complex, whereas with older peers they become more so (Katz, Evangelou, & Hartman, 1990). In contrast, elementary studies focus on affective and academic outcomes in comparisons of mixed-age groups.

Reviews of this research are mixed. According to Veenman's analysis (1995), there are no or inconsistent differences between multigrade and single-grade and multi-age and single-age groups. This is interpreted by the author to mean that there is no support for concern about student achievement in non–age-segregated programs. Furthermore, exploring grade-level effects, Veenman (1996) found a small positive effect of multigrade programs, with diminishing effects as students got older. Focusing on multigrade classes, Mason and Burns (1996) disputed the no difference finding, asserting that these programs have a small negative effect on both student achievement and teacher motivation based on a critique of Veenman's explanations for his findings and their own analysis.

The efficacy of longer student–teacher relationships—either through multi-age grouping or through looping—is largely unassessed. There are no data on the number of classes/teachers that practice looping (Jacobson, 1997), and the literature is more likely to be comprised of testimonials and suggestions for implementation aimed at practitioners than reports of empirical work. A search of the ERIC database (by both an ERIC information specialist and this author) yielded a number of articles and books that described the experiences of teachers who employ looping, rather than presenting evidence of the efficacy of the practice. From the attention that looping has been given, with articles in *Phi Delta Kappan* and *Educational Leadership*, it is clear that it is a strategy that has captured the imagination of many educators. Conceptually, why it would be chosen and what values and practices it tends to endorse are known, but knowledge of its efficacy, or even of the range of its implementation, is still quite underdeveloped.

More research and more varied types of inquiry are necessary. Mason and Burns (1996) suggested performing field experiments of affect and achievement, with random assignment of both teachers and students to treatment conditions. In addition, the measures of outcomes employed in such studies must be carefully contemplated. Most tests are age or grade leveled and, thus, do not match the notions of curriculum generation in multi-age programs. For example, with K-1 students, do you use the K or 1 version of a test if the program does not differentiate children by grade, and what is the appropriate comparison group? We also need to take a hint from the early childhood studies and gain a better understanding of what happens in multi-age programs through interpretive research (Mason & Burns, 1996). These studies need to address not only the nature of the curriculum developed but also the conditions grouping students of different ages by exploring teacher workload and preparation. Furthermore, other outcomes for students could enrich our understanding of alternative grouping strategies. For example, how are issues of "youngness" so prominent in single-age early childhood settings negotiated in multi-age settings? How do outcomes such as retention relate to the philosophy and practice of multi-aging?

Within-Class Groupings   Reviews of ability grouping at the classroom level, which focus on forming subsets of students according to perceptions about skills or innate abilities, have found little support for its implementation across age levels of students studied (Gamoran, 1992; Mosteller, Light, & Sachs, 1996; Slavin, 1987; Wilkinson, 1988–1989). Grouping students across and within classes has mixed outcomes, with effects in specific curriculum content areas. Effects in the early grades are relatively small, and positive effects have been shown in mathematics and science (Lou, Abrami, Spence, Poulsen, Chambers, & d'Apollonia, 1996).

A variety of explanations can be asserted for these findings. One explanation is the selection problem; that is, any time one variable is selected, another is deselected. Although this is an attempt to sort children on some criterion, the outcome could be a relatively heterogeneous group. The identification of children on one reading variable might be unrelated to another dimension of reading, which could have a serious impact on the entire process of learning to read. Because the ability to measure most educationally relevant characteristics is so faulty, it is little wonder that our sorting does not produce the desired homogeneity. Another reason could be the nature of the content. Some forms of content, by their structure, might need more or less variability to facilitate student achievement. The positive effects in mathematics and science could be related to our ability to test and sort in those content areas, or they could be a matter of structure of intellectual content. It is not known which explanation is most plausible.

Studies of the process of instruction find that higher-ability students receive richer, more complex instruction (Wilkinson, 1988–1989). It is not surprising then that studies of outcomes (Lou et al., 1996; Mosteller et al., 1996) found variable effects by student ability, with higher-ability students benefiting more than moderate or low-ability students. An ethical issue then arises: How can the benefits of strategies that are differentially effective be assessed? What is the nature of the treatment that produced advantages for high-ability students: the instruction they receive, the grouping itself, or an interaction between the two in terms of expectations? Slavin (1987) asserted that the key to the grouping issue is not the grouping itself, it is what happens afterward, in the day-to-day life in the classroom. Instruction leverages change in student knowledge, and thus a solid understanding of this is necessary if grouping research is to be interpreted (Gamoran, 1987; Hiebert, 1987).

Our understanding of grouping would be enriched by a diverse array of approaches to inquiry. Rich interpretive research would allow us to understand the process dimension of teaching and learning in grouped settings. High-quality, randomized, controlled field studies to assess the effects of within-class instructional groupings across a broad array of students and grade levels would provide information about outcomes. As this research base is developed, existing practices need to be compared with the empirical knowledge base. One practice that would come into question at the kindergarten level would be the development of special programs for students marked as readiness risks. In some contexts, students are placed in specially developed programs with more "developmental" curriculum, sometimes in full-day programs rather than half-day programs. Although the motivations of these programs have merit—the matching of students with curriculum—they also have other, unintended effects. These programs segregate one group of children from their same-age peers, setting up a two-tiered system for our youngest students. Rather than separating children by perceived readiness levels, it may be more effective to develop more inclusive curriculum within the kindergarten program and include more targeted instruction within that setting, or in add-on programming, to focus effort on areas of child challenge (Shepard & Graue, 1993).

This topic provides a wonderful challenge for teacher educators. The three-group ability model is such a part of the institutional history of U.S. schooling that it provides almost an unspoken grammar to most discussions on teaching. One basic obstacle to teaching outside ability grouping is the lack of alternative models. Theorization of cognition in psychological approaches to teaching and learning could help both prospective and in-service teachers rethink their practice. Teacher educators can contribute much to the potential for change by providing theoretical and field-based orientations to models of instruction that work from both homogeneity and heterogeneity.

Class Size

Traditional early childhood researchers believed that working in small groups advanced development more than working in settings in which there were more children per teacher. Early research on class size (Glass, Cahen, Smith, & Filby, 1982) indicated that significant reductions in class size for typical elementary settings (15 or fewer students) yielded impressive increases in academic achievement as well as improvement in students' and teachers' attitudes, regardless of the level of schooling examined. Large-scale field studies on class size for students in kindergarten through grade 3 in Tennessee maintained this finding (Mosteller, 1995; Mosteller et al., 1996). Interestingly, most state initiatives for smaller classes are focused on the early years and in settings with children experiencing significant challenges, typically those related to poverty. Tennessee and Wisconsin also invested funds in the reduction of class size. The Wisconsin program, Student Achievement Guarantee in Education (SAGE), had impressive results in its first year of implementation. First-graders who participated in the program, which reduced student–teacher ratios to 15:1 for kindergarten and first grade, scored significantly higher on standardized measures of literacy and mathematics than students in comparison schools. Classroom observations and interviews with teachers indicated reductions in discipline problems, more content coverage, and better assessment of individual student need (Department of Public Instruction, 1997). These results, considered in concert with the broader literature on class size, indicated that the investment in personnel, space, and materials necessary to decrease the number of students per teacher might be worth it. Future research should focus on how these results are produced and should address the optimal class size as well as the number of years this kind of investment should be undertaken.

The policy and teacher education dimensions of this issue cannot be ignored if anything is to be determined regarding the advantage of smaller teacher–student ratios. Policies on class size reduction need to be more involved than throwing an extra adult into an already crowded classroom. The costs of class size reduction will probably include classroom space and materials. They will also involve re-thinking how a teacher interacts with individual students and the class as a whole. The same practice that is effective in managing a 25-student classroom does not necessarily make sense when the group size is reduced to 15. To make the most out of this reduction in ratio, teachers will need to do things in different ways, maximizing whatever is most potent about this model of teaching.

Summary

Children are put within our pedagogical reach by the parameters set for practice. The converse is also true—the threshold for our responsibility is determined by conceptualizing who does not fit our model of the teachable child. This is framed implicitly by the way that the question, *Who can we teach?* is answered. The as-sumptions that are made about children, their needs, and the actions that must be taken to meet them are inscribed in instructional organization. These assumptions can be seen in the rules made about when children may enter school and how they move from grade to grade, the strategies used for grouping, and resources de-voted to the student–teacher ratio.

Conversations about buried assumptions need to be encouraged, and how the teaching practice is supported or not supported by existing literature needs to be examined. Creative approaches to reworking policy need to be considered so that more children are included in the answer to this first question through edu-cation, resources, and institutional change.

HOW CAN WE TEACH?

When the second question, *How can we teach?* is pondered, assumptions about what children need to grow and learn and how to best facilitate those processes are being addressed. It is an enactment of philosophy that serves as a framework for the structures of classroom practice and for the research that works to gener-ate understandings about classroom practices. In this section I discuss how re-search on classroom practices is shaped by assumptions made about what matters and how the literature must be read with that in mind. In addition, the literature is examined by reading it for patterns.

Research as Rhetorical Argument

Early educators seem to love dichotomies. Programs and individuals are placed into opposing camps, pitting those who pledge allegiance to one kind against another. For example, educators speak of developmentally appropriate and devel-opmentally inappropriate, academic versus social, whole child or basic skills, phon-ics versus whole language, teacher directed or child centered, and ready children or ready schools. These labels represent not only programmatic issues and cur-riculum materials and activities but also passionately held conceptions of what children are, what they need, and what our roles should be in their development and education. Assessing what teachers contribute to children's lives is less a matter of comparing one type of teacher with another than of untangling the assumptions about learning and development that are embedded in the programs and in the measures used to depict outcomes. Attempting to answer *How we teach?* addresses this complex muddle, looking at how various program types position children and teachers philosophically, how these philosophies are enacted, and how the consequences of placing children in them might be interpreted.

First, it is important to note that these dichotomies are in many ways artificial. They are oversimplified depictions of the interactions that occur among children and the adults who care for them. Rarely are programs pure enactments of a single philosophy because programs are experienced by people—people who are complex, contradictory, pragmatic, and political. They do what they need to do and what they want to do to achieve their ends, both expressed and unconscious.

Second, it is vital to acknowledge that the assessment of program orientations is driven by the implicit values embedded in their measurement. A cynic might say that scholars rig the race so that outcomes privileged in a model are used to judge who wins. It could be argued also that assessment is aligned with the instructional frames that are most valued. Whatever the interpretation, it is almost as important to look carefully at the outcome measure as it is to understand the treatment. When a researcher argues that practice "x" is better than practice "y," it is a good bet that measure "x" will produce a more flattering picture than measure "y" and that you can predict which was chosen. The entire chain of argument needs to be examined to understand embedded assumptions, unintended blind spots, and unspoken alternatives.

Relations Between Research Structure and Philosophy

Discussion of early childhood curriculum breaks down into two camps, the first endorsing a child-centered approach, typically through play and social activity, and the other supporting a teacher-directed or academic approach, through direct instruction on academic skills such as letter and number recognition. This contrast is not only instructional but also an essentially philosophical debate on what children need to learn and develop.

Advocates of child-centered approaches premise classroom practice on developmental philosophies that suggest that children's experiences and developmental needs should direct activity. A focus on play-oriented, socially based, integrated approaches is seen as necessary to provide a context for children to develop the skills needed for learning and the dispositions that make them learners (Katz, 1985). Within this model, adults provide opportunities for students to make choices from which they learn consequences. It is within these contexts that skills are developed. Facilitating learning is the role for the teacher, who sometimes sets up learning situations that involve indirect teaching. Other times he or she uses more direct instructional approaches, depending on the needs of the content and the learners involved. This approach has been most thoroughly described by early childhood experts (Elkind, 1987) and in position statements of early childhood groups, such as the National Association for the Education of Young Children (NAEYC) (Bredekamp, 1987; Bredekamp & Copple, 1997).

In contrast, those who advocate direct teaching of specific skills seek to increase instructional interaction time among teachers and students, defined in terms of adult-orchestrated activities. Diverse perspectives shape this view from those who think in terms of increasing time on task (Gersten, Darch, & Gleason, 1988) to those who advocate providing access to basic skills and the culture of power (Delpit, 1995). The turn toward direct instruction engages teachers in the transmission of knowledge and skills to students on which they can then build educational foundations.

The differences between the child-centered and the direct approach to teaching are related to what forms the best foundation for learning—indirect, child-initiated activities or direct, teacher-structured lessons. The battle lines (and they are rather war like) are often drawn as though these ways of teaching are mutually exclusive—that child centered means no direction and teacher directed means no child initiative.

A growing body of research has attempted to examine the relationship between program type and student outcomes. Scholars have described the nature of the programs in terms of types of interactions, student affect, and academic achievement, attempting to prove which type of program is better for children. This research has focused primarily on preschool and kindergarten years, with much less attention paid to the early elementary grades. Although political documents advocating developmental approaches extend discussion for Years 6 to 8, little work has been done in grades 1 to 3 to examine the effects of specific differences in initiation to formal schooling.

Examining the research since the late 1970s shows shifting sentiments and meanings for concepts such as readiness for kindergarten, academics, teacher direction, and child-centered instruction. It seems that society has come to terms with the idea that kindergarten is no longer a place of pure play and social development but still struggles with the tension that changing that curricular focus has for children. The academic "bootcamp" that was described in the early 1980s seems to have moderated in most settings, in large part due to the intense and continued political groundwork by groups such as NAEYC. This shift is important to set the context for examining the literature on the nature of kindergarten programs. When child-centered programs are compared with didactic programs, it is difficult to discern what those labels mean in various eras. A program that is considered to be child centered at one point in time might easily be seen as teacher directed during another.

One key sign that indicates that the way people look at learning and development has been broadened is the addition of a dimension to the concept of *developmental appropriateness*. In the first set of guidelines developed by the NAEYC, two dimensions were suggested: age appropriateness and individual appropriateness. These dimensions portrayed the patterned nature of growth and development, while calling attention to the ways that individual children lived those patterns (Bredekamp, 1987). The revised statement (Bredekamp & Copple, 1997) broadened this notion of regularity and individuality by bringing attention to the social and cultural contexts in which children live. By understanding the interrelations among these three sources of influence, teachers can generate rich, situated understandings of children.

In addition, the theoretical foundations for interpreting kindergarten practice have changed. One of the main changes in theory informing early childhood education has been the broadening from perspectives based on Piaget's theories to those influenced by the social constructivism most readily identified with Vygotsky. Enactments[1] of Piaget's work tended to be more child initiated, with the assumption that individual children reach out to the environment to construct knowledge of the world. This kind of approach developed from the assumption that

> Learning and development are separate entities—that development is the dominant process, and that learning follows after it and has little impact on the structure or maturity of children's thinking. . . . School learning, in the form of direct teaching of scientific concepts, was assumed to have little determining effect on development. . . . In a Piaget-based classroom, teachers de-emphasize conveying knowledge verbally, through didactic instruction. Instead, they provide a rich variety of activities designed to promote exploration and encourage children to choose freely among them. . . . Because Piaget's theory stresses the supremacy of development over learning, the teacher's contribution to the process of acquiring new knowledge is reduced relative to the child's. (Berk & Winsler, 1995, pp. 101–103)

In contrast, sociocultural perspectives such as Vygotsky's consider learning and development to be mutually constitutive so that instruction leads development. Followers of Piaget's thinking place the individual in the foreground and the environment in the background, whereas Vygotskians reverse the emphasis, highlighting the role of teachers in advancing children's development:

> Vygotsky emphasized that teachers must collaborate with children in joint cognitive activities carefully chosen to fit the child's *level of potential development,* thereby advancing the child's actual development . . . instead of advocating either discovery learning in its purest form or didactic teaching, the Vygotskian approach to education is one of *assisted discovery.* (Berk & Winsler, 1995, pp. 107–108)

The changing conceptions of learning provide a way to look at the research on instructional implications of varied strategies for teaching young children.

A first step in looking at this literature is related to the issue of labels. The studies discussed in the next section signal to the reader the values that researchers have for the teaching practices they are studying. Contrasting the concepts of developmentally appropriate and developmentally inappropriate definitely telegraphs which pedagogical strategy is preferred. Aligning basic skills with a context that lacks nurturance and promotes stress signals a perspective that limits its acceptability in traditional early childhood circles. These are measurement issues as much as they are findings. The search for optimal settings is limited by the way in which contrasts are framed and processes and outcomes are measured. The labels are connected to systems of value, which influence the instruments used to prove efficacy. Understanding this issue, patterns in the literature on early school curriculum are readily visible.

In the next sections, research that addresses the question, *How can we teach?* with regard to kindergarten scheduling, teacher-directed versus child-centered instruction, curriculum organization, and models of child guidance is examined.

---

[1]Work enactments are used here because most researchers familiar with Piaget's work would call for attention to the complexity of his treatment of the relations between child and context. As with most uses of theory, it has been rather unidimensional and stereotypical.

Scheduling

Length of Day Originally, kindergarten was meant to be an introduction to settings outside the home for the vast majority of children and was primarily a half-day program focused on play and socialization. Today's kindergarten is not quite like that. One of the key issues for kindergarten today is what kind of scheduling kindergartens should adopt. The issue of length of day is a perfect example of the complexity of causal elements in early childhood policy research. The question of whether full-day kindergarten is effective requires considerable dancing among all the elements of influence: the array of full-day kindergarten types, the goals and clientele of the program, the curriculum employed, and the standards and measures used to assess success. There are many types of full-day kindergartens for many types of children, serving a variety of goals and working toward diverse outcomes. Whether full-day kindergarten is effective depends on the child and the circumstances. A kindergarten program badly run in 2½ hours will do even less for children in 5–6 hours per day. However, a growing body of research indicates that good-quality, full-day programs have positive effects for a variety of students.

The first question to consider is how can various kindergarten schedules be assessed? The simplest, most typical way is to examine student outcomes. From this perspective, we must compare student achievement. A key concern is determining what types of achievement. Furthermore, the effects of the achievement in the short term as well as the long term can be assessed. One of the most comprehensive analyses of the achievement–scheduling link was performed by Karweit (1987) using a best evidence synthesis. Studies of full-day kindergarten were examined, looking explicitly at the effects along three dimensions: adequacy of study design, student risk status, and longevity of effects. In this analysis, students identified as disadvantaged were most likely to have increased achievement at the end of their kindergarten year on varied measures of reading, mathematics, and general achievement. These effects were not maintained beyond the kindergarten year. In contrast, groups who were not disadvantaged did not outperform controls in short- or long-term studies. These general patterns are similar to those found by Puleo (1988), although he pointed out that achievement differences always favor full-day programs. Sheehan, Cryan, Weichel, and Bandy (1991) argued that full-day programs achieved broader and more long-lived effects (through first grade), with full-day kindergarten students scoring better on standardized tests than students in half-day programs (or alternate full-day programs). In addition, full-day kindergarten students were less likely to receive Chapter 1 services or to be retained. A subsequent study found that full-day students were rated more positively on social behaviors on a standardized scale of child behavior (Cryan, Sheehan, Weichel, & Bandy-Hedden, 1992).

One issue that was not explicitly addressed in these syntheses was the various forms a full-day program could take. A full-day program could be an extended-day program, which adds additional services onto regular half-day attendance. This add-on could be targeted instructional time, general enrichment, or a self-standing program with a particular curriculum related to length of day. It would be advantageous for subsequent syntheses to address the issue of program type, along with student characteristics.

A picture of the types of activities and the nature of curriculum generated in full-day kindergartens is beginning to emerge. This is where the effects literature does not tell the whole story and where identifying commitments to early child-hood philosophy seem to have the most salience. People who oppose full-day kindergarten suggest that it will rob kindergarten of its special status as a place that prizes social interaction and play and would irrevocably move toward aca-demic and structured activity. However, this argument does not appear to hold its ground. The full-day and half-day programs are more alike than different (Meyer, 1985), and at least one study found a reversal of this expectation—that half-day programs had children spending a greater proportion of their time in teacher-directed large-group activity and full-day students spending more of their time in free play (Cryan et al., 1992).

A key policy issue in this debate is how to think about kindergarten schedul-ing. Are changes in social structure in which the majority of children have already had an out-of-home experience, which might require rethinking the role of kinder-garten, being considered? Can a cost–benefit analysis be done to determine whether the considerable cost of teacher salary, space, and materials leverages a particular outcome? Furthermore, what is the desired outcome? There is spirited argument about this issue, and consensus will be hard to achieve until the questions are more clearly defined.

Didactic or Child-Centered Methods   Who is the leader and who is the fol-lower in student–teacher interactions? Comparisons of didactic and child-centered programs are a mixed lot. Results generally favor child-centered approaches, but patterns that indicate that effects are not unidimensional do exist. One way to un-derstand the work is to know researchers philosophically. Constructivists (De-Vries, Reese-Learned, & Morgan, 1991) who compared didactic (Direct Instruction System for Teaching Arithmetic and Reading [DISTAR]) and child-initiated pro-grams (constructivist) found that initial academic advantage for didactic program participants diminished by third grade and that social interactions among chil-dren were more prominent in the constructivist program. Didactic proponents compared a direct instruction component (DISTAR) in a more traditionally ori-ented program for children with disadvantages to a direct instruction program for children who began the program at grade 1. They found that achievement was greater for the students who began academically oriented programs earlier (Ger-sten et al., 1988). Levels of stress for boys and for African American children have been found to be greater in programs classified as developmentally inappropriate by researchers working within the model of developmentally appropriate practice (Burts, Hart, Charlesworth, & Kirk, 1990). Comparison of didactic and child-centered programs (Stipek, Feiler, Daniels, & Milburn, 1995) differentiated be-tween the two using scales that associated basic skills and a focus on performance and evaluation with negative social climate.

Findings in works that compare child-centered and teacher-directed ap-proaches can be examined in three categories: process, dispositional outcomes, and skills outcomes. The process findings relate to the types of interactions and ac-tivities employed in varied programs. Constructivist programs were character-ized by more social interaction (DeVries et al., 1991), and developmentally appro-priate or child-centered programs scored higher on measures of implementation of developmental appropriateness (Burts et al., 1992; Burts et al., 1990; Stipek et al., 1995), such as more center, group story, and transition activity.

Dispositional outcomes, which are affective outcomes of program configura-tion, examine the ways that students interact with classroom activity. Comparisons have noted that child-centered approaches are less likely to produce children who exhibit stress and dependency (Burts et al., 1992; Burts et al., 1990; Stipek et al., 1995) and are more likely to produce children who are more confident about their abilities, have higher expectations for their success, enjoy school more, and are more proud of their accomplishments. However, these findings are not universal. When Goldenberg (1994) compared programs on the affective dispositions of self-confidence, motivation, and enjoyment, he found no differences among classes using small books at home and in school, standard kindergarten classes, and highly structured academic kindergartens. These dispositional categorizations are important; they help us to understand how we produce students in classrooms.

However, the cultural loadings within these labels must not be ignored. For example, Stipek et al. (1995) interpreted children waiting for permission to begin a task or approval upon completion as being dependent on adults. This is one possible characterization, but another would be that these are children who have learned not to be impulsive in their actions and to wait for instructions so that they can do what is expected of them. For children who are not part of the dominant cultural practices of American elementary schools—cultural practices that have been described as mirroring the values of Caucasian, middle-class families (Delpit, 1995; Lareau, 1989)—interpretation of their place in the power structure is critical to school success. Therefore, in addition to describing the dispositions enacted by children in various classroom configurations, it is vital to consider divergent interpretations of behavior, including those of teachers and children.

This discussion is not to point to weaknesses in good research. Instead, it is to heighten attention to the importance of meaning in research with children (Graue & Walsh, 1998). If the territory of affect and interpretation (making sense of the meaning of a child's actions) is to be considered, it is vital to go beyond our *own* sense of activity. One of the gifts left by Piaget is the conception that children see the world differently than adults. Adding in the complexity of cultural difference requires us to situate our readings within emic understandings of the way the world works. The indirect teaching that is so much a part of privileged early childhood practice is linked to cultural patterns related to race and socioeconomic status (SES) (Heath, 1983; Lareau, 1989). It is important to understand that the interpretations of practices made by relevant participants cannot be made in a one-size-fits-all manner. There are multiple ways of being a good teacher, just as there are multiple ways that children can have positive, albeit different, kindergarten experiences.

For example, Delpit (1995) explained that student descriptions of what to white liberals would be a "mean" teacher are actually to some an indication of pride about the teacher's methods. What many people would see as developmentally inappropriate or harsh is, in the eye of the beholder, a matter of tradition and power. Pertaining to this, Delpit stated:

> I suggest that although all "explicit" black teachers are not also good teachers, there are different attitudes in different cultural groups about what characteristics make for a good teacher. Thus, it is impossible to create a model for the good teacher without taking issues of culture and community context into account. (p. 37)

The outcome–program type relationship appears multidimensional, with child-focused programs facilitating greater growth in some areas than others when compared with more didactic approaches. Didactic approaches have been linked with higher performance on measures of letters/reading achievement than traditional child-centered programs (Goldenberg, 1994; Stipek et al., 1995), and there are mixed results related to mathematics (Gersten et al, 1988; Rawl & O'Tuel, 1982; Stipek et al., 1995). However, the explanations for differential effects reflect the perspectives of the interpreters so that there are a variety of ways to look at outcomes. From a content-oriented or psychological perspective, the differential findings are related to the nature of the curriculum content. Stipek et al. (1995) surmised that the advantages provided by didactic instruction in reading skills are related to the amenability of acquisition through memorization of skills such as letter recognition. In contrast, other types of literacy or mathematics skills require more than memorization and would benefit from broader instruction than is provided in narrow didactic programs.

A cultural or power critique provides a different interpretation. Goldenberg's (1994) finding that academic programs produced higher-achieving students in every area except recognition of letter names and sounds and oral language skills situated explanations outside the structure of content. Rather than discipline related, the differences are generated by differences in power. He suggested that indirect methods can leave significant numbers of children without access to the tools of literacy. For some members of ethnic minority groups, this is very much a matter of power. His discussion is provocative:

> Although I am not necessarily making a case for academic kindergartens, I am suggesting that the current, mainstream revulsion at teaching academic skills to 5-year-olds merits reexamination, particularly when there is evidence that children can benefit from such learning while suffering no adverse side effects. A lot depends on the teaching and the context in which academic learning is expected to take place. The last words go to one of the two teachers in the academic kindergartens, who confounded some of my most cherished assumptions about early literacy development:
> "Teachers think these kids are so deprived we need to let them play all day here. That really makes me mad because I came from a background like this. [Teachers make assumptions about children's backgrounds] to allow letting kids play all day rather than taking responsibility for teaching them what they need to know so they can be academically successful. These kids can learn, but they have to be taught. If more teachers realized this and did what they were supposed to do, more of these kids would go to college." (Goldenberg, 1994, p. 185)

From yet another perspective, these differences are related to the measures used to depict achievement. Standardized measures of young children's learning have used simplified content to reduce the psychometric complexity of the testing task. Most measures reflected readiness conceptions of early literacy that predate the infusion of more context-oriented and socially oriented approaches (Stallman & Pearson, 1990). The outcomes portrayed in many standardized instruments used with young children favor programs that teach skills that can be measured with simple items (e.g., letter recognition, word identification). Skills requiring more complex treatment, such as inferences from stories or generating text as an author, are not captured. Therefore, the advantage of one program type over another is related to what content is used in the measures that assess the advantage.

There is no final answer in the child-centered, teacher-directed conversation. The results are mixed, depending on the orientation of the researcher who does the work, the focus of the study, and the measures used. Balance between the two poles of activity is probably more of the norm than work at either end and seems sensible given the state of our knowledge.

The Shape of Curriculum Content   Another way to think about curriculum and instruction for young children is according to organizing principles. How is curriculum framed, and what shape does it take within this framing? What categories are used to build and read curriculum, and how does this set up relationships between the child and activity? Kindergarten is a pivotal transition point for these questions as it represents a change in the way that people think about curriculum as children are placed into elementary contexts.

One way of organizing curriculum is by the area of development targeted for instruction. Many programs generate curriculum within categories, such as language development, fine motor skills, and social skills. From this model, activities are developed that target particular areas of growth. This is a typical way of categorizing work in early education settings and illustrates the notion that children are complex beings with dimensions of development that can be addressed explicitly by instructional activities. In contrast, we can think in terms of disciplines or content perspectives. A typical way of segmenting the schedule and activities in elementary schools, this model frames work in terms of literacy (reading, language arts), mathematics, social studies, and so on. Thinking about these content areas takes on a variety of forms, from separate times and activities for content areas (with coverage typically uneven, focused mostly on literacy) to various ways of connecting the content areas through thematic work.

The locus of curriculum is also varied. Curriculum can be generated from developmental notions of how skills are grown within children, it can be framed from themes seen as appropriate for a given age/grade, or it can be formed from the interests and experiences of a given group of children. Given this array of choices, what kinds of curriculum organization will facilitate the transition of students into elementary school?

A strong value in the early childhood community is that curriculum should be 1) multifaceted, to increase the likelihood that diverse students will find connections to it; 2) integrated, because content categories are artificial constructions of adults; and 3) close to child interests, so that it is relevant. The literature is increasingly rich in its resources to teachers interested in teaching within this model; the resources range from theoretical to practitioner reports of integrated projects (Bredekamp & Rosegrant, 1995; Fogarty, 1993; Katz & Chard, 1989; Seely, 1995). This literature is interesting in that it is primarily inferential in nature—it originates from particular ways of thinking about how children grow and develop. The vast majority of work delineates theoretical and philosophical foundations for curriculum integration or provides models for implementing it. Missing are empirical assessments of the process or products of this way of working with children. The theoretical assertions, though inferential, are well grounded. They develop from diverse schools of thought on how knowledge and expertise evolved. However, it is surprising how little we know about the implementation of integration.

One issue is how the various forms of curriculum organization would be evaluated. Can a horse race of content-segregated versus developmentally designed versus integrated approaches be set up to see which gets farther faster? Should the ease with which each approach is developed or implemented be assessed? A multifaceted approach to evaluating forms of curriculum is necessary to understand the various ways of organizing instructional activities for young children. The process of instruction under different models—what kinds of knowledge are generated, what types of relations are fostered, and what connections are made to activities such as assessment—needs to be known. Evaluating how assessment formats frame what can be known about student learning in various curriculum formats is very important. With the current focus on standards and benchmarks, student-initiated, integrated curriculum is often threatened because the measures used to assess achievement of standards are mapped in a unilinear way. The basic values and structures of intellectual content are seen as different in various models of curriculum, and whether the measures need to vary as well needs to be decided.

Research- and practice-oriented inquiry should also address short- and long-term outcomes of curriculum models, in terms of academic achievement, intellectual dispositions, and interpersonal relationships. How the conditions of teaching constrain or facilitate models of teaching needs further exploration, and it is not enough to find which is most efficient. This knowledge must be weighed against the findings in the other areas to assess the costs and benefits of structuring programs in various ways.

In many universities, teacher education is structured to support segregated notions of curriculum content. Methods courses are taught within subject areas such as language arts, mathematics, and science. Thinking and working outside those boundaries is not facilitated by this structure, and curriculum integration is seen as diminishing attention to the content of the course. Structural changes will be required if attention is to be focused on curriculum integration, at the least, collaborating activities among methods courses. At the same time, concerns for the structure of disciplinary content need to be addressed to ensure that prospective teachers have adequate grounding in the discipline they are teaching, regardless of the structure of the curriculum they choose.

Guiding Children's Activity

The idea of managing a classroom is often at the top of the educational agenda. For novice teachers, it is one of their greatest concerns; for the public, it is seen as a barometer of educational adequacy; and for researchers, it is a perennial focus of inquiry. We worry a lot about losing control of classrooms; therefore, it is important to pay attention to what research tells us about how to get the best out of children in all domains. This issue is at the heart of the question, *How can we teach?* because for many people, it is seen as a prerequisite to teaching. Whether this work is seen as classroom management, child guidance, or school socialization, it is clear that children do not learn in chaos. How to avoid chaos, or even wasted time for children, is the focus of work on child guidance. This brief overview of the topic explores three different frameworks for understanding classroom behavior and its management. These frameworks are typically presented by three different groups of scholars, but increasingly they are borrowing each other's logic to frame integrative views.

Curriculum-Focused Classroom Management This genre of research has turned the focus away from what teachers do as they keep control to what teachers do within instructional practices to engage students at the highest level for the largest proportion of time. A review by Evertson and Harris summarized the literature in this way:

Teachers who are effective managers: use time as effectively as possible; implement group strategies with high levels of involvement and low levels of misbehavior; choose lesson formats and academic tasks conducive to high student engagement; communicate clearly rules of participation; prevent problems by
implementing a system at the beginning of the school year. (1992, p. 76)

These authors pointed to the idea that management is a matter of providing
educationally rich contexts for learning that engage children in consistently productive activity. These activities are without the cracks that trap students in down-
time that leads to troublesome interactions. They also frame expectations in ways
that are clear and shared by all involved. This kind of guidance is not brought off
the shelf as an add-on to a program. In fact, although programs such as Assertive
Discipline or Teacher Effectiveness Training provide generic strategies for dealing
with infractions, they are not capable of integrating the complex terrain of classroom interactions that are the core of teacher–student relationships (Emmer &
Aussiker, 1990) and classroom management. In addition, from this perspective,
self-standing courses on classroom management within teacher education courses
would make no sense. It would be like having a course on using a pencil when
what you wanted to teach was writing. Constructing content that captures all students is intellectually focused rather than management focused.

Engagement is not a one-size-fits all concept. What is engaging to one student
will be irritating to another. Teaching will need to move beyond planning guidance
with a generic student who fits the profile of a particular age or grade. Generating
authentically engaging activities that will maximize student involvement and not
waste time will require teachers to get to know their students and to find out what
interests them and how to leverage growth for them in that context. This is a much
more personal connection between teacher and student, one that melds the need
for good rules and routines with diagnosing needs and tailoring instruction.

Developmental Perspectives on Child Guidance   The early childhood community has favored perspectives on classroom management that use developmental
explanations for management strategies—the general patterns in child growth
and development that can be used to understand the reasoning and interactions
of young children. For example, Hyson and Christiansen (1997) framed the discussion of developmentally appropriate guidance in terms of the knowledge base
related to early emotional development, motivation, and sociomoral understanding and prosocial development. Using these conceptions of children's development, a framework for facilitating their actions can be inferred. The constraints
and possibilities for child reasoning and responsibility for behavior imply that
"guidance strategies should foster self-regulation, self-efficacy and self-respect,
emotional understanding, and sociocultural competence" (Hyson & Christiansen,
1997, p. 307). Specifically, this would involve 1) creating a secure emotional environment; 2) helping children understand feelings; 3) modeling genuine, appropriate emotional responses; 4) supporting children's emotional regulation; 5) identifying and respecting children's emotional styles; and 6) uniting learning and
positive emotions (Hyson & Christiansen, 1997).

One of the most interesting aspects of Hyson and Christiansen's (1997) discussion is their acknowledgment that models for guiding children's actions are related to general philosophical positions on education. Understanding the consis-
tencies or gaps between guidance and other forms of teacher action is key to

understanding how a program works as a unit or, conversely, how it might work to adapt to the needs of individual children. In addition, Hyson and Christiansen (1997) noted that guidance is by its nature a cultural phenomenon, shaped by the values and practices of teachers and students. Creating a cultural context that bridges disparate views of how adults and children should act would be one of the first building blocks of developmentally appropriate guidance. This is more than making children learn the teacher's rules; it is dialogic, requiring the development of in-depth understanding of both individual children and their culturally shaped patterns of interaction.

Cultural Perspectives on Guidance   A third way to examine the issue of child guidance in classrooms is to look at it as a cultural practice—one that is shaped by communication traditions, cultural values, social pressures, political power, and so on. This perspective has been used in a variety of ways as educators and researchers have attempted to understand the interactions of increasingly diverse dyads of teachers and students (Erickson, 1993). It has played out in sociolinguistic explanations of cultural differences, focusing on communication strategies (Erickson & Mohatt, 1982; Mehan, 1982) and labor market explanations, which argue that perceived constraints on student success narrow the expectations of students of color (Ogbu, 1978). Much of this work has focused on how to use cultural patterns of students for the development of culturally relevant teaching. This chapter focuses on the importance of the cultural meanings that teachers generate for students' actions and behavior. Because guidance of students' actions in the classroom is highly dependent on teachers' judgments about what children are doing, this is a pivotal issue.

Cultural interpretation is not easy. We tend to use our own explanations to understand the actions of others. With children, it is especially difficult because developmental issues come into play. Early childhood educators are often attuned to the developmental aspect of interpretation. We have learned that children's thinking is different from our own as adults. However, thinking across cultural borders, that is, unpacking how our interpretations put children in the center or in the margins in ways that have nothing to do with their actions, has been more difficult for us to learn. Expectations for meaning tend to put children of color, particularly boys, on the edge of disciplinary action, even when they are "doing" approximately the same thing as their Caucasian and usually male peers. Some children are given organic interpretations for their perceived pathology, whereas others' problems are interpreted as the results of living in a culturally deprived setting. For example, some children are seen as developmentally immature and would benefit from an additional year in a home or preschool environment. Their readiness problems are viewed as biological and amenable to more time for development. These children tend to be Caucasian and middle class. In contrast, other children are seen to have readiness problems that are the result of inadequate socialization or preparation for school. For these children, school entry is the answer, the idea being to push them along until they fail enough to qualify for special services. This group tends to be living in poverty and tends to be members of a racial/ethnic minority group. What is troubling about these differences is that they appear to be systemic, working to disadvantage groups of children in patterned ways that go beyond the correlational (Wilcox, 1982).

The moral of the story of cultural interpretations for child guidance is that adults (often from a culture different from their students) must learn to understand children from a child's perspective, understanding their behavior from a nonadult perspective. Ladson-Billings (1994) suggested the relations that might facilitate this kind of relationship between teachers and students in her analysis of successful teachers of African American students. Although she does not address management particularly, her focus on humane equity, connectedness with all students, the development of community, and high expectations shows how teachers must reach outside themselves to understand the nature of student action both in and out of school.

How can these three ways of viewing child guidance be used to set out a plan for research, policy, and teacher action? It is clear that no package of strategies will work to put perfect behavior in place in every classroom context. An off-the-shelf system cannot be developed or bought to help maintain classroom harmony. More examples of good practice that work to the potential rather than the detriment of all children are needed. There are probably multiple ways that teachers can meet the needs of children, using one or all of the models described previously. How are they enacted in the day-to-day interactions of teachers who are successful with diverse groups of students? Do certain models of child guidance benefit some groups more than others?

More needs to be understood about the professional development strategies that allow educators to see across cultures or developmental levels, and the long-term implications of helping children to become members of an educational community, while respecting what they bring to that community, also need to be understood. Assimilation, where all children will end up looking or acting the same, is not the desired end result. Instead, transformation that will build on the best of what children bring with them to the classroom, while helping them to develop the skills needed to be viable members of settings that have particular expectations, needs to be the prerogative.

Summary

When the question, *How can we teach?* is discussed, particular assumptions about development and learning and what teachers need to do within those assumptions are made. These ideas can be read in the ways that researchers approach their inquiry and must be understood if the evidence for various approaches to teaching is going to be sorted out. Situating findings within perspectives allows us to understand the responsibilities that reside within choices of teaching strategies and structures.

WHAT CAN WE TEACH?

The question, *What can we teach?* is the foundation for numerous books, courses, workshops, and curriculum arguments. It is the fodder of lesson plans, textbook development, and program evaluation. It is the most concrete question that is derivative of the other two questions posed in this chapter. What is taught is related foundationally to who is being taught and how they are being taught. When discussing what is going to be taught, we wrestle with the nature of curriculum content and its related elements in teaching. In this section I explore the kindergarten content and the knowledge that should be used to construct content.

Curriculum Content

The notion of curriculum content for kindergarten has been the subject of much debate related to the purposes of kindergarten. This in turn is related to the social and political context in which kindergarten has existed (Walsh, 1989). When kindergarten was seen as the place to get ready for the rigors of real education and as a place of transition from home to school, the focus was much more on the social aspects of developing children. From this perspective, the main purpose was to become part of the school and the secondary purpose was to build the basic skills that would allow children to succeed in the academic activities with which they are confronted in first grade and beyond.

However, somewhere along the line the world changed. Children entered educational institutions in the preschool years rather than in kindergarten, giving many of them a start on their learning to be students. Changing conceptions of early learning made us aware of the potential for additional academic learning in the pre-elementary years. This learning could be achieved by giving a head start to children with developmental delays, by working to bridge the gap between children whose culture is not represented in most schools, and by helping those children who are already in the mainstream to reach an even higher academic level. Kindergarten teachers, finding that their students were entering school with knowledge of the basic concepts, such as shapes and colors, were able to move to more "advanced" material sooner (Graue, 1993b).

How do we think about the content of the kindergarten curriculum in a context in which its focus, constituency, and ethos are changing? This is not only an educational question, but also a question with political, social, and cultural dimensions. How do we think about curriculum so that it is inclusive of all children, not just those who are easy to teach or who fit our models of success?

As mentioned previously, the discussion is often enacted in terms of teacher-directed versus child-centered approaches. In Karweit's (1994) review of research on kindergarten curriculum, this discussion is represented by the phonics versus whole language debate, illustrating the power that literacy has in the tug-of-war over kindergarten curriculum—it is clearly seen as a prime focus of early schooling, given its correlates with later success. But before going down that road, it is important to think about what it means to take that focus for granted. Literacy can be conceptualized as a relatively narrow domain of academic inquiry and educational practice (as in reading), or it can be viewed as an encompassing way of being that involves all forms of communication (including mathematical, scientific, and artistic forms). The second view is not universally held, so if we think of literacy as the development of written and oral communication, we might jump to the conclusion that literacy is what kindergarten is about if we want children to make a good transition into multiple forms of content and knowledge.

What is gained or missed by choosing literacy as the goal of kindergarten, particularly if it is chosen by default, needs to be carefully contemplated. Where do we place mathematics, social studies, science, or the arts, and what does it mean that these disciplines are grouped together? Where do we negotiate a place for the social, emotional, and physical aspects of child growth and development? I address this problem by calling attention to the difficulty of organizing a way to think about the curriculum that is inclusive and politically savvy enough to garner support from all quarters. The only way to do this is to stay within a general discussion, with brief forays into specific content areas.

There are some general patterns in the work on curriculum content. The first pattern is that there is very limited knowledge about the efficacy of specific curricular packages. It can be surmised that this is partly due to the focus on generating curriculum within children's experiences, rather than depending on externally developed programs of activities. One analysis reviewed an array of kindergarten curriculum programs that ranged in intensity, focus, and cost. In a summary of this work, Karweit (1994) presented four examples with evidence of their effectiveness: Kindergarten Integrated Thematic Experiences (KITE), Early Prevention of School Failure (EPSF), Writing to Read (WTR), and Story Telling and Retelling (STAR). Karweit (1994) noted positive effect sizes for KITE, WTR, and STAR, as well as diversity in the approaches these programs represent, from thematic instruction paired with systematic introduction to letter–sound correspondence to interactive story reading. She also noted the paucity of evidence for most curriculum packages and urged developers to put energy into research to support the use of various programs.

Although a broad knowledge base for kindergarten curriculum has not developed, there is an increasingly rich foundation of work that maps the terrain of children's learning within specific content areas (e.g., literacy: Adams, 1990; Bissex, 1980; Clay, 1979; Dyson, 1989; Mason & Sinha, 1993; math: Baroody, 1993; Ginsburg & Baron, 1993; Hiebert & Carpenter, 1992). This work has looked carefully at the regularities that exist in children's learning as well as the specific contextual supports that foster that learning. Interpretations of this research suggest instructional approaches that will provide conceptually congruent activities to foster development. For example, the standards for practice suggested by the National Council of Teachers of Mathematics (NCTM) were generated from research on learning, as well as implied from the philosophical frameworks of constructivism (NCTM, 1989). Work on whole language learning originated from Vygotskian inquiry on literacy and research on the development of literacy practice and skills acquisition.

As theories and practices have become increasingly diverse, the polarization among groups advocating for approaches and philosophies has intensified. Inquiry into approaches to teaching has mirrored this trend with researchers, policy makers, and practitioners evaluating research within standards that match their own perspectives, while discounting those with different assumptions (e.g., see exchanges related to literacy approaches, McGee & Lormax, 1990; Schickedanz, 1990; Stahl, 1990; Stahl & Miller, 1989). Parsimony is hard to come by in such a setting and is increasingly less sought. Again, our inquiry has been shaped by the assumptions and implicit theories we have for children and their lives, which have left imprints in the outcomes of this research.

Careful readings find a few patterns across content areas and between poles of argument. For example, patterns are much less pronounced than one would think. There are regularities across large numbers of children in terms of the general ways they learn, and knowing about these regularities makes teaching much stronger. For example, the patterned nature of learning to write provides a helpful roadmap to teachers as they think about ways to structure experiences so that development continues for children beginning to express themselves on paper. It is hard to help children work on the leading edge of development if one does not know what that edge is or how to find it. However, the means and manners of learning are not enacted in the same fashion by all children. The diversity of children in virtually any dimension chosen by researchers (age, SES, ethnic group membership, temperament, adult construction) produces different results in response to different instructional approaches. There is not a one-size-fits-all approach in any content area. Children vary and, therefore, so do the instructional approaches that facilitate their learning. The locus of the differences could be seen as attributable to the researcher who is doing the analysis. For some, the focus is developmental, coming out of patterned unfolding of skills that dictate specific interactions at various points; for others, it is related to individual learning styles or temperaments. For still others, it is related to cultural and social practices that shape what resources individuals have for interaction.

Within this pattern of diversity among students is a parallel focus on diverse instruction—moving from the ends of instructional perspectives toward blended approaches. Teachers neither drill and kill nor let students sink or swim. Instead, they attend closely to children's emerging development, providing activities that embed developmental tasks within contexts connected to real-life experiences. Active intervention that is focused on needs that are established through the careful collection of evidence provides children with instructional contexts that challenge their potential. An example of this approach can be seen in Cognitively Guided Instruction (CGI), developed by mathematics educators at the University of Wisconsin. In this program, students learn the strategies of mathematics through self-generated problems that are carefully assessed and extended by teachers who know the generalized patterns in mathematical content learning (Carpenter, Fennema, Peterson, Chiang, & Loef, 1989).

Knowledge Bases for Strong Curriculum Content   Three related dimensions of knowledge/practice come to the forefront when considering ways of teaching that use contemporary conceptions of curriculum content: knowledge of development, knowledge of goals, and knowledge of students. Curriculum content that is inclusive has within it awareness of regularities in patterns of learning, a goal in mind for instructional interactions, and ways of assessing children's knowledge and experience relative to these goals. These three patterns are interwoven and must be considered foundational aspects of content.

Knowledge of Development   Knowledge of the generally expected patterns of development in content domains—from literacy to social development and from numeracy to artistic expression—provides a concrete way to orient decision making when constructing curriculum. Understanding what to expect next helps teachers to support students in making the connections necessary to advance. But this knowledge must be used to challenge children, not hold them back. Thinking developmentally, when done from a deficit model, can be a straightjacket rather than a productive tool. When teachers have inflexible expectations for age-level competencies, this can translate into judgments of inadequacy for children who do not fit the model. This can be paired with lower expectations for children below age expectancies, resulting in less challenging instruction that produces less complex learning. Developmental patterns are complex and are increasingly acknowledged as being related to cultural resources in a given setting. The key is to use this knowledge to enhance a child's potential rather than as a rationale for determining failure.

Knowledge of generalized patterns of development should never inhibit learning; consequently, it needs to be paired with an acknowledgment of its fallibility and bias toward particular ways of looking at the world. The use of developmental knowledge must recognize the ways in which it is doubly situated in cultural contexts. On the one hand, its generation is culturally determined within particular groups and resources by researchers with particular cultural interpretations. On the other hand, within individuals, the portrayal of developmental status is culturally located as well, developed by children within cultural contexts and also used by teachers within cultural contexts. That makes judgments about development more complex, more interpretive, and more requisite of responsibility on the part of professionals. This skepticism does not mean that developmental knowledge is not useful; it means that it must be used wisely. The early childhood community (at least the part represented by NAEYC) has invested a great deal of faith in developmentally guided practice, and researchers need to examine the outcomes and process of using this knowledge to enhance learning and teaching. It also needs to extend beyond correlational work that examines the relationship among courses in child development and indices of developmentally appropriate practice. It is necessary to explore 1) how knowledge of development is portrayed in teacher preparation programs and in professional experience, 2) how it is used in decision making, and 3) what student outcomes it produces (and for whom).

Standards for Learning   The second dimension of knowledge pertains to goals for students—standards for learning developed by communities that represent aspirations for child learning. Standards and benchmarks are highly touted in today's political rhetoric in education, framed variously for accountability purposes and goals that raise expectations for all students. Their potential benefits are related to their ability to guide action. But they have potential downsides as well. Bredekamp and Rosegrant pointed to these possibilities and pitfalls:

> [Standards of learning] can serve as a beacon to direct curriculum development in general. At their best standards are visionary, compelling the field to follow toward shared, lofty goals. At the local level, standards can serve almost as flashlights, focusing the direction of teachers and children in classrooms, helping them figure out where they are in relation to where they want to go. . . . [P]otential negative effects of national standards include the threat to both integrated curriculum and emergent curriculum, the risk of expectations becoming standardized without regard for individual and cultural differences, and the danger of establishing inappropriate performance standards. (1995, pp. 8, 11)

For standards to benefit young children, it is necessary to pay close attention to three forms of standards. Development of these three types is uneven, particularly for the education of young children. The first, standards for the resources needed to attain our goals, also called "opportunity to learn," recognizes that contexts must be set for adequate teaching and learning to occur. Not only does opportunity to learn address a teaching context that must be in place to facilitate learning, but it also focuses on the need for material resources of all kinds. In the early years, these resources might include adequate health and nutrition, appropriate compensation and professional development for educators, and relevant programming for children. The second type of standard is most closely related to the content itself—the stated goals for learning and teaching. These goals must be stated in ways that are specific but inclusive, to guide action without reducing teaching activity to the level of a cookbook. The third type of standard addresses the levels of proficiency chosen to indicate attainment of goals (performance).

To maximize successful transitions, the opportunity to learn standards may be the most important because they will include attention to issues of developmental appropriateness and the dynamic nature of curriculum generation for our youngest learners. Overall, our use of standards needs to be multidimensional, recognizing that there is not a single notion of appropriate curriculum and learning, with multiple benchmarks to ensure attention to all levels of student development (McLaughlin & Shepard, 1995).

Standards are different from curriculum. Standards are endpoints, or goals that we have for the intense work of teaching. The way we achieve those goals in curriculum—the interactions that we use to promote learning—do not correspond one-to-one to the goals. The means of education are much more complex, multifaceted, and generative. When we simplify one to the other, we lose all that most early childhood educators value about the field: attention to the local, child-centered dimensions that make teaching relevant to the lives of those being taught. The problems of high-stakes assessment-based reform—where standards inform curriculum too heavily, thereby turning testing into teaching—should be carefully guarded against. The challenge is to find out how exactly to use standards as a way to guide action without determining it. One suggestion might be to involve relevant stakeholders in the development of standards, including professionals in the classroom.

Assessment as a Way of Knowing   The third type of knowledge is the bridge between the expectations for child development and the goals for child learning—that aspect of curriculum that provides direction for teacher action, in other words, assessment. In approaches to learning and development that take children's lived experiences and developmental status as foundational, teacher knowledge of certain children at various times in specific contexts is vital. One does not teach generic children. Instead, good teaching is linked to knowledge derived from assessed information about each child's status and strategies across time. Assessing beyond performance or status by looking at ways that children learn and interact provides a much richer portrait of a child than just identifying his or her level(s) of skill (Lunt, 1993). It also requires a different model for assessment than is typically enacted in research, policy, or practice (see Chapter 3).

Attention to assessment issues has been important in the early childhood community because of past and continuing misuse of tests in the education of young children. I do not discuss the ground that has been covered by others (e.g., Meisels, 1987; Shepard, 1994; Shepard & Graue, 1993). The focus on assessment has been enriched by emerging knowledge about how children grow and develop during this period. Sameroff and McDonough pointed to the links between knowledge of children and their success in school:

> Understanding the nature of the 5- to 7-year shift is a major prerequisite if educators are to help children make a successful transition into the elementary school. The timing and quality of this shift is influenced by characteristics of the child, the home environment, the cultural context, and previous experiences with group learning. When the resulting heterogeneity of children's characteristics and capacities is met by a uniformity of teacher expectations and behavior, many children become cognitive and social casualties. If we wish to change these outcomes, then the elementary school must become much more attuned to the individuality that each child brings to the classroom. (1994, p. 193)

To perform the kind of work suggested by Sameroff and McDonough (1994), assessment is a key factor. My discussion of assessment will, of necessity, be brief.

It focuses on guidelines that have been developed by researchers interested in the testing of young children and makes suggestions about goals for assessment that will maximize the success of children moving from informal to formal educational environments.

For those outside the measurement community, assessment or testing is a relatively simple task; it is a tool for getting information. But like any tool, its utility is very much related to the job. Attending to the jobs that assessment does, Shepard (1994) provided principles for early childhood assessment that highlight responsible assessment practices with young children. Three uses of assessment comprise this model: instructional practice (including home–school communication), identification of special needs, and program evaluation.

- Testing of young children should not occur unless it can be shown to lead to beneficial results.

- Methods of assessment, especially the language used, must be appropriate to the development and experiences of young children.

- Features of assessment—content, form, evidence of validity, and standards for interpretation—must be tailored to the specific purposes of assessment.

- Identification of children for special education is a legitimate purpose for assessment and still requires the use of curriculum-free, aptitude-like measures and normative comparisons. However, because disabling conditions are rare, the diagnostic model used by special education professionals should not be generalized to a larger population of below-average learners.

- For both instructional and public policy-making purposes, the content of assessments should embody the important dimensions of early learning and development. The tasks and skills children are asked to perform should reflect and model progress toward important learning goals.

Using these principles, assessment is a task that is undertaken to enrich teacher–student interactions and child learning in ways that are shaped by the local setting. Assessment is authentic in that it is linked to actual curriculum content and the relationships developed between teachers and students. In the past, much assessment has been in the form of anecdotal observations of student activity over time or through the use of a variety of off-the-shelf tests that describe readiness for instruction or achievement. Because these forms lacked a systematic connection to experience in the classroom, they were not able to be authentic. New forms of assessment work to enlarge the role of the teacher in assessment practices, heightening the utility of information derived from instructional interactions for decision making (Grace & Shores, 1991; Hills, 1992; Wolf, Bixby, Glenn, & Gardner, 1991).

Enacting these new forms has not been easy. The amount of time needed to generate assessment practice, and then information, is a great burden on teachers who do not see this as one of their prime activities. Guides that provide a balance between assistance for assessment, while keeping the practice within local interactions, have been slow in coming. An interesting example of materials that provide this kind of support is the Work Sampling System (Meisels, 1996), which involves documenting student work and evaluating its approximation of standards.

Using developmental checklists, portfolios, and summary reports, this system is based on professional development that provides a supportive foundation for good assessment practice. Results from psychometric studies of its reliability and criterion validity have been positive.

Much interest in assessment peaked in the early 1990s, and there has been some retrenchment as practitioners and policy makers have come to understand the time and professional development requirements of this kind of reform. However, much is still unknown about how to support teachers conducting assessment-leveraged teaching. One contribution that research could make would be in the preservice and in-service assessment needs of teachers. More information also needs to be generated about how this kind of work can fit into the already overburdened life of teachers of young children. Given the political nature of assessment, we need to examine how to maximize the instructional payoffs of assessment activities and the various uses this information might have beyond teaching decisions. We also need to develop strategies of assessment that do more than mirror teachers' visions of the world—ways of helping teachers see potential in children rather than reinscribing the biases inherent in all of us. This is especially important as teachers meet more children who are different from themselves and work to understand the cultural context for development in all its complexity.

Summary

The notions of curriculum content outlined here are in some ways more diverse because they recognize that there are multiple ways to address the needs of children. At the same time, they are more coherent in that they share a core set of principles for action. One aspect that is quite clear is that we must work to have curriculum that is more intentional, that is related to a growing knowledge base about how children learn, that is planful and goal oriented, and that is reflexive in its use of appropriate information to chart growth and evaluate the adequacy of our efforts. This model of curriculum comes from knowledge of the general and the specific and of principled ideas about how children learn and how they might be taught, but most important, from locally generated knowledge of specific children. Pulling out that unit on bears that has been the substance of teaching for the last 15 Octobers or marching through the letters of the week does not address either the general or specific aspects of curriculum generation. This concept of *planfulness* will need to be fully integrated into notions of teaching to avoid being seen as an add-on responsibility. Professional development for both preservice and inservice teachers should work through successful models of purposeful teaching, providing resources and support that allow teachers to take on these responsibilities successfully.

CONCLUSION

The practice of education is complex. It represents the aspirations, values, energies, and knowledge of diverse individuals and groups who generally want the best for children. The practice of kindergarten is no different. In fact, its symbolic importance in U.S. education fills it with emotion and hope in ways that focus attention on all relevant parties. Because of the complexity inherent in the subject, our inquiry needs to be equally intricate, taking advantage of the strengths that different ways of knowing can bring to our understanding. Attention needs to be focused on process and outcomes, beliefs, and practices to help us leverage change that will make schools become better places for all children.

Three broad questions were used to organize this discussion. However, these questions are more than organizational tools for the purpose of writing this chapter. They are framed to heighten attention to the questions that can be used to analyze practice with young children and to look for buried assumptions and unintended consequences of our actions. Working from these questions, what kinds of recommendations can be made to make transitions into kindergarten contexts smoother and more successful for all children?

When the question, *Who can we teach?* is asked, the focus should be on the responsibilities inherent in any policy that includes some children while excluding others. In assessing literature related to this question some observations and suggestions can be made. Actions taken to increase the readiness of children entering elementary schools have been regressive for the most part, blaming children for not meeting expectations set (in many cases, arbitrarily) by communities and schools. More potential-building programming that focuses on what children bring to school is needed to replace deficit model systems that focus on what children lack. Building on existing and emerging competence and looking forward to more complex development provide opportunities. Once in our care, we need to examine carefully how decisions are made about the size and nature of student groups. The understanding of the research on grouping is mixed, but evidence that higher-ability students receive higher-quality, more complex instruction does exist. Although differentiated instruction is an important factor in meeting children's needs, the equity issues related to quality cannot be ignored. High expectations for all students, regardless of their skills, should be an integral part of the grouping rationale and process. Finally, the late 1990s are a political period during which there is much interest in the relation between class size and achievement. Much faith exists, in both political and early education circles, in the power of smaller classroom groups. To capitalize on this opportunity, staffing policies, instructional practices, and research designs that use the potential of smaller group sizes need to be developed. A substantial public investment in this innovation will be wasted if this issue is not approached carefully.

The question, *How can we teach?* provides an opportunity to look at the way we structure learning interactions in classrooms. A key skill to attain is learning to read the research in this area, which is very much shaped by the philosophical orientation of the researcher. As decision makers use the literature, it is vital that they read results realizing that the outcomes of research come out of frameworks that promote certain answers. One lesson from the research is that there is more than one way to facilitate learning for young children. There are values to be found in most models of curriculum content; the key is to understand what they are and how they promote certain opportunities for children. The research community would contribute much to practice (and itself) by developing strategies for understanding the complexities of various forms of instruction. For example, in developing an understanding of the efficacy of the varied scheduling formats, there needs to be recognition that length of day is a small piece of the production of student outcomes in kindergarten. The type and quality of instructional practice, as it relates to length of day, need to be addressed in this literature as well as in the areas of professional preparation and practice. More complex measures of process and effects of instructional practice, from teacher- to child-centered models to disciplinary to integrated models, would allow researchers to differentiate among the array of possibilities for children. More information about practices, such as curriculum integration, is needed to move discussions of this strategy beyond the level of testimonials.

Asking *What can we teach?* often seems to be the first question that occupies the imagination of educators who must plan the day-to-day activity in classrooms and policy makers and researchers who use this as a way to assess instructional effectiveness. Realizing that it is a question that is derived from our answers to the two previous questions helps to prioritize our thinking about teaching. Acknowledging that three forms of knowledge—of development, of goals, and of particular children—form the foundation of strong content points to the centrality of planfulness in curriculum generation. We need to work harder to invest in content that represents what is generally known about how children learn but that is relevant and responsive to the children in our care. Consequently, the fact that off-the-shelf, teacher–child proof curriculum will not meet anyone's needs has been accepted. Policy and professional development needs to support the use of developmentally based curriculum generation that stays open to diversity within those developmental patterns. Models that generate good practice in others are needed, that is, models of teacher development that promote ideas without a simple make-and-take mentality. Doing this kind of work requires teachers to be thinkers who constantly question their practice. It is hard work, but it is what keeps good teachers alive as professionals. We need to support that kind of professionalism structurally, contractually, and emotionally.

In this chapter, I have attempted to pull together diverse ways of looking at teaching and learning to highlight the connections between the ways that questions are asked and answers generated. A lot is known but there are few definitive answers. For some, this lack of parsimony could be maddening. But looked at in another way, it could be seen as an opportunity. The multiple answers provided by the existing literature point to the complexity of the system of education and force us to realize that as much may be learned from the spaces between questions and answers as may be learned from the answers themselves. It turns our attention to the importance and intensity of local interactions between children and their teachers and highlights the responsibility that is entailed within those interactions. If this can be used to broaden our focus to include many viewpoints on teaching and learning, the center and margins of our discussions could be shifted so that fewer children are outside our expectations and reach.

REFERENCES

Adams, M.M. (1990). *Beginning to read: Thinking and learning about print.* Cambridge, MA: MIT Press.

Baroody, AJ. (1993). Fostering the mathematical learning of young children. In B. Spodek (Ed.), *Handbook of research on the education of young children* (pp. 151–175). Indianapolis, IN: Macmillan Publishing USA.

Berk, L.E., & Winsler, A. (1995). *Scaffolding children's learning: Vygotsky and early childhood education* (Vol. 7). Washington, DC: National Association for the Education of Young Children.

Bissex, G. (1980). *Gnys at work: A child learns to read and write.* Cambridge, MA: Harvard University Press.

Bredekamp, S. (Ed.). (1987). *Developmentally appropriate practice in early childhood programs serving children from birth through age 8* (Exp. ed.). Washington, DC: National Association for the Education of Young Children.

Bredekamp, S., & Copple, C. (Eds.). (1997). *Developmentally appropriate practice in early child-hood programs* (Rev. ed.). Washington, DC: National Association for the Education of Young Children.

Bredekamp, S., & Rosegrant, T. (1995). Transforming curriculum organization. In S. Bredekamp & T. Rosegrant (Eds.), *Reaching potentials: Transforming early childhood curriculum and assessment* (Vol. 2, pp. 167–176). Washington, DC: National Association for the Education of Young Children.

Burts, D.C., Hart, C.H., Charlesworth, R., Fleege, P.O., Mosely, J., & Thomasson, R.H. (1992). Observed activities and stress behaviors of children in developmentally appropriate and inappropriate kindergarten classrooms. *Early Childhood Research Quarterly, 7*(2), 297–318.

Burts, D.C., Hart, C.H., Charlesworth, R., & Kirk, L. (1990). A comparison of frequencies of stress behaviors observed in kindergarten children in classrooms with developmentally appropriate versus developmentally inappropriate instructional practices. *Early Childhood Research Quarterly, 5*(3), 407–423.

Byrd, R.S., Weitzman, M., & Auinger, P. (1997). Increased behavior problems associated with delayed school entry and delayed school progress. *Pediatrics, 100,* 654–661.

Byrnes, D.A. (1989). Attitudes of students, parents, and educators toward repeating a grade. In L.A.S.M.L. Smith (Ed.), *Flunking grades: Research and policies on retention* (pp. 108–131). London: Falmer Press.

Cameron, M.B., & Wilson, B.J. (1990). The effects of chronological age, gender, and delay of entry on academic achievement and retention: Implications for academic red-shirting. *Psychology in the Schools, 27,* 260–263.

Carpenter, T.P., Fennema, E., Peterson, P.L., Chiang, C.P., & Loef, M. (1989). Using knowledge of children's mathematics thinking in classroom teaching: An experimental study. *American Educational Research Journal, 26,* 499–532.

Clay, M. (1979). *Reading: The patterning of complex behavior.* Portsmouth, NH: Heinemann.

Cryan, J.R., Sheehan, R., Wiechel, J., & Bandy-Hedden, I.G. (1992). Success outcomes of full-day kindergarten: More positive social behavior and increased achievement in the years after. *Early Childhood Research Quarterly, 7*(2), 187–204.

Delpit, L. (1995). *Other people's children: Cultural conflict in the classroom.* New York: The New Press.

Department of Public Instruction. (1997). *First-year SAGE report shows promising increases in student learning.* Madison, WI: DPI Information.

DeVries, R., Reese-Learned, H., & Morgan, P. (1991). Sociomoral atmosphere in direct-instruction, eclectic, and constructivist kindergartens: A study of children's enacted personal understanding. *Early Childhood Research Quarterly, 6*(4), 473–518.

Dyson, A.H. (1989). *Multiple worlds of child writers: Friends learning to write.* New York: Teachers College Press.

Elkind, D. (1987). *Mideducation: Preschoolers at risk.* New York: Alfred A. Knopf.

Emmer, E.T., & Aussiker, A. (1990). School and classroom discipline programs: How well do they work? In O.C. Moles (Ed.), *Student discipline strategies.* Albany: State University of New York Press.

Erickson, F. (1993). Transformation and school success: The politics and culture of educational achievement. In E. Jacob & C. Jordan (Eds.), *Minority education: Anthropological perspectives.* Greenwich, CT: Ablex Publishing Corp.

Erickson, F.D., & Mohatt, G. (1982). Cultural organization of participation structures in two classrooms of Indian students. In G.D. Spindler (Ed.), *Doing the ethnography of schooling: Educational anthropology in action.* Austin, TX: Holt, Rinehart & Winston.

Evertson, C.M., & Harris, A.H. (1992). What we know about managing classrooms. *Educational Leadership, 49*(7), 74–78.

Fogarty, R. (Ed.). (1993). *Integrating the curricula: A collection.* Palatine, IL: IRI Skylight.

Gamoran, A. (1987). Organization, instruction, and the effects of ability grouping: Comments on Slavin's "best evidence synthesis." *Review of Educational Research, 57*(3), 341–345.

Gamoran, A. (1992). Is ability grouping equitable? *Educational Leadership, 50*(2), 11–17.

Gersten, R., Darch, C., & Gleason, M. (1988). Effectiveness of a direct instruction academic kindergarten for low-income students. *The Elementary School Journal, 89*(2), 227–240.

Ginsburg, H.P., & Baron, J. (1993). Cognition: Young children's construction of mathematics. In R.J. Jensen (Ed.), *Research ideas for the classroom: Early childhood mathematics* (pp. 3–21). Reston, VA: National Council of Teachers of Mathematics.

Glass, G.V., Cahen, N., Smith, M.L., & Filby, N. (1982). *School class size: Research and policy.* Thousand Oaks, CA: Sage Publications.

Goldenberg, C. (1994). Promoting early literacy development among Spanish-speaking children: Lessons from two studies. In E.H. Hiebert & B.M. Taylor (Eds.), *Getting reading right from the start: Effective early literacy interventions* (pp. 171–200). Needham Heights, MA: Allyn & Bacon.

Grace, C., & Shores, E.F. (1991). *The portfolio and its use: Developmentally appropriate assessment of young children.* Little Rock, AR: Southern Association on Children Under Six.

Graue, M.E. (1993a). Expectations and ideas coming to school. *Early Childhood Research Quarterly, 8*(1), 53–76.

Graue, M.E. (1993b). *Ready for what? Constructing meanings of readiness for kindergarten.* Albany: State University of New York Press.

Graue, M.E., DiPerna, J.C., & Dixson, A. (1998). *Academic redshirting: A backdoor policy in need of review.* A paper presented at the annual meeting of the American Educational Research Association, San Diego.

Graue, M.E., & Walsh, D.J. (1998). *Studying children in context: Theories, methods, and ethics.* Thousand Oaks, CA: Sage Publications.

Gredler, G.R. (1984). Transition classes: A viable alternative for the at-risk child? *Psychology in the Schools, 21*, 463–470.

Grissom, J.B., & Shepard, L.A. (1989). Repeating and dropping out of school. In L.A.S.M.L. Smith (Ed.), *Flunking grades: Research and policies on retention* (pp. 34–63). London: Falmer Press.

Heath, S.B. (1983). *Ways with words: Language, life, and work in communities and classrooms.* Cambridge, UK: Cambridge University Press.

Hiebert, E. (1987). The context of instruction and student learning: An examination of Slavin's assumptions. *Review of Educational Research, 57*(3), 337–340.

Hiebert, J., & Carpenter, T.P. (1992). Learning and teaching with understanding. In D.A. Grouws (Ed.), *Handbook of research on mathematics teaching and learning* (pp. 65–97). Indianapolis, IN: Macmillan Publishing USA.

Hills, T. (1992). Reaching potentials through appropriate assessment. In S.B.T. Rosegrant (Ed.), *Reaching potentials: Appropriate curriculum and assessment for young children* (Vol. 1). Washington, DC: National Association for the Education of Young Children.

Hyson, M.C., & Christiansen, S.L. (1997). Developmentally appropriate guidance and integrated curriculum. In C.H. Hart, D.C. Burts, & R. Charlesworth (Eds.), *Integrated curriculum and developmentally appropriate practice. Birth to age eight.* Albany: State University of New York Press.

Jacobson, L. (1997). "Looping" catches on as a way to build strong ties. *Education Week XVII,* 1, 18–19.

Karweit, N. (1987). *Full day or half day kindergarten: Does it matter?* Baltimore: The Johns Hopkins University, Center for Research on Elementary and Middle Schools.

Karweit, N. (1994). Issues in kindergarten organization and curriculum. In R.E. Slavin, N.L. Karweit, & B.A. Wasik (Eds.), *Preventing early school failure: Research, policy, and practice.* Needham Heights, MA: Allyn & Bacon.

Katz, L. (1985). Dispositions in early childhood education. *ERIC/EECE Bulletin, 18*(2), 1, 3.

Katz, L. (1992). *Nongraded and mixed-age grouping in early childhood programs.* (ERIC Digest EDO-PS-92-9). Urbana-Champaign, IL: ERIC Clearinghouse on Elementary and Early Childhood Education.

Katz, L., & Chard, S. (1989). *Engaging children's minds: The project approach.* Greenwich, CT: Ablex Publishing Corp.

Katz, L.G., Evangelou, D., & Hartman, J.A. (1990). *The case for mixed-age grouping in early education.* Washington, DC: National Association for the Education of Young Children.

Ladson-Billings, G. (1994). *The dreamkeepers.* San Francisco: Jossey-Bass.

Lareau, A. (1989). *Home advantage.* London: Falmer Press.

Lawton, M. (1997). AFT report assails schools' promotion, retention policies. *Education Week*, pp. 8–9.

Leinhardt, G. (1980). Transition rooms: Promoting maturation or reducing education? *Journal of Educational Psychology, 72*, 55–61.

Lou, Y., Abrami, P.C., Spence, J.C., Poulsen, C., Chambers, B., & d'Apollonia, S. (1996). Within-class grouping: A meta analysis. *Review of Educational Research, 66*(4), 423–458.

Lunt, I. (1993). The practice of assessment. In H. Daniels (Ed.), *Charting the agenda: Educational activity after Vygotsky*. New York: Routledge.

Mason, D.A., & Burns, R.B. (1996). "Simply no worse and simply no better" may simply be wrong: A critique of Veenman's conclusion about multigrade classes. *Review of Educational Research, 66*(3), 307–322.

Mason, J.M., & Sinha, S. (1993). Emerging literacy in the early childhood years: Applying a Vygotskian model of learning and development. In B. Spodek (Ed.), *Handbook of research on the education of young children* (pp. 137–150). Indianapolis, IN: Macmillan Publishing USA.

McGee, L.M., & Lormax, R.G. (1990). On combining apples and oranges: A response to Stahl and Miller. *Review of Educational Research, 60* (1), 133–140.

McLaughlin, M.W., & Shepard, L.A. (1995). *Improving education through standards-based reform*. Stanford, CA: National Academy of Education.

Mehan, H. (1982). The structure of classroom events and their consequences for student performance. In P. Gilmore & A.A. Glatthorn (Eds.), *Children in and out of school: Ethnography and education* (Vol. 2, pp. 59–87). New York: Harcourt Brace & Co.

Meisels, S.J. (1987). Uses and abuses of developmental screening and school readiness testing. *Young Children, 42*, 4–6, 68–73.

Meisels, S.J. (1996). Using work sampling in authentic assessments. *Educational Leadership*, 60–65.

Meyer, L. (1985). *A look at instruction in kindergarten: Observations of interactions in three school districts*. (ERIC Document Reproduction Service No. ED 268 489)

Morrison, F.J., Griffith, E.M., & Alberts, D.M. (1997). Nature-nurture in the classroom: Entrance age, school readiness, and learning in children. *Developmental Psychology, 33*(2), 254–262.

Mosteller, F. (1995). The Tennessee study of class size in the early school grades. *Future of Children, 5*(2), 113–127.

Mosteller, F., Light, R.J., & Sachs, J.A. (1996). Sustained inquiry in education: Lessons from skills grouping and class size. *Harvard Educational Review, 66*(4), 797–842.

National Council of Teachers of Mathematics (NCTM). (1989). *Curriculum and evaluation standards for school mathematics*. Reston, VA: Author.

Ogbu, J. (1978). *Minority education and caste: The American system in cross-cultural perspective*. San Diego, CA: Academic Press.

Puleo, V. (1988). A review and critique of research on full-day kindergarten. *The Elementary School Journal, 88*(4), 427–439.

Rawl, R., & O'Tuel, F. (1982). A comparison of three prereading approaches for kindergarten students. *Reading Improvement, 19*, 205–211.

Sameroff, A., & McDonough, S. (1994). Educational implications of developmental transitions: Revisiting the 5- to 7-year shift. *Phi Delta Kappan, 76*(3), 188–193.

Schickedanz, J.A. (1990). The jury is still out on the effects of whole language and language experience approaches for beginning reading: A critique of Stahl and Miller's study. *Review of Educational Research, 60*(1), 127–131.

Seely, A.E. (1995). *Integrated thematic units*. Westminster, CA: Teacher Created Materials.

Sheehan, R., Cryan, J.R., Weichel, J., & Bandy, I.G. (1991). Factors contributing to success in elementary school: Research findings for early childhood educators. *Journal of Research in Childhood Education, 6*(1), 66–75.

Shepard, L.A. (1989). A review of research on kindergarten retention. In L.A.S.M.L. Smith (Ed.), *Flunking grades: Research and policies on retention* (pp. 64–78). London: Falmer Press.

Shepard, L.A. (1990). Readiness testing in local school districts: An analysis of backdoor policies. *Politics of Education Association Yearbook*, 159–179.

Shepard, L.A. (1994). The challenges of assessing young children appropriately. *Phi Delta Kappan, 76*(3), 206–213.

Shepard, L.A., & Graue, M.E. (1993). The morass of school readiness screening: Research on test use and test validity. In B. Spodek (Ed.), *The handbook of research on the education of young children*. Indianapolis, IN: Macmillan Publishing USA.

Shepard, L.A., & Smith, M.L. (1986). Synthesis of research on school readiness and kindergarten retention. *Educational Leadership, 44,* 78–86.

Shepard, L.A., & Smith, M.L. (1989). Academic and emotional effects of kindergarten retention in one school district. In L.A.S.M.L. Smith (Ed.), *Flunking grades: Research and policies on retention* (pp. 79–107). London: Falmer Press.

Slavin, R.E. (1987). Ability grouping and student achievement in elementary schools: A best-evidence synthesis. *Review of Educational Research, 57,* 293–336.

Stahl, S.A. (1990). Riding the pendulum: A rejoinder to Schickedanz and McGee and Lormax. *Review of Educational Research, 60*(1), 141–151.

Stahl, S.A., & Miller, P.D. (1990). Whole language and language experience approaches for beginning reading: A quantitative research synthesis. *Review of Educational Research, 59* (1), 87–116.

Stallman, A.C., & Pearson, P.D. (1990). Formal measures of early literacy. In L.M. Morrow & J.K. Smith (Eds.), *Assessment for instruction in early literacy* (pp. 7–44). Upper Saddle River, NJ: Prentice-Hall.

Stipek, D., Feiler, R., Daniels, D., & Milburn, S. (1995). Effects of different instructional approaches on young children's achievement and motivation. *Child Development, 66,* 209–223.

Veenman, S. (1995). Cognitive and noncognitive effects of multigrade and multi-age classes: A best evidence synthesis. *Review of Educational Research, 65*(4), 319–381.

Veenman, S. (1996). Effects of multigrade and multi-age classes reconsidered. *Review of Educational Research, 66*(3), 323–340.

Walsh, D.J. (1989). Changes in kindergarten. Why here? Why now? *Early Childhood Research Quarterly, 4,* 377–391.

Wilcox, K. (1982). Differential socialization in the classroom: Implications for equal opportunity. In G. Spindler (Ed.), *Doing the ethnography of schooling.* (pp. 268–308). Prospect Heights, IL: Waveland Press.

Wilkinson, L.C. (1988–89). Grouping children for learning: Implications for kindergarten education. In E.Z. Rothkopf (Ed.), *Review of research in education* (Vol. 15, pp. 203–223). Washington, DC: American Educational Research Association.

Wolf, D.P., Bixby, J., Glenn, J., & Gardner, H. (1991). To use their minds well: Investigating new forms of student assessment. *Review of Research in Education, 17,* 31–74.

Zill, N., Loomis, L.S., & West, J. (1997). *The elementary school performance and adjustment of children who enter kindergarten late or repeat kindergarten: Findings from national surveys.* (NCES 98-097). Washington, DC: U.S. Department of Education, National Center for Education Statistics.

Chapter 6

Families and Schools

Rights, Responsibilities, Resources, and Relationships

Sandra L. Christenson

Students spend 91% of their time from birth to age 18 outside school (Usdan, 1991, cited in Ooms & Hara, 1991). Once they start school, they spend 70% of their waking hours outside it (Clark, 1990). The impact of out-of-school time—exposure to messages about learning, use of time, and congruence with the school environment—must be acknowledged in discussions about students' school performance and productivity.

Therefore, the importance of partnerships among family, school, and community for encouraging children and youth to be lifelong learners cannot be ignored. Two National Education Goals—Goals 1 and 8—explicitly link families and schools. These goals, which intersect at the point of children's transition to school, propose that by the year 2000 every child will start school ready to learn and every school will promote partnerships that increase parent participation in facilitating the social, emotional, and academic growth of children (National Education Goals Panel, 1998). Implicit in these goals is the recognition that both families and schools are needed to promote development and educational outcomes for children. Philosophically, individuals tend to agree that families and school personnel are essential strands in the safety net for children's optimal development and educational performance, and with the absence of either strand, the net is substantially weakened. As noted by Kellaghan, Sloane, Alvarez, and Bloom, educators agree with the goal of working with parents as partners; however, in practice, they often find themselves "trapped in blaming families or viewing the home as auxiliary, merely providing supplemental support for the work of the school" (1993, p. 135).

The empirical base for family involvement in education is strong (Christenson, Rounds, & Gorney, 1992). Sloane succinctly described the conclusion of family–school researchers about the effect of the home's influence on children's educational performance when she stated, "It is now well accepted that the home plays an important role in children's learning and achievement. Some children learn values, attitudes, skills, and behaviors in the home that prepare them well for the tasks of school" (1991, p. 155). Almost a decade earlier, Hess and Holloway (1984) conducted a comprehensive literature review of the family's effect on cognitive, social, and motivational aspects of student behavior and their relationship to classroom performance. They concluded that consensus between home and school about the goals of education is essential to counter information from competing sources, such as television and peers, and that discontinuities between families and schools compromise the effectiveness of either parents or educators as socializing agents. Entwisle and Alexander (Chapter 2) demonstrate the success of schools in fostering the academic growth of young children of all socioeconomic levels and find that differences in children's achievement are the result of the psychological resources provided by the family during the summer months. Zill and Nord (1994) reinforced the importance of the home–school safety net for adolescents, who report that parents should be more involved with their children's schooling. Finally, the influence of adolescents' perspectives about family and school on their school performance has been investigated by Phelan, Yu, and Davidson (1994). They found that all students, even those who describe their home, peer, and school contexts as congruent with respect to academic expectations, report psychosocial pressure and stress. However, students whose peer, school, and family worlds are different experienced greater adversity in navigating across borders of diverse expectations. Students in this group reported a low probability of graduating from high school and perceived their personal futures as bleak.

Although the centrality of the home environment on children's school learning has long been recognized, there has been a renewed interest in the development of programs to increase family involvement in education. Reasons for this surge of development include the cumulative impact of research findings that underlie the importance of the home in contributing to children's school progress; reform efforts focused on school and teacher practices, such as new curricula and strategies, have not been as successful in improving achievement as had been hoped; and dramatic changes in the structure and function of families have given rise to concern about families' abilities to provide the conditions that foster children's school interest and learning (Kellaghan et al., 1993). Although family involvement in education is an empirically supported practice and different models and strategies have been developed, there continues to be more rhetoric than reality about family–school connections (Christenson, 1995; Epstein, 1995). Perhaps part of the reason for the "rhetoric rut" is that family–school relationships are complex and multifaceted.

This chapter reviews the literature on family involvement in education for school-age children with the intent of identifying critical issues for families and schools, particularly in the context of children's transition to school. This transition provides a unique opportunity to develop positive family–school relationships to enhance children's learning and development. In this chapter, the following issues and topics are discussed: transition to school; alternate conceptualizations of family–school connections; the current knowledge base, including six conclusions from research conducted since the late 1970s; the family–school interface in special education; and models for family–school collaboration. Empirical support for the home and school contextual influences that enhance learning from the Live and Learn Project is described. A major contention of this chapter is that the *relationship* between families and schools—not the *roles*—is critical for children's learning. The chapter concludes with identification of specific issues to be addressed to advance understanding of the effect of family–school linkages on children's learning and development.

TRANSITION TO SCHOOL ISSUES

Parents are always implicated in education, either as silent, passive partners or as vocal, active partners. Homes can provide support for or distraction from children's learning. As children make the transition to school, it is important to recognize differences between the sending system (preschool) and the receiving system (kindergarten)—differences that may influence family–school relationships.

Since the professionalization of teaching, home and school are two microsystems that have been used to operating autonomously, and this autonomy contributes a sense of social distance between parents and teachers. In contrast to preschool programs that foster parent–teacher relationships through ongoing, informal contact and interaction, kindergarten is the beginning of increased formal interaction, almost bureaucratic in nature, between families and school personnel. Limited opportunity for dialogue and frequency of ritualized contacts between families and schools may partly explain the decrease in parent involvement across grade levels. School norms and structures do not naturally support building relationships between families and educators. Although it is true that schools have the formal responsibility for educating children, the voiced but too often forgotten factor in terms of school practices is that the informal education that takes place in the family is a powerful prerequisite for success in formal education (Bronfenbrenner, 1991).

Although home–school relationships, as rated by teachers and parents from diverse backgrounds, reveal greater satisfaction than dissatisfaction, results also reveal that the relationship is less than optimal. Data from more than 2,000 parents and 1,000 teachers on the 1987 Metropolitan Life Survey of the American Teacher showed that 77% of parents and teachers rated the relationship as good or excellent and less than 8% rated the relationship as poor. However, only 60% felt mutual support (Olson, 1990). In a national interview of 217 parents, Christenson, Hurley, Sheridan, and Fenstermacher (1997) found that most parents described their contacts with school personnel as cooperative (93%) rather than conflictual (7%). Some parents described their contacts as mistrusting (11%), stressful (16%), or uncomfortable (16%). Mutual reluctance between parents and teachers was also noted. Olson (1990) reported that 19% of parents felt awkward or were reluctant to talk to school officials, whereas 55% of teachers felt uneasy or were reluctant to approach parents to discuss their child. Hurley (1996) found that non-Caucasian parents reported feeling less welcome at their children's school than Caucasian parents and, regardless of ethnicity, parents who reported getting involved with their children's schooling felt more welcome than parents who waited to be asked to be involved. Her findings are consistent with Delgado-Gaitan's (1991) contention that the difference between parents who participate and those who do not is that those who do have recognized that they play a critical role in their children's education.

Collectively, these data suggest that a cause of concern for enhancing children's learning is the nature of the family–school relationship. Mutual reluctance is exacerbated by the fact that few schools have meaningful contact with parents before children enter kindergarten, a pattern that exists at other transition points for children and youth in grades 3 through 12. In a national survey, Early and Pianta (1998) found that one of the least used practices related to the transition to kindergarten involved contact between the family and the school. Family–school contact occurred for less than 15% of teachers surveyed. It appears that even for the youngest students, educators may not think of the importance of building a relationship with families as a means to enhance learner outcomes. According to Pianta, Rimm-Kaufman, and Cox (Chapter 1), the development of supportive family–school relationships should not be considered a correlate or antecedent but rather an outcome of school transition. Therefore, a child's competence in kindergarten "may not be the only, or the best outcome measure of a successful transition" to schooling; the quality of the parent's relationship with the teacher and school personnel may be "an equally valid indicator of transition outcome, and one that may forecast later school success" (Early & Pianta, 1998, p. 36). This chapter concurs with this statement and suggests greater consideration must be given to the effect of family–school relationships, because parents may be more useful in the educational process than in the educational outcome.

Changes in society (e.g., urbanization, migration, labor force, growth in technology) and in families (e.g., structure, working parents, cultural background) have numerous and important implications for children's education, in general, and for the educational role of the family, in particular. According to Hodgkinson (1991), approximately one third of U.S. preschool children are at risk of school failure even before they enter kindergarten because of poverty, neglect, sickness, and lack of adult nurturance and protection. There is a recognition that it is difficult for many families to cope with the educational needs of their children and that the combination of problematic circumstances often works to undermine children's formal education and development (Kellaghan et al., 1993). Although our understanding of the family–school interface in relation to children's learning is still limited, there is increased speculation that issues of psychological capital provided by the family (see Chapter 2), cultural capital (Phelan et al., 1994), and social capital (Coleman, 1987) must be addressed.

This chapter makes two assumptions: 1) both parents and teachers are agents of socialization and, therefore, have important roles related to the school performance of children and youth; and 2) how students spend their time in and out of school influences their opportunity to learn. Coleman (1987) contended that home and school provide different inputs for the socialization process of children. One class of inputs—opportunities, demands, and rewards—comes from schools, whereas the second class of inputs—attitudes, effort, and conception of self—comes from the social environment of the household. Educational outcomes result from the interaction of the qualities that the child brings from home with qualities of the school. Schools do make a difference for children; however, they do not have an equal effect on all children. According to Coleman,

Schools, of whatever quality, are more effective for children from strong family backgrounds than for children from weak ones. The resources devoted by the family to the child's education interact with resources provided by the school—and there is greater variation in the former resources than the latter. (1987, p. 35)

Schools can reward and demand and provide opportunities for children to learn; however, Coleman (1987) viewed families as providing the building blocks that make learning possible. Families provide the social capital needed by schools to enhance learner outcomes.

Social capital refers to the amount of adult–child interaction about academic and personal matters as well as the social and community support system for families. Coleman (1987) argued that as social capital in homes shrinks, due to single-parent and dual-income families and a sense of alienation in community, school achievement will not be maintained or increased if educators simply replace these resources with more school-like resources—those that produce opportunities, demands, and rewards. Rather, academic and developmental outcomes for children are maintained or increased by enhancing resources that provide attitudes, effort, and conception of self—those qualities from the home that interact with those provided by the school.

APPROACHES TO FAMILY–SCHOOL CONNECTIONS

Educators in grades K through 12 have always valued parent involvement in education (Berger, 1991), which is also referred to as family involvement (Davies, 1991). The changing demographics of American families have given rise, in part, to two approaches to family involvement. Referred to as traditional and partnership approaches, both are viable means, however qualitatively different, for involving families in education. Depending on the characteristics and needs of students, parents, and teachers, either approach may be effective. Differences in the approaches are worthy of examination because successful family–school relationships demand site-specific development (National Association of State Boards of Education, 1992).

Traditional Approach

The traditional approach to family involvement is by far the most commonly used approach. Parents' and educators' perspectives offer insight into both the characteristics and drawbacks of this approach for many American families. Consider these commonly heard comments from parents: teachers send home bad news, schools don't make parents feel welcome, educators don't do what they say they will, parent–teacher conferences are routine and unproductive, teachers teach too much by rote, and teachers care more about discipline than teaching. Also consider these comments from educators: parents don't seem interested in school, parents promise but don't follow through, parents don't show up, parents only pretend to understand, parents do children's work for them, parents worry too much about how other kids are doing, and I never see the parents I really need to see (Henderson, Marburger, & Ooms, 1988).

In a traditional approach, much emphasis is placed on involving parents in ways that address the school's agenda. Schools designate prescribed roles for parents, which are often traditional roles such as volunteering, fundraising, or homework helper. These roles are described in the context that parent help is needed to accomplish a task for the school; therefore, parents are seen as desirable in *specific* situations. Another defining feature of the traditional approach relates to the underlying assumption that families and educators have separate roles and responsibilities in educating and socializing children and youth. There tends to be ritualized contact at prescribed times (e.g., back-to-school nights, 20-minute parent–teacher conferences) or limited contact; sometimes contact is precipitated by a child concern or crisis. In addition, one-way communication is the norm; the direction of communication is mostly from schools to homes, often in the form of school-determined recommendations for parents. Finally, it is helpful to examine who is involved when a traditional approach is used. Generally, parents of primary-grade children or those for whom there is a match between the approach of the school and the family (e.g., culture, attitude, style, philosophy) tend to be most involved. Educators measure success of their family involvement efforts in terms of the number of parents, or which parents, attend school functions and participate at school.

A conservative estimate would suggest that 90% of family involvement in America's schools is characterized by the traditional approach, which has been most successful for children of middle-class families where there is continuity between the needs, beliefs, and knowledge about education of schools and families. However, it has been critiqued mostly in terms of maintaining social and physical distance between the essential socializing agents. Rich has appropriately reminded us that "families and teachers might wish that the school could do the job alone. But today's school needs families and today's families need the school. In many ways, this mutual need may be the greatest hope for change" (1987, p. 62). Given that families are facing many challenges—making ends meet in a changing economy, combating negative peer influences, and maintaining control as children grow older (Zill & Nord, 1994)—while children are experiencing a reduction in social, cultural, and/or psychological capital, the traditional approach is less relevant for today's society.

Partnership Approach

The goal of a partnership approach irrespective of the specific model is to improve educational experiences and outcomes for all children. Because this approach is characterized by a belief in shared responsibility for educating and socializing children and youth, families and educators recognize the need to share information and resources. Although both families and educators have legitimate roles and responsibilities, the emphasis is not on the roles families can play for schools. Rather, the emphasis is on relationships; specifically, how families and educators work together to promote the academic and social development of children. The partnership approach underscores that the attitude between partners is integral to the success of the relationship. Many options for families to contribute to children's education exist, and the contributions of families are valued even when they are not perceived as meeting a present need at school. In this approach, families and educators interact differently. They model collaboration by listening to each other's perspective and viewing differences as strengths; sharing information to co-construct the "bigger picture" about children's performance; respecting the skills and knowledge of each other; and planning and making decisions cooperatively that address the needs of parents, teachers, and students. A partnership approach focuses the goal of family involvement on enhanced success for students, develops a relationship based on shared decision making and mutual contributions, and strives to provide students with a consistent message about their schoolwork and behavior.

Family–school collaboration, therefore, is an attitude, not merely an activity. The goal of family–school collaboration is to change the interface between home and school to support students as learners, not merely to arrive at a solution for the immediate school-based concern (Weiss & Edwards, 1992). Finally, shared responsibility is understood to mean that the product of education—learning—is not produced by schools but by students with the help of parents, educators, peers, and community professionals who support learners (Seeley, 1985). Thus, in a partnership approach, students learn because of what students do, but students "do" because of a supportive safety net. According to Swap (1993), four elements of a true partnership are creating two-way communication, enhancing learning at home and at school, providing mutual support, and making joint decisions for the benefit of students' development.

The view that parents are essential for children's school progress is certainly an implicit assumption of the partnership orientation to family involvement; a missing piece is the explicit acknowledgment, particularly in school attitudes, policies, and practices, that parents are essential partners. In the contextual systems model for the socialization of youth, Pianta and Walsh (1997) described a necessary belief system for educators, one in which it is understood that children develop and learn in the context of the family and that that system must interface in a positive way with the school system and schooling issues for a child's educational performance to be optimal. Not all educators recognize families and schools as contexts for children's development or believe interventions should encompass the child/family system. This chapter contends that this is the difference between looking at families as partners and looking at families as extras.

The view that families and schools are essential contexts for children's learning and development raises issues about the "3 Rs"—not "readin, ritin, and rithmetic," but rights, responsibilities, and resources. In essence, how can sustaining relationships between families and schools be constructed while addressing these critical issues?

CURRENT KNOWLEDGE BASE

Conclusions of Family Involvement Studies

Several recurring findings are evident in even a cursory review of the research conducted since the late 1970s regarding family involvement in education. First, the conceptualization of parent involvement has broadened. Parent involvement refers to participation in a child's learning at school and at home. In fact, because of work demands and situational family barriers (e.g., transportation, child care), more parents are available to participate at home. This is a broader definition of parent involvement than recognized by some educators, who tend to use a traditional definition that includes fundraising and attendance at school functions. New definitions, particularly in urban settings, replace "parent" with "family," because the most significant adults in the lives of many children may be siblings, relatives, or even neighbors who provide child care (Davies, 1991). Options for involvement have moved beyond the "big three" (i.e., fundraising, volunteer, homework helper) to include roles for parents as teachers, decision makers, advocates, and supporters (Henderson & Berla, 1994).

In addition, school performance indicators are considered broader than achievement and include classroom and school participation, attendance, graduating from high school, and less discipline referrals and suspensions. Although the majority of research has been conducted with lower-income families or in reference to students at risk for educational failure, the goal of family–school partnerships is to enhance the school success of all students. In fact, the possibility exists that achievement for average students would be elevated significantly if collaboration between families and schools were the norm. This, of course, is one of the goals of the federal program, Partnership for Family Involvement in Education, wherein families and schools have a 13-year contract.

Finally, the burgeoning interest in family involvement in education is evident from many directions and sources. For example, 40% of parents believe that they are not devoting enough time to their children's education; teachers ranked strengthening parents' roles in their children's learning as the issue that should receive the highest priority in public education policy in the 1990s; 72% of students ages 10–13 and 48% of students ages 14–17 said they would like to talk to their parents about schoolwork; and 89% of business executives identified lack of parent involvement as the biggest obstacle to school reform (U.S. Department of Education, 1994). In a survey conducted by Connors and Epstein (1994), 82% of high school students agreed that parent involvement was needed at the high school level: 80% of parents indicated that they wanted to be more involved; more than 50% of students indicated that they wanted their parents involved. Only 32% of the teachers, however, thought that it was their responsibility to involve parents.

Second, variables that affect the involvement of parents in education point to attitudes, practices, and knowledge of families and school personnel. School and teacher practices have been found to be the most important predictor of parent involvement and participation in their child's schooling (Epstein, 1991; Smith, Connell, Wright, Sizer, & Norman, 1997). School practices were a stronger predictor of parent involvement than were parents' educational level, income status, or ethnic background. Also, parents are involved to a greater and more consistent degree when they view their participation as directly linked to the achievement of their children, which Comer (1995) referred to as *meaningful parent involvement*. Parent attitudes toward education are a salient factor in parent involvement, suggesting programs that provide parents with information about the association between their involvement and achievement may be helpful (Smith et al., 1997). However, the extent to which information alone modifies attitudes and behavior has yet to be demonstrated. A high sense of self-efficacy among teachers (Hoover-Dempsey, Bassler, & Brissie, 1987), a positive school climate and schoolwide effort to work with families (Dauber & Epstein, 1993), and the degree to which family members feel influential and view their roles as that of teachers (Grolnick, Benjet, Kurowski, & Apostoleris, 1997) are positive correlates of parent involvement.

Regardless of educational level, ethnic background, or income level, parents want their children to be successful in school; however, they do not know how to assist their children. Parents consistently report that they would be willing to spend more time on activities with children if educators gave them more guidance (Epstein, 1986). Parents want information on how schools function, child/adolescent development, ways to support student learning at home, ways to improve behavior and social skills of children, and opportunities to consult with school psychologists about personal concerns for their children (Christenson et al., 1997).

Most parents also rated the item, *time for parents and teachers to share information about children, school requirements, and family needs,* as an activity they value and would use. Joyce Epstein speculated that only a "relatively small percentage of parents, approximately 10%, have personal problems so severe that they cannot work as partners with schools, given the proper assistance." She contended that "parent educational level and family social class are influential factors for which families become involved in education only if school personnel do not work to involve all parents" (1996, personal communication).

Barriers for developing home–school partnership programs are well articulated (Liontos, 1992). The barriers receiving the greatest attention include the following:

- Lack of teacher and administrator training for working with parents as partners
- Parent and educator lack of skills and knowledge about effective interpersonal interaction
- Lack of opportunity for family–school interaction
- Psychological and cultural barriers that serve to divide parents and school personnel
- No routine communication system
- Failure to examine school practices that "fail" families (e.g., responding only in a crisis, viewing families as deficient, defining families based solely on structure)
- A narrow conceptualization of the roles that parents can play in schooling (Epstein, 1989; Moles, 1993; Weiss & Edwards, 1992)

In their interview study examining home–school partnership barriers with 29 core subject teachers and 60 parents from two low-income junior high schools, Leitch and Tangri concluded, "It isn't misperceptions of each other that are the root of home–school problems; it is the lack of specific planning, or, at a more basic level, the lack of knowledge about how each can use the other person more effectively that is a major barrier" (1988, p. 70).

Lack of clarity for roles and responsibilities often emerges as a barrier for parents and schools, regardless of demographic characteristics. However, educators' use of students' background characteristics (e.g., parent educational level, family social class) as an explanation of students' school performance has influenced which families become involved in education (Epstein, 1991). There is no question that social background is moderately correlated with school achievement (e.g., White, 1982). However, the effect of family process is cogently stated by Clark: "Of the many studies that have shown a statistical correlation between background, life chances, and life achievements, few seem to explain adequately the fact that many youngsters with disadvantaged backgrounds perform very well in school and in later life" (1990, p. 18). Background or contextual factors may be useful in identifying target students, that is, students who are most likely to be at risk for not succeeding in school. Under no conditions, however, should it be inferred that background characteristics are the reason why students do not succeed. It is noteworthy that alternative ways of conceptualizing the demographic characteristics of family contexts have begun to appear in the literature. For example, Conger et al. (1992) suggested that a measure of economic hardship in homes should replace socioeconomic status (SES) in research. Similarly, it may be more important to understand the number of adults available to support children's learning, what Coleman (1987) referred to as "social capital," than to conduct data analyses with the more commonly used variable, family structure.

Third, parent involvement in schooling is positively associated with many desirable benefits for students and key stakeholders. When parents are involved, students show improvement in the following:

- Grades (Fehrmann, Keith, & Reimers, 1987)
- Test scores, including reading achievement (Clark, 1988; Epstein, 1991; Stevenson & Baker, 1987) and math achievement (Epstein, 1986)
- Attitude toward schoolwork (Kellaghan et al., 1993)
- Behavior (Comer & Haynes, 1991; Steinberg, Mounts, Lamborn, & Dornbusch, 1991)
- Self-esteem (Collins, Moles, & Cross, 1982; Sattes, 1985)
- Completion of homework (Clark, 1993; Epstein & Becker, 1982)
- Academic perseverance (Estrada, Arsenio, Hess, & Holloway, 1987)
- Participation in classroom learning activities (Collins et al., 1982; Sattes, 1985)
- Fewer placements in special education (Lazar & Darlington, 1978)
- Greater enrollment in postsecondary education (Baker & Stevenson, 1986; Eagle, 1989; Marjoribanks, 1988)
- Higher attendance rates (Collins et al., 1982)
- Lower dropout rates (Rumberger, 1995)
- Fewer suspensions (Comer & Haynes, 1991)
- Realization of exceptional talents (Bloom, 1985)

Benefits of parent participation in education are evident for key stakeholders, suggesting that they help create conditions that facilitate home–school connections. For example, benefits for teachers include recognition by parents for better interpersonal and teaching skills, higher ratings of teaching performance by principals, and greater satisfaction with their jobs, requesting fewer transfers (Christenson, 1995). Parent benefits include an increased sense of influence (Davies, 1993; Kagan & Schraft, 1982), increased understanding of the school program (Epstein, 1986), greater appreciation for the role they play in their children's education (Davies, 1993), and improved communication with their children about schoolwork (Becher, 1984).

Benefits for students, parents, and teachers vary as a function of the specific family involvement activity. Epstein (1995) demonstrated that expected results for key stakeholders are different for different activities and that student achievement is not influenced by all types of family involvement. For example, parenting activities have been shown to be associated with improved attendance for students, greater awareness of the inherent challenges of parenting, and more respect for families' strengths and the efforts of teachers. Home learning activities have resulted in greater homework completion or gains in skills for students, increased knowledge of how to support and help students at home for parents, and better design of homework assignments and respect of family time for teachers. Finally, decision-making activities have resulted in awareness of family influence on school decisions for students, feeling of school ownership for parents, and awareness of parent perspectives as a factor in policy development and decisions for teachers. The differential effects of varied forms of family involvement reinforce the centrality of asking, family involvement for what purpose?

Studies that correlate levels of parent involvement with gains in student achievement invariably find that the more extensive the involvement, the higher the student achievement. In programs that are designed to be full partnerships, achievement for students from low-income families not only improves but also reaches levels that are standard for children from middle-income families (Comer, 1995; Comer & Haynes, 1991). Children who are the farthest behind make the greatest gains (Henderson & Berla, 1994). Programs and practices were stronger in schools where teachers perceived that they, their colleagues, and parents all felt strongly about the importance of parent involvement (Dauber & Epstein, 1993).

Fourth, home environmental influences are positive correlates of students' academic achievement and school performance. Family process variables (what parents do to support learning) predict scholastic ability better than family status variables (who families are). Social class or family configuration predicts up to 25% of variance in achievement, whereas family support for learning or interaction style predicts up to 60% of variance in achievement (Walberg, 1984). There is a moderate-to-strong correlation between income level and student achievement when data are aggregated; however, this correlation is substantially reduced when family processes are also considered. White (1982) analyzed 101 studies and concluded that these aspects of the home environment had a greater impact than SES on students' school performance: parents' attitudes, guidance, and expectations for their children's education; quality of verbal interaction; participation in cultural and learning-related activities; and overall stability in the home. Also, the considerable variation in family environments within social class has led to the conclusion that what parents do vis-à-vis their children's education is more important than who they are. Milne stated, "Family structures are not inherently good or evil per se; what is important is the ability of the parent to provide pro-educational resources for children—be they financial, material, or experiential" (1989, p. 58).

The specific activities that families perform to facilitate their children's educational success, referred to as "the curriculum of the home" by Walberg (1984), include informed parent–child conversations about everyday events, encouragement and discussion of leisure reading, monitoring and joint analysis of television viewing, expression of affection, interest in children's academic and personal growth, and delay of immediate gratification to accomplish long-term goals. In his intensive observational study of the home environment of 10 high-achieving and 10 low-achieving secondary-level students, all of whom were from low-income, African American families, Clark (1983) identified the home variables that differentiated high and low achievers. Family life of high-achieving, low-income students was characterized by frequent dialogues between parents and children,

strong parental encouragement of academic pursuits, warm and nurturing interactions, clear and consistent limits, and consistent monitoring of how time was
spent. Parents of high achievers felt personally responsible for helping their children to gain knowledge and basic literacy skills, communicated regularly with
school personnel, and were involved in school functions and activities. Both parents' attitudes (i.e., I expect you to do well in school) and behavior (i.e., I will communicate and support your learning) toward schooling for their children were
evident. Across several studies of families with varying income and ethnic backgrounds, the presence of three factors in the homes was strongly associated with
student achievement: strong, consistent values about the importance of education;
willingness to help children and intervene at schools; and ability to become involved (Mitrsomwang & Hawley, 1993).

Other findings are also noteworthy. For example, three factors over which
parents exercise authority—attendance, variety of reading materials in the home,
and amount of television watching—explained almost 90% of the difference in
mean achievement of students in 37 states and the District of Columbia on the National Assessment of Educational Progress (Barton & Coley, 1992). Although the
definitive family process variables for student achievement gains are unknown,
Peng and Lee (1992) identified parental educational expectations, talking with students about school, providing learning materials, and providing learning opportunities outside school as family process variables that showed the strongest relationship with student achievement. Although the database is replete with
correlational studies, to attribute a causal link between family environments and
educational performance would be inappropriate.

Finally, the use of out-of-school time—or how and with whom students spend
time—helps to explain school performance differences. In addition, supportive
guidance from adults, not just families, is a determining factor. High-achieving
students from all backgrounds spend approximately 25–35 hours per week in constructive learning activities outside school according to Clark, who stated,

> The attitudes and relationships between youngsters and their parents, relatives,
> teachers, ministers, coaches, instructors, and tutors can be among the most im-
> portant factors in creating an environment that will maximize the chances for suc-
> cess during their school years and throughout their lives. (1990, p. 23)

In addition, the degree of match between home and school contexts is a contributing factor for students' school success. Hansen (1986) demonstrated achievement gains from third to fifth grades for those students who experienced congruence in rules and interaction styles across home and school environments. He also
found that the greater the discontinuity between home and school, the more students' academic grades declined. As a result, he concluded that there was no preferred classroom (e.g., open, traditional) or home (e.g., permissive, restrictive)
type; rather the match in the message received by students between home and
school contexts was the critical factor for children's academic success.

Gains in student performance are greater when home and school interventions in contrast to classroom- or parent-only interventions are used. There is evidence that performance for preschoolers is best when family interventions, in
addition to child interventions, are implemented (Ramey & Campbell, 1984). Sim-

ilarly, Heller and Fantuzzo (1993) demonstrated that fourth- and fifth-grade African American students who receive reciprocal peer tutoring (RPT) and parent involvement (PI) evidenced greater math gains than similar students who received only RPT. Based on teacher ratings, students in the RPT and PI groups demonstrated better work habits, higher levels of motivation, more task orientation, less disruptive behavior, and were more interpersonally confident. Mesosystemic interventions using conjoint behavioral consultation have shown promise in improving students' performance in academic and social areas (Sheridan, Kratochwill, & Bergan, 1996). With respect to mesosystemic interventions, Bronfenbrenner (1974, cited in Henderson & Berla, 1994) noted, "To use a chemical analogy, parent intervention functions as a kind of fixative, which stabilizes effects produced by other processes" (p. 34).

The elements of a collaborative partnership are not unrecognized by educators. These key elements of collaboration were identified by special education teachers of and parents of children with emotional problems: mutual respect for skills and knowledge, honest and clear communication, open and two-way sharing of information, mutually agreed-on goals, and shared planning and decision making (Vosler-Hunter, 1989). Similarly, Dunst, Johanson, Rounds, Trivette, and Hamby (1992) identified trust, open communication, mutual respect, active listening, and honesty as essential characteristics of the parent–professional relationship. Although it is relatively easy to list the elements of collaboration (i.e., speak the language), in practice it is more difficult to implement a collaborative relationship (i.e., walk the talk). In part, this is due to time constraints. The availability of time for dialogue and interaction, particularly where there is physical and social distance between families and schools, is an issue.

A study (Adams & Christenson, 1998) of trust between parents and general and special education teachers suggested that the elements of collaboration may be difficult, if not impossible, to implement, particularly if the partners are unknown to each other and especially when a child is demonstrating any deviance from the norm for expected school behavior. The trust data raised many questions about whether it is reasonable to expect family–school collaboration without adequate trust-building opportunities. It was found that parents whose children were in middle school in an urban education environment trust teachers more than teachers trust parents. Parent trust for teachers did not differ as a function of social strata, educational level, or ethnicity, and high-trust parents were more involved in education than moderate- or low-trust parents. It was also found that parents of students receiving more intensive special education services displayed significantly higher levels of trust than parents of students receiving less intensive services, suggesting that increased interaction may foster trust between partners and increase confident expectations for a positive outcome. Trust can be viewed as a prerequisite for collaboration and involvement or as an outcome of involvement. The study data support Don Davies' (1990, personal communication) belief that trust is "essential lubrication for more serious intervention." Because many of the critical elements of collaboration, such as communication and mutual goal setting, are firmly rooted in trust and basic to their success, it is important to view trust as a prerequisite for collaboration.

Finally, effective communication between families and schools is considered to be the foundation of all family involvement programs. Although there has been little empirical investigation of communication strategies, there appears to be consensus in the literature that good communication is needed to share information about children's progress, needs, and interests; establish shared goals for children's education; inform parents of school expectations in terms of student behavior and achievement; inform teachers of parent expectations relative to curriculum and discipline; inform parents of classroom activities and events; avoid misunderstandings; and help parents to reinforce school instruction at home (Cale, 1993). Both frequency and content of the messages are important. According to McAfee (1993), home–school partnerships are dependent on communication of the message "that mutual respect and interdependence of home, school, and community are essential to children's development" (p. 21). Emphasis is placed on establishing and maintaining two-way communication between home and school and using a positive orientation rather than a deficit-based or crisis orientation. Principles underlying successful partnership programs include the following:

- A no-fault model where blame is not attributed to the family or school because there is not a single cause for the presenting concern

- A nondeficit approach where assets and strengths of individuals are emphasized

- The importance of empowerment where families are actively involved in decision making and choices for their personal lives

- An ecological approach where there is recognition that the school context influences the family and the family context influences the school (Cochran, 1987; Comer, Haynes, Joyner, & Ben-Avie, 1996; Ooms & Hara, 1991)

Also, school personnel actively initiate outreach to families. Families tend to wait for schools to take the lead in developing the partnership and to articulate roles for parents. Successful school "reaching out" efforts are characterized by the following new beliefs about families: All families have strengths, parents can learn ways to help their children if provided with the opportunity and necessary support, and parents have important information and perspectives about children (Liontos, 1992). Lindle (1989) showed that parents want a person-to-person relationship not a "professional–client" relationship with schools. Parents overwhelmingly reported their desire for opportunities to speak with educators about their child's education, to share perceptions about their child with educators, and to receive timely information about their child's school performance on an informal basis. The personal touch from the teacher was reported as the most important factor in encouraging their involvement and support with schools. Lindle's (1989) findings are consistent with parents who have children with special learning needs. For example, Peterson and Cooper (1989) found that parents of children with developmental disabilities overwhelmingly desired information, training, time off, informal contact, and a support network from the parent–professional relationship.

Parental desire is one thing; achieving equality when there is little to no provision for parents to be enfranchised as equal partners in the educational process is quite different. In most schools, professional educators are responsible for fiscal, personal, curricular, and disciplinary activities of schools. For example, studies about roles for families tend to find the greatest disagreement between parents and teachers or administrators to be in the area of shared decision making, especially related to curricular decisions (Chavkin & Williams, 1993).

Families and Special Education

Wolery (Chapter 9) indicates that, despite specific procedures and mandates for involvement, parents of children with disabilities in early elementary school years are not active participants in the individualized education program (IEP) process and generally do not perceive being in a positive partnership with schools. Wolery reports that family-centered services are seldom used by early elementary school personnel. Yet, families want the school to be responsive to their requests for information about their child's progress, to be included in decisions that affect their child, and to feel respected and welcome at school. The aspects of the family–school relationship desired by families of children with special learning needs, according to Wolery, are not surprising; they are also similar to those desired by all families.

There is substantial evidence that the current state of the family–school relationship is not the desired state for families whose children are in special education programs. In her summary of minority family involvement in special education, Harry reported three commonly found characteristics of the family–school relationship: "An expressed sense of isolation and helplessness; low self-confidence in interaction with professionals; and professionals' implicit or explicit discouragement of parents' participation in the special education process" (1992, p. 100). Similarly, Kalyanpur and Rao's (1991) interviews with parents about their perspective of experiences at school and with an outreach worker revealed two relationship types: traditional-unempowering and collaborative-supportive. Traditional-unempowering relationships were described by parents as disrespectful because of their focus on children's deficits and because they discounted parental skills and knowledge, primarily because they were different than those of professionals. In contrast, the collaborative-supportive relationship was characterized by responsiveness to families' needs for emotional support, specific services, and two-way communication.

Finally, in a 3-year study of 24 African American families with children receiving early childhood special education in a large, urban school district, Harry, Allen, and McLaughlin (1995) found that parents became less satisfied with special education over time because of inappropriate peer groups, labeling, and isolation of the programs. There was a dramatic drop in family involvement during the 3-year-period, with parents reporting that the atmosphere in schools was less open and welcoming over time. Approximately one quarter of the parents were able to influence decisions about their child, and most parents found advocacy quite challenging. They reported these deterrents to advocacy in parent conferences: late notices and inflexible scheduling, limited time, emphasis on paperwork rather than participation and interaction, use of jargon, and the structure of power that favored school professionals.

Special education provides a requirement for parent participation but does not require a truly collaborative partnership between parents and professionals, one based on communication with and empowerment of families. Harry (1992) identified several aspects of the family–school relationship that are especially critical for children's transition to kindergarten. First, a collaborative approach for understanding children's difficulties in school is needed. According to Harry, not involving families collaboratively in the identification of children's learning problems "creates an avenue not for dialogue but rather an adversarial type of contest"

(1992, p. 163). Second, parents want their children to do well in school, but it is hard for parents to challenge authority when they also need to entrust their children's welfare to educators. Harry (1992) noted that it is difficult for parents to challenge professionals in the absence of information, particularly when there is a lack of understanding of the importance or meaning of an event within the special education system. Third, parents expected and wanted to trust the school and were more comfortable when relationships with professionals had a personal tone. Knowing little about the system, some parents were intimidated and fearful of finding out more, in part because their participation seldom resulted in what they desired. Furthermore, each additional communication added a source of confusion and frustration.

A major conclusion of this study is that professionals' goals and parents' needs must be coordinated. Harry stated,

> I would like to suggest that perhaps there is indeed low motivation—not with regard to their children's needs but with regard to participation in activities whose form and style fail to address parents' real information needs or utilize a learning style with which parents can be comfortable. (1992, p. 234)

Harry (1992) recommended restructuring the way discourse between parents and professionals is structured, which means moving parents from a primarily singular role of consent giver to one including four roles: assessors, presenters of reports, policy makers, and advocates/peer supporters. The provision of reciprocal rather than one-way discourse provides an opportunity for professionals to begin the process of developing collaborative practice.

Models for Family–School Connections

One of the main conclusions from family–school research is that there is no prescription for developing family involvement programs in education. After an extensive review of the literature, Kagan (1984) appropriately suggested instead that educators and parents need to be guided by two questions, what forms of parent participation are desirable and feasible and what strategies can we employ to achieve them? According to Schorr, "Successful programs find interventions cannot be routinized or applied uniformly. . . . Successful programs see the child in the context of the family and the family in the context of its surroundings" (1989, p. 257). Family involvement programs are no exception. Two well-researched models of family–school partnerships emphasize the importance of roles and responsibilities and the relationship between families and school personnel. However, this chapter contends that they differ in the weighting given to each in their approaches.

Epstein (1995), who conceptualized the relationship between family and school as one of overlapping spheres of influence that exist for the benefit of children's learning, socialization, and development, also contended that a comprehensive partnership program includes six types of family involvement. These six types are as follows: parenting, communicating, volunteering, learning at home, decision making, and collaborating with community groups. In her framework, she employed an action team comprised of parent and teacher representatives, community professionals, and students to guide the development of a comprehensive, unified, and integrated program to organize, implement, and evaluate options for the six types. Epstein (1995) offered a structured process, including specific steps to take and questions to ask, for the team developing the program. In particular, she encouraged the team to focus on present strengths for involving families (e.g., What practices of school/family/community partnerships are now working well for the school?); needed changes (e.g., How do we want school/family/community partnerships to work in 3 years?); expectations (e.g., What do teachers expect of families?, What do families expect of school personnel?); sense of community (e.g., Which families are we reaching? Which families have we yet to reach?); and links to goals (e.g., How might family/school/community connections assist the school in helping more students to perform with greater success?). Her recommended structure places the onus on the school for reaching out to all families. A major contribution she has made in her work is that educators now are focused on examining why and how families are systematically excluded because of current school practices.

Epstein's (1995) framework, primarily concerned with a mechanism for schools to develop integrated family–school partnership programs to enhance the success of all students, placed a major focus on the roles and responsibilities of families and schools. With the recognition that the process takes 3–5 years, Epstein (1995) suggested that teams need to address two questions: How can the process ensure that the school–family–community partnership will continue to improve its structure, processes, and practices in order to increase the number of families that are partners with the school in their children's education, and what opportunities will teachers, parents, and students have to share information on successful practices as well as to strengthen and maintain their efforts?

In contrast, Comer (1995) placed greater emphasis on the relationship between parents and teachers—and families and schools—than on the structural aspects for creating the relationship. He proposed that "it is the attachment and identification with a meaningful adult that motivates or reinforces a child's desire to learn" (Comer, 1984, p. 327). He also argued that schools can and should be redesigned to reduce alienation and negative interaction among staff, administrators, and parents in an effort to promote a strong, positive attachment for students to school. In the School Development Program, or what is often referred to as the Comer process, "the organizational or management system between family and school is based on knowledge of child development and relationship issues" (Comer et al., 1996, p. 8). Changing the interface between family and school, according to Comer and his colleagues (1996), requires trust; interventions demand a new way of working and a new way of thinking, which is a relatively tall task because individuals do not change easily, especially when they feel like strangers. The three guiding principles of the program—consensus, collaboration, and no fault—nurture a positive climate between families and school personnel.

Three mechanisms are used to facilitate the family–school connection, especially the orientation that both systems must accept responsibility for change. The School Planning and Management Team—usually facilitated by the principal and comprised of three parents, three teachers, and a school psychologist or social worker—sets policies and procedures, coordinates activities, and engages in strategic planning with key stakeholders. In this model of shared governance, the needs of students, parents, and educators are addressed. The team does not simply include parents and assume their physical presence represents parent input. Parents are valued, active participants in problem solving for ways to enhance children's development on six pathways: psychological, social, cognitive, ethical, language, and physical. The Parent Team involves parents at every level of school activity (classroom assistant, decision making), and the Student and Staff Support Team addresses schoolwide prevention issues and manages individual student cases. These teams operate with the philosophy of consensus, collaboration, and no fault and coordinate with the comprehensive school plan; staff development opportunities, which include parents and teachers as colearners; and a schoolwide student assessment and monitoring system.

The Comer process represents changes in the structural relationship between family and school. One theoretical base for his process is ecological, that is, Comer believed that to change students' attitudes, achievement, and behavior, one must change interactions within the system or parts of the system that have an impact on the individual. Structure as defined by roles and responsibilities is not the cornerstone of this model. Rather, relationships vis-à-vis children's/adolescents' development dominate; "the three teams in the Comer model use consensus, collaboration, and no-fault with the aim of the optimal development of each child along the six developmental pathways" (Comer et al., 1996, p. 30).

The work of two other individuals is also noteworthy. Swap's (1993) analysis of the assumptions, as well as merits and limitations, of four models of home–school relationships (protective, school-to-home transmission, curriculum enrichment, and partnership) underscored the significance of a philosophical orientation and/or policy for explaining qualitatively different practices across families and schools. Her categorization highlighted the importance of families and schools deciding together what kind of relationship works. The assumption that continuity of learning between home and school is of critical importance for encouraging children's learning is a defining feature of three of the models; however, each model implements unique parent involvement strategies. For example, educators have the primary responsibility to communicate with families about their children's progress, school policies and programs, and parent involvement opportunities in the school-to-home transmission model. Interactive learning and involving parents from the community is very characteristic of the curriculum enrichment model. Similar to Comer, only in the partnership model do collaborative relationships permeate all areas of school culture. Implementation of this model requires a progressive paradigm shift for parents and educators alike, because parents, educators, and the community work together to determine goals for education, with a focus on local autonomy and control. Swap's analysis suggested the need to work as partners regardless of whether a traditionally oriented approach (i.e., school-to-home transmission model) or a partnership-oriented approach (i.e., partnership model) is selected.

Weiss, Director of the Family–School Collaboration Center in New York City, argued that family–school relationships must focus first and foremost on the interface between family and school so that a collaborative climate becomes the norm (Weiss & Edwards, 1992). This norm applies to interactions between parents and educators regarding both issues for an individual child as well as those for group problem solving, which allows families and educators an opportunity for mutual support in finding solutions to schooling problems (e.g., school vandalism). Prerequisites for successful partnership efforts include administrative support for partnerships and a zeal for relaying this message to teachers; use of a home–school partnership coordinating council, staffed by administrators, teachers, support staff, and parents, to map the course for the school's efforts; and a family–school coordinator, who has the immediate responsibility for organization and implementation of activities.

It should be clear that partnership, regardless of the individual approach, goes well beyond the view that families have an impact on children's learning and, therefore, a place in the school, toward advocating mutual contributions of parents and teachers to children's learning. Parents are not merely supporters of the school; rather, they are vital and irreplaceable partners in the educative process. It should also be clear that the focus of these models is on gains for students. What may not be as clear is that the approaches differ in their "weighting" of the centrality given to roles/responsibilities and the relationship.

Summary

Empirical support for family involvement in education as a means for enhancing student achievement and performance in school is strong. Family involvement is a positive correlate of several school performance indicators. Opportunities for family involvement are important, and Epstein's (1995) typology of family–school partnership activities is becoming a common organizational structure for K through 12 schools. The value of a family–school team for guiding the process of developing programs, as well as the elements of collaboration and characteristics of effective programs, is known. Yet, school practices for family involvement in education, particularly for working with families as partners, are defined more by rhetoric than reality.

The issue is not whether family involvement in education works or whether there is consensus about family influences on children's learning (see Chapter 2). The question, at this point, is not, what the factors are that help to increase the probability of student success in school. Research has demonstrated the significance of families in children's learning and development. Although family factors or out-of-school time influences on various indicators of children's school performance can be readily listed, the continuing influence of the family learning environment on students' attitudes, behavior, and achievement through grade 12 is not so often acknowledged. Much more is known about the effect of families on students' schooling experiences, whereas much less is known about the process of implementing family–school partnerships, especially from a mesosystemic orientation. Systematic investigation of the effect of a partnership approach on students' development and school performance is warranted.

LIVE AND LEARN PROJECT

A contention of the Live and Learn Project, a University of Minnesota project funded by the Minnesota Extension Service, is that many family involvement efforts have not been grounded in theory, particularly those related to the development of children and youth. It seems that researchers are not asking (and answering) what contextual influences enhance learning and development for children and youth, what conditions facilitate students' learning and achievement, or what it takes for a child to develop an identity as a learner. The field of medicine routinely tells individuals what to eat to reduce the probability of having colon cancer, or what foods increase the probability of having coronary heart disease. This medical analogy is consistent with the goal of the Live and Learn Project, which is to disseminate empirically supported information about conditions that help school-age children to be responsible, productive learners.

Project personnel have assumed that school is children's work. Additional assumptions that underlie the project's conceptualization of developing learners are as follows:

- Student success in school is mutually determined by student characteristics, the family environment, and the school environment.

- Out-of-school time provides important learning opportunities.

- Both parents and teachers are educators, but not all of education is schooling.

- The stronger the knowledge of each other, the stronger the bond is between home and school.

- Children perform in school according to how they see the importance of education.

- There are many ways in which teachers and families address students' needs for fostering learning.

The first task of the project was to identify alterable family, school, and community influences on children's learning in grades K through 12. As literature from the three areas was read simultaneously, remarkable similarities were found in the kinds of contextual influences that enhance student learning (Christenson & Christenson, 1998). Based on a comprehensive review, it was found that students perform best when they have standards to work toward, support for learning, opportunity to learn, a structure to work within, positive relationships with adults, and good role models for learning from families and schools. Thus, there is evidence for a common set of factors regardless of the child's microsystem.

It was also found that family and school databases consist of primarily correlational studies, with reported significant correlations generally in the low-to-moderate to moderate range. A major strength of these databases is replication of findings. The size of the correlation is not as important as the consistency and direction of findings, which suggest convergence in the family and school factors critical for children's learning. Returning to the medical analogy, identification of correlates of students' school performance allows one to speak only in terms of probabilities, either creating conditions that increase the likelihood that the student will be more successful in school or reducing the student's risk of school failure. The six factors for family and school influences—standards and expectations, structure, opportunity to learn, support, climate/relationships, and modeling—are summarized in this section.

Standards and Expectations

Standards and expectations refer to the level of expected performance held by key adults for youth. Student success in school is facilitated when parents and teachers clearly state expectations for student performance, set specific goals and standards for desired behavior and performance, discuss expectations with youth, emphasize children's effort when completing tasks, and ensure that youth understand the consequences for not meeting expectations. Academic achievement is positively correlated with realistic, high parent and teacher expectations for children's school performance. The following is known regarding standards and expectations:

- Parents' estimates of their children's abilities have long-term effects on achievement (Entwisle & Hayduk, 1988).

- Realistic and accurate parent expectations (i.e., those close to the child's actual performance) are associated with children's superior performance on cognitive tasks (Scott-Jones, 1988).

- Parent expectations for children to read, to learn math, and to request verbal responses from their children (Hess & Holloway, 1984), for postsecondary outcomes (Clark, 1993; Eagle, 1989), and for continued achievement and hard work in school—defined as "press for achievement" by Marjoribanks (1979)—are associated with better academic performance.

- Parents' use of effort attributions is related to positive academic performance (Stevenson & Lee, 1990).

- Student performance is higher in classrooms in which teacher expectations for the student's learning (i.e., lesson goal) and the student's performance (i.e., following instructions) are explicitly stated (Kagan, 1992).

- Student achievement is improved when instructors hold high expectations for all students and expect students to respond (Brophy & Good, 1986).

- Goal ambitiousness is associated positively with achievement gains for both special education (Fuchs, Fuchs, & Deno, 1985) and mainstreamed youth (Levin, 1987).

Structure

Structure refers to the overall routine and monitoring provided by key adults for youth. Students' success in school is facilitated when both families and schools provide a consistent pattern of events and age-appropriate monitoring and supervision. Students perform better in school when they understand their schedule of daily activities, directions for schoolwork, rules for behavior, and so on. The following regarding structure and student performance is known:

- A regular family routine and priority given to schoolwork to ensure adequate time for reading, studying, and completion of schoolwork are associated with better academic performance (Kellaghan et al., 1993).

- Parental monitoring of the use of children's out-of-school time (Clark, 1983), homework completion (Cooper, 1989), television viewing (Keith, Reimers, Fehrmann, Pottebaum, & Aubrey, 1986), and students' performance in school (Fehrmann et al., 1987) is also significantly related to better grades.

- Authoritative parenting is positively associated with achievement and psychosocial maturity for elementary and secondary students (Dornbusch, Ritter, Leiderman, Roberts, & Fraleigh, 1987; Steinberg, Elmen, & Mounts, 1989).

In addition, high-achieving classrooms are characterized by the following:

- An academic, task-oriented focus (Rosenshine & Stevens, 1986)

- High rates of academic learning time (Marliave & Filby, 1985)

- Systematic use of effective classroom strategies for regular and special education students (Anderson, Evertson, & Brophy, 1979; Englert & Thomas, 1982)

- Teacher monitoring of student progress toward the intended goal (Gettinger, 1984; Waxman, Wang, Anderson, & Walberg, 1985)

Opportunity to Learn

Opportunity to learn refers to the variety of learning options available to youth in the home, at school, and within the community. Student success in school is facilitated when youth are provided with various tools for learning, such as reading materials, access to clubs and organizations, varied teaching strategies, and time to practice and master new skills. Also, it is enhanced when the key adults in the youth's life communicate with each other. The following correlations can be made regarding opportunity and youth:

- The involvement of youth in constructive learning activities outside school is associated with higher achievement (Clark, 1990).

- High levels of verbal guidance, exposure to vocabulary, complex language usage, and frequent dialogue between parents and children are associated with academic achievement (Hart & Risley, 1995; Kellaghan et al., 1993).

- The availability of learning resources (Bradley & Caldwell, 1976; Hess, Holloway, Price, & Dickson, 1982) and learning opportunities in homes (Peng & Lee, 1992) is correlated with achievement.

- The amount, encouragement, and discussion of leisure reading are associated with reading performance (Graue, Weinstein, & Walberg, 1983).

- Time spent with parents and siblings completing family tasks is associated with healthier youth development (Benson, 1997).

- The amount of time allocated to instruction and spent on academic pursuits positively correlates to academic achievement for all students, regardless of whether they are labeled at risk, typical, or in need of special education (Greenwood, 1991).

- The opportunity to respond in classrooms is associated with reading and math gains for at-risk and nonrisk students (Greenwood, Delquadri, & Hall, 1984).

- The time needed to learn contributes significantly to learning (Gettinger, 1984).

- Regularly assigned, checked, and graded homework that is related to daily lessons is correlated with student achievement (Walberg, Paschal, & Weinstein, 1985).

Support

Support refers to the guidance provided by, the communication between, and the interest shown by adults to facilitate student progress in school. This progress is facilitated when adults give frequent verbal support and praise; provide youth with regular, explicit feedback; talk directly to youth about schoolwork and activities; and teach problem-solving and negotiation skills. It is what adults do on an ongoing basis to help youth learn and achieve. Positive family correlates of academic achievement for elementary- and secondary-level students include the following:

- Parental interest in children's academic and personal growth (Walberg, 1984)

- Strong parental encouragement of academic pursuits (Clark, 1983) and a supportive learning environment when grades are lower than desired (Dornbusch & Ritter, 1992)

- Fostering children's interest and skill in reading and math (Hess & Holloway, 1984)
- Orienting a student's attention to learning opportunities (Hess & Holloway, 1984)
- Recognizing and encouraging the child's special talents (Bloom, 1985)
- Talking with children about schoolwork (Peng & Lee, 1992) and participating in meaningful ways with their children's school (Comer, 1984, 1995)
- Amount of additional supportive behaviors related to homework completion (Clark, 1993)
- Discussing the value of a good education and possible career options (Mitrsomwang & Hawley, 1993)

Other important correlates include the following:

- Neutral, task-specific, immediate, and frequent praise is related positively to student achievement (Brophy & Good, 1986).
- Feedback based on continuous monitoring and appropriate instructional modifications for student skill level are associated with learning gains for students with and without special learning needs (Fuchs & Fuchs, 1986).
- Students who are directly taught thinking skills and use learning strategies complete more schoolwork and have higher grades (Weinstein & Mayer, 1986).
- Motivational strategies that emphasize personal effort (Dweck, 1991), setting goals (Fuchs & Fuchs, 1986), maintaining student engagement with the learning task (Ainley, 1993), and teacher emphasis on knowledge or skills to be gained from completion of the learning task (Brophy, 1983) have been shown to enhance academic performance.

Climate/Relationships

Climate/relationships refers to the amount of warmth and friendliness and praise and recognition received and the degree to which the adult–youth relationship is positive and respectful. These relationships are facilitated by cooperative, accepting environments; a nonblaming relationship between home and school; and encouragement, praise, and involvement in the youth's life from key adults. The degree of continuity of these relationships and interactions, between adults at home and at school, will greatly influence the degree of academic achievement of the youth. Climate/relationships is how adults in the home, school, and community help youths to be learners.

The following observations can be made regarding climate/relationships and academic achievement in children:

- A parent–child relationship characterized by parental acceptance, nurturance, encouragement, involvement, and responsiveness to the child's needs and level of development is positively associated with academic achievement (Hess & Holloway, 1984) and the likelihood children will initiate and persist in challenging and intellectual tasks (Estrada et al., 1987).
- Positive self-esteem and low anxiety for youth from eight cultures was correlated with family harmony and nurturance (Scott, Scott, & McCabe, 1991).
- Continuity between home and school environments and use of a nonblaming, problem-solving approach to resolve concerns and develop programs are re-

lated positively to students' academic and social functioning (Comer, 1995; Hansen, 1986).

- Students, regardless of age, ability, subject area, or learning task, achieve more in cooperative rather than competitive, individualistic learning structures (Johnson, Maruyama, Johnson, Nelson, & Skon, 1981).

- A positive teacher–student relationship where the student feels supported and connected to school has been successful in reducing the probability of dropping out (Whelage & Rutter, 1986).

- Support, encouragement, and gentle, positive praise were more influential factors than challenging tasks and high expectations in motivating students from low SES backgrounds (Brophy & Good, 1986).

Other researchers have found that positive adult–student relationships have an impact on students' achievement-related beliefs, academic performance, and engagement in school (Clark, 1990; Connell, Halpern-Felsher, Clifford, Crichlow, & Usinger, 1995).

Modeling

Modeling refers to how adults demonstrate desired behaviors and commitment/ value toward learning and working hard in their daily lives. Student success at school is enhanced when teachers establish an academically demanding classroom that has clearly defined objectives, explicit instructions, and an orderly and efficient environment, and when the parent(s) or other adults read, ask questions, discuss the importance/value of education, set long-term goals, and are able to intervene and be involved with youth's schooling. Modeling appears to be influenced by both the attitudes and behaviors of parents and teachers. According to Maccoby and Martin (1984), children attend to, respond to, and follow the behavior of salient models more often than models whose words and actions are incongruent. The following regarding modeling is known:

- A positive family correlate of academic achievement is the degree to which parents model learning by using reading or math at home (Eagle, 1989; Hess & Holloway, 1984) and appreciating learning, self-discipline, and hard work by asking questions and engaging in conversations about achievement resulting from hard work (Clark, 1993; Mitrsomwang & Hawley, 1993; Rumberger, 1995).

- Teachers who establish academic objectives and model a task-oriented attitude for their students elicit higher student achievement than those who fail to establish clear objectives, are unable to accomplish academic objectives due to poor management skills, or establish primarily affective objectives (Brophy, 1986).

- Teachers who used instructional talk that made "visible their invisible thinking" while teaching reading comprehension had students who performed better on reading assignments and achievement tests (Duffy et al., 1986).

Summary

These six factors are readily applied to children from birth to school entrance. Based on a review of the literature for preschoolers, it appears that home and school influences that help to facilitate the development of preschool children, particularly for school-related tasks, are the following:

- An enriching environment (e.g., material and personal resources, interaction with others, play, amount of reading)
- Management/discipline practices (e.g., understanding family rules; guidance in teaching, such as reasoning and explanation; affirmations)
- Responsivity/support (e.g., warm, nurturing relationship; positive adult–child relationship when teaching)
- Language (e.g., exposure, interaction with others, use of language facilitators) (Christenson, 1996)

In addition, preschoolers benefit (or are being prepared for school-related tasks) from specific interactions with caregivers. Caregivers positively affect the learning of preschoolers when they

- Model reading and writing to children frequently
- Talk to children frequently, provide positive feedback, and foster vocabulary development by explaining the meaning of words and describing objects in the environment
- Incorporate language, reading, and writing into play themes with children, such as singing silly songs that substitute sounds and playing rhyming games
- Develop environments that are "literacy rich," with print materials and learning resources available to children to help foster their identities as learners and prepare them for the tasks of school

In summary, families and educators have a shared vested interest in children and youth when they are students: Both homes and schools provide opportunities for students to learn. Schools and teachers alone seldom help students achieve their full academic potential. This is not an indictment of schools or teachers but a fact of child development. Students' personal investment in and interest for learning are influenced by the degree to which home and school environments—in concert—create optimal conditions for learning. Six factors have been suggested as an empirically supported framework for creating shared meaning between families and schools. A way to conceptualize family–school relationships is considering the presence of two curricula—the curriculum of the school and the curriculum of the home—as well as the significance of communication between families and schools to maintain a consistency of influence and to handle conflict. Because children traverse family and school contexts, the degree to which their primary socializing agents—parents and teachers—have developed a sense of shared meaning (Pianta & Walsh, 1996) or a common language about conditions that enhance children's learning may be integral to the success of collaborative relationships.

THE FUTURE: RESEARCH, TRAINING, AND POLICY

Based on the information presented in this chapter, the nature of the family–school relationship vis-à-vis student learning is the seminal issue for the future. The critical question is, How can sustaining relationships between educators and parents be constructed to enhance children's learning and development? The lack of an ecological, systems perspective for understanding children's development and learning in practice is a barrier. It is seldom asked what contextual influences enhance learning and development of children and youth or what conditions help children to make a personal investment in learning. Much more is known about the outcomes of family involvement in education than about the process of implementation. The focus is more often on what schools do, can do, and/or should do to achieve higher student achievement. Such a focus suggests the responsibility for educational outcomes lies with schools, ignoring that the informal education in homes is a prerequisite for formal education in schools (Bronfenbrenner, 1991). Roles for families and schools exist; each system contributes to the educational performance of children. To date, the approach to understanding the significance of families and the contributions of schools to children's learning has been too fragmented. Restructuring the relationship between home and schools to create mutual support for addressing child-related concerns will require a serious examination of issues related to the rights, responsibilities, and resources of students, families, and schools.

The clear demarcation between early intervention and K through 12 education defies the notion of constructing sustaining relationships between families and schools for children's development and learning. As children make the transition to kindergarten, it is important to note that the receiving system, K through 12, has characteristically been less ready to interface with families from a partnership approach than the early intervention system. This is no small matter. For example, children's acquisition of language is both a visible expression of development and a key to subsequent learning and school achievement. Not only is there evidence that children need to be prepared for school learning (Campbell & Ramey, 1994), but there also is evidence that K through 12 education could benefit from aligning with the family support principles that are characteristic of early intervention practices. The transition to school may be the linchpin in establishing a strong family–school connection for learning; therefore, the comprehensive program recommended by the family support movement makes sense. It recommends that family–school connections be organized as a continuum across development, that they address unique circumstances to enhance success for all students, and that they consist of the following three components: school readiness; parent involvement, which empowers parents to take an active role in education of children in grades K through 12; and school-linked services aimed at improving achievement by ensuring that the health and social needs of all children are met.

Roles and relationships for families and schools must be differentiated. To be serious about sustained relationships between families and schools for children's learning and development, it must be recognized that each system has a role to play and that each system has to accept responsibility. Families and schools have always played a role in children's learning. In practice, communication about roles based on a partnership approach, however, has occurred infrequently. It is noteworthy that roles recommended by the U.S. Department of Education training materials reflect mutuality, specifically recommending that home and school act as co-advisors, advocates, and decision makers; co-teachers; co-learners; co-supporters; and co-communicators (Moles, 1993). Also, the value of a common language (i.e., six Live and Learn factors) is that it assumes families and schools have active roles to play and encourages families, school personnel, and students to discuss each other's responsibilities. A specific responsibility for families or schools is not designated because of the need to be sensitive to the rights of families and schools and the availability of differential resources from families and schools for fostering children's learning.

Throughout the literature, references to roles often reflect those for the school or the family. When roles are coordinated and complementary across family and school contexts, a relationship between the partners is evident. Acknowledging the rights, responsibilities, and resources of parents, teachers, and students helps them think of their relationship differently—one which moves from the concept of relationships in terms of service delivery—of "provider" and "client"; of "professionals" and "target populations"—to one of complementary efforts toward common goals (Seeley, 1985). The issue of time as a barrier can no longer be ignored. That is, time is often found to handle a crisis or conflict between families and schools, but usually at the expense perhaps of not having time for dialogue, learning from each other, interaction, and building a relationship.

Research

Our understanding of the potential effect of the family–school interface on children's learning is limited and students' transition to school is an ideal time to conduct longitudinal research using a mesosystemic perspective. Studies examining attitudes, perceptions, or behaviors in the family or school microsystem in relation to children's learning or studies that provide evidence for the additive effects of parent involvement have been primarily conducted. To advance the knowledge of the effect of the family–school interface on children's learning, research must move beyond these preexisting models. The effect of the reciprocal influence of family and school messages about learning and practices on student motivation and behavior must be examined.

Because the understanding of what constitutes an effective family–school relationship under specific conditions and for varied populations is limited, systematic examination of process-related variables in intervention studies is warranted. The current database is replete with descriptive studies, suggesting positive outcomes when families are involved in education. Building relationships between families and schools is complex and multifaceted but feasible. Much like partners in business, partners in education must work hard to clarify their mutual interests in the children they share (Rutherford, 1995). It is suggested that these critical process variables for understanding how to develop sustaining relationships between families and schools—rights, responsibilities, and resources for the partners—must be better understood. What are parents', teachers', and students' rights, responsibilities, and resources? How are these three variables interrelated? How do they influence interventions implemented?

These, however, are not the only questions. First, there are many questions related to the conditions for connecting families and schools. For example, why are some educators so wary of families? Or, what are the consequences of implementing a family involvement program before trust between home and school is established? Perhaps the field needs to recognize that the research is moving in a direction of mandating family involvement (e.g., Goal 8), raising issues about whether what really matters in the family–school relationship can be mandated. Is it possible to respect each other, make joint decisions, and engage in honest, clear two-way communication, all defining features of collaboration, without trust? What is the relationship between trust and school performance? Other related questions are, how are attitudes about family involvement in education acquired, and do our attitudes influence the types of activities supported at the school? Finally, given their skills, knowledge, and time constraints, what are meaningful roles for all families in education? Some families need information; some need information and attention to unique family circumstances; and some need information, attention, and ongoing support to be active participants in facilitating their children's learning and development. Could the same be said of educators—whether teachers, administrators, or support personnel—with respect to the relationship with families?

Second, there are questions related to the significance of family involvement in education. How should the significance of family involvement in education be communicated? Although programs that provide parents with information about the significance of their involvement and its impact on levels of achievement appear to be a viable approach, the extent to which information alone alters parent attitudes, and subsequently behavior, remains to be demonstrated. In addition, the distinction between achievement and learning is relevant. Is it the case that school reform discussions that include parent involvement overemphasize academic performance? Do we really want family involvement at school, or is the real need a universal recognition of the essential role the family plays in enhancing student success? Could it be that enhancing learning at home and valuing learning in out-of-school time may be more important for child outcomes than establishing a comprehensive family–school partnership program? Thinking of achievement as the product of education may reinforce exclusive responsibility on schools, whereas thinking of learning as the product of education, as suggested by Seeley (1985), may reinforce shared responsibility between families and schools for the educational status of youth.

Third, many questions relate to communication between home and school. For example, how do we address the social and physical distance between home and school, and what kinds of opportunities for dialogue (not monologue) are feasible, relevant, or efficient? We know personal contact between home and school is identified as an essential feature for developing a home–school connection for many families and educators. This raises the question, how can preferences for style of communication be addressed and still result in a doable program for families and school personnel?

In a collaborative family–school relationship, educators consider the family's viewpoint and encourage the family to consider the school's viewpoint to attain a mutual, shared understanding of student behavior across environments. To develop sustaining relationships between families and schools the key elements of problem solving must be better understood. Although problem-solving structures exist, they often omit what may be crucial elements, such as perspective taking, opportunity to learn from each other, and sharing constraints of each system (e.g., available resources). Without an opportunity for families and educators to co-construct the "bigger picture" to understand child performance and the presence of a cooperating attitude between the partners, which means partners strive to attain a common goal while coordinating their feelings and perspective with awareness of another's feelings and perspective, finger pointing and blame across the socializing agents may continue. For example, one of the objectives of the National Education Goal 1 is to recognize parents as their children's first teachers and as having a lifelong influence on their children's values, attitudes, and aspirations. The assessment of progress in relation to this objective involves indexing how many parents read to their children daily. At best, this index would seem to provide a narrow picture and is contrary to the flexibility needed to develop sustaining relationships for children's learning. All families and schools have a responsibility to create a nation of readers, but the specific responsibility for the family and school needs to be negotiated depending on the resources (e.g., reading ability of family) available. In some cases the schools will need to take the lead to eliminate or reduce barriers to parents' involvement with reading at home by providing opportunities for the parents to learn ways to provide support for their children's learning. Clearly, effective problem-solving skills are fundamental.

Finally, questions about the appropriate boundary between families and school are often asked. Establishing the goal of the family–school partnership as working together to enhance school success for students provides a permeable boundary. Although it is helpful to always maintain the relationship around educational issues, it is acknowledged that some students also need family-based barriers to learning removed (Adelman, 1996). Schools that make linkages with resources in the community help involve parents with their child's education as well as meet other needs in the family that might impede the healthy development of children (Brice-Heath & McLaughlin, 1987). Although service integration appears to be a promising approach, the effect of this approach on children's learning is yet to be documented.

Policy and Training

According to Rutherford (1995), "current school-level policies and expectations tend to center on what parents can provide for teachers and schools rather than what teachers and schools can provide for parents" (p. 15). If school personnel are serious about sustaining relationships between families and schools for children, the focus of a policy, as suggested by Brice-Heath and McLaughlin (1987), should be on children and the conditions that help children develop. Policy, evident in National Education Goals 1 and 8, must be understood as a framework that requires supportive mechanisms to be successful. For example, policy without training for school personnel on how to communicate with parents as partners is meaningless. Training extends beyond sharing a list of 10 easy ways to involve families; it must focus primarily on strategies for establishing a mutual understanding of the family–school relationship for children's learning through dialogue about families' and educators' desires, rights, responsibilities, and resources.

CONCLUDING REMARKS

Children's transition to kindergarten marks a critical juncture for focusing on the family–school relationship to enhance children's learning. Altering the current "rhetoric rut" about family involvement in grades K through 12 demands training, policies, and practices based on an understanding of the ecological development of children and youth. According to Coleman (1987), the impact of the erosion of social capital is that a growing number of children are unprepared to perform successfully in school. It has been suggested that addressing the question, how can social capital be generated where it does not naturally occur, ought to be the premier policy question of the 1990s. A constructive relationship between families and schools is one way to provide an opportunity to increase social capital for children and youth.

In this chapter, it is suggested that a constructive, sustained relationship between families and schools depends on creating a common language to discuss the roles of families and schools and shaping the relationship through dialogue about rights, responsibilities, and available resources for the developing child. Finally, conceptualizing a constructive family–school relationship as an outcome of students' successful transition to school, one to be maintained across subsequent years, offers much promise for attaining the safety net desired for children and youth.

REFERENCES

Adams, K.S., & Christenson, S.L. (1998). Differences in parent and teacher trust levels: Implications for creating collaborative family–school relationships. *Special Services in the Schools, 14*(1/2), 1–22.

Adelman, H.S. (1996). Restructuring education support services and integrating community resources: Beyond the full service model. *School Psychology Review, 25*(4), 418–430.

Ainley, D.D. (1993). Styles of engagement with learning: Multidimensional assessment of their relationship with strategy use and school achievement. *Journal of Educational Psychology, 85*(3), 395–405.

Anderson, L., Evertson, C., & Brophy, J. (1979). An experimental study of effective teaching in first-grade reading groups. *The Elementary School Journal, 79*, 193–223.

Baker, D.P., & Stevenson, D.L. (1986). Mothers' strategies for children's school achievement: Managing the transition to high school. *Sociology of Education, 59*, 156–166.

Barton, P.E., & Coley, R.J. (1992). *America's smallest school: The family.* Princeton, NJ: Educational Testing Service.

Becher, R.M. (1984). *Parent involvement: A review of research and principles for successful practice.* Urbana, IL: ERIC Clearinghouse on Elementary and Early Childhood Education. (ERIC Document Reproduction Service No. ED 247-032)

Berger, E.H. (1991). Parent involvement: Yesterday and today. *The Elementary School Journal, 91*(3), 209–220.

Bloom, B.S. (1985). *Developing talents in young people.* New York: Ballantine Books.

Bradley, R.H., & Caldwell, B.M. (1976). The relation of infants' home environments to mental test performance at fifty-four months: A follow-up study. *Child Development, 47*, 1172–1174.

Brice-Heath, S.B., & McLaughlin, M.W. (1987). A child resource policy: Moving beyond dependence on school and family. *Phi Delta Kappan, 68*, 576–580.

Bronfenbrenner, U. (1991). What do families do? Parts 1 and 2. *Teaching Thinking and Problem Solving, 4*(1–2).

Brophy, J.E. (1983). Fostering student learning and motivation in the elementary school classroom. In S.G. Paris, G.M. Olson, & H.W. Stevenson (Eds.), *Learning and motivation in the classroom* (pp. 283–305). Mahwah, NJ: Lawrence Erlbaum Associates.

Brophy, J.E., & Good, T.L. (1986). Teacher behavior and student achievement. In M.L. Wittrock (Ed.), *Handbook of research on teaching* (3rd ed., pp. 328–375). Indianapolis, IN: Macmillan Publishing USA.

Cale, L.B. (1993). Communication skills and strategies. In O. Moles (Ed.), *Building school–family partnerships for learning: Workshops for urban educators.* Washington, DC: U.S. Department of Education, Office of Research and Educational Improvement.

Campbell, F.A., & Ramey, C.T. (1994). Effects of early intervention on intellectual and academic achievement: A follow-up study of children from low income families. *Child Development, 65*, 684–698.

Chavkin, N.F., & Williams, D.L., Jr. (1993). Minority parents and the elementary schools: Attitudes and practices. In N.F. Chavkin (Eds.), *Families and schools in a pluralistic society* (pp. 73–84). Albany: State University of New York Press.

Christenson, S.L. (1995). Best practices in supporting home–school collaboration. In A. Thomas & J. Grimes (Eds.), *Best practices in school psychology III* (pp. 253–267). Silver Spring, MD: National Association of School Psychologists.

Christenson, S.L. (1996, November). *The importance of learning environments for preschoolers' development and school success: Description of home and school influences.* Keynote address for observing and assessing the preschool learner, Teachers College, Columbia University, New York.

Christenson, S.L., & Christenson, C.J. (1998). *Family, school and community influences on children's learning: A literature review* (Report No. 1). Minneapolis: University of Minnesota, Live and Learn Project.

Christenson, S.L., Hurley, C.M., Sheridan, S.M., & Fenstermacher, K. (1997). Parents' and school psychologists' perspectives on parent involvement activities. *School Psychology Review, 26*(1), 111–130.

Christenson, S.L., Rounds, T., & Gorney, D. (1992). Family factors and student achievement: An avenue to increase students' success. *School Psychology Quarterly, 7*(3), 178–206.

Clark, R.M. (1983). *Family life and school achievement.* Chicago: University of Chicago Press.

Clark, R.M. (1988). Parents as providers of linguistic and social capital: How do the literacy skills of low achievers and high achievers differ, and how do parents influence these differences? *Educational Horizons, 66*(2), 93–95.

Clark, R.M. (1990). Why disadvantaged students succeed: What happens outside school is critical. *Public Welfare,* 17–23.

Clark, R.M. (1993). Homework-focused parenting practices that positively affect student achievement. In N.F. Chavkin (Ed.), *Families and schools in a pluralistic society* (pp. 85–105). Albany: State University of New York Press.

Cochran, M. (1987). The parental empowerment process: Building on family strengths. *Equity and Choice, 4*(1), 9–23.

Coleman, J.S. (1987, August–September). Families and schools. *Educational Researcher,* 32–38.

Collins, C.H., Moles, O., & Cross, M. (1982). *The home–school connection: Selected partnership programs in large cities.* Boston: Institute for Responsive Education.

Comer, J.P. (1984). Home–school relationships as they affect the academic success of children. *Education and Urban Society, 16*(3), 323–337.

Comer, J.P. (1995). *School power: Implications of an intervention project.* New York: The Free Press.

Comer, J.P., & Haynes, N.M. (1991). Parent involvement in schools: An ecological approach. *The Elementary School Journal, 91*(3), 271–278.

Comer, J.P., Haynes, N.M., Joyner, E.T., & Ben-Avie, M. (1996). *Rallying the whole village: The Comer process for reforming education.* New York: Teachers College Press.

Conger, R.D., Conger, K.J., Elder, G.H., Jr., Lorenz, F.O., Simmons, R.L., & Whitbeck, L.B. (1992). A family process model of economic hardship and adjustment of early adolescent boys. *Child Development, 68,* 526–541.

Connell, J.P., Halpern-Felsher, B.L., Clifford, E., Crichlow, W., & Usinger, P. (1995). Hanging in there: Behavioral, psychological, and contextual factors affecting whether African American adolescents stay in high school. *Journal of Adolescent Research, 10*(1), 41–63.

Connors, L.J., & Epstein, J.L. (1994). *Taking stock: Views of teachers, parents, and students on school, family, and community partnerships in high school* (Report No. 25). Baltimore: The Johns Hopkins University, Center on Families, Communities, Schools, and Children's Learning.

Cooper, H. (1989). Synthesis of research on homework. *Educational Leadership, 47,* 85–91.

Dauber, S.L., & Epstein, J.L. (1993). Parents' attitudes and practices of involvement in inner-city elementary and middle schools. In N.F. Chavkin (Eds.), *Families and schools in a pluralistic society* (pp. 53–72). Albany: State University of New York Press.

Davies, D. (1991). Schools reaching out: Family, school, and community partnerships for student success. *Phi Delta Kappan, 72*(5), 376–382.

Davies, D. (1993). Benefits and barriers to parent involvement: From Portugal to Boston to Liverpool. In N.F. Chavkin (Ed.), *Families and schools in a pluralistic society* (pp. 53–72). Albany: State University of New York Press.

Delgado-Gaitan, C. (1991). Involving parents in the schools: A process of empowerment. *American Journal of Education, 100*(10), 20–46.

Dornbusch , S.M., & Ritter, P.L. (1992). Home–school processes in diverse ethnic groups, social classes, and family structures. In S.L. Christenson & J.C. Conoley (Eds.), *Home–school
collaboration: Enhancing children's academic and social competence* (pp. 111–126). Silver
Spring, MD: National Association of School Psychologists.

Dornbusch, S.M., Ritter, P.L., Leiderman, P.H., Roberts, D.F., & Fraleigh, J.J. (1987). The
relation of parenting style to adolescent school performance. *Child Development, 58,*
1244–1257.

Duffy, G.G., Roehler, L.R., Meloth, M.S., Vavrus, L.G., Book, C., Putnam, J., & Wesselman,
R. (1986). The relationship between explicit verbal explanations during reading skills in-
struction and student awareness and achievement: A study of reading teacher effects.
Reading Research Quarterly, 21(3), 237–252.

Dunst, C.J., Johanson, C., Rounds, T., Trivette, C.M., & Hamby, D. (1992). Characteristics of
parent–professional relationships. In S.L. Christenson & J.C. Conoley (Eds.), *Home–school
collaboration: Enhancing children's academic and social competence* (pp. 157–174). Silver Spring,
MD: National Association of School Psychologists.

Dweck, C.S. (1991). Self-theories and goals: Their role in motivation, personality, and development. In R.A. Dienstbier (Ed.), *Nebraska symposium on motivation* (pp. 63–84). Lin-
coln: University of Nebraska Press.

Eagle, E. (1989, April). *Socioeconomic status, family structure, and parental involvement: The correlates of achievement.* Paper presented at the annual meeting of the American Educational
Research Association, San Francisco. (ERIC Document Reproduction Service No. ED
307-332)

Early, D.M., & Pianta, R.C. (1998, April). *Kindergarten transition practices: Relations with
teacher and classroom characteristics.* Paper presented at the annual meeting of the American Educational Research Association, San Diego.

Englert, C.S., & Thomas, C.C. (1982). Management of task involvement in special education
classrooms: Implications for teacher preparation. *Teacher Education and Special Education,
5,* 3–10.

Entwisle, D.R., & Hayduk, L.A. (1988). Lasting effects of elementary school. *Sociology of Education, 61,* 147–159.

Epstein, J.L. (1986). Parents' reactions to teacher practices of parent involvement. *The Elementary School Journal, 86,* 277–294.

Epstein, J.L. (1989). Building parent–teacher partnerships in inner-city schools. *Family Resource Coalition, 8,* 7.

Epstein, J.L. (1991). Effects on student achievement of teachers' practices of parent involvement. In S.B. Silvern (Ed.), *Advances in reading/language research: Vol. 5. Literacy through
family, community, and school interaction* (pp. 261–276). Greenwich, CT: JAI Press.

Epstein, J.L. (1995). School/family/community partnerships: Caring for children we share.
Phi Delta Kappan, 76(9), 701–712.

Epstein, J.L., & Becker, H.J. (1982). Teacher practices of parent involvement. *The Elementary
School Journal, 83,* 103–113.

Estrada, P., Arsenio, W.F., Hess, R.D., & Holloway, S. (1987). Affective quality of the
mother–child relationship: Longitudinal consequences for children's school-relevant,
cognitive-functioning. *Developmental Psychology, 23,* 210–215.

Fehrmann, P.G., Keith, T.Z., & Reimers, T.M. (1987). Home influences on school learning:
Direct and indirect effects of parent involvement on high school grades. *Journal of Educational Research, 80,* 330–337.

Fuchs, L., & Fuchs, D. (1986). Effects of systematic formative evaluation in student achievement: A meta-analysis. *Exceptional Children, 51,* 199–208.

Fuchs, L.S., Fuchs, D., & Deno, S.L. (1985). Importance of goal ambitiousness and goal mastery to student achievement. *Exceptional Children, 52,* 63–71.

Gettinger, M. (1984). Measuring time needed for learning to predict learning outcomes. *Exceptional Children, 53*(1), 17–31.

Graue, M.E., Weinstein, T., & Walberg, H.J. (1983). School-based home instruction and
learning: A quantitative synthesis. *Journal of Educational Research, 76*(6), 351–360.

Greenwood, C.R. (1991). Longitudinal analysis of time, engagement, and achievement in
at-risk and non at-risk students. *Exceptional Children, 57,* 521–535.

Greenwood, C.R., Delquadri, J., & Hall, R.V. (1984). Opportunity to respond and student
academic performance. In W.L. Heward, T.E. Heron, J. Trap-Porter, & D.S. Hill (Eds.),
Focus on behavior analysis in education (pp. 58–88). Upper Saddle River, NJ: Merrill.

Grolnick, W.S., Benjet, C., Kurowski, C.O., & Apostoleris, N.H. (1997). Predictors of parent involvement in children's schooling. *Journal of Educational Psychology, 89*(3), 538–548.

Hansen, D.A. (1986). Family–school articulations: The effects of interaction rule mismatch. *American Educational Research Journal, 23*(4), 643–659.

Harry, B. (1992). *Cultural diversity, families, and the special education system: Communication and empowerment.* New York: Teachers College Press.

Harry, B., Allen, N., & McLaughlin, M. (1995). Communication versus compliance: African American parents' involvement in special education. *Exceptional Children, 61*(4), 364–377.

Hart, B., & Risley, T.R. (1995). *Meaningful differences in the everyday experience of young American children.* Baltimore: Paul H. Brookes Publishing Co.

Heller, L.R., & Fantuzzo, J.W. (1993). Reciprocal peer tutoring and parent partnership: Does parent involvement make a difference? *School Psychology Review, 22*(3), 517–534.

Henderson, A.T., & Berla, N. (Eds.). (1994). *A new generation of evidence: The family is critical to student achievement.* Washington, DC: National Committee for Citizens in Education.

Henderson, A.T., Marburger, C.L., & Ooms, T. (1988). *Beyond the bake sale: An educator's guide to working with parents.* Columbia, MD: National Committee for Citizens in Education.

Hess, R.D., & Holloway, S.D. (1984). Family and schools as educational institutions. In R.D. Parke, R.M. Emde, H.P. McAdoo, & G.P. Sackett (Eds.), *Review of child development research: Volume 7. The family* (pp. 179–222). Chicago: University of Chicago Press.

Hess, R.D., Holloway, S.D., Price, G.G., & Dickson, W.P. (1982). Family environments and acquisition of reading skills: Toward a more precise analysis. In L.M. Laosa & I. Siegel (Eds.), *Families as learning environments for children* (pp. 87–113). New York: Plenum Publishing Corp.

Hodgkinson, H. (1991). Reform versus reality. *Phi Delta Kappan, 73,* 9–16.

Hoover-Dempsey, K.V., Bassler, O.C., & Brissie, J.S. (1987). Parent involvement: Contributions of teacher efficacy, school socioeconomic status, and other school characteristics. *American Education Research Journal, 24*(3), 417–435.

Hurley, C.M. (1996). *The effects of parental welcome status on desired family involvement activities.* Unpublished master's thesis, University of Minnesota, Minneapolis.

Johnson, D.W., Maruyama, G., Johnson, R., Nelson, D., & Skon, L. (1981). The effects of cooperative, competitive, and individualistic goal structures on achievement: A meta-analysis. *Psychological Bulletin, 89,* 47–62.

Kagan, D.M. (1992). Implications of research on teacher beliefs. *Educational Psychologist, 27*(1), 65–90.

Kagan, S.L. (1984). *Parent involvement research: A field in search of itself.* Boston: Institute for Responsive Education.

Kagan, S.L., & Schraft, C.M. (1982). *When parents and schools come together: Differential outcomes of parent involvement in urban schools.* Boston: Institute for Responsive Education. (ERIC Document Reproduction Service No. ED 281-951)

Kalyanpur, M., & Rao, S.S. (1991). Empowering low income Black families of handicapped children. *American Journal of Orthopsychiatry, 61*(4), 523–532.

Keith, T.Z., Reimers, T., Fehrmann, P.G., Pottebaum, S.M., & Aubrey, L.W. (1986). Parental involvement, homework, and TV time: Direct and indirect effects on high school involvement. *Journal of Educational Psychology, 78,* 373–380.

Kellaghan, T., Sloane, K., Alvarez, B., & Bloom, B.S. (1993). *The home environment and school learning: Promoting parental involvement in the education of children.* San Francisco: Jossey-Bass.

Lazar, L., & Darlington, R.B. (1978). *Summary: Lasting effects after preschool.* Ithaca, NY: Cornell University Consortium for Longitudinal Studies. (ERIC Document Reproduction Service No. ED 175-523)

Leitch, M.L., & Tangri, S.S. (1988). Barriers to home–school collaboration. *Educational Horizons, 66,* 70–71.

Levin, H. (1987). Accelerated school for disadvantaged students. *Educational Leadership, 44*(6), 19–21.

Lindle, J.C. (1989). What do parents want from principals and teachers? *Educational Leadership, 47*(2), 8–10.

Liontos, L.B. (1992). *At-risk families and schools: Becoming partners.* Eugene, OR: University of Oregon, College of Education, ERIC Clearinghouse on Educational Management.

Maccoby, E.E., & Martin, J.A. (1984). Socialization in the context of the family: Parent–child interaction. In P.H. Mussen (Ed.), *Handbook of child psychology: Socialization, personality, and social development* (Vol. 5). New York: John Wiley & Sons.

Marjoribanks, K. (1979). Family environments. In H.J. Walberg (Ed.), *Educational environments and effects* (pp. 15–37). Berkeley, CA: McCutchan Publishing Corp.

Marjoribanks, K. (1988). Perceptions of family environments, educational and occupational outcomes: Social-status differences. *Perceptual and Motor Skills, 66,* 3–9.

Marliave, R., & Filby, N.N. (1985). Success rate: A measurement of task appropriateness. In C.W. Fisher & D.C. Berliner (Eds.), *Perspectives on instructional time* (pp. 217–235). New York: Addison Wesley Longman.

McAfee, O. (1993). Communication: The key to effective partnerships. In R.C. Burns (Ed.), *Parent and schools: From visitors to partners* (pp. 21–34). Washington, DC: National Education Association.

Milne, A.M. (1989). Family structure and the achievement of children. In W.J. Weston (Ed.), *Education and the American family* (pp. 32–65). New York: New York University Press.

Mitrsomwang, S., & Hawley, W. (1993). *Cultural adaptation and the effects of family values and behavior on the academic achievement and persistence of Indochinese students.* Final report (#R117E00045) to Office of Educational Research and Improvement, U.S. Department of Education, Washington, DC.

Moles, O.C. (1993). *Building home–school partnerships for learning: Workshops for urban educators.* Washington, DC: U.S. Department of Education, Office of Educational Research and Improvement.

National Association of State Boards of Education. (1992). *Parent involvement in education.* (Technical Report No. NCES 92-042). Washington, DC: U.S. Government Printing Office.

National Education Goals Panel. (1998). *The National Education Goals report: Building a nation of teachers, 1998.* Washington, DC: Author.

Olson, L. (1990, April). Parents as partners: Redefining the social contract between parents and schools [Special issue]. *Education Week, 9*(28), 17–24.

Ooms, T., & Hara, S. (1991). *The family–school partnership: A critical component of school reform.* Washington, DC: The Family Impact Seminar.

Peng, S.S., & Lee, R.M. (1992, April). *Home variables, parent-child activities, and academic achievement: A study of 1988 eighth graders.* Paper presented at the annual meeting of the American Educational Research Association, San Francisco.

Peterson, J.L., & Cooper, C.S. (1989). Parent education and involvement in early intervention programs for handicapped children: A different perspective on parent needs and the parent-professional relationship. In M.J. Fine (Ed.), *The second handbook on parent education: Contemporary perspectives* (pp. 197–236). San Diego, CA: Academic Press.

Phelan, P., Yu, H.C., & Davidson, A.L. (1994). Navigating the psychosocial pressures of adolescence: The voices and experiences of high school youth. *American Educational Research Journal, 31*(2), 415–447.

Pianta, R., & Walsh, D.B. (1996). *High-risk children in schools: Constructing sustaining relationships.* New York: Routledge.

Ramey, C.T., & Campbell, F.A. (1984). Preventive education for high-risk children: Cognitive sequences of the Carolina Abecedarian Project. *American Journal of Mental Deficiency, 88*(55), 515–523.

Rich, D. (1987). *Teachers and parents: An adult-to-adult approach.* Washington, DC: National Education Association.

Rosenshine, B.V., & Stevens, R. (1986). Teaching functions. In M.C. Wittrock (Ed.), *Handbook of research on teaching* (3rd ed., pp. 376–391). Indianapolis, IN: Macmillan Publishing USA.

Rumberger, R.W. (1995). Dropping out of middle school: A multilevel analysis of students and schools. *American Educational Research Journal, 32*(3), 583–625.

Rutherford, B. (Ed.). (1995). *Creating family–school partnerships.* Columbus, OH: National Middle School Association.

Sattes, B. (1985). *Parent involvement: A review of the literature.* (Report No. 21). Charleston, WV: Appalachia Educational Laboratory.

Schorr, L.B. (1989). *Within our reach: Breaking the cycle of disadvantage.* New York: Doubleday.

Scott, W.A., Scott, R., & McCabe, M. (1991). Family relationships and children's personality: A cross-cultural, cross-source comparison. *British Journal of Social Psychology, 30,* 1–20.

Scott-Jones, D. (1988). Families as educators. *Educational Horizons, 6*, 66–69.

Seeley, D.S. (1985). *Education through partnership*. Washington, DC: American Enterprise Institute for Public Policy Research.

Sheridan, S.M., Kratochwill, T.R., & Bergan, J.R. (1996). *Conjoint behavioral consultation: A procedural manual*. New York: Plenum Publishing Corp.

Sloane, K.D. (1991). Home support for successful learning. In S.B. Silvern (Ed.), *Advances in reading/language research: Vol. 5. Literacy through family, community, and school interaction* (pp. 153–172). Greenwich, CT: JAI Press.

Smith, E.P., Connell, C.M., Wright, G., Sizer, M., & Norman, J.M. (1997). An ecological model of home, school, and community partnerships: Implications for research and practice. *Journal of Educational and Psychological Consultation, 8*(4), 339–360.

Steinberg, L., Elmen, J.D., & Mounts, N.S. (1989). Authoritative parenting, psychosocial maturity, and academic success among adolescents. *Child Development, 60*, 1424–1436.

Steinberg, L., Mounts, N.S., Lamborn, S.D., & Dornbusch, S.M. (1991). Authoritative parenting and adolescent adjustment across varied ecological niches. *Journal of Research on Adolescence, 1*(1), 19–36.

Stevenson, D., & Baker, D. (1987). The family–school relation and the child's school performance. *Child Development, 58*, 1348–1357.

Stevenson, D., & Lee, S. (1990). Contexts of achievement: A study of American, Chinese, and Japanese children. *Monographs of the Society for Research in Child Development, 55*, 1–106.

Swap, S.M. (1993). *Developing home–school partnerships: From concepts to practice*. New York: Teachers College Press.

U.S. Department of Education. (1994). *Strong families, strong schools: Building community partnerships for learning*. Washington, DC: U.S. Government Printing Office.

Vosler-Hunter, R.W. (1989). Families and professionals working together: Issues and opportunities. *Focal Point, 4*(1), 1–4.

Walberg, H.J. (1984). Families as partners in educational productivity. *Phi Delta Kappan, 65*, 397–400.

Walberg, H.J., Paschal, R.A., & Weinstein, T. (1985). Homework's powerful effects on learning. *Educational Leadership, 42*(7), 76–79.

Waxman, H.C., Wang, M.C., Anderson, K.A., & Walberg, H.J. (1985). Synthesis of research on the effects of adaptive instruction. *Educational Leadership, 43*, 26–29.

Weinstein, C.E., & Mayer, R.E. (1986). The teaching of learning strategies. In M.C. Wittrock (Ed.), *Handbook of research on teaching* (3rd ed., pp. 315–327). Indianapolis, IN: Macmillan Publishing USA.

Weiss, H.M., & Edwards, M.E. (1992). The family–school collaboration project: Systemic interventions for school improvement. In S.L. Christenson & J.C. Conoley (Eds.), *Home–school collaboration: Enhancing children's academic and social competence* (pp. 215–243). Silver Spring, MD: National Association of School Psychologists.

Whelage, H.J., & Rutter, R.A. (1986). Dropping out: How much do schools contribute to the problem? *Teachers College Record, 87*, 374–392.

White, K.R. (1982). The relationship between socioeconomic status and academic achievement. *Psychological Bulletin, 91*, 461–481.

Zill, N., & Nord, C.W. (1994). *Running in place*. Washington, DC: Child Trends.

Chapter 7

Changing Schools for Changing Families

Gary B. Melton
Susan P. Limber
Terri L. Teague

THE CHANGING CONTEXT

In the last generation of the 20th century, extraordinary changes in family structure took place in the United States. Between 1960 and 1989, the fertility rate declined by one half, the rate of births outside marriage quadrupled, the number of married mothers of children younger than age 6 working outside the home tripled, and the divorce rate quadrupled (Popenoe, 1990, 1993).

At the same time that the number of adults per household has been declining, the demands on parents have been increasing. The time available for family life continues to decrease (Mellman, Lazarus, & Rivlin, 1990), and young mothers experience more stress than any other segment of the population (Mirowsky & Ross, 1989).

Furthermore, young families commonly experience frequent major disruptions in their social support. One in four young children lives in a different home from his or her residence a year ago (Bureau of the Census, 1990). In communities experiencing high mobility (e.g., many communities in the West), this figure is substantially higher. Among families with few economic assets, mobility is even higher still. For example, among apartment residents, the annual turnover rate is 65% (Szymanski, 1996).

Correspondence should be addressed to Susan P. Limber, Ph.D., M.L.S., at the Institute on Family and Neighborhood Life, Clemson University, Poole Agricultural Center, Clemson, SC 29634 (phone: 864-656-6271; fax: 864-656-6281).

This decrease in adult human resources in young families is occurring at the same time that their average material support is diminishing (for reviews, see Garbarino, 1992, & Voyndanoff, 1991). Since the 1960s, poverty has become substantially more sustained and geographically concentrated (see, e.g., Coulton & Pandey, 1992). These trends (i.e., sustained poverty, geographic concentration of poverty) have been particularly pronounced among young families. For the first time in U.S. history, the economic outlook for children is bleaker than any other age group (Moynihan, 1987; National Commission on Children, 1991). Furthermore, the fact that most young families cannot yet afford to own their own homes (Johnson, Sumi, & Weill, 1988), combined with the high geographic mobility already common among families just getting started, may mean that they are even less likely to develop relationships with their neighbors—a specific example of a more general trend.

The Age of Alienation

While many young American families are threatened by economic poverty or near-poverty, social poverty—weak ties among neighbors and kin—has become endemic. In an exceptionally broad and insightful integration of political and social trends, comparative political scientist Robert Putnam (1995) summarized the contemporary American situation as "bowling alone," a situation that he regards as threatening democracy in the United States and perhaps other industrialized countries.

"Bowling alone" is the encapsulation of a sharp decline in Americans' involvement in civic life (Putnam, 1995). Between 1980 and 1993, the total number of bowlers in the United States increased by 10% to 80 million, but league bowling decreased by 40%. Since the 1970s, membership has dropped precipitously in political, religious, fraternal, educational, humanitarian, and civic organizations—virtually every kind of organization that demands social interaction or volunteer service. Whether the venue is the voting booth, the union hall, or the Parent–Teacher Association meeting, many fewer Americans are present than were in attendance a generation ago. As Putnam acerbically noted, "multitudes of Red Cross aides and Boy Scout troop leaders [are] now missing in action" (1995, p. 70).

However, membership has grown rapidly in mass membership organizations, such as the American Association of Retired Persons, the Sierra Club, and the National Rifle Association, which require no more effort from their members than writing a check. Putnam succinctly described the kind of organizations that they are and, by extension, the kind of society that the United States has become:

> Few ever attend meetings of such organizations, and most are unlikely ever (knowingly) to encounter any other member. The bond between any two members of the Sierra Club is less like the bond between any two members of a gardening club and more like the bond between any two Red Sox fans (or perhaps any two devoted Honda owners): they root for the same team and they share some of the same interests, but they are unaware of each other's existence. Their ties, in short, are to common symbols, common leaders, and perhaps common ideals, but not to one another. . . . From the point of view of social connectedness, the Environmental Defense Fund and a bowling league are just not in the same category. (1995, p. 71)

Social capital, "features of social organization such as networks, norms, and social trust that facilitate coordination and cooperation for mutual benefit" (Putnam, 1995, p. 67), is not only highly correlated with the vitality of democratic institutions (Putnam, 1993, 1995), but it also has long been a primary marker of American culture (de Toqueville, 1835/1990). If the contemporary decline in social capital continues at the same rate, however, by 2030, the United States will be at the current midpoint of nations in social capital and within two generations will be at the current level of nations with virtually no democratic tradition (Putnam, 1995).

If the trend is not interrupted, the decline in social capital thus portends a dire future for the integrity of the United States. Although this long-term possibility is troubling enough, the immediate concern is about the direct and rapidly developing catastrophic consequences for child development and family life—effects that may indirectly ensure that the broader long-term social disaster occurs. Consider the following example:

> What is most striking about parents today is how isolated many of them are from other families and from each other, and how hungry they are for new ways of making contact. "Sometimes I feel like the last person on earth," one PTA president told me. Isolation among parents helps create isolated kids—or more specifically, kids isolated from the adult world, more vulnerable to their peers. Why are parents so isolated? Longer commutes; both parents working ever longer hours; the new urban form; the fading of older networks—coffee klatches, churches, neighborhood schools. In the work place, parents seldom discuss parenting because parenting is too often considered a career hindrance. Instead of support from the society, we get advice, a booming how-to-parent industry. "I'm *afraid* of other parents," said one mother. "You never know what kind of weirdos are raising your child's friends." As lonely parents fear their environment and doubt their own competence, *community*—the real preventer of child abuse and other violence—diminishes. (Louv, 1991, p. 6)

This is an age of alienation in which fear, distrust, and isolation are the order of the day. Despite its statistical rarity, child abduction tops the fears of American parents (Whitehead, 1991). Adults, in general, name crime and the well-being of children as the United States' top two problems (Cannon, 1996a, 1996b; Montgomery, 1996). American adults further perceive their leaders as both inept and cynical in dealing with these problems (Slevin, 1996). Perhaps even more disturbing, they doubt whether average citizens care for each other very much anymore (Cannon, 1996b). Today's parents, unlike parents of just a generation ago, report that they look for help for their families primarily from professionals whose time they buy and that adults in their community rarely are involved in the lives of children outside their own families (Melton, 1992). Increasingly, these psychological walls are concretized—literally—in brick walls, as 28 million Americans now live in gated communities or privately guarded apartment complexes (Boaz, 1996; Diamond, 1997); to an alarming degree, contemporary America is replicating the medieval landscape.

When the attitudes and behavior of contemporary young people are considered, the prospect of rapidly declining social capital becomes even more stark.

Compared with all previous classes since the 1960s for which the annual national survey of entering college freshmen has been conducted, the respondents in 1995 and 1996 reported less interest in political affairs, less involvement in student groups, less involvement in discussions with teachers, and more boredom in class (Kelley, 1996; Sax, Astin, Korn, & Mahoney, 1996). Thus, there is ample reason to doubt that the next generation of parents will be tightly interwoven in the social fabric.

Consequences for Children

The potential costs of such alienation and isolation are profound. Only economic poverty (Duncan & Brooks-Gunn, 1997) exceeds social poverty—weak ties among neighbors and kin—as a factor in the prevalence of social ills involving children and families, such as juvenile delinquency (Maccoby, Johnson, & Church, 1958; Sampson, Raudenbush, & Earls, 1997; Simcha-Fagan & Schwartz, 1986; Skogan, 1990) and child maltreatment (Cotterill, 1988; Coulton, Korbin, Su, & Chow, 1995; Drake & Pandey, 1996; Garbarino & Crouter, 1978; Garbarino & Kostelny, 1992, 1994; Garbarino & Sherman, 1980; U.S. Advisory Board on Child Abuse and Neglect, 1993; Vinson, Baldry, & Hargreaves, 1996; Young & Gately, 1988). When economic poverty and social poverty are combined (probably an inevitable outcome of the increasing concentration of economic poverty), the power of each is perniciously magnified (see Panel on High-Risk Youth, 1993).

Increased alienation and isolation are particularly costly for young families experiencing the stress of life transitions, including the transition of children into kindergarten. Although the importance of this period curiously has received little attention by social scientists, educators, and policy makers (see Chapter 2), evidence suggests that this transition is a critical time in the lives of children and their parents. As Zill (Chapter 4) describes, parents of kindergartners are relatively young adults whose work experience and incomes are more limited than those of parents of older children. Indeed, nearly 25% of the families of kindergartners in the class of 1995/1996 had household incomes below the poverty level (see Chapter 4). Moreover, these parents are less experienced at parenting than are parents of somewhat older children, and many are learning to assume new roles as parents within the school system. Parents of kindergartners also struggle to juggle child care arrangements to a greater extent than parents of somewhat older elementary school children. Although many children are enrolled in full-day kindergarten, most attend part-day programs (55%, see Chapter 4) and require alternative forms of care for the remaining hours of the day.

The transition to kindergarten is also a time of particular stress for many children. As Entwisle and Alexander (Chapter 2) note, a child's entry to elementary school is marked by changes in his or her self-concept (from a "home child" to a "school child"). He or she must learn to operate away from the familiarity of his or her home during the school day and develop many new interpersonal relationships among classmates and adults at school. In addition, children entering kindergarten experience stress related to evaluation of their behavior and scholastic performance as well as other factors (including social class and ethnicity) by school staff. The importance of this transition is highlighted by findings that reveal that relatively small differences among children's performance and school adjustment are apparent upon their entry into school, and these differences enlarge during the next several years (see Chapter 2).

In an age of alienation, the general significance for children of strong community–family linkages is clear. Developmentally, children's "wealth" might be measured in social capital as much as the material resources of their families. In that regard, the strength of the connections between the two most central entities in the life of a child—the family and the school—is likely to be a particularly potent factor in the child's well-being, particularly during times of stressful life transitions, such as the entry into formal schooling.

SIGNIFICANCE OF PARENT INVOLVEMENT IN PRIMARY EDUCATION

Although the importance of the family–school linkage for children's well-being alone would justify concerted efforts to strengthen the ties between home and school, such work also serves schools' institutional interests. The educational benefits of the involvement of parents in their children's schools are well documented (see, e.g., Adelman, 1994; Bogenschneider, 1997; Comer & Haynes, 1991; Eccles & Harold, 1993, 1996; Epstein & Dauber, 1991; Hoover-Dempsey & Sandler, 1997; Seeley, 1989; Vickers & Minke, 1995; see also Chapter 6). As a leading researcher on family–school relations has summarized: "Students at all grade levels (including, of course, the primary grades [Epstein & Dauber, 1991]) do better in their academic work and have more positive school attitudes if their parents are aware, knowledgeable, and encouraging about school" (Epstein, 1990, p. 105).

The mechanisms by which such outcomes occur are varied. Perhaps the broadest and most fundamental effect of a strong connection between family and school is that, when parents are intimately aware of the current foci in a child's formal education, they can maximize the use of the home as a venue for generalization of new knowledge (Epstein, 1990). By the same token, family-based experiences serve as a foundation for school achievement. In particular, educators and parents need to understand education in year-round terms. The increasing social class gap in achievement across the school years is largely a function of differential gains during the summer months (Alexander & Entwisle, 1996; see also Chapter 2). More systematic efforts by schools to bridge across time and space—in effect, to prepare parents for their role as teachers in the years prior to kindergarten and in the summer months—might diminish this disparity. Clearly, such efforts must begin before a child enters kindergarten. Poor children exhibit lower scores on achievement tests than do children who are better off financially; after formal schooling begins, this initial disparity increases substantially during the summer months (see Chapter 2). Analogously, the provision to parents of encouragement and information about programs for children with special needs facilitates talented female and ethnic minority children's use of such opportunities (Eccles & Harold, 1996).

Investment in home–school partnerships is striking in its win–win character. Students, teachers, parents, and schools are all better off when parents are involved in the schools. Elaborating this point in her Lightner Witmer Address to the American Psychological Association Division of School Psychology, Christenson summarized the benefits of parent participation:

- Students show improvement in grades, test scores, attitudes, and behavior, complete more homework, are more engaged in classroom learning activities, and have higher attendance rates and a reduction in suspension rates.

- Teachers are recognized by parents for better interpersonal and teaching skills, evaluated higher on teaching performance by principals, and indicate greater satisfaction with their jobs, requesting fewer transfers.

- Parents show a greater understanding of the work of schools, improve their communication with their children in general and about school work in particular, increase their communication with educators, and are more involved in learning activities at home.

- Schools are rated as more effective, and there are more successful school programs. (1995, p. 120)

Epstein and Dauber provided an even more succinct summary of the specific benefits that schools' efforts to elicit parent participation bring:

When teachers make parent involvement part of their regular teaching practice, parents increase their interactions with their children at home, feel more positive about their abilities to help their children in the elementary grades, and rate the teachers as better teachers overall; and students improve their attitudes and achievement. (1991, p. 289)

Nature of Parent Involvement

Parent involvement of all types is especially common in the early grades. Epstein's typology (see, e.g., Becker & Epstein, 1982; Epstein, 1982, 1984, 1986, 1990, 1996; Epstein & Dauber, 1991) is widely cited. Specifically, Epstein distinguished parental involvement manifested in

- The basic obligations of families (e.g., preparing children for school by providing a safe, healthy, and intellectually stimulating home environment)
- The basic obligations of schools (e.g., schools' normative communication with parents, such as report cards and notices of special events)
- Volunteer work in the schools
- Educational work in the home (e.g., monitoring of homework, family visits to museums)
- Participation in school decision making

Epstein's typology—similar to much of the discussion of parent involvement—tends to present the parent–school relationship as a one-way relationship: parents in service of the schools. Commentary (e.g., Christenson, 1995; National Education Goals Panel, 1995) increasingly is framing the desired relationship in terms of a *partnership* or *collaboration*.

Zill (Chapter 4) observes that the level of parent involvement exhibited by parents of kindergartners was slightly lower than for parents of students in elementary school grades. However, he notes that the observed difference may be due to the fact that the survey questions were less applicable to kindergarten activities than for activities in higher elementary grades. Thus, drawing conclusions from these comparisons should be done with caution.

As children move into and through middle and high school, substantially less parent involvement occurs (see, e.g., Eccles & Harold, 1993; Epstein, 1986; Epstein & Dauber, 1991; Vaden-Kiernan, 1996). For example, parents do more monitoring of their children's schoolwork in first grade and second grade than even fifth grade (Eccles & Harold, 1996). Compared with secondary schools, elementary schools have more volunteers in school and more programs to involve parents in children's education at home (Epstein & Dauber, 1991).

The change across school levels in parent involvement occurs even though it is a factor in the academic success of adolescents (Bogenschneider, 1997), just as it is with children in the primary grades. This reduced involvement is probably a reflection in part of developmental changes in family life. Parents may perceive their participation in their adolescent children's secondary schools as unduly intrusive or simply unnecessary.

It is likely, however, that parents' reduced participation in secondary schools also is the product of structure. For example, parents of fifth graders in middle schools are commonly less involved than are parents of fifth graders in elementary schools (Eccles & Harold, 1996). Just as large size and complex bureaucracy have long been known to impede active participation by students in secondary schools (see, e.g., Barker & Gump, 1964; Eccles et al., 1993; Felner & Adan, 1988; Rogeness, Bednar, & Diesenhaus, 1974), such structural features may also result in the alienation of parents in middle schools.

In contrast, parents are likely to feel a sense of connection to their children's elementary schools. Psychologically, schools may be centers of the community even when they make little effort in that capacity. For example,

> Parents who are involved in neighborhood elementary schools may see this involvement as a connection with their community and friends. The home elementary school may seem like an extension of the family, particularly in neighborhoods where the population is relatively stable. Parents and teachers get to know each other well over the years their children are in the school. As children leave their home schools and several elementary schools merge into one middle school, there may be a decrease in the extent to which the families feel connected to the school. Junior high and middle schools expand the physical community but may not expand the emotional sense of community. The sense of belonging and investment may decrease and, as a result, parents may feel less able and less inclined to be involved and/or try to affect change in the educational experiences of their children. Additionally, children typically spend 6 or 7 years in an elementary school and only 2 or 3 in a middle school. The attachments, which often form over the elementary years when parent help seems more essential, have less time to form and may feel less necessary in the middle and upper grades. (Eccles & Harold, 1996, p. 11)

Although school officials seeking parent involvement—and parents seeking to become involved in their children's education—have a relatively easy task in the primary grades, the belief that such involvement is natural or inevitable is mistaken. Just as the movement into the early school grades marks a major transition in the lives of children, it is also a time for parents to settle into new roles in relation to the settings of which their child is a part. To use the jargon, the parental mesosystem—the child-related connections between the parents and other peo-ple—is transformed when children enter school. Thus, the primary grades present a pivotal stage in the evolution of parents' involvement in their children's educa-tion and indeed their children's social world as a whole. Thus there is especially pronounced variation (both individual and contextual differences) in parent in-volvement in the early years of formal schooling.

An illustration of the transitional nature of parent involvement in the primary grades is the fact that monitoring of schoolwork actually increases from kinder-garten to third grade, when parent involvement begins to decline (Eccles & Harold, 1996). Overall parent involvement declines, however, from preschool to elementary school, just as it does from elementary to middle school and middle to high school (Epstein, 1996).

Even in elementary schools, the paradox of parent involvement—a phenom-enon that both research and common sense show to be an almost universally positive event—is just how unnatural it is. As one research team summarized, "parents and educators frequently seem like islands in the lives of children, sur-rounded by competing agendas, often without visible connections to one another" (Norman & Smith, 1997, p. 5).

Barriers to Parent Involvement

A number of factors have been identified that may hamper the development of healthy connections between parents and schools, including differences in teach-ers' and parents' perceptions of parent involvement, logistical difficulties for par-ents, resistance of school staff, and characteristics of parents themselves.

Conflicts in Perception of Role   Efforts to build bridges between the "islands" are hampered by the fact that teachers and parents typically do not even share a common understanding about what parent involvement is (Norman & Smith, 1997). Many educators lament parents' minimal involvement in school-based ac-tivities and their nonresponsiveness to invitations, invitations that both parents and students say seldom come (Eccles & Harold, 1996; Epstein, 1986; Norman & Smith, 1997). At the same time, parents tend to view involvement in their chil-dren's education as something that occurs primarily in the home.

Teachers view parents as apathetic when parents do not make appearances in the school for meetings or volunteer work (Norman & Smith, 1997). Very few par-ents, even in elementary schools, spend much time at the school that their child attends (Epstein, 1990). However, parents perceive themselves as highly involved in the school when they use their scarce time at home to monitor and assist with homework and when they stimulate conversations about their children's day at school (Norman & Smith, 1997). Parents are commonly much more involved with their children's education at home than at school (Eccles & Harold, 1996; Epstein, 1986). From their perspective, schools can build a collaborative relationship by of-fering tools for educational activities at home; opportunities for parents to be in-volved in events in the school building are less important.

Although parents' definitions of school involvement in terms of home-based activities undoubtedly reflect the realities of their time and resources, they are also typically a product of their perspectives. In that respect, the chasm between teach-ers and parents is often widened when their perceptual discrepancies are magni-fied by differences in social class (Epstein & Dauber, 1991). Working-class parents commonly view their educational role as being providers of emotional support and preparation for school. Their involvement consists in significant part, therefore, of "ensuring that children have good manners and getting them to school on time" (Hoover-Dempsey & Sandler, 1997, p. 15). Working-class parents often passively accept the education that is being offered to their children at school, because they believe that education professionals bear the responsibility for their children's progress in school and the expertise needed to effect such development.

Logistical Problems   When parents themselves define the reasons that they are not involved in "visible" forms of participation in their children's education (e.g., parent–teacher organization meetings, field trips), logistical problems top the list. The simple fact is that most parents work outside the home during school hours (Eccles & Harold, 1996; Norman & Smith, 1997). Even when parents do not have to take a leave from their jobs to attend functions or volunteer in the schools, they often report that their involvement is impeded by other practical concerns, such as child care and transportation (Norman & Smith, 1997). Such gaps in resources may seem particularly formidable for single parents who may face extraordinary demands on their time as well as tight budgets (Norman & Smith, 1997).

Although such problems are not trivial, they need not be overwhelming. For example, leaders of the School Development Program (SDP) developed by James Comer (described later in this chapter) argued that when parents' participation is perceived as integral to a program, "even work commitments are not seen as obstacles but rather as logistical problems in need of solving" (Haynes & Ben-Avie, 1996, p. 47). Thus, SDP staff negotiate directly with parent council members' employers to facilitate parents' attendance with minimal hassles and without penalties.

School Resistance   In contrast to the affirmative effort made by SDP staff, the most difficult obstacle to parent involvement is probably staff resistance, whether overt or passive. On average, teachers take remarkably few steps to encourage parent participation or to offer tips to parents about ways to enhance their children's education (Eccles & Harold, 1996; Norman & Smith, 1997), although such solicitations are more common in elementary than in secondary schools (Dornbusch & Glasgow, 1996). When communication does occur, it is often perceived as punitive (Mannan & Blackwell, 1992) or meaningless (Hoover-Dempsey & Sandler, 1997).

In such a context, it should not be surprising that many parents report that they do not feel welcome at their children's school (Norman & Smith, 1997; see also Harry, 1992a, 1992b, on related cultural issues). This is illustrated by research undertaken for the Kettering Foundation as background for the foundation's effort to put the "public" into the public schools. This study showed that people tend to have markedly different reactions to the words *education*, which is viewed warmly and perceived to occur in many settings, and *schools*, which evokes images of unpleasant experiences, stories of incompetent and unresponsive teachers and administrators, and associations with social problems, such as violence and teen pregnancy (Mathews, 1996).

Characteristics of Parents   The conventional wisdom about the low level of parental involvement in many schools is simply that many parents are difficult to reach. Numerous parental characteristics (e.g., educational level, income, marital status, ethnicity) do relate to parental involvement in the schools. However, even more remarkable, perhaps not so remarkable when the evidence about school resistance to meaningful parent involvement is considered, is how weak these correlations are (Eccles & Harold, 1996). Analogously, family process variables (the "curriculum of the home"—e.g., discussion of homework, consistent routines) are more significant factors in children's achievement than are family status variables (Christenson, 1995). Children's school performance is less dependent on who their parents are than what they do. In that regard, class differences in achievement to some measure reflect class differences in parents' ability to manage the "system," the accuracy of their expectations about schools' expectations, and the strength of their belief that they do and should have a say in shaping their children's education (Alexander & Entwisle, 1996; Hoover-Dempsey & Sandler, 1997).

What Schools Must Do

The evidence is clear that most parents, regardless of their social class, want information about the best ways for them to facilitate and enhance their children's education (see, e.g., Norman & Smith, 1997). Schools are in a good position to provide such information.

Indeed, the big message of research on parent involvement in the schools is that the barriers to parents' participation are to a large extent within the control of schools. The school itself has substantially greater influence on parent involvement than do parent characteristics (see, e.g., Epstein & Dauber, 1991):

> The strongest predictors in several studies are the specific school programs and teacher practices being used (or not used) to encourage parent involvement: When parents feel schools are doing things to involve them, they are more involved in their children's education. (Eccles & Harold, 1996, p. 10)

The most important leverage point in increasing parental involvement is teachers' own worldviews (Epstein & Dauber, 1991). The level of parent involvement in schools serving low-income communities varies widely, the key factor being teachers' practices. Furthermore, whether teachers are effective in involving parents appears to be based largely on whether they psychologically "write off" parents as likely not to take a positive and significant role in their children's education. Whether parents demonstrate a sense of efficacy in regard to their role as partners in education is dependent in large part on whether teachers demonstrate a sense of efficacy in regard to their side of the home–school partnership (see Hoover-Dempsey & Sandler, 1997). Teachers who are leaders in use of parent involvement—for example, those who frequently contact parents—rarely make stereotypic judgments about low-income, poorly educated, or single parents. Such teachers also perceive a high level of congruity between their own expectations for their students and parents' expectations for their children. In essence, teachers who engage parents successfully are those who adopt a parental analogue of a "zero-reject" policy for children. Such teachers believe that parents want to be involved in the schools, they regard such involvement as an important element in the school program, and they actively seek parental involvement in multiple and varied ways, including ways that do not require physical presence in the school building.

To look one step further into the problem, teachers' attitudes and practices in regard to parental involvement often mirror those of their supervisors. Teachers are more likely to engage parents when they perceive support by the principal for doing so (Epstein, 1982; Epstein & Dauber, 1991). Thus, ultimately, the major step to a strong home–school partnership is an educational altar call: School administrators must make clear that parental participation is a core element of education.

For example, leaders of the SDP program (the Comer initiative) stated that the most important lessons from their experience are that:

> [A] parent program needs to be part of a comprehensive school change initiative and that the other key players in the school community, such as the central office, the principal, the teachers, and other staff need to be oriented to the program. (Haynes & Ben-Avie, 1996, p. 54)

It is not surprising, therefore, that virtually without exception, model school-based family programs have had strong leadership, with an unequivocal buy-in by the school administration (General Accounting Office, 1993). This buy-in can be demonstrated by a partial surrender of administrative control. Meaningful participation by parents in school governance offers tangible proof that parents are important players on the educational team (Haynes & Ben-Avie, 1996).

In that regard, policy makers would be wise to place their highest priority on building a commitment to parent participation by elementary school principals and the central office administrators to whom they report. Although elementary schools, especially in the primary grades, can claim substantially greater parent involvement than can secondary schools, it is important to remember that the curve for level of parent involvement slopes downward almost from the beginning and that the curve becomes precipitously steeper at transitions between types of schools. Experience in transition of families from elementary to middle school suggests that conscientious efforts to provide bridges from preschool to elementary school (e.g., parent orientation prior to their children's leaving preschool) would result in less decline in parent involvement (Epstein, 1996).

Then administrative attention needs to be placed on sustained maintenance of the relatively high level of parent involvement in their children's education in the primary grades. Just as the schools must never write off parents at the beginning of their children's education, the schools must never accept parents' slipping away—or, more aptly, being excluded—as their children mature.

INNOVATIONS IN SCHOOL-BASED SUPPORT FOR FAMILIES

Trends

As the preceding section illustrates, strong connections between families and schools are an important, perhaps even necessary, ingredient in any program to fulfill schools' core educational mission. However, there are other important goals of school-based support for families. We argue later in this chapter that the trends noted in the introduction demand a transformation in the role of schools in the communities of which they are a part. Less ambitiously, schools provide a convenient, relatively nonstigmatizing venue for delivery of health and social services to children and families.

Since the late 1980s, therefore, there has been a dramatic increase in the number and variety of school-based and school-linked initiatives that have developed across the United States (for illustrative programs, see Levy & Shepardson, 1992, and Wilson, 1993; for a description of their common elements and their policy foundations, see Epstein, 1991). For example, Dryfoos (1994) identified approximately 500 clinics based in school buildings, and numerous others are emerging each year.

Although the desire to address adolescent social and health problems has been the primary motivation for many of these programs (Dryfoos, 1994), efforts have often begun instead in the elementary schools, with a particular focus on the primary grades. Just as there is relative ease in building family involvement in primary schools, there also is relative ease in constructing programs to facilitate such involvement. Political problems that sometimes accompany school-based family support and health programs occur much less frequently when the target population is young children than when the intent is to serve adolescents. Besides the fact that developers of programs for primary-grade children and their families need not utter the "C" word ("condoms"), the importance of family connections and related support services may be intuitively clearer for younger children. Just as basic health services (e.g., dental screenings) have historically been a feature of many elementary schools (but seldom of secondary schools), planners anxious to take the path of least resistance commonly adopt primary schools as the first venues for school-based health and social services (General Accounting Office, 1993).

These new efforts have a common thrust—namely, the expansion and collaboration of services to children and families, with the school as the hub. Most also feature at least some effort to reshape the relationships among school, family, and student. Themes commonly include "providing success for all children," "serving the whole child," and "sharing responsibility" with parents, community groups, and health and social services agencies (Davies, 1991, p. 377). Such programs often involve parents at home, in the neighborhood, and in school. The new programs typically include or even target "hard-to-reach" families, but in so doing they emphasize family and community assets rather than personal pathology. Consistent with that perspective, they typically enable families to set at least part of the agenda for services.

Although such themes are common, the heterogeneity of the programs and the initiatives of which they are a part is also striking. School-based and school-linked programs vary widely along several dimensions (Adelman & Taylor, 1997a; Goldman, 1997):

- Purpose (e.g., Is the initiative intended to reform the human services system, the school system, or both, or simply to provide specific programs or services?)

- Location (e.g., Is the initiative located within a school or in a community organization or agency?)

- Scope (e.g., What is the number and variety of programs and services?)

- Ownership (e.g., Is the program owned by the school, the community, or multiple entities? Is there both public and private ownership?)

- Integration (e.g., Are the services unconnected, communicating, cooperating, coordinated, or fully integrated?)

- Population (e.g., Is the program directed at disadvantaged communities? Is the focus on elementary school students, middle school students, or high school students?)

- Empirical foundation (e.g., Has the program been systematically evaluated?)

Unintegrated Services

The answers to these questions most often reveal that the program is on the limited end of all these dimensions. The vast majority of the thousands of school-based or school-linked programs involve simple, one-component partnerships between a school and an outside agency or organization without broader community governance. Such programs often focus on a specific, sometimes small target population, and they provide services that are largely uncoordinated and unintegrated with school activities and other services that the family may receive. For example, a school system may contract with a speech and hearing clinic to provide speech-language therapy and audiological services that are necessary to meet the district's legal obligation to provide "related services" for children with disabilities. Similarly, a mental health center anxious to reduce its no-show rate may "outstation" a clinician at a school to deliver diagnostic and therapeutic services.

Such limited measures usually increase the accessibility of services and sometimes their efficiency. For example, of the elementary schoolchildren in six schools who were randomly assigned to school- or center-based mental health services, 98% of children in schools with on-site mental health programs who were referred for services actually received them (Catron & Weiss, 1994). In contrast, only 17% of children referred to community mental health centers entered treatment. The authors' evaluation studies showed similarly dramatic effects of program location on *parents'* rates of attendance at appointments with mental health professionals. However, simple shifts of service location to the school have little, if any, direct effect on the school program or the service itself. Far too often, school-based mental health services, for example, have the same form and content as those that are delivered at a traditional mental health clinic.

In other instances, discrete school-specific services are delivered because of the educational necessity of addressing particular problems. Thus, a psychologist might be asked to design a behavior modification plan to reduce a distractible child's off-task behavior, or a physical therapist may suggest particular kinds of motor activities to be incorporated into the physical education class of a child with mild cerebral palsy. This clinical approach obviously does not typically involve significant change in the classroom, the school as a whole, or the community, and it usually does not even involve family members other than the affected child.

Nonetheless, this genre of services potentially could serve as a repertoire for integration into broader family support services. The range of alternatives is huge. For example, the *Handbook of School-Based Interventions* (Cohen & Fish, 1993) provides digests of approximately 200 articles on specific behavioral therapies in the schools, with brief abstracts of scores more. The range of problems of primary-grade children addressed by these therapies is quite diverse (e.g., shyness, aggression, impulsivity, inattentiveness, hyperactivity, anxiety, phobias, poor self-esteem, enuresis).

Integrated Service Models

Of course, some initiatives have substantially more ambitious goals. Perhaps the most significant is a set of initiatives developed at Yale: psychiatrist James Comer's SDP, psychologist Edward Zigler's Schools of the 21st Century (21C), and the merger of these efforts as CoZi. (See also the Abecedarian Project and the Head Start/Public School Early Childhood Transition Demonstration Project, two model comprehensive programs for at-risk children, described in detail in Chapter 8.)

Comer's School Development Program   Established in more than 550 participating schools since its inception in 1968 (Comer, Haynes, Joyner, & Ben-Avie,
1996), SDP is "designed to rebuild learning communities by connecting the significant adults in children's lives through a collaborative process of systemic reform and school improvement" (Haynes & Comer, 1996, p. 501). Thus, SDP is intended to *transform* a school by building a sense of community within and beyond
its walls—a social climate and a social network that are regarded as fundamental
to children's healthy cognitive and social development. SDP builds on the theory
that connections among families, schools, and other community institutions form
the fabric that supports children's development (cf. Cochran & Brassard, 1979;
Cochran, Larner, Riley, Gunnarsson, & Henderson, 1990). Accordingly, the pervasive features of SDP are parent involvement, including parent leadership (Comer
& Haynes, 1991), and community linkages.

The developers of SDP perceive parent involvement "as a necessary asset in
school communities":

> Parents bring a wealth of knowledge and understanding about their communities
> and children which helps to strengthen the "personalization" we seek to embed in
> our curriculum, instruction, and assessment activities in school. As we build trust,
> plan well, and empower parents, we create school communities that nourish the
> minds of our children, and warm and shape their hearts to become the citizens
> and adult leaders of tomorrow that our nation and our world need. (Haynes &
> Comer, 1996, p. 502)

At the same time, parents and schools "need other elements of our community to join us in this noble mission":

> Community involvement entails expanding the focus of education beyond the
> walls of the school building to embrace and include groups and organizations in
> the community that are willing and able to support the total development of chil-
> dren. This is a two-way process: community resources are brought into schools,
> and students and staff in SDP schools travel into the community to provide ser-
> vices, to learn, and to receive services. (Haynes, Ben-Avie, Squires, et al., 1996, p. 54)

Within the framework of SDP, the broader community includes those community organizations, institutions, agencies, and businesses in the immediate area
with which students, staff, and parents can interact regularly. Community also is
defined to include more distant entities that may affect teaching, learning, and
assessment processes (e.g., corporations and foundations that contribute to the
school's work).

Conceptualized as a *process* (Comer et al., 1996) rather than a content-based
program, the cornerstones of SDP are three teams at each school. Governance of
the program is vested in the School Planning and Management Team (SPMT),
which includes representative teachers, administrators, parents, and support staff.
With the primary responsibility for creation of a healthy learning community, the
SPMT generates and implements a school-specific plan to build a climate and a
network of relationships consistent with the core theory underlying the SDP pro-

gram. Among other activities, the SPMT is responsible for program planning, public relations, staff development, and periodic needs assessment and program evaluation.

The other two teams focus on the school's core constituencies. The Student and Staff Support Team responds to referrals for services for individual students and their families, and it continuously informs the SPMT about the school climate as experienced by students, teachers, and other staff. The Parent Team develops means of overcoming obstacles to parents' involvement and deepening their sense of connection to the school.

Initial evaluations of SDP suggest that the program has significant effects on school climate, student attendance, student behavior, student participation, and student achievement (Haynes, Emmons, Gebreyesus, & Ben-Avie, 1996). Compared with parents of children in similar schools, parents of children in SDP schools perceive the school climate positively. Interviews in 10 SDP schools of participants drawn from all the principal constituencies—parents, students, teachers, and administrators—showed further that they did believe that the process increased involvement by parents and other community members (Yale Child Study Center, 1997).

Zigler's Schools of the 21st Century   Another widely disseminated model of school-based services developed at Yale is the School of the 21st Century (21C; Zigler, Finn-Stevenson, & Linkins, 1992), a school-based child care and family support initiative "that transforms the school into a community hub of coordinated programs" (Zigler, Finn-Stevenson, & Stern, 1997, p. 396). 21C, which is in operation in more than 400 schools in 13 states, is a primary prevention strategy intended to promote mental health and prevent behavioral and emotional problems in children. The model is based on the recognition that public schools have a critical role to play in alleviating the stressors associated with poverty and the lack of high-quality, affordable child care and can contribute to improving both school readiness and academic success.

21C includes a full-day (6:00 A.M. to 6:00 P.M.), year-round child care program for 3- to 5-year-olds, and before and after-school child care and vacation care for school children as old as age 12. Outreach components of the initiative include home visitation to new parents (beginning in the third trimester); information and referral services for families regarding child care, health care, and other community-based services; health and developmental screening; nutrition education; and training, support, and other services for child care workers within 21C schools. In preliminary evaluations of the program, parents using 21C services reported significantly less stress than did parents in a comparable school district (Finn-Stevenson, Desimont, & Chung, 1997).

CoZi Schools   The CoZi initiative is a collaboration of the School Development Program (founded by Comer) and the 21C program (founded by Zigler). The goal of the CoZi model is not simply to add child care and family support services to the school setting, but rather to change the very nature of a school, broadening its scope to include children from birth though age 5 and their parents.

Providing services to families of children from birth through early adolescence, CoZi schools combine the child care, after-school, and outreach components of the 21C model with the planning and parent involvement mechanisms of SDP schools. Representatives of all adult stakeholders (teachers, parents, outreach workers, child care personnel, and health care services providers) participate on a

SPMT, which sets the mission of the school, coordinates school and community activities, and evaluates the usefulness of programs and services.

CoZi was originally implemented in 1991 in Norfolk, Virginia, at the Bowling Park Elementary School, a predominantly African American school serving a public housing community (see Donnelly, 1997a, for a detailed description of the Bowling Park program). Thus, unlike the early 21C schools that provided child care for predominantly middle-class communities, the CoZi pilot combined child care with classes designed to build job skills. CoZi currently is being implemented and evaluated in three additional elementary schools in Connecticut and Missouri (Finn-Stevenson & Stern, 1996).

Schools of the Future   Another derivative of Comer's and Zigler's work is the Schools of the Future program developed by the Hogg Foundation in four cities in Texas (for descriptions of the evolution and results of the program, see Donnelly, 1997b; Holtzman, 1997; Iscoe, 1996; Iscoe & Keir, 1997; Keir & Millea, 1997). In each city, the foundation provided the school district with $50,000 annually for 5 years to establish a School of the Future at a middle school and one or two of its elementary feeder schools. The foundation also set aside $1,000,000 for technical assistance and evaluation.

The key addition to CoZi in each School of the Future was a full-time project coordinator who worked to promote parent involvement and to stimulate and sustain community linkages. Evaluations of the Schools of the Future have shown that the participants in the projects regard the availability of the project coordinator as having been critical to their successful implementation and maintenance of the program, including elements continued after foundation funding ceased (Iscoe, 1996; Iscoe & Keir, 1997).

Similar observations have been made about other well-known school-based programs (Epstein, 1991; General Accounting Office, 1993). Simply put, the establishment and maintenance of multiple collaborative relationships are time consuming. Agreements must be negotiated, programs must be designed and implemented, and problems must be resolved as they arise. Moreover, the integration of staff from multiple agencies requires a "traffic cop" who ensures that schedules are made and kept, distributes resources, maintains records, and so on. Even more important, it requires a creative and trusted leader, who can help to establish a vision for the program and to resolve the political, legal, bureaucratic, and financial problems of service integration.

The range of programs offered in each School of the Future has been shaped to fit the needs identified in community assessments. However, the list is typically diverse, with the following categories ordinarily covered: mental health, physical health, early childhood, parent involvement, prevention (e.g., intended to reduce drug abuse, violence, and dropping out), problem solving (e.g., peer mediation, conflict resolution), and recreation (Iscoe & Keir, 1997). Examples of specific programs in Schools of the Future include a support group for Spanish-speaking parents, a family support program for African American families, legal aid, health and social services for preschoolers, job training for parents, mental health services, and mentoring.

On Board Early   On Board Early (Swick et al., 1997) is an SDP-like program in Baltimore County, Maryland, that is intended to serve families of children in transition to elementary school—specifically, those in prekindergarten and kindergarten. Similar to SDP and CoZi, On Board Early has a central focus on parent involvement. Parents are included in programmatic decision making (e.g., budget allocations), and teachers maintain regular communication with parents through frequent conferences and daily or weekly two-way logs. In addition, some staff members' work is dedicated exclusively to facilitation of family involvement; they make regular home visits. In the various means of communication by teachers and home visitors, they offer specific home learning activities and strategies. There also are formal classes on parenting. Furthermore, parents serve as volunteers in the school.

Primary Mental Health Project   Perhaps the oldest and most extensively studied large-scale school-based human services program for primary-grade children is the Primary Mental Health Project (PMHP) at the University of Rochester, Rochester, New York. The research on PMHP has filled two books (Cowen et al., 1996; Cowen et al., 1975). Begun in the 1950s, PMHP is found in more than 700 school districts around the world. It is the subject of statewide initiatives in four states, in most instances with a statutory foundation.

PMHP is more child focused than the newer broad-based programs such as CoZi, which define themselves as family support programs. PMHP is a secondary prevention program with four core elements: a focus on children in the primary grades; an emphasis on early detection of behavior problems (red-tagging of children identified by primary-grade teachers and peers as having adjustment problems); use of nonprofessionals (child associates), typically former housewives, as service providers; and modification of the role of mental health professionals in the schools ("quarterbacking," that is, training and supervising the child associates and consulting with other school staff as part of a team). Child associates build a continuing relationship, often based in the playroom, with children red-tagged through teachers' behavior ratings and other means.

Relative to children who were red-tagged who were untreated or assisted by college volunteers, children helped by the child associates improved in social skills, interpersonal relationships, self-esteem, and academic performance. Perhaps because of the influence of the team process, PMHP has also changed school climates.

A BROADER VISION

Building a Community

Dryfoos described her widely cited treatise on school-based services as having a focus on "the transition from school-based clinics to full-service schools" (1994, p. xvii). Our perspective is still broader, envisioning the transformation of schools, both as communities in themselves and as centers of the broader community. With their goal of fostering learning communities, CoZi and related initiatives come closer, but they also are constrained by relatively narrow, yet ambitious, objectives (e.g., increasing access to quality child care).

The grand vision of this chapter's authors is based on two premises, one empirical and the other normative. Empirically, as noted in the introduction to this chapter, there is a profound need to build social capital if children are to have healthy communities in which to grow. Normatively, the goal is to build a community in which children are taken seriously as people—in which the relationships that are most important to them are protected, their participation is valued, their personal and cultural identities are respected, and the requisites for "development of [their] personality, talents, and mental and physical abilities to their fullest potential" and for "responsible life in a free society" (United Nations Convention on the Rights of the Child, 1989, art. 29, §§ 1[a] & 1[d]) are provided.

At the Institute for Families in Society (IFS) at the University of South Carolina (USC), these premises were integrated into a slogan that guides the work of providing services to families: *Families should be able to get help where they are, when they need it, and in a form that they can use with ease and without stigma.* Concretely and succinctly, this maxim can be reduced to five words: *People shouldn't have to ask.*

This overarching principle to guide program and policy development has two corollaries. First, help should be built into natural settings in the community. From such a perspective, location of services in the schools is not enough. Rather, schools and other community institutions should be transformed so that people notice when others are having problems and respond accordingly. Thus, a service system in which families need not define themselves as clients or patients to obtain help is the goal.

To the extent that formal services are necessary to meet families' needs, those services should be designed so that they are not only located in natural settings in the community but that they also seem "natural" in those settings. School-based services should look as though they belong in schools.

Furthermore, efforts in developing programs should be focused on the constellation of programs that look as though they belong in neighborhoods, including neighborhood institutions, such as elementary schools. In an age of alienation, efforts need to be concentrated on the development and sustenance of primary services (Wynn, Costello, Halpern, & Richman, 1994)—the set of organized associations (e.g., children's clubs and scout troops, hobby clubs, mutual assistance groups [see Simoni & Adelman, 1993], service organizations, religious organizations, neighborhood associations) that provide the structure for the social fabric. These basic services should be designed in ways so that they are flexible enough to incorporate and respond even to those families that are "hard to reach" or have multiple and severe needs.

The second corollary to some degree subsumes the first: Fundamental community institutions (including, but not limited to, the schools) should be humane environments for both children and families. Children, no less than other people, are entitled to dignity (see United Nations Convention on the Rights of the Child, 1989). Children (and their parents and other family members) should believe that they have a say in the programs of which they are a part, and they should be treated with politeness and respect. A large body of research has shown that perceived control and "ethical propriety" (politeness) are the key ingredients in perceived justice (Lind & Tyler, 1988).

This idea subsumes the first corollary, because everyone wants the people with whom they work, study, and play to notice and respond accordingly when they and the people closest to them are facing difficult challenges or, in contrast, experiencing personal triumphs. In effect, community institutions should be designed so that they "demand" attentive and caring responses—making it easy to follow the Golden Rule.

The term *demand* is being applied to the social environment in the way that environmental psychologists use the word to describe behavior elicited by the physical environment. Thus, for example, an attractive play area surrounded by homes with front porches "demands" watchful behavior by parents and neighbors.

Similarly, a small "underpopulated" school demands involvement by students in diverse activities (Barker & Gump, 1964). Otherwise, roles in the school play and positions on the track team will go unfilled, and instruments in the band will go unplayed. It is worthwhile to consider other features of the school environment that can be altered to demand the development of social capital. For example, some aspects of the Nordic model of education, which emphasizes group constancy and cooperation, may facilitate a sense of social stability and dependability (see Ogden & Backe-Hansen, 1997).

Designing community institutions so that they demand attentive and caring responses enhances children's achievement, promotes their mental health, and increases their investment in school (see, e.g., Tremper & Kelly, 1987). Hence, this approach should be followed because it is closely connected to schools' institutional mission. More important, however, it should be pursued because it is the right thing to do.

Personal attention has particular significance at times of developmental transition. In moving to new settings and confronting new tasks, everyone wants to reduce the anxiety that comes from the ambiguity associated with the unfamiliar (see Dibner, 1954) and to learn ways of adapting. In many neighborhoods, young families are extremely mobile. For example, Catron and Weiss (1994) found that one in five children receiving mental health services in one of six Nashville schools moved to another school outside the study project within its first year (presumably, the first academic year). To ease their transition to new communities, a "welcome wagon" for children and families who have recently moved into the attendance area—or simply who have entered kindergarten—ought to be a feature of every elementary school (see, e.g., Adelman, 1997; Cárdenas, Taylor, & Adelman, 1993; Epstein, 1990; see also Felner & Adan, 1988, showing the effectiveness of preparation for the transition from elementary to middle school and of having an assigned older "buddy" in promoting school adaptation and preventing dropout).

The importance of systematic attention to such transitions is amplified by the instability in the staff of many schools in distressed neighborhoods. For example, the Schools of the Future in Texas were hampered by high staff turnover (Iscoe, 1996). One school had a 50% turnover rate for teachers. Only 2 of the 10 schools in the project had no change in principal during a 5-year period. Mirroring the staff instability, one elementary school experienced 30% annual turnover among its pupils.

Preventing Violence

The significance of reforming schools' norms and organization to increase responsiveness to pupils and their families can be demonstrated by examination of school violence, a problem that has received enormous public and professional attention in recent years. However, this attention has often not been thoughtful (Conoley, Hindmand, Jacobs, & Gagnon, 1997).

Although school violence is typically viewed as a problem of secondary schools, Conoley et al. (1997) persuasively described a context for school violence that places equal emphasis on elementary schools and even preschools. In noting 10 common errors in schools' violence prevention plans, Conoley et al. (1997) asserted that schools frequently assume a reactive posture ("Let's wait until there's trouble") in regard to school violence, undermining any chance of early intervention. Specifically, noting the early origin and persistent course of aggressive behavior, Conoley et al. argued that "early intervention with parents prior to children coming to kindergarten may be the best strategy schools have to promote the safety and health of students" (1997, p. 8).

> When teachers and administrators wait until a child in early grades misbehaves before contacting parents and then assume that parents have the skills to respond effectively, they are often disappointed. Preschool interventions that focus on skill building for parents are critically important. Aversive patterns among children (e.g., bullying, victimization, etc.) are quite stable over time and so the "stitch in time" must be offered before such interactions become the basis for negative interactions throughout a child's school career. (Conoley et al., 1997, p. 8)

Consistent with the overall perspective being presented in this chapter, Conoley et al. noted that not only must action take place prior to children's entry into kindergarten to be maximally effective in preventing school violence, but that it also must be broad based. Schools need to involve parents and the community as a whole in their violence prevention efforts. Furthermore, the focus must not be simply on changing the child; rather, the culture of the school must be reshaped so that children feel safe:

> Schools cannot keep violence out by constructing higher walls or using sophisticated monitoring/alarm systems. They must build relationships among community members that promote peaceful interactions, mutual respect, and investment in the good of the community. (Conoley et al., 1997, p. 10)

Illustrative Projects in the Institute for Families in Society

Transforming the School Environment   The level of transformation that is sought—to a large extent, the establishment of the network of positive relationships that Conoley et al. (1997) argued should be a major objective for schools—is an ambitious (some might say grandiose) goal. Its accomplishment will not come easily or quickly, particularly given that society seeks such a result for schools in general, not just a demonstration school here and there. Faculty at the Institute for Families in Society are attempting to apply their general injunction that "people shouldn't have to ask" in a number of different ways in elementary schools (Limber & Motes, 1996; Melton, 1996).

The School-Based Mental Health Project   IFS has worked with several state agencies and local school districts to establish school-based mental health services in more than 20 schools in largely rural, underserved communities in South Carolina (Motes, 1997). Although this initiative has focused primarily on middle schools, it is applicable in concept to schools at all levels, and several community mental health centers (CMHCs) have extended their programs to include elementary schools. Indeed, such a program may be particularly appropriate for supporting families whose children are making the transition into formal education. Recognized by the federally supported Center for School Mental Health Assistance at the University of Maryland at Baltimore as a "program that works," the School-Based Mental Health Project relies on teams of CMHC clinicians and graduate assistants drawn from several colleges at USC.

IFS also provides training and technical assistance to other school-based mental health service providers in South Carolina. Approximately 100 clinicians employed by the state Department of Mental Health (DMH) are school-based for at least part of their work; they now provide services in more than 150 schools across the state (South Carolina Department of Mental Health, 1997).

Whether in the IFS-administered project or the other school-based mental health programs, the challenge faced by our faculty has been to ensure that such services match the school setting (that clinicians do not rely largely or even exclusively on traditional 30- or 50-minute sessions of psychotherapy). Rather, clinicians are encouraged to move into the "quarterback" role applied by Cowen and his colleagues (1996) in the Primary Mental Health Project and thus to use school staff or resources in the community whenever possible to serve as the support people for children having problems. Clinicians are also urged to apply primary and secondary prevention programs that fit well with the school culture (e.g., social skills training, school transition programs, programs to facilitate parent involvement).

Even in the delivery of therapeutic services, clinicians are encouraged to shape their work to fit the opportunities and constraints in the school environment. For example, clinicians might see students in small blocks of time on a daily basis to facilitate the children's *in vivo* practice of key social or behavioral skills or to offer support at times of personal or family crisis. Similarly, clinicians might check periodically with teachers to monitor how a particular child is doing and to make prompt changes in treatment and consultation plans accordingly.

To enable such flexible practice and to provide incentives for preventive work, IFS worked with the Department of Mental Health and the state Department of Health and Human Services (the state Medicaid authority) to develop a new Medicaid standard for school-based mental health services. A bundled service, the new service code enables CMHCs to receive a daily fee if any of a range of services is delivered to a child or those working with him or her (e.g., teachers) on a given day.

Well Baby Plus   IFS also has collaborated with state and community agencies to establish several school-based projects that are designed to facilitate family and community connections—in effect, to build not only more humane schools but also stronger families and communities. For example, Well Baby Plus (Rushton, 1998) is a collaborative program established by health and education professionals in Beaufort, South Carolina. Initially, the program used no new resources; rather, it was a common-sense solution to the problem of how to serve young families (primarily families headed by single mothers) with multiple needs. Well Baby Plus now has support from the Duke Endowment to permit its expansion and replication.

Based in an elementary school, Well Baby Plus strives to enroll all the families of newborns in the school attendance area and to follow them until they make the transition to kindergarten. The linchpin of the program is group well child care. Each family visits the program at the ordinary ages for well child visits, including immunizations. They come, however, to the school for a 90-minute group visit rather than to the doctor's office for the typical 5- or 10-minute examination and immunizations.

The groups, which include parents and often grandparents of children of the same age as well, of course, as the children themselves, offer opportunities for anticipatory guidance, modeling, and mutual assistance (e.g., babysitting exchanges). Furthermore, the families have the same health- and school-based home visitors, and the group visits also provide opportunities for linkages with family literacy, adult education, and child care programs that are also based in the school. Thus, the service embodies a normalized, universal approach that enables integration of health, educational, and social services; that permits prompt "natural" preventive and therapeutic responses; and that facilitates connections between families and both formal and informal resources in the community, including other parents and grandparents.

The Golden Strip Human Resource Center   Located in a rapidly growing suburban and small town area south of Greenville, South Carolina, the Golden Strip Human Resource Center is the product of several years of planning by a group affiliated with the local United Way. Rather than spend a huge sum to build a new family resource center, the group developed an agreement with the school district for the rent-free lease of an abandoned elementary school campus adjacent to the new elementary school. Integrating the resources in the community, volunteers fully renovated the campus buildings, and volunteers now play important roles in the management and programs of the center.

In some respects, the Golden Strip Center is an "ordinary" multiservice center in which approximately a dozen agencies have co-located. It is "extraordinary," however, in a number of respects:

- The level of investment of volunteer labor, combined with monetary gifts by local governments and community organizations and donation of staff time by community agencies, is exceptional. Accordingly, the level of new funds that have been required to organize the center is amazingly low.

- The range of services offered is unusually broad: counseling, education and training, health, employment, housing, emergency relief, family support, and information and referral.

- Relying on an IFS community development specialist to direct the center, the cooperating agencies have made important steps toward a unitary program that integrates their resources.

- The center is the home for a kindergarten program for 200 4-year-olds. Building on the resources provided by the school district's own teachers (who do regular home visits) and family literacy staff, the center has made a commitment to make a special effort each year to connect with the families of children in the kindergarten program. The plan is to follow each cohort across the school years, with the primary planning objective each year to be maintenance of family involvement.

The Lancaster Family Resource Network   A "virtual organization" established by IFS in collaboration with the school district, the various human services agencies (especially the district office of the state health department), and a regional campus of USC, the Lancaster Family Resource Network serves the families in the attendance areas of a middle school and two elementary schools in Lancaster, South Carolina. Lancaster is a town of approximately 9,000 people; its economy is dominated by textile manufacturing.

The establishment of school attendance areas as the boundaries for the program had several purposes. It enabled special attention to high-need neighborhoods in which the schools are located, it provided opportunities for services to a diverse population (not focusing just on communities with the highest need), and it offered possibilities for increased responsiveness to the needs of children and families in the schools themselves. Furthermore, the focus on the schools offered opportunities to address education issues that community groups nearly universally had at the top of their list of priorities and to bring together communities divided by race and class.

Relying almost completely thus far on contributed (integrated) human resources, the Lancaster Family Resource Network has emphasized the development of positive communication among families, the schools, and community leaders (cf. Christenson, 1995). Besides sponsoring periodic community forums to address issues of common concern, the network is undertaking several projects in pursuit of the general goal of community responsiveness to family needs.

In one instance, professionals drawn from community agencies and volunteer paraprofessionals are offering in-home support for the purpose of strengthening family involvement in education. The project is patterned after Jesse Jackson's PUSH for Excellence program, which has been shown to result in long-term gains in both academic skills and achievement motivation (see Rodick & Henggeler, 1980). The "helpers" meet with the family in the home and develop a contract for parental involvement, with progress monitored through weekly telephone and biweekly home contacts.

Building on informal programs that some parents in the community had initiated and incorporating volunteers identified through a school phone-a-thon, the Family Resource Network has established neighborhood homework clubs. The clubs meet in homes, churches, a community center, the library, and other easily accessible and nonstigmatizing community sites.

Easing the transition to school and providing an opportunity to use "experts" (natural helpers) as well as professionals in the community, the network is sponsoring a back-to-school day of workshops for parents and other family members. With child care and transportation provided, community leaders are offering workshops on a variety of topics: parenting skills, family finances, homework monitoring, drug education, rites of passage, grandparents as parents, and neighbors helping neighbors (also the focus for a communitywide public information campaign that the network is organizing). In the same vein, the network is sponsoring school–community forums to facilitate communication among school administrators, teachers, parents, and leaders of community organizations.

The cooperating agencies are establishing family resource teams that integrate contributed time. Building a noncategorical, flexible approach to service delivery, the goal is ultimately to have a resource person for every family in the target area that wants one. This approach should enable responses to families at the times and places that they need help and should provide for early intervention before problems become serious. Opportunities will be available for families to become acquainted "naturally" (e.g., outreach at times of developmental transitions) so that supportive relationships are already established on which families can rely when problems do arise.

THE CHALLENGES IN FULFILLING A BROADER VISION

The Enormity of the Task

The experience in the IFS projects mirrors that in other comprehensive school-based programs designed to promote family–school–community connections—in effect, to build social capital from which families can draw. These examples show that it is possible to go beyond simple co-location models to establish true partnerships intended to build more humane schools and more responsive, family-friendly communities, so that children and families can obtain help without asking.

Furthermore, notwithstanding the occasional brouhaha about provision of health and social services in the schools, it is not difficult to reach at least a superficial consensus about the importance of strong ties between families and schools and even of school-based family support services, especially in the preschool years and the primary grades. Reflecting that consensus, in 1994, the U.S. Congress added a goal on parent participation (Goal 8) to the National Education Goals: *By the year 2000, every school will promote partnerships that will increase parental involvement and participation in promoting the social, emotional, and academic growth of children* (National Education Goals Panel, 1995, p. 13). The National Education Goals Panel concluded,

> A . . . reason for increasing and strengthening family-school-community partnerships is that they are essential to achieving the National Education Goals. Practically speaking, no single group is likely to attain the Goals without the assistance and support of others. For example, it is unrealistic to expect that without the assistance of parents, schools alone can attain the first Goal—that all children will start school ready to learn—since parents are chiefly responsible for their children's health and well-being and their earliest learning experiences prior to school entry. Likewise, it is unrealistic to expect that parents alone can ensure that schools are safe, disciplined environments for learning which are free of drugs and alcohol unless they have the backing and commitment of the school administration and staff. Although it is difficult to envision that the National Education Goals could easily be attained by teachers alone, schools alone, parents alone, or government alone, by working together as partners we can greatly improve our chances of attaining all of the Goals. (1995, pp. 64–65)

Because of the centrality of Goal 8 in the fulfillment of other National Education Goals, that goal was framed broadly to encourage every state to undertake policies and every school district to develop programs to build and enhance partnerships between schools and families. Involvement was perceived as insufficient. Thus, one of the objectives under Goal 8 is that *every school will actively engage parents and families in a partnership which supports the academic work of children at home and shared educational decisionmaking at school* (p. 13).

At the same time, the gap between conventional practice and Goal 8 is enormous. Although there has been substantial expansion of school-based family support services, institutionalization and systematization of these programs are still largely lacking (Kagan & Neville, 1993). Most programs remain at the demonstration level; they are small-scale, their funding is scant and unstable, and few program evaluations have been completed (General Accounting Office, 1993). In addition, most programs address single problems in isolation (Adelman & Taylor, 1998; Dryfoos, 1994).

In the conclusion to her review of full-service schools, Dryfoos (1994) noted the magnitude of the change necessary to make even those programs widely available, although they typically fall short of the level of transformation that is needed. She stated, "Going to scale—opening thousands of new sites—requires more than money. A lot of work has to be done to turn this array of serendipitous programs into a solid field of endeavor" (Dryfoos, 1994, p. 211). Dryfoos lamented, however, that few communities have even begun to understand, much less to complete, the work that needs to be done:

> I have observed in many communities a kind of mystical belief that if everyone talks to everyone else, a collaborative project will emerge; but when the discussion turns to the technical expertise needed to manage complex programs, interest flags. This reflects the "it" problem—many potential community agencies and school systems have not a clue as to what this thing is that they might put together. If the full-service school movement is to grow, much greater access to technical assistance must be developed, with specific training in issues such as accounting, reporting, quality control, personnel management, and outreach. (1994, p. 211)

The Need for Supportive Policies

Although the failure to recognize—much less to take—the steps that must be taken if demonstration programs are to go to scale is common in service system reform efforts (Melton, 1997), there are some particular challenges that must be addressed if school-based service systems are to be built. Perhaps the most fundamental is that supportive policies have yet to be developed. Few states have even established a comprehensive program for parent involvement in the schools: "Insufficient and inappropriate expenditures and allocations of staff characterize many states' efforts, and the programs in most states lack coherence" (Epstein, 1991, p. 349). Even traditional school-based services have been vulnerable during periods of retrenchment to "the basics." For example, only 15% of schools have full-time nurses, a proportion that dramatically declined during the 1980s (Dryfoos, 1994).

At root, the problem is that family support has yet to become identified as a necessary element—perhaps indeed the central element—of any effective effort to reform schools, much less to transform communities. Although there are some notable exceptions (e.g., Goetz, 1993), reform has usually focused narrowly on school management and curriculum—"limited efforts [that] will not accomplish the main goal of restructuring: improvement in academic achievement" (Jehl & Kirst, 1992, p. 98). Making the same point, Adelman and Taylor (1998) lamented that reformers have failed to recognize that schools must transform themselves to address barriers to learning:

> In the naïve belief that a few health and social services will do the trick, [reformers] talk of "integrated health and social services" (usually in terms of linking community services to school sites). There is little talk of restructuring school programs and services designed to support and enable learning, and this neglect continues to marginalize activity that is essential to improving school achievement.
>
> Ultimately, addressing barriers to learning must be approached from a societal perspective and requires fundamental systemic reforms designed to improve efforts to support and enable learning. This calls for developing a comprehensive, integrated continuum of community and school programs. Such a continuum must be multifaceted and woven into three overlapping systems: systems of pre-

vention; systems of early intervention to address problems as soon after onset as feasible; and systems of care for those with chronic and severe problems. All of this encompasses an array of programmatic activity that (a) enhances regular classroom strategies to improve instruction for students with mild-to-moderate behavior and learning problems, (b) assists students and families as they negotiate the many school-related transitions, (c) increases home and community involvement with schools, (d) responds to and prevents crises, and (e) offers additional assistance to students and their families when necessary. It is unfortunate that most school reformers seem unaware that schools must play a major role in developing such programs and systems if all students are to benefit from higher standards and improved instruction.

As educators, Adelman and Taylor (1997a, 1997b, 1998) have been particularly chagrined that school policy makers have not recognized that schools themselves must change. A family support agenda or, for that matter, a student achievement agenda that leaves out guidance counselors and other existing "pupil personnel services" is missing key resources. (The nomenclature itself suggests the need for change.) Moreover, traditional hierarchical, bureaucratic school administration is incompatible with the kind of leadership that is needed to be responsive to families' needs (Finn-Stevenson & Stern, 1996; Gardner, 1992; Jehl & Kirst, 1992; Kagan & Neville, 1993). Indeed, many schools have far to go simply to welcome parents, much less to share power with them. For example, a 1992 poll for the Kettering Foundation showed that only 15% of school administrators and 26% of teachers, in contrast with about 60% of the general public, believed that parents and other citizens should have more say in administrative decisions, such as allocation of funds and choice of curriculum (Mathews, 1996).

Although Adelman and Taylor (1997a, 1997b, 1998) focused on the change that must occur in schools, similar points could be made about health and social services professionals. For example, innovations in services for children and families historically subject to the various public human service systems are based largely on common-sense principles:

- When people have a multiplicity of serious problems, develop a multifaceted service plan.

- To maximize client involvement, go where the clients are, address problems that they find significant in their everyday lives, and do so in a form that minimizes stigma.

- To maximize the service efficacy and efficiency, work on multiple aspects of an individual's problems in the settings in which problems arise. For example, enhance the school's capacity to serve children with serious emotional disturbances, build the child client's competence in adapting to teachers' expectations and forming and maintaining peer relationships, and build the parents' competence in maneuvering through the school system.

- To maximize the long-term efficacy and efficiency of services, design services in a manner that enhances client responsibility, that builds skills in obtaining help at times when it is needed, that develops a stable support system, and that assures a decent standard of living in a stable environment. (Melton, 1997, pp. 352–353)

These principles comport not only with common sense but also with outcome research. For example, the Fort Bragg experiment (e.g., Bickman et al., 1995) stands not for the proposition that its investigators argue—that systems of care do not work. Rather, the experiment illustrates common sense—that traditional out-patient psychotherapy (the service that was provided to the vast majority of the Fort Bragg clients) is ill matched to the needs of children and families with significant problems in the real world (see also Weisz & Weiss, 1993). Nonetheless, in the authors' experience, the usual inclination of mental health professionals when they are out-stationed to a school (still in itself a relatively uncommon event) is to do the same thing that they did at the clinic. They stay in their offices, take referrals, and provide hour or half-hour units of psychotherapy (mostly individual therapy, often without significant family involvement). It is, as they say, hard to teach old dogs new tricks. It is especially hard when their leaders give no sign that they will reinforce staff for creativity in service delivery.

In the health and social services agencies, as much as the schools, there is usually a great need for:

1. Policy makers' commitment to integration of services into the schools

2. Administrative leadership in transforming services to fit the school context and to respond to the needs of children and families

3. Professional creativity in resolving the programmatic and bureaucratic problems that inhibit the growth of meaningful partnerships among the agencies, the schools, and the families that they are supposed to serve

At the top of most administrators' lists in regard to breaking down barriers to meaningful partnerships is the problem of financing.

Financing

In the introduction to the David and Lucille Packard Foundation's monograph on school-linked services (Larson, Gomby, Shiono, Lewit, & Behrman, 1992), the editors argued that each agency involved in such programs should redirect funds to support such efforts and that governance should also be shared across sectors. The Packard staff further lamented that the need for collective redistribution of funds "may seem obvious, but most current efforts at integrating services through schools have relied primarily on new, short-term funding" (Larson et al., 1992, p. 10), with the result that such programs are almost invariably fragile. Describing today's school-linked programs as "minuscule experiments in the massive health, education, and social services systems that have been built up over the last several decades" (Larson et al., 1992, p. 14), the Packard staff concluded that "the financing of school-linked services is the area that most critically needs attention before school-linked services can be broadly implemented" (Larson et al., 1992, p. 13).

Echoing the need for attention to financing, Farrow and Joe contended:

> Focusing on financing . . . guarantees that the toughest issues involved in implementing new patterns of service delivery will be raised. To be successful, comprehensive school-linked service strategies require change. Service agencies must operate differently, professionals must change their day-to-day practices, and dollars must be spent in new ways. Though everyone, at some level, is in favor of better "integration" between schools and other human services, asking How will we pay

for it? puts their commitment to the test. Are agencies willing to redirect funds from existing services to achieve this goal? Are administrators willing to share "their" dollars, giving up exclusive control in the interest of shared authority over a broader resource pool? Assuming that a major goal of school-linked services is to ensure that children succeed in school, are human services providers willing to make that goal theirs, devote money to it, and be judged accordingly? In short, many of the issues that surround the financing of school-linked services are really issues of priorities, authority, and control over resources. (1992, p. 57)

It is agreed that the core issues around financing are not really about that topic, at least insofar as "financing" refers to availability of money. In fact, with some creativity and thoughtfulness and, most important, with a strong administrative commitment, many existing funding streams can be redirected to school-based services and other family–school–community partnerships. Zigler and Finn-Stevenson's (1996) summary of the funding streams used to support Schools of the 21st Century is illustrative (see Table 7.1), although they did argue that states ought to establish grant programs to provide school districts with necessary startup funds (approximately $425,000 per district, over 3 years).

For example, the Health Care Financing Administration (1997) published a technical assistance guide on the use of Medicaid for school-based services. States that are savvy in using Medicaid to draw federal dollars can "save" and then redirect state and local dollars through Medicaid (Farrow & Joe, 1992). Thus, the funds potentially available for school-based services can be multiplied. To that end, the 1997 Amendments to the Individuals with Disabilities Education Act (IDEA; PL 105-17) provide in part that states must develop interagency agreements and reimbursement programs to ensure that noneducational sources such as Medicaid are available to facilitate a free appropriate public education for children with disabilities (see "Special Education," 1997). Traditional sources of funding for educational support services (e.g., Title I) can also be used to enhance home–school–community partnerships (Chavkin, 1993).

The amount of money available for development of school-based family support services thus may be less problematic than administrators' skill or zeal in obtaining it. That point stated, however, problems do remain of incompatibility of existing funding streams with school-based services, especially those that are intended broadly to make the school a more responsive, family-friendly environment (Farrow & Joe, 1992). Existing funding streams often are based on a fee-for-service model that is case focused, crisis oriented, and problem targeted. Such streams tend not to be well matched to flexible, individualized services, and they often offer no support for early intervention, prevention, or health ("wellness") promotion. That they often require case-focused billing is itself ill matched to the school culture, which has a universal entitlement to education as its core strength, at least in the United States.

Furthermore, even if administrators and policy makers are willing to trade ideological purity for dollars, they may be left behind in the rapidly changing health care environment. For example, school-based service providers are rarely included as preferred providers in health maintenance organizations (Brellochs, 1997). Therefore, if policy makers and administrators are serious about school-based family support, they must begin diligently and skillfully to co-opt the ex-

Table 7.1.   Revenue sources used to fund child care and parent outreach components of the
Schools of the 21st Century

Component	Funding source
Before- and after-school child care for school-age children	Sliding-scale fees (paid by parents) AFDC vouchers State grants Foundation grants Drug-Free Schools grant Employer subsidies for child care Family Resource Center grants (in Kentucky and Connecticut)
Preschool child care	Sliding-scale fees (paid by parents) Special education funds AFDC vouchers State grants Head Start Foundation grants Child Care and Development Block Grant Town Council Employer subsidies for child care Title I of Elementary and Secondary Education Act Department of Education funds Family Resource Center grants (in Kentucky and Connecticut)
Parent outreach	State grants Department of Education funds Department of Human Services grants Foundation grants Title I of Elementary and Secondary Education Act Drug-Free Schools grant Child Care and Development Block Grant Family Resource Center grants (in Kentucky and Connecticut)
Family child care provider network	Supported by other components Child Care and Development Block Grant
Information and referral	Partnerships with local child care resource and referral agencies Supported by other components State grants Foundation grants Title I of Elementary and Secondary Education Act State Department of Education funds

From Zigler, E.F., & Finn-Stevenson, M. (1996). Funding child care and public education. *Future of Children*, 6(2), 111; reprinted with permission of the David and Lucille Packard Foundation.

isting funding streams or, perhaps better, to seek redirection of funds on a program (rather than a fee-for-service) basis.

A Concluding Paradox

Probably the most difficult challenge to be faced, however, is the intrinsic difficulty of the task. In essence, the creation of natural helping is being attempted. Moreover, this logical conundrum is trying to be overcome, even in communities where the overarching social and economic trends have been magnified by long-standing decline—in Garbarino and Kostelny's (1994) vivid term, *negative social momentum*. When families are facing threats to their safety and their economic survival, the physical environment is decaying, inspiring leaders are absent, and the most competent or lucky neighbors are leaving, families and those who serve them are apt understandably to be overwhelmed.

Despite the acknowledgment of the paradox inherent in this goal and the practical challenges in meeting it, it cannot be abandoned. If the social capital needed for children's healthy development is to be present, then it means that affirmative efforts must be undertaken to reshape the community institutions that purport to serve children and families. Absent concerted action, the prevailing trends will lead to weaker and weaker ties among people and, therefore, increasingly greater threats to the well-being of children and families. Therefore, schools and other community institutions should be redesigned so that they demand caring responses and that they foster new connections between families and communities.

This premise is especially applicable at times of transition, whether of individuals (e.g., the transition to kindergarten) or communities (e.g., a sudden shift in the economic base). At such times, people are most likely to need skills, guidance, and reassurance in confronting unfamiliar challenges.

The approach being advocated here can be implemented on a large scale. The several broad-based model programs that have been applied in diverse school districts suggest the possibilities.

Perhaps the ultimate reason for this optimism, though, is that care is contagious. When norms are established for mutual assistance, help goes both ways; it becomes self-sustaining (see Reissman & Carroll, 1995). The result will be that children are better prepared to learn. Perhaps even more important, they will feel that they are being taken seriously, and they themselves will be better prepared to watch out for others. *People shouldn't have to ask!*

REFERENCES

Adelman, H. (Ed.). (1997). Easing the impact of student mobility: Welcoming and social support. *Addressing Barriers to Learning, 2*(4), 1–2, 5–9.

Adelman, H.S. (1994). Intervening to enhance home involvement in schooling. *Intervention in School and Clinic, 29,* 276–287.

Adelman, H.S., & Taylor, L. (1997a). Addressing barriers to learning: Beyond school-linked services and full-service schools. *American Journal of Orthopsychiatry, 67,* 408–421.

Adelman, H.S., & Taylor, L. (1997b, September). *Addressing barriers to student learning: Closing gaps in school/community policy and practice.* Los Angeles: University of California, Mental Health in Schools Training and Technical Assistance Center.

Adelman, H.S., & Taylor, L. (1998, January 29). *School reform is failing to address barriers in learning. School Mental Health ENEWS Bulletin* [On-line]. Available: smhp@ucla.edu; also available at http://smhp.psych.ucla.edu

Alexander, K.L., & Entwisle, D.R. (1996). Schools and children at risk. In A. Booth & J.F. Dunn (Eds.), *Family-school links: How do they affect educational outcomes?* (pp. 67–88). Mahwah, NJ: Lawrence Erlbaum Associates.

Barker, R.G., & Gump, P.H. (1964). *Big school, small school.* Stanford, CA: Stanford University Press.

Becker, H.J., & Epstein, J.L. (1982). Parent involvement: A study of teacher practices. *The Elementary School Journal, 83,* 85–102.

Bickman, L., Guthrie, P.R., Foster, E.M., Lambert, E.W., Summerfelt, W.T., Breda, C.S., & Heflinger, C.A. (1995). *Evaluating managed mental health services: The Fort Bragg experiment.* New York: Plenum Publishing Corp.

Boaz, D. (1996, January 7). Gates of wrath: Angry about crime, people have good reason to fence out the world. *Washington Post,* pp. C1–C2.

Bogenschneider, K. (1997). Parental involvement in adolescent schooling: A proximal process with transcontextual validity. *Journal of Marriage and the Family, 59,* 718–733.

Brellochs, C. (1997). Paying for school health services. *Family Futures, 1*(1), 19–22.

Bureau of the Census. (1990). *Statistical abstract of the United States.* Washington, DC: U.S. Government Printing Office.

Cannon, A. (1996a, February 11). Little ones are big concern: Three-quarters of Americans worry about children's issues. *The State,* p. D9.

Cannon, A. (1996b, February 11). Political center still attractive: Survey uncovers tolerance, optimism. *The State,* pp. D1, D8.

Cárdenas, J., Taylor, L., & Adelman, H.S. (1993). Transition support for immigrant students. *Journal of Multicultural Counseling and Development, 21,* 203–210.

Catron, T., & Weiss, B. (1994). The Vanderbilt school-based counseling program: An interagency, primary-care model of mental health services. *Journal of Emotional and Behavioral Disorders, 2,* 247–253.

Chavkin, N.F. (1993). Developing family and community involvement policies: Guidelines for school districts. *Family Resource Coalition Report, 12*(3/4), 25–27.

Christenson, S. L. (1995). Families and schools: What is the role of the school psychologist? *School Psychology Quarterly, 10,* 118–132.

Cochran, M., & Brassard, J.A. (1979). Child development and personal social networks. *Child Development, 50,* 601–616.

Cochran, M., Larner, M., Riley, D., Gunnarsson, L., & Henderson, C.R. (Eds.). (1990). *Extending families: The social networks of parents and their children.* Cambridge, UK: Cambridge University Press.

Cohen, J.J., & Fish, M.C. (1993). *Handbook of school-based interventions: Resolving student problems and promoting healthy educational environments.* San Francisco: Jossey-Bass.

Comer, J.P., & Haynes, N.M. (1991). Parent involvement in schools: An ecological approach. *The Elementary School Journal, 91,* 271–277.

Comer, J.P., Haynes, N.M., Joyner, E.T., & Ben-Avie, M. (Eds.). (1996). *Rallying the whole village: The Comer process for reforming education.* New York: Teachers College Press.

Conoley, J.C., Hindmand, R., Jacobs, Y., & Gagnon, W.A. (1997). How schools promote violence. *Family Futures, 1*(1), 8–11.

Cotterill, A.M. (1988). The geographic distribution of child abuse in an inner city borough. *Child Abuse and Neglect, 12,* 461–467.

Coulton, C., Korbin, J., Su, M., & Chow, J. (1995). Community level factors and child maltreatment rates. *Child Development, 66,* 1262–1276.

Coulton, C.J., & Pandey, S. (1992). Geographic concentration of poverty and risk to children in urban neighborhoods. *American Behavioral Scientist, 35,* 238–257.

Cowen, E.L., Hightower, D.A., Pedro-Carroll, J.L., Work, W.C., Wyman, P.A., & Haffey, W.G. (1996). *School-based prevention for children at risk: The Primary Mental Health Project.* Washington, DC: American Psychological Association.

Cowen, E.L., Trost, M.A., Lorion, R.P., Dorr, D., Izzo, L.D., & Issacson, R.V. (1975). *New ways in school mental health: Early detection and prevention of school maladaptation.* New York: Human Sciences Press.

Davies, D. (1991). Schools reaching out: Family, school, and community partnerships for student success. *Phi Delta Kappan, 72*(5), 376–382.

de Toqueville, A. (1990). *Democracy in America*. New York: Vintage Books. (Original work published 1835).

Diamond, D. (1997, January 31–February 2). Behind closed gates. *USA Weekend*, p. 4.

Dibner, A.S. (1954). Ambiguity and anxiety. *Journal of Abnormal and Social Psychology, 56*, 165–174.

Donnelly, M. (1997a). Bowling Park Elementary: A caring community school. *Family Futures, 1*(1), 15–17.

Donnelly, M. (1997b). School of the Future Project. *Family Futures, 1*(1), 12–14.

Dornbusch, S.M., & Glasgow, K.L. (1996). The structural context of family-school relations. In A. Booth & J.F. Dunn (Eds.), *Family-school links: How do they affect educational outcomes?* (pp. 35–44). Mahwah, NJ: Lawrence Erlbaum Associates.

Drake, B., & Pandey, S. (1996). Understanding the relationship between neighborhood poverty and specific types of child maltreatment. *Child Abuse and Neglect, 20*, 1003–1018.

Dryfoos, J.G. (1994). *Full-service schools: A revolution in health and social services for children, youth, and families*. San Francisco: Jossey-Bass.

Duncan, G.J., & Brooks-Gunn, J. (Eds.). (1997). *Consequences of growing up poor*. New York: Russell Sage Foundation.

Eccles, J.S., & Harold, R.D. (1993). Parent-school involvement during the early adolescent years. *Teachers College Record, 94*, 568–587.

Eccles, J.S., & Harold, R.D. (1996). Family involvement in children's and adolescents' schooling. In A. Booth & J.F. Dunn (Eds.), *Family-school links: How do they affect educational outcomes?* (pp. 3–34). Mahwah, NJ: Lawrence Erlbaum Associates.

Eccles, J.S., Midgley, C., Wigfield, A., Buchanan, C.M., Reuman, D., Flanagan, C., & Mac Iver, D. (1993). Development during adolescence: The impact of stage-environment fit on young adolescents' experiences in schools and in families. *American Psychologist, 48*, 90–101.

Epstein, J.L. (1982). Teachers' reported practices of parent involvement: Problems and possibilities. *The Elementary School Journal, 83*, 103–113.

Epstein, J.L. (1984). School policy and parent involvement: Research results. *Educational Horizons, 62*, 70–72.

Epstein, J.L. (1986). Parents' reactions to teacher practices of parent involvement. *The Elementary School Journal, 86*, 277–294.

Epstein, J.L. (1990). School and family connections: Theory, research, and implications for integrating sociologies of education and family. *Marriage and Family Review, 15*, 99–126.

Epstein, J.L. (1991). Paths to partnership: What we can learn from federal, state, district, and school initiatives. *Phi Delta Kappan, 72*, 344–349.

Epstein, J.L. (1996). Perspectives and previews on research and policy for school, family, and community partnerships. In A. Booth & J.F. Dunn (Eds.), *Family-school links: How do they affect educational outcomes?* (pp. 209–246). Mahwah, NJ: Lawrence Erlbaum Associates.

Epstein, J.L., & Dauber, S.L. (1991). School programs and teacher practices of parent involvement in inner-city elementary and middle schools. *The Elementary School Journal, 91*, 289–305.

Farrow, F., & Joe, T. (1992). Financing school-linked, integrated services. *Future of Children, 2*(1), 56–67.

Felner, R.D., & Adan, A.M. (1988). The School Transition Environment Project: An ecological intervention and evaluation. In R.H. Price, E.L. Cowen, R.P. Lorion, & J. Ramos-McKay (Eds.), *Fourteen ounces of prevention: A casebook for practitioners* (pp. 111–122). Washington, DC: American Psychological Association.

Finn-Stevenson, M., Desimont, L., & Chung, A. (1997). *Linking child care and support services with the school: Pilot evaluation of the school of the 21st century*. New Haven, CT: Yale University, Bush Center in Children Development and Social Policy.

Finn-Stevenson, M., & Stern, B.M. (1996, May). CoZi: Linking early childhood and family support services. *Principal*, 6–10.

Garbarino, J. (1992). The meaning of poverty in the world of children. *American Behavioral Scientist, 35*, 220–237.

Garbarino, J., & Crouter, A. (1978). Defining the community context of parent-child relations. *Child Development, 49*, 604–616.

Garbarino, J., & Kostelny, K. (1992). Child maltreatment as a community problem. *Child Abuse and Neglect, 16*, 455–464.

Garbarino, J., & Kostelny, K. (1994). Neighborhood-based programs. In G.B. Melton & F.D. Barry (Eds.), *Protecting children from abuse and neglect: Foundations for a new national strategy* (pp. 304–352). New York: Plenum Publishing Corp.

Garbarino, J., & Sherman, D. (1980). High-risk neighborhoods and high-risk families: The human ecology of child maltreatment. *Child Development, 51*, 188–198.

Gardner, S. (1992). Key issues in developing school-linked, integrated services. *Future of Children, 2*(1), 85–94.

General Accounting Office. (1993). *School-linked human services: A comprehensive strategy for aiding students at risk of school failure* (Report No. GAO/HRD-94–21). Washington, DC: Author.

Goetz, C. (Ed.) (1993). Kentucky looks at the first year of its statewide program and charts a course for the future. *Family Resource Coalition Report, 12*(3/4), 47–48.

Goldman, R.K. (1997). Model mental health programs and educational reform: Introduction. *American Journal of Orthopsychiatry, 67*, 344–348.

Harry, B. (1992a). *Cultural diversity, families, and the special education system: Communication and empowerment.* New York: Teachers College Press.

Harry, B. (1992b). Restructuring the participation of African-American parents in special education. *Exceptional Children, 59*, 123–131.

Haynes, N.M., & Ben-Avie, M. (1996). Parents as full partners in education. In A. Booth & J.F. Dunn (Eds.), *Family-school links: How do they affect educational outcomes?* (pp. 43–55). Mahwah, NJ: Lawrence Erlbaum Associates.

Haynes, N.M., Ben-Avie, M., Squires, D.A., Howley, J.P., Negron, E.N., & Corbin, J.N. (1996). It takes a whole village: The SDP school. In J.P. Comer, N.M. Haynes, E.T. Joyner, & M. Ben-Avie (Eds.), *Rallying the whole village: The Comer process for reforming education* (pp. 42–71). New York: Teachers College Press.

Haynes, N.M., & Comer, J.P. (1996). Integrating schools, families, and communities through successful school reform: The School Development Program. *School Psychology Review, 25*, 501–506.

Haynes, N.M., Emmons, C.L., Gebreyesus, S., & Ben-Avie, M. (1996). In J.P. Comer, N.M. Haynes, E.T. Joyner, & M. Ben-Avie (Eds.), *Rallying the whole village: The Comer process for reforming education* (pp. 123–146). New York: Teachers College Press.

Health Care Financing Administration. (1997). *Medicaid and school health.* Washington, DC: Author.

Holtzman, W.H. (1997). Community psychology and full-service schools in different cultures. *American Psychologist, 52*, 381–389.

Hoover-Dempsey, K.V., & Sandler, H.M. (1997). Why do parents become involved in their children's education? *Review of Educational Research, 67*, 3–42.

Individuals with Disabilities Education Act Amendments of 1997, PL 105-17, 20 U.S.C. §§ 1400 *et seq.*

Iscoe, L.K. (1996). *Beyond the classroom: Experiences of a school-based services project.* Austin, TX: Hogg Foundation for Mental Health.

Iscoe, L.K., & Keir, S.S. (1997). *Revisiting the School of the Future: The evolution of a school-based services project.* Austin, TX: Hogg Foundation for Mental Health.

Jehl, J., & Kirst, M. (1992). Getting ready to provide school-linked services: What schools must do. *Future of Children, 2*(1), 95–106.

Johnson, C.M., Sumi, A.M., & Weill, J.D. (1988). *Vanishing dreams: The growing economic plight of America's young families.* Washington, DC: Children's Defense Fund.

Kagan, S.L., & Neville, P.R. (1993). Family support and school-linked services: Variations on a theme. *Family Resource Coalition Report, 12*(3/4), 4–6.

Keir, S., & Millea, S. (1997). *Challenges and realities: Evaluating a school-based service project.* Austin, TX: Hogg Foundation for Mental Health.

Kelley, P. (1996, January 8). Survey: College students changing. *Charlotte Observer*, p. C1.

Larson, C.P., Gomby, D.S., Shiono, P.H., Lewit, E.M., & Behrman, R.E. (1992). Analysis. *Future of Children, 2*(1), 6–18.

Levy, J.E., & Shepardson, W. (1992). A look at current school-linked service efforts. *Future of Children, 2*(1), 44–55.

Limber, S.P., & Motes, P.S. (1996). Schools as neighborhood safe havens. *Child, Youth, and Family Services Quarterly, 19*(3), 4–6.

Lind, E.A., & Tyler, T.R. (1988). *The social psychology of procedural justice.* New York: Plenum Publishing Corp.

Louv, R. (1991). Weaving a new web. *Family Affairs, 4,* 6.

Maccoby, E., Johnson, J., & Church, R. (1958). Community integration and the social control of juvenile delinquency. *Journal of Social Issues, 14,* 38–51.

Mannan, G., & Blackwell, J. (1992). Parent involvement: Barriers and opportunities. *Urban Review, 24,* 219–226.

Mathews, D. (1996). *Is there a public for public schools?* Dayton, OH: Kettering Foundation Press.

Mellman, M., Lazarus, E., & Rivlin, A. (1990). Family time, family values. In D. Blankenhorn, S. Bayme, & J.B. Elshtain (Eds.), *Rebuilding the nest: A new commitment to the American family* (pp. 73–92). Milwaukee: Family Service America.

Melton, G.B. (1992). It's time for neighborhood research and action. *Child Abuse and Neglect, 16,* 909–913.

Melton, G.B. (1996). "People shouldn't have to ask": The vision of the Institute for Families in Society. *Child, Youth, and Family Services Quarterly, 19*(3), 1–3.

Melton, G.B. (1997). Why don't the knuckleheads use common sense? In S.W. Henggeler & A.B. Santos (Eds.), *Innovative services for difficult-to-treat populations* (pp. 351–370). Washington, DC: American Psychiatric Press.

Mirowsky, J., & Ross, C.E. (1989). *Social causes of psychological distress.* New York: Aldine de Gruyter.

Montgomery, L. (1996, February 11). Survey shows crime tops Americans' list of fears. *The State,* p. D9.

Motes, P.S. (1997). Reaching out to teachers and families: A school-based mental health project. *Family Futures, 1*(1), 18–19.

Moynihan, D.P. (1987). *Family and nation.* New York: Harvest/HBJ. (Original work published 1986.)

National Commission on Children. (1991). *Beyond rhetoric: A new American agenda for children and families.* Washington, DC: U.S. Government Printing Office.

National Education Goals Panel. (1995). *The National Education Goals report: Building a nation of learners.* Washington, DC: U.S. Government Printing Office.

Norman, J.M., & Smith, E.P. (1997). Families and schools, islands unto themselves: Opportunities to construct bridges. *Family Futures, 1*(1), 5–7.

Ogden, T., & Backe-Hansen, E. (1997). The group is the thing: The Nordic educational model. *Family Futures, 1*(1), 25–26.

Panel on High-Risk Youth. (1993). *Losing generations: Adolescents in high-risk settings.* Washington, DC: National Academy Press.

Popenoe, D. (1990). Family decline in America. In D. Blankenhorn, S. Bayme, & J.B. Elshtain (Eds.), *Rebuilding the nest: A new commitment to the American family* (pp. 39–51). Milwaukee, WI: Family Service America.

Popenoe, D. (1993). American family decline, 1960–1990: A review and appraisal. *Journal of Marriage and the Family, 55,* 527–555.

Putnam, R.D. (1993). *Making democracy work: Civic traditions in modern Italy.* Princeton, NJ: Princeton University Press.

Putnam, R.D. (1995). Bowling alone: America's declining social capital. *Journal of Democracy, 6,* 65–78.

Reissman, F., & Carroll, D. (1995). *Redefining self-help: Policy and practice.* San Francisco: Jossey-Bass.

Rodick, J.D., & Henggeler, S.W. (1980). The short-term and long-term amelioration of academic and motivational deficiencies among low-achieving inner-city adolescents. *Child Development,* 1126–1132.

Rogeness, G.A., Bednar, R.A., & Diesenhaus, H. (1974). The social system and children's behavior problems. *American Journal of Orthopsychiatry, 44,* 497–502.

Rushton, F. (Ed.). (1998). *Family support in community pediatrics: Confronting the challenge.* Westport, CT: Praeger Publishers.

Sampson, R.J., Raudenbush, S.W., & Earls, F. (1997). Neighborhood and violent crime: A multi-level study of collective efficacy. *Science, 277,* 918–924.

Sax, L.J., Astin, A.W., Korn, W.S., & Mahoney, K.M. (1996). *The American freshman: National norms for fall 1996.* Los Angeles: University of California, Higher Education Research Institute.

Seeley, D.S. (1989). A new paradigm for parent involvement. *Educational Leadership, 47,* 46–48.

Simcha-Fagan, O., & Schwartz, J.E. (1986). Neighborhood and delinquency: An assessment of contextual effects. *Criminology, 24,* 667–703.

Simoni, J., & Adelman, H.S. (1993). School-based mutual support groups for low income parents. *Urban Review, 25,* 335–350.

Skogan, W. (1990). *Disorder and decline: Crime and the spiral of decay in American neighborhoods.* Berkeley: University of California Press.

Slevin, P. (1996, February 11). Voters on government: It's not evil, just inept. *The State,* pp. D1, D8.

South Carolina Department of Mental Health. (1997). *Annual report: 1996–97.* Columbia, SC: Author.

Special education: You can use the system to get services for qualified abused and neglected children. (1997). *Children's Law Report, 2*(7), 1–3.

Swick, K.J., Grafwallner, R., Cocky, M., Roach, J., Davidson, S., Mayor, M., & Gardner, N. (1997). On board early: Building strong family-school relations. *Early Childhood Education Journal, 24,* 269–273.

Szymanski, K. (1996, May 4). Apartment communities strive to become good neighbors. *Charlotte Observer,* p. 14E.

Tremper, C.R., & Kelly, M.P. (1987). The mental health rationale for policies fostering minors' autonomy. *International Journal of Law and Psychiatry, 10,* 111–127.

United Nations Convention on the Rights of the Child, U.N. Doc. A/Res/44/25 (1989).

U.S. Advisory Board on Child Abuse and Neglect. (1993). *Neighbors helping neighbors: A new national strategy for the protection of children.* Washington, DC: U.S. Government Printing Office.

Vaden-Kiernan, N. (1996). *Parents' reports of school practices to involve families.* Washington, DC: U.S. Department of Education, Office of Educational Research and Improvement.

Vickers, H.S., & Minke, K.M. (1995). Exploring parent–teacher relationships: Joining and communication to others. *School Psychology Quarterly, 10,* 133–150.

Vinson, T., Baldry, E., & Hargreaves, J. (1996). Neighbourhoods, networks and child abuse. *British Journal of Social Work, 26,* 523–543.

Voyndanoff, P. (1991). Economic distress and family relations: A review of the Eighties. In A. Booth (Ed.), *Contemporary families: Looking forward, looking back* (pp. 429–445). Minneapolis, MN: National Council on Family Relations.

Weisz, J.R., & Weiss, B. (1993). *Effects of psychotherapy with children and families.* Thousand Oaks, CA: Sage Publications.

Whitehead, B.D. (1991). Why are parents afraid? *Family Affairs, 4,* 15.

Wilson, B. (Ed.). (1993). Family support and school-linked services [Special issue]. *Family Resource Coalition Report, 12*(3/4).

Wynn, J., Costello, J., Halpern, R., & Richman, H. (1994). *Children, families, and communities: A new approach to social services.* Chicago: University of Chicago, Chapin Hall Center for Children.

Yale Child Study Center. (1997). *Comer School Development Program overview.* New Haven, CT: Author.

Young, G., & Gately, T. (1988). Neighborhood impoverishment and child maltreatment: An analysis from the ecological perspective. *Journal of Family Issues, 9,* 240–254.

Zigler, E.F., & Finn-Stevenson, M. (1996). Funding child care and public education. *Future of Children, 6*(2), 104–121.

Zigler, E.F., Finn-Stevenson, M., & Linkins, K.W. (1992). Meeting the needs of children and families with Schools of the 21st Century. *Yale Law and Policy Review, 10,* 69–81.

Zigler, E.F., Finn-Stevenson, M., & Stern, B.M. (1997). Supporting children and families in the schools: The School of the 21st Century. *American Journal of Orthopsychiatry, 67,* 396–407.

TRANSITIONS FOR CHILDREN WITH DIVERSE BACKGROUNDS

Chapter 8

Beginning School for Children at Risk

Craig T. Ramey
Sharon L. Ramey

One of the few universals of childhood is the transition to school. As each child crosses the threshold of the school, he or she embarks on a remarkable course of learning accompanied inevitably by successes, failures, friends made and lost, and interests turned on and off. Make no mistake, school is the real world for children and what happens there matters—now and forever.

After the family, the school is likely to be the most profound influence in a child's life. Moreover, the family–school relationship greatly influences how well a child adjusts to school and how much a child benefits from school. In fact, the family–school relationship really begins before the child enters the classroom and is expressed in the way the family talks about and prepares the child for school. For children with only minimal preparation prior to entering school—a situation that applies to an increasing number of children in American society—specific compensatory strategies are likely to be needed (Alexander & Entwistle, 1988).

This chapter reviews the reasons why the transition to school is considered an important period for scientific inquiry, educational improvement, and societal concern. The literature underscores the multiplicity of influences on children's social and academic progress. What is notably lacking in the current research literature is a multimethod, multivariate longitudinal approach to studying the early elementary school years, taking into account diverse, simultaneous influences on

Research reported in this chapter was supported by grants from the National Institute of Child Health and Human Development, the Maternal and Child Health Bureau of the Public Health Service, the Department of Education, and the Administration for Children, Youth, and Families. We gratefully acknowledge that support and the children and families who have so generously given of their time and effort.

children, parents, teachers, schools, and communities. In addition, the relatively limited types of outcomes—focused almost exclusively on the child—that have been included in studies are noted. In part, the challenge in reviewing the existing literature is that it is not connected by a cohesive, practical, conceptual framework that can inform both practice and policy. Ramey and Ramey (1992) proposed the beginning of such a framework for understanding and studying the transition to school. In this chapter, a revised and expanded conceptual framework is presented that incorporates new findings and that is being used to guide longitudinal research on students at risk and their families. The final section of this chapter identifies key issues for policy and practice and proposes promising directions for future research.

TRANSITION TO SCHOOL AS A CONSTRUCT

The transition to school has emerged as a new construct in the early childhood and elementary school education fields as well as in the developmental psychology field. Transition is replacing the earlier construct of school readiness. Kagan has been one of the most articulate spokespersons for the need for revising the thinking about children's school readiness. In a special issue of *Phi Delta Kappan* on early care and education, she wrote the following:

> Acknowledging increased attention to young children and their families and to the issue of school readiness, I confront the polemics and priorities that need to be considered as schools and their communities ready themselves for young children. I suggest that a nascent early care and education movement exists and that, by harnessing it along with other current social movements and lessons from the long history of school reform, we can create "ready schools" that exist within "ready communities." (Kagan, 1994, p. 187)

An interdisciplinary conference, sponsored by the Maternal and Child Health Bureau in 1994 (cf. Crnic & Lamberty, 1994), also provided compelling evidence that the traditional construct of school readiness was severely flawed by a disproportionate focus on the child's skills per se. There was not adequate consideration of the contribution of the family and school environments to a child's early adaptation to school. That is, much of the research was acontextual and implicitly assumed that schools were comparable in their expectations, practices, and evaluations of children. Similarly, the extent to which early experiences contributed to children's readiness upon entry into kindergarten was often overlooked in the analysis and interpretation of findings. The consensus reached was that the traditional school readiness construct needed to be replaced with a transition-to-school framework that viewed the child within a broader contextual and developmental perspective. Furthermore, this new construct of the transition to school was proposed to be a multiyear window on school adjustment, rather than a single snapshot of adjustment arbitrarily limited to kindergarten or first grade. For most children and families, as well as for schools and communities, the first several years in school represent an important introductory phase, theoretically postulated to establish crucial attitudes, behaviors, and competencies that help to determine the subsequent academic and social successes of a child throughout the school years and into adulthood.

The current perspective on the transition to school builds on the early experience paradigm and incorporates the vast literature associated with early interventions and their public policy embodiments including Head Start (in its various forms including Follow Through), as well as the multitude of programs stemming from the legislation for children with disabilities (see reviews by Guralnick, 1997, and Ramey & Ramey, 1998, for a fuller treatment of this history).

DEFINITION OF TRANSITION TO SCHOOL

Within the conceptual framework, *transition to school* refers to an ongoing process that occurs during the first several years of life when children, families, and schools are making mutual adaptations to facilitate the eventual success of the child, family, and school in the early elementary school years. This definition, however, begs the question of what a successful transition to school is.

Successful transitions during this age period have been characterized by Ramey and Ramey (1995) as consisting of multiple features, including

1. Children's positive attitudes toward learning, school, teachers, and peers

2. Children's maintenance of prior skills and acquisition of new academic and social skills

3. Parents' positive attitudes toward and active involvement with their children's school and learning

4. Teachers' provision of developmentally appropriate experiences for individual children and creation of a classroom environment that positively values individual differences and cultural diversity

5. A community that provides the supports for positive transition experiences, such as increased cooperation and coordination across agencies and service providers in promoting children's health, social development, academic progress, and positive self-esteem

Figure 8.1 displays schematically the general framework that is used for successful transitions. Later in this chapter, this framework is incorporated into a larger conceptualization that emphasizes systematic variations in children, families, schools, and communities.

Importance of the Transition to School for Children at Risk and Their Families

Ramey and Ramey (1997) delineated five major reasons for the increased level of national interest in the transition to school:

1. Changes have occurred in the United States' demography, which have had an impact on schools. The diversity of children and families served by schools is greater than at any time in United States history, presenting powerful new challenges for teachers and schools (see Chapter 4).

2. Schools now serve all children, including those with disabilities beginning at age 3 (see the Individuals with Disabilities Education Act [IDEA] of 1990, summarized by Ramey & Ramey, 1996), and increasingly do so in inclusive educational settings (see Chapter 9 for a more detailed discussion). For both children at risk and their families, including those with identified disabilities,

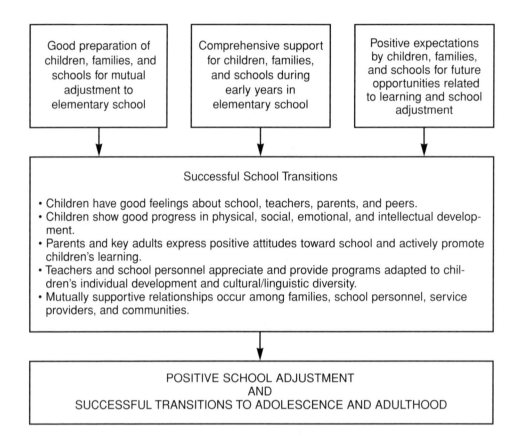

Figure 8.1. A framework showing successful transitions to school as a function of preparation, comprehensive support, and positive expectations for the future.

additional educational, social, and health supports often are viewed as crucial to a successful transition to school.

3. New and more comprehensive paradigms in early childhood education and developmental psychology are available that build on advances in systems theory, transactional analysis, social ecology, and resilience theory (see Ramey & Ramey, 1998, for a brief overview of these perspectives). Collectively, these theoretical and conceptual shifts emphasize that a child's development should not be studied out of context, but rather such studies should explicitly recognize that important developmental milestones, such as the transition to school, are embedded in a developmental, ecological, and dynamic set of interactive systems. Most notable are the family, school, peer, neighborhood, and community systems and their interrelationships.

4. A dramatic increase has occurred in the availability of sophisticated measurement procedures and analytical techniques to model the transition to school (see, e.g., Bryk & Raudenbush, 1987; Burchinal & Appelbaum, 1991).

5. The Congressional mandate, enactment, and completion of a 31-site randomized trial to promote positive transition to school experiences for children at risk and their families, as well as for their classmates, school, and communi-

ties, have taken place. This intervention extended comprehensive, Head Start–like supports from kindergarten through third grade for former Head Start children and their classmates who were not participants in Head Start (cf. Ramey, Ramey, & Phillips, 1996).

For children judged at risk for poor school progress, by a variety of indicators, the existing literature confirms that by third grade, their long-term success as students and as productive citizens can be predicted with alarming accuracy (Alexander & Entwistle, 1988). Moreover, there has been a widely held belief stemming from the Westinghouse report on the long-term impact of Head Start (Cicirelli, 1969) that early intervention benefits "fade out" by the third grade. Although many reports contain evidence for longer-term positive effects of early intervention, particularly with respect to reduced grade retention and special education placement (see, e.g., Campbell & Ramey, 1995; Lazar, Darlington, Murray, Royce, & Snipper, 1982), many people persist in inaccurately characterizing the results of early intervention as small and fleeting (e.g., Hernstein & Murray, 1994). This issue is discussed later in this chapter when the Abecedarian Project and its long-term findings are presented.

An urgent issue is determining to what degree transition to school can be altered for children at risk and their families, such that these children are not "doomed" by the demographic and environmental variables that characterize their life circumstances at birth. The challenge for educators and developmentalists has become to test whether certain patterns of support within and across the family, school, and community contexts in which children learn and grow can yield better developmental outcomes for children at risk. This new conceptual framework encourages collaboration, coordination, and creativity in meeting children's developmental and educational needs and emphasizes nonacademic factors, such as persistent and untreated health problems, abuse and neglect, family or neighborhood disruptions, and the child's school progress.

THE TRANSITION CONCEPTUAL MODEL

In recognition of the many and diverse forces that have an impact on the likelihood of successful school transitions, and as a guide for more comprehensive research into the transition process, the Transition Conceptual Model was created (Ramey & Ramey, 1992, 1996).

This model derives from a social-ecological perspective on the development of children within a developmental systems theory framework. Figure 8.2 presents a composite picture of the multiple contemporary influences hypothesized as important in determining the developmental quality of children's and families' transition experiences. Represented within this figure are the key concepts of developmental systems theory, namely context, process, and outcomes. Child outcomes are shown as embedded within and influenced by the family's outcomes. Both the child and family are shown as embedded within the context of the community, especially the availability and quality of preschool and school programs, social and health services, and community resources related to learning (e.g., libraries). A basic premise in this framework is that the child, family, school, and the community are all involved in this transition. Furthermore, the successful adjustment of both the family and the child as well as the school and the community is

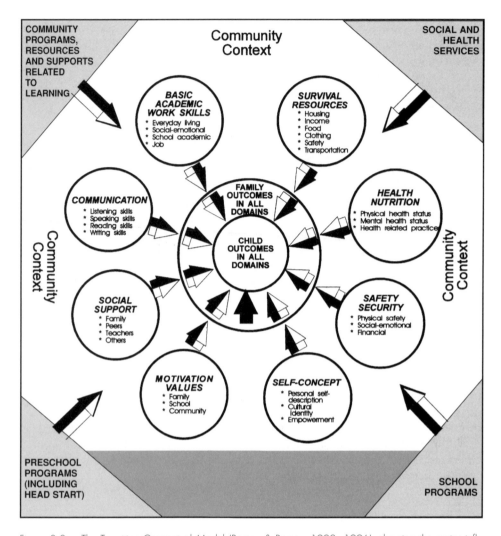

Figure 8.2.   The Transition Conceptual Model (Ramey & Ramey, 1992, 1996), showing the major influences on children and families during the school years. *Note:* Children and families are recognized as influences on schools, programs, and communities. These bidirectional or mutual influences are not shown, however, because the major focus is on ways to improve child and family outcomes. (Key: ➤ supportive influences and protective factors, ⇨ stressors and risk factors.)

assumed to be affected by similar mediating influences. These mediating influences have been grouped into eight major domains (spheres), although these are recognized as nondiscrete and overlapping to some unknown degree. Accordingly, positive transition outcomes for children and families are expected to relate to the degree to which these eight domains of functioning (indicated by capital letters in Figure 8.2) are present in their lives, as evidenced by the following list:

1.   SURVIVAL RESOURCES are adequate to meet the child's and family's needs.

2.   Good physical and mental HEALTH and health practices prevail.

3.   Individuals have a sense of SECURITY.

4.   The child and family have a positive and realistic SELF-CONCEPT.

5. Positive MOTIVATION, EXPECTATIONS, AND VALUES exist to do well in school.

6. Individuals have good SOCIAL SUPPORT to facilitate the transition to school.

7. The child and family have GOOD COMMUNICATION, both among themselves and with those concerned with the transition to school (e.g., teachers, peers, service providers).

8. The child and family have those BASIC SKILLS that are considered essential to do well, such as everyday living, social-emotional, school and academic, and job-related skills.

In the Transition Conceptual Model, these eight domains of influence are thought of as the proximal factors in the overall system. In turn, these domains are conceptualized as intertwined with and directly influenced by the everyday supports and community resources referred to as the *community context*. The processes in this model include the behavioral and cognitively mediated transactions that occur among children and families with individuals and agencies (broadly construed) in their communities. In Figure 8.2, these transactions are graphically represented as arrows—potentially involving supportive processes or protective factors and/or stressors or risk factors. For example, there may be some aspects of school programs that directly enhance the development of children and families in one or more of the eight spheres of influence (that is, supportive processes), while other aspects of the same school program may cause stress and contribute to negative outcomes for the child or family. Similarly, some of the transactional processes that occur between children and parents may contribute to positive developmental outcomes, whereas others may have negative effects or may prevent a child from benefiting from other available supports outside the family. The number and extent of these factors are empirical issues for particular populations at given points in history.

Obviously, in such a complex web of influences, the notion of simple, linear models of causality is challenged. These authors believe that the model (particularly when applied in a longitudinal repeated measures framework) helps to organize the data analysis process. From that analytical process, new insights might be generated concerning causal pathways that might help to refine the Transition Conceptual Model into a more time-distributed model with a more refined cascade of causal influences among the domains. At present, lacking directly relevant and adequate data, specification of that cascade would be premature. Ultimately, the developmental cascade is an empirical issue.

The Transition Conceptual Model is intended to illustrate the importance of thinking about development in terms of both environmental context and specific spheres of influence mediated by specific developmental processes. What is not illustrated are direct lines of influence between specific contextual factors and specific outcomes, because multiple processes in all likelihood affect more than one outcome. Thus, this conceptual framework underscores the importance of assessing a family's and a child's initial status and their community context, so that what they need for a successful transition can be identified and provided. For families with excellent health and good health care practices, for example, there may be no measurable benefits over time associated with the extra provision of readily available free medical care. Similarly, not all families at an economic disadvantage need additional supports to improve their basic skills or their communication skills, whereas for others, improvement in these domains may be vital for their future success in school and in community settings. In addition to supporting the provision of individualized interventions, this framework is also compatible with the idea that outcomes need to be interpreted in a more differentiated or individualized family- and child-specific manner than they have been traditionally. That is, the statistical analyses must go beyond simply testing for overall group differences and, instead, seek to identify which types of families and children benefit from which types of programs and services. Interventions should not be judged by the expectation that all families and children will benefit to the same extent in all domains. At the same time, more rigorous scientific inquiry is vital to increase the knowledge base about why some interventions and some families show more positive outcomes than do others. In the next section, two attempts at improving transitions to school for children at risk that were derived from the Transition Conceptual Model are described.

EXAMPLES OF TRANSITION INTERVENTION PROGRAMS FOR CHILDREN AT RISK

Because the Transition Conceptual Model is both multifaceted and somewhat abstract, two examples of projects that have been guided by it or an earlier version are presented. The first example is the Abecedarian Project (Ramey & Campbell, 1992), which is now in a posttreatment, long-term, follow-up phase. The second project is the just-completed Head Start/Public School Transition Demonstration Project, which is at the beginning of its initial analysis phase (Ramey et al., 1996). Both of these transition projects focused on socially and economically defined high-risk children and built on the findings of previous early intervention programs. Both projects conducted a transition support program after children had participated in earlier preschool programs. To the authors' knowledge, these two projects are the only ones to date to have used randomized research designs to test the efficacy of specific transition practices to affect the developmental outcomes of children and families during the early elementary school years.

THE ABECEDARIAN PROJECT

The first example of a transition-to-school project for children at high risk has been described in detail elsewhere and is described here only briefly (see, e.g., Ramey & Haskins, 1981, and Ramey & Campbell, 1992, for more complete descriptions). This project compared the efficacy of a kindergarten through second-grade Transition Program (K-2 Transition Program) with improved school outcomes with and without an intensive birth-to-age 5 early intervention program. Figure 8.3 illustrates the research design. Children were assigned to conditions at random.

Abecedarian Preschool Program

The Abecedarian preschool treatment and control conditions are summarized in Table 8.1. In general, the Abecedarian preschool program was a comprehensive health, education, and family support program that provided an individualized approach to families at risk and their children.

The primary goal of the preschool phase was to improve the likelihood of greater school readiness and, thus, to establish a better base for a successful transition consistent with the ideas in Figure 8.1. It is important to note that the Abecedarian Project was located in a generally affluent and well-educated college

K-2 Transition Program

	Yes	No
Yes	Birth to Age 8 Intervention (*N*=25)	Birth to Age 5 Intervention (*N*=24)
No	Age 5 to Age 8 Intervention (*N*=24)	Controls* (*N*=23)

Preschool In-
tervention
(birth to age 5)

Figure 8.3.   Experimental design of the Abecedarian Project. (Key: * = Children received additional social services, medical care and referral, and nutritional supplements and were not deprived of any available service of the community, which was highly resourceful.)

town in which there were few families at socioeconomic risk. The town also had a socially progressive stance toward disadvantaged families and, therefore, provided many public and private services that these families needed. Because these services in all likelihood improved the performance of the control group children over what would have occurred in a poorer community context and the Abecedarian Project provided additional services to both treated and control group children and families on top of those generally offered, it is reasonable to view the research design as a conservative test of the power of educationally oriented early intervention.

In summary, it should be noted that although the preschool treatment condition was comprehensive and intensive, the main difference between it and the control condition was the addition of the early childhood education component that began at 6 weeks of age. In fact, the comparison of these two groups is quite conservative, considering that the control condition was more intensive and comprehensive than many early intervention programs that are being implemented throughout the United States (see Guralnick, 1997, for an extensive review of current early intervention practices).

To place the Abecedarian K-2 transition program and its empirical findings in context, salient findings from the preschool period are summarized as follows:

- Early intervention reduced the incidence and magnitude of developmental delay during the preschool years. This delay became detectable in the control group in the second year of life on standardized developmental assessments and persisted until kindergarten entry (Ramey & Campbell, 1984).

- The most vulnerable children (as measured by maternal cognitive status, home environment, and mother–child interaction patterns) benefited the most as measured by child cognitive assessments (Ramey, Farran, & Campbell, 1979; Martin, Ramey, & Ramey, 1990).

Table 8.1.   Summary of Abecedarian preschool treatment and control conditions

Control treatment (N = 54)
   Nutritional supplements
   Family social services
   Pediatric care and referral
Preschool treatment (N = 57)
   Nutritional supplements
   Family social services
   Pediatric care and referral
   Early childhood education
- 6 weeks to 5 years of age
- Good teacher–child ratios and a year-round program that met or exceeded NAEYC standards
- Developmentally appropriate practices
- Hours of operation: 7:30 A.M. to 5:30 P.M.
- Partners for Learning curriculum plus other documented approaches
   Preservice and in-service training
   Individualized learning experiences in natural preschool atmosphere
   Emphasis on language, cognition, social, emotional, and physical development
   Promotion and support for parent involvement
- Daily transportation

From Ramey, C.T., & Campbell, F.A. (1992). Poverty, early childhood education, and academic competence: The Abecedarian experiment. In A. Huston (Ed.), *Children in poverty* (pp. 190–221). New York: Cambridge University Press; reprinted by permission.

NAEYC, National Association for the Education of Young Children.

- Early intervention acted as an additive influence in conjunction with important family influences including maternal IQ and home environments to co-determine child preschool developmental outcomes (Ramey, Yeates, & Short, 1984).

- Early intervention increased high-risk children's resilience to nonoptimal biological conditions such as low Apgar scores (Breitmayer & Ramey, 1986), difficult temperament (Ramey, MacPhee, & Yeates, 1982), and fetal undernourishment (Zeskind & Ramey, 1978).

- Some control group children benefited from exposure to good quality, early childhood education but not as much as did children in the Abecedarian Preschool Program (Burchinal, Lee, & Ramey, 1989).

- High-quality early intervention did not harm the mother–child attachment bond (Burchinal, Bryant, Lee, & Ramey, 1992).

- Teenage mothers of children receiving early intervention had an increased likelihood of completing high school, obtaining postsecondary training, and becoming self-supporting by the time that their children entered kindergarten (Campbell, Breitmayer, & Ramey, 1986).

The Abecedarian K-2 Transition Program

Given the positive preschool effects on children and families at kindergarten entry, there was a dilemma. Should these children's progress in school be followed to see how they fared or should a special transition program be provided to aid their transition to school? Because there were no directly relevant data from randomized designs to serve as a guide, it was decided to do both and to do so within the randomized design presented in Figure 8.3. This decision was made despite the realization that a relatively small group of children and families were being subdivided, and, therefore, the statistical power to detect group differences was being reduced. On balance, however, it was believed that the experimental design allowed the direct test of some basic hypotheses and, therefore, the potential benefits of the design outweighed the risks. However, the basic statistical approach was revised, and it was hypothesized that benefits should be proportional to the duration of the intervention as tested by linear trend analyses of variances (for continuously distributed outcome variables), across the four groups. This was done in acknowledgment of the low power to detect significant differences among each of the four groups.

Consistent with the question of whether effects of the preschool program that began in infancy would fade after children entered public school, the school-age intervention program can be thought of as a 2–2 factorial experiment. The factors are preschool educational treatment versus no preschool treatment and K-2 transition treatment versus no K-2 transition treatment. At school entry, children were ranked from highest to lowest according to their 48-month scores on the Stanford-Binet Intelligence Scale within both the preschool experimental and control groups. One member of each consecutive pair within each group was then assigned randomly to the Abecedarian K-2 Transition Program. This design provided the opportunity to examine and compare the long-term effects of early and continuing intervention, of early intervention only, and of late intervention only, relative to control group participants.

Based largely on the view that parent involvement in and support of academic work and the school more generally is an important factor in public school success, and consistent with the hypothesis that supplementary intervention programs potentially can influence both individual children and some level of their social environment, the Abecedarian K-2 Transition Program was designed to influence both the child's home and school environments. The primary objective of the Abecedarian K-2 program was to provide children with additional help on teacher-chosen academic tasks. Specific activities focused on basic skills in reading, writing, and arithmetic. The Abecedarian K-2 Transition Program was implemented by Home-School Resource Teachers. As the name implies, the Home-School Resource Teachers were the principal liaison between home and school. They coordinated home and school academic activities and served as educational resources for both parents and teachers. As advocates on behalf of children, they helped procure educational services and supports for children, teachers, and families. These activities by the Home-School Teachers were conceptualized as supplemental to the regular educational program provided by the public schools. The child remained a pupil of the school that he or she attended and was therefore available for special service referrals or any other aspect of the regular school program. No part of the intervention program was intended to preclude the child's regular school program. It should be noted that the public schools in this university town were generally well regarded and consistently performed near or at the top of public schools throughout the state on measures of student performance. Furthermore, because students at risk made up only a small portion of the student body there was a high level of resources devoted to their education and general welfare.

Meetings with Classroom Teachers   Regular classroom academic activities served as a major focus of the home educational activities. This was done to ensure generality of concepts across settings and to increase the opportunity to practice the academic skills that teachers used to judge academic performance. Meetings with classroom teachers were held biweekly. The Home-School Teacher obtained information from the classroom teacher concerning the curriculum and child's progress. This information was used to construct materials for home activities. The Home-School Teachers then shared with the classroom teachers a report of the most recent home contact, as well as suggestions about educational approaches or behavior management. Finally, the Home-School Teacher and the classroom teacher discussed the child's attainment of previously set objectives and established new objectives.

The specific functions of the Home-School Resource Teacher, in relation to the classroom teacher, were as follows:

1. To generate behavioral objectives, individually tailored for each child, that were consistent with the classroom teacher's lesson plans and classroom goals

2. To provide classroom materials and suggestions of techniques for working with an individual child in the Transition Program

3. To foster and assist in communication between the home and school

4. To obtain whatever services were perceived as necessary in consultation with the classroom teacher

Meetings with Caregivers   The second major part of the Home-School Teachers' responsibilities was to involve the child's primary caregivers, whether parents, grandparents, or siblings, in the child's education. Approximately every 2 weeks, a Home-School Teacher met with a primary caregiver to accomplish three ends:

1. To provide information concerning the child's curriculum and progress in school

2. To communicate the objectives previously established in meetings with the classroom teacher and to provide home activities designed to attain these objectives

3. To assist parents in developing techniques for working with their children in response to school-related problems

4. To encourage parents to be active participants in their child's school

Each home visit followed a general pattern involving three activities by the Home-School Resource Teacher and three activities by the parent. The Home-School Teacher's first activity was giving the parent positive information about the school, focusing on the child's successes and accomplishments. Second, the teacher inquired about the child's degree of success with the previous home activities. If the parent reported a problem with an activity, the Home-School Teacher made suggestions for additional work or returned later with a home activity designed to address the problem. Third, the teacher introduced new home learning activities by explaining why a particular activity was important and what academic skills it would help to develop; rehearsing the task with the child or mother (modeling for the mother if the child was present, role-playing with the mother if the child was absent); and teaching positive correction techniques that could be used if the child had difficulty with the activity.

The parent also had three primary activities during the home visits. First, the parent reported results of the previous home activities. Second, the parent informed the Home-School Resource Teacher of any problems encountered in using the home activity. Third, the parent rehearsed the new activity with the Home-School Teacher. The parent then worked and played with the child on a regular basis and documented that work on a special calendar. Once a month, the calendar was picked up by the Home-School Resource Teacher and exchanged for family gift certificates at a local restaurant if the parent and child had worked together at least five times each week. The parents were encouraged to let the child "treat the family" for having worked together successfully for the past month.

It is important for parents to be active participants in the child's learning. Thus, a major goal of this program was to have parents view themselves as an important educator of the child and, particularly, to take advantage of the many learning situations that occur daily around the home.

Learning Activities   A major component of the home program was the learning activities. These activities were based on objectives established in conjunction with the classroom teacher, as well as on the classroom curriculum. Occasionally, the objectives selected for home learning varied from those set by the classroom teacher. Modifications were made at the discretion of the Home-School Resource Teacher to avoid overwhelming a parent with too many activities or to avoid having children attempt activities that were beyond their ability. A task-analysis approach was taken to each objective so that activities focused on component skills necessary to achieve the objective. The sequencing of small and manageable steps characteristic of the task-analysis approach helped to ensure successful experiences for the child and avoided the failure that could result from working on remedial tasks (tasks with which the child was having difficulty in school). Home learning activities were individualized for each child, developed in a sequential manner, based on specific goals and objectives, and used materials readily available or provided by the Home-School Resource Teacher. Usually, the activities were developed around materials the Home-School Teacher brought into the home.

The format of a home activity consisted of four parts. First, the objective of the activity was stated in behavioral terms. Second, the materials necessary to complete the activity were listed. Third, directions for conducting the activity were specified. Fourth, suggestions were provided for supplementary activities, using materials available in the home, that extended and reinforced the objective of the activity.

The overall rationale for the Abecedarian K-2 Transition Program was that children at high risk might otherwise learn more slowly than average during the early elementary school years and, thus, could potentially benefit from increased exposure to and mentoring in basic concepts in two key academic subjects: reading and mathematics. In addition, it was expected that the children would profit from having their parents become more directly involved in their educational program, and their classroom experiences could be enhanced by working directly with their teachers to maximize individualized developmentally appropriate practices. Because all the parents had had difficulty when they were in school, it was clear from interviews with them that they wanted and needed practical and specific suggestions for how they could help their children succeed in school. The intervention program during the primary grades thus consisted of providing the children with extra exposure to academic concepts by having their parents engage in specific supplemental educational activities at home. Materials for this supplemental curriculum were developed by master-level Home-School Resource Teachers. These resource teachers also provided emotional, social, and instrumental support to parents and individualized consultation to classroom teachers on a biweekly basis for 3 years.

To guarantee that the materials were of high quality and to enhance the program's credibility with classroom teachers, master teachers with extensive and successful backgrounds in primary education, and particularly with children at risk and their families, were recruited for the positions of Home-School Resource Teachers. Typically, a Home-School Resource Teacher worked each year with 12 children, their families, and their classroom teachers.

It was hypothesized that regular visits by a professional educator who had specific knowledge about the child's classroom opportunities and performance, and who demonstrated and explained specific materials and procedures and answered parents' questions and discussed concerns, would help high-risk parents who themselves had had difficulty in school to have a clearer idea of how to help their children have a successful transition to school. It was also expected that this process might lead the parent to be better informed, to take a more substantive interest in and to place greater value on the child's academic accomplishments, and to be more encouraging of the child's efforts. Another important goal of the program was to facilitate effective and timely communication and to establish trust and understanding between the high-risk family and the school system. In the Home-School Resource Teacher's dual role, working with home and school, the educator became an advocate for the family within the school and community systems and for the school within the family.

Summer Program   In addition to the Abecedarian Home-School Transition Program, the children attended camp throughout the summer months that, while containing traditional summer camp experiences, also had a "hidden curriculum" that emphasized enjoyable reading and math experiences. Summer camps were typically 8 weeks in duration, were based in an elementary school, and made extensive use of community facilities. The camps were staffed by the Home-School Resource Teachers and supplemented by paid and volunteer students and adults. The daily programs contained arts and crafts, music, games, and sports. The following list contains a brief summary of the Abecedarian K-2 Transition Program:

- Individualized focus on academically related activities in school and at home
- Emphasis on reading, mathematics, and writing
- Master Home-School Resource Teachers with 12 children and families per year
- Development of an individualized and documented supplemental curriculum for each child
- Explicit attention and action relevant to family circumstances, as needed
- Summer camps with academically relevant experiences

A brief summary of the implementation data of the Home-School Resources Program is presented in Table 8.2. The Home-School Resource Teacher met approximately every other week with the parent, usually in the home but occasionally at the parent's workplace or some other location. The Home-School Resource Teacher conveyed any special messages from the classroom teacher regarding the child's academic interests and achievements or behavior in class and introduced new activities to be carried out at home. Family life and adult issues were also discussed at the parents' request. Mothers sometimes revealed personal problems and sought advice. Counselors and other helping professionals were available to the teachers and parents on a consultative basis.

Accordingly, Home-School Teachers helped families with situations that, unattended, might have made it difficult or impossible for parents to devote energy to their child's school progress. Parents were helped to find jobs and housing as well as to secure appropriate social and health services. In one case, for example, a Home-School Resource Teacher arranged for a custodial grandparent to take adult literacy classes so that the child and his guardian learned to read at the same time.

Home-School Resource Teachers also met approximately every other week with the classroom teachers. Telephone calls and written notes to teachers and parents were used frequently to increase efficiency and timeliness of communication.

In a typical year, approximately 60 different learning activities were designed for each child. These activities were maintained in notebooks to document the curriculum. Many of these activities were original games created by Home-School Resource Teachers. In addition, ready-made activities to give practice in handwriting, phonics, and math concepts and facts were provided. Parents always were asked for feedback on these activities, including how much time they had spent doing them during the previous 2 weeks. Parents reported that they averaged about 15 minutes per day.

The activities were generally popular with parents and well received. Parents especially liked the specificity of the activities because they "took the guess work out of what to do." Most parents reported high levels of success and satisfaction in using them. Overall, the parents participated enthusiastically and frequently; at the project's end, all parents reported that they had found it an extremely positive experience and would have liked to continue to participate if the program had lasted longer. Throughout the program, the opinions and ideas of parents were so-

Table 8.2.   Summary of Home-School Resources Program contacts by years

	Year 1	Year 2	Year 3
Grade level	Kindergarten	Grade 1	Grade 2
Number of children served	46	46	45
Mean school visits	18.3	17.6	13.9
Mean home visits	15.4	14.2	12.5
Mean total contacts[a]	42.4	40.3	35.0
Ratings of parental acceptance of activities			
Positive	84%	82%	83%
Neutral	15%	16%	16%
Negative	1%	1%	0%

[a] Includes all telephone calls, special visits to home, and "other" contacts for each family but does not include summer camp activities.

licited, and the parents' contribution to their child's development was emphasized. Parents were encouraged and assisted in their role as advocates for their
children's welfare and development.

Educational Outcomes   Consistent with the Transition Conceptual Model
presented in Figure 8.2, outcomes were assessed at the levels of the child and the
family in each of the eight domains. In this chapter, due to space limitations, only
measures of basic skills, including academic achievement in reading and mathematics and retention in grade, are addressed. These are the real-world performance measures used in most school districts, and they are likely to be used in the
foreseeable future. Of course, consistent with the conceptual model, many other
domains of performance are important, such as academic self-concept, classroom
behaviors, and enjoyment of school. Nevertheless, the measures to be discussed
represent a practical summative evaluation of the Abecedarian K-2 Transition Program. In the interest of parsimony, performance at the endpoint of the program is
emphasized (i.e., after 3 years in school).

Academic Achievement   Academic outcomes during the primary grades represent a practical test of the efficacy of the transition program as well as a test of
the duration of earlier intervention effects. Achievement in two basic subjects,
reading and mathematics, was considered most important because these subjects
had been the primary focus of the Home-School Transition Program, and they
teach the skills to which teachers, school administrators, and the public pay particular attention. These data are presented in greater detail in articles by Campbell
and Ramey (1994); Horacek, Ramey, Campbell, Hoffmann, and Fletcher (1987);
and Ramey and Campbell (1992). Both age- and grade-referenced measures were
used to compare academic outcomes among the four experimental groups, and
they yielded similar conclusions. The age-referenced measure held years of exposure to school constant when children were tested and consisted of age-referenced
standard scores for reading and mathematics on the Woodcock-Johnson Psychoeducational Battery, Part 2: Test of Academic Achievement (Woodcock & Johnson,
1977), which was individually administered to all children at the end of 3 years in
school. In this chapter, standard scores with means of 100 and standard deviations
of 15 are presented. As noted previously, a linear trend of performance as a function of duration of intervention is hypothesized as well as academic achievement
scores, which were believed to vary positively across the four experimental
groups by the end of the program at second grade. The standard score results for
age-referenced reading and mathematics performance are presented graphically
in Figures 8.4 and 8.5.

Effect sizes for the three treatment conditions were calculated relative to the
mean and standard deviation for participants in the control condition. Social and
educational programs generally regard effect size estimates of ≥.2 as practically
significant. Effect sizes of .4 are generally regarded as moderate and >.6 as large.

In Figure 8.4, the effect sizes for reading achievement vary from .28 to 1.04 for
the treatment conditions and are consistent with the hypothesis about duration of
the program. The most effective treatment condition was the preschool program
followed by the K-2 Transition Program. A similar pattern of findings was obtained for mathematics achievement with somewhat more modest effect (i.e., effect sizes ranging from .11 to .64). Consistent with the reading scores, the largest
effect was attributable to the Abecedarian Preschool Program followed by the
K-2 Transition Program, and those scores, similar to the reading scores, were near

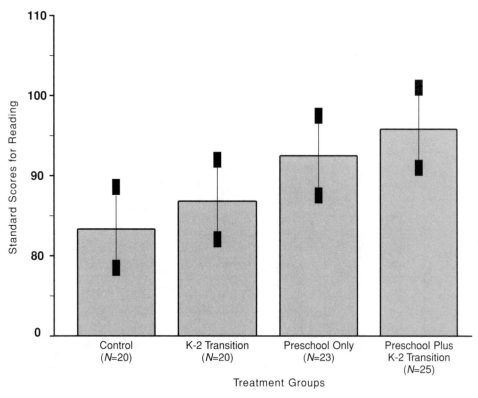

Figure 8.4.   Woodcock-Johnson age-referenced reading standard scores from spring of school year 3. Reading achievement linear trend, $p < .001$.

national average. The effect sizes for the K-2 Transition Program by itself were marginal, at best, being .28 for reading and .11 for math (Figure 8.5).

The conclusion, with respect to scholastic achievement as measured by standardized tests, is that the hypothesized trend across groups from lowest to highest scores as a function of increasing amounts of intervention is supported for both reading and mathematics achievement. Furthermore, these differences are educationally meaningful and of practical magnitude.

Retention in Grade   One real-world measure of a child's lack of adequate progress in school is whether the child is retained in grade. Independently of whether this is an effective remedial practice, it clearly indicates great concern for the child's readiness for a more advanced curriculum. Figure 8.6 shows the percentage of children in each treatment group retained in grade during the first 3 years in public school. Previously reported by Horacek et al. (1987), these data show that the children at high risk overall fared much worse (i.e., 50% retention) than the local systemwide average for retentions in the early grades (13%), confirming the initial high-risk status of this sample, which was determined at birth.

Comparing the grade-retention rates among the high-risk groups in Figure 8.6, the highest failure rate occurred in the control group (50%) and the lowest rate in the preschool plus K-2 Transition Group (16%). In fact, the rate for the preschool plus K-2 Transition Group (16%) is similar to that for the local population base rate of 13%. The K-2 program by itself reduced the failure rate by a modest amount

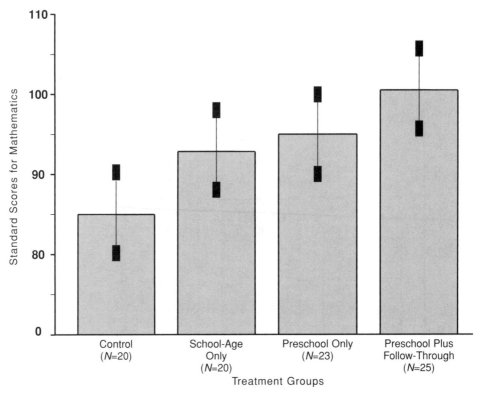

Figure 8.5.   Woodcock-Johnson age-referenced mathematics standard scores from spring of school year 3. Mathematics achievement linear trend, $p < .05$.

from 50% to 38%. Thus, the failure rate exhibits a decreasing pattern with increase in duration and intensity of intervention.

Overall, the addition of an intensive transition program after an intensive preschool program facilitated the successful transition to school for these high-risk children in basic skills, and these increased skills resulted in meaningful reductions in academic failure. Thus, an intensive K-2 Transition Program, coupled with an intensive preschool intervention, was a powerful positive influence on the school performance of these children from low resource and undereducated families during the early elementary school years.

Abecedarian K-2 Transition Conclusions

The K-2 Transition Program had a consistently positive effect on academic achievement in both reading and mathematics as well as in reducing grade retention. Although the program's effects were modest when it constituted the sole educational treatment, its effects were positive and large when combined with an intensive, high-quality preschool experience. The policy implication is clear. Even in a high-resource community such as the one in which the Abecedarian Project was conducted, with a high-quality public school system, very high-risk children needed and benefited from an individualized transition support program during the first 3 years of school.

The school system liked the program, the parents participated in and enjoyed it, and the children benefited academically. This program's results helped to under-

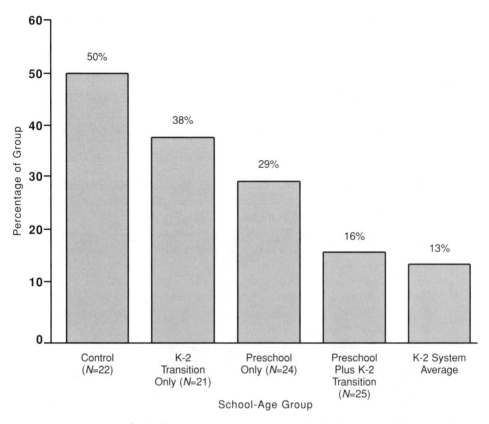

Figure 8.6.   Percentage of school-age intervention groups retained in kindergarten and grades 1 and 2.

gird the rationale for the program to be discussed next—the Head Start/Public School Early Childhood Transition Demonstration Program.

THE HEAD START/PUBLIC SCHOOL EARLY CHILDHOOD TRANSITION DEMONSTRATION PROGRAM

The Head Start/Public School Early Childhood Transition Demonstration Program is a 31-site randomized trial involving more than 8,400 former Head Start children, families, schools, and communities. It has four essential components at each local site. These include

1. Implementation of developmentally appropriate practices to maximize the continuity and integrity of children's learning experiences
2. The provision of supportive social services for all families in need, including the availability of special family workers to help facilitate positive family–school interactions and to assist in coordinating services across agencies
3. The implementation of programs to increase parent involvement in their children's transition experiences and to provide parents with representation on advisory boards for the Transition Demonstration Programs
4. The offering of essential health services to all families and children to promote physical and mental health.

Each local site had autonomy in adapting these four key components to their local needs and resources. The following text box elaborates the specific program elements of the Transition Demonstration Program.

National Transition Demonstration Study Primary Questions

The National Transition Demonstration Study, of which the authors of this article are the Principal Investigators, has two major goals: to look at the process and the outcomes of the National Head Start/Public School Early Childhood Transition

---

COMPONENT 1: DEVELOPMENTALLY APPROPRIATE CURRICULA

1a. Enact assessment procedures for the determination of the child's functional level and measurement of the child's progress.

1b. Incorporate a set of activities into the Transition Demonstration appropriate for the various cultural groups represented in the demonstration site.

1c. Provide for the mainstreaming of children with disabilities.

1d. Provide assurances that the supportive services team will be equipped to assist children and families with limited English proficiency and disabilities, if appropriate.

1e. Conduct a meeting of the early childhood development program teacher with the kindergarten teacher and the child's parents to discuss the transition of each child and to address any particular educational needs of such child.

1f. Develop procedures for the transfer of knowledge about the child, including the transfer (with parental consent) of written records from the early childhood development program teacher to become part of the school record of the child.

1g. Conduct home visits (see description under Parent Involvement).

COMPONENT 2: HEALTH

2a. Assist families, administrators, and teachers to respond to health, immunization, mental health, nutrition, social service, and educational needs of students.

2b. Conduct a self-assessment of the Head Start agency's and local education agency's programs to address health, immunization, mental health, and nutrition.

COMPONENT 3: PARENT INVOLVEMENT

3a. Develop individual family support plans based on family intake interviews. The family support plans shall detail services needed and plans for providing or accessing these services.

3b. Conduct home visits and help students and their families to obtain health, immunization, mental health, nutrition, parenting education, literacy education (including tutoring and remedial services), and social services (including substance abuse treatment, education, and prevention), for which such students and their families are eligible.

3c. Provide a family outreach and support program, including a plan for involving parents in the management of the program, in cooperation with parental involvement efforts undertaken pursuant to the Follow Through Act, Chapter I of the Elementary and Secondary Education Act of 1965, the Head Start Act, Part B of Chapter I of Title I of the Elementary and Secondary Act of 1965 (Even Start), and the Education of the Handicapped Act of 1975.

3d. Assist families, administrators, and teachers in enhancing developmental continuity between the programs assisted under the Head Start Act and elementary school classes.

3e. Assure that families will be involved in the design and operation of the program. Develop a plan describing how families will be involved.

COMPONENT 4: SOCIAL SERVICES

4a. Provide social services (including substance abuse treatment, education, and prevention).

4b. Provide assurances that state agencies, local agencies, and community-based organizations that provide supportive services to low-income students served by programs such as Head Start or local educational agency will designate an individual who will act as liaison to the supportive services team.

4c. Provide a plan for the development of a supportive services team of family service coordinators.

4d. Conduct home visits (see description under Parent Involvement).

Demonstration Programs. The National Transition Demonstration Study is guided by a set of primary questions related to understanding successful transitions and the effects of the Transition Demonstration Program. These research questions are as follows:

Question 1: How have the Head Start/Public School Early Childhood Transition Demonstration Programs been implemented?

Question 2: To what extent have comprehensive, continuous Head Start–like services been provided to participating children and families?

Question 3: What have been the barriers and difficulties encountered in implementing the Transition Demonstration Program?

Question 4: What characteristics of local sites are associated with more (or less) successful implementation of the Transition Demonstration Program?

Question 5: As a result of the Head Start/Public School Early Childhood Transition Demonstration Programs, what institutional and systemic changes are evident at local sites? Specifically, what systemic changes are noted in how Head Start programs, schools, service providers, and communities offer transition supports?

Question 6: To what extent do families participating in the Transition Demonstration Program show expected positive outcomes? Specifically, is there evidence of significantly increased parental involvement in children's school, improved family and parent functioning, and increased self-sufficiency as a function of program participation?

Question 7: To what extent do children in the Transition Demonstration Program show expected positive outcomes? Specifically, do children in the Transition Demonstration group, compared to those in the comparison group, show more positive attitudes toward school, better social-emotional adjustment, higher rates of progress in academic and language skills, and lower rates of school failure or special education placement?

Question 8: Are there some identifiable families and children who appear to benefit *more* from participating in the Transition Demonstration Program than do others? If yes, then who are they and what are the likely reasons (mediating processes) why they benefit more (or less) from program participation?

Question 9: Which families and children appear more likely to have poor transition experiences during the transition years? What are their characteristics, their service needs, and their challenging life circumstances?

Thus, there are many similarities in goals and practices between the Abecedarian Project and the National Transition Demonstration Program and some important differences. Noteworthy similarities include intensive and multicomponent programs, strong encouragement of parent involvement, and a focus on the beginning years of formal schooling. Some of the most noticeable positive differences are listed:

1. A much larger and more ethnically and culturally diverse sample in the Transition Demonstration Program

2. A multiplicity of sites in the Transition Demonstration Program that permits an examination of variation in community contextual factors and their relationships to developmental processes and outcomes identified within the Transitional Conceptual Model in Figure 8.2

As transition programs go to national scale and are implemented in diverse sites, the Transition Conceptual Model (Figure 8.2) is useful in explicitly acknowledging the importance of taking into account the resulting increased diversity in children, families, schools, and communities. What works in one place, with some families, in a given community may or may not work in other circumstances. To begin an exploration of the importance of these diversities, family diversity is being examined in ways that are hoped to be productive.

Perhaps one example might illustrate how the larger and more diverse sample of participants is an advantage analytically. Ramey, Ramey, and Gaines (1998) developed a family typology that is useful in understanding risk variation within the Head Start population. In the next section, this typology is discussed and related to some measures of children's readiness for school.

TOWARD A USEFUL TYPOLOGY OF FAMILIES AT RISK

Although there is tremendous variability in attributes among families living in poverty, few studies have sought to better understand the meaningfulness of that variability. Relatively few studies have compared familial variations with poverty and children's outcome, yet there is a wide spectrum of children's developmental outcomes among families at risk. Thus, although familial poverty predicts high rates of school failure relative to families who are not in poverty, not all or even most poor children fail in school. This lack of predictive precision suggests that within economic poverty other variables or factors are playing important roles in determining success or failure in school. Determining those factors and how to incorporate them into the risk models and, more important, into the service delivery models and public policies is a major issue of national urgency. Targeting services to families who do not fundamentally need them or who do not benefit from them is both bad science and bad public policy.

A long-standing area of deliberation and scientific concern has been how to adequately capture important dimensions of diversity within the general population of children and families. Historically, most research has contrasted low-income children and families with their middle-income counterparts. What has been lacking is a useful classification of families, in terms of their demographic and functional characteristics, who fall within poverty and thus under the classification of "at risk."

To increase understanding of educationally meaningful variations among families in poverty, a line of research that uses a cluster analysis statistical technique to develop and refine a typology of poverty families has been started. Preliminary work was begun by Ramey, Yeates, and MacPhee (1984) in the early 1980s. A sample that combined the 111 children from the Abecedarian Project with 63 children from a subsequent early intervention program for high-risk children called Project CARE (Ramey, Bryant, Sparling, & Wasik, 1985) is used in this chapter. The same eligibility requirements, including poverty status, were used in both studies and both were conducted in the same community.

Even though most previous research has considered children and families in poverty as relatively homogenous, data indicated that children from poor families with young mothers who lacked formal education and who had low assessed intelligence were at highest risk for cognitive, social, and academic problems. Conversely, children from families with older mothers, who were somewhat more educated and had higher IQs, as well as who provided a more supportive home environment for the child, were shown to be at "lesser" risk for poor academic and social development. Most important, for public policy, the children of the highest risk families were the ones who most benefited from the preschool program (Martin et al., 1990; Ramey et al., 1984).

There were, however, at least two important limitations to the preliminary work. First, information obtained was gathered at a single site in the United States. The lack of a national sample impeded adequate representation of diverse social, economic, and political influences as well as the accompanying variation in life circumstances, both for control families as well as for families receiving supplemental intervention supports. Second, the relatively small sample size ($N = 174$) hindered the ability to perform certain complex analyses to understand underlying processes regulating outcomes within and across subtypes. In short, the previous typology results were provocative but not conclusive due primarily to technical limitations that could not be addressed in a single-site intervention study no matter how large. The Transition Demonstration Program allowed these two limitations to be overcome.

The general strategy used for developing the family typology in the much larger-scale Transition Demonstration Program was as follows. First, 13 widely used variables known to describe important aspects of family characteristics were selected. These variables were as follows:

1.   Maternal education

2.   Presence of father in the home

3.   Maternal age at the time of child's entry into kindergarten

4.   Number of children in the home

5.   Number of adults in the home

6.   Mean household annual income

7.   Mother's employment status

8.   Maternal U.S. citizenship

9.   Whether the family had been homeless in the last year

10.   Whether the mother reported parenting assistance in the home

11.   Whether the mother self-reported chronic health problems

12.   Whether the mother received Aid to Families with Dependent Children (AFDC; now called Temporary Assistance for Needy Families) benefits

13.   Whether the mother reported English as the primary language spoken in the home

To develop reliable and valid family clusters, the data set was randomly divided into two equal groups. Then, the same cluster procedure was applied to each data set independently using the 13 variables to determine if similar solutions were obtained. In applying the SAS cluster criterion (SAS, 1996), six identical clusters were found and replicated in both data sets.

A theoretically important finding is that each family type occurred in all major ethnic/cultural groups studied: Caucasian, African American, Latino, and Native American. Thus, it appears that the six types are not simply markers for sociological-level molar variables. These family types are summarized in the following sections.

Family Type A: Traditional Family Configuration   This family type represents 30% of the former Head Start families. Fathers are present in more than 90% of these homes. In approximately 95% of these homes, mothers report that someone else helps regularly in caring for their child/family. The average educational level of these mothers is above high school (12.4 years), and they typically were 24 or 25 years old when the child in the study was born. This family type has also the highest average income although still below the federal poverty level. (Note: In describing each family type, it is important to recognize that there are some families that do not conform in terms of some characteristics. For example, for Family Type A, about 10% do not have fathers present in the homes and some mothers have less than a high school education. This is simply a limitation of present statistical clustering techniques.)

Family Type B: Single Unemployed Mother, Larger Family   This group represents the next largest family type (29%). Typically, the father is not present in these families (the father absence rate is 72%) and the mother is not employed (95% unemployment rate). Overwhelmingly, the mothers received AFDC (92%). Virtually all these families have mothers born in the United States who speak English at home, and none of these mothers report having chronic health problems themselves. The mothers' average educational level is slightly less than high school (11.3 years), and these families have on average the largest number of children (an average of 3.1) of any family type.

Family Type C: Working Mother, Usually Single, Smaller Family   The third major family type represents 24% of the families studied and may be distinguished primarily by high rates of maternal employment (72%) and by corresponding much lower rates of receiving AFDC (18%). All the mothers were born in the United States, and the fathers are present in only 24% of these families although they may not be married to the mother. All these families speak English at home, and the mothers have no chronic maternal health problems.

Family Type D: Traditional Family Configuration, Foreign-Born, Non-English Speaking at Home   The most important feature that differentiates this family type is that more than 99% do not speak English as their primarily language at home, and 80% of the mothers were not born in the United States. Fathers are present in 70% of these families, although only 57% of the mothers report that they have someone who helps them in major parenting duties. These mothers report having the least amount of formal schooling (average years of schooling is 10). This group represents 10% of the sample participating in the National Transition Demonstration Study.

Family Type E: Chronic Maternal Health Problems, Older Mothers   This family type represents only 3% of the study families. In all these families, the mother has chronic major health problems. These mothers are, on average, 2–4 years older than the mothers in the other family types, and their family income is very low (comparable to Group F, the very lowest). Fathers are present in only 39% of these homes, although 69% of the mothers report that someone else in their home helps them with child rearing. The mothers in this group have an average educational level of 11.5 years.

Family Type F: Homeless in Last Year, Unemployed   This family type represents 3% of the study sample. All these families were homeless at least some time in the past 12 months. On average, they have more than three children, and most mothers are not employed (unemployment rate is 74%). AFDC is received by 60% of these families. More than 92% speak English as their first language at home. These mothers have less than a high school education (on average, 11.5 years).

The next step in the exploration of family diversity was to ask if there were functional consequences for children's development related to the family types. Illustrated next are results using kindergarten measures of children's recapture language status and level of social skills as proxy variables for other, even more important outcomes, which are being vigorously pursued (consistent with the Transitional Conceptual Model) but which are not yet available for analysis.

Receptive Language Related to Family Type

Children's receptive language in kindergarten was assessed by the Peabody Picture Vocabulary Test–Revised (PPVT-R; Dunn & Dunn, 1981). An analysis indicated that, understandably, Type D children (from traditional, foreign-born, non–English-speaking families) had the lowest receptive language scores. Type F children from homeless, unemployed families and Type B children from single, unemployed, larger families significantly scored the next lowest. The families that scored the highest were those from the Type A "traditional" families (i.e., both parents present in the home and not on welfare). Thus, the family types relate systematically to the important domain of language development. Other domains of functioning of importance are continuing to be explored.

Social Skills

Children's social skills were assessed by the Social Skills Rating System developed by Gresham and Elliott (1990) for use by teachers and parents. The teacher questionnaire focuses on social skills and behaviors observed in the classroom, behavior problems, and academic performance and motivation.

Analysis of variance indicated that teacher ratings of children's social skills varied as a function of family type. Children from both of the "traditional" families (both parents in the home, not on welfare), Types A and D, were rated as having significantly more positive social skills than were the other children. Children's social skills from homeless families (Type F); older mothers with chronic health problems families (Type E); and single, unemployed mothers with larger families (Type B) were rated by their teachers as significantly lower than were those of other children.

Overall, these findings indicate that there are systematic and, perhaps, practically important differences among poverty families with respect to their children's levels of academic and social competence risk. This finding is a necessary prelude to the more intriguing question of whether the Transition Demonstration Project will have differential benefits on some of the subtypes. These authors hope to create a transition program typology in a fashion analogous to the family typology. By crossing the family typology with the program typology, they want to address empirically the question of what works best for whom.

CHILDREN'S PERSPECTIVE ON THE TRANSITION TO SCHOOL

Consistent with the definition of a successful transition to school presented in Figure 8.1, considerable effort has been devoted to determining children's attitudes toward school. For example, Ramey, Gaines, Phillips, and Ramey (1998) reported children's attitudes as they completed kindergarten.

Children themselves have provided information about their early school experiences via a questionnaire titled *What I Think of School* (Reid & Landesman, 1988). With this procedure, individual Vygotskian-style dialogues with children yield information on how much the child likes school, how hard the child tries in school, how well the child gets along with teachers and peers, how important it is to the child and to his or her parents to do well in school, how well the child is doing academically, and how much the teacher helps the child learn new things. (For a description of the rationale and procedures used to develop this child dialogue, see Reid, Ramey, & Burchinal, 1990.) Children indicate their responses on a three-point scale. Based on an independent sample of 337 children, this instrument has a test–retest reliability of .84 for all items and an internal consistency via Cronbach's alpha of .69 (Reid, Ramey, & Kerns, 1999). The items divide into two orthogonal factors: one composed of the two items concerning the importance of doing well in school to the child and to the parent, and the other containing the remaining items about school experiences.

The first set of analyses concerns children's perceptions of their first year in school. The overwhelming majority of former Head Start children (76%) reported liking school "a lot," with only 12% saying they liked school "not very much." Concerning how good their school work was, just more than two thirds (68%) said "great"; one fourth (24%), "sort of good"; and less than one tenth (8%), "not very good." Children had highly favorable impressions about how good their teacher was at helping them learn new things: 81% rated their teacher "very good"; 13%, "sort of good"; and 6%, "not very good." A large majority of children perceived that they got along very well with their teacher (78%) and other children (70%). Most children reported that to them doing well in school was "very important" (78%), with only 9% stating this was "not very important." Similarly, they perceived that their parents also highly valued doing well in school: More than 80% stated it was "very important" to their parents, and only 7% thought it was "not very important." Most children (83%) reported that they tried "very hard" to do well, and only 6% said they "did not really try hard."

Girls were significantly more positive than boys in their responses concerning how well they get along with the other children, how much they like school, how important doing well in school is to them, and how well they get along with their teachers. The magnitude of the differences, however, was relatively small (1%–5%).

Children Who Reported More and Less Positive School Perceptions

Although children's perceptions were generally highly positive, some children did report less favorable impressions. Two primary groups can be differentiated on the basis of responses to the questions, "How much do you like school?" and "How well do you do in school?" Seven percent of the children provided the lowest ratings for one or both questions and no highest rating for either question, with 3% providing the lowest ratings to both questions.

To explore possible factors that differentiated these groups—namely, those with more and less positive ratings of liking school and doing well—two sets of analyses were conducted. The first focused on whether children's responses to these questions were associated with other perceptions of school. The second tested hypotheses about whether certain child characteristics and family ecology variables differed between the two groups.

How Liking School and Doing Well Relate to Other School Perceptions

For all remaining items from the questionnaire *What I Think of School*, the two groups differed significantly and dramatically. Specifically, the children who were less positive reported that they did not try as hard in school, responding "I do not really try hard at all to do well in school" five times more often than students in the more positive group. They also believed that their teachers were less skilled in helping them learn new things, and many more said they did not get along very well with their teacher relative to more positive children. Children in the less positive group further reported that they did not get along very well with other children at school at a rate five times higher than children in the more positive group. Furthermore, only 43% of the children said they got along "very well" with peers, compared with 71% among the most positive group. Less than half (47%) of those in the less positive group said doing well in school was "very important" to them, with more than one third (34%) indicating that school was "not very important at all." Similarly, they believed that doing well in school was significantly less important to their parents than did children in the more positive group.

Factors Associated with More and Less Positive School Perceptions

To evaluate the contribution of child and family characteristics, correlational analyses and independent *t*-tests and chi-squares were conducted. Second, a logistic regression analysis, including variables significant at $p < .01$ from the first analyses, was conducted.

Individual Child Characteristics   Significant individual child characteristics were gender and children's Peabody Picture Vocabulary Test (PPVT) scores. Boys (60%) were significantly more likely than girls (40%) to be in the less positive group. Also, the more positive group had significantly higher PPVT scores than did the less positive group. Rates of special education placement in kindergarten and children's age at school entry did not differ significantly between the two groups.

Overwhelmingly, Asian or Pacific Islander (97%), Alaskan Native (100%), and Latino (96%) children were in the more positive group. Somewhat fewer Native American (92%), Caucasian (93%), African American (93%), and "other" (93%) children were in the more positive group.

Family Ecology   Children in the less positive group differed significantly from those in the more positive group for only two family risk variables: maternal age and homes in which English was not the primary language. Specifically, the mean maternal age in the more positive group was 30.2 years (SD = 5.45), slightly higher than in the less positive group (M = 29.4 years, SD = 5.41). In the more positive group, 8% used English as a second language, whereas only 4% did in the less positive group. Maternal educational level, employment status, whether a father was present in the home, presence of a chronic health problem in the primary caregiver, family income level (less than or more than $18,000 per year), and maternal depression did not differ significantly between the two groups.

It is important to note that family ecology might be better represented by a composite risk score rather than individual variables (e.g., Sameroff & McDonough, 1994). Thus, a Family Risk Index was created that counted the number of the following risk conditions present: poverty, low income, maternal education less than high school, maternal depression, English as a second language, parental chronic health problem, single-parent household with no additional parenting assistance, teen mother, homelessness, receiving AFDC, receiving Supplemental Security Income (SSI), and parental unemployment. Family Risk Index scores could range from 0 to 11. Children in the less positive group came from families with slightly higher risk scores than did those in the more positive group. Another aspect of family ecology considered was whether the child's primary caregiver anticipated school adjustment problems prior to school entry. In fact, significantly more caregivers of the less positive children reported that they had anticipated problems. Forty-five percent of the parents in the more positive group thought about possible adjustment problems, whereas fifty-three percent of those in the less positive group had. These numbers indicate that many parents anticipated the possibility of school adjustment problems, although on an individual basis parental anticipation was not highly predictive of children's school perceptions.

Logistic regression results revealed that boys were 1.4 times more likely to have negative school perceptions than were girls. Children in homes where English was the primary spoken language were more than three times less likely to be in the less positive group than were children in homes where another language was spoken. In addition, children with lower receptive language skills (as measured by the PPVT-R) were more likely to be in the less positive group.

Academic Competence and Attitude Toward School

Teachers' standardized ratings (M = 100, SD = 15) from the Academic Competence Scale of the Social Skills Rating System (Gresham & Elliott, 1990) were examined in kindergarten. Teachers rated children in the more positive group significantly higher than those in the less positive group.

Parents' Perceptions of Children's School Adjustment

Although parents of children with more and less positive school perceptions generally rated their children's attitudes as positive, there were statistically significant differences between these groups in their ratings for all items from *Your Child's Adjustment to School* (Reid & Landesman, 1988). Specifically, parents of children with more positive views reported greater child adjustment in terms of liking school, doing well in school, trying hard, overall adjustment, getting along with other children, and having a good relationship with their teacher. Thus, at the beginning of public school, former Head Start children generally like school. Those who do not are in a small minority and have some readily identifiable family and teacher characteristics. What these attitudes toward school portend for the child's progress through school and whether the Transition Demonstration Program will exert its hypothesized positive effect is now being investigated and will be reported in the coming year as the full dataset becomes available for analysis.

FUTURE RESEARCH

Based on the findings about the transition to school from the Abecedarian Project and the National Transition Demonstration Study, as well as from the information presented at "The Transition to Kindergarten: A Synthesis Conference" (Charlottesville, Virginia, February 18–20, 1998) sponsored by the Office of Educational Research and Improvement (OERI), some needed research that should be given high priority has been recognized.

The gaps in a relatively new field of inquiry inevitably are numerous. Accordingly, an attempt has been made to specify those most crucial for advancing understanding about what contributes to more successful transitions and how the obstacles or factors that hinder successful transitions can be minimized. To the extent possible, these gaps have been linked to theoretical underpinnings and to potential practical significance. Furthermore, promising and alternative ways to address these gaps in knowledge are suggested.

There are five central issues that must be addressed vigorously to obtain a holistic, integrated, and contextual understanding of the transition to school especially for children at risk. These issues have been framed in terms of known principles of human behavior (Ramey & Ramey, 1998) and then derivative questions about the transition process have been asked.

Principle 1: The Primacy of Early Experience

Vast amounts of scientific data endorse the principle that early experiences are highly influential for later performance. There is increasing evidence about the significance of the first 5 years of life for early brain and behavioral development. Concerning the transition to school, what is not known is precisely how children's early school experiences and their early adjustment (both academic and social-emotional) directly influence later school experiences and progress. This question can be asked in terms of children's attitudes toward school and learning; their engagement in learning activities within the school context and outside school (at home and in the community); their academic gains; and their social-emotional well-being (e.g., behavioral adjustment versus behavior problems, friendships, social skills with peers, social skills with adults). Which particular early school experiences are the most important? That is, are there some events or experiences that are highly facilitative of later successes in school or of school failures?

Recommendation   Research in this area can benefit from large-scale, population-based prospective studies of diverse groups of children, families, schools, and communities, but it can also be informed by targeted studies of extreme groups of children, families, schools, or communities. Short-term prospective longitudinal studies that assess closely the variations in early school experiences and ascertain their primacy in determining child and family outcomes are needed. Participant observation, systematic classroom and family observations, and frequent interviews with all participants will provide much needed data about the transition process.

Principle 2: The Principle of Transactional Influences

This influential theory about transactions posits that partners are changed via their transactions with one another, rather than relationships being unidirectional (Sameroff & Haith, 1996). In other words, what occurs through the process of transition is hypothesized to change not only the child, but also the other partners in the child's learning environment. Is there evidence that teachers are changed during the year, or from year to year, by their encounters with particular types of children and families or by changes in how communities support what occurs in the classroom? It is one thing to have children and families perceive that their concerns and needs are met (certainly, an important perception). Yet it is quite another to demonstrate that teachers and other educators actually change in their attitudes, skills, and practices because of the transactions they have had. Similarly, the same questions can be asked about parents, principals, and communities. If schools seek to be responsive and adaptable, and if families seek to support their children's progress in school and positive attitudes toward learning, then evidence of this transactional principle in operation is needed. Such data will be invaluable in helping to specify what types of transactions promote more positive changes and participation in mutually supportive activities at the level of child, parents, educators, and communities and what types lead to major problems (e.g., withdrawal, obstructive behavior, aggression, lack of cooperation).

Recommendation   Because transactional influences are at the core of a systems approach to development it is recommended that they be studied directly at all of the levels that shape children's transition to school: child, family, school, and community. Furthermore, it is recommended that serious investments be made in developing better research instruments and methods to capture these changing influences. Reliance on questionnaires and rating scales needs to be complemented by methodological innovation and increased sophistication.

Principle 3: The Principle of Historical Change and Contextualism

The principle of historical change states that all societal institutions are in flux. Just as families are changing in terms of how they are structured, how they function, and what their values and goals are for their children, so are schools in a state of change. It cannot be anticipated that what will be learned from studying transition at one time of history will necessarily apply to other times. This necessitates a critical reanalysis and reinterpretation of findings from cohorts studied 10, 20, or even 50 years ago. It also serves as a reminder of the value of placing present-day study within its full context, including historical, geographical, economic, and political. All too often, educational and developmental research concerning children's school adjustment has ignored where the study occurred, when it occurred, and what the major societal forces were that could have influenced who was studied, what was happening in their lives, and the degree to which certain findings were obtained. This additional demand—that research be placed within a historical and contextual perspective—is not for the sake of mere academic completeness, nor is it to appease certain political or social movements. Rather, asking questions about the extent to which certain findings transcend different time periods and contexts versus depending heavily on the complex array of contextual conditions is central to developing a useful theory of what school transitions represent in the lives of children, families, schools, and communities. This is a case in which systematic study of these contextual forces will inform practices, so that correlation from a few narrow studies will not be inappropriately mistaken for causation or inappropriately generalized to other places. In many states and cities, public education is described as in a major crisis.

Public confidence in our ability to "fix" education or significantly improve the outcome of public education is not high. The research must take into account current issues. Some research will address practices or problems that plague particular communities, such as the now popular tendency among upper–middle-class families to have their children enter kindergarten a year later (referred to as "academic red-shirting") so their children will be at an advantage relative to peers or the converse tendency among Head Start–eligible families to have children enter school at the earliest age possible, because there are no other community educational alternatives for them. In communities where Head Start children and upper–middle-class children are in the same kindergarten classrooms, a divergence in the skill level of the children is created that is even greater than the disparity observed when children are the same age. These examples are included to illustrate the importance of conducting studies with a full awareness of community factors affecting what is seen at the classroom level or the level of adjustment of individual children and families. The seminal work of Entwisle and Alexander (Chapter 2) looked beyond simply monitoring year-end academic performance of children and discovered that children from economically impoverished homes disproportionately lost many of their gains from school because they did not have summer experiences that furthered their intellectual skills (as did more advantaged peers). This finding, grounded in a contextual view of children's lives, led to a radically different appraisal of what schools achieved and what they could accomplish alone in their traditional mode of operation.

Recommendation It is recommended that a set of standard descriptors be gathered in studies of school transitions so that findings from different cohorts and across locations can be systematically compared. This will facilitate conducting meta-analyses and addressing the degree of similarity or difference across studies to facilitate more thoughtful reviews of the empirical work. It is likely that studies that appear to yield discrepant findings may, in fact, not be discrepant but instead reflect important differences in who was studied and identifiable features of the school and community contexts. Knowing the full context in which transitions occur, as well as methodological variations across studies, is vital to interpreting findings usefully.

Principle 4: The Principle of Systematic Individual Differences

This principle is somewhat analogous to the principle of historical change and contextualism. Extensive data confirms that individuals vary systematically in their response to the same situation and that these differences can be attributed, at least in part, to biological and social factors. The idea of the "match" between children and environments or environmental expectations is not new (see Hunt, 1961), nor uniquely associated with any one branch of the human disciplines (see Miller, 1978). In education, child–setting interactions have been recognized and studied since the 1970s (see Cronbach, 1975). This principle reiterates that there is unlikely to be a set of transition strategies that work best or are needed for all types of children, families, schools, or communities. Of particular interest, however, is the identification of groups of children at risk for the poorest quality school transitions and careful study of their needs and adaptation. Theoretically, it is quite likely that what comprises an optimal set of supports and transactions for highly gifted children during the transition to school may not be the same as for children who come from a foreign country, who have social or behavioral adjustment problems, or who enter school significantly delayed in their language and intellectual skills.

Recommendation   It is vital that individual differences be studied vigorously so that schools, communities, and families do not adopt a "one size fits all" strategy when not appropriate. At the same time, excessive individualization of the transition process for every child and family may not be feasible or particularly beneficial to certain types or even the majority of children entering school.

Principle 5: The Principle of Codetermination

The codetermination principle states that a child's developmental progress is codetermined by many factors, ranging from genetic and biological influences to family-, peer-, and neighborhood-level influences. In some ways, this reality makes the study of transition seem like an overwhelming task to perform thoroughly or accurately. Nonetheless, awareness of this principle serves to inform the selection of variables to be measured and decisions about the timing of when to collect data. For many people in American society, the questions about children's well-being and their academic achievement have been reduced to an either–or situation in which either parents or the schools are blamed. This type of simplistic blame is reminiscent of the outmoded heredity versus environment controversy that has hindered the study of the growth of intelligence (see Shore, 1997). Codetermination is implicitly assumed in the definition of successful transitions to school because cooperation, collaboration, and partnerships among children, families, schools, and communities are included as hallmarks of successful transitions.

Educators and developmentalists do not deny that there are potentially powerful early influences on a child's development and readiness to learn. Parents are widely acknowledged to be the child's first and foremost teachers. Furthermore, family factors—from demography to literacy—have always accounted for a large amount of the variance in observed competency differences among children. What has been overlooked in most empirical research is the codetermination that undergirds children's learning. Typically, studies of effective schools and best classroom practices have ignored who the children and families are. Similarly, studies of family influences and the value of family participation in children's schooling often fail to consider what is happening in the classroom or at the level of the school and school district. Narrow study of only a few factors influencing children's progress is unlikely to result in substantial gains in knowledge.

A central issue here concerns the resources any one study has to explore the process of transition. Not every potentially relevant factor can be measured. More important, many carefully conducted prospective, longitudinal studies have gathered rich descriptive datasets yet failed to analyze these thoroughly. In addition to conducting new studies, it is likely that certain valuable databases can be identified for continued analysis as germane to questions about the transition process. Cross-study comparisons might be highly informative. Some of these datasets may have been collected as part of evaluating interventions (such as randomized trials to prevent aggressiveness in high-risk children, studies to maximize the gains from Head Start through third grade, studies of children followed from birth who participated in early intervention). Sophisticated data analysis now permits more integrated approaches to using these rich databases, yet these approaches are rarely applied to existing datasets. Furthermore, the history of conducting large-scale evaluations or research projects has been that few ever are fully analyzed, because funding and timing do not permit these after the primary study questions are answered. This is especially true of large government evaluation projects conducted outside university settings where the priority seldom is on presenting findings widely and pursuing data analyses beyond the formal requirements of the evaluation contract.

Recommendation   The study of transitions will benefit from multiple investigators having access to rich databases to answer particular questions about the transition to school. In addition, new longitudinal research of population-based samples representing different school and community ecologies is needed, with an explicit focus on the mechanisms responsible for more or less successful transitions. The limitations of existing databases must, of course, be acknowledged; nonetheless, these are likely to inform future research in terms of design; choice of measures; timing of measurement; and subgroups of children, families, schools, and communities to study in greater depth.

CONCLUSION

The quality of the transition to school is important to each and every child. It is a cultural universal that is remembered with fondness or despair well into adulthood and frequently passed on as a legacy to the next generation. Too many children from poor and undereducated families are not doing as well as expected. The reasons for this situation are complex and only partially understood. A substantial body of literature, both theoretical and empirical, provides reason for optimism that flexible, individualized, comprehensive programs can improve the developmental trajectory and school performance of youth at risk. It is a central tenet of this chapter that a solid partnership of program developers and researchers is a key ingredient in improving the lives and futures of children, schools, and communities.

REFERENCES

Alexander, K.L., & Entwisle, D.R. (1988). Achievement in the first 2 years of school: Patterns and processes. *Monographs of the Society for Research in Child Development, 53*, 1–157 (Serial No. 218).

Breitmayer, B.J., & Ramey, C.T. (1986). Biological nonoptimality and quality of postnatal environment as codeterminants of intellectual development. *Child Development, 57*, 1151–1165.

Bryk, A.S., & Raudenbush, S.W. (1987). Application of hierarchical linear models to assessing change. *Psychological Bulletin, 101*, 147–158.

Burchinal, M., Lee, M., & Ramey, C.T. (1989). Type of day care and preschool intellectual development in disadvantaged children. *Child Development, 60*, 128–137.

Burchinal, M.R., & Appelbaum, M.I. (1991). Estimating individual developmental functions: Methods and their assumptions. *Child Development, 62*, 23–43.

Burchinal, M.R., Bryant, D.M., Lee, M.W., & Ramey, C.T. (1992). Early day care, infant–mother attachment, and maternal responsiveness in the infant's first year. *Early Childhood Research Quarterly, 7*, 383–396.

Campbell, F.A., Breitmayer, B.J., & Ramey, C.T. (1986). Disadvantaged single teenage mothers and their children: Consequences of free educational day care. *Family Relations, 35*, 63–68.

Campbell, F.A., & Ramey, C.T. (1994). Effects of early intervention on intellectual and academic achievement: A follow-up study of children from low-income families. *Child Development, 65*, 684–698.

Campbell, F.A., & Ramey, C.T. (1995). Cognitive and school outcomes for high risk African-American students at middle adolescence: Positive effects of early intervention. *American Educational Research Journal, 32*, 743–772.

Cicirelli, V.G. (1969). *The impact of Head Start: An evaluation of the effects of Head Start on children's cognitive and affective development*. Athens, OH: Westinghouse Learning Corp.

Crnic, K., & Lamberty, G. (1994). Reconsidering school readiness: Conceptual and applied perspectives. *Early Education and Development, 5*, 91–105.

Cronbach, L.J. (1975). Beyond the two disciplines of scientific psychology. *American Psychology, 30*, 116–127.

Dunn, L., & Dunn, L. (1981). *PPVT-R manual for Forms L and M*. Circle Pines, MN: American Guidance Service.

Gresham, F.M., & Elliott, S.N. (1990). *Social Skills Rating System*. Circle Pines, MN: American Guidance Service.

Guralnick, M.J. (Ed.). (1997). *The effectiveness of early intervention*. Baltimore: Paul H. Brookes Publishing Co.

Hernstein, R.J., & Murray, C. (1994). *The bell curve: Intelligence and class structure in American life*. New York: The Free Press.

Horacek, H.J., Ramey, C.T., Campbell, F.A., Hoffmann, K.P., & Fletcher, R.H. (1987). Predicting school failure and assessing early intervention with high-risk children. *American Academy of Child and Adolescent Psychiatry, 26*, 758–763.

Hunt, J.M. (1961). *Intelligence and experience*. New York: Ronald Press.

Individuals with Disabilities Education Act (IDEA) of 1990, PL 101-476. (October 30, 1990). Title 20, U.S.C. 1400 et seq: *U.S. Statutes at Large, 104*, 1103–1151.

Kagan, S.L. (1994). Early care and education: Beyond the fishbowl. *Phi Delta Kappan, 76*, 184–187.

Lazar, I., Darlington, R., Murray, H., Royce, J., & Snipper, A. (1982). Lasting effects of early education: A report from the Consortium for Longitudinal Studies. *Monographs of the Society for Research in Child Development, 47*(2–3, Serial No. 195).

Martin, S.L., Ramey, C.T., & Ramey, S.L. (1990). The prevention of intellectual impairment in children of impoverished families: Findings of a randomized trial of educational day care. *American Journal of Public Health, 80*, 844–847.

Miller, J.G. (1978). *Living systems*. New York: McGraw-Hill.

Ramey, C.T., Bryant, D., Sparling, J.J., & Wasik, B.H. (1985). Educational interventions to enhance intellectual development: Comprehensive day care versus family education. In S. Harel & N.J. Anastasiow (Eds.), *The at-risk infant: Psycho-socio-medical aspects* (pp. 75–85). Baltimore: Paul H. Brookes Publishing Co.

Ramey, C.T., & Campbell, F.A. (1984). Preventive education for high-risk children: Cognitive consequences of the Carolina Abecedarian Project. *American Journal of Mental Deficiency, 88*, 515–523.

Ramey, C.T., & Campbell, F.A. (1992). Poverty, early childhood education, and academic competence: The Abecedarian experiment. In A. Huston (Ed.), *Children in poverty* (pp. 190–221). New York: Cambridge University Press.

Ramey, C.T., Farran, D.C., & Campbell, F.A. (1979). Early intervention: From research to practice. In B. Darby & M.J. May (Eds.), *Infant assessment: Issues and applications* (pp. 215–232). Seattle, WA: Westar.

Ramey, C.T., & Haskins, R. (1981). The modification of intelligence through early experience. *Intelligence, 5,* 21–27.

Ramey, C.T., MacPhee, D., & Yeates, K.O. (1982). Preventing developmental retardation: A general systems model. In J.M. Joffee & L.A. Bond (Eds.), *Facilitating infant and early childhood development* (pp. 343–401). Hanover, NH: University Press of New England.

Ramey, C.T., & Ramey, S.L. (1995). Successful early interventions for children at high risk for failure in school. In G. Demko & M. Jaspoan (Eds.), *Populations at risk in America at the end of the 20th century* (pp. 129–145). Boulder, CO: Westview Press.

Ramey, C.T., & Ramey, S.L. (1996). Early intervention: Optimizing development for children with disabilities and risk conditions. In M. Wolraich (Ed.), *Disorders of development and learning: A practical guide to assessment and management* (2nd ed., pp. 141–158). St. Louis, MO: Mosby.

Ramey, C.T., & Ramey, S.L. (1998). Early intervention and early experience. *American Psychologist, 53,* 109–120.

Ramey, C.T., Ramey, S.L., & Gaines, R. (1998). Differentiating developmental risk levels for families in poverty: Creating a family typology. In M. Lewis & C. Feiring (Eds.), *Families, risk, and competence.* (pp. 187–205). Mahwah, NJ: Lawrence Erlbaum Associates.

Ramey, C.T., Yeates, K.O., & MacPhee, D. (1984). Risk for retarded development among disadvantaged families: A systems theory approach to preventive intervention. In B. Keogh (Ed.), *Advances in special education* (pp. 249–272). Greenwich, CT: JAI Press.

Ramey, C.T., Yeates, K.O., & Short, E.J. (1984). The plasticity of intellectual development: Insights from preventive intervention. *Child Development, 55,* 1913–1925.

Ramey, S.L., Gaines, R., Phillips, M., & Ramey, C.T. (1998). Perspectives of former Head Start children and their parents on the transition to school. *The Elementary School Journal, 98,* 311–328.

Ramey, S.L., & Ramey, C.T. (1992). *The National Head Start/Public School Early Childhood Transition Study: An overview.* Washington, DC: Administration on Children, Youth, and Families.

Ramey, S.L., & Ramey, C.T. (1997). Evaluating educational programs: Strategies to understand and enhance educational effectiveness. In C. Seefeldt & A. Galper (Eds.), *Continuing issues in early childhood education* (2nd ed., pp. 274–292). Upper Saddle River, NJ: Prentice-Hall.

Ramey, S.L., Ramey, C.T., & Phillips, M.M. (1996). *Head Start children's entry into public school: An interim report on the National Head Start–Public School Early Childhood Transition Demonstration Study.* Washington, DC: U.S. Department of Health & Human Services.

Reid, M., & Landesman, S. (1988). *Your child's adjustment to school.* Seattle, WA: University of Washington.

Reid, M.K., Ramey, S.L., & Kerns, K. (1999). What I think of school: 6- to 12-year old children's perceptions of their school adjustment. Manuscript submitted for publication.

Reid, M.K., Ramey, S.L., & Burchinal, M. (1990). Dialogues with children about their families. In I. Bretherton & M. Watson (Eds.), *Children's perspectives on their families: New directions for child development* (pp. 5–28). San Francisco: Jossey-Bass.

Sameroff, A.J., & Haith, M.M. (Eds.). (1996). *The five to seven year shift: The age of reason and responsibility.* Chicago: University of Chicago Press.

Sameroff, A., & McDonough, S.C. (1994). Educational implications of developmental transitions: Revisiting the 5- to 7-year shift. *Phi Delta Kappan, 76,* 188–193.

SAS Institute. (1996). SAS© Software, version 6.11. Cary, NC: SAS Institute, Inc.

Shore, R. (1997). *Rethinking the brain: New insights into early development.* New York: Families and Work Institute.

Woodcock, R.W., & Johnson, M.B. (1977). *Woodcock-Johnson Psychoeducational Battery. Part 2: Test of academic achievement.* Hingham: Teaching Resources.

Zeskind, P.S., & Ramey, C.T. (1978). Fetal malnutrition: An experimental study of its consequences on infant development in two caregiving environments. *Child Development, 49,* 1155–1162.

Chapter 9

Children with Disabilities in Early Elementary School

Mark Wolery

Young children with disabilities and children at substantial risk for disabilities and their families often face a number of significant transitions during the children's first 8 years. The shift to school-age services is one of several transitions children and their families experience. In this chapter, conclusions are drawn from research and practices related to the transition to school-age services. When appropriate, recommendations related to transition practices for children without disabilities are suggested and the class placements of children with disabilities in the early elementary grades are discussed. Finally, this chapter focuses on issues related to serving children with disabilities who are in their early elementary school years.

The most common transitions faced by families of children with disabilities are identified and defined in the following section. Service goals related to these transitions are described; and challenges to transition, as well as recommended practices for addressing those challenges and promoting smooth transitions, are identified.

COMMON TRANSITIONS FOR CHILDREN WITH DISABILITIES

Many disabling conditions are evident at birth. Some of these conditions threaten infants' survival, whereas some, but not all, require infants with disabilities to stay

Development of this chapter was supported by the U.S. Department of Education, Office of Special Education and Rehabilitative Services (Grant No. HO24Q70001). However, the opinions expressed do not necessarily reflect the policy of the U.S. Department of Education, and no official endorsement should be inferred.

in neonatal intensive care nurseries for an extended period. For these infants, the transition from hospital to home may be sufficiently challenging to require specific assistance for the family (Thurman, Cornwell, & Korteland, 1989). This assistance may include helping families learn how to care for their infant, providing social support for the parents, connecting parents with community agencies and programs, and continuing interventions and therapeutic practices initiated in the hospital.

Once at home, some infants and toddlers with disabilities attend a center-based intervention program (Mowder, 1997; Stayton & Karnes, 1994), family day care (Golbeck & Harlan, 1997), or child care center (Craig, 1997). Such services may be needed to allow the mother to return to work, to provide parents with daily respite, or to deliver early intervention services. Other infants and toddlers, of course, may be served in their homes (Sandall, 1997a). Families of infants and toddlers with disabilities receive services from Part C (formerly Part H) of the Individuals with Disabilities Education Act (IDEA) of 1997 (PL 105-17). As part of these services, an individualized family service plan (IFSP) must be developed, which must specify how both the child and the family will make the transition to preschool services (Part B) (Sandall, 1997b; Turbiville, Turnbull, Garland, & Lee, 1996).

Children served through the infant and toddler program (Part C) and who are eligible for preschool services (Part B) often undergo a transition at age 3. This transition is often challenging because it may involve changing service providers, having different operating procedures and regulations, and experiencing new service delivery options (Bruder & Chandler, 1996). Although preschool services for children ages 3 through 5 years are under the auspices of public education, children with disabilities and their families often face another transition into school-age services (Atwater, Orth-Lopes, Elliott, Carta, & Schwartz, 1994). A transition at this point often occurs because many schools do not provide direct preschool services in elementary schools; rather, those services occur in a variety of programs (e.g., child care programs, Head Start programs, early intervention programs, home visiting programs). Thus, young children with disabilities and their families may face a transition from the hospital to home, from home to a group care arrangement for infants and toddlers, from the infant/toddler program to a preschool program, and from the preschool program into public school at age 5 or 6. These transitions, of course, occur in the context of the family adapting to caring for, and living with, a child with disabilities.

Many young children without disabilities also experience multiple transitions during the early childhood years. Specifically, they may make the transition from home care to family day care, to a Head Start program, or to a community child care center before enrolling in public school, usually at kindergarten entry age. However, these transitions are often made for family reasons rather than to receive specific services for the child requiring them.

TRANSITIONS: DEFINITIONS AND GOALS

Young children experience a variety of different transitions: from program to program, daily transitions from home to program to home, and transitions within programs. The program to program transitions should be planned carefully around specific goals. These transitions and transition goals are discussed in this section.

Defining Transitions

At least three types of transitions related to young children need to be defined. First, as presented in the preceding section, transitions involve movement from one setting to another, including from one service agency or arrangement to another and from one set of formal supports to another. Thus, this includes transitions having a "sending" agency, group, person, or service arrangement and transitions having a "receiving" agency, group, person, or service arrangement (Atwater et al., 1994). Defined as such, transitions involve children and families moving from one program to another, and transition services involve preparing families and children for this move, supporting them during the move, and maintaining contact with them to address problems that may arise immediately after the move.

Second, when children participate in group care or therapy outside the home, they experience daily transitions. These transitions involve leaving parental care, entering care by another adult, and returning to parental care. Daily transitions are difficult for many young children regardless of their ability status, and these transitions may present particular difficulties for children with disabilities. Group care early intervention programs do not always occur every day; thus, children's daily schedules vary throughout the typical week. For example, they may attend a group intervention program two or three mornings per week, go to a child or family day care program for those afternoons, go to even another group care arrangement on other days of the week, or stay home with a parent on some days. For some young children with disabilities, they may see a therapist (e.g., occupational therapist, physical therapist, speech-language pathologist) one or two times per week for an hour or so. This variation in daily schedule may lead to less predictability about daily events and thus less adaptation to them. Furthermore, some children with disabilities (e.g., those with autism) may become disruptive or upset when they are required to change settings or situations. For early elementary school age children with disabilities, daily transitions may occur between a general education class, special education class, and special subject classes (e.g., art, music, physical education). A range of challenges to children and their teachers can accompany these daily transitions. These daily transitions for children with and without disabilities have not been thoroughly studied.

Third, within each setting transitions occur. For example, in a classroom, the child may move (transition) from one play area to another and from one activity to another (e.g., snack time to free play); these are called *in-class transitions* (Wolery, Anthony, & Heckathorn, 1998). Some of these in-class transitions involve only the child with disabilities, whereas others include the entire group. These transitions are often difficult for teachers, and children can spend significant portions of their classroom time in such transitions (Sainato, 1990). These transitions can also occur in homes; for example, the child can move from dinner to playing with siblings and from playing to taking a bath and going to bed. These transitions can be problematic times for all parents and young children, including families with children who have disabilities.

For the remainder of this section, transitions of the first type (from program to program) are discussed with emphasis placed on the transition from preschool services to elementary school age services. The term *school age* is used broadly and refers to the time when the child is no longer considered to be part of the preschool program but to be part of the elementary program. The precise age for this classification shift varies across localities. In some cases, a major transition occurs before children's kindergarten year; for others, it occurs after kindergarten; and in other cases, it occurs after some postkindergarten transition class. Nonetheless, sometime between the age of 5 and 7 years, children are seen as being part of the elementary school program rather than part of the preschool program.

Rosenkoetter, Hains, and Fowler (1994) identified six statements that reflect the general knowledge about transitions:

- "Transition is a lifelong process" (p. 4). All people experience transition during childhood, adolescence, and adulthood. Transitions are not a uniquely early childhood event or process.

- "Transitions are inevitable" (p. 5). Children and families in early childhood special education programs move to other programs based on the age of the children. Thus, some transitions are going to occur and cannot be eliminated; they are a basic component of the current service structure.

- "Transition is a continuous process" (p. 5). Because the early childhood years progress quickly, the child and family are often in an almost continuous process of adapting to one program and getting ready to move on to another program. Furthermore, preparing the child, family, and staff of both the sending and receiving programs requires time, which in turn extends the duration of the transition process.

- "Early transitions are significant" (p. 5). Because children are young, they and their families often have little experience with these types of transitions. As a result, the transitions may produce a significant amount of discomfort and uncertainty. The transition into elementary school, including kindergarten, is a critical event in the lives of many families, and such events are associated with increased stress, reflection, and disruption to family life (Bailey, 1988).

- "Transitions involve change" (p. 5). Often the transition from preschool to school-age services involves different service providers, schedules, settings, and expectations. This requires the child and family to understand and to adapt to these differences. Also, for families, different amounts and modes of communication may exist with the new professionals. This sets the stage for misunderstanding and for miscommunication between the home and the school.

- "Transitions are usually stressful" (p. 6). Because of the nature of change involved in transitions, the child and, in particular, the family may experience a fairly substantial amount of stress.

These general statements about transitions are likely to be applicable to all young children and their families, perhaps in varying levels of intensity. Special consideration for children with disabilities may be needed, and schools and preschool programs involved in transitions should examine their practices in light of these statements. For example, recognizing that transition to elementary school is inevitable and that it may be a critical event for families, child care centers should engage in specific practices to help children adjust to the transition (e.g., visiting an elementary school, going on joint field trips with early elementary classes). Likewise, child care programs should assist families in understanding the kindergarten registration process used in their communities. Similarly, the public schools can communicate with community child care programs about the transition process and about the nature of the early elementary curriculum.

Goals of Transition Services

Although individual goals for children may vary and specific program goals can be established, at least four broad goals can be stated for transitions from one program to another: "(1) to ensure continuity of services . . . (2) to minimize disruptions to the family system by facilitating adaptation to change . . . (3) to ensure that children are prepared to function in the receiving program . . . [and] (4) to fulfill, in some cases, the legal requirements of P. L. 99-457" (Wolery, 1989, pp. 2–3). Continuity of services involves making sure that the needed services are provided to both the child and the family. This includes ensuring that needed therapy and specialized services are continued, only necessary assessments are conducted, teaching practices that were successful in the sending program are communicated to those in the receiving program, and important goals in the sending program are communicated to those in the receiving program.

As noted previously, transitions involve changes, some of which can be disruptive to the family system. Transition from the preschool status to school entry is a normative critical event for families (Bailey et al., 1986). This event or process, though normative, may be associated with a substantial amount of change, uncertainty, and concern (Hanline, 1988), and this stress may be increased when the child has a disability (Bailey et al., 1986). Of course, the transition to school programs can also be associated with decreased demands and decreased stress on families. For example, if the child has participated in a part-day program during the preschool years, child care would need to be secured for the remaining portions of the parents' work day, which may involve added expense, transportation needs, and difficulties in finding adequate child care. Thus, having a full-day school program may eliminate some of these stressful events. However, such benefits tend to be realized only after a smooth transition is completed.

Ensuring that children can function in the new setting is necessary because preschool classes tend to be quite different from early elementary classes. Preschool classes tend to have lower child-to-staff ratios, more individual and small-group instruction and activities, less demand on the child to adhere to a fixed schedule, less need for independence on the part of the child, and more teacher assistance and support. Thus, the conditions under which the child must function in the receiving program can be quite different from those to which the child is accustomed. Even when conditions across the sending and receiving programs are similar, lack of skill maintenance and generalization (transfer) may occur with rather minor shifts in settings (Warren & Horn, 1996). Thus, practices that promote both maintenance and generalization should be used.

Engaging in transition services to meet the requirements of the IDEA is particularly important for transitions from infant and toddler services to preschool services (Part C to Part B), because transition plans are required. Having transition goals on the individualized plans for preschoolers is a defensible and desired practice, but such plans are not required. Nonetheless, all children with disabilities and their families have specific due process rights that exist throughout children's public education. These rights and the procedures used to ensure these rights are protected and require careful consideration in planning transitions. In some cases, attempts to comply with procedural requirements of IDEA may unwittingly lead to increased family stress and inconvenience. For example, in some systems, children who undergo an eligibility assessment at age 4 experience another one at age 5 prior to entry into elementary services. Minimizing duplicative assessments is important in reducing disruption to families and ensuring continuity of services (Shotts, Rosenkoetter, Streufert, & Rosenkoetter, 1994).

These goals were specified for programs that work with children with disabilities and their families. Nonetheless, variations of these goals may be relevant for child care programs that are primarily designed to work with children without disabilities. For example, preparing children for school entry is a major national goal that has undergone significant debate and discussion (see Chapter 3). However, ensuring that the transition is not stressful for children, that it fosters eagerness for school activities and learning, and that it promotes children's perceptions of themselves as competent learners are goals to which most early childhood educators assign value. Discussions are appropriate between community child care programs and public school personnel about what constitutes appropriate preparation of children for entry into the school-age program. Similarly, schools clearly have a vested interest in families doing well, and promoting the smooth transition of children into elementary programs may be a means of generally supporting families. Thus, early childhood programs for children without disabilities and public schools should consider establishing goals related to the transition into the school program. Establishing joint goals between schools and community early childhood programs is recommended.

Transition Challenges and Recommended Practices

A host of events and conditions reduces the probability that children's services will be continuous, family systems will be disrupted minimally, and children will be prepared to function in the receiving program. These challenges exist at the systemic levels and at the individual child and family levels. Comprehensive transition programs often target their efforts on the following areas: 1) administrative and interagency issues, 2) issues related to the staff of the sending and receiving programs, 3) issues related to families, and 4) issues related to children (Bruder & Chandler, 1996; Rous, Hemmeter, & Schuster, 1994). In the following sections, the challenges and resulting recommendations for these four areas are identified.

Administrative and Interagency Issues   Administrative challenges vary by community, but a common difficulty is having multiple sending and receiving agencies. Although public education is responsible for ensuring that appropriate special education and related services are provided to eligible preschoolers with disabilities, a broader array of arrangements is used to provide those services at the preschool level than at the school-age level. At the school-age level, most public schools provide their own special education and related services. At the preschool level, a variety of arrangements is used. Some preschoolers receive services in their homes, whereas others receive theirs from Head Start, inclusive child care programs, private not-for-profit intervention programs, public school preschool programs, and different combinations of these arrangements. As a result, a single public school may be the receiving program and may be required to interact with multiple sending programs. Thus, the school personnel must interact with many different individuals. Each preschool program may have different record-keeping systems, time lines for addressing transitions, levels of involvement in the transition process, staff, and relationships with the receiving school personnel. A commonly recommended solution to deal with this situation is to establish a communitywide, interagency transition policy (Rous et al., 1994). The transition policy may include time lines for referrals, clear specification of the transition steps and process, specific personnel to contact to receive information, meetings for parents of children in the transition process, and a mechanism for regularly reviewing the agreement. Sometimes communities, including sending and receiving programs, establish a joint transition committee that reviews the transition process yearly and attempts to solve problems that arise. The converse, of course, is also true. A given preschool intervention program may send children to multiple school districts. In such cases, a given program may be involved in multiple interagency agreements.

A related administrative issue, when preschoolers from agencies other than public schools are moving to the public schools, is the transfer of confidential records and other confidential information. Clearly, parental permission is required for the transfer of confidential records, and parents should understand to whom the records are being sent, who will have access to those records, and what use will be made of those records. Thus, specifying what records are needed in the transition agreement assists in clarifying this issue.

Another administrative problem can be the use of different eligibility criteria for preschoolers and for school-age children (Shotts et al., 1994). Three potential issues arise. First, although the state definitions are used for preschoolers and school-age children, different diagnoses are sometimes employed. Until the late 1990s, states were able to use the category of "developmental delay" for preschoolers but not for school-age children. Although the latest amendments to IDEA (1997, PL 105-17) allow states to determine whether to use the developmental delay category for determining eligibility during the primary grades, some states may not adopt this flexibility. Similarly, in some states, preschoolers are not eligible to receive a learning disability diagnosis, but this diagnosis is available for school-age children. Second, even within the same diagnosis, different criteria may be applied for preschoolers and school-age children. This seems most evident in categories such as speech-language disorders and behavior disorders (Mallory & Kerns, 1988). For example, more professional judgment is allowed with preschoolers than with school-age children. Third, in some cases children will be eligible for preschool services but will not be eligible at entry to school. This may be due to the positive effects of early intervention or to slight differences in assessment procedures and results (Barnett, Macmann, & Carey, 1992; Boyd, 1989). The common solution to this issue can take two forms. First, agreements about eligibility issues can be established through interagency work and policy review, which often require participation with the department of public instruction at the state level (Rosenkoetter et al., 1994). Second, depending on the patterns of disagreements that may occur, preschool staff should prepare parents for the possibility that the child's eligibility and/or diagnostic category may shift as the child reaches school age.

Administrative issues are often resolved through interagency collaboration (Rous et al., 1994). Rosenkoetter et al. (1994) suggested that good transitions require 1) some joint planning among the sending and receiving agencies, 2) flexible transition procedures to allow the ability to respond to individual situations, 3) information sharing between the sending and receiving programs, 4) promotion of trust through ongoing communication, 5) encouragement for parents to advocate in proactive ways for their child, and 6) regular reviews of the transition policies and procedures.

Staff Issues   Staff in the sending and receiving programs may face unique and shared challenges during the transition process. As a shared difficulty, staff may have decidedly different philosophies about the education of young children with disabilities. For example, preschool programs are often operated in compliance with the guidelines of developmentally appropriate practices (Bredekamp & Copple, 1997). Whereas some primary-age classes are conducted using these guidelines, early elementary teachers and principals report in national survey data that they engage in fewer of these practices than they consider ideal (Wolery, Werts, Caldwell, et al., 1997). Early elementary staff are also under substantially more pressure than preschool staff to ensure that children perform to some specified standard. Thus, the two sets of staff may hold decidedly different philosophies about practice and may work under decidedly different expectations. This difference can lead to concerns on the part of the preschool staff about the future well-being of the child, and concerns on the part of the school-age staff about how well children were prepared for school-age programs. Attempts to resolve such philosophical differences are not likely to be successful. However, focusing on the needs of individual children with disabilities and on the practices that appear to be effective for that child is a tactic that is likely to result in more consensus about practices (Carta, 1994; Wolery & Bredekamp, 1994).

Training of both groups of staff is often necessary. Preschool staff members often have inaccurate perceptions about the demands of schooling in the primary grades and about the limited flexibility available to staff in the elementary schools. Elementary school teachers, particularly those who have no or limited special education preparation, report needing knowledge about teaching students with disabilities, particularly those with sensory impairments or severe mental retardation (Werts, Wolery, Snyder, & Caldwell, 1996; Wolery, Werts, Caldwell, Snyder, & Lisowski, 1995). The type of training, however, that is most useful to such teachers is ongoing technical assistance related to the children with disabilities who are in their classes, as compared with general training in special education or awareness training about disabilities. Furthermore, the transition procedures, interagency agreements related to transitions, and service options in elementary schools should be explained to the preschool staff, and the staff in both programs should visit each others' classes (Bruder & Chandler, 1996).

Family Issues   Major transition issues for families include concerns that they have about the loss of the support network they established when their child was a preschooler, how professionals in the elementary school will treat their child, and how their child will fit into the social climate of the school (i.e., will he or she be teased?). These concerns, of course, are well founded. Many parents who have children with disabilities in the early elementary grades report that 1) they have little ongoing communication with elementary school staff, 2) they do not participate fully in decisions about their child's education, 3) they do not feel welcome in the schools, and 4) they have little information about their child's program and progress (Schuster, Ault, & Hemmeter, 1998; Trivette & Dunst, 1997).

During the transition to school services, it appears that families may move from service agencies that view family support as a legitimate program function to a situation where the service agency (i.e., public school) sees families as a support for their work with the child (e.g., help in completing homework). This shift in perceived roles may cause significant problems for parents. Remedies for the family concerns include the following:

1. Promoting strong informal support systems for the parents while the child is still in preschool

2. Providing families with comprehensive information about the transition process and the elementary school

3. Allowing pretransition visits to the classrooms targeted for the child

4. Providing pretransition meetings with the parents and the staff of the sending and receiving programs

5. Identifying an elementary school staff member with whom the family can readily communicate (i.e., single point of contact during and after the transition)

6. Connecting parents with other parents of older children with disabilities

7. Continuing some social support from the staff at the preschool program after the transition

8. Using a number of simple means (i.e., telephone messages, daily notebooks) to maintain communication with elementary school staff (Bruder & Chandler, 1996; Rosenkoetter et al., 1994; Wolery, 1989)

Another problem for families is the failure to have a flexible and individualized transition policy (Rosenkoetter et al., 1994). The remedy to this problem, of course, involves identifying the aspects of the transition policy that are inflexible and work against individualization, and then establishing procedures to correct those deficits. Clearly, this requires ongoing review of the transition procedures and securing information from parents after they have completed the transition process (Bruder & Chandler, 1996; Rosenkoetter et al., 1994).

Child Issues   As noted previously, a major goal of transition services is to ensure that children function successfully in the receiving program. As a result, a number of studies have focused on identifying skills that preschoolers with disabilities need to be successful in inclusive classes and in kindergarten classes (for summaries, see Atwater et al., 1994, and Chandler, 1992). Some studies used interviews and written questionnaires with experienced teachers in receiving sites, and other studies employed direct observation of those classrooms. The results of these studies

> Provide consistent evidence that preparing a child with special needs for early childhood transitions does not entail teaching specific preacademic or readiness skills. . . . Rather, it involves teaching generic, functional skills that move a child toward increasing independence and increasingly active, appropriate engagement, alongside typically developing peers, in the instructional, play, and social activities of early childhood programs. (Atwater et al., 1994, p. 173)

Atwater et al. (1994) classified these desirable skills into four broad categories, which are shown in Table 9.1. Rosenkoetter et al. (1994) presented a similar list of skills, which are shown in Table 9.2.

Table 9.1.   Criteria for generic and functional skills to increase success in receiving programs

1.   They are useful to the child across diverse settings and situations and will continue to
be useful as the child moves to new educational programs. For example, the ability to
locate and replace one's materials is functional at home, in classrooms, during play and
educational activities, and throughout the life span.

2.   They are "keystone skills" that enable a child to learn more complex skills. For instance,
the ability to attend and follow instructions in group activities enables a child to acquire
new knowledge; expand linguistic skills; and learn interactive skills, such as turn taking
with peers.

3.   They move a child toward increasing independence in inclusive environments. The ability
to interact socially with peers, for example, provides the child with natural opportunities to
observe and practice age-appropriate play skills rather than being dependent on direct
instruction by adults.

4.   They facilitate a child's active engagement in learning activities. The ability to complete
tasks without frequent teacher prompting enables a child to spend more time actively
engaged in child-directed tasks and less time passively attending to teacher direction.
The critical importance of active engagement to a child's optimal development has been
well documented.

From Atwater, J.B., Orth-Lopes, L., Elliott, M., Carta, J.J., & Schwartz, I.S. (1994). Completing the circle:
Planning and implementing transitions to other programs. In M. Wolery & J.S. Wilbers (Eds.), *Including children with special needs in early childhood programs* (pp. 175–178). Washington, DC: National Association for the Education of Young Children; reprinted by permission.

Classrooms, however, can vary a great deal from one another (Carta, Sainato,
& Greenwood, 1988; Fleming, Wolery, Weinzierl, Venn, & Schroeder, 1991; Sainato
& Lyon, 1989). Thus, to prepare children to function in receiving classrooms, skills
that are idiosyncratic to that setting should be identified. Such identification can
occur by engaging in ecological assessments of those classrooms (Barnett, Carey,
& Hall, 1993; Thurman & Widerstrom, 1990), usually well before the transition actually occurs. This assessment includes identifying the tasks and activities that
occur regularly in the receiving class, noting the types of skills children need to be
competent in those tasks and activities, noting the level of competence needed to
be accepted in that class, and then teaching those skills to the child who is preparing for transition. It is important to note, however, that readiness skills; language
skills; self-care skills (toileting and self-feeding skills); and generic skills related to
independence, compliance with group activities, appropriate peer interactive behavior, and play should *not* be considered prerequisites for enrollment in elementary school classes, including kindergarten classes (Atwater et al., 1994; Salisbury
& Vincent, 1990). Decisions about placement consider a number of factors, one of
which is children's competence. Other factors include parents' preferences, presence of adaptive peer models, the potential for developing social relationships
with peers who do not have disabilities, and so forth. Similarly, whereas preschool
programs should prepare children for successful functioning in the receiving class
and in other settings where children spend time, early elementary programs are
responsible for providing children with appropriate educational experiences.
Early intervention programs are not likely to inoculate children from the inade-
quacies of future environments (Zigler & Hunsinger, 1979).

     In addition to teaching the generic and functional skills noted in the previous
paragraph and in Tables 9.1 and 9.2 and teaching skills that are idiosyncratic to
particular receiving classes, other practices in preschool classes may help prepare

Table 9.2.   Nonacademic skills useful for transition into kindergartens

Playing and Working Independently and Collaboratively
1. Plays and works appropriately with and without peers
2. Completes activities approximately on time
3. Stays with an activity for an appropriate amount of time
4. Plays and works with few individual prompts from the teacher

Interacting with Peers
1. Imitates peers' actions when learning new routines
2. Initiates and maintains contact with peers
3. Responds to peers' initiations
4. Learns and uses names of peers
5. Shares objects and takes turns with peers
6. Plans activities with peers

Following Directions
1. Responds to adults' questions
2. Responds appropriately to multi-step verbal directions
3. Responds appropriately to verbal directions that include common school-related prepositions, nouns, and verbs
4. Complies with group as well as individual instructions
5. Modifies behavior as needed when given verbal feedback
6. Recalls and follows directions for tasks previously discussed or demonstrated
7. Watches others or seeks help if he or she doesn't understand directions

Responding to Routines
1. Learns new routines after limited practice
2. Moves quickly and quietly from one activity to another without individual reminders
3. Reacts appropriately to changes in routine
4. Cares for personal belongings

Conducting Oneself According to Classroom Rules
1. Waits appropriately
2. Lines up if teacher requests that he or she do so
3. Sits appropriately
4. Focuses attention on the speaker, shifts attention appropriately, and participates in class activities in a manner that is relevant to the task or topic
5. Seeks attention or assistance in acceptable ways
6. Separates from parents and accepts the authority of school personnel
7. Expresses emotions and feelings appropriately

From Rosenkoetter, S.E., Hains, A.H., & Fowler, S.A. (1994). *Bridging early services for children with special needs and their families: A practical guide for transition planning* (p. 143). Baltimore: Paul H. Brookes Publishing Co.; reprinted by permission.

Note: The following skills may be useful for goal writing, if they are developmentally appropriate for a given child. They should *never* be used as entrance criteria or to exclude any child from a classroom.

children with disabilities for the transition. These practices include using strategies that can be implemented with large groups of children, promoting skill transfer, sharing information about children between sending and receiving programs, allowing children to visit their receiving classrooms, and adapting familiar preschool activities to be more like the receiving classroom activities (Atwater et al., 1994). Of course, families should be involved in planning the transition so that they also can promote acquisition of skills that are likely to be useful to children in the receiving class (Atwater et al., 1994; Bruder & Chandler, 1996).

Another issue related to children's transitions—particularly to the continuity of services—deals with the provision of related services, particularly occupational therapy, physical therapy, and speech-language therapy (Rosenkoetter et al., 1994). Such services, among others (e.g., audiology, adapted physical education), must be provided to preschoolers and school-age children if they are to have educational benefit. Two issues arise: whether to provide those services and how those services are delivered when they are provided. Despite difficulties, such as staff shortages and high costs (McWilliam, Young, & Harville, 1996), specialized services for preschoolers are generally provided to promote the children's development. In elementary schools, academic achievement may take precedence over developmental advancement. During transitions, the issue is often raised as to whether specialized services will have educational benefit. Thus, children who received specialized services during the preschool years may not be eligible for the same services or the same level of services during the early elementary years.

The manner in which these services are provided may also become an issue. For example, the current recommended practice in early childhood programs is to integrate such services into the ongoing classroom activities (McWilliam, 1996b). The more usual pattern in elementary schools, however, is to provide such services through pull-out arrangements (Wolery, Bailey, et al., 1997). Thus, conflicts may arise over which related services are necessary (Rosenkoetter et al., 1994) and about the manner in which those services are delivered. McWilliam (1996a) provided a number of suggestions for addressing conflicts over the way services are provided, including building integrated specialized services into children's individualized plans, building integrated specialized services into school contracts with therapists and therapist groups, and making integrated specialized service provision a priority in personnel preparation programs. Although this issue is included under the heading of "child issues," it clearly has its roots and ramifications in "administrative issues," "staff issues" for both the sending and the receiving programs, and "family issues."

In summary, a number of challenges exist to providing effective transitions for children. These include administrative challenges, deficiencies in the skills of the staff in both the sending and receiving programs, difficulties related to families in the transition process and family concerns about the transition, and challenges in preparing children to function successfully in the receiving program.

Major issues related to transitions were identified by families of young children with disabilities who experienced difficult transitions from preschool to school-age services. These difficulties also became apparent to the preschool staff who were attempting to ensure continuity of services for children with disabilities. As a result, effort has been devoted to identifying the transition problems and generating and evaluating strategies to deal with those problems. The recommendations and practices listed here are specific to children with disabilities; however, they may have broader applications. As a recommendation for children without disabilities and their families, perhaps the most useful action schools and community early childhood programs could take is to identify areas of concern around transitions. In some communities, significant issues may relate to the preparation of children for the early elementary program; in other cases, the difficulties may focus on how families are treated during the transition or on how administrative difficulties between community early childhood programs and the public schools may exist. Once these problems and concerns are identified, potential solutions can be devised. The literature related to transitions for children with disabilities may be a starting point for devising solutions, but other recommendations and practices may also emerge.

PLACEMENT OF CHILDREN WITH DISABILITIES IN THE PRIMARY GRADES

A legitimate question is, What are the placements for children with disabilities during their kindergarten, first-, second-, and third-grade years? Without the answer to this question, recommendations about continuity of services across the transition and about preparing children for the receiving program are difficult to generate. This question, of course, is not easy to answer. Potential placements range from a special education class in a school that exclusively serves children with disabilities to full-time inclusion in a general education class in a public school. Experience suggests that many children with disabilities spend time in multiple classes (e.g., a resource room and a general education class). Although each state reports annually the number of children with disabilities served by placement, questions have been raised about the accuracy of these data (Gerber, 1984; Roach, Halvorsen, Zeph, Giugno, & Caruso, 1997) and about the limited number of reporting choices related to placement.

According to Sawyer, McLaughlin, and Winglee (1994), states reported the number of students enrolled by placement using six categories:

1. General education class—students receive most of their education in a general education class but could be outside that class up to 21% of the school day.

2. Resource room—students receive education 21%–60% of the school day outside the general education class.

3. Separate class—students receive more than 60% of their education outside the general education class.

4. Separate school facility—students receive at least 50% of their education in a special day school.

5. Residential facility—students receive at least 50% of their education in a residential facility.

6. Homebound/hospital environment—students are in a hospital or are homebound (apparently receiving 100% of their education in those settings).

From aggregated data using these reporting categories, it is difficult to determine the extent to which students with disabilities are participating in general education classes. For example, if a student spends 55% of his or her school day in a separate facility and 45% of the day in a general education class, this could count as a separate facility placement. Also, general education classes apparently include special subject classes such as music, art, library, and physical education, and it is unclear how classes such as transitional kindergartens are reported. Tracing historical trends in placement is complicated by changing diagnostic criteria, the addition of new diagnostic categories (e.g., traumatic brain injury, autism), and changes in the ages of students who are eligible for special education services. Furthermore, the number of children identified as having disabilities has increased since the 1970s, particularly in the area of learning disabilities (Gresham, 1997).

Using the state reported data, however, it appears that nearly all (i.e., more than 93%) the children with disabilities (all types of disabilities combined) are served in regular public schools as compared with segregated placements outside the public schools (Sawyer et al., 1994). For all disabilities combined, the proportion of students with disabilities served in public schools has changed relatively little since the passage of PL 94-142. An increase, however, appears to have occurred in the percentage of students with orthopedic impairments and sensory (hearing, visual) impairments being served in public schools. However, a decrease in the percentage of students with serious emotional disturbances being served in public schools has occurred during the same period. This decrease may reflect shifts in the severity of the problems of students with this diagnostic label (Sawyer et al., 1994). Inclusion advocates have argued for placement exclusively in children's home schools (i.e., the school the student would have attended if he or she did not have disabilities) (Brown, Long, Udvari-Solner, Davis, et al., 1989; Brown, Long, Udvari-Solner, Schwarz, et al., 1989). The state data are not useful in determining whether any changes have occurred in the percentage of students being served in such schools.

The state data have been used to determine whether participation in general education classes in the public schools is changing. Sawyer et al. (1994) indicated that substantial increases have occurred since the 1980s in the percentage of students with disabilities who are attending general education classes in the public schools. Furthermore, these increases appear to be occurring across each diagnostic category. The authors do not, however, present these data by age levels; thus, it is impossible to determine from their analyses the extent to which 5- to 8-year-old children with disabilities are spending time in general education classes.

An alternative method of determining whether students with disabilities are attending early elementary classes is to survey general educators. Four studies using randomly selected national samples have adopted this tactic. The first study focused on preschool mainstreaming, but it included public school kindergarten teachers (Wolery et al., 1993). A total of 203 kindergarten teachers were mailed questionnaires, and 124 (61.1%) responded with a usable questionnaire. The teachers were asked to report whether they had students with disabilities in their class (part- or full-time) during the survey year (1989/1990), and whether they had students with disabilities in each of the previous 4 years. For the survey year, 81.5% indicated that they had a student with disabilities in their class; the trends during the previous years showed steady increase from a low of about 35% in the earliest reported study year (1985/1986).

The second study focused on supports for the inclusion of children in kindergarten through grade 6. Questionnaires were mailed to 2,100 public school teachers (300 per grade level) during the 1992/1993 school year (Wolery, 1996). The overall return rate of usable questionnaires was 68.1%. For the grades of interest to this chapter (kindergarten through grade 3), the return rate of usable questionnaires was at or higher than 70%. The percentage of teachers with at least one child enrolled with disabilities by grade and the percentage with at least one child enrolled full time are presented in Table 9.3. As shown, a substantial majority of the teachers at each grade level indicated that they had at least one child with a

Table 9.3.   Percentage of teachers with at least one child enrolled with a disability

Grade	At least one child with a disability in class		At least one child with a disability enrolled full time	
	Number	Percentage	Number	Percentage
Kindergarten (N = 200)	145	73	132	67
First grade (N = 196)	159	81	130	66
Second grade (N = 188)	154	82	115	61
Third grade (N = 197)	165	84	115	58

Source: Wolery (1996).

disability, and a majority also indicated that they had at least one child with a disability who was enrolled full time.

The third study assessed kindergarten through third-grade teachers' and principals' perceptions about individualization practices for students with disabilities and the use of developmentally appropriate practices during the 1995/1996 school year (Wolery, Werts, Caldwell, et al., 1997). Approximately 500 questionnaires were mailed to each grade level (kindergarten through grade 3) and about 500 to principals. The return rates of usable questionnaires across groups ranged from 43% to 52%. Teachers were asked to indicate the number of children with disabilities in their classes. Of the 969 responding teachers, 707 (73%) indicated they had at least one student with a disability enrolled in their class. The percentages of teachers by grade (kindergarten, first, second, and third grades) who had at least one child with disabilities enrolled were 61%, 68%, 79%, and 87%, respectively. These teachers were also asked whether the students with disabilities in their classes attended special education classes. Of the 707 who reported having a student with a disability, 582 (82%) indicated that the student also attended a special education class.

In this study, principals were asked a series of questions about the placement of students with disabilities in their schools. In one question, they were asked where a majority of the 5- to 8-year-old students with disabilities were taught. They were given three choices: only in special education, in special and general education, and only in general education. Almost all the principals (84%) indicated that the majority of the 5- to 8-year-old students with disabilities was taught in special and general education. Two percent selected only in special education, and 14% selected only in general education. The principals also were asked four binary questions about the placement of 5- to 8-year-old students with disabilities. In the first question, they were asked if *any* students spent their entire day in special education; 25% selected "yes." In the second question, they were asked if *any* students spent their entire day in general education; 66.5% selected "yes." In the third question, they were asked, do *any* students go to art, music, or physical education classes with general education students; 97% selected "yes." In the final question, they were asked whether a *majority* of the students went to art, music, or physical education classes with general education students; 96% selected "yes."

The final study surveyed art, music, and physical education teachers about the enrollment of 5- to 8-year-old students with disabilities in their classes during the 1995/1996 school year (Wolery, Werts, & Dunst, 1997). Slightly more than 500 teachers from each of the three groups were sent questionnaires. The return rates of usable questionnaires were 56% for art teachers, 61% for music teachers, and 52% for physical education teachers—all of whom taught children in the early elementary grades, often in addition to teaching students in more advanced grades. They were asked whether 5- to 8-year-old students with disabilities were enrolled in the primary classes (K–3) that they taught. Of the 866 responding teachers, 793 (91%) indicated that students with disabilities were in their primary-grade classes. By type of teacher, the percentages were 90% for art, 93% for music, and 88% for physical education.

These four studies, as a whole, indicated that large percentages of the early elementary teachers (general education class teachers; art, music, and physical education teachers) have students with disabilities enrolled in their classes. It is important to note that the reported percentages are the percentage of teachers, not the percentage of students with disabilities. In each of these survey studies, however, the questionnaires had multiple questions related to students with disabilities. Thus, it is possible that teachers who had students with disabilities were more likely to respond, thereby inflating the proportion of teachers who have students with disabilities in their classes. However, even when the number of teachers with students who have disabilities in their classes is divided by the total number of questionnaires mailed, as compared with the number of questionnaires returned, more than one third of the teachers in all studies, and sometimes more than one half of the teachers overall, reported having students with disabilities in their classes. Another limitation of these studies is that we do not know what definitions the teachers used in responding to the questions. In two studies (Wolery, 1996; Wolery et al., 1993), teachers were asked to list students by their diagnosis. In the remaining two studies (Wolery, Werts, Caldwell, et al., 1997; Wolery, Werts, & Dunst, 1997), the terminology *students with individualized education programs (IEPs) but not gifted or talented* was used.

In summary, it appears that most students with disabilities are served in the public schools, and students with disabilities across diagnostic categories are increasingly being served in general education classes in those schools (Sawyer et al., 1994). Many kindergarten through third-grade teachers reported having students with disabilities in their classes. Principals indicated that most primary-age students with disabilities in their schools attend both special and general education classes. Nearly all the principals also reported that the majority of primary-age students with disabilities attend special subject classes (art, music, or physical education) with general education students. Art, music, and physical education teachers concurred by indicating that nearly all of them have students with disabilities in the primary classes they teach.

In terms of transitions, a few implications seemed unavoidable. First, preschoolers with disabilities are likely to attend public schools for their early elementary education. Thus, contact between preschool programs and the elementary program is warranted. Second, many preschoolers with disabilities are likely to transition into multiple, rather than single, classes in the early elementary program. Relatively little research attention has been given to the fact that young children with disabilities and their families must negotiate a transition from a preschool to an elementary program that is comprised of multiple classes, potentially a general education class, a special education class, an art class, a computer class, a physical education class, a music class, and perhaps others. Each class may involve different teachers. We do not know what effect this has on children's learning, their adjustment to new settings, or the overall continuity of services.

ISSUES IN EDUCATING CHILDREN WITH DISABILITIES IN THE PRIMARY GRADES

Many young children with disabilities make the transition to public elementary schools, and many of them receive services in general elementary classroom placements. In this section, five issues that are central to educating students with disabilities in public schools, particularly in the early elementary grades, are addressed. These issues are related to 1) identifying outcomes for students with disabilities, 2) the students' parents, 3) service coordination and integration, 4) curriculum and instruction, and 5) supporting the teaching and therapeutic staff. Other issues, of course, could be addressed. For example, a section of this chapter could be devoted to the inclusion of students with disabilities in general education classes. This issue is not directly addressed for two reasons. First, a great deal of inclusion appears to be occurring in elementary schools as evidenced by the first part of this chapter. Given this fact, the task at hand seems to be ensuring that the existing efforts to include students with disabilities are supported sufficiently to produce the desired outcomes. Second, the issue of inclusion has undergone a great deal of discussion in other sources (e.g., Fuchs & Fuchs, 1994; Hunt & Goetz, 1997), and an additional discussion is not likely to produce consensus on the topic or to change the minds of many people.

The five issues listed here are addressed because they are central to the transition process. They highlight some of the concerns that emerge during the transition process when children with disabilities leave the preschool program and enter the elementary program. If these issues are not addressed satisfactorily, then problems will continue to emerge during the transition process.

Outcomes for Children with Disabilities

Each child who receives special education and related services must have an IEP. This program is to be devised by a team of individuals, including those with expertise in the child's disabilities and the child's parents or guardians. This plan should specify the goals that are to be achieved. PL 105-17 (the 1997 amendments to IDEA) made some significant changes to the requirements related to this plan. Specifically, the goals must reference the general education curriculum, parents of children with disabilities must be informed about children's progress at least as often as parents of children without disabilities are informed, and parents' concerns must be considered in the development of the IEP.

Thus, a discussion of the outcomes for children with disabilities as a result of the participation in public education is relevant for at least three reasons. First, identifying broad outcomes for most children with disabilities puts the individualized goals in a broader contextual framework while not restricting idiosyncratic variations that are likely necessary for some children. Having a contextual framework provides some definition of, and expectations for, activities that constitute legitimate educational endeavors. Second, there has been strong sentiment among politicians and the mass media that setting standards for student achievement and for schools' performance is desirable (e.g., Kantrowitz, 1997). Examples of this movement include the Goals 2000 initiatives (Short & Talley, 1997). In fact, the 1997 amendments to IDEA require that students with disabilities be included in statewide testing efforts. If such standards are too narrowly focused, then educational efforts may not serve children with disabilities well. Setting standards and involving students with disabilities in statewide assessment activities may profoundly influence the definition of outcomes and curriculum content for students with disabilities. If individualized programs are needed as required by law and regulation for students with disabilities, then logic suggests that some outcomes may be different from those specified for students without disabilities. If this is the case, then attention must be given to identifying those outcomes to ensure that curriculum and instructional efforts are devoted to those broader outcomes. Third, agreement on outcomes across the age span may result in smoother more productive transition planning.

Many outcomes for children without disabilities may be relevant and important to many, perhaps even most, students with disabilities. This seems more likely for students with mild disabilities as compared with students with moderate and severe disabilities. The fundamental assumption underlying the identification of outcomes is the realization that schools are funded, in large part, to prepare students for life outside schools. In this vein, Billingsley, Gallucci, Peck, Schwartz, and Staub (1996) articulated a framework with three broad areas of outcomes: membership, social relationships, and competence. Membership involves affiliation with or belonging to a group and engaging in joint activities with other individuals in that group. This outcome reflects the basic notion that humans are social entities, recognizes the extent to which group activity is central to community life, and acknowledges the importance of affiliation and group responsibility in modern democracies. Education, then, should provide students with opportunities to form groups, assist students in becoming part of groups, allow students to practice being a part of groups, and encourage group activity—including joint goal setting and problem solving. These groups may be comprised of children in a single class and children across classes and may include community organizations and resources. Because students with disabilities are members of the broader community, they should be included in efforts to promote membership. The outcome of membership, however, extends beyond formal groups to include informal groups.

The second major outcome area is social relationships (Billingsley et al., 1996). This area includes social interactions, social competence, friendship formation, and many related constructs. The point is that schooling should provide a context for social relationships to occur; assist students in establishing and maintaining social relationships; and encourage students to have relationships with others of different races, economic statuses, and ability levels. This outcome is particularly critical for many students with disabilities because the quality of their lives will be dependent on the extent to which others recognize their value and the extent to which they have stable and varied social networks (Newton, Ard, Horner, & Toews, 1996; Newton, Olson, Horner, & Ard, 1996).

The third major outcome area is competence (Billingsley et al., 1996). This outcome focuses on traditional academic areas, social and communicative behavior, and functional life skills. For many primary-age students with disabilities, this includes language arts, mathematics, and science. For other primary-age students with disabilities, the focus should be on communication skills, locomotion, self-care skills, domestic skills, and leisure skills (Westling & Fox, 1995).

The weight that is given to each broad area would be determined by the student's IEP team. However, in nearly all cases, some goals and objectives in each area seem relevant. The move toward documenting educational accountability through systemwide testing schemes has the potential of focusing exclusively on the competence domain, and doing so in a narrow fashion. Realization of this potential may substantially devalue the worth of educational participation for students with disabilities; specifically, they will not be prepared to function outside the school context.

This framework has some positive aspects for transitions. It is not age specific; it is applicable for preschool programs and for elementary school programs. If both preschool and early elementary programs used this framework of outcomes, then continuity of services would be more likely. The framework is not philosophy or approach dependent. Preschool teachers using a developmentally appropriate approach and early elementary schools using a more traditional academic approach can work within the conceptual assumptions and parameters of the framework. This should help resolve some of the difficulties that arise in transitions as a result of philosophical differences.

Parent Issues

Parents (guardians) of children with disabilities have a right to shared decision making related to their child's IEP, and the 1997 amendments to IDEA require that parents' concerns be considered in developing the IEP. This right includes being able to participate in planning the assessment activities conducted to develop the goals and objectives, participating in that assessment, participating in discussions and meetings about the goals and objectives, and implementing the IEP (Turnbull, 1990). Despite these rights, parents have historically faced substantial barriers in actually being involved in IEP development and implementation (Goldstein, Strickland, Turnbull, & Curry, 1980), and this state of affairs apparently continues to exist (Schuster et al., 1998). A number of models and processes have emerged for resolving these issues and for providing parents with a central role in planning. Examples include Personal Futures Planning (Mount & Zwernik, 1988), the McGill Action Planning System (MAPS) (Vandercook, York, & Forest, 1989), the Choosing Outcomes and Accommodations for Children (COACH) model (Giangreco, Cloninger, & Iverson, 1998), and person-centered planning (Miner & Bates, 1997). Thus, the issue may be less one of finding procedures and processes for involving families in IEPs and more one of studying how to get schools to adopt those practices and processes and ensuring that schools use those processes. Furthermore, application of these processes during transition planning may increase family commitment to schools and reduce difficulties faced in those transitions.

Beyond the IEP process, an important parental issue is the extent to which a positive family–school relationship is established. With students who have disabilities, this process is initiated when the student begins the transition into the elementary-age program, continues through the development of the IEP, and is then played out in the manner in which communication occurs as the IEP is implemented. The aspects of the family–school relationship desired by families are not surprising. These include issues such as feeling welcome in the school, having the school be responsive to their requests (e.g., providing information about the child's progress), believing the school staff cares about their child, being included in decisions that affect their child, and feeling mutual trust and respect (Trivette & Dunst, 1997), among others. Establishing positive family–school relationships clearly has benefits for families but also may have benefits for schools. For example, parental involvement appears to be related to increased student achievement on standardized tests (Griffith, 1996). At the preschool level, a large literature exists on how to support families of children with disabilities (e.g., Bailey, Buysse, Edmondson, & Smith, 1992; Bailey, Buysse, Smith, & Elam, 1992; Dunst, Trivette, & Deal, 1988, 1994). Many of the assumptions, procedures, and practices represented in this literature appear relevant during the early elementary years and particularly to the transition process. However, early elementary teachers, administrators, and related service personnel report that practices associated with family-centered services are infrequently employed (Wolery, Bailey, et al., 1997). Thus, future research should focus on how family-centered principles and practices can be implemented during the transition to the early elementary years, and how those practices affect family–school relationships and students' achievements.

Issues of Service Coordination and Integration

In addition to having an IEP, each child with disabilities has an IEP team. This team consists of the group of individuals who are to work together to carry out the plan, monitor its effects, and make any needed adjustments (Bruder, 1996). Many primary-age children with disabilities attend general and special education classes as well as special subject classes (art, music, and physical education). Many of these students also receive related services, such as physical, occupational, and speech-language therapy. Furthermore, many students with disabilities have daily contact with paraprofessionals, and some students may have contact with one paraprofessional in the general class and another in the special education class (Jones & Bender, 1993; Wolery, Werts, & Snyder, 1997). Thus, as few as 2 staff members, but probably 8–10 individuals, will have regular contact with each student who has disabilities. Although all these individuals may not be on the child's IEP team, each plays a role in the child's education. Thus, if the services are to be integrated and coordinated, communication must exist between them, with the child's parents, and with other service providers outside the school.

Early elementary teachers, special education teachers, administrators, and related services staff indicate that a number of barriers interfere with their ability to communicate with one another. These include large class sizes for teachers, large caseloads for therapists, minimal time set aside for regular planning, conflicting schedules, and the demands of carrying out other responsibilities (Wolery, Bailey, et al., 1997). Although such issues can be addressed, the solutions often involve additional resources (e.g., more staff, more time for planning), someone to coordinate the efforts, and better mechanisms for sharing relevant information. Participation on the IEP team, at least for special subject teachers, is related to increased knowledge of the IEP content, more involvement with families, greater satisfaction with teaching students who have disabilities, and more frequent communication with other school personnel about students with disabilities (Wolery, Werts, & Dunst, 1997).

Taken together, these findings appear to indicate that coordination of services within elementary schools is a significant challenge. If this is the case, then coordination with community preschool programs to facilitate smooth transitions may pose a substantial strain on the system. Clearly, planning and executing smooth transitions can take staff time and effort for both the sending and receiving programs. Thus, policies related to providing additional staff for elementary schools and how staff are deployed seem relevant.

Issues of Curriculum and Instruction

A great deal of instructional research has addressed teaching students with disabilities. This research has focused on teaching different types of skills, including academic skills such as

- Reading (Kameenui, Simmons, Chard, & Dickson, 1997; Rohena-Diaz & Browder, 1996)

- Spelling (Gordon, Vaughn, & Schumn, 1993; Grskovic & Belfiore, 1996)

- Writing (Englert & Rozendal, 1996)

- Mathematics (Bentz & Fuchs, 1996)

- Developmental skills such as language (Kaiser & Gray, 1993; Warren & Reichle, 1992) and social interactions and relationships (Kennedy, Cushing, & Itkonen, 1997; Kennedy & Shukla, 1989)

- Other adaptive responses such as safety skills (Gast, Wellons, & Collins, 1994), self-feeding, and toileting (Westling & Fox, 1995)

Research has also focused on different instructional issues, such as

- Peer-assisted instruction (Fuchs, Fuchs, Mathes, & Simmons, 1997)

- Cooperative learning groups (Dugan et al., 1995)

- Small-group instruction (curriculum-based and performance measurement) (Elliott & Fuchs, 1997; Fuchs & Fuchs, 1996)

- Ecobehavioral analysis of classrooms (Greenwood, Carta, & Atwater, 1991)

- Embedding instructional strategies into ongoing classroom activities (Wolery, Anthony, Snyder, Werts, & Katzenmeyer, 1997)

- Using procedures such as mnemonic strategies (Mastropieri, Scruggs, & Whedon, 1997)

- Adapting textbooks and other materials (Bean, Zigmond, & Hartman, 1994)

- Teaching children cognitive strategies (Duchardt, Deshler, & Schumaker, 1995)

- A variety of direct instruction strategies (Wolery & Schuster, 1997)

In addition, a substantial amount of research has focused on children's problematic behaviors, including identification of environmental variables related to the occurrence of those behaviors, assessment of the motivational properties of those behaviors, and development of nonpunitive treatment approaches (Singh, 1997).

Despite the advances that have been made, a great deal remains to be learned. Although research exists on how to teach many important skills, increasing the efficiency of that instruction and promoting greater generalization of the acquired behaviors are areas for future research. Likewise, many of the instructional arrangements and strategies noted previously were evaluated in isolation from the entire milieu of classroom routines and activities. Thus, future research should focus on how to ensure that the practices and strategies can be used in the context of teachers' other instructional duties. Furthermore, the application of some of the special education instructional technology needs to be studied in inclusive classrooms, if students with disabilities are to continue in those classrooms. Finally, little research has focused on special subject classes, such as art and music, although primary-age students with disabilities are often included in those classes.

Issues in Supporting the Teaching and Therapy Staff

In general, elementary teachers are willing to provide services to children with disabilities, assuming behavior problems are under control, and they are willing to allow modifications of testing procedures and assignment requirements (Schumm & Vaughn, 1992). However, general elementary teachers who have children with disabilities in their classes report having no more supports available to them than teachers who do not have children with disabilities; they do, however, report needing more resources and supports (Werts, Wolery, Snyder, Caldwell, & Salisbury, 1996). Thus, although teachers are willing to include students, they may perceive themselves as being in an ongoing state of need. Such a situation is not likely to promote success or feelings of efficacy on the teachers' part. Thus, a legitimate question becomes, What do teachers report needing to teach children with disabilities effectively?

When teachers who have included students with disabilities are asked, What supports and resources are critical to successful teaching of students with disabilities? some consistent responses emerge (Scruggs & Mastropieri, 1996; Werts, Wolery, Snyder, & Caldwell, 1996). These include needing time to plan for children with disabilities and time to meet with others who have expertise related to the child with disabilities. Teachers also report needing additional training. This training must be intensive, focused on the children with disabilities who are in their classrooms, and include ongoing support from a team of professionals who have expertise related to teaching students with disabilities. Teachers also report needing additional in-class help from teaching assistants and volunteers. Reduced class size is a perceived need when children with disabilities are enrolled, as is having adequate curricular materials. Furthermore, a repeated finding is that when children have more significant disabilities, more of these supports are required.

In successful efforts, it appears that the issue of who is responsible for the child with disabilities is also resolved. For example, in some cases, general education teachers are willing to use adapted tests, but they are less willing to devote planning time to make adaptations of tests and instructional materials (Schumm & Vaughn, 1992). Thus, if the special educator or a paraprofessional adapts the tests and materials, the teacher is willing to continue with the child who has disabilities. Wood (1998) suggested general and special education teachers initially work out an informal, but defined, division of labor related to children with disabilities. Over the course of a few months, more cooperative activities are initiated and the roles that were initially established become less distinct.

If children with disabilities are to make the transition into the elementary program and still have their needs met, then consideration must be given to meeting the needs of the staff members who teach them. Transitions are likely to be unsuccessful if general education teachers in the receiving program are given increased demands (i.e., including a child with disabilities) without the needed supports and resources (Werts, Wolery, Snyder, Caldwell, & Salisbury, 1996). Thus, policy decisions to make these supports and resources available are necessary. Without such supports, teachers in the receiving programs are likely to become more resistant to accepting children with disabilities, and children's education in the receiving programs is likely to be of lower quality.

CONCLUSION

Children with disabilities and their families may undergo a number of significant transitions from one program to another. Although the transition from preschool programs to early elementary schools includes a number of challenges, these can be addressed by establishing interagency transition teams and policies, addressing the staff needs of both the sending and receiving programs, responding to families' concerns about the transition through a variety of strategies, and preparing children for the receiving program. Although future research could evaluate strategies for accomplishing these tasks, the more pressing need is to identify the forces and conditions that will ensure that preschools and elementary schools engage in practices that already appear to be effective.

Most early elementary-age students with disabilities are served in public schools and since the mid 1980s there appears to be an increase in the proportion who are served in general education classes. Many kindergarten through third-grade teachers and art, music, and physical education teachers report having primary-age students with disabilities in their classes. Most principals indicate that primary-age students with disabilities attend both special and general education classes, including art, music, or physical education classes with their peers without disabilities.

A number of issues arise related to teaching students with disabilities in early elementary classes. Among others, the identification of legitimate outcomes for students with disabilities is seen as an issue requiring consideration. Billingsley et al.'s (1996) three-part framework (promoting membership, social relationships, and competence) appears to be useful, flexible, and sufficiently comprehensive. Another issue focuses on parents of students with disabilities, and two points seem pertinent. First, despite available processes and procedures, parents do not appear to be integral parts of the IEP process. Second, parents on average do not perceive being in a positive partnership with the schools. These issues appear to require fairly major adjustments to practices used by schools; understanding how to promote adoption of different practices and identifying how to initiate and sustain positive family–school relationships are clearly research priorities. Given the large number of adults who have regular contact with children who have disabilities, the demands on these adults, and the constraints of their situations, serious questions emerge about whether services for students with disabilities are adequately coordinated. Understanding how to promote and sustain coordination practices is clearly needed. Although a great deal is known about teaching students with disabilities, research continues to be needed to improve the efficiency of that instruction and its application in inclusive classrooms. Finally, some evidence speaks to the supports that teachers need to provide instruction to students with disabilities; unfortunately, such supports do not, at least from the teachers' perspectives, appear to be widespread. Thus, research aimed at making such supports more common seems important; however, as with other issues, such investigations should focus on how schools can adopt and sustain the use of known supports and resources.

Although this discussion has focused on children with disabilities, applications for those without disabilities may exist. For example, interagency efforts between schools and community early childhood programs could be used to identify problems that exist related to the transition into kindergarten for children who are developing typically. Also, input from families about their transition experiences is warranted. Once particular problems in the transition process have been identified, concentrated effort (e.g., through interagency agreements) could be used to address the problems. This strategy, of course, places the school in partnership with other organizations in the community. Such a partnership has ramifications beyond the transition into kindergarten and holds potential benefits for children, families, schools, and community programs.

REFERENCES

Atwater, J.B., Orth-Lopes, L., Elliott, M., Carta, J.J., & Schwartz, I.S. (1994). Completing the circle: Planning and implementing transitions to other programs. In M. Wolery & J.S. Wilbers (Eds.), *Including children with special needs in early childhood programs* (pp. 167–188). Washington, DC: National Association for the Education of Young Children.
Bailey, D.B. (1988). Assessing critical events. In D.B. Bailey & R.J. Simeonsson (Eds.), *Family assessment in early intervention* (pp. 119–138). Upper Saddle River, NJ: Merrill.
Bailey, D.B., Buysse, V., Edmondson, R., & Smith, T.M. (1992). Creating family-centered services in early intervention: Perceptions of professionals in four states. *Exceptional Children, 58,* 298–309.
Bailey, D.B., Buysse, V., Smith, T., & Elam, J. (1992). The effects and perceptions of family involvement in program decisions about family-centered practices. *Evaluation and Program Planning, 15,* 23–32.
Bailey, D.B., Simeonsson, R.J., Winton, P.J., Huntington, G.S., Comfort, M., Isbell, P., O'Donnell, K.J., & Helm, J.M. (1986). Family-focused intervention: A functional model for planning, implementing, and evaluating individualized family services in early intervention. *Journal of the Division for Early Childhood, 10,* 156–171.
Barnett, D.W., Carey, K.T., & Hall, J.D. (1993). Naturalistic intervention design for young children: Foundations, rationales, and strategies. *Topics in Early Childhood Special Education, 13,* 430–444.
Barnett, D.W., Macmann, G.M., & Carey, K.T. (1992). Early intervention and the assessment of developmental skills: Challenges and directions. *Topics in Early Childhood Special Education, 12,* 21–43.
Bean, R.M., Zigmond, N., & Hartman, D.K. (1994). Adapted use of social studies textbooks in elementary classrooms: Views of classroom teachers. *Remedial and Special Education, 15,* 216–226.
Bentz, J.L., & Fuchs, L.S. (1996). Improving peers' helping behavior to students with learning disabilities during mathematics peer tutoring. *Learning Disability Quarterly, 19,* 202–215.
Billingsley, F.F., Gallucci, C., Peck, C.A., Schwartz, I.S., & Staub, D. (1996). "But those kids can't even do math": An alternative conceptualization of outcomes for inclusive education. *Special Education Leadership Review, 3,* 43–55.
Boyd, R.D. (1989). What a difference a day makes: Age-related discontinuities and the Battelle Developmental Inventory. *Journal of Early Intervention, 13,* 114–119.
Bredekamp, S., & Copple, C. (Eds.). (1997). *Developmentally appropriate practice in early childhood programs* (Rev. ed.). Washington, DC: National Association for the Education of Young Children.
Brown, L., Long, E., Udvari-Solner, A., Davis, L., VanDeventer, P., Ahlgren, C., Johnson, F., Gruenwald, L., & Jorgensen, J. (1989). The home school: Why students with severe intellectual disabilities must attend the schools of their brothers, sisters, friends, and neighbors. *Journal of The Association for Persons with Severe Handicaps, 14,* 1–7.
Brown, L., Long, E., Udvari-Solner, A., Schwarz, P., VanDeventer, P., Ahlgren, C., Johnson, F., Gruenwald, L., & Jorgensen, J. (1989). Should students with severe intellectual disabilities be based in regular or in special education classrooms in their home schools? *Journal of The Association for Persons with Severe Handicaps, 14,* 8–12.
Bruder, M.B. (1996). Interdisciplinary collaboration in service delivery. In R.A. McWilliam (Ed.), *Rethinking pull-out services in early intervention: A professional resource* (pp. 27–48). Baltimore: Paul H. Brookes Publishing Co.
Bruder, M.B., & Chandler, L. (1996). Transition. In S.L. Odom & M.E. McLean (Eds.), *Early intervention/early childhood special education: Recommended practices* (pp. 287–307). Austin, TX: PRO-ED.

Carta, J.J. (1994). Developmentally appropriate practices: Shifting the emphasis to individual appropriateness. *Journal of Early Intervention, 18,* 342–343.

Carta, J.J., Sainato, D.M., & Greenwood, C.R. (1988). Advances in the ecological assessment of classroom instruction for young children with handicaps. In S.L. Odom & M.B. Karnes (Eds.), *Early intervention for infants and children with handicaps: An empirical base* (pp. 217–239). Baltimore: Paul H. Brookes Publishing Co.

Chandler, L.K. (1992). Promoting children's social/survival skills as a strategy for transition to mainstreamed kindergarten programs. In S.L. Odom, S.R. McConnell, & M.A. McEvoy (Eds.), *Social competence of young children with disabilities: Issues and strategies for intervention* (pp. 245–276). Baltimore: Paul H. Brookes Publishing Co.

Craig, S.E. (1997). Child care centers. In S.K. Thurman, J.R. Cornwell, & S.R. Gottwald (Eds.), *Contexts of early intervention: Systems and settings* (pp. 191–200). Baltimore: Paul H. Brookes Publishing Co.

Duchardt, B.A., Deshler, D.D., & Schumaker, J.B. (1995). A strategic intervention for enabling students with learning disabilities to identify and change their ineffective beliefs. *Learning Disability Quarterly, 18,* 186–201.

Dugan, E., Kamps, D., Leonard, B., Watkins, N., Rheinberger, A., & Stackhaus, J. (1995). Effects of cooperative learning groups during social studies for students with autism and fourth-grade peers. *Journal of Applied Behavior Analysis, 28,* 175–188.

Dunst, C.J., Trivette, C.M., & Deal, A.G. (1988). *Enabling and empowering families: Principals and guidelines for practice.* Cambridge, MA: Brookline Books.

Dunst, C.J., Trivette, C.M., & Deal, A.G. (1994). *Supporting and strengthening families: Vol. 1: Methods, strategies and practices.* Cambridge, MA: Brookline Books.

Elliott, S.N., & Fuchs, L.S. (1997). The utility of curriculum-based measurement and performance assessment as alternatives to traditional intelligence and achievement tests. *School Psychology Review, 26,* 224–233.

Englert, C.S., & Rozendal, M.S. (1996). Nonreaders and nonwriters in special education: Crossing new literacy thresholds. *Reading and Writing, 8,* 87–103.

Fleming, L.A., Wolery, M., Weinzierl, C., Venn, M.L., & Schroeder, C. (1991). Model for assessing and adapting teachers' roles in mainstreamed settings. *Topics in Early Childhood Special Education, 11*(1), 85–98.

Fuchs, D., & Fuchs, L.S. (1994). Inclusive schools movement and the radicalization of special education reform. *Exceptional Children, 60,* 294–309.

Fuchs, D., Fuchs, L.S., Mathes, P.G., & Simmons, D.C. (1997). Peer-assisted learning strategies: Making classrooms more responsive to diversity. *American Educational Research Journal, 34,* 174–206.

Fuchs, L.S., & Fuchs, D. (1996). Combining performance assessment and curriculum-based measurement to strengthen instructional planning. *Learning Disabilities Research and Practice, 11,* 183–192.

Gast, D.L., Wellons, J., & Collins, B. (1994). Home and community safety skills. In M. Agran, N.E. Marchand-Martella, & R.C. Martella (Eds.), *Promoting health and safety: Skills for independent living* (pp. 11–32). Baltimore: Paul H. Brookes Publishing Co.

Gerber, M.M. (1984). Is Congress getting the full story? *Exceptional Children, 51,* 209–224.

Giangreco, M.F., Cloninger, C.J., & Iverson, V.S. (1998). *Choosing Outcomes and Accommodations for Children (COACH): A guide to educational planning for students with disabilities* (2nd ed.). Baltimore: Paul H. Brookes Publishing Co.

Golbeck, S.L., & Harlan, S. (1997). Family child care. In S.K. Thurman, J.R. Cornwell, & S.R. Gottwald (Eds.), *Contexts of early intervention: Systems and settings* (pp. 165–189). Baltimore: Paul H. Brookes Publishing Co.

Goldstein, S., Strickland, B., Turnbull, A.P., & Curry, L. (1980). An observational analysis of the IEP conference. *Exceptional Children, 46,* 278–286.

Gordon, J., Vaughn, S., & Schumm, J.S. (1993). Spelling interventions: A review of the literature and implications for instruction for students with learning disabilities. *Learning Disabilities Research and Practice, 8,* 175–181.

Greenwood, C.R., Carta, J.J., & Atwater, J. (1991). Ecobehavioral analysis in the classroom: Review and implications. *Journal of Behavioral Education, 1,* 59–77.

Gresham, F.M. (1997). We need a better way to identify students with learning disabilities. *CEC Today, 4*(5), 14.

Griffith, J. (1996). Relation of parental involvement, empowerment, and school traits to student academic performance. *Journal of Educational Research, 90,* 33–41.

Grskovic, J.A., & Belfiore, P. (1996). Improving the spelling performance of students with disabilities. *Journal of Behavioral Education, 6,* 343–354.

Hanline, M.F. (1988). Making the transition to preschool: Identification of parent needs. *Journal of the Division for Early Childhood, 12,* 98–107.

Hunt, P., & Goetz, L. (1997). Research on inclusive educational programs: Practices and outcomes for students with severe disabilities. *Journal of Special Education, 31,* 3–29.

Individuals with Disabilities Education Act (IDEA) of 1990, PL 101-476. 20, U.S.C. §§ 1400 *et seq.*

Individuals with Disabilities Education Act Amendments of 1997, PL 105-17, 20 U.S.C. §§ 1400 *et seq.*

Jones, K.H., & Bender, W.N. (1993). Utilization of paraprofessionals in special education: A review of the literature. *Remedial and Special Education, 14,* 7–14.

Kaiser, A.P., & Gray, D.B. (Eds.). (1993). *Enhancing children's communication: Research foundations for intervention.* In S.F. Warren & J.R. Reichle (Series Eds.), *Communication and Language Intervention Series: Vol. 2.* Baltimore: Paul H. Brookes Publishing Co.

Kameenui, E.J., Simmons, D.C., Chard, D., & Dickson, S. (1997). Direct instruction reading. In S.A. Stahl & D.A. Hayes (Eds.), *Instructional models in reading* (pp. 59–84). Mahwah, NJ: Lawrence Erlbaum Associates.

Kantrowitz, B. (1997). Why Johnny stayed home: On test days some schools encourage absences. *Newsweek, 30*(14), 60.

Kennedy, C.H., Cushing, L.S., & Itkonen, T. (1997). General education participation improves the social contacts and friendship networks of students with severe disabilities. *Journal of Behavioral Education, 7,* 167–189.

Kennedy, C.H., & Shukla, S. (1989). Social interaction research for people with autism as a set of past, current, and emerging propositions. *Behavior Disorders, 14*(4), 21–35.

Mallory, B.L., & Kerns, G.M. (1988). Consequences of categorical labeling of preschool children. *Topics in Early Childhood Special Education, 8*(3), 39–50.

Mastropieri, M.A., Scruggs, T.E., & Whedon, C. (1997). Using mnemonic strategies to teach information about U.S. Presidents: A classroom-based investigation. *Learning Disability Quarterly, 20,* 13–21.

McWilliam, R.A. (1996a). Implications for the future of integrating specialized services. In R.A. McWilliam (Ed.), *Rethinking pull-out services in early intervention: A professional resource* (pp. 343–371). Baltimore: Paul H. Brookes Publishing Co.

McWilliam, R.A. (Ed.). (1996b). *Rethinking pull-out services in early intervention: A professional resource.* Baltimore: Paul H. Brookes Publishing Co.

McWilliam, R.A., Young, H.J., & Harville, K. (1996). Therapy services in early intervention: Current status, barriers, and recommendations. *Topics in Early Childhood Special Education, 16,* 348–374.

Miner, C.A., & Bates, P.E. (1997). The effect of person centered planing activities on the IEP/transition planning process. *Education and Training in Mental Retardation and Developmental Disabilities, 32,* 105–112.

Mount, B., & Zwernik, K. (1988). *It's never too early, it's never too late. A booklet about personal futures planning.* St. Paul, MN: Metropolitan Council.

Mowder, B.A. (1997). Early intervention program models. In A.H. Widerstrom, B.A. Mowder, & S.R. Sandall, *Infant development and risk: An introduction* (2nd ed.) (pp. 289–312). Baltimore: Paul H. Brookes Publishing Co.

Newton, J.S., Ard, W.R., Horner, R.H., & Toews, J.D. (1996). Focusing on values and lifestyle outcomes in an effort to improve the quality of residential services in Oregon. *Mental Retardation, 34,* 1–12.

Newton, J.S., Olson, D., Horner, R.H., & Ard, W.R. (1996). Social skills and the stability of social relationships between individuals with intellectual disabilities and other community members. *Research in Developmental Disabilities, 17,* 15–26.

Roach, V., Halvorsen, A., Zeph, L., Giugno, M., & Caruso, M. (1997). Providing accurate placement data on students with disabilities in general education settings. *CISP Issue Brief, 2*(3), 1–10.

Rohena-Diaz, E.I., & Browder, D.M. (1996). Functional reading for students with developmental disabilities who are linguistically diverse. *Journal of Behavioral Education, 6,* 25–33.

Rosenkoetter, S.E., Hains, A.H., & Fowler, S.A. (1994). *Bridging early services for children with special needs and their families: A practical guide for transition planning.* Baltimore: Paul H. Brookes Publishing Co.

Rous, B., Hemmeter, M.L., & Schuster, J.W. (1994). Sequenced transition to education in the public schools: A systems approach to transition planning. *Topics in Early Childhood Special Education, 14,* 374–393.

Sainato, D.M. (1990). Classroom transitions: Organizing environments to promote independent performance in preschool children with disabilities. *Education and Treatment of Children, 13,* 288–297.

Sainato, D.M., & Lyon, S.R. (1989). Promoting successful mainstreaming transitions for handicapped preschool children. *Journal of Early Intervention, 13,* 305–314.

Salisbury, C.L., & Vincent, L.J. (1990). Criterion of the next environment and best practices: Mainstreaming and integration 10 years later. *Topics in Early Childhood Special Education, 10*(2), 78–89.

Sandall, S.R. (1997a). Home-based services and supports. In A.H. Widerstrom, B.A. Mowder, & S.R. Sandall, *Infant development and risk: An introduction* (2nd ed.) (pp. 315–333). Baltimore: Paul H. Brookes Publishing Co.

Sandall, S.R. (1997b). The individualized family service plan. In A.H. Widerstrom, B.A. Mowder, & S.R. Sandall, *Infant development and risk: An introduction* (2nd ed.) (pp. 237–257). Baltimore: Paul H. Brookes Publishing Co.

Sawyer, R.J., McLaughlin, M.J., & Winglee, M. (1994). Is integration of students with disabilities happening?: An analysis of national data trends over time. *Remedial and Special Education, 15,* 204–215.

Schumm, J.S., & Vaughn, S. (1992). Planning for mainstreamed special education students: Perceptions of general classroom teachers. *Exceptionality, 3,* 81–98.

Schuster, J.W., Ault, M.J., & Hemmeter, M.L. (1998). *Integrated therapy: Supports, barriers, and state of the practice.* Manuscript submitted for publication.

Scruggs, T.E., & Mastropieri, M.A. (1996). Teacher perceptions of mainstreaming/inclusion, 1958–1995: A research synthesis. *Exceptional Children, 63,* 59–74.

Short, R.J., & Talley, R.C. (1997). Rethinking psychology and the schools: Implications of recent national policy. *American Psychologist, 53,* 234–240.

Shotts, C.K., Rosenkoetter, S.E., Streufert, C.A., & Rosenkoetter, L.I. (1994). Transition policy and issues: A view from the states. *Topics in Early Childhood Special Education, 14,* 395–411.

Singh, N.N. (Ed.). (1997). *Prevention and treatment of severe behavior problems: Models and methods in developmental disabilities.* Pacific Grove, CA: Brooks/Cole.

Stayton, V.D., & Karnes, M.B. (1994). Model programs for infants and toddlers with disabilities and their families. In L.J. Johnson, R.J. Gallagher, M.J. La Montagne, J.B. Jordan, J.J. Gallagher, P.L. Hutinger, & M.B. Karnes (Eds.), *Meeting early intervention challenges: Issues from birth to three* (2nd ed.) (pp. 33–58). Baltimore: Paul H. Brookes Publishing Co.

Thurman, S.K., Cornwell, J.R., & Korteland, C. (1989). The Liaison Infant Family Team (LIFT) project: An example of case study evaluation. *Infants and Young Children, 2*(2), 74–82.

Thurman, S.K., & Widerstrom, A.H. (1990). *Infants and young children with special needs: A developmental and ecological approach* (2nd ed.). Baltimore: Paul H. Brookes Publishing Co.

Trivette, C.M., & Dunst, C.J. (1997). *Family perceptions of barriers and supports in early elementary schools.* (Unpublished progress report, Grant No. HO24Q50001). Asheville, NC: Orelena Hawks Puckett Institute.

Turbiville, V.P., Turnbull, A.P., Garland, C.W., & Lee, I.M. (1996). Development and implementation of IFSPs and IEPs: Opportunities for empowerment. In S.L. Odom & M.E. McLean (Eds.), *Early intervention/early childhood special education: Recommended practices* (pp. 77–100). Austin, TX: PRO-ED.

Turnbull, R.H. (1990). *Free appropriate public education: The law and children with disabilities* (3rd ed.). Denver, CO: Love Publishing Co.

Vandercook, T., York, J., & Forest, M. (1989). The McGill Action Planning System (MAPS): A strategy for building the vision. *Journal of The Association for Persons with Severe Handicaps, 14,* 205–215.

Warren, S.F., & Horn, E.M. (1996). Generalization issues in providing integrated services. In R.A. McWilliam (Ed.), *Rethinking pull-out services in early intervention: A professional resource* (pp. 121–143). Baltimore: Paul H. Brookes Publishing Co.

Warren, S.F., & Reichle, J. (Eds.). (1992). *Causes and effects in communication and language intervention.* In S.F. Warren & J. Reichle (Series Eds.), *Communication and Language Intervention Series: Vol. 1.* Baltimore: Paul H. Brookes Publishing Co.

Werts, M.G., Wolery, M., Snyder, E.D., & Caldwell, N.K. (1996). Teachers' perceptions of the supports critical to the success of inclusion programs. *Journal of The Association for Persons with Severe Handicaps, 21,* 9–21.

Werts, M.G., Wolery, M., Snyder, E.D., Caldwell, N.K., & Salisbury, C.L. (1996). Supports and resources associated with inclusive schooling: Perceptions of elementary school teachers about need and availability. *Journal of Special Education, 30,* 187–203.

Westling, D.L., & Fox, L. (1995). *Teaching students with severe disabilities.* Upper Saddle River, NJ: Prentice Hall.

Wolery, M. (1989). Transitions in early childhood special education: Issues and procedures. *Focus on Exceptional Children, 22,* 1–16.

Wolery, M. (1996). *Final report: Providing effective instruction in inclusive classrooms.* (Grant No. HO86D20005). Pittsburgh: Allegheny-Singer Research Institute.

Wolery, M., Anthony, L., & Heckathorn, J. (1998). Transition-based teaching: Effects on transitions, teachers' behavior, and children's learning. *Journal of Early Intervention, 21,* 117–131.

Wolery, M., Anthony, L., Snyder, E.D., Werts, M.G., & Katzenmeyer, J. (1997). Training elementary teachers to embed instruction during classroom activities. *Education and Treatment of Children, 20,* 40–58.

Wolery, M., Bailey, D.B., Dunst, C.J., Schuster, J.W., McWilliam, R.A., Trivette, C.M., Hemmeter, M.L., & Maxwell, K.L. (1997). *Early Childhood Follow-Through Research Institute: Year 2 progress report.* (Grant No. HO24Q50001). Chapel Hill: University of North Carolina.

Wolery, M., & Bredekamp, S. (1994). Developmentally appropriate practice and young children with special needs: Contextual issues in the discussion. *Journal of Early Intervention, 18,* 331–341.

Wolery, M., Holcombe, A., Brookfield, J., Huffman, K., Schroeder, C., Martin, C.G., Venn, M.L., Werts, M.G., & Fleming, L.A. (1993). The extent and nature of preschool mainstreaming: A survey of general early educators. *Journal of Special Education, 27,* 222–234.

Wolery, M., & Schuster, J.W. (1997). Instructional methods with students who have significant disabilities. *Journal of Special Education, 31,* 61–79.

Wolery, M., Werts, M.G., Caldwell, N.K., Dunst, C.J., McWilliam, R.A., Maxwell, K.L., & Bailey, D.B. (1997). *National survey concerning individualization and developmentally appropriate practices for students with disabilities in early elementary classes.* (Unpublished progress report, Grant No. HO24Q50001). Chapel Hill: University of North Carolina.

Wolery, M., Werts, M.G., Caldwell, N.K., Snyder, E.D., & Lisowski, L. (1995). Experienced teachers' perceptions of resources and supports for inclusion. *Education and Training in Mental Retardation and Developmental Disabilities, 30,* 15–26.

Wolery, M., Werts, M.G., & Dunst, C.J. (1997). *National survey of art, music, and physical education teachers about students with disabilities in early elementary classes.* (Unpublished progress report, Grant No. HO24Q50001). Chapel Hill: University of North Carolina.

Wolery, M., Werts, M.G., & Snyder, E.D. (1997). *National survey about the use of paraprofessionals in early elementary classrooms.* (Unpublished progress report, Grant No. HO24Q50001). Chapel Hill: University of North Carolina.

Wood, M. (1998). Whose job is it anyway? Educational roles in inclusion. *Exceptional Children, 64,* 181–195.

Zigler, E., & Hunsinger, S. (1979). Look at the state of America's children in the Year of the Child. *Young Children, 34,* 2–3.

Chapter 10

Kindergarten Practices with Children from Low-Income Families

Barbara T. Bowman

Many American children are not succeeding in school. One group of under-achievers lives in persistent poverty (Brooks-Gunn, Klebanov, & Duncan, 1996) and is disproportionately made up of minorities—African American, Native American, and Latino children (National Center for Education Statistics, 1995). These children score lower on standardized tests, repeat grades more often, and drop out of school at higher rates than other children and are overrepresented in special education programs. Their high incidence of school failure is a threat to the economic and social stability of the United States and, therefore, is the focus of attention of educators, policy makers, and business and civic leaders.

Schools and teachers are essential players in altering the educational experience of low-income children, and changes in their practices are essential. Kindergarten, the first step on the academic ladder, represents an almost universal challenge for American children. It is a time of shifting demands for social, cognitive, and emotional behavior (Sameroff & Haith, 1996) as children move from learning informally in the home and community to mastering abstract and complex disciplines taught in formal settings. It is a critical time, in particular, for children who are at an economic disadvantage.

Learning in school depends on 1) the characteristics of the classroom (curricula and pedagogy) and school (climate and resources) and 2) the capabilities of young children to learn in the school setting. Problems for low-income children exist on both fronts: Classrooms frequently fail to adapt to their specific needs, and they, as well as their families, are often poorly prepared for the school experience. These are not separate problems, but interrelated ones; achievement is related to the "goodness of fit" between the child and the school. When the mix of child, family, and community characteristics and classroom demands is too disparate, kindergarten is the beginning of a downward spiral of which failure is the result.

A number of early preschool programs have successfully altered both short- and long-term educational trajectories for low-income children (Berrueta-Clement, Schweinhart, Barnett, Epstein, & Weikart, 1984; Campbell & Ramey, 1995; Campbell & Taylor, 1996; Comer, 1980; Shorr, 1988). The primary findings of this research are 1) interventions should begin as early as possible, and 2) interventions should address child, family, and community variables. Despite the positive evidence, so far, few large-scale programs have been uniformly successful across sites or have brought the school performance of low-income children up to the level of other children (Barnes, Goodson, & Layzer, 1995/1996; Barnett, 1995; Halpern, in press; Haskins, 1989). Thus, preschool intervention still falls well short of its goal and many young children arrive at kindergarten unprepared for success.

This chapter examines factors identified in the research on low-income children and families and discusses their implications for schools and classrooms. Its purpose is to alert teacher educators, school administrators, and teachers to what it will take to change school achievement for these children. Translating research into practice is hazardous because it is only one source of knowledge about teaching (Stott & Bowman, 1996). The daily lives of teachers rarely fit easily with the advice emanating from academe (Gersten & Brengelman, 1996). Research studies and theoretical models, however, can set parameters, if not the blueprints, for practice (Stott & Bowman, 1996), alerting practitioners to areas for potential improvement. Nevertheless, it is important to pass recommendations through the filter of practice, examining the usefulness of our advice and the probability of it being implemented. This chapter, therefore, strives to include some of the realities faced by teachers and administrators as they try to implement recommended practices.

Three interrelated topics are considered: 1) developmental dysfunction and stress-related behavioral problems, 2) social and emotional well-being and school success, and 3) cultural differences between home and school. Using the knowledge base of the field—much of which is represented in this book—expectations for kindergarten are examined. This chapter concludes with recommendations for school and classroom policies and practices that could improve outcomes for low-income children.

POVERTY INCREASES THE INCIDENCE OF DEVELOPMENTAL PATHOLOGY

Historically, developmental pathology conceived of health and pathology as discontinuous variables. This point of view has been modified as theorists and clinicians have been increasingly inclined to view development as more complex, differentiated, and variable. Current views focus on the interplay between children's biologically driven characteristics and the resources of the physical and interpersonal environment (Sameroff & Chandler, 1975). Consequently, the notion of pathology as a condition found inside the child is less consistent with current research than a perspective that sees problems lodged in the relationship between the child (with whatever strengths and weaknesses) and his or her interpersonal world (with whatever its resources or limitations) (Bowman, 1993).

A number of factors that correlate with developmental difficulties and psychological dysfunction are found more frequently in low-income families and communities. These include preterm and low birth weight infants, hunger, physically inadequate and overcrowded housing, unsafe environments, and inadequate medical care (Department of Health and Human Services, 1997). In addition, abuse and neglect are reported more frequently in low-income homes. Although there is undoubtedly overreporting of child mistreatment in poor and minority families, the stress of living poor exacerbates anxiety, depression, substance abuse, and poor physical and mental health, making low-income parents and caregivers more likely to be irritable, explosive, and punitive (Hann, Ray, Bernstein, & Halpern, 1995).

For a number of reasons, then, children from low-income families are more likely to have physical, social, and psychological dysfunction and disabilities (Garbarino, Dubrow, Kostelny, & Pardo, 1992; McLoyd, 1990). Also, many such children, by belonging to marginalized groups in American society (low income and minority), are more likely to have their symptoms intensified by a hostile and unforgiving environment, thus worsening their developmental status and school learning. When school is yet another stressful environment, it can intensify dysfunction or can itself produce long-term social and emotional challenges. Given this perspective, even children who have incurred developmental insults can have their symptoms tempered by the resources available in their schools, or the interaction between the classroom teacher and the child can create or intensify developmental problems. (See Chapter 9 for a more complete discussion of children with developmental disabilities.)

Implications for Schools and Teachers

School personnel can play an important role in preventing developmental difficulties that compromise educational achievement. The research on children with developmental difficulties suggests that administrators and teachers should 1) work with other community institutions to help alleviate threats to healthy development, 2) assess children quickly for evidence of developmental delay or unrecognized disability, and 3) manage classrooms to support the positive development of children.

Working with Community Institutions   Working with community institutions has not been a high priority with schools (Dryfoos, 1994). To avert children failing, schools should work with public health and social services agencies and organizations, the courts, child care and early intervention programs, and community activists to improve conditions for them (Kagan, 1991; Shorr, 1988; Wang, Haertel, & Walberg, 1997).

Although there is good reason to include the school in the panoply of agencies responsible for meeting family and community social needs, many teachers believe that the school should restrict itself to academic concerns, despite evidence of the interrelatedness of educational achievement and other domains of children's lives. Their reluctance to be involved is not wholly capricious. In some instances, teachers share the view, pervasive in American society, that schools are for learning academic subjects and not for solving social problems. Dryfoos (1998) pointed out that this value is relatively new in American society where, until the last generation or two, the school was embedded in the civic and religious life of the community. Nonetheless, since mid-century, schools in low-income communities have not been heavily involved in community activities.

Another reason for teacher hesitation to engage in activities outside school is the position of the administration regarding school responsibilities. Where administrators are struggling with in-school problems, they may be doubtful about the value of work outside the school. Even when convinced of its value, some administrators do not have the time or knowledge to design and implement effective collaborations. Teachers, therefore, see little reason to extend themselves; instead, they follow the lead of the administration in setting priorities and allocating their time and energy.

One of the primary impediments to teacher involvement in community activities is the discomfort many teachers experience when interacting with low-income families. The public school record for engaging low-income parents is far from outstanding (Bowman, 1994), which puts teachers at a disadvantage in reaching out to these families. In addition, teachers have had little preparation for engaging low-income parents, having had neither coursework nor experience working with adults, much less adults from different socioeconomic, racial, or ethnic groups (Bowman, 1997a). In some low-income communities, kindergarten teachers have been encouraged to become more involved with preschools, to coordinate curricula and transition activities.

Assessment   Children with developmental difficulties and serious behavior problems need to be identified quickly, but teachers are often unable to distinguish between children with serious problems and those who are developing typically. As Meisels points out in Chapter 3, assessing young children is a complicated and difficult process, made more difficult when cultural differences (to be discussed later in this chapter) confound the assessment of developmental accomplishments. The distinctions between 1) disease and dysfunction, 2) disturbances due to environmental stress and temporary physical conditions, and 3) normal variations in development and culture are often blurred. For example, a child may be inattentive, easily distracted by extraneous stimuli, and excessively active. These symptoms may signal attention-deficit/hyperactivity disorder, an overwhelmingly stressful environment, cultural disorientation, an impulsive temperament, or a temporary separation anxiety. Determining developmental status requires considerable diagnostic skill, especially when children are young. Consequently, teachers either refer large numbers of students for formal evaluation, thereby wasting valuable time by slowing the process of determining who is eligible for special education services, or they refer too few and miss the opportunity for arranging special education resources.

Few schools have sufficient resource professionals to assist teachers in making developmental assessment and referrals, and there are few transdisciplinary coaches and mentors for teachers striving to cope. To help teachers to be more responsive to the range of special needs of children calls for reforming both pre-service and in-service education. Coursework stressing assessments of typical development across individual and cultural differences should have much more prominence in schools of education than it does (Bowman, 1997a). Schools also need to put in place a consultation and planning resource within the school to assist teachers to quickly identify and refer children with disabilities.

Classroom Management   Referrals may also take considerable time to arrange, leaving the teacher to cope—but with few resources at his or her disposal. Even after testing, children may remain in the general classroom, with teachers none the wiser about how to respond to them. Although inclusion may provide a less restrictive environment for children with developmental dysfunction and delay or serious behavior problems, it often constitutes an overwhelming burden for teachers. When there are four or five children with disabilities in classrooms, teachers have difficulty managing the classroom and providing effective instruction. Children with disabilities miss out on their own education, and their presence frequently interferes with the education of other children by placing an unmanageable burden on classrooms—both teachers and children. Although training for teachers can be helpful, there is also a need for more realistic expectations. It is unlikely that the arrangements commonly used in kindergarten—20–30 children per class, double sessions, 10-month school years, and annual changes in classroom teachers and children—will promote more effective management.

Probably the most needed and least attended to facet of improving teacher management is their need for psychological support. Many teachers are immobilized by the same conditions that exact a toll on children and families. In high crime areas, in neighborhoods where violence is a daily occurrence, where depression and anger are close to the surface of everyday activities, the strain on teachers is enormous, often eroding their ability to be empathic and responsive. Yet, few schools routinely provide support for the staff, and turnover is high, regularly bringing the least experienced teachers into the most challenging educational environments. Support is essential if teachers are to create an effective learning environment, one that maximizes children's strengths and permits all children to learn.

SOCIAL AND EMOTIONAL FACTORS AFFECT SCHOOL LEARNING

Underlying academic competence are social and emotional characteristics that relate to children's school performance and social relationships (Birch & Ladd, 1996, 1997; Howes, 1996; Howes, Hamilton, & Matheson, 1994; Pianta, 1992, 1994). Ideally, two facets of development—emotional and social—operate in a mutually congruent manner, such that there is a match between feeling states and social expectations for behavior. There exists, however, a potential for tension between the two; thus, maladjustment is, at times, a reflection of the dissonance between internal feeling and external social expectations for behavior. When the conflict between feelings and social demands becomes too great, children may regress to earlier intrapsychic organizations and develop inappropriate social behavior. Winnicott (1988) used the term "false self" to indicate such a conflict and pointed out the potential for harm in the misfit between children's inner selves and their social world. School readiness connotes that the child's intrapsychic organization and behavior is in close approximation to the demands made by the social environment in which the child lives.

Children who experience greater academic success in their early school years demonstrate compliance with rules and requests, are cooperative, have positive attitudes and confidence in their approach to learning, and have the ability to appropriately regulate emotions and postpone gratification (Alexander & Entwisle, 1988). Given the importance of these social and emotional characteristics, one cannot help but be struck by the relative paucity of research on social and emotional development in early childhood programs in comparison with the wealth of research available on the cognitive or skill-based aspects of learning. Indeed, with the exception of the work of Comer and Levin, few school reform movements have paid much attention to the social and emotional components in reforming schools (Boyd & Shouse, 1997). In the next section, three aspects of children's social and emotional development are considered: primary relationships, individual differences, and self-esteem and self-awareness.

Primary Relationships

It is assumed that when children come to school they are already able to use adults as sources of information, discipline, and enjoyment. This is only the case if the stage has been set by families or other consistent caregivers who have engaged in such relationships with them. The quality of early care lays the groundwork for the capacity to love and to use other humans as a source of comfort, hope, and guidance and lays the basis for a sense of well-being and an interest in social engagement.

A central theme in current developmental theories is the importance of the first infant–caregiver relationships in shaping later social and emotional development and behavior. Both animal and developmental research scientists have found strong connections between the quality of the relationship between mother (caregiver) and child and the child's later development and learning. Not only do social interactions stimulate the development of more complex neural patterning of the brain, but they also act to protect the brain from overdoses of stress-related chemicals (Perry, 1995). Many researchers see this first social relationship as setting the stage for later interpersonal characteristics (Pianta, Smith, & Reeve, 1991), and the relationship is often used as a predictive marker for development (Ainsworth, 1973; Carlson & Earls, 1997). Chief, then, among the ingredients necessary for development are emotionally and socially supportive relationships. Such relationships are the bedrock on which school learning and adjustment depend.

Parents experiencing economic hardship are more likely to be psychologically stressed and less able to respond positively to their children, exposing children to punitive discipline and violence (Weiss, Dodge, Bates, & Petit, 1992). Furthermore, with less sustained positive interaction with the parent, the child has fewer opportunities to learn strategies that help in initiating and maintaining positive social interactions. Thus, social and emotional competence, conveyed through early caregiving relationships, has a direct impact on characteristics likely to promote school learning (Wang et al., 1997), primarily children's ability to develop healthy relationships with their teachers and peers.

Although the ability to establish satisfying interpersonal relationships with primary caregivers (attachment) remains an important developmental accomplishment during infancy and contributes to the quality of later interpersonal relationships, its adequacy must be assessed within particular sociocultural contexts (LeVine & Miller, 1990). Relationships must be judged by how well they work in the world in which the parent and the child live. This means that there is no single exemplar of the relationships that predict competence. Nonetheless, the quality of parent interactions with their children does contribute to school success (Wang et al., 1997).

Parental relationships are not the only important relationships. Teachers and caregivers can also buffer (or intensify) a child's experience so that a child can escape relatively unscathed from events that might otherwise severely affect him or her (Sroufe, 1988). Although parental relationships are most predictive of later relationships, other important adults in a child's life may also influence him or her. Howes et al. (1994) and Pianta (1994) reported that the quality of teachers' relationships affects how children adapt to school and learn. Thus, children's learning is tied to the kind of relationship they have with their mothers and their prior teachers, indicating the strength of all early relationships in mediating learning.

Implications for Teachers   The previous findings are relevant to children's kindergarten adjustment in two ways. First, they speak to the importance of understanding and accepting the bond between children and their primary caregivers. Regardless of whether parents carry out their responsibilities in ways that are consistent with the expectations of teachers, the relationship is essential to the children's well-being and forms the basis for their expectations of other adults. Although parent education and support programs have shown only modest effects, children whose low-income parents participate actively in their children's schools are more likely to influence the school performance of their children (Halpern, in press; Pfannenstiel & Seltzer, 1989). This suggests that teachers must create welcoming environments if they expect to form alliances with primary caregivers in setting expectations for children's behavior. When teachers' and parents' notions of how and what children ought to learn are at odds, it is less likely that children will respond to school expectations.

Second, the relationship between kindergarten teacher and child echoes the parent–child relationship (Pianta, 1994). Children whose primary relationships were problematic may seek to reproduce or ameliorate earlier unsatisfying ones, often creating an emotional drain on teachers as they are caught up in children's attempts to deal with their attachment issues. Even when children have arrived at school emotionally and socially stable, establishing relationships requires a high level of emotional commitment from teachers. For many teachers, the strain of becoming a role model for children, of accepting behavior that conflicts with their own values, and of committing themselves emotionally is overwhelming and leads them to limit their relationships with children. Facilitating and supporting teachers' abilities to sustain important relationships with children require preservice and in-service education that focuses on relationship building, as well as on curriculum and management, and group sizes that are small enough for teachers to establish meaningful relationships (Howes, 1996, 1988).

Individual Differences

Children's age-related biological and neurodevelopmental timetables affect the sequence by which knowledge is acquired and the style of learning most likely to be used (Peterson, 1994). Maturation proceeds in spurts and plateaus as growth and experience reconfigure neurobiological capacities. This process is orderly but shows considerable individual variation because it is influenced by both genes and environment. From infancy on, individuals are constitutionally predisposed to vary widely along dimensions such as affect, attention, and motor activity—or more succinctly, *temperament.*

In some cases, children's early temperament has been associated with later social and emotional difficulty. Children who have developed behavioral problems, such as aggressiveness, high anxiety, and sleep difficulties, were found as infants to have been temperamentally quite different from children not evidencing these symptoms. Some of the characteristics of children's "readiness" to learn in school may be as much, if not more, of a reflection of temperamental features as of socioemotional maturity. This research emphasizes the importance of the "goodness of fit" between the school environment and individual characteristics of the child. Some children's temperaments may enable them to adapt more easily to the social environment of school, whereas others are predestined to social and academic dissonance.

Recognizing the number and complexity of biological, psychological, and so-cial factors that affect development has led some researchers to use concepts of re-silience and vulnerability to explain differences in children's response to chal-lenging environments (Werner, 1989). Vulnerable children have psychological experiences and/or biological predispositions that push them to respond nega-tively to stresses that other children do not find challenging. Resilient children, be-cause of their social and biological resources, are able to avoid negative outcomes from situations and events that profoundly affect other children. For instance, Weiss et al. (1992) found that although harsh discipline correlates with children's negative social and emotional adaptation, the effects are not large, indicating the great variability of children's reactions to this stressful factor.

One of the more helpful conceptualizations of what makes children effective learners is contained in *The Emotional Foundations of School Readiness* (National Center for Clinical Infant Programs, 1992). The following characteristics are listed therein:

1. Confidence—a sense of control and mastery of one's body, behavior, and world; the child's sense that he or she is more likely than not to succeed at what he or she undertakes and that adults will be helpful

2. Curiosity—the sense that finding out about things is positive and leads to pleasure

3. Intentionality—the desire and capacity to have an impact and to act with persistence

4. Self-control—the ability to modulate and control one's own actions in age-appropriate ways; a sense of inner control

5. Relatedness—the ability to engage with others based on the sense of being understood by and understanding others

6. Capacity to communicate—the desire and ability to verbally exchange ideas, feelings, and concepts with others, which is related to a sense of trust in oth-ers and of pleasure in engaging with others, including adults

7. Cooperativeness—the ability to balance one's own needs with those of others in a group activity

The framework of resilience and vulnerability is useful for classroom teachers who often are unduly influenced by the litany of pathology in low-income families and communities. It is too easy to assume that all children will be overwhelmed by deprivations in their personal and physical environments, but in fact, children are remarkably resilient, and there is little evidence that large numbers of low-income and minority children are pathology ridden.

Implications for Teachers   This foregoing research suggests that although or-dinary environments may not be a challenge for most children, and certainly not for resilient children, nevertheless, some children will be hurt and their learning compromised in fairly benign settings. It is the responsibility of the teacher to rec-ognize those sensitive or vulnerable children for whom special care is needed.

More attention also needs to be given to the normal variations in individual development. The degree of convergence inherent in normative scales for young children fails to sufficiently reflect the broad range in typical development. As a consequence, children are penalized for relatively unimportant differences in developmental trajectories (Shepard & Smith, 1986). Expectations for individual behavior and lock-step curricula—the curricula often recommended for low-income children—may hinder learning for many young children and place them under unnecessary stress (Elkind, 1987).

Using the classroom as a supportive environment for individual children is a formidable task for kindergarten teachers, particularly for children whose temperaments—impassive or shy, for instance—make them difficult members of a group. The need to match learning opportunities to different ways in which individual children learn is essential; yet, class size, curriculum pressures, and the culture of schools mitigate against this type of personalized and supportive environment, particularly in schools that are serving low-income children (Darling-Hammond, 1994). Furthermore, teachers rarely focus on the mental health quality of the classroom environment as a factor in children's learning. Consequently, children who do not fit easily into the group are frequently further disadvantaged. Clearly, many structural changes are necessary if teachers are to respond to individual differences among children.

Self-Esteem and Self-Awareness

Self-esteem in children has received considerable attention because of its correlation with school success (Beane, 1991) and the reports of low self-image among children of color (Delpit, 1988; Garcia, 1988; Jipson ,1991; Otheguy, 1982; Spencer, 1985).

Harter (1996) noted that children experience a shift in self-understanding between 5 and 7 years of age and that this shift moves children to evaluate their performance by the standards set by others. Children at this age are becoming aware of the regard of others and gradually integrate their assessment into their own thinking. They are particularly vulnerable, therefore, to judgments that picture them as inadequate and failing. Confidence in their ability to achieve, viewing school knowledge as useful and worthwhile, and seeing school subjects as related to their personal and cultural identity are factors that predict academic strength.

Some studies depict young African American children as highly self-valuing within their own families and communities but as having negative views about their own group (Spencer, 1985). When they enroll in school, self-confidence diminishes, but it is not clear whether self-esteem deteriorates. As children expand their horizons to include other adults and peers, socially valued attributes would be expected to play an increasingly important role in self-image and could account for decreasing self-esteem and explain declining school achievement and school avoidance by students academically at risk.

Implications for Teachers   Experiences that build self-confidence and self-esteem are considered particularly important for children from low-status groups because of their vulnerability to self-doubt (Steele, 1989). Beane described two classroom orientations toward self-esteem. One, the "tetanus shot" theory of mental health, views high self-esteem as teachable by exhortation and praise and as conferring "immunity to problem situations" (1991, p. 154). Some teachers who use this approach praise children's performance frequently and create opportunities for them to "show off" as ways to bolster self-evaluation. Others create slogans and songs that emphasize the child's value.

The second orientation toward self-esteem is what Beane (1991) called the "free market" approach, in which self-esteem is earned through the individual's own effort in a narrow range of socially approved activities. Accordingly, high academic and behavioral standards and the involvement of parents and communities in setting and reinforcing standards are considered important. This approach fits the rationale of many advocates of school reform who recommend direct instruction of basic skills as the best way to improve performance.

Another perspective recommends embedding curricula in the cultural traditions of various communities, thus the development of a number of racial-, linguistic-, and gender-centric curricula and programs. These approaches, particularly early home language instruction and curricula, have shown some success, as have antibias curriculum (Derman-Sparks & Phillips, 1997). As yet, definitive studies that demonstrate a clear connection among self-esteem, classroom curricula, and student achievement have not been done. Nevertheless, attention to children's beliefs and feelings about themselves, their families, and communities cannot do harm and may contribute to young children's confidence and competence.

CULTURAL DIFFERENCES ARE CONFUSED WITH DEVELOPMENTAL AND BEHAVIORAL PROBLEMS

Although many low-income children are exposed to noxious environments and, therefore, have a higher incidence of developmental pathology and stress-related conditions than is found in more economically advantaged populations, the majority of low-income children are not so affected. Most low-income young children are developing typically, although they may not have learned the social behavior or cognitive skills required by schools and expected by teachers. They are often, therefore, mistakenly described as having developmental delays.

The assumption in the United States that children who do not belong to mainstream culture groups—particularly children of color—are in some way deficient in their development is ubiquitous (Gould, 1981). The explanation for the poorer school performance of low-income, minority children (primarily African American, Latino, and Native American) is not in the children's biological characteristics but in the cultural surround. Attributing differences in performance to developmental inadequacy reinforces the deficit hypothesis that permits us to undervalue children who do not fit the expected mold. Development is an interactive process shaped by a variety of factors, including cultural beliefs and practices, residence patterns, and situational factors (Rogoff, Gauvain, & Ellis, 1984). These differences have profound implications for how children learn to organize their environment, the language they learn to speak, how they occupy their leisure time, the kinds of problems they will see, and the strategies they will use to solve them.

Social interactions are not haphazard. Although cultures may be highly complex and constantly changing as groups adapt to new challenges, the meaning individuals in a group attribute to experience is relatively stable and represents almost unconscious definitions of what is right and, therefore, normal human behavior (Bowman & Stott, 1994). Slobin noted, "patterns of culture are extraordinarily persistent because they are laid down in childhood through structured interaction with the bearers of culture"(1990, p. 250). Research on development of minority infants shows that they are exposed to different patterns of affective and social interactions, different modes of communication, different means of exploring their environment, and alternative cognitive skills (Cole & Bruner, 1972; Coll, 1990; Florio-Ruane, 1987; Labov, 1995). Therefore, children who are developing typically from different cultural groups may achieve developmental benchmarks at different ages, learn different skills, and have different relational styles than their mainstream peers. They organize knowledge and respond to stimuli in somewhat different ways than is expected by schools (Ashton-Warner, 1964; Florio-Ruane, 1987; Hale, 1982). Accordingly, school, based on mainstream expectations, constitutes a greater challenge for these children than for others (Bowman & Stott, 1994).

Patterns of interaction guide the developing children, but they also become the basis for children's definitions of themselves—their identities. Children become what they live. They select from a pool of possible behaviors depending on their personal capabilities and inclinations and their understanding of what the situation (context) requires. Because children choose a particular response in a given situation does not mean that they are incapable of another, only that the response chosen is consistent with the requirements of the situation as they understand it (Bowman & Stott, 1994). Culture shapes the social world in which children develop, and there are multiple formulations of what it means to be human. Children learn whether to pay attention to gang symbols or the alphabet, to play basketball or soccer, to prefer to talk rather than read books, and to play drums or violins. These preferences and accomplishments are related to children's culture, not their development. Accordingly, there is no universally optimum teaching strategy; there are only strategies that better deal with the factors to which the child and teacher must adapt (Hinde, 1983).

Developmental accomplishments and cultural manifestation are inextricably bound together and, as a consequence, specific behaviors come to be synonymous with development itself. However, when comparing development across cultural settings and social practices, it is easy to be led astray. Similar developmental accomplishments may look quite different from one group to another. Black English, for instance, represents the same benchmark for an African American child as standard English or a foreign language does for other children. All are languages or dialects that permit children to communicate within their own families and communities—an equivalent developmental accomplishment. Because learned behavior and development are intertwined, it is quite easy to mistakenly attribute children's inability to perform particular tasks to developmental delay rather than cultural difference.

The confusion of development with specific cultural accomplishments has led to the misunderstanding of children's abilities and, therefore, to poorly designed educational programs and practices. By equating a child's developmental competence with a particular form of behavior, teachers misread the meaning of the child's behavior and are often led toward practices that compromise the child's potential for learning. It is not happenstance, then, that children who are poor and who are minorities are overrepresented in certain types of early intervention and special education programs.

Although families generally teach their children the culture of their community, the community may independently exert pressure on families, sometimes reinforcing, sometimes contradicting, parental teaching. For instance, Garbarino, Dubrow, Kostelny, and Pardo (1992) reported that most 5-year-olds living in housing projects knew someone who had been murdered and had personally witnessed violence and abuse, experiences that inevitably affect children's ideas about their own safety, the value of life, and their future potential. Community pressure can overwhelm the benefits and disadvantages of family influence (Sampson, Rau-

denbush, & Earls, 1997). With increasing age, children become much more suscep-
tible to the efficacy of their community culture, taking on identities and attributes
of role models outside the family. Even when families value school achievement,
the social environment in many low-income neighborhoods impinges on their values and affects children's motivation. Thus, low-income children may begin school
with quite different worldviews from those of their teachers.

The social distance between minorities of color and whites also affects school
achievement. Ogbu (1996), who noted that all classes of African Americans
achieved more poorly in school than white Americans of the same class, attributed
the lower achievement to the "disconnect" between the values of home and school
communities. The extent of alienation can be drawn from opinion surveys that consistently show differences in perceptions of the openness of the American system.
Most white Americans believe that there are equal opportunities for African Americans, whereas African Americans see prejudice and discrimination as pervasive.

Children must be supported in both their home and school cultures if they are
to learn well in school. Children from ethnic and racial groups that are most different from and most excluded from the mainstream society live in two separate
worlds: in their own ethnic enclaves and in the larger community. They can become bicultural and able to switch culturally encoded behavior depending on the
context in which they find themselves, but they need support to maintain a positive identity in both worlds. Research on cultural difference indicates that, to ameliorate effects of poverty on low-income children's school performance, schools
need to bridge the gap between home and school. Three areas of particular concern are 1) differences in beliefs and values between home and school culture,
2) teaching bias, and 3) selecting appropriate curricula and assessment strategies.

Differences in Beliefs and Values Between Home and School

School learning is most likely to occur when family values reinforce school expectations. This does not mean that parents must teach the same things at home that
teachers do in school. It does mean, however, that parents and community must
project school achievement as a desirable and attainable ideal if children are to
build it into their own sense of self and their identity constructs. Parents who are
afraid of the power of school, who are defensive about their possible shortcomings in relation to school, and who do not trust schools to meet their children's
needs are not likely to send their children with the explicit message—learn.

Most teachers are unanimous in wanting a partnership with parents, yet this
is not easy to obtain. Although teachers want a partnership, they tend to want it
on their own terms. Frequently, they devalue the home-generated knowledge of
low-income and minority communities (Jipson, 1991; Lubeck, 1994). Differences
occur over worldviews, the desirable qualities in interpersonal relationships, standards of behavior, and the goals and objectives of education (Bowman, 1994).

Low-income parents and community members often have different ideas
about appropriate developmental goals and educational objectives from those
guided by a formal knowledge base (Lubeck, 1994). Unfortunately, teachers often
dismiss these perspectives as uninformed. Although on the surface, the debate appears to be between those who are well informed by current research in child development and pedagogy and those who are not, it is, in reality, a debate between
individuals who hold different values about the purposes of schooling, what
counts as legitimate knowledge, and presumably the nature of the good life (Bow-

man & Stott, 1994). For example, when social orientations that emphasize individualism are presented as the norm for people raised in communities that sponsor interdependent behavior, normal behavior seems deviant, making what is ideal in one community unacceptable in another. Ethnotheoretical assumptions of superiority are often little more than preferences for one's own way of doing things.

When the social distance between families and the school prevents parents from supporting the school experience, children's emotional resiliency is diminished. When children do not have the support of their caregivers for school learning, they may disregard school rules of social engagement. Consider what might happen when children who are accustomed to families who are authoritarian, personal, and expressive encounter teachers who are indirect, impersonal, and not given to highly emotional displays. They may direct their attention to trying the teacher's limits—that is, eliciting a response from him or her—instead of learning the content of the lesson. Even more serious, by devaluing the culture of poor and minority children, teachers encourage an ominous cultural choice: Identify with family and friends and disavow the school, or embrace school culture and face emotional and social isolation. The result is that many young children opt for family and friends and become unwilling participants in school culture.

To create partnerships with low-income parents, teachers and administrators will need to approach their outreach efforts in a radically different manner. Instead of confining themselves to explaining their own views and demands, they will need to solicit and deal with those of the parent community. Creating a partnership with parents is as important, perhaps more important, than many of the tasks on which teachers spend their time. During the preschool and primary years, teachers should think of themselves as having two clients—parents and children—and they need to invest effort in engaging both.

Teaching Bias

Teaching consists of "meaning-making" episodes as adults and children create common interpretations of events and actions and standard ways of representing these interpretations. Teachers are often disadvantaged as they try to teach low-income children in communities where they work and seldom live. When adults and children do not share common experiences or do not hold common beliefs about the meaning of experiences, many misunderstand culturally encoded interchanges (Bowman, 1989a). Thus, teachers fail to appreciate real similarities and differences between their understanding of the world and that of children and families who come from different backgrounds. They become victims of their own naive and culture-bound conceptions.

Teachers understand that the meaning of children's behavior is derived, in part, from their own experiences. Their subjective understanding is essential because young children have limited ability to say how they think and feel and why they behave as they do. They are dependent on teachers' abilities to understand without words—an empathic understanding (Bowman, 1989b). Anna Freud, in describing the needs of young children, wrote, "We have to rely upon the capacity of the normal adult to remember things" (1963, p. 22) to supplement their understanding of children. Because they have access to their own memories, they can make sense of the behavior of young children and develop interpretive connections between their acts of teaching and the meaning their behavior will have for children (Bowman, 1989b).

Teachers have difficulty incorporating new visions of reality when these visions conflict with their own personal beliefs and experience. When confronted with discrepancies, teachers cling to their own "meaning-making" theories, forcing evidence to the contrary to fit their old beliefs. Thus, behavior that does not fit their preconceived notions is doctored to conform to their sense-making hypotheses. This makes it difficult to interpret the behavior of children from cultures different from their own. New strategies need to be employed to help teachers and administrators overcome their cultural biases. This means helping them to learn about children's past experiences, their families, their neighborhoods, and their culture. Unfortunately, the way schools are currently structured (teachers with little released time and teaching in isolation) does not offer great stimulus for change. Teachers need to observe and to be observed by their peers and supervisors, and to reflect with others to protect themselves from biased teaching. Opening the school to community residents, convening focus and reflection groups, providing coaches, and establishing multiyear placements for teachers and children can help teachers to develop more sensitivity to their own teaching biases.

Selecting Appropriate Curricula and Assessment Strategies

There are sharp differences of opinion about how to structure curricula for low-income children to improve their achievement. Psychologists, educators, politicians, and the general public have staked out positions that reflect their theoretical bias and their worldviews. In Chapter 5, Graue characterizes the opposing views on curricula as either direct instruction or child-centered instruction. She notes that the controversies between advocates of these two positions are heated, obscuring the practices that are "complex, contradictory, pragmatic, and political." The research on curricula is driven by different theoretical models and parents, politicians, and the general public often support one curricula over another because they believe it reflects their values about the nature of schooling and the responsibilities of various levels of government.

Supporters of a direct instruction and basic skills position look to behavioral psychology for theoretical support and the history of public education for traditions. Some minority educators and parents, who believe their children are not being given the tools they need to succeed in the broader American society (Delpit, 1988), are strong supporters of the notion of directly teaching children what is to be tested. However, the child-centered approach uses child development as its research base, contending that learning is age related and curricula should follow maturation and the inclinations of the child. This perspective reflects the influence of both normative and genetic psychologists and the philosophical biases of Rousseau and Montessori. It also defines the model of education used in most preschool programs for middle-class children (Bowman, 1997b).

As Graue notes in Chapter 5, these polar positions have been tempered by the National Association for the Education of Young Children's (NAEYC's) publication of *Developmentally Appropriate Practice in Early Childhood Programs* (Bredekamp & Copple, 1997). NAEYC continues to direct teachers' attention to children's individual differences, age-related abilities and learning styles, and cultural differences (Bredekamp & Copple, 1997) but recommends a balance at the same time. This balance requires neither content nor methods to be decided on *a priori* but suggests that they be decided on in response to the strengths and needs of particular children. According to this perspective, teaching consists of "meaning-making" episodes as adults and children create common interpretations of events and actions and standard ways of representing these interpretations. Children, then, need to learn academic content and they need to understand and see the relevance of the content to themselves and their lives. Polarizing "into either/or choices many questions that are more fruitfully seen as both/and" is believed to compromise children's opportunities to learn (Bredekamp & Copple, 1997, p. 3). The Committee on the Prevention of Reading Difficulties of the National Research Council (Snow, Burns, & Griffin, 1998) took a similarly balanced position, recommending the end of the reading wars and promoting both direct instruction and child-motivated reading for meaning.

Another area of disagreement is the extent to which educational arrangements should be culturally embedded. Some research suggests that when schools become more culturally and linguistically relevant to children and families, children's achievement improves (Au & Kawakami, 1991; Garcia, 1988; Labov, 1995). Bilingual programs are the most controversial of these culturally focused programs for a variety of reasons but primarily because parents fear that, if their children participate in these programs, they will be disadvantaged on high-stakes educational tests. Thus, the political climate may make such programs unworkable.

When standardized tests are used to track children or to retain them, inevitably low-income children are in the lowest groups, from which it is often impossible to escape. Retention, even if it is euphemistically called "developmental," is generally considered counterproductive, predicting school dropout better than it predicts school success (Shepard & Smith, 1986).

There are no easy answers as to how to bridge between low-income, minority children's experience and school expectations; however, when teachers fail to appreciate culturally equivalent behaviors of children from low-income, minority communities, they misdiagnose, mislabel, and misteach children who belong to these culturally different groups. There is little evidence that either preservice or in-service education of teachers addresses these issues.

Cultural differences cannot be ignored, but they also should not cloud the individuality of culturally different children. Low-income, minority children learn by the same developmental rules as other children. They need to construct their own knowledge, to be active learners, to be interested and motivated to learn, and to have teachers who they love and admire and who love and respect them in turn.

Teaching in a multicultural society requires knowledge; understanding; compromise; and the merging of beliefs, attitudes, and perspectives, so that as a community a new consensus is created and each person's differences are respected. The challenge, it seems, is to accept the legitimacy of culturally and personally embedded thinking and feeling—others' as well as the teacher's own—and to integrate or negotiate these with a professional knowledge base (Bowman & Stott, 1994). It requires adopting role definitions, curriculum, and teaching practices that may not reflect the values of the wider society or of the teacher but that do connect with the children.

CONCLUSION

The risks for children living in poverty are an important consideration for policy revisions and resource allocation; however, risks to groups are not the same as effects on individuals. Often, statistical risk is accepted as both diagnosis and prognosis, without considering their effects on the particular children and families being assessed. Many classroom interventions are planned as "one size fits all" rather than matching the intervention with the causes of children's difficulty. For example, children with developmental dysfunction and developmental delay may require specialized therapies, psychologically overstressed children may require social services, individual differences in development may require differences in the pacing of instruction, cultural differences may require bridging between home and school cultures, and emotional and social challenges may require mental health support as well as changes in classroom practices. Decisions about classroom practices should be tempered by knowing what is required for whom and under what circumstances.

Activities for parents and children can help ease the transition into school for low-income children. Although schools with high populations of children who are poor tend to provide more transition activities than is the case in other schools, these activities are usually superficial and confined to giving information about school requirements (Love, Trydeaym, Thayer, & Logue, 1990). Teachers need to rethink some of their conventional practices and learn new teaching techniques if they are to provide a stable, inclusive environment for children marginalized by poverty. Following are some general recommendations to improve school achievement for low-income children:

1. *Use risks as public health markers for the school to define the quality of life of the community and to predict the incidence of pathology in a community.* Assessment of poverty, the quality of housing and health care, the availability of substance abuse treatment centers, and incidences of child abuse and foster home placement is useful in planning community and school collaborations. In addition, risk assessments can stimulate the development of preschool programs, higher standards for child care, and more family resource and support services. Risk assessments should not be used in making classroom decisions.

2. *The degree of convergence inherent in normative scales for young children fails to sufficiently reflect the broad range in typical development.* As a consequence, children are penalized for relatively unimportant differences in developmental trajectories. Too narrow developmental criteria conflicts with the uneven pace of development in young children and leads to inappropriate placement decisions. Too rigid expectations for individual behavior and lock-step curricula limits learning for many young children and places them under unnecessary stress (Elkind, 1987).

3. *Place more weight on understanding cultural differences and engaging parents and communities in the process of setting standards and determining school practices.* Misfits occur from developmental criteria that are too narrow, expectations for individual performance that are too rigid, and definitions of appropriate behavior that are too exclusive for children from various culture groups. The policy choice is either to broaden schools' approach to teaching or to continue to follow traditional policies, which allows many children to remain unready and makes their failure inevitable.

4. *Direct attention to supporting children's emotional and social health, particularly in their relationships with their parents and teachers.* The relationships between program qualities and child outcomes are well established. As noted previously, social and emotional development in early childhood depends on the match between children's feelings and social knowledge and the expectations of the social situations in which they find themselves. States need to set standards and require

schools to monitor the health of the school environment, as well as children's academic standards performance.

5. *Provide more training and support for teachers.* More attention needs to be given to the quality of preservice and in-service training and to requirements for teachers' lifelong learning. In addition, school boards and state departments of education should promote and reward excellence, such as providing support and salary increments. Practicing teachers will need time and resources to work with a range of children, they will need consultation and curricula support to work effectively with children who come from different socioeconomic and cultural backgrounds, and they will need to be held accountable using assessment strategies that are based on children's performance in authentic contexts.

6. *Make a greater commitment of resources for the education of low-income children.* In 1983, the High/Scope Foundation startled the educational policy world by pointing out that the long-term effects of a fairly expensive preschool intervention program resulted in financial savings by decreasing other educational and social costs (Berrueta et al., 1984). Although the argument for early intervention for children from low-income families has proven persuasive, as indicated by increases in Head Start, Title 1, and state funding, there is still considerable resistance to investing at the level that assures that interventions are successful. Whether the schools and the public can build the political will to make the investment necessary to ensure the achievement of all children remains to be seen.

Improving educational outcomes for children who live in poverty will require understanding and hard work. Attention to the change process, assessing barriers and resources, and involving teachers more directly in research can stimulate new classroom practices. However, these teaching practices must be realistic and achievable and part of a larger and systemic effort that includes in-service education, coaching, and mentoring, and of sufficient interest to engage both teachers and administrators (Gersten & Brengelman, 1996). St. Pierre, Layzer, Goodson, and Bernstein warned us that instead "of being advocates for a particular program, we need to be advocates for solving the problem. Instead of advocating in the absence of research evidence we need to be intellectually curious about finding the best approaches" (1997, p. 24). Teachers and researchers need to work together to improve the lives of low-income children.

REFERENCES

Ainsworth, M. (1973). Development of infant–mother attachment. In B. Caldwell & H. Ricciuti (Eds.), *Review of Child Development Research,* (pp. 1–94). Chicago: University of Chicago Press.

Alexander, K., & Entwisle, D. (1998). Achievement in the first 2 years of school: Patterns and processes. *Monographs of the Society for Research in Child Development, 53*(2, Serial No. 218).

Ashton-Warner, S. (1964). *Teacher.* New York: Bantam Doubleday Dell Publishing Group.

Au, K.H., & Kawakami, A.J. (1991). Culture and ownership. *Childhood Education, 67*(5), 280–284.

Barnes, H., Goodson, B., & Layzer, J. (1995/1996). *Review of research on supportive interventions for children and families* (Vols. 1 & 2). Cambridge, MA: Abt Associates.

Barnett, S. (1995). Long term effects of early childhood programs on cognitive and school outcomes. *The Future of Children: Long-Term Outcomes of Early Childhood Programs, 5,* 25–50.

Beane, J.A. (1991). Enhancing children's self-esteem: Illusion and possibility. *Early Education and Development, 2*(2), 153–160.

Berrueta-Clement, J., Schweinhart, L., Barnett, W., Epstein, A., & Weikart, D. (1984). *Changed lives: The effects of the Perrry Preschool Program on youths through age 19*. Ypsilanti, MI: High/Scope Press.

Birch, S., & Ladd, G. (1996). Interpersonal relationships in the school environment and children's early school adjustment: The role of teachers and peers. In K. Wentzel & J. Juvenen (Eds.), *Social motivation: Understanding children's school adjustment*. New York: Cambridge University Press.

Birch, S., & Ladd, G. (1997). The teacher–child relationship and children's early school adjustment. *Journal of School Psychology, 35*(1), 612–679.

Bowman, B. (1989a). The challenge of diversity. *Phi Delta Kappan, 76*(3), 218–224.

Bowman, B. (1989b). Self reflection as an element in professionalism. *Teachers College Record, 90*(3), 444–451.

Bowman, B. (1993). Early childhood education. In L. Darling-Hammond (Ed.), *Review of research in education* (Vol. 19, pp. 101–134). Washington DC: American Educational Research Association.

Bowman, B. (1994). Home and school: The unresolved relationship. In S. Kagan & B. Weissbourd (Eds.), *Putting families first* (pp. 51–73). San Francisco: Jossey-Bass.

Bowman, B. (1997a). How higher education is meeting the challenge of early care and education. In L. Kagan & B. Bowman (Eds.), *New directions in teacher education* (pp. 107–118). Washington, DC: National Association for the Education of Young Children.

Bowman, B. (1997b). Preschool as family support. In S. Reifel & M. Wolery (Eds.), *Advances in early education and day care: Family policy and practice in early child care* (Vol. 9, pp. 157–170). Greenwich, CT: JAI Press.

Bowman, B., & Stott, F. (1994). Understanding development in a cultural context. In B. Mallory & R. New (Eds.), *Diversity and developmentally appropriate practices* (pp. 119–134). New York: Teachers College Press.

Boyd, W., & Shouse, R. (1997). The problems and promise of urban schools. In H. Walberg, O. Reyes, & R. Weissberg (Eds.), *Children and youth: Interdisciplinary perspectives* (pp. 141–166). Thousand Oaks, CA: Sage Publications.

Bredekamp, S., & Copple, C. (Eds.). (1997). *Developmentally appropriate practice in early childhood programs*. Washington DC: National Association for the Education of Young Children.

Brooks-Gunn, J., Klebanov, P., & Duncan, G. (1996). Ethnic differences in children's intelligence test scores: Role of economic deprivation, home environment, and maternal characteristics. *Child Development, 67*, 396–408.

Campbell, F., & Ramey, C. (1995). Cognitive and social outcomes for high-risk African-American students at middle adolescence: Positive effects of early intervention. *American Educational Research Journal, 32*(4), 743–772.

Campbell, F., & Taylor, K. (1996). Early childhood programs that work for children from economically disadvantaged families. *Young Children, 51*, 74–80.

Carlson, M., & Earls, F. (1997). Psychological and neuroendocrinological sequelae of early social deprivation in institutionalized children in Romania. In C. Carter, B. Lederhendler, & B. Kirkpatrick (Eds.), *Integrative neurobiology of affiliation: Annals of the New York Academy of Science* (pp. 419–428). New York: New York Academy of Science.

Cole, M., & Bruner, J.S. (1972). Cultural differences and inferences about psychological processes. *American Psychologist, 26*, 867–876.

Coll, C. (1990). Developmental outcomes of minority infants: A process-oriented look into our beginnings. *Child Development, 61*, 270–289.

Comer, J. (1980). *School power: Implications of an intervention program*. New York: Free Press.

Darling-Hammond, L. (1994). *The current status of teaching and teacher development in the United States*. Background paper prepared for the National Commission on Teaching and America's Future.

Delpit, L.D. (1988). The silenced dialogue: Power and pedagogy in educating other people's children. *Harvard Educational Review, 58*(3), 280–298.

Department of Health and Human Services. (1997). *Trends in the well-being of America's children and youth*. Washington, DC: U.S. Department of Health and Human Services.

Derman-Sparks, L., & Phillips, C. (1997). *Teaching/learning anti-racism: A developmental approach.* New York: Teachers College Press.

Dryfoos, J. (1994). *Full-service schools: A revolution in health and social services.* San Francisco: Jossey-Bass.

Dryfoos, J. (1998). *A look at community schools in 1998.* (Occassional paper #2). New York: National Center for Schools and Communities at Fordham University.

Elkind, D. (1987). *Miseducation: Preschoolers at risk.* New York: Alfred A. Knopf.

Florio-Ruane, S. (1987). Sociolinguistics for educational researchers. *American Education Research Journal, 24*(2), 185–197.

Freud, A. (1963). *Psychoanalysis for teachers and parents.* Boston: Beacon Press.

Garbarino, J., Dubrow, N., Kostelny, K., & Pardo, C. (1992). *Children in danger.* San Francisco: Jossey-Bass.

Garcia, E. (1988). Attributes of effective schools for language minority students. *Education and Urban Society, 20*(4), 387–398.

Gersten, R., & Brengelman, S. (1996). The quest to translate research into classroom practice. *Remedial and Special Education, 17,* 67–74.

Gould, S.J. (1981). *The mismeasure of man.* New York: W.W. Norton.

Hakuta, K., & Garcia, E. (1989). Bilingualism and education. *American Psychologist, 44*(2), 374–379.

Hale, J. (1982). *Black children.* Provo, UT: Brigham Young University Press.

Halpern, R. (in press). Early childhood intervention for low-income children and families. In S. Meisels & J. Shonkoff (Eds.), *Handbook of early childhood intervention* (pp. 469–498). New York: Oxford University Press.

Hann, S., Ray, A., Bernstein, V., & Halpern, R. (1995). *Caregiving in the inner city: A final report to the Carnegie Corporation of New York and the Charles Stuart Mott Foundation.* New York: Carnegie Corporation.

Harter, S. (1996). Developmental changes in self-understanding across the 5 to 7 shift. In A. Sameroff & M. Haith (Eds.), *The five to seven year shift.* Chicago: University of Chicago Press.

Haskins, R. (1989). Beyond metaphor: The efficacy of early childhood education. *American Psychologist, 44*(2), 274–282.

Hinde, R.A. (1983). *Biological bases of the mother–child relationship.* Unpublished manuscript, Medical Research Council Unit on the Development and Integration of Behavior, Madingley, Cambridge, England.

Howes, C. (1988). Relations between early child care and schooling. *Developmental Psychology, 24,* 53–57.

Howes, C. (1996). *Children's experiences in center based child care as a function of teacher background and adult:child ratio.* Unpublished paper, University of California at Los Angeles.

Howes, C., Hamilton, C., & Matheson, C. (1994). Children's relationships with peers: Differential associations with aspects of the teacher–child relationship. *Child Development, 65,* 253–263.

Jipson, J. (1991). Extending the discourse on developmental appropriateness: A developmental perspective. *Early Education and Development, 2*(2), 95–108.

Kagan, S.L. (1991). *United we stand: Collaboration for child care and early education services.* New York: Teachers College Press.

Labov, W. (1995). Can reading failure be reversed?: A linguistic approach to the question. In V. Gadsden & D. Wagner (Eds.), *Literacy among African American youth: Issues in learning, teaching, and schooling* (pp. 39–68). Cresskill, NJ: Hampton Press.

LeVine, R.A., & Miller, P.M. (1990). Commentary. *Human Development, 33,* 73–80.

Love, J., Trydeaym, H., Thayer, K., & Logue, M. (1990). *Connecting with preschools: How our schools help (and fail to help) entering kindergartners. Final report of the National Study of Children's Transition from Preschool to Kindergarten.* Washington, DC: RMC Research Corporation.

Lubeck, S. (1994). The politics of developmentally appropriate practice: Exploring issues of culture, class, and curriculum. In B. Mallory & R. New (Eds.), *Diversity and developmentally appropriate practices* (pp. 17–43). New York: Teachers College Press.

McLoyd, V. (1990). The impact of economic hardship on black families and children: Psychological distress, parenting, and social-emotional development. *Child Development, 61*(2), 311–346.

National Center for Clinical Infant Programs. (1992). *The emotional foundations of school readiness.* Washington, DC: ZERO TO THREE: National Center for Clinical Infant Programs.

National Center for Education Statistics. (1995). *Approaching kindergarten: A look at preschoolers in the United States.* Washington, DC: U.S. Department of Education, Office of Educational Research and Improvement.

Ogbu, J. (1996). Understanding the school performance of urban blacks. In H. Walberg, O. Reyes, & R. Weissberg (Eds.), *Children and youth: Interdisciplinary perspectives* (pp. 190–222). Thousand Oaks, CA: Sage Publications.

Otheguy, R. (1982). Thinking about bilingual education: A critical appraisal. *Harvard Educational Review, 52*(3), 301–314.

Perry, B. (1995). Incubated in terror: Neurodevelopmental factors in the "cycle of violence." In J. Osofsky (Ed.), *Children, youth and violence: Searching for solutions.* New York: The Guilford Press.

Peterson, R. (1994). School readiness considered from a neuro-cognitive perspective. *Early Education and Development, 5*(2), 120–140.

Pfannenstiel, J., & Seltzer, D. (1989). New parents as teachers: Evaluation of an early parent education program. *Early Childhood Research Quarterly, 4,* 1–18.

Pianta, R. (Ed.). (1992). *Beyond the parent: The role of other adults in children's lives: New directions in child development* (Vol. 58). San Francisco: Jossey-Bass.

Pianta, R. (1994). Patterns of relationships between children and kindergarten teachers. *Journal of School Psychology, 32,* 1–16.

Pianta, R., Smith, N., & Reeve, R. (1991). Observing mother and child behavior in a problem-solving situation at school entry: Relations with classroom adjustment. *School Psychology Quarterly, 6*(1), 1–15.

Rogoff, B., Gauvain, M., & Ellis, S. (1984). Development viewed in its cultural context. In M.H. Bornstein & M.E. Lamb (Eds.), *Developmental psychology* (pp. 533–571). Mahwah, NJ: Lawrence Erlbaum Associates.

Sameroff, A.J., & Chandler, M.J. (1975). Reproductive risk and the continuum of caretaking casualty. In F.D. Horowitz, M. Hethrington, S. Scarr-Salapatek, & G. Sigel (Eds.), *Review of child development research* (Vol. 4, pp. 187–244). Chicago: University of Chicago Press.

Sameroff, A., & Haith, M. (1996). *The five to seven year shift.* Chicago: University of Chicago Press.

Sampson, R., Raudenbush, S., & Earls, F. (1997). Neighborhood and violent crime: A multilevel study of collective efficacy. *Science, 277,* 918–924.

Shepard, L.A., & Smith, M. (1986). Synthesis of research on school readiness and kindergarten retention. *Educational Leadership, 44*(33), 78–86.

Shorr, L. (1988). *Within our reach: Breaking the cycle of disadvantage.* New York: Anchor Press.

Slobin, D. (1990). The development from child speaker to native speaker. In J. Stigler, R. Shweder, & G. Herdt (Eds.), *Cultural psychology* (pp. 233–256). Cambridge, UK: Cambridge University Press.

Snow, C., Burns, S., & Griffin, P. (Eds.). (1998). *Preventing reading difficulties in young children.* Washington, DC: National Academy Press.

Spencer, M. (1985). Cultural cognition and social cognition as identity correlates of Black children's personal-social development. In M. Spencer, G. Brookins, & W. Allen (Eds.), *Beginnings: The social and affective development of Black children* (pp. 215–230). Mahwah, NJ: Lawrence Erlbaum Associates.

Stroufe, L. (1988). The role of infant–caregiver attachment in development. In J. Belsky & T. Negworski (Eds.), *Clinical implications of attachment* (pp. 18–38). Mahwah, NJ: Lawrence Erlbaum Associates.

St. Pierre, R., Layzer, J., Goodson, B., & Bernstein, L. (1997). *The effectiveness of comprehensive care management interventions: Findings for the national evaluation of the comprehensive child development program.* Cambridge, MA: ABT Associates.

Stott, F., & Bowman, B. (1996). Child development knowledge: A slippery base for practice. *Early Childhood Research Quarterly, 11,* 169–183.

Steele, S. (1989). Being black and feeling blue. *American Scholar, 58*(4), 497–508.

Thomas, H. (1998). The shame response to rejection triggers primitive, physical reactions. *The Brown University Child and Adolescent Behavior Newsletter, 14,* 1.

Wang, M., Haertel, G., & Walberg, H. (1997). Fostering educational resilience in inner-city schools. In W. Walberg, O. Reyes, & R. Weissberg (Eds.), *Children and youth: Interdisciplinary perspective* (pp. 119–140). Thousand Oaks, CA: Sage Publications.

Weiss, B., Dodge, K., Bates, J., & Petit, G. (1992). Some consequences of early harsh discipline: Child aggression and a maladaptive social information processing style. *Child Development, 63,* 1321–1336.

Werner, L. (1989). *Vulnerable but invincible: A longitudinal study of resilient children and youth.* New York: Adams, Bannister, & Cox.

Winnicott, D. (1988). *Human nature.* New York: Schocken.

IMPLICATIONS FOR THE KINDERGARTEN TRANSITION

Chapter 11

Research on the
Transition to Kindergarten

John Wills Lloyd
Donna R. Steinberg
Mary K. Wilhelm-Chapin

Many contemporary social and educational initiatives are undergirded by an emphasis on early childhood. Not since the 1960s has the United States participated in such a sustained effort to finance services to young children and their families. As this chapter indicates, evidence of this emphasis abounds.

At the national level, the federal government began their declaration of educational goals, *A Nation of Learners*, with statements about all young children having access to important health care, developmentally appropriate preschool programs, and parental help with early learning activities (National Education Goals Panel, 1995). The Secretary of Education hosted a discussion entitled "Ready to Learn: Preparing Young Children for School Success" and, in 1996, First Lady Hillary Rodham Clinton called on America to ensure that young children's welfare is secure. In addition, the U.S. Department of Education has made significant efforts to identify and serve young children with disabilities (for example, by passage of the Education of the Handicapped Children Act Amendments of 1986 [PL 99-457]).

The authors appreciate the opportunity to work with the research synthesis group at "The Transition to Kindergarten: A Synthesis Conference" conducted under the auspices of the National Center for Early Development and Learning (NCEDL). Members of that group included Anne Casey, Diane Early, Doris R. Entwisle, James Griffin, Susan P. Limber, Frederick Morrison, Craig T. Ramey, and Mary Bruce Webb. The discussions of this group contributed significantly to the development of this chapter.

At the state level, in the 1990s, many governments initiated programs designed expressly to provide services to young children (and their families) who are not participating in Head Start and similar federally supported programs. For example, the North Carolina Partnership for Children, a public–private collaboration, has served tens of thousands of children in the "Smart Start" program. New York provides pre-kindergarten opportunities to all children and families who desire them. The Virginia Preschool Initiative annually enrolls more than 6,000 4-year-olds. These children would be eligible for free- or reduced-price lunch if they were in school but not receiving services under Chapter I or Head Start. In many ways, the public schools are becoming heavily involved in providing educational services to children before they are mandated.

At the local level, governments have also initiated programs for young children in hopes of easing their transition to kindergarten. Typically these programs have been funded using local government money and are aimed at serving a fairly small group of children and families.

Although policies, programs, and public statements are one set of indices of public concern about young children and the transition to kindergarten, another indicator is the investment in research on this topic. The U.S. Department of Education has provided substantial support for research on the transition to kindergarten through the Office of Educational Research and Improvement's National Center on Early Development and Learning. Similarly, the Department of Health and Human Services has funded some of the largest projects addressing transition since the massive Follow Through Project of the 1960s and 1970s, including Phase Two of the Study of Early Child Care Project (through the National Institute of Child Health and Human Development), the Early Childhood Longitudinal Study, and the National Head Start/Public School Early Childhood Transition Demonstration Study.

These initiatives not only illustrate the importance that early childhood education has assumed in contemporary America, but they also demonstrate the need for research on early childhood programs and policies. Research is so intimately interwoven into initiatives that it can be difficult to separate the research and programmatic functions of a given activity. For example, in the Head Start Transition Study, basic research on kindergarten transition is being conducted at the same time and place that the program for enhancing transition outcomes is being implemented (see Chapter 8).

Research serves many functions in the early childhood field. Legislators routinely call for research on which decisions about public policy initiatives can be based. Funding for research depends on budgetary decisions by policy makers. Researchers debate methods for developing empirical approaches to problems faced by practitioners. Teachers ask for practices that have demonstrated effectiveness. Teacher educators wonder how to translate sometimes obtuse research findings into terms that can be communicated to and implemented by young people just beginning to work with young children. Parents of children with disabilities demand that legislators include funding for research on best practices. Clearly, research, policy, preparation of personnel, and practice are dependent on and inform each other. Because of these relationships, efforts are needed to coordinate research, policy, personnel preparation, and practice.

This chapter provides a general overview of the current state of knowledge in research on transition to kindergarten, describes the major gaps in our knowledge about this transition, and recommends in broad terms an agenda for research on the transition during the early 21st century. "The Transition to Kindergarten: A Synthesis Conference" (Charlottesville, Virginia, February 18–20, 1998) provided the impetus for this chapter, which represents an integration of the themes and ideas reflected in discussions held at that time. The conference participants were a diverse population of academic researchers, state policy makers, teachers, program directors, parents, and graduate students; thus, consumers and generators of research knowledge were represented, and their opinions are reflected in this chapter. This chapter's approach is founded on the notion that understanding the transition to school is of fundamental importance in understanding the social and cognitive development of children (Ramey & Ramey, 1994) and that research on aspects of this transition not only will affect policy and practice but is also affected by them.

CURRENT KNOWLEDGE BASE

The contemporary state of knowledge about transition to kindergarten is, at once, remarkably extensive and substantially inadequate. As the previous chapters indicate, a lot is known about this transition and the factors that influence it. For example, early childhood educators have remarkable follow-up data about children attending particular schools in Baltimore (see Chapter 2) or participating in carefully controlled combinations of home and school interventions during preschool and primary-grade years (see Chapter 8). However, at the same time, the knowledge is incomplete and spotty; for example, early childhood educators still struggle with defining "readiness" (see Chapter 3) and have little clear evidence about the consequences of the diverse programs that characterize experience in kindergartens (see Chapters 4 & 5).

The previous chapters, in pointing out the gaps and overlaps in the knowledge base, reflect a great deal about what is known of children's transition to kindergarten. Because these chapters synthesize the state of the knowledge, it is not necessary to review the evidence again. Rather, it is important to examine that knowledge base more generally.

A broad perspective reveals several general conclusions that form the basis of the knowledge about children's transition to kindergarten. Among these are the following:

1. Transition to school and subsequent success is influenced by a complex set of variables.

2. Early education can facilitate transition and reduce some of the untoward effects of other factors in children's lives.

3. The context for transition appears to have powerful, but incompletely understood, influences on transition.

4. Assessment of transition—both readiness and outcomes—is still unsettled.

Each of these facets of the available knowledge base is both a product of, and foundation for, needed research.

Complexity

Many factors—child, parent, family, teacher, school, or community characteristics—affect outcomes, and no single factor controls so much variance in outcomes that it overshadows all the others. Instead, there are complex interactions of factors that are poorly understood and rarely identified in empirical studies. Even when a study highlights a specific factor, firm conclusions cannot be drawn because that factor does not work in isolation. For example, reducing class size has received a great deal of attention because small class size has been found to be an important element in improving children's academic achievement and attitudes toward school (Glass, Cahen, Smith, & Filby, 1982; Mosteller, 1995). However, the statement that small class size increases children's achievement is decontextualized. That is, although reduction in class size benefits children, the specific mechanisms producing these results are not well understood (Slavin, 1989).

Everyone understands that researchers carefully control some variables while studying others. They use metaphorical lenses to focus on a particular factor. However, the lenses often serve also as blinders, preventing researchers and consumers of research from seeing important contextual factors. This book illustrates the importance of maintaining a focus on these multiple factors. For example, parents' concerns about their children's safety may result in declining participation in community activities and may operate to reduce involvement in early schooling. As Christenson (Chapter 6) and Melton, Limber, and Teague (Chapter 7) indicate, given the importance of parental involvement, particularly for children of impoverished families, such decrements in participation may have deleterious effects on outcomes. Although it is tempting to view low levels of parental participation as a fault in parents, it is probably more accurate to consider the possibility that their lack of involvement may be the combined result of several factors.

The complex interactions among child, family, and school factors are critical when early childhood educators discuss children with disabilities. Too often, people ignore the complexity of factors and reflexively focus on child characteristics when considering transition to school for young children with severe disabilities. As discussed by Wolery (Chapter 9), there are substantial data identifying characteristics of services—administrative organizations, staff training, and family collaboration—that can facilitate successful transition. Adapting environments on the basis of only one of these factors is a recipe for failure, as recognized in the rationale for individualized family service plans. Unfortunately, these modifications are often reserved for children with obvious disabilities. Many children come to the kindergarten transition with less easily recognized learning and behavior problems that are still affected by the complicated web of child, family, school, and community factors. For example, in educators' haste to work with families, they may overlook the importance of friendships among young children and the effects of those friendships on transition (Ladd & Kochenderfer, 1996). In their haste to provide, for example, family-friendly services, overlooking children's friendships may prevent early childhood educators from designing effective transition programs, especially among children who later develop behavior problems. Students with incipient learning and behavior problems would almost surely benefit from many of the services described by Wolery (Chapter 9).

The complex relationships among factors affecting transition demand that research questions and methods reflect more than simple child-, family-, teacher-, school-, or community-based influences or even bivariate relationships among these influences and outcomes. Basic research will serve early childhood education far better when it reflects this complexity. Analyses and interpretations of research will also be stronger when they routinely take complexity into account.

Early Intervention

In addition to examining complex interactions of factors, there has been a great deal of attention given to early intervention as a way of enhancing the transition to formal schooling. Historically, there has been debate in the field about whether early intervention is worthwhile. Some observers emphasize study results, stating that cognitive benefits from programs such as Head Start diminish by the third grade, as evidence that such programs do not work (Hernstein & Murray, 1994). However, there are many studies that suggest that early intervention provides benefits to children's physical, intellectual, and emotional development under some conditions, for limited periods of time, and when certain practices are used (Lazar, Darlington, Murray, Royce, & Snipper, 1982). For example, it has repeatedly been found that attending preschool leads to a reduction in retention rates during the school years (Barnett, 1996). Similarly, longitudinal studies, such as the Perry Preschool Program (Berrueta-Clement, Schweinhart, Barnett, Epstein, & Weikart, 1984), the Syracuse University Family Development Research Program (Lally, Mangione, & Honig, 1988), the Yale Child Welfare Research Program (Provence & Naylor, 1983), and the Houston Parent-Child Development Center (Johnson, 1988), indicate that early childhood intervention programs may reduce juvenile delinquency and predeliquent behavior.

Clearly, early intervention that might benefit many students—whether they have obvious disabilities, moderate learning disabilities or behavior problems, or modest problems that seem simply related to one factor such as the stress of adapting to new routines—is emphasized in this book. Providing early intervention raises the problem of identifying students to whom such specialized services should be provided. There seems to be a reluctance to identify individual students as needing special services, but there are no logical means short of primary prevention (Pianta, 1990) by which an individual or agency can allocate services to some children and not others without identifying those who will receive the services.

Despite the convergence of evidence about the beneficial effects of early intervention, there are still important issues for research: 1) conducting sustained studies of practices and their effects, 2) incorporating into studies multiple dependent measures assessing differing outcomes, 3) enlarging practices to the scale required by public policy, and 4) complimenting experimental research with process-oriented studies of practices.

Sustaining Interventions   Unfortunately, too much literature on early intervention continues to be predicated on the idea that a brief exposure to a well-meant program will inoculate children against subsequent difficulties. Alterations of preschool environments, for example, may be helpful but can hardly be considered sufficient. As research by Entwisle and Alexander (Chapter 2) indicates, schools differ across the long run, not just at the beginning of children's school careers. Thus, it is important to conceptualize continuing efforts to intervene, as is reflected in the Head Start Transition Project described by Ramey and Ramey (Chapter 8).

Studies find that early intervention provides benefits to children's development when it integrates child, family, school and community factors into an intervention package. This more complex approach probably accounts for many of the differences among disparate study outcomes. For intervention to be effective, risk populations must receive supplemental and continuing services. Not only must intervention address multiple factors (see Chapters 6 & 9), but it must also capture developmentally sensitive information over long periods of time to accurately illuminate sustained effects.

Measuring Broadly   Given the immediate importance of developing social competence and the influence of social competence on subsequent peer relations and school progress (Pianta & Walsh, 1996), early childhood educators are rightly concerned about children's social development. In addition to improving children's social outcomes, a goal of early education for many policy makers, practitioners, researchers, and parents is to enhance academic achievement. Large and sustained improvements in intelligence scores were achieved by the Abecedarian Project (Ramey & Campbell, 1991), which provided at-risk children with enriched environments (home and school) for an extended period of time. Reading and math achievement scores increased as children received greater amounts of intervention. In addition, retention rates were highest in the group of children receiving no intervention, and progressively decreased as intensity of intervention increased (see Chapter 8). Test scores of children in enriched environments were already higher than controls by age 2. Seven years after the end of the intervention, at age 12, test scores were still about 5 points higher.

Concern about multiple outcomes parallels the previously described concern about the benefits of considering complex relationships among the factors influencing transition. Research that measures multiple outcome variables provides greater understanding of the phenomena. Furthermore, it is important that the measures come from different domains of measurement. Just as few early childhood educators would settle for a paper-and-pencil measure of arithmetic computation as the sole measure of an early intervention program's effects, they should not settle only for a teacher rating of social skills. Measures need to reflect the effects of programs on children's actual social and academic competence as well as assess potential epiphenominal effects (e.g., changes in parent participation or outlook on schooling).

Studies that include measurements of multiple variables tend to use small samples because of the difficulties inherent in collecting large amounts of data. However, small-sample studies present additional problems, not the least of which is the extent to which their results are representative and can be generalized. Because of the need for research to provide information necessary for the policy, training, and programmatic functions of educating young children, the need for comprehensive, longitudinal study of large, population-based samples is considerable. Small-sample studies, although useful for exploring new ideas, may simply not be sufficient for providing the information needed at the national level.

Going to Scale   Research that uses well-designed measures to assess diverse effects of intensive intervention programs may not transfer to a larger scale. Although procedures have worked for specific populations, programs such as the Abecedarian Project may be much more difficult to implement successfully when used for entire populations. The fact that programs do not transfer easily to other populations suggests that community factors cannot be ignored, pointing again to the idea that complex relationships among factors must be examined. Researchers seeking to replicate studies and practitioners seeking to implement programs from other communities may find that contextual factors inhibit their efforts.

Most important, the inability to replicate programs and their effects is a function of complex, developmental systems and ought to be embraced in research, not just controlled out of research (Pianta & Walsh, 1996). Research that uses systems theory and principles as a way of capturing and understanding the complexities involved may provide an important way out of the conundrum of replication.

Studying Processes   Consistent with a systems theory orientation, one way for early childhood researchers to address the complexity introduced by consideration of contextual factors is to adopt a more process-oriented approach. Although random assignment is still critical to experimental studies, researchers can examine the contributions of multiple factors, including context, by studying naturally occurring variation in programs. By developing measures of important independent variables (e.g., essential features from the National Association for the Education of Young Children [NAEYC] guidelines) and measuring those features in large numbers of classrooms, researchers will be able to assess their effects (and interactions among them and contextual features) on children's outcomes. Wisely conceptualized and judiciously executed combinations of process and experimental studies should provide rich and trustworthy data about early intervention programs and principles.

Context for Transition

As noted previously, locating problems within children and examining interventions as if they were inoculations have not served early childhood research (or programs) well. Context matters. Two important features of context are the effects of communities on outcomes and the environments into which young children move when they begin school.

Community Effects   When children begin formal schooling in kindergarten, factors other than the academic program itself affect how successful a child is in school. Early childhood researchers are only beginning to investigate the contributions of community factors. Children who are more advantaged score higher on standardized achievement tests than do children who are disadvantaged. However, the Beginning School Study shows that both children who are advantaged and children who are disadvantaged make similar gains on achievement test scores during the school year (see Chapter 2). In other words, although there is a discrepancy between groups in achievement scores, children make equal gains regardless of group membership. It is during the summer, when children are not attending school, that the disparities in the test scores of the advantaged and disadvantaged groups increase. As a result, Entwisle and Alexander (Chapter 2) attribute the difference in test scores to family and community factors. Unlike children who are advantaged, children who are disadvantaged are not exposed to a quantity and diversity of experiences and, therefore, do not have the same opportunities for learning.

The current consensus regarding the role of communities and families in children's transitions to kindergarten leads directly to specific recommendations for future research. For example, early childhood educators need much more extensive information about when and how children come into contact with extra-school resources; how those resources promote the acquisition of competence in school, at home, and in the wider community; and what factors moderate the effects of these resources.

School Context   Another key issue for researchers, policy makers, school personnel, and parents is how little is known about current early elementary teaching and transition practices and their effects on various groups of children (see

Chapter 5). The effects of practices, such as grouping children of similar ages, keeping teachers with the same children from one year to another (looping), waiting an additional year before school entry (academic red-shirting), and retaining students, are not carefully and empirically documented and rely heavily on teacher report. Educators do not have clear information about the differences across kindergartens. That is, although nearly all educators may claim to use developmentally appropriate practices, the character and quality of their implementation remains more a matter of conjecture than fact.

In other words, early childhood educators have little empirical basis on which to decide into what context children move when they begin kindergarten. In addition, the extent to which kindergarten classrooms conform to recommendations about best practices has not been addressed. A research program designed to describe the current state of kindergartens (and variations among them) would be particularly helpful. Of course, such a program of studies would have to adopt high-quality sampling and measurement procedures. However, well-designed and executed studies would permit educators not only to describe the environments into which young children move when they begin school but also to help design preschool environments that will prepare children to succeed in kindergarten.

ASSESSMENT

Unfortunately, assessment tools are often seen as a separate aspect of schooling instead of a continual and integral part of teaching and learning. This division creates problems with their development and use, as well as with interpretation of information gleaned from them. Yet, assessment often dominates discourse, policy, and practice in early childhood. For example, in the early 1990s, 13 states use developmental screening instruments with 5- and 6-year olds (Shepard, Taylor, & Kagan, 1996). In addition, assessments are frequently used to determine school placement and grouping prior to or upon entrance to kindergarten. Although there are legitimate reasons to downplay assessment of young children, it seems likely that the topic of assessment will continue to be on the United States' early childhood agenda for the foreseeable future.

What, then, is the role of research in relation to assessment? In the educational standards domain, there is a pressing need for a strong research enterprise. As education moves further toward standards-based assessments, questions about the technical adequacy, appropriateness, use, and interpretation of assessment become more and more salient. For example, Shepard et al. (1996) questioned the use of screening instruments to deny children, particularly those with disabilities, admission to schools. The movement toward standards clearly carries with it issues of equity, eligibility, and access. Access will in part be determined by the tools used to assess and describe children in relation to these standards.

Furthermore, even when there is a strong database to guide practice in assessment, it is often ignored. Although it has been cogently argued that the construct of readiness can best be assessed over time and in context (see Chapter 3) and the resulting data need to be tied to services, there is little evidence that these procedures occur in practice. In a best-case scenario, for example, programs that screen for problems in phonological awareness can be linked to provision of developmentally appropriate instruction in this and related skills critical for early literacy (e.g., Invernizzi, Meier, Juel, & Swank, 1997; Swank, Meier, Invernizzi, &

Juel, 1997). However, the gap between what educators know about the pros and cons of assessment (see Chapter 3) and what actually occurs in practice suggests a need for research on factors influencing teachers' assessment practices.

FUTURE DIRECTIONS

This chapter illustrates some of the shortcomings of contemporary research on the transition to kindergarten for children at risk for later social and academic problems. These drawbacks—some resulting from omissions and others resulting from inadequate methods—lead directly to recommendations about future research on the transition to kindergarten. The critical outcomes and activities for a research agenda on the transition to kindergarten should include the following:

1. Identify what constitutes a successful transition and define successful transition in a way that captures important dimensions and is open to measurement.
2. Conduct comprehensive, large-scale studies of factors affecting transition.
3. Carry out smaller studies of intensive interventions.
4. Coordinate efforts among researchers and research projects.

Although there are certainly overlaps among these ideas, they are separated here for emphasis and the sake of clarity. This final section highlights these issues and some of their components.

Characterizing Successful Transitions

In identifying what constitutes successful transition to kindergarten, not only must many factors be considered, but they also must be considered in relation to each other. As previously stated, transition occurs on many interwoven levels (i.e., child, family, school, community). Examination of the transition to kindergarten should include identification of the aspects of transition to new or different environments that create risk or opportunity. Similarly, transition outcomes must be conceptualized in terms of context.

With contemporary emphasis on basic skills, it is important to note also that evaluations of what constitutes successful transition should not be based solely on notions of accomplishment. This idea reemphasizes the earlier point about measurement methods. Achievement should be one part of a larger metric used to assess whether transitions are successful. Social and behavioral factors are as, if not more, important than achievement. It is also important to factor into the metric of success such concerns as parents' satisfaction with their children's schooling experiences. In statistical terms, to judge the success of transition, researchers need a canonical variable that is composed of a broad array of conceptually important component variables.

Comprehensive Research Strategies

Comprehensive studies are essential for establishing the factors that affect transition itself as well as the actual outcomes of transition to kindergarten. One lesson from the Abecedarian Project, Beginning School Study, and other longitudinal work is that research should implement and examine the integration of many factors on many levels (i.e., child, family, school, community) at many points in time.

Without carefully conceived longitudinal research, it will be impossible to assess contributions of these multiple factors to transition success.

Studies of substantial scope are required to understand the contributions of various factors to transition. A study conducted in one or two local educational agencies is bound by that context and may or may not reflect what can be expected to occur on a statewide or regional basis. Similarly, before research can provide clear recommendations about policies, researchers must have assessed these recommendations on a broad scale. Thus, we need population-based studies.

These studies need to use objective measures of both dependent and independent variables, in addition to survey or other self-report methods. Objective measures (e.g., observations) will allow researchers to understand processes, not simply correlations, between children and various conditions. Clearly, measures that are drawn from just one domain—for example, teacher evaluations—are insufficient bases for building dependable models of factors that contribute to transition.

Attrition must be carefully scrutinized when developing studies and analyzing results because it is likely that the portion of the sample lost in most studies is not random. Attrition probably separates the least vulnerable group from the highest risk group in the sample. A concerted effort needs to be made to maintain high-risk members of the sample. Another alternative, albeit difficult, is to design studies exclusively targeting populations at especially high risk.

In addition, to aid in a comprehensive understanding of the transition to kindergarten, national assessments of current transition practices and their effects on children need to be conducted. As mentioned previously, insufficient information is known about the environments into which young children move when they begin kindergarten. As a part of understanding this context, researchers should systematically investigate motivation to change and to sustain changes at both the individual and programwide levels. For example, findings may indicate that contacting children's families prior to kindergarten entry reduces the risk of school failure. If so, the obstacles to teachers making contact with parents must be identified and studied. Although most researchers would agree that teachers intend to enhance their students' learning, there is an inherent reluctance among many professionals to try new techniques. The benefit of research on teaching practices is of little use if the results cannot be transferred to the classroom.

Focused Research

As a complement to large-scale longitudinal work, smaller, more highly focused studies of intensive interventions are needed. Intensive evaluations of innovations are essential prior to their broader implementation. When it is necessary to study practices intensively, costs for measurement and other aspects of the research effort constrain the research; such evaluations can only be undertaken at the level of a few classrooms, educational agencies, or families. However, intensive evaluations should not sacrifice rigor. For example, randomized longitudinal designs are essential so that longer-term effects can be gauged.

The efficacy of different field trials, such as using parent advocates, needs to be determined. Because parent influences are important (see Chapters 6 & 7) and research aimed at changing parent behaviors has not been as effective as hoped, it is important to continue to improve research targeting parent involvement. The contributions of parent motivation for change, and how to increase parent motivation, will be important areas of focus. Small field trials will be of added benefit if common metrics are used, which would allow multiple small studies to be integrated. In addition to continued services, studies also need to be customized for each unique population prior to intervention.

Coordination of Effort

The expenses of time and effort to collect and analyze data make those data a valuable commodity. To enhance the usefulness of these data, it is important to coordinate efforts among researchers. Sharing of data should be encouraged by stipulating common metrics across studies. Funding agencies should assemble a diverse panel of researchers and research consumers and charge the panel with identifying a brief list of measures that should be routinely incorporated into studies. The Marker Variable Project in learning disabilities (Keogh, Major, Reid, Gándara, & Omori, 1978) illustrates what should be a profitable model.

Proposals and data resulting from funded projects must be subject to peer review. Too often, reports of research are issued through public media prior to careful scrutiny by knowledgeable peers. Weak but intuitively appealing results should not be allowed to dominate recommendations based on carefully developed evidence. In addition, coordination among research projects that have been reviewed carefully for scientific merit should help to promote connections among research; these connections will help to overcome the sometimes piecemeal, spotty nature that seems to characterize early childhood research (and much of educational research, in general).

SUMMARY

The opportunity for consensus about a research agenda on the transition to kindergarten is at hand. However, in light of this consensus, researchers need to proceed carefully. Because the types of research conditions outlined here are expensive, researchers need to ask policy makers for appropriate and adequate funding. Partial or inadequate funding not only restricts but can also confuse conclusions and progress. One option for providing adequate funding may be to promote collaboration among funding agencies.

In sum, although they may not completely mitigate prior differences on socioeconomic factions, school- and community-based educational experiences enhance children's achievement in academic as well as social realms under some conditions, for limited lengths of time, and when certain practices are used. Comprehensive research provides the best avenue for understanding the processes behind efforts to increase the rate of successful transition to kindergarten. Researchers should identify what constitutes a successful transition; conduct a combination of comprehensive, large-scale studies and smaller, intensive studies; coordinate efforts among researchers and research projects; and establish findings through a system of carefully organized and rigorous peer review. Such provisions should help stabilize the foundation for providing appropriate services to aid transition to kindergarten and provide a firm basis for policy.

REFERENCES

Barnett, W.S. (1996). Long-term effects of early childhood care and education on disadvantaged children's cognitive development and school success. *The Future of Children, 5*(3), 25–50.

Berrueta-Clement, J., Schweinhart, L., Barnett, W., Epstein, A., & Weikart, D.C. (1984). *Changed lives: The effects of the Perry Preschool Program on youths through age 19.* Ypsilanti, MI: High/Scope Press.

Education of the Handicapped Children Act Amendments of 1986 (PL 99-457). 20 U.S.C. §§ 1400 *et seq.*

Glass, G.V., Cahen, L.S., Smith, M.L., & Filby, N.N. (1982). *School class size: Research and policy.* Thousand Oaks, CA: Sage Publications.

Hernstein, R.J., & Murray, C. (1994). *The bell curve: Intelligence and class structure in American life.* New York: Free Press.

Invernizzi, M., Meier, J.D., Juel, C., & Swank, L. (1997). *PALS II: Phonological awareness & literacy screening.* Charlottesville: University of Virginia.

Johnson, D.L. (1988). Primary prevention of behavior problems in young children: The Houston Parent-Child Development Center. In E.L. Cowen, R.P. Lorion, & J. Ramos-McKay (Eds.), *Fourteen ounces of prevention: A handbook for practitioners* (pp. 44–52). Washington, DC: American Psychological Association.

Keogh, B.K., Major, S.M., Reid, H.P., Gándara, P., & Omori, H. (1978). Marker variables: A search for comparability and generalizability in the field of learning disabilities. *Learning Disability Quarterly, 1*(3), 5–11.

Ladd, G.W., & Kochenderfer, B.J. (1996). Linkages between friendship and adjustment during early school transitions. In W.M. Bukowski, A.F. Newcomb, & W.W. Hartup (Eds.), *The company they keep: Friendship in childhood and adolescence* (pp. 322–345). New York: Cambridge University Press.

Lally, R.J., Mangione, P.L., & Honig, A.S. (1988). The Syracuse University Family Development Research Program: Long-range impact on an early intervention with low-income children and their families. In D. Powell (Ed.), *Parent education as early childhood intervention: Emerging directions in theory, research and practice* (pp. 79–104), Greenwich, CT: Ablex Publishing Corp.

Lazar, I., Darlington, R., Murray, H., Royce, J., & Snipper, A. (1982). Lasting effects of early education: A report for the Consortium for Longitudinal Studies. *Monographs of the Society for Research in Child Development, 47*(2–3, Serial No. 194).

Mosteller, F. (1995). The Tennessee study of class size in the early school grades. *The Future of Children, 5*(2), 113–127.

National Education Goals Panel. (1995). *A national of learners.* Washington, DC: U.S. Department of Education.

Pianta, R.C. (1990). Widening the debate on educational reform: Prevention as a viable alternative. *Exceptional Children, 56*, 306–313.

Pianta, R.C., & Walsh, D.J. (1996). *High-risk children in schools: Constructing sustaining relationships.* New York: Routledge.

Provence, S., & Naylor, A. (1983). *Working with disadvantaged parents and children: Scientific issues and practice.* New Haven, CT: Yale University Press.

Ramey, C.T., & Campbell, F.A. (1991). *Poverty, early childhood education and academic competence: The Abecedarian Project.* Cambridge, UK: Cambridge University Press.

Ramey, S.L., & Ramey, C.T. (1994). The transition to school: Why the first few years matter for a lifetime. *Phi Delta Kappan, 76*, 194–198.

Shepard, L.A., Taylor, G.A., & Kagan, S.L. (1996). *Trends in early childhood assessment policies and practices.* Washington, DC: U.S. Department of Education, Office of Educational Research and Improvement.

Slavin, R. (1989). Class size and student achievement: Small effects of small classes. *Educational Psychologist, 24*, 99–110.

Swank, L., Meier, J.D., Invernizzi, M., & Juel, C. (1997). *PALS I: Phonological awareness & literacy screening.* Charlottesville: University of Virginia.

Chapter 12

Personnel Preparation and the Transition to Kindergarten

Richard M. Clifford

As attested to by a number of the previous chapters in this book, transition to kindergarten has changed markedly in the last half of the 20th century. According to Zill (Chapter 4), approximately 98% of all children now attend either public or private kindergarten in the United States. Kindergarten has become the start of formal schooling even though states generally do not legally require children to attend kindergarten. The make up of the kindergarten population is changing, with teachers in kindergarten facing a more diverse group of children and families (see Chapters 4 & 7). In addition, more and more children are having group experiences outside the home (i.e., preschool) for significant periods before coming to kindergarten. This situation does not automatically mean that children are more prepared for school. In fact, there is some evidence that children with preschool experience are more likely to have reported behavior problems (see Chapter 4). The concept of readiness for kindergarten is even more an issue now than in the past, and there is no general agreement as to what readiness means (see Chapter 3). The personnel who are responsible for groups of children in preschool compared with personnel in school environments employ different teaching strategies and have different expectations of children (see Chapter 9). Although

This chapter relies heavily on the work of the personnel preparation synthesis group at "The Transition to Kindergarten: A Synthesis Conference" conducted under the auspices of the National Center for Early Development and Learning (NCEDL). Special thanks are due to Bridget Hamre of the University of Virginia for compiling the notes from the meetings and to the entire group for the excellent ideas, many of which are incorporated in this chapter. In addition, Gisele Crawford made important contributions to the final version of this chapter.

this book pays little direct attention to issues of personnel preparation at either the preschool level or the kindergarten and early school level, one implication of the many issues that this book raises is that a rethinking of the preparation of teachers and other staff serving children and their families is in order.

In examining the preparation of personnel at this critical period in the lives of young children, several issues related to personnel preparation are especially important. Who needs to be trained? What should be the content of the training? How can this training best be provided? How can support be provided to encourage young adults to enter the field and to keep them in the profession?

WHO NEEDS TO BE TRAINED

Differences in the teaching staff in preschool settings and in the more formal school settings where most kindergartens are located are obvious. Education at the bachelor's level or beyond, with some form of teaching credential, is almost universal for teachers in public kindergartens (see, e.g., Bryant, Clifford, & Peisner-Feinberg, 1991). The National Center for Education Statistics' Schools and Staffing Survey indicated that nearly 40% of kindergarten teachers have a master's degree or higher (Early, Pianta, & Cox, 1999). Teachers in child care and other prekindergarten programs are much less likely to have education at the bachelor's level. For example, the National Child Care Staffing Study found that only 21% of the teaching staff in the sample of centers in five metropolitan areas in the United States had a bachelor's degree or higher, including all fields of study (Whitebook, Howes, & Phillips, 1989). The Profile of Child Care Settings Study found higher education levels, with a reported 47% of center-based teachers having completed a 4-year degree, and an additional 13% having completed a 2-year degree. However, only 11% of teachers in home-based programs had a 4-year degree, and 9% a 2-year degree (Kisker, Hofferth, Phillips, & Farquhar, 1991). Discrepancies exist between these two studies, but it is clear that dramatic differences exist in the training of personnel in early school settings compared with personnel in the preschool settings. Any recommendations relating to who should be trained or the most effective timing, location, and content of the training must take these differences into account. The differences in training may contribute to a lack of continuity across these settings for children and their families.

Diversity Among Families

A theme echoed in a number of the chapters in this book relates to the diversity of children and families being served in both preschool and kindergarten settings (see Chapters 4, 6, 7, 9, & 10). Teachers serving children in typical child care settings appear to be more representative of the children and families served than teachers in the more formal school settings of most kindergarten classes. For example, a national survey of kindergarten teachers indicated that only 13.9% of kindergarten teachers belong to minority groups (Pianta, Cox, Taylor, & Early, in press), whereas 1995 U.S. Bureau of the Census (1996) data indicated that 25.5% of the adult population are minorities. In child care centers, 26% of paid classroom staff belong to minority groups (Kisker et al., 1991). In a study of a random sample of public school kindergartens in North Carolina, 31.6% of the children were non-Caucasian, whereas only 16.5% of the teachers were non-Caucasian (Bryant et al., 1991). In a study of typical child care in the central portion of North Carolina, approximately 35% of children were non-Caucasian with 36% of the program staff being non-Caucasian (Helburn, 1995). In both cases, the large majority of teachers were female, with only a smattering of teachers of young children being male. (The figures for non-Caucasian children are quite close to the proportions of non-Hispanic Caucasians cited in Chapter 4 for the 1995/1996 school year in kindergarten in the United States.) Phillips (1994) and Williams (1994) argued that values, interpersonal behavior, and language are grounded in the context of a person's culture and that students will be better understood by teachers who share their culture (Early et al., 1999). Schools of education in the United States need to become much more active in recruiting minorities into their programs. Similarly, efforts are needed to induce more males to enter the early childhood field.

Other issues of diversity also come into play. More children with disabilities are being served in typical early childhood settings since the implementation of the Individuals with Disabilities Education Act (IDEA) of 1990 (PL 101-476). As noted by Zill in Chapter 4, the mix of family settings where young children are being reared has changed. In particular, more children are being reared in single-parent families and by people other than their biological parents. Children in the early years are more likely to be reared in homes with limited economic means than the general population (Duncan & Brooks-Gunn, 1997). All of these factors should be taken into account in looking at who should be trained to work with young children and in recruiting people into preservice training programs.

Diversity in Function and Role

It is clear that many types of professionals come into contact with children during the transition to school period. The most obvious, and the group that this chapter deals with primarily, is teachers. However, many others in the early childhood settings of kindergarten, child care, and other preschool programs have an influence on these young children. Teaching assistants or aides are prevalent in early childhood settings and in many ways serve as teachers for the children in these programs. Only 18.5% of teaching assistants in child care settings have completed a 4-year degree, and 10.8% have less than a high school diploma (Whitebook et al., 1989). Other significant people for children include bus drivers, food services staff, and administrators. In addition, health professionals are actively involved in providing services to children in the early years, with increasing attention being paid to health and hygiene issues in preschool settings. With the emphasis on serving children and their families as a unit—as described by Christenson (Chapter 6) and by Melton et al. (Chapter 7)—family support personnel are increasingly a part of the lives of young children and their families in early childhood programs. Training of these personnel tends to be even more limited than for lead teachers (Cost, Quality, and Child Outcomes Team, 1995).

WHAT SHOULD BE THE CONTENT OF TRAINING

Considering the range of staff discussed in the previous section and the substantial differences in the nature of the early childhood work force across the types of early childhood settings, there are no simple answers to this question. Obviously, the needs of preschool teachers with little preservice training are quite different from those of kindergarten teachers with extensive preparation before beginning to teach. In a chapter such as this, it is impossible to deal with the full range of content of training for teachers of young children. However, there are some critical issues regarding professional preparation that emerged from the work of a synthesis group on professional preparation during "The Transition to Kindergarten: A Synthesis Conference" (Charlottesville, Virginia, February 18–20, 1998). The discussion of professional preparation is categorized into three broad areas for consideration: relationships, rights and responsibilities, and the general content of professional preparation.

Relationships

At the heart of work with young children is the need to establish and maintain effective working relationships. First, of course, is the need to establish effective relationships with the children in the program. Here, the cultural and ethnic differences of teachers and children in kindergarten present serious challenges for professional development. In both preservice and in-service venues, the focus must be on bridging the cultural gaps that are present in almost every early childhood setting. Even in child care, Head Start, and other preschool environments, the increasingly diverse mix of children requires staff to develop new understandings of the rich mixture of cultural backgrounds and values in children. Although the racial mix of teachers of preschoolers may closely reflect that of children served at both the individual teacher and the group level, all teachers have to acquire the skills and knowledge of working with children from differing backgrounds. Valuing differences is important to developing good working relationships. The same issues exist in considering the development of effective relationships with the families of the children in early childhood programs. Teachers must respect and take advantage of the many cultures that exist in the families with which they work, and professional preparation programs must improve their capacity to prepare teachers to work in diverse environments.

Although no attempt is made to address the specifics of the impact of children and families who come to early childhood settings with different abilities in the English language, teachers must be aware of the range of professional positions, family sentiments, and emotions involved in working with children with a primary language other than the predominant one in the school or preschool culture. In preparing professionals, nothing can take the place of firsthand experience in dealing with issues of race, class, culture, and language. Educational settings that reflect the diversity in the population provide opportunities for dealing constructively with the differences and in broadening understanding across a range of specific issues.

Finally, the importance of working relationships with other professionals in the early childhood field cannot be overlooked. In a study of kindergarten teachers and the transition to school, it is clear that there are serious gaps in communication across the preschool–school boundaries (Pianta et al., in press). Schools are not reaching out to preschool providers, and, similarly, preschool personnel are not seeking opportunities to ease the transition for their children as they move to school. Placing blame is not a responsible approach to dealing with this problem. Neither side has effectively sought solutions to the difficulties of providing assistance to the children and their families at this critical juncture in the lives of young children. The starting point is to build the capabilities in staff to develop long-term working relationships with colleagues in different settings. In-service training, which brings together personnel from preschool and kindergarten settings, offers rich opportunities for jointly developing knowledge of the various early childhood delivery systems and skills in working with people from these different agencies and organizations. For many teachers and administrators, there is a basic lack of understanding of the extent and nature of other types of providers and services. Wolery (Chapter 9) points out this lack of knowledge and the differences in points of view of the "sending" and "receiving" teachers in the transition to school for children with disabilities, but the differences affect all children, not just those with disabilities.

Working with others includes working with other professionals inside as well as outside the given setting. Typically, effective teaching is done as part of a team of people within a given program. Knowledgeable people within early childhood settings are needed to assist with identifying special learning needs of children. Other people with special skills at designing safe and secure environments are also needed, as well as a team of people prepared to work together to provide the best possible programs for young children and their families. Yet, little is done in professional development at either the preservice or in-service levels to help prepare professionals to work as part of a team. However, some good models are coming out of special education to develop individual family service plans and individualized education programs for children with disabilities and their families (Bailey, McWilliam, Winton, & Simeonsson, 1992). These models require the families to be a part of the planning for services for their children and involve multiple professional perspectives. The models are only beginning to make their way into the mainstream of professional development as it relates to all children.

Rights and Responsibilities

Although the United States is one of the few developed nations that has not adopted the United Nations Convention on the Rights of Children, there is general acceptance of many of the principles contained in the document. Yet these issues are not dealt with systematically in the preparation of teachers of young children. Families have rights and responsibilities as well, and an understanding of the relative roles of professionals and families is key to successful program implementation.

At the heart of understanding the relative roles of professionals and families is the question of who owns the school or preschool program. Sharing ownership of the program among children, their families, and the staff is important to successful programs, and professional preparation in this area of interest is critical to achieving effective transition practices.

Content of Professional Preparation

No attempt is made in this chapter to outline the content of professional preparation programs at either the preservice or the in-service levels. There are, however, a series of issues that should be addressed, many of which are discussed in this book.

Graue (Chapter 5) discusses issues related to developmentally appropriate practice at length. She highlights the importance of not being hamstrung by any one point of view and correctly points out that no one conceptualization of practice is adequate. She also states that there is much to learn from understanding a range of different developmental perspectives, regardless of whether they are in vogue at any given point in time. A thorough understanding of a variety of developmental perspectives is important for professionals. Inherent in her discussion is the importance of a depth of knowledge that goes beyond a surface understanding of the principles of any one approach. The knowledge of child development must cut across a relatively wide age range. That is, teachers should not be seen as being prepared to teach only a narrow age spectrum but rather be given knowledge of a range of development. During this transition period when children begin formal schooling, they change substantially in how they acquire and process information. Because the change is gradual and occurs in various ways in different children, teachers and others working with children during this transition need to understand the full range of development they are likely to encounter. Knowledge of development must also be expanded to consider the development of families. The ways in which families grow and change as children mature and parents develop new skills themselves is also an essential element of professional preparation.

In this book, little attention is paid to the various content domains and the degree to which preparation in these is important. Language development and preparation for instruction in reading is often seen as a central element of working with young children; however, just how language development occurs and the appropriateness of specific instructional practices is not as well understood as some would like to believe. Indeed, contrary to current trends in the United States, teaching children to read in kindergarten in some countries is considered inappropriate. In Germany, a country with very high literacy rates, kindergarten teachers (kindergarten is for children 3–5 years of age) are prohibited from teaching reading. This role is reserved for teachers of children beginning at about age 6. More training for teachers in the early childhood years of appropriate methods for teaching early skills in math and science is certainly needed.

No one model of child development and no one model for teaching children is adequate to prepare teachers and related personnel to work effectively in today's preschool and kindergarten settings. The fact that many kindergarten teachers have been prepared to work with children in grades K through 6 means that the preservice training of most kindergarten teachers gives little attention to very young children's development. Preschool teachers have, on average, relatively much less preservice training. Both of these situations mean that in-service training will be a vital component of preparing a teaching work force to work with children and with one another during children's transition to kindergarten.

HOW CAN PROFESSIONAL PREPARATION BEST BE PROVIDED?

It is natural to turn to in-service training as the way to deal with the professional preparation needs of the staff working with young children. However, there is evidence that for teachers in child care, the patchwork of workshops offered to meet state training requirements has major limitations (Cost, Quality, and Child Outcomes Team, 1995). In addition, the extremely high turnover rate of teachers in child care centers (Whitebook et al., 1989) offers a serious challenge to the goal of a broad based, deep understanding of children's development and of various approaches to practice. For preschool teachers, a systematically organized approach to in-service training, preferably one organized to lead toward formal degrees, offers the best hope for improving their level of preparation. For teachers in kindergarten, preservice training needs to be modified to provide extensive work in understanding the development of children well before the age of entry into kindergarten, as well as in the complex system (or nonsystem) of delivery of care and education services prior to school entry age. Obtaining this extra information may require an extension of the time needed to complete training for the basic teaching certificate for kindergarten teachers.

Professional preparation must take multiple forms and be delivered in multiple settings. Universities will continue to play a vital role in providing teacher education for school-based personnel. They will play an increasing role in providing training opportunities for prekindergarten teachers as well. Community and technical colleges are increasingly seen as the primary deliverers of educational services to practicing professionals in the early childhood work force. Links between these institutions and 4-year institutions are beginning to allow teachers in preschool settings to complete the traditional preservice programs while maintaining jobs in preschool settings. These links need to move more toward bringing the current cadre of kindergarten teachers together physically with teachers in child care, Head Start, and early intervention services. New technologies, including the World Wide Web, offer interesting possibilities for meeting current preservice and in-service training needs.

One final point should be made regarding the delivery of professional preparation for people working with young children. The training should reflect both the research base and the experience base available. The delivery of the training also needs to take place both in the classroom and in practical settings. Although there are constants across both content and settings, there are important unique features of the preschool and school settings that can be learned only by being there. This means that school-based personnel need training in the preschool settings so that they experience first hand the realities faced by preschool personnel, and, similarly, preschool personnel need to experience the realities of the school environments.

HOW ARE EARLY CHILDHOOD PERSONNEL SUPPORTED?

It is impossible to discuss professional preparation completely without dealing with the financial realities affecting this field. There are wide disparities in income between professionals practicing in schools and those practicing in preschool settings. These differences affect the relative abilities of the people in these settings to get additional training. They even affect the degree to which training is a viable avenue for improving practice.

In schools in general, salaries are not adequate but do at least provide a living wage. For school personnel, normal pay incentives suffice to encourage active participation in meaningful professional development initiatives. In many preschools, however, salaries of teachers are so low as to place the teachers in poverty. Just to get the staff to make serious efforts to engage in meaningful professional development activities requires providing some financial incentives. Loan forgiveness programs for preservice training and substantial pay incentives are needed to encourage participation. Current turnover rates for child care professionals in particular are so great that even major investments will be wasted as the teachers leave the field in rapid succession. Investments in professional preparation efforts must be coupled with compensation increases of a magnitude to reasonably expect the trained personnel to remain in the profession. Such changes will also bring about more parity between the two sectors of early childhood professionals making cooperative work on effective transition activities more likely.

Professional preparation for improving the transition experiences for young children moving into kindergarten is clearly needed. The preparation must bridge the gaps in the services that children and families receive in the two, mostly separate, worlds of kindergarten in the schools and the various preschool settings to which children are exposed. This chapter deals almost exclusively with issues related to the transition of children from some form of extraparental care and education to the beginning of the formal school experience. It is true that a minority of children are reared at home without substantial experience in group settings prior to entry into kindergarten. The schools have a long history of dealing with such transitions. This chapter was designed to address the new reality being faced by school personnel, preschool practitioners, and the families themselves. There is much to learn about making the transition a successful and enriching experience for America's young children and their families.

REFERENCES

Bailey, D.M., McWilliam, P.J., Winton, P.J., & Simeonsson, R.J. (1992). *Implementing family-centered services in early intervention: A team-based model for change.* Cambridge, MA: Brookline Books.

Bryant, D.M., Clifford, R.M., & Peisner-Feinberg, E.S. (1991). Best practices for beginners: Developmental appropriateness in kindergarten. *American Educational Research Journal, 28*(4), 783–803.

Cost, Quality, and Child Outcomes Team. (1995). *Cost, quality, and child outcomes in child care centers, Public report.* Denver: University of Colorado at Denver, Department of Economics.

Duncan, G., & Brooks-Gunn, J. (1997). *Consequences of growing up poor.* New York: Russell Sage Foundation.

Early, D., Pianta, R., & Cox, M. (1999). Kindergarten teachers and classrooms: A transition context. *Early Education and Development, 10,* 25–46.

Helburn, S.W. (Ed.). (1995). *Cost, quality, and child outcomes in child care centers, Technical report.* Denver: University of Colorado at Denver, Department of Economics.

Individuals with Disabilities Education Act (IDEA) of 1990, PL 101-476. 20 U.S.C.A. §§ 1400 *et seq.*

Kisker, E., Hofferth, S., Phillips, D., & Farquhar, E. (1991). *A profile of child care settings: Early education and care in 1990.* Princeton, N.J.: Mathematica Policy Research.

Phillips, C. (1994). The movement of African-American children through sociocultural contexts. In B. Mallory & R. New (Eds.), *Diversity and developmentally appropriate practices: Challenges for early childhood education* (pp. 137–154). New York: Teachers College Press.

Pianta, R.C., Cox, M.J., Early, D., & Taylor, L. (in press). Kindergarten teachers' practices related to the transition to school: Results of a national survey. *The Elementary School Journal.*

U.S. Bureau of Census (1996). 1996 Statistical Abstract of the United States. (pp. 22–23).

Whitebook, M., Howes, C., & Phillips, D. (1989). *Who cares? Child care teachers and the quality of care in America.* Oakland, CA: The Child Care Employee Project.

Williams, L. (1994). Developmentally appropriate practice and cultural values: A case in point. In B. Mallory & R. New (Eds.), *Diversity and developmentally appropriate practices: Challenges for early childhood education* (pp. 155–165). New York: Teachers College Press.

Chapter 13

The Practice of Effective Transitions

Players Who Make a Winning Team

Laura B. Smolkin

Consuela Ramirez, the Head Start's speech-language therapist, is talking about her great desire to follow her Head Start students up to the "big school." She speaks animatedly about how her students have been progressing and how their scores on a test of phonemic awareness outstripped those of other 4-year-olds. Then she frets. She tells me that when the children begin kindergarten at the "big school," 99% of them "fall silent"; they will say little to nothing for 4–5 months. Their native culture and their native language—so much a part of their Head Start experience—are painfully absent from instruction in this elementary school. This is the school in which their parents first met their educational limitations, were told not to speak their native language, and were made to feel as outsiders in their own land. They are not comfortable to go to the "big school" on their children's behalf. Many think, "What does it matter, anyway? The White Man's school is there to teach the White Man's ways." (Field notes, L. Smolkin, February 16, 1998)

Young children are involved in numerous transitions each day. Some children have complicated schedules; they are awakened at their homes, are dressed and

This research was conducted as part of CIERA, the Center for the Improvement of Early Reading Achievement, and supported under the Educational Research and Development Centers Program, PR/Award No. R305R70004, as administered by the Office of Educational Research and Improvement, U.S. Department of Education. However, the contents of the described report do not necessarily represent the positions or policies of the National Institute on Student Achievement, Curriculum, and Assessment; the National Institute on Early Childhood Development; or the U.S. Department of Education, and you should not assume endorsement by the federal government.

taken to a babysitter's home, are picked up by a Head Start bus, spend part of their Head Start time in one language and part in another, are delivered by their Head Start buses to their babysitters' homes, and are finally carried home late at night. In addition to these daily transitions, major changes often await these soon-to-be 5- and 6-year-olds. If, for example, they have even been attending preschool, the kindergarten to which they advance may hold a completely different philosophy of how children should speak, how they should behave, and what they are responsible for knowing and doing. It is well known that transitions frequently involve stress; clearly, some are more stressful than others. Although not all transitions from preschool to kindergarten are quite as dire as the picture painted here, much can be done to improve the general practice of transitions. As the field notes at the beginning of this chapter imply, there are many parties involved in the children's transition from the Head Start program to the elementary school. In this instance, there are teachers, administrators, ancillary staff, families, and local Native American tribal officials who represent the community. Transition programs, which are subject to turf wars, resistance to change, and funding concerns, are rare. This chapter includes recommendations and rationales for practices for all those involved in children's transition to kindergarten. If the practices suggested in this chapter are followed, continuities in children's lives can be enhanced; if they are not, children's transitions to school can be disruptive and damaging, endangering the future success of America's children.

THE TEAM OF ADULTS ON THE CHILDREN'S TRANSITION TO KINDERGARTEN PLAYING FIELD

Practice, as it relates to the child making the transition from home or preschool to kindergarten, operates in a complex world of unequal players. Three educational entities are found in most young children's lives—the home, the preschool, and the elementary school—and all three entities are, generally, located within the context of a particular community. The community is the site of organizations to which families belong, such as churches, synagogues, and mosques. Such religious institutions frequently house weekly preschool programs. Often, there may be recreation or community centers and social services and health provider locations as well. Within each of these settings are particular groups of people, the "players," who comprise the adult supports for children's kindergarten transition. These entities and players are important to consider in conceptualizing kindergarten transition with an ecologically sound perspective (Chapter 1). A brief overview of the roles of the adults in each context appears in the following sections.

Families

Home, regardless of whether it is a tenement building, row house, trailer home, or house, is where children interact with families or caregivers. Although the closeness of social networks outside the nuclear family varies among differing ethnic groups (MacPhee, Fritz, & Miller-Heyl, 1996) and the networks and the social capital they afford may, as Melton, Limber, and Teague express in Chapter 7, be shrinking in today's age of alienation, both nuclear and extended families are, without a doubt, the first educators in their children's lives. Social networks communicate to children what has value and what does not, what is acceptable behavior and what is not, and which skills are important and which are not. Families, spending days and nights together, know a great deal about their preschool child. They are well acquainted with their children's strengths and weaknesses; they know the activities their children enjoy and the topics that interest them. Such information should be important to professionals involved in children's transition from home or preschool to kindergarten, not only for the design of appropriate instruction but also for the provision of emotional support.

Families are concerned with the quality of education their children will receive in the elementary school setting. Some families are quite comfortable advocating for their child. However, many other families hesitate to make their feelings known. According to Katz (1995; Katz, Aidman, Reese, & Clark, 1996), the reasons for this hesitancy may range from cultural orientations that regard teachers as authority figures to personal memories of school failures to concerns that their intercession will cause problems for their child. Simich-Dudgeon (1986) noted that Hispanic migrant parents have expressed fear that their involvement would be construed as interference and thus would receive a negative response. The Mexican-American families in Nicolau and Ramos' (1993) study viewed themselves as providers of their children's basic needs as well as the source from which their children learned respect and proper behavior. They viewed schools as the instillers of knowledge and stated their belief that neither schools nor families should interfere with the other's domain. Thus, for many of these families, the idea of participating in their children's education represents an unknown cultural concept.

In addition, poor and minority families are frequently reported in the literature as believing that schools are not run to benefit their children (e.g., Ascher, 1987). Chavkin and Gonzalez (1995) cataloged the many barriers for Mexican-American parents, which include the parents' sense that schools are bureaucracies controlled by non-Hispanics. Still, as Entwisle and Alexander indicate in Chapter 2, certain families will go to great lengths to move their children into higher socioeconomic status schools, which they believe will better serve their children's education.

Wolery, in Chapter 9, cites the findings of Trivette and Dunst (1997) that clearly show the nature of the relationship families want to have with school personnel. They want themselves, their concerns, and their children to be warmly received and respected, and they want to be given the information they request and require. Given that most elementary schools pay scant attention to family-centered services, as Wolery's own research demonstrates, it is little wonder that the concept of a "full-service" elementary school has not occurred to families. That ecologically sound programs, such as those discussed by Christenson in Chapter 6 and Melton et al. in Chapter 7, might possibly exist is beyond the dreams of most families.

Preschools

Although most of America's children remain exclusively within the care of their families prior to beginning kindergarten, as noted by both Entwisle and Alexander (Chapter 2) and Ramey and Ramey (Chapter 8), preschool attendance is particularly important for economically disadvantaged children. Notably, it leads to a reduction in children's retention rates in the elementary school.

Preschools generally are significantly smaller than the elementary school into which they feed. They vary considerably in their philosophies, their funding, their size, and their organizational structure. They vary even more in the curriculum, teaching strategies, and assessment that their classes offer preschoolers. Their owners may lack an educational background, or may, as in some large Head Start operations, even have educational administrative licensure.

Preschool teachers, more frequently than elementary school teachers, come from the community in which they are located. Their orientations, expectations, and language backgrounds often match well with the families and caregivers of the children they serve. Although federally funded programs such as Head Start are mandated to have parental involvement, most preschools, either formally or informally, maintain considerable contact with the families of the children they serve. However, unless they also serve as child care centers for children's after-school care, preschools have little to no contact with the elementary school that the children will attend. Although their staff, such as Consuela Ramirez, the Head Start speech-language therapist mentioned at the beginning of this chapter, may recognize that transition can be a source of trouble to children, they generally lack the resources or the power to launch effective transition programs.

Elementary School Principals

Elementary schools generally begin their instruction at the kindergarten level and run through fifth or sixth grade, although that picture is now changing as certain preschool programs are attached to elementary schools. As Entwisle and Alexander note in Chapter 2, much variability is found in the nature of the elementary school experience from one community to another. Although funding per child often varies from school to school within given districts, most are relatively well-funded and public elementary school principals, usually in charge of these institutions, may be seen as the powerful giants on the transition playing field. Of all entities discussed so far, it is the elementary school that is most frequently viewed with trepidation by communities, families, and their children.

Schools that receive Title I funding under the revised guidelines are now required to foster parental and community involvement in schools, with special attention paid to the school–parent contract requirement. Beyond that, elementary schools' home–school partnerships range from the old standard "Come join the PTA" to programs that entail a complete range of opportunities for and levels of parental participation, such as those discussed by Christenson in Chapter 6.

Given that Williams and Chavkin's (1986) survey of school administrators revealed principals favoring "traditional parental roles," such as participating in open house, over parental involvement in schools' decision-making activities, there remains, in general, a considerable gap between current practice and genuine family–school collaboration. Their survey further suggests that parental involvement is directly related to principals' attitudes and sincerity. Families need and want to feel truly welcome in their children's schools and to be given a clear indication that their contributions to their children's education are positive and significant. With the principal attitudes described by Williams and Chavkin, it is unlikely that most families receive either of these messages.

Schools, guided by their principals, need to present a range of participation opportunities for families. Williams and Chavkin (1989) indicated that effective school–home partnerships, at the minimum, require a strong commitment on the part of the school so that policies regarding the partnership appear in written form, administrative support continues, teacher training for work with families is ongoing, and regular evaluation of the success of parental efforts occurs. Approaching the maximum level of parent participation are models such as Comer's School Development Program (Comer, Haynes, Joyner, & Ben-Avie, 1996), presented in Chapters 6 and 7.

Given the research reviewed by Christenson (Chapter 6) on families and schools which consistently showed a positive correlation between parent involvement and children's school success, schools that fail to involve families clearly do so at the peril of their students' well-being. Furthermore, in light of Eccles and Harold's finding discussed in Chapter 7 that parental involvement decreases as children grow older, the most critical time for coordinated, multidirectional parental involvement efforts would seem to be during children's transition to kindergarten.

Kindergarten Teachers

Kindergarten teachers and their classrooms represent the first major link between children and the elementary schools that serve them. Although there are increasing numbers of elementary schools that feature full-day kindergarten classrooms, virtually one half of America's kindergarten teachers continue to operate two distinct sessions for children each day (Smith et al., 1994). Even if those classes were the ones with 15 or fewer students that Graue (Chapter 5) reports as producing better achievement scores, kindergarten teachers with two sessions per day would still have more students and more families with whom they need to communicate than other elementary grade teachers. Clearly, this restricts the amount of time teachers have to communicate with families about their children.

Furthermore, given that elementary school teachers, unlike preschool teachers, are much less commonly members of the community in which their school is located, their ability to correctly interpret families' communications is sometimes hindered. Often, as Christenson (Chapter 6) reports, teachers admit to feeling awkward, uneasy, and reluctant with the families of their students. They feel particularly uncomfortable when families question their pedagogical practices (Allen, 1997; Anderson-Clark, 1996). Their lack of knowledge of the home lives and families of their increasingly diverse student body often causes them to misconstrue parent actions. Findings, as Entwisle and Alexander (Chapter 2) suggest, seem consistent over time that many teachers particularly underestimate the interest of ethnic and racial minority families in the education of their children. This misperception, in turn, has an impact on the information that these teachers choose to share with these families (e.g., Epstein & Dauber, 1989; Holden, 1996) and the ways in which they move to include them in their children's education.

Another potential source of discomfort for kindergarten teachers, as Graue (Chapter 5) established, is the curriculum of their classrooms (e.g., Reynolds, 1998). Many kindergarten teachers are members of the National Association for the Education of Young Children (NAEYC), adopting and working to implement its philosophy of developmentally appropriate practice (Bredekamp & Copple, 1997). When families question the value of "play" in the classroom or when upper-grade colleagues and administrators advocate the "push down" curriculum (a practice that Meisels [Chapter 3] links to the release of the *Nation at Risk* report), many kindergarten teachers who embrace a child-centered approach feel that they and their philosophies are under attack.

Although kindergarten teachers are aware that their efforts at establishing links to preschools that feed into their elementary classrooms would ease children's transition to kindergarten, many of them, similar to other elementary school teachers, are overwhelmed by the number of expectations already placed on them. However, there are certainly many kindergarten teachers who extend themselves far beyond their school day and community setting to improve educational opportunities for children (e.g., Burchby, 1992).

These four groups—families, preschools, principals of elementary schools (representing personal as well as school board and higher-level administrative stances), and kindergarten teachers—comprise the major players in children's transitions, although there are additional agencies and services (social services, health care providers) that become part of the transition constellation as sound practices commence. The four key groups are clearly unequal in the power they hold and the resources they command, yet, similar to the members of any team, they each hold certain responsibilities and must coordinate their efforts for transitions to kindergarten to be effective.

The next sections of this chapter consider the practices those responsibilities entail and highlight practices essential to successful kindergarten transition efforts. Although practices appear under the headings of particular players, kindergarten transition should be conceptualized as an ecological system, as suggested by Melton et al. (Chapter 7) and Pianta, Rimm-Kaufman, and Cox (Chapter 1). The team cannot win the game without working together as a unit, attentive to each other's moves on the field. It is pointless, for example, for preschool teachers to make the effort to inform families about assessment if the elementary school their children will attend has an unwritten policy of divulging as little assessment information as possible. This chapter's abundant use of "reaching out" and "welcoming in" metaphors (R. Pianta, personal communication, April 16, 1998) signals the importance of relationships to transition success. The order of examination will proceed from the most powerful but most distant from the child, the principal, to those with whom the first section began, those far less powerful but considerably closer to the transitioning child, the family.

THE ROLE OF ELEMENTARY SCHOOL
PRINCIPALS IN PROMOTING EFFECTIVE TRANSITIONS

Melton et al. (Chapter 7) cite Dryfoos as commenting on "a kind of mystical belief that if everyone talks to everyone else, a collaborative project will emerge" (1994, p. 211). Clearly, effective transitions will never occur if each of the four players in the lives of the beginning kindergartner waits for the others to start their collaborative efforts. Of the four, it is the elementary school that is best funded and most powerful; it is the elementary school principal who can affect the most individuals by his or her decisions. For this reason, this section begins by focusing, as suggested by Epstein and Connors (1992), on the elementary school principal and the leadership that individual must provide for successful transitions to kindergarten.

Effective schools research (e.g., Findley & Findley, 1992) attaches great significance to principals' roles in any type of change. For schools to be effective in improving the abilities of the children they serve, principals must be able to envision the changes that are needed as well as the best situations for effecting those changes. Although such work will ultimately involve the entire range of school personnel, principals can begin by reconfiguring their own understandings of their roles in maximizing successful transitions to kindergarten.

Although this chapter is limited to the community within which any given elementary school is located, attention still must be paid to the complex question of how to make kindergarten transitions and the playing field they entail important to principals. If principals do not recognize an issue as significant, they are unlikely to extend their leadership efforts to addressing it. That is, to influence principals' orientation toward kindergarten transitions, it seems important to recognize that elementary school principals appear to fall into two distinct categories based on their career histories (Crow, 1990, 1992). Those principals whose careers have entailed greater mobility appear to have a greater sense of themselves as leaders and, simultaneously, have an orientation toward community connections. Principals whose careers have included less mobility seem more likely to conceive of themselves as subordinates of school districts' central offices. Any meaningful national, state, and district efforts to transform principals into transition advocates for their schools and communities would need to recognize these differences and offer incentives appropriate to each of these groups.

With this caveat, the following sections outline the four critical roles and actions that principals can take to enhance successful transitions to kindergarten for America's children. These include being liaisons to communities and their institutions, champions of home–school partnerships, leaders of schools' instructional practices, and administrators of effective policies.

Liaisons to Communities and Their Institutions

As other chapters have established, only a small number of children attend formal preschools; the rest remain at home with families and caregivers. As noted previously in this chapter, principals, in general, have not placed a high priority on family–school partnerships; similarly, only a few give much thought to community contacts. To have the most impact on effective transitions, principals can begin by considering how they, as liaisons, and their faculty should reach out to and welcome each institution and organization that influences the lives of preschoolers and their families. The "how" of these interactions may determine their durability: Seeking partners rather than issuing edicts appears to be the best route. Whether through face-to-face meetings or through written correspondence, all communication should be a two-way, rather than a one-way, transmission of ideas. This is definitely an instance where the process may be as important as its product.

Creating and Supporting Interfacing Processes with Preschools   Though relatively small numbers of children attend formal preschools, preschools are the community organizations most similar in structure and purpose to elementary schools. A relatively simple way to begin the process of effective transitions, then, is for principals to reach out to these formal institutions through a series of communicative efforts with their directors.

Initial meetings can highlight the importance of smooth transitions to kindergarten. Presentations of successful transition programs may serve to focus the dialogue so that private preschool and Head Start directors are comfortable participating in a dialogue. Possible action plans may be outlined, and future meetings and their content can be considered. Locally made videos that show a day in kindergarten at "the big school" might also be supplied at this time so that preschool teachers and their students can see what to expect from the transition to the elementary school.

Subsequent meetings may welcome preschool teachers and directors into the *weltanschauung* (world view) of public elementary school education. Principals might consider opening staff development meetings at the elementary school to interested preschool and Head Start teachers. This could have a quick impact on effective transitions in that preschool teachers, learning of a new program or a new orientation toward teaching, might immediately begin to orient their students toward those practices. Or, principals could schedule special transition meetings between kindergarten teachers and preschool staff. Information on daily organization might be exchanged to address Zill's finding (Chapter 4) that children who attend center-based preschools are more likely to get critical reports from kindergarten teachers. Also, curricula and current forms of assessment in both the preschool and the kindergarten might be described. An elementary school might want, for example, to demonstrate portfolio assessment (e.g., Balm, 1995) so that preschool students' work samples might inform kindergarten teachers' instructional planning.

Contacting Families Whose Children Do Not Attend a Formal Preschool   Principals need to consider how to best reach out to the families of the majority of preschool-age children who are not found in formal educational settings. Because it is not feasible to contact individuals, principals might start by assessing which community institutions would most readily welcome the elementary school's transition efforts.

Community health care and social services providers as agencies of government, for instance, seem logical locations for linkages to begin. Local churches, synagogues, and mosques represent another possible avenue for establishing contact with families. Many of these institutions may have organized preschools that children attend, so their directors would already have been included in the types of meetings proposed here. Others offer "babysitting" options, such as Mother's Day Out, or child care while families attend religious functions. As Melton et al. (Chapter 7) note, although connections to religious institutions may be fading in today's age of alienation, any possible path for contacting large numbers of families merits strong consideration.

Having established these community connections, principals can create a series of pamphlets for families. These might describe a typical day in kindergarten or communicate the value of organized preschool experiences in aiding children in their transition to school (e.g., Gullo & Burton, 1993) as well as in leading to increased academic school success (see Chapter 2). Pamphlets that feature the elementary school's kindergarten teachers with their personal suggestions for activities in which families may want to engage their preschoolers might have particular appeal.

Principals may also want to consider outreach efforts particularly suited to local businesses' endeavors. For example, establishments that rent videos might be willing to manage the promotion, distribution, and maintenance of videotapes that feature a typical kindergarten day in the local elementary school classroom or that introduce families to interactions that are particularly important in preparing children for schooling success.

The ways in which creative principals can establish community connections are considerable. These suggestions are those that seem easiest to accomplish for principals who are not accustomed to reaching out.

Champions of Home–School Partnerships

As Epstein (1992) pointed out, solid home–school partnerships are developmental. This chapter clearly conceptualizes partnerships that are developmental for each party. First, principals and teachers must consider that family involvement entails a greater range of options than volunteering in the classroom or accompanying the class on a field trip. Second, families must feel that schools welcome them and their involvement in their children's educational experiences.

The community linkages suggested in the previous section are designed to inform families that their children's future school is thinking of them long before their children ever enroll in kindergarten classrooms. This is the reason that the distribution of locally prepared pamphlets and locally created video materials is stressed—to establish and enhance early connections between families and the public elementary school in their community.

Welcoming families and their involvement, however, requires more than reaching out to distribute factual information. Because principals' and teachers' attitudes have an impact on the amount of family involvement that occurs (Dauber & Epstein, 1993), principals who want to go beyond advocating home–school relationships into actually fostering them can set the stage for families to feel comfortable in their encounters with and at the school. This means that all school personnel need to consider whether their current actions and stances welcome families or push them away.

As Melton et al. (Chapter 7) stress, when principals put families' participation near the top of their schools' priority lists, teachers are much more likely to include families in their children's education. Principals may assist this process by encouraging their teaching staff to surface their reservations about families' involvement, then supplying them the information and training Bowman advocates in Chapter 10. Principals can prepare to support changes eliminating the mismatch between families' and teachers' perceptions of parental involvement cited by Melton and colleagues (Chapter 7).

This, in fact, is not so easy to accomplish, and principals need to be realistically prepared for objections to these efforts. Given the results of the Williams and Chavkin's (1986) survey described previously, principals might begin by considering and then making public their own reasons for prior resistance to parental involvement and the new types of thinking in which they are engaging. In short, this is the time to lead by example. While continually stressing that family–school partnerships will ultimately bring an entire community's commitment and resources to bear in enhancing children's learning, principals can move to address concerns teachers have raised.

After heightening teachers' knowledge of the benefits of family involvement, principals can present a developmental picture of home–school partnerships. Teachers can be made aware of models such as Epstein's (1995) six types of family involvement noted in Chapter 6. Examples of success, such as Comer's School Development Program, should be made available for teachers to consider what may be ultimately possible. Finally, principals can stress for their teachers the finding noted by Christenson in Chapter 6—that school and teacher practices are the greatest predictor of families' involvement.

A possible next step might be to supply teachers with guidelines that can improve individual teacher–family (microsystemic) relationships so that each can be individually implementing simple changes while the school moves forward on its mesosystemic intervention. For instance, Katz et al. (1996) set forth some basic principles while stressing the notion of two-way communication. Principals can also prepare themselves to create and continue contexts where teacher–family contact comfortably occurs.

Following the preparatory work described previously for the school staff, principals can begin to implement both the principles and processes of family inclusion. Attending to the forms of messages from the school represents an important starting point. Instead of relying on notes sent home with children as the single source of communication, principals can "get their word out" through community connections. Notices for school events may be posted at food markets and community centers. Religious leaders may be requested to include upcoming school events in their announcements. All forms of communication, however, ought to be created with the various literacy levels and spoken languages of families in mind (Nicolau & Ramos, 1993).

Messages from the school—written, spoken, and even unspoken signals—can communicate clearly that any type and any degree of family involvement is welcomed, wanted, and needed. For example, for those families whose work schedules or transportation difficulties do not allow them to visit their children's schools, the message that even brief, school-related conversations with children at home constitute partnership in their children's education should be communicated. Whatever form they take, messages should highlight the two-way communication that will now be the norm. School personnel can emphasize that listening will be as high a priority as telling, and that Comer's "no fault" principle will undergird every communicative act.

Principals may also begin contacting those families already known to be actively involved in their children's education to assist in establishing home–school ties. This clearly conveys a, "Hey, can you help us with this?" attitude, an important first step in a genuine partnership. For instance, family-run "welcoming committees" (e.g., Ortner, 1994) that have included home visits as part of their efforts have been found to increase minority family involvement and to reduce student mobility. "Unofficial" family networks often supply each other information on matters related to their children's education, such as how best to work with a given classroom teacher. In addition, as Nicolau and Ramos (1993) suggested, families already involved with schools can be asked to bring three acquaintances to any meetings at the school, communicating a "we want you with us" message.

Principals and staff can also recognize that families' concerns often extend beyond the academic needs of the children and into emotional and physical health as well. Families are often unsure of how best to help their children; any questions they pose about how and what they might be doing at home ought to be given serious attention. Family education programs, offered at times families have indicated they will be available to participate, may be created to advise families on how best to help their children, whether through the preparation of nutritional meals or through monitoring children's television viewing or through effective forms of discipline. Every school-related interaction affords opportunities for practicing reaching-out and welcoming-in stances, and principals can stress this repeatedly as they communicate with their staffs.

Leaders of Effective Instructional Practice

Principals are far more than liaisons to communities and champions of family–school partnerships; they are also the instructional leaders for their schools. Although teachers often come to principals to share ideas for instructional change, it is the principal who is ultimately responsible to explain the adoption of practices to the central office. The following sections describe instructional practices that seem most important to children's successful transitions to school. These include class size, the length of the school day, summer experiences for children, early intervention programs, and meaningful forms of assessment.

Reducing Kindergarten Class Size   Although some researchers may question the lasting effects of small class sizes at all elementary grade levels (e.g., Harvey, 1994; see also Chapter 5), the long-term results of Tennessee's small classes at the kindergarten level policy clearly indicate that reduced class size leads to increased academic achievement, fewer grade retentions, more on-task time for teachers, higher levels of student engagement, and a reduction in the gap of minority student achievement. Undoubtedly these results arise from the increased attention teachers can offer to each child, an important factor in children's effective transitions from their preschool or home settings to the kindergarten classroom.

Lengthening the Kindergarten Day   Although there have been mixed reviews in the past concerning the outcomes of full-day kindergartens, research (Entwisle & Alexander, 1998; Fusaro, 1997; Fusaro & Royce, 1995) appears to establish the superiority of extended day kindergartens over half-day kindergartens in preparing children for school success. If effective transitions minimize stress, full-day kindergartens that feature extended child care may possibly represent an ideal situation. Children of working parents would not have to go to child care settings after school, reducing their required number of transitions per day to two—to school and back to home.

Creating Summer Programs   Given Entwisle and Alexander's (Chapter 2) findings on the dire impact of summers on the achievement of poor children, it behooves all principals and their faculties, along with the families and community of the children the school serves, to contemplate summer programs. In her speech at "The Transition to Kindergarten: A Synthesis Conference" (Charlottesville, Virginia, February 18–20, 1998), Entwisle indicated that standard summer school, simply a repetition of the content of the school year, did not appear as effective for children's growth as did enrichment experiences such as going to the zoo or participating in a summer read-a-thon at a library. Brief summer programs for incoming kindergartners would serve a trifold purpose. They would allow children contact with their classrooms and peers, eliminating much of the strangeness of school when the school year actually begins. They would ensure the early establishment of personal relationships—teachers and families, teachers and children, and children and children. They would also give children access to enrichment opportunities. Given current thinking that the most critical transition may be, in fact, between kindergarten and first grade (e.g., Entwisle & Alexander, 1998), intensified summer programming efforts might be created for these young members of the elementary school community.

Establishing Effective Early Intervention Programs   As Entwisle and Alexander point out, "the short-term pay-offs for interventions designed to help children in the early years are likely to be greater than interventions later on" (1998, p. 16). Slavin, Karweit, and Wasik (1992–1993) provided a cogent review of the research on programs designed to improve children's school success. They contended that early intervention programs that involve one-on-one tutoring in first-grade reading may, in fact, be more effective than preschool experience, reduction in class size, or extended kindergarten days in improving children's third-grade reading achievement. Although their findings in general may be open to question, attention still must be paid to early intervention efforts.

Slavin and colleagues' (1992–1993) negative assessment of the practice termed *transitional first grade* or *developmental kindergarten* seems to find frequent support in the literature (e.g., Ferguson & Streib, 1996; Wang & Johnstone, 1997). In a sense, these programs function exactly the same as special education placements; they permanently pull children out of their normal trajectory. As Entwisle and Alexander (Chapter 2) comment, once placed in special education classes or retained, children seldom move back with the classmates with whom they began. Principals, their primary-grade staffs, and families will need to carefully consider the relative merits of early intervention programs (e.g., Success for All versus Reading Recovery) and whether these efforts should be focused on kindergarten, first grade, or both.

Promoting Meaningful Assessments   Both Meisels (Chapter 3) and Graue (Chapter 5) call attention to assessment practices and their potential hazards. Clearly, principals, supported by appropriate school staff members, should aid kindergarten teachers and families in understanding the distinction between developmental screening tests and readiness tests, which are frequently a pale reflection of the range of abilities that children actually have. Thinking about assessments should move beyond those things that we struggle through in the fall and in the spring to a vision of assessments as supplying information about a child's progress and needs throughout the school year. Such a model already exists in the field of special education through the federally mandated individualized education program (IEP), mentioned in Chapter 9. The IEP documents the child's current ability level, while also indicating what the expected level is for that child's particular age or grade level. However, what is used to determine success for the child is the improvement shown in his or her own goals and abilities. The IEP is then referred to periodically throughout the year to mark the progress toward the goals. Principals may want to encourage kindergarten teachers to consider such a model in assessing their students.

Administrators of Effective Policies

This section addresses the administrative actions that principals might take to enhance successful transitions. These include reconfiguring kindergarten teachers' time; springtime creation of fall kindergarten class lists; and producing clearly stated, readily available school policies.

Reconfiguring Teachers' Time   If kindergarten teachers are to conduct preschool visits and if they are to more regularly initiate face-to-face interactions with the families of their students to ease transitions to the elementary school, then they will need additional time for these tasks. Many school districts already have designated 1 day per week as a shortened day. A variation for kindergarten may be allowing teachers to have the afternoon off, then returning to school to be available at times when more families can visit. Optimal situations can be designed only after all involved parties—families and teachers—have had the opportunity to voice their needs and concerns. Principals, then, must initiate time rearrangement efforts, bearing in mind that teachers, too, have families and lives outside the school buildings in which they teach.

Creating Opportunities for Teacher Visits to Preschools   Kindergarten teachers' visits to community preschools are, as noted previously, an important possible action in aiding transition efforts. As preschool days are concurrent with elementary school days, such visits would necessitate either substitute teachers for their classrooms or a distribution of their students among other classrooms on that day (possibly a day to visit first-grade classes in action). Principals would need to meet with teachers to determine a plan of action.

Generating Fall Classes in the Spring   Elementary schools can support preschoolers' transition to kindergarten by allowing children and their families to establish relationships with the future kindergarten teacher months before the new school year begins. To accomplish this goal, in order to make possible any sort of meaningful summertime contacts, principals can arrange for kindergarten registration to take place in the early spring instead of in late spring or summer. This early registration, in turn, allows kindergarten teachers to welcome students and their families into the existing kindergarten world, facilitating familiarity with teachers, their classrooms, and their practices.

Creating and Making Available Clearly Stated School Policies and Goals   Research (e.g., Hoffman, 1991; Purkey & Smith, 1983) has repeatedly shown the importance of clearly stated goals to children's success. Policies and goals supply a common path toward which both teachers and families can guide a child's efforts and attention. Consistency of message is critical to easing transition stress for children as well as adults; principals must guide their staff to ensure that they are communicating linked goals. As Hiebert and Raphael noted, "after classroom, Title I, and other resource (special education, speech and language, bilingual) teachers shared the goals and benchmarks for focused Right Start in Reading instruction, the levels of literacy in schools rose remarkably" (1998, p. 224). Known and shared expectations enhance the types of information and communication families can offer their school partners.

In summary, principals can serve as liaisons to the community, champions of home–school partnerships, leaders of instructional change, and administrators of effective policies. Each of these roles is critical for enabling young children's successful kindergarten transitions.

THE ROLE OF KINDERGARTEN
TEACHERS IN PROMOTING EFFECTIVE TRANSITIONS

Although the public may picture kindergarten teachers as serving milk and cookies for snacks, joyfully singing songs with children while playing the piano, and refilling paint jars at the classroom easels, their jobs are infinitely more complex. They must establish individual relationships with children and their families.

Each fall, most kindergarten teachers greet groups of more than 20 children whose prior experiences with schooling vary more widely than those at any other grade level. Some entering kindergartners have spent their preschool years at home with their families; their socialization with peers may have been limited to playing occasionally with cousins or neighborhood children. Other kindergartners may have been in child care settings virtually since birth; these settings vary impressively from the neighbor who keeps three or four children to efficiently organized institutions serving professional establishments such as hospitals or businesses. Still other kindergarten children have been attending preschool since 2 years of age; as with child care, preschools also vary considerably in the ways they are structured, the educational backgrounds of the teachers, and their orientations toward experiences for the preschool child.

Regardless of their students' backgrounds, kindergarten teachers must orient their students toward the social and academic behaviors necessary for children's ultimate successful schooling. Their students must learn to follow group instructions, to work independently for periods of time, and to see that both peers and adults can serve as sources of information.

Children's success in these endeavors is made easier when kindergarten teachers consider their students within an ecologically sound model that involves the transition field players. Table 13.1 shows the model expressed within an 18-month, time-related framework that indicates the cyclical nature of kindergarten teachers' transition-related efforts. The following sections address the human and institutional relationships as well as the curricular and assessment issues that kindergarten teachers can consider as they plan for children's smooth transitions to the elementary school.

Reaching Out to Preschools

Once principals have welcomed preschools to the transition playing field, put springtime class creation policies into effect, and created situations to allow visits to preschools, kindergarten teachers' links to preschools can serve two purposes. The first is to participate in the increased communication with their preschool colleagues resulting from the principal's agenda, including knowing about each other's instructional practices. For example, Papierz, Hiebert, and DiStefano (1990) reported that the kindergarten teachers in their study made no inquiries about the literacy experiences their students had in their former child care or preschool settings. In fact, they reported that the kindergarten teachers initiated no contact concerning children unless a child was having severe behavior problems. Because one of the preschools involved had a strongly developed agenda, which included copying letters, it contrasted markedly with the kindergarten program in which children were encouraged in invented writings and participated in many book reading experiences. In their linking efforts, then, kindergarten teachers should learn about any literacy-related practices or philosophies (see Wolery's discussion of staff issues in Chapter 9) to which their students have become accustomed in preschool and make sure that early kindergarten practices incorporate some aspect of what has been learned. They should also describe their literacy programs to preschool teachers, explaining their rationales for their decisions and giving suggestions of what earlier experiences might assist with the kindergarten literacy program.

The second linkage serves to set the stage for individual children's entry into kindergarten. Table 13.1 shows that visits to the preschools of their incoming students serve not only to allow children to meet their future teachers in a familiar setting, but also to gather and share information. Kindergarten teachers may observe and interact with the incoming kindergarten child, creating anecdotal records that address interaction styles, participation patterns, and topics of interest. They may also gather work samples and records as they chat with preschool teachers about individual children. Kindergarten and preschool teachers may want to use this opportunity to show children videotapes or slide presentations to let them see what kindergarten looks like. Kindergarten teachers must communicate to their incoming students that they are looking forward to working with them. They must establish the legitimate importance of future two-way communication, so that preschool teachers will feel free to call kindergarten teachers to

Table 13.1. A time-related framework for kindergarten teachers' transition practices

Practices	Spring	Summer	Fall	Winter
Reaching out to preschools	Visits to preschools to observe incoming students in class Show videotape or slides of kindergarten Gather work samples		Participate in principal's reaching out and welcoming agenda Work with preschool colleagues	Participate in principal's reaching out and welcoming agenda Work with preschool colleagues
Welcoming families and their children	Begin contact with children and their families Letters to children begin at this time Invitations to new students and families to visit classrooms	Continue letters to children and their families Send "Tips for Families" Introduce two-way communication approach to reinforce the notion of partnership Home visits—perhaps an alphabet book and a story book for each child Families discuss what child likes to do Leave a learning packet (to be returned when school begins)	Where possible, schedule family member visiting days Create special classroom space for "our families" Schedule several open houses to accommodate family members' schedules Encourage families to be involved in larger home-school partnership efforts Learning packets distributed on a weekly basis Books from classroom library sets to be sent home for reading aloud twice weekly Other materials requested by families	Where possible, schedule family member visiting days Continue "our families" space Schedule several open houses to accommodate family members' schedules Ask for volunteers to visit incoming children and families Learning packets distributed on a weekly basis Books from classroom library sets to be sent home for reading aloud twice weekly Other materials requested by families
Enrichment experiences—stress those that will introduce new vocabulary and concepts	Prepare for summer enrichment program	Summer enrichment weeks Half-class grouping each attends 1 week in June and July Whole class attends 1 week in early August		

(continued)

Table 13.1. (continued)

Practices	Spring	Summer	Fall	Winter
Curriculum creation	Curriculum stresses progress for all children in school literacies, social skills, and language development Plan first-grade visits for each child in the class	Use information gathered from home visits to plan topics for upcoming year's curriculum Begin planning individualized instruction as indicated	Use information gathered from anecdotal records and families to plan topics for spring semester	
Assessment	Assessment of children's progress will be ongoing, with an eye to forms that will assist families Begin folders of information on incoming students Collect school information for those incoming students who have been in formal preschool settings Share information with first-grade teachers	Enter information from family interview sheets Plan for testing of children who may have displayed special needs Enter anecdotal records from observations of child during summer enrichment	Assess phonological awareness Use three child per day emphasis to enter regularly scheduled anecdotal observations	Use three child per day emphasis to enter regularly scheduled anecdotal observations

340

inform them of any particularly important happenings in a child's life and kindergarten teachers will feel free to contact the preschool teacher if his or her help is needed to support a beginning kindergartner.

Reaching Across to First Grade

It has been suggested that the transition from kindergarten to first grade might be almost as important as the transition to kindergarten. Often in schools, one of the greatest divides lies between the classroom organization and philosophies of kindergarten teachers and those of first-grade teachers. Increased dialogue between kindergarten and first-grade teachers may not necessarily resolve philosophical differences (see Wolery's comments in Chapter 9), but it certainly could lead to opportunities for kindergarten students to visit their springtime-assigned first-grade teachers' classrooms and for their current and new teachers to discuss teaching and learning practices that support individual children. It could also lead to well-crafted summertime experiences between the kindergarten and first-grade years. Just as preschool teachers have shared their records and impressions with kindergarten teachers, so, too, might kindergarten teachers share theirs with first-grade teachers.

Welcoming Children and Their Families

Perhaps nothing is more important for children's future elementary school success than the kindergarten teacher's welcoming of both future students and their families. This section concentrates on the establishment and maintenance of home–school partnerships and the nature of teacher–child relationships prior to the start of the kindergarten year.

Establishing and Maintaining Home–School Partnerships Kindergarten teachers can begin their contacts with families immediately after they receive their fall class lists. Kindergarten teachers can mail letters (keeping language differences in mind) to their incoming students' homes, introducing themselves and inviting families to bring their preschooler to kindergarten for a day. Such letters may serve as the start of communication prior to the child's entrance to school. During summer, for example, teachers may choose to enclose, in the letters they write to their incoming students, "Tips for Families" sheets discussing topics such as television viewing and sleep habits and offering summertime activity suggestions.

Once they establish communication, kindergarten teachers can work with families to schedule home visits to occur most likely during the summer months. Such home visits permit teachers to learn about their new students both through observation and through discussion with family members. They also afford teachers the opportunity to describe the summer enrichment experiences noted in Table 13.1 and to schedule which sessions the child will attend. Teachers can leave learning packets, such as those described by Reutzel and Fawson (1990), that contain school-related activities, books, and possibly video- or audiotapes, for families to complete with children over the summer. They can also present outstanding pieces of literature as gifts for children's home libraries as they stress to families the importance of reading aloud.

Once school has begun, kindergarten teachers can signal that families are welcome by scheduling family daytime visits as well as multiple open house opportunities. They can also create "our families" corners that include places for visiting family members to hang coats, look at their children's work samples, and serve as display areas for individual children's family photographs and artifacts. Such corners may contain multilingual audiotapes made by community members that describe the kindergarten classroom so that family members feel welcome, regardless of whether they understand English. As the year progresses, teachers may want to suggest that families volunteer to visit and support the families of next year's incoming kindergarten students.

As in summer, teachers can continue to involve families in school-related home activities. Learning packets can continue their route from school to home and back to school. Many teachers have found that including a Comment Sheet for families to complete encourages children to describe what they have learned and what they like and gives them an opportunity to watch writing in their homes. Such activities clearly foster the school-related talk that Christenson describes in Chapter 6. Other kindergarten teachers initiate a book club and send home books with their students for capable family members to read aloud to their kindergartners. Neuman (1996) found that, even for Head Start children whose families have low reading proficiency, participation in reading aloud significantly improved children's receptive language and their concepts of print.

When teachers manifest sincere interest, families begin to feel welcome to share concerns they have on child rearing. Such statements can lead to miniworkshops, prepared either by the teacher or a family volunteer, that have genuine significance for their audience, or they can lead to suggestions that families contact other families that have been concerned with similar issues. Any response serves to further intensify home–school partnerships.

Creating Meaningful Teacher–Child Relationships   Perhaps most important of all for helping children to make an effective transition to kindergarten is the nature of kindergarten teachers' relationships with their students. Their interactions with children should be designed to support children's emotional development—listening carefully when children have something to say, responding in a fashion that indicates the child's communicative effort has been taken seriously, guiding children in appropriate ways to conduct themselves with their peers, and letting them know that they are cared for and welcomed in their class. These interactions, beginning with the teacher's earliest contacts with the child during the spring and summer prior to kindergarten entry, should also support and extend children's intellectual development. Kindergarten teachers must pay careful attention to the reactions of their young students whose verbal abilities may not allow them to express frustration with their work. Talk with children in response to their efforts—written, drawn, built, painted, and sculpted—plays a critical role in communicating methods of problem solving, increasing language competence, and demonstrating the teacher's desire to assist and support every kindergarten child.

Equally important as assistance may be insistence. Entwisle and Alexander, in Chapter 2, allude to the critical issue of high teacher expectations. At all times, teachers' interactions with children should be purposeful with the intent to guide, teach, and help students reach beyond what they can presently do.

Ensuring that Assessment Meets the Needs of All Children

If teachers' goals include helping children to reach beyond their current abilities, then determining what a child is now able to do—in playing with peers, in completing tasks, and in terms of literacy—is essential to creating instructional settings. As the value of readiness testing is under question (see Chapters 3 and 5), the logical place for kindergarten teachers to focus their energies is on informal, ongoing assessments that are easily shared with families and children throughout the school year. Table 13.1 displays the ongoing nature of assessment, with kindergarten teachers creating entries as early as the spring prior to the child's arrival in the kindergarten classroom. Teachers, at that time, may use the Rosenkoetter and colleagues' (1994) skill assessment guide discussed in Chapter 9 to begin considering what to stress for families and for themselves during interactions with the child over summer break. The Rosenkoetter et al. list, incidentally, is exactly the type of assessment that teachers should share with their preschool colleagues.

To maintain ongoing assessment entries for their students during the course of hectic school weeks, teachers can create a system for following children. Cunningham (1991) suggested that the class be divided according to the days of the week, so that, for example, every Monday the teacher attends to the behaviors of three particular children in the class.

Starting with their first intensive teacher contact during summer home visits, families can be introduced to assessment portfolios and the notion that assessment influences instruction, if they have not had the opportunity to learn about these during their children's preschool experiences. Teachers, soliciting information from families at that time, can demonstrate that families' input is valued by inserting sheets with interview data into the child's file and discussing the creation of curriculum and instruction to meet those expressed concerns.

Crafting Effective Curriculum and Goals

Controversy swirls around the exact nature of kindergarten curricula. Although few teachers would advocate that kindergarten children should sit at small desks, toiling hour after hour on worksheets, the question of what should be taught in kindergarten remains. Most professionals in early childhood education would tend to agree with Wolery's statement that all children should leave kindergarten more literate, should know more about science and math, should be more socialized to group and cooperative work, and should be more capable at solving social problems and conflicts than when they began their kindergarten years.

Such a statement regarding the outcomes of a kindergarten curriculum recognizes families' concerns that their children "learn something" (e.g., Anderson-Clark, 1996) and respects teacher concerns that learning in kindergarten be accomplished through child-centered, developmentally appropriate approaches (e.g., Rusher, McGriven, & Lambiotte, 1992). Such a statement would also be consonant with current NAEYC positions (see Bredekamp & Rosegrant, 1995) that address content found in national standards, discussed in Chapter 5, by setting these in a developmental perspective.

The actual nature of the curriculum, given the input of families and preschool teachers, realistically ought to vary considerably from year to year. Instruction based on assessment, with careful tailoring of standards-mandated content as suggested by Seefeldt (1995), could recognize what all this year's children have actually come to school "ready to learn," even if what each child were ready to learn differs to some degree. Whatever curriculum goals teachers create based on family, field, and community input need to be shared with families as quickly as possible so that children will find the same expectations at home as at school. This would result in a reduction of stress for kindergarten children and an increase in their likelihood for success.

In sum, kindergarten teachers' roles are quite different from principals' roles. All their efforts are focused on creating the best possible learning environments for the individual children who make up their kindergarten class, whether those efforts entail reaching back in time to preschool teachers, forward in time to first-grade teachers, or out to children and their families before and after kindergarten has begun.

THE ROLE OF PRESCHOOLS IN PROMOTING EFFECTIVE TRANSITIONS

Much of what preschools might do to enhance children's transitions to school has been described in the preceding sections. These suggestions have assumed, however, that the elementary school and its kindergarten teachers have initiated the transition agenda. If that does not happen, what might preschools, less powerful than their public school counterparts yet concerned with effective transitions for their students to the elementary school, do? Because preschool directors are frequently school owners, are often teachers of a class as well as a director, or have relatively small numbers of staff (many of whom have had little formal preparation for their jobs), this section focuses on the preschool director's actions. To create effective transitions, preschool directors can seek community support, guide their staff in supporting strong home–school partnerships, and prepare children and their families for the move to kindergarten.

Seeking Community Support

Arranging a meeting with the principal to which directors of several preschools are invited would communicate that effective transitions are of great concern to those who guide children's earliest schooling experiences. Such a meeting would provide an ideal time to welcome elementary school personnel to administer early developmental screening tests (see Chapter 3). If the elementary school principal remains unresponsive, however, preschool directors can turn to community leaders and/or families for their support in the quest for carefully considered and crafted transitions. Preschool directors who are committed to successful transitions should be prepared to persist even if their initial efforts prove unproductive. Regardless of whether their efforts are successful, directors should next plan to foster successful transitions by working with their staff and with families.

Guiding Staff in Fostering Families' Involvement

As preschool staff are often members of the children's community, they have frequently interacted with families long before their children enroll in the institution. Then, too, families are generally more visible and accessible in preschool settings. They escort their small child to a classroom door, exchanging a few words with the teacher and/or the assistant, or they chat with a Head Start bus driver as their child leaves for school. In such ways, preschools and their staff tend to be more aware of the concerns of families than their elementary school counterparts. In many ways, this makes family–school partnerships a much less daunting agenda item for preschools, but school-related links that serve families and their children remain extremely important. Directors who understand the role their institution plays in socializing families into relationships with schools will want to ensure that they and their staff are actively fostering family-school links.

Although receiving relatively little attention, a strong place to begin family programs and staff development is with the assessment of children's progress (e.g., Bagley, 1995; Nevada State Department of Human Resources, Early Childhood Services, 1997; Williams & Lundsteen, 1997). All families want their children to do well in school, but most have no operationalized definition of what "doing well" might mean. Preschool programs that, early in the year, present the curriculum-embedded performance assessments advocated by Meisels in Chapter 3, in terms and concepts that preschool teachers and children's families can comfortably understand and use, enable families to discern what their children are working toward in preschool. Early involvement in their children's assessment ultimately helps families become better informed consumers of assessments gauging their children's success in elementary school.

Determining what performance-based information the elementary school's kindergarten teachers would like before children begin fall kindergarten classes can guide preschool assessment to a degree that engenders more successful transitions but should not necessarily constitute the entire assessment focus in the preschool. Good preschools generally have established their own objectives, and conveying to families how these objectives have been achieved compels directors, teachers, and even families to contemplate what constitutes success. Certainly, the characteristics of effective learners noted in Chapters 3 and 10—confidence, curiosity, intentionality, self-control, relatedness, capacity to communicate, and co-operativeness—merit being operationalized every year by families, teachers, and the director of the preschool. Including assessments in children's kindergarten-bound portfolios that value the home-generated knowledge of minority communities' children (see Chapter 10) may eventually heighten kindergarten teachers' awareness of what their incoming students actually *can* do.

To support families' understanding of assessment, preschool staff will need assistance. They, too, need guidance in observing their students' progress; tools such as anecdotal records and family/school-generated checklists will serve them well as they assess and plan for children's learning environments. They, as well as families, must understand that development follows different paths for different children.

In their work in Texas, Williams and Lundsteen (1997) found that parents involved in assessing their children's progress through a home literacy portfolio not only increased their awareness of literacy development but also found the portfolio a useful support for discussions with their children's teachers. Families who have watched for signs of a child's developing ability are more likely to make suggestions to teachers and/or the director about curricular activities. This likelihood increases when families understand, as Dodge and Phinney (1990) stressed in their parents' guide, that successful learning experiences occur when adults have attended to children's interests (whether these interests are dinosaurs in the virtual world of movies or the tools their grandfather uses in his garden) and created situations in which children can further explore and learn about their interests.

As they look for their own children's interests to contribute to the preschool curriculum, families are likely to recognize that there is some aspect of their children's learning or their own parenting that they would like to know more about. They can mention these issues as the basis for future preschool programs; directors and teachers can encourage them to continue this type of input once their children are in kindergarten.

Preparing Families and Their Children for the Transition to Kindergarten

An important form of assistance that preschools can offer families and their children is insight into the ways that elementary school differs from preschool. Directors can afford families insight into kindergarten through several channels. Perhaps the most useful way is to have a family member of a current kindergartner and a current first grader speak to the preschool families on a regular basis throughout the school year. This not only informs them of the differences but also serves to establish a local family–school "advisor" and family networking as well (e.g., Thompson et al., 1997). Another possibility is to invite a kindergarten teacher or the principal from the local elementary school to speak with the families. The director might also arrange family visits to the elementary school for open house events or daytime visits.

Assistance to children would entail basically the same formats. Directors could arrange small-group visits to kindergarten classrooms, or they could ask one of their graduates, now a kindergartner, to accompany his or her classroom teacher on a visit to the preschool. They may also have teachers set up learning centers similar to those found in the kindergarten so that children will have a familiar task when they arrive in their new schools. Whether working with children, families, or staff, directors can stress the preschool's willingness to listen should any problems occur during the child's transition to kindergarten (e.g., Helms, 1997).

Preschool directors, in summary, can reach forward in time, connecting with the elementary school to create greater congruence between institutions. They can reach out to their communities to support them in their efforts. They can welcome the families of their students, encouraging all staff members to take the time to be attentive listeners as families and children communicate their needs and concerns. They can equip families with an understanding of children's development and how it is measured, and they can pave the way for successful transitions by enabling both families and children to anticipate the changes in their lives.

THE ROLE OF FAMILIES IN PROMOTING EFFECTIVE TRANSITIONS

Of all players on the transition field, it is almost always the family that has the fewest resources to enable successful transitions for their children. If their children have not been attending a preschool, if they are new to a neighborhood, or if their elementary school has not instituted a reaching out policy or spring registration for kindergartners, how, then, can they support their beginning kindergartner?

This is a difficult and troublesome question to answer. Lesko et al. (1998) revealed that a concerted, well-funded government effort aimed at reducing the numbers of sudden infant death syndrome (SIDS) deaths in infants failed to meet its goal. The goal was to have 90% of the families put their infants to sleep in a supine position (on their backs). The particularly bad news was that 43% of African American and Hispanic families put their children to sleep on their stomachs at 3 months of age, the time when the risk of SIDS is greatest, despite the government's campaign and their being enrolled in a study investigating infant care practices. In short, a strongly supported effort to change one family practice—the position in which infants are put to sleep—was least successful for the very population (i.e., African American) in which the greatest numbers of SIDS-related deaths occur. If it is this difficult to change one simple physical practice, despite the counsel of medical professionals and the pamphlets distributed to their patients, then how successful will be random admonishments by neighbors to families to participate in their children's transition to kindergarten? How likely is it that families who currently believe that schools are responsible for children's education will take the initiative to advocate for effective transition practices? The simple, sad answer is that families that are not cocooned in the coordinated transition efforts of elementary school principals, preschool directors, and kindergarten and preschool teachers are extraordinarily unlikely to effect positive transitions on their own.

This realization makes it absolutely imperative for those concerned with preschoolers' successful transition to kindergarten to continue their research, advocacy, and funding efforts. The following statement was made by a transition director at the Head Start where the author is currently involved in an early literacy research effort:

> What a disappointing day! The kindergarten teacher's comments about what "those parents" need to understand seemed so inflexible. And Consuela says the plans for the Head Start's first summer-before-kindergarten session have fallen through. Their grant didn't materialize. She says, though, that the transition director has already begun working on securing funds for next year. (Field notes, L. Smolkin, May 24, 1998)

Successful transitions are critical. Researchers and teachers must recognize the difficulty of transforming long-term, ineffectual habits and actions. The successful practices of the key players on the transition field must continue to be fostered so that they can become a true Cinderella story, a winning support team for America's young children.

REFERENCES

Allen, L.L. (1997). Food for thought. Do you resent and stonewall parents?—Matthew's line. *Young Children, 52*(4), 72–74.

Anderson-Clark, J. (1996). *The development and implementation of a developmentally appropriate curriculum that meets the expectations of African American parents.* Master's practicum, Nova Southeastern University, Fort Lauderdale, FL. (Eric Document Reproduction Service No. ED 404 383)

Ascher, C. (1987). *Improving the school-home connection for poor and minority urban students* (ERIC/CUE Trends and Issues Series, Number 8). (Eric Document Reproduction Service No. ED 300 484)

Bagley, D.M. (1995). Supporting families during the transition into kindergarten. *Day Care and Early Education, 22,* 24–27.

Balm, S. (1995). Using portfolio assessment in a kindergarten classroom. *Teaching and Change, 2,* 141–151.

Bredekamp, S., & Copple, C. (Eds.). (1997). *Developmentally appropriate practice in early childhood programs* (Rev. ed.). Washington, DC: National Association for the Education of Young Children.

Bredekamp, S., & Rosegrant, T. (Eds.). (1995). *Reaching potentials: Transforming early childhood curriculum and assessment* (Vol. 2). Washington, DC: National Association for the Education of Young Children.

Burchby, M. (1992). Food for thought: A kindergarten teacher speaks to the governors: A story of effective advocacy. *Young Children, 47,* 40–43.

Chavkin, N.F., & Gonzalez, D.L. (1995). *Forging partnerships between Mexican American parents and the schools.* Charleston, WV: ERIC Clearinghouse on Rural Education and Small Schools. (Eric Document Reproduction Service No. ED 388 489)

Comer, J.P., Haynes, N.M., Joyner, E.T., & Ben-Avie, M. (Eds.) (1996). *Rallying the whole village: The Comer process for reforming education.* New York: Teachers College Press.

Crow, G.M. (1990). Perceived career incentives of suburban elementary school principals. *Journal of Educational Administration, 28*(1), 38–52.

Crow, G.M. (1992). Career history and orientation to work: The case of the elementary school principal. *Journal of Research and Development in Education, 25*(2), 82–88.

Cunningham, P.M. (1991). Non-ability grouped, multilevel instruction: A year in a first-grade classroom. *Reading Teacher, 44*, 566–571.

Dauber, S.L., & Epstein, J.L. (1993). Parents' attitudes and practices of involvement in inner-city elementary and middle schools. In N.F. Chavkin (Ed.), *Families and schools in a pluralistic society.* Albany: State University of New York Press.

Dodge, D.T., & Phinney, J. (1990). *A parent's guide to early childhood education.* Washington, DC: Teaching Strategies, Inc.

Dryfoos, J.G. (1994). *Full service schools: A revolution in health and social services for children, youth, and families.* San Francisco: Jossey-Bass.

Entwisle, D., & Alexander, K.L. (1998). Facilitating the transition to first grade: The nature of transition and research on factors affecting it. *The Elementary School Journal, 98*, 351–364

Epstein, J.L. (1992). *School and family partnerships.* (Report No. 6). Baltimore: Johns Hopkins University, Center on Families, Communities, Schools and Children's Learning. (Eric Document Reproduction Service No. ED 343 715)

Epstein, J.L. (1995). School/family/community partnerships: Caring for children we share. *Phi Delta Kappan, 76*(9), 701–712.

Epstein, J.L., & Connors, L. (1992). School and family partnerships. *Practitioners, 18*(4), 22–55.

Epstein, J.L., & Dauber, S.L. (1989). *Teacher attitudes and practices of parent involvement in inner city elementary and middle schools. Report No. 32.* (Grant No. OERI-G-90006.) Baltimore, MD: Center for Research on Elementary and Middle Schools.

Ferguson, P., & Streib, M.M. (1996). Longitudinal outcome effects of non-at-risk and at-risk first grade samples: A follow-up study and further analysis. *Psychology in the Schools, 33*, 38–45.

Findley, D., & Findley, B. (1992). Effective schools: The role of the principal. *Contemporary Education, 63*(2), 102–104.

Fusaro, J.A. (1997). The effect of full-day kindergarten on student achievement: A meta-analysis. *Child Study Journal, 27*, 269–277

Fusaro, J.A., & Royce, C.A. (1995). A reanalysis of research data. *Perceptual and Motor Skills, 81*, 858.

Gullo, D.F., & Burton, C.B. (1993). The effects of social class, class size and prekindergarten experience on early school adjustment. *Early Child Development and Care, 88*, 43–51.

Harvey, B.H. (1994). *The effect of class size on achievement and retention in the primary grades: Implications for policy makers.* Paper presented at the Annual Meeting of the North Carolina Association for Research in Education. (Greensboro, NC, March 1994).

Helms, J.H. (1997). Easing the way to kindergarten. *Scholastic Early Childhood Today, 11*, 11.

Hiebert, E.H., & Raphael, T.E. (1998). *Early literacy instruction.* San Diego: Harcourt Brace & Co.

Hoffman, J.V. (1991). Teacher and school effects in learning to read. In R. Barr, M. Kamil, P. Mosenthal, & P.D. Pearson (Eds.), *Handbook of reading research* (pp. 911–950). New York: Longman.

Holden, C. (1996). Equally informed? Ethnic minority parents, schools and assessment. *Multicultural Teaching, 14*(3), 16–20.

Katz, L.G. (1995). *Talks with teachers of young children: A collection.* Norwood, NJ: Ablex.

Katz, L.G., Aidman, A., Reese, D.A., & Clark, A.M. (1996). *Preventing and resolving parent-teacher differences.* Washington, DC: Office of Educational Research and Improvement. (Eric Document Reproduction Service No. ED401048)

Lesko, S.M., Corwin, M.J., Vezina, R.M., Hunt, C.E., Mandell, F., McClain, M., Heeren, R., & Mitchell, A.A. (1998). Changes in sleep position during infancy. *Journal of the American Medical Association, 280*, 336–340.

MacPhee, D., Fritz, J., & Miller-Heyl, J. (1996). Ethnic variations in personal social networks and parenting. *Child Development, 67*, 3278–3295.

Neuman, S.B. (1996). Children engaging in storybook reading: The influence of access to print resources, opportunity, and parental interaction. *Early Childhood Research Quarterly, 11*, 495–513.

Nevada State Department of Human Resources, Early Childhood Services. (1997). *HAPPY Rural Outreach Project.* (Final Report). Reno: Author. (Eric Document Reproduction Service No. ED 412 666)

Nicolau, S., & Ramos, C.L. (1993). *Together is better: Building strong relationships between schools and Hispanic parents.* New York: Hispanic Policy Development Project, Inc. (Eric Document Reproduction Service No. ED 325 543)

Ortner, M.L. (1994). *An alternative approach to increase parent involvement among culturally diverse families.* Ed.D. practicum, Fort Lauderdale, FL. (Eric Document Reproduction Service No. ED 374 195)

Papierz, J.M., Hiebert, E.H., & DiStefano, D.D. (1990, December). *Literacy experiences of preschool children.* Paper presented at the annual meeting of the National Reading Conference, Miami.

Purkey, S.C., & Smith, M.S. (1983). Effective schools: A review. *The Elementary School Journal, 83*, 427–452.

Reutzel, D.R., & Fawson, P.C. (1990). Traveling tales: Connecting parents and children through writing. *Reading Teacher, 44*, 222–227.

Reynolds, B. (1998). To teach or not to teach reading in the preschool. . . . That is the question. In R. Campbell (Ed.), *Facilitating preschoool literacy* (pp. 155–168). Newark, DE: International Reading Association.

Rosenkoetter, S.E., Hains, A.H., & Fowler, S.A. (1994). *Bridging early services for children with special needs and their families: A practical guide for transition planning.* Baltimore: Paul H. Brookes Publishing Co.

Rusher, A.S., McGriven, C.Z., & Lambiotte, J.G. (1992). Belief systems of early childhood teachers and their principals regarding early childhood education. *Early Childhood Research Quarterly, 7*(2), 277–296.

Seefeldt, C. (1995). Ready to learn! But what? *Contemporary Education, 66*(3), 134–138.

Simich-Dudgeon, C. (1986). *Parent involvement and the education of limited English proficient students.* Washington, DC: ERIC Clearinghouse on Languages and Linguistics. (ERIC Document Reproduction Service No. ED 279 205)

Slavin, R.E., Karweit, N.L., & Wasik, B.A. (1992–1993). Preventing early school failure: What works? *Educational Leadership, 50*(4), 10–18.

Smith, T., Rogers, G., Alsalam, N., Perie, M., Mahoney, R., & Martin, V. (1994). *The condition of education, 1994.* Washington, DC: National Center for Educational Statistics. (Eric Document Reproduction Service No. ED 371 491)

Thompson, L., Lobb, C., Elling, R., Herman, S., Jurkiewicz, T., & Hulleza, C. (1997). Pathways to family empowerment: Effects of family-centered delivery of early intervention services. *Exceptional Children, 64*, 99–113.

Trivette, C.M., & Dunst, C.J. (1997). *Family perceptions of barriers and supports in early elementary schools.* (Unpublished progress report, Grant No. H024Q50001). Asheville, NC: Orleana Hawks Pucket Institute.

Wang, Y.L., & Johnstone, W. (1997). *Evaluation of pre-first grade.* Paper presented at the annual meeting of the American Educational Research Association, Chicago.

Williams, D.L., Jr., & Chavkin, N.F. (1986). Strengthening parent involvement. *Streamlined Seminar, 4*(5), 1–6.

Williams, D.L., Jr., & Chavkin, N.F. (1989). Essential elements of strong parent involvement programs. *Educational Leadership, 47*(2), 18–20.

Williams, P., & Lundsteen, S.W. (1997). *Home literacy portfolios: Cooperative tools for assessing parents' involvement in their prekindergarten child's literacy development.* Paper presented at the annual meeting of the American Educational Research Association, Chicago.

Chapter 14

Policy and the Transition Process

James J. Gallagher

The transition to kindergarten involves a range of local, state, and federal rules and regulations, or policies, that create a foundation for the contexts and practices that children, families, and teachers experience as each cohort of 5-year-olds enters elementary school for the first time. These policies range from those that affect class size and teacher credentialing to those that determine the age of children at entry to kindergarten, whether retention in kindergarten is a desired outcome for children, whether screening tests are used for placement decisions, or how and when class lists are generated. Many more policies could be added to this list and debates concerning them (e.g., class size, readiness assessment, retention) seem to never go away (for examples of these debates, see Chapters 3 & 5).

Almost all the chapters in this book generate a list of policy-related topics and concerns. For example, in discussing the relationship between families and schools, various chapters touch on pre- and in-service teacher training (Should teachers be required to receive training on how to interact with families?), administrative functions (Can class lists be generated early enough so that teachers and families could have contact prior to kindergarten? Can schools be open in the summer?), the utility and effectiveness of the range of transition practices (open houses, communications about expectations) that typically occur in schools, and how assessment and curriculum function with respect to facilitating connections with families (see, e.g., Chapters 6 & 7).

Thus, Chapters 2–10 raise important policy-related issues that in turn relate to other facets of the transition process. Policies related to fostering relationships with families are affected by assessment and placement policies, and vice versa. In this way, analysis of policies related to kindergarten transition must attempt to focus at a macro level and, without becoming too fixed on one or another policy, attempt to generate a set of principles by which policy can be set and evaluated.

In this chapter, the goal is to identify a set of practices and principles by which policy related to kindergarten transition can be examined. In the following sections, policy and rules for examining policy are defined, specific issues related to the transition to kindergarten that have policy implications are discussed, and finally, a set of principles for the analysis of policy related to kindergarten transition is advanced.

DEFINING AND ANALYZING POLICY

Establishing a working definition of social policy can provide the springboard for meaningful analysis. Gallagher provides the following definition:

> [Social policy comprises] the rules and standards by which scarce resources are allocated to meet almost unlimited needs. Policies should state the following: 1) Who receives the resources? 2) Who delivers the resources? 3) What resources are to be delivered? 4) What are the conditions under which the resources are delivered? (1994, p. 337)

These questions, properly answered, deal with the eligibility for resources, who the resource deliverer should be (and their qualifications), the nature of the resources to be delivered, and the setting in which resources are delivered. According to this definition, policy serves as a means of directing decision making and actions pertaining to a particular issue. In the case of the transition to kindergarten, policies concerning age of entry, for example, are directly influenced by the answers to these questions. The movement of public schools to offer educational services and programs for 4-year-olds indicates a shift in policy concerning the age at which public education resources can be delivered to children. Staffing, hours, location, and curricular decisions regarding these programs for 4-year-olds are a set of associated policy matters as well. Thus, in using this definition of social policy and the related questions, the public and its representatives on decision-making bodies create a blueprint for actions.

In this example, one role of public policy has been to clearly state the expectations of the society to those most involved with the issue at hand. Rules derived from policy on what the education of a day care director should be, for example, communicate expectations for that position and role. Similarly, rules that stress accountability emphasize the importance of collecting valid information on the outcomes of various services or programs. But policy also functions to provide society with information about itself, its decision makers, and its priorities.

In this way, policy serves a feedback function in society. Whether considering the licensing of barbers, the certification of teachers, or the standards for the practicing lawyer, the rules reveal a great deal about what society expects of individuals in certain professional positions. So public policy is a mirror in which expectations are reflected (Basharov, 1996; Gallagher, 1994; Gormley, 1997). Analysis of policy related to the transition to kindergarten communicates beliefs on the importance of families in schools (see Chapter 6), priorities for child development (see Chapters 3 & 5; Kagan & Cohen, 1997), the role of communities in relation to schools (see Chapter 7), and how the social structure is reflected in schools (see Chapters 2 & 10).

Having defined policy, it becomes possible to begin examining and analyzing policies. In the case of kindergarten transition, researchers are interested in the proposition that changing the rules and standards by which transition policy is carried out will change and improve the situation for the new entrant into kindergarten. Such rules need to be clear on the use of resources and who delivers them and receives them. However, in order to examine policy, it is important to determine and define essential key policy issues, such as transition.

Consistent with the definitions offered for the transition to kindergarten by the contributors to this book (e.g., Chapter 9), the transition process can be defined as having three major components: the child, the kindergarten itself with its social environment and activities, and the match between child and institution (kindergarten). This definition, however simple it may seem, allows for discussion of policy in a less abstract fashion—it contextualizes the analysis of policy. Given this definition, the basic purpose of transition policies can be stated as follows: Transition policies should enhance or create opportunities whereby a child can view the transition to kindergarten as a warm and exciting adventure. A child's transition to kindergarten should be a reassuring experience for parents and should allow the teacher to teach important knowledge and skills. This statement regarding the purposes of policies related to the transition to kindergarten serves as a means of analyzing and making policy.

For example, when considering policies related to screening assessments or class size, the previous statement provides a framework for the ensuing discussions. How does screening enhance or create opportunity for children? How does current practice related to transition (e.g., schools closed in summer, group orientations in the first week of school, numerous flyers and written communication) offer a reassuring experience for parents? How do class size and placement policies related to gender, ability, and so on affect the extent to which a teacher can facilitate the developing child's skills? At which level of public discourse and regulation (local, state, federal) are these policies and analyses best located?

In moving past these broad statements of the goals of policies related to kindergarten transition, it is important to recognize that policy making and analysis related to transition are intimately tied to the state of knowledge regarding transition. There has often been a serious gap between professional knowledge and public policy (Heclo, 1996), and one of the purposes of this volume is to narrow that gap and to bring policies more in line with what is known about children and the institutions that serve them. Identifying how particular issues related to the state of knowledge on the transition to kindergarten affect policy analysis is critical in order to generate creative and effective policy.

POLICY ANALYSIS AND ISSUES
RELATED TO THE TRANSITION TO KINDERGARTEN

The chapters in this book each describe the state of knowledge, and specifically, the gap in knowledge regarding a particular aspect of the transition to kindergarten (see Chapter 15). Consequently, it is evident that making and analyzing policy hinges on the existing state of knowledge. Although numerous knowledge gaps exist, four are focused on here: conceptualizing and measuring readiness, the role of families in transition, the lack of research on kindergarten transition, and the limitations of policy.

Conceptualizing Readiness

There are many anecdotal reports and other evidence of the failure of numerous children to make a smooth adjustment during the transition from prekindergarten to kindergarten. Some of these children may have spent 2–3 years in early child care settings, whereas others are experiencing this complex social transition for the first time. The National Household Education Survey showed that 5% of first and second graders in 1995 and 6% in 1993 had to repeat kindergarten or attend a transition class before first grade. These proportions projected to almost 383,000 children who had repeated kindergarten in 1995 (see Chapter 4). Thus, there are critical concerns regarding individual and group differences in children as they enter school, how to best conceptualize and understand those differences, and what, if anything, can and should be done about them (see Chapters 2, 3, & 8).

For example, some children come from economically advantaged homes where the parents have made major efforts to prepare their child for this initiation into formal schooling. Other parents, more economically limited, may not have had the opportunity to provide their children with such preparation so that these children from low-income families enter at a genuine disadvantage in language development, social skills, and cooperative work habits (Scarr, 1998). How these differences among children (and families) are understood has a significant impact on policies pertaining to readiness for school and whether readiness can be assessed and influenced. This knowledge gap influences attempts to close the readiness gap through providing programs for high-risk 4-year-olds as well as policies related to associated assessment and eligibility mechanisms.

Ramey and Ramey (Chapter 8) make an explicit statement regarding how to understand individual and group differences in children as they enter school which they call the principle of codetermination. This principle states that "a child's developmental progress is codetermined by many factors, ranging from genetic and biological influences to family-, peer-, and neighborhood-level influences" (page 248). Similarly, Entwisle and Alexander (Chapter 2) note that schools are not the problem. Instead, they suggest that it is the distribution of resources across families and neighborhoods which is the problem, and that problems in families and neighborhoods cannot be solved by simply changing schools.

These points, consistent with Meisels' view of readiness, suggest that the state of knowledge concerning child development is such that any product of development (e.g., performance in school) must be viewed not solely as a consequence of the developmental level of the child but as a result of complex interactions involving many different settings and environments (Gomby, Larner, Stevenson, Lewitt, & Behrman, 1995). Consistent with this formulation, policies related to describing and assessing readiness (and, similarly, school entry and eligibility for services) should prescribe practices that are contextually sensitive.

There has been an enormous effort to develop policies that would aid in creating a level playing field for the children entering kindergarten. One of the oft-stated goals of national education policy is that all children shall be ready to learn when they enter kindergarten (National Education Goals Panel, 1995). Because many children appear not ready due to factors in the family, the neighborhood, and the society, the social policy indicates that there must be some investment of resources devoted to assuring that goal. The question then becomes what level of investment and for what purpose?

Measurement Tools

Any effort to close the knowledge gap concerning issues in the transition to kindergarten is faced with problems measuring the phenomenon of concern. This extends to measuring readiness, measuring relationships between families and schools, and measuring the quality of the kindergarten environment. Unless, and until, well-accepted measurement tools are devised for these tasks, policy will be made based on a flawed knowledge base.

There is enough evidence about the limitations of measuring instruments at this age (younger than 6 years) to cause concern about meaningful assessment of young children. There have been efforts to develop more effective tools that could inform the kindergarten staff in advance that there were some students arriving with inadequate skills and knowledge (Meisels, Liaw, Dorfman, & Nelson, 1995). Yet, despite some progress in being able to adequately measure child readiness, some vexing problems remain, such as determining whether the child should necessarily be ready for school, or whether the school should be ready for the child (see Chapter 3). These questions clearly suggest that, if a view of readiness as both a function of the child's competencies and opportunities available to the child in school (or at home) is adopted, then a parallel effort should be made to design and conduct assessments of these contexts and the opportunities afforded for child development in them. The current state of knowledge concerning the quality of kindergarten contexts is extremely limited, in part because of the absence of adequate assessment tools.

Most important, even if the quality of classroom contexts could be assessed, there would still be the difficulty of deciding what child outcomes should be a function of experiences in those contexts (see Chapter 5). To improve outcomes for children in kindergarten, there needs to be some reliable way to identify children who are likely to struggle in making an easy transition from preschool to school and environments that may contribute to that struggle. However, at the level of policy making and analysis, more pleasure seems to be taken in complaining about the limitations of existing diagnostic or classification instruments than in following up such discussions with a commitment to invest resources in the construction of more adequate instruments. Thus, the lack of such instrumentation reflects a lack of policy in directing resources to develop such instruments. It seldom seems to occur to policy makers or professionals that the building of a good diagnostic instrument takes years, even given a major commitment of resources from some funding source. If such a commitment is not made, it seems likely that future generations of professionals can make the same disappointed noises when the available instruments are inadequate for what they require.

The Role of Families in Transition

In the available knowledge base there is general agreement on two important points. First, families are often the key to helping children adjust to the school environment (Hayes & Bon-Avie, 1996). Second, the schools have not always done a good job in cultivating and gaining cooperation from parents (Harry, 1992). The policy-making implications of these points are numerous and wide-ranging. For example, Christenson (Chapter 6) describes how families often have the power to transform institutions as they are brought into power and responsibility-sharing arrangements, as has happened in the early intervention field. She suggests that schools often have difficulty with discussions of power and responsibility and often promote policies and practices that, in the name of increasing parent involvement, actually diminish parental responsibility and power within the school. Christenson's analysis of the family–school relationship immediately changes the basis on which schools' policies related to families must be considered.

Melton and colleagues (Chapter 7), with years of experience working to implement policies facilitating and empowering families, rely on a simple philosophy regarding these policies: *"Families should be able to get help where they are, when they need it, and in a form that they can use with ease and without stigma"* (p. 196).

How would this idea reshape discussions of policy related to kindergarten transition? Presumably, it might influence discussions of how and where community-based resources are located; for example, it might lead to policies supporting full-service schools or schools in which a holistic approach to family development shapes the nature and form of resources available (e.g., day care, job training). In the context of these types of schools, the transition to kindergarten takes on new meaning and form, as families often have numerous contacts with the school and school personnel long before their child enters school.

In short, how do policies help create a "family-friendly" atmosphere in the schools? Many parents who have been quite satisfied with their child's adjustment to child care or other preschool experiences become quite nervous as their child faces his or her first contact with the public schools. In particular, parents of students who have been receiving some special programming, such as Head Start or programs for children with disabilities, worry that such individualized attention will no longer be given to their child in kindergarten (Bailey, Buysse, Smith, & Elam, 1992). If the next experience for their child is vastly different from their previous treatment, then there are good reasons for such parents to dread the "first day of school." There are a number of reasons to look further into possible "parent empowerment" measures so that the parents may not, individually or collectively, feel so helpless in the face of huge and apparently implacable institutions (Hayes & Comer, 1996).

Interestingly, there is evidence that even when policies direct specific actions linking parents with schools, including mandating parental influence, responsibility, and power sharing, the outcomes of such policies do not approximate their intent to foster collaboration and mutuality. According to Wolery (with regard to children with disabilities),

> Despite available processes and procedures, parents do not appear to be integral parts of the IEP process. Second, parents . . . do not perceive being in a positive partnership with the schools. . . . Understanding how to promote adoption of different practices and identifying how to initiate and sustain positive family–school relationships are clearly research priorities. (Chapter 9, p. 275)

Discussions of the relationship between families and schools are really part of a larger focus on schools and the communities they serve. From one perspective, part of the failure of many children to adapt to kindergarten could be ascribed to the fact that the school environment waiting for them has yet to respond to the needs of the community (see Chapter 10). Melton and colleagues (Chapter 7) suggest that if the schools do not respond to the cultures of the communities within which they are situated, that children will continue to suffer.

Thus, policy analysis and policy making are complicated by familial, cultural, and economic forces that shape the transition process and transition outcomes. Unfortunately, little is known about these forces as the knowledge base on transition has been largely derived from studies that have failed to adequately measure or sample family and community factors.

The ecological forces at work on the child and the institution mean that possible causes for poor transition need to be explored far beyond the characteristics of the single child in question. The model designed by Bronfenbrenner (1989), which shows interaction among child, family, neighborhood, and society, is being increasingly referred to as holding the secret to the causes of transition failure. Some of the possible solutions may go beyond offering some remedial training to offering instead wraparound (comprehensive, multidisciplinary) community and school services. In fact, according to Christenson (Chapter 6), successful family–school partnerships require significant, meaningful parent involvement; culturally sensitive and responsive schools; and comprehensive school-linked services.

Lack of Research on Kindergarten Transition

The period of transition to school has largely been ignored by researchers in education. Although specific research needs are discussed in Chapter 11, it is important to note that policy making is very dependent on the available knowledge base; therefore, limitations present in research are also constraints on the making of good policy.

Thus, policy related to the transition process is often made on the basis of data available from elementary school research or from the preschool years. In fact, Pianta, Rimm-Kaufman, and Cox (Chapter 1) argue that the absence of research on kindergarten transition has in part been related to the absence of a model with which to conceptualize the transition process. In addition, Ramey and Ramey (Chapter 8) point out that even in the studies of children making the transition to school, there are numerous flaws that prevent solid policy making. One of these is the reliance of such studies on small and special samples. As is the case with the absence of measuring instruments, there is also an absence of solid research that applies directly to the transition issue or of knowledge that could be derived from related research. Perhaps this reflects some bias by researchers in their choice of topics to pursue. Thus, even if researchers are given their choice of what projects or questions they want to pursue, it is not likely that transition would be an early choice. Transition may be a practical matter of concern to the schools but not necessarily to the research community. Yet, if the schools want to discover more about the issue, then some form of a request for proposal would need to be designed and funded that would ask investigators to bid on projects relevant to the issue that the schools want to be investigated.

The Limitations of Policy

It should be clear that the establishment of rules and standards about certain expected behaviors can be a positive step toward reaching such standards. However, policies only provide opportunities for success; they cannot, in themselves, guarantee success. For example, a limit to class size can be established in kindergarten to keep the class at a manageable level, for example, 10 children per adult per classroom. By establishing such a standard, the opportunity is provided for staff to interact more frequently and effectively with the children, to establish one-to-one relationships with them, and to cope more adequately with the range of individual differences that inevitably appear in most kindergartens. But the policies themselves cannot guarantee that these desirable interactions will occur. A poorly conducted kindergarten can always be found, even with the most desirable class size.

. Similarly, standards can be established for personnel preparation that will create a favorable set of conditions for educating children. Although such personnel standards increase the probability of obtaining well-prepared staff, they do not guarantee that, in each and every case, the personnel will be outstanding, exceptional, or even totally qualified.

Therefore, establishing policy for early childhood is a necessary step in the process of building a quality program but cannot be considered the total process. Policy can set the stage for adequate physical facilities, appropriate curriculum material, and quality personnel preparation programs, but in the end the teacher must teach, and teach well, if the kindergarten is to work. Policies, unsupported by professional action or implementation, cannot guarantee that that will happen.

SEVEN PRINCIPLES FOR POLICY MAKING AND ANALYSIS IN THE TRANSITION TO KINDERGARTEN

The issues noted previously shape the form and nature of many discussions concerning policy. Rather than simply prescribing specific policy regarding the transition to kindergarten here, it is perhaps more constructive to provide recommendations for how these policies should be made and analyzed. This is a different focus than recommending certain practices and requires attention to a broader and more abstract set of concerns and issues. In that context, the following seven principles can be used to guide policy making and analysis at local, state, and federal levels.

1. *Policies for young children should be universal.* Although policies typically direct specialized resources toward children with special needs or limited economic conditions, there is strong sentiment for accepting the universal need of children for assistance (e.g., transition services) and agreement that such services should be available to all children as they are now available to subsets of children with special needs. Thus, policies related to the transition to kindergarten should mandate resources that enable practices to be available to the entire population of children and families.

2. *Policies should enhance both equity and excellence.* Resources should be allocated to ensure equal opportunity for all children to develop to the maximum of their potential and, at the same time, should recognize the range of individual differences present in the current population, allowing those with special abilities and talents to flourish as well. The policies should provide a floor for all children without placing a ceiling on possible development. Thus, minimal competency policies or standards on their own are inadequate because they only ensure equity. Such efforts to define minimal competencies for kindergarten entry or promotion to first grade must also be linked with policies that encourage, and perhaps mandate, practices that also extend the range of expectation and opportunity upward.

3. *Accept the proposition that differential resources will be required for differential needs.* This principle refers to the great imbalance in the allocation of educational

and other resources in most states, with some school districts having greater resources and others having limited or none. It would be possible to provide additional subsidies for districts that fell below a certain standard or to provide extra technical assistance for such economically disadvantaged districts, to ensure that their children would reach a particular level of proficiency. Thus, policies related to funding mechanisms and levels must provide the means to direct disproportionate resources to those constituencies experiencing the greatest challenges.

4. *Need for monitoring instruments.* Resources should be allocated for the construction of better measuring instruments for child progress, for program evaluation, and to assess community involvement. One of the essential limitations of existing programs has been the inability to carefully monitor the child and family outcomes with instruments that are both valid and reliable. The construction of such instruments requires intensive and long-term attention, and substantial resources are needed for their creation. It is important that agencies with responsibilities in early childhood recognize this as a need and allocate resources over a multiyear period to professionals interested in the construction of such instruments.

5. *Demonstration of effective practices.* These policies would represent an active effort on the part of supporting agencies to encourage a variety of methods for improving prekindergarten and kindergarten environments as an aid to easing the transition process. Examples of such demonstration would be making full use of community resources, adapting kindergarten programs to children who are developmentally slow or children with disabilities, effectively coordinating existing community resources, designing summer programs for children from low-income families, or recasting the school calendar to prevent the manifest summer losses suffered by young children.

   Such demonstrations can illustrate to a broader constituency some of the possible innovations that could be productively adapted to their own communities. The basic principle here is not to tell local communities specifically what to do, accompanied by restrictive rules and standards, but to provide resources that would allow for creative and innovative local actions, based on local conditions and values, that otherwise could not be supported because of resource limitations.

6. *Support long-term research on effective practices, on community influences, and on promising innovations.* This basically recognizes the significance of following children developmentally during the early years to establish the influence and impact of resources and other factors, over time, and to establish which variables predict more effective development and which do not. Policies regarding young children and their education often focus too narrowly with respect to time. Policy making and analysis must take a long-term view of the child and his or her education.

7. *Minimal competency standards should be phased or layered, recognizing individual differences.* A great deal of policy making at the local, state, and federal levels regarding education has concerned the development and implementation of standards for minimal competencies. The importance of layered standards was stressed in recognition of the enormous range of individual differences in any age cohort so that some children will be able to reach a basic standard,

whereas others can reach an advanced level of proficiency on whatever the particular standard deals with. Setting a single standard (e.g., mastering reading skills) ignores the enormous range of aptitude and experience among children and would inevitably harm students who did not meet the standard. However, if the standards are to mean anything at all, they must show expectation for an increase in performance on the part of many or all students, but on a performance ladder that allows for individual graduated progress.

WHO IS RESPONSIBLE?

In the end, discussions of policy often rest on identifying the person, agency, or unit responsible for ensuring that certain rules and regulations are stated and enforced. The seven principles of policy making just discussed encompass activities across the range of governmental levels from local to state to federal. For example, the federal government has been the clear sponsor for organized research activities. States have been central in setting up personnel standards and technical assistance for local programs and have an important policy role to play here. The local governmental level seems to be the point at which collaboration across agencies and interests can most easily be implemented, which implies a policy role.

What seems clearly indicated from what is now known about early childhood policy, as well as about policy related to kindergarten transition, is that although an integrated system of early childhood policies and associated services is needed, only isolated, individual policies and services currently exist. Policies on class size are made without considering curricular issues, and policies regarding how best to engage families are made without considering policies that influence the personnel with whom these families interact. None of these integrations are reflected in research priorities.

A more integrated policy approach, encompassing a blending of research, demonstration, development, personnel preparation, technical assistance, and communication networks, can bring quality to a field in clear need of it. Transition to kindergarten is merely one example of the lack of infrastructure, organizational planning, and systems operations in the early childhood field. Future policy efforts need to focus on this lack of infrastructure if there is to be more consistent and reliable quality child care in the United States.

REFERENCES

Bailey, D.B., Buysse, V., Smith, T., & Elam, J. (1992). The effects and perceptions of family involvement in program decisions about family-centered practices. *Evaluation and Program Planning, 15,* 23–32.
Basharov, D. (1996). *Enhanced early childhood programs: Burdens and opportunities.* Washington, DC: CWLA Press and American Enterprise Institute.
Bronfenbrenner, U. (1989). Ecological systems theory. *Annals of Child Development, 6,* 187–249.
Gallagher, J. (1994). Policy designed for diversity: New initiatives for children with disabilities. In D. Bryant & M. Graham (Eds.), *Implementing early intervention* (pp. 336–350). New York: Guilford Press.
Gomby, D.S., Larner, M.B., Stevenson, J.D., Lewitt, E.M., & Behrman, R.E. (1995). Long-term outcomes of early childhood programs: Analysis and recommendations. *The Future of Children, 5*(3), 6–24.
Gormley, W. (1997). *Everybody's children.* Washington, DC: The Brookings Institute.

Harry, B. (1992). *Cultural diversity, families and the special education system: Communication and empowerment*. New York: Teachers College Press.

Hayes, N.M., & Bon-Avie, M. (1996). Parents as full partners in education. In A. Booth & J.F. Dunn (Eds.), *Family-school links: How do they affect educational outcomes?* (pp. 43–55). Mahwah, NJ: Lawrence Erlbaum Associates.

Hayes, N.M., & Comer, J.P. (1996). Integrating schools, families, and communities through successful school reform: The School Development Program. *School Psychology Review, 25,* 501–506.

Heclo, H. (1996). Coming into a new land: The changing context of American social policy. In S. Kamerman & A. Kahn (Eds.), *Whither American social policy* (pp. 1–42). New York: Columbia University School of Social Work.

Kagan, S.L., & Cohen, N.E. (1997). *Not by chance: Creating an early care and education system for America's children: Executive summary*. New Haven, CT: Bush Center in Child Development and Social Policy at Yale.

Meisels, S.J., Liaw, F.R., Dorfman, A., & Nelson, R. (1995). The Work Sampling System: Reliability and validity of a performance assessment for young children. *Early Childhood Research Quarterly, 10*(3), 277–296.

National Education Goals Panel. (1997). *The National Education Goals report: Summary*. Washington, DC: U.S. Department of Education.

Scarr, S. (1998). American child care today. *American Psychologist, 53*(2), 95–108.

Chapter 15

The Changing Nature of the Transition to School

Trends for the Next Decade

Robert C. Pianta
Martha J. Cox

In this chapter, the various perspectives described in previous chapters are integrated with trends in American society and education to derive implications for work in the area of the transition to kindergarten. Although there are many ways in which society and schools are changing as the 21st century approaches, four trends have been chosen to be examined in relation to their effect on the transition of children into American schools for the foreseeable future.

1. There is an emerging conceptual base that integrates developmental psychology and education. This conceptual base, solidly grounded in empirical work, has fueled increasing recognition by educators that 1) the development of young children (younger than age 8) relies greatly on contexts and 2) the early grades of school are a different, and somewhat critical, period for later school success. Thus, a new conceptual model for understanding the role of the school as a context for development is emerging and will likely influence how educators think about and prepare for the transition to school as they come to understand the role of various contexts in development.

2. The diversity of America's families and school population is increasing rapidly and is likely to be most pronounced among the younger age groups of children. Challenges of culture, language, family background and processes, and differences in the way families view schools, all of which are formidable

even for children entering school today, will be exacerbated by these demographic shifts. These shifts raise issues of how schools will face the challenges of educating a diverse population, how communities will work to support families and schools working collaboratively, and how the teacher work force will need to respond to student and family diversity.

3. Public school programs for young children (ages 3 and 4) will continue to increase. Universal prekindergarten programs for 4-year-olds will be the norm, programs for 3-year-olds will be common, and the age for entering school will be 1–2 years earlier than it now is for nearly all American children. Clearly, the phenomenon of public schools offering programs for 4-year-olds, which was started in the 1980s mostly for children with high-risk backgrounds, will expand to near-universal status and radically change the nature of the transition to school. The elementary school of the future is likely to run from age 3 through third grade. Such schools will need to be more family friendly, will need to integrate diverse curricula and instructional practices, and will need to be linked more closely with communities. Policies concerning the age at and circumstances under which children enter schools will be transformed in response to whether prekindergarten programs are universal or offered only on a selective basis. Transformations of readiness definitions and assessment will also occur as programs are implemented for younger children.

4. A movement for accountability has emerged in American education in response to pressures, political and substantive, from all sides. From one perspective, such a movement holds potential for enhancing the quality of education offered to American children and for ensuring their performance at higher levels. Clear communication of expectations, for example, can actually enhance transition processes when these expectations form the basis for constructive communication about a child between home and school and between programs and grades. However, dangers also lurk in the accountability movement. For the most part, this movement has ushered in a rash of new testing and assessment for children of all ages. Children in school are now tested with group-administered standardized tests and other "high-stakes" devices more than ever before. Such practices are not consistent with the emerging conceptual model that underlies most educational practice for young children. Thus, the accountability movement is likely to produce serious tensions for educators interested in this period of school transition.

In the remainder of this chapter, these four trends are expanded on in relation to the material presented by the other authors in this book. By bringing their perspectives on the transition to school to bear on these emerging trends in American education and society, it is hoped that a framework for research, policy, professional development, and practice can be provided that will ultimately enable these endeavors to enhance the quality of children's transitions into school.

ADVANCES IN THE CONCEPTUAL BASE FOR UNDERSTANDING THE TRANSITION TO SCHOOL

Since the early 1980s, the beginnings of a change can be seen in the way the development of young children is understood. As Entwisle and Alexander (Chapter 2) note, in the mid-1950s, the National Collaborative Perinatal Study examined children in 50,000 families to understand how medical events in the perinatal period affected long-term development. The conclusion from the follow-up of that study was that the primary causes of poor performance in those children were not related to biomedical history but rather to the social context of development. Findings such as these both supported and spurred the increasing influence of new paradigms that build on advances in developmental theories and models. Many different, although often complementary, perspectives, which emphasize the study of relationships, individuals, and contexts, have influenced the way in which researchers are coming to understand how normative development proceeds and how difficulties or disorders arise and are maintained. These perspectives include developmental systems theories (Ford & Lerner, 1992; Pianta & Walsh, 1996; Sameroff, 1983; Sroufe, 1989) and ecological theory (Bronfenbrenner, 1979; Bronfenbrenner & Morris, 1998).

The Importance of Social Processes

A common thread in these perspectives is that development is seen as occurring in the context of relationships. Each child faces a set of developmental challenges that form core themes for adaptation in the early years. Such challenges are not faced by the child alone but by the child in relationships with parents, peers, and teachers. From this perspective, it makes little sense to talk about "competence" in early childhood as residing only in the child. To consider the "child's readiness for school" without considering the ways in which the child's adaptation is facilitated or impeded by relationships in the family and school narrows the scope of understanding and impedes efforts to help the child. Likewise, it makes little sense to assess "readiness" by asking the child to perform isolated, preacademic skills. Early school outcomes are products of social processes and are embedded in a social context. It is becoming increasingly clear that this emphasis on social processes, contexts, and systems, which has guided much of early childhood education, is also applicable to education in the early elementary grades and over time is likely to lead to reformulation of instructional practices, staffing, and socialization in the classroom.

Multifactorial and Dynamic: Development in Context

Developmental systems models can help shape research, interpretation of research, and the formation of research-based policies. Advances in developmental theory coupled with prevailing ideas regarding socially mediated educational experiences (e.g., applications of Vygotsky's theories to early childhood education) result in two heuristics for guiding research and policy related to the transition to elementary school environments: 1) that behavior is multidetermined, a function of interactions across multiple systems and contexts and 2) that these interactions change over time. Thus, important emphasis is placed on interactions, contexts for development, social processes, and developmental pathways. For example, one area of work that has been prominent in the literature on the transition to school has been understanding the preschool predictors of success and failure in elementary school (e.g., Pianta & McCoy, 1997). Often, family poverty has been identified as one of these predictors. However, a multifactorial, dynamic view of the relation between poverty and school failure suggests that instead of focusing on single predictors of school failure (e.g., poverty), there must be consideration of the variety of mechanisms by which poverty comes to be associated with school failure.

Research that focuses on factors associated with positive or negative school outcomes often neglects the multiple processes that account for child adaptation. As a consequence, policy and intervention can be informed by "single-factor models" that embrace isolated variables, such as poverty, as explanations for risk or as intervention goals (Pianta & Walsh, 1996). For example, growing up in a violent neighborhood is a risk factor for "failure" in school, but only when violence erodes relationships in the home (Richters & Martinez, 1993) is this effect seen. Thus, relationships within the family mediate the effect of community violence; when family relationships are of high quality, violent neighborhoods appear not to increase child risk.

A new generation of research must advance understanding of the multifactor mechanisms by which risk factors such as poverty or violence are translated into school failure (e.g., Ramey & Campbell, 1991; see also Chapter 8) and embrace the fact that no single outcome (e.g., IQ or academic test scores) represents the success or failure of a child in school (Schweinhart, Weikart, & Larner, 1986). Using a multifactorial, dynamic model, the conceptual base for understanding and influencing children's transitions to school is as complex as that used for understanding development. This conceptual model allows researchers to study early schooling using the tools that are used to study contextual influences on development prior to school entry.

The Importance of Transitions

Developmental models are particularly important in understanding how children are affected by transitions. Transition periods are those in which considerable change occurs. Development is reorganized and new competencies emerge, often with consequences for the child that mark qualitative change. When the competencies of the preschooler interact with the demands of the school environment a "new" child can emerge—socially competent, literate, and capable of higher levels of mastery and self-reliance (or the converse can also occur).

Transitions are accomplished in an ecological context. The processes responsible for regulating development across transition points are distributed in these contexts (Rogoff, 1990). Thus, cognitive competencies that emerge in the preschool and early school years are socially mediated: a function of resources for cognition that are afforded to the child—in context—by parents, teachers, peers, and materials (Resnick, 1994). Transition periods are periods of relative fluidity, out of which emerge new organizational patterns, and they are windows for the influence of context in shaping these emerging patterns.

A second reason for a focus on early transitions is their importance for later competencies. A developmental view suggests that early experience and early organization biases later development (Greenspan, 1989; Sroufe, 1989). Development remains open to input but nonetheless carries with it the influence of its own history. A longitudinal view emphasizes that adjustment in the early school years cannot be understood fully without reference to adjustment and experience in infancy, toddlerhood, and the preschool years (Ramey & Campbell, 1991). Models of early schooling that do not incorporate developmental history are ineffective largely because of a narrow frame of reference (Pianta & Walsh, 1996). Thus, a developmentally informed conceptual model brings tools for understanding change and the relation of contexts and experience to change.

Transitions to Formal Schooling

Clearly, a key transition point for children is the transition to formal schooling. Entwisle and Alexander's (Chapter 2) landmark study stands as a stark reminder of the importance of this transition. In this study, the trajectories of children's school adjustment (among both children at risk and not at risk) were nearly fixed by third grade. The influence of schools in modifying individual differences in children's competencies had declined considerably by third grade. This early school transition period can be thought of as a sensitive period (Bornstein, 1989) for developing the skills, knowledge, and attitudes critical to later school success. As a sensitive period, these years take on unique importance in establishing the developmental "infrastructure" on which later experience will build. Minor adjustments in the trajectory of child adjustment in this period may have disproportionate effects on the direction of the child's school career.

Because a sensitive period is one in which considerable fluidity occurs, both positive and negative consequences can be strongly influenced. Retention, peer problems, difficult relationships with teachers, and problems learning to read are just some of the early "downward" deflections that can easily be translated into increasingly intransigent patterns of failure (e.g., Pianta, Steinberg, & Rollins, 1995; Shepard & Smith, 1989). However, evidence strongly suggests that "upward" deflections of school outcome pathways can also be initiated during the early childhood period and have long-lasting effects (e.g., Lazar, Darlington, Murray, Royce, & Snipper, 1982; Ramey & Campbell, 1991; Schweinhart et al., 1986).

Viewing formal schooling as a context for development and melding developmental with educational research and theory is a conceptual leap that may enhance previous efforts to understand this important period. Such an approach puts the child, family, and school at center stage; leads to the recognition that individual indicators of the child have limited usefulness; and focuses attention on the processes and mechanisms accounting for child outcomes that are considered to be desirable. How do early developmental functions emerge in the transition to formal schooling? What are the roles of family, school, and community in the transition process? How is the transition process influenced by the quality of adaptation in earlier transition periods? These are the major questions that such a framework suggests and that a new generation of research must address.

THE INCREASING DIVERSITY OF AMERICA'S SCHOOL CHILDREN

The questions raised in this book regarding the importance of the transition to school must be addressed for an increasingly diverse group of children. As Zill (Chapter 4) notes, the demographic characteristics of today's kindergartners highlight the challenges that educators face in meeting the dual goals of equity and excellence. Educators must provide environments in which children from diverse backgrounds can succeed and must establish connections with an increasingly diverse group of families. Zill (Chapter 4) reports several important characteristics of children entering formal schooling: 1) One in four kindergartners come from families with incomes below the official poverty line; 2) higher proportions of today's young children come from Hispanic or African American families; and 3) there are increasing numbers of families in which a language other than English is spoken in the home, due to high immigration rates, especially among people from Mexico and Central America. These groups have traditionally had greater ed-ucational difficulties and will challenge the school systems to respond to the indi-vidual needs of children and the specific characteristics of families.

Several issues need to be considered with regard to educating a diverse group of young children. First, larger numbers of immigrant children from other cultures will certainly increase the already wide variety in knowledge and skills that teach-ers find in their kindergarten students. How will schools and their classrooms ac-commodate to this diversity? Are traditional methods appropriate for a more di-verse set of children? Are teachers equipped to provide an effective instructional atmosphere for all children? Second, parental involvement and collaboration be-tween parents and schools is associated with academic success for children. Thus, how will schools and parents find common ground and bases for communication if the cultural backgrounds of parents and teachers are quite different? Third, rates of poverty among young children are increasing. Because poverty is associated with less school success, what are the implications of these changes for schools and teachers? Fourth, family structures and roles have changed dramatically since the early 1980s. What are the implications of these changes for schools and teachers?

The Changing Ethnic Composition of the United States

Zill (Chapter 4) notes that the racial and ethnic make-up of today's kindergartens reflects the changing demography of the United States and foreshadows trends that will continue into the 21st century. The Caucasian majority is increasingly smaller, and the Hispanic minority increasingly larger. In 1960, fewer than 600,000 U.S. residents were Mexican born; in 1994, the Mexican-born population had in-creased to nearly 6.2 million (a tenfold increase, whereas the U.S.-born population increased by less than 40% in that period) (Goldenberg, 1996). Between 300,000 and 350,000 Hispanic immigrants, mostly from Mexico and South America, are projected to arrive in the United States yearly during the next half century. This will mean that, by the year 2010, Hispanics will number more than 40 million and by the year 2040, more than 80 million. By the year 2050, the Bureau of the Cen-sus expects that 25% of the U.S. population will be Latino (Goldenberg, 1996). These are dramatic changes, especially in particular states such as California, Flor-ida, New York, and Texas. Many Latino immigrants come to the United States with low levels of education and are more likely to be living in poverty than U.S.-born residents.

The challenges posed by the large numbers of immigrant and language-minority children are great. Zill (Chapter 4) notes that according to the Bureau of the Census' Current Population Survey, 31% of Hispanic children had difficulty speaking English in 1995 and 74% of these children spoke Spanish at home. Like-wise, 14% of children of other races (including Asians) found speaking English difficult and 46% of these children spoke a language other than English at home. The United States has not resolved how to deal with the challenges these groups pose; this is evidenced by the continuing controversies over bilingual education and state propositions that would limit educational access to illegal immigrants. The United States is not completely unified as a nation in its opinions toward the necessity of educating all these children; and even if it was agreed on, it is unsure what is the best approach. What is almost certainly true is that greater numbers of children from diverse cultures will result in greater diversity in the skills, knowl-edge, and behaviors of children in many classrooms. Zill (Chapter 4) suggests that schools must be prepared to offer a variety of activities and materials to their kindergarten students. Individual attention to children will likely become increasingly important. However, kindergarten class sizes in the United States are large, and potentially preclude the level of individual attention students will need. Surveys find that kindergarten class sizes in the United States average about 22 or 23 children but that schools with more minority students have larger class sizes than those with fewer minority students (Pianta, 1998; see also Chapter 4).

Beyond the need for individual attention, there is also concern that the cultural attitudes and behavior patterns of these children will not be understood in the classroom. Bowman (Chapter 10) suggests that schools and classroom teachers do not put enough emphasis on understanding cultural differences. As a consequence, what is considered appropriate behavior in the classroom is too narrowly and rigidly defined. Bowman proposes that teachers be provided consultation and curricula support to work effectively with children from various socioeconomic and cultural backgrounds. Her viewpoint is supported by findings from a survey by the National Center for Early Development and Learning (Pianta, 1998). Caucasian teachers in schools with higher percentages of minority students report more behavior problems among their students than do Caucasian teachers in schools with lower percentages of minority students. In contrast, minority teachers with higher percentages of minority students do not report more behavior problems among their students when compared with minority teachers at schools with lower percentages of minority students. One obvious conclusion is that minority teachers have a broader and perhaps more culturally relevant view of what is appropriate behavior in their classrooms. In addition, the survey found that more experienced teachers were also less likely to report behavior problems among students. These data seem to support Bowman's contention that teachers need more training to work effectively with children of diverse backgrounds and cultures, in that the more experienced teachers and teachers from a minority background were less likely to see problems in the behavior of minority children.

In line with these concerns that the perceptions of teachers may not serve minority or immigrant children well, Skinner, Bryant, Coffman, and Campbell (1998) noted that ethnographies of minority children's school performance have long recognized that these children do not necessarily lack personal capabilities or caring families. Rather, they do not conform to the speech patterns, interaction styles, family structure, rules and routines, and other cultural knowledge characteristics of the Caucasian middle class, the culture that is validated and accepted as desirable in most U.S. schools. Making teachers more aware of these cultural differences is one solution.

However, the real problems arise when perceptions of children lead to an acceptance of failure in these children because they do not have the requisite "skills" and "behaviors" to succeed in the classroom. One way to deal with this issue, Skinner and her colleagues (1998) suggested, is for schools to take a different approach to failure. They noted that learning activities can be reorganized for children not to fail, and when children do not succeed in school, educators need to examine how learning is organized to understand practices that help to create and maintain failure. These ideas highlight the need for change not only in classroom practices, with more emphasis on individual attention, but also in perceptions of students and understanding of success and failure.

Another solution to increase cultural sensitivity in schools is to perhaps increase the diversity of school faculty and administrators. This could take some time. Almost all kindergarten teachers are women (98%) and most of them are also

Caucasian (85%), with only 8% or 9% African American and 5% Hispanic (Chapter 4). Undergraduate teacher training programs have had great difficulty in recruiting and retaining potential African American teachers whose cultural backgrounds are more similar to those of the children and families with whom they will interact. This situation is not likely to change soon. Thus, Bowman's (Chapter 10) suggestion that preservice and in-service training be provided for teachers is one of the few possible immediate solutions to problems teachers may have in working effectively with children from a variety of socioeconomic and cultural backgrounds.

The issue of cultural sensitivity is relevant to the concern that families are involved in the education of their children. It is likely that more experienced and better trained (especially when there is training specific to cultural issues) teachers will be better able to promote communication and cooperation with families. In addition, a growing number of initiatives across the United States, such as the School Change Project (Goldenberg, 1996), are specifically focused on bringing educators and, in this case, Latino families together to effect change for children. Such projects may represent an important avenue for change in the schools to create more understanding of cultural issues.

Poverty and Education

Although one of the wealthiest nations in the world, the United States has a higher rate of poverty than most other Western industrialized nations (Smeeding & Rainwater, 1995). The number of children living in poverty is particularly concerning. Although the United States made strides in reducing childhood poverty between the end of World War II and the 1960s, that trend has reversed throughout the 1970s, 1980s, and into the 1990s (Hernandez, 1993). This is troubling for the nation's schools because numerous studies show that children raised in low-income families score lower than children from more affluent families on assessments of health, cognitive development, school achievement, and emotional well-being (Brooks-Gunn, Duncan, & Maritato, 1997). Brooks-Gunn and her colleagues also noted that African American and Hispanic children are much more likely to be poor, and for longer periods of time, than are Caucasian children. Research suggests that income matters because lower income is associated with the provision of a less-rich home learning environment for children (Brooks-Gunn et al., 1997) and the purchase of lower-quality preschool learning environments for children (National Institute of Child Health and Human Development [NICHD] Early Child Care Research Network, 1997). Thus, schools must be ready to receive children into kindergarten who, compared with their more affluent counterparts, are less prepared by their preschool experiences for the demands of the school environment, and the numbers of these children are growing. Entwisle and Alexander (Chapter 2) note that these differences in children's achievement at the beginning of school are further exacerbated by differential progress during the summer months between children from less affluent and more affluent homes.

Changes in Maternal Work Force Participation and in Family Structure

Other changes in U.S. families are also relevant to the challenges faced by schools. There have been dramatic increases since the early 1980s in mothers' labor force participation and in the incidence of mother–child families with no father present (Hernandez, 1993). The increase of mothers' labor force participation has meant that more children have preschool experience before entering kindergarten than in the past, but because of the shortage of high-quality preschool programs, many children spend time in programs of low quality. The increase in maternal labor force participation also puts added pressure on schools to provide before- and after-school programs.

Greater numbers of mother-headed families, partly because of the association with lower family income, increase the numbers of children who are at risk for lower success in school. In 1996, only 65% of kindergarten students were from homes with both birth parents or two adoptive parents; whereas 24% were living with the mother only, 6% were living with a birth parent and a stepparent, 3% with a father only, and 2% were living with grandparents or other relatives or guardians or were in foster care.

These percentages represent dramatic changes in the families and children that use U.S. schools and provide great challenges for the provision of equitable and excellent schooling. How schools face these challenges, how teachers can be prepared to respond to an increasingly diverse group of students, how communities can foster collaboration between schools and an increasingly diverse group of families will be crucial to the success of the nation's children in the twenty-first century.

EXPANSION OF PUBLIC SCHOOL PROGRAMS FOR PREKINDERGARTEN CHILDREN

Throughout this book, frequent references have been made to the first national education goal (National Education Goals Panel, 1995), which emphasizes that children should start school ready to learn. One objective intended to facilitate progress toward this goal, and by which progress is measured, is that all children will have access to high-quality and developmentally appropriate preschool programs, which will help to prepare them for school. Thus, clearly, the national reformers who considered the early school success of children to be so important as to attempt to ensure it also believed that access to preschool programs was a primary means of achieving this goal.

However, universal participation in (or availability of) high-quality preschool programs is not evident in the data available to track progress toward Goal 1. Through 1996, the disparity in preschool participation rates for 3- to 5-year-olds for high- and low-income families was 29%, a level that remained stable since 1991 (National Education Goals Panel, 1997). These data reflect estimates of participation in *all* nursery schools, prekindergarten programs, day care centers, and Head Start, regardless of the quality of these environments. Thus, it is likely that access to high-quality, developmentally appropriate preschools is even lower, and that the disparity in access for high- and low-income families is even greater. For example, a study demonstrated that children from high-income homes were more likely to be in child care programs of higher quality than children from lower incomes homes (NICHD Early Child Care Research Network, 1997).

Although it was likely the original intent of the Goal 1 work group that preschool programs would be available via a variety of support and eligibility mechanisms (e.g., public, private), it is increasingly clear that states throughout America are moving to assume responsibility and offer prekindergarten programs on a universal, publicly supported basis. Increasingly, school is starting when a child reaches 4 years of age in many states. Presumably, such a movement would reduce the gap between high- and low-income families' access to preschools. The last couple of years have seen state-led initiatives to offer publicly supported programs for all 4-year-old children in the public schools in California, Georgia, and New York, whereas states such as Virginia operate programs for 4-year-old children from a range of less-advantaged backgrounds under the auspices of the public schools or other public agencies.

The emergence of prekindergarten programs at such widespread and near-universal levels is the consequence of years of effort supported by 1) research on early intervention programs such as the Abecedarian Project (Chapter 8), the Perry Preschool Project (Schweinart et al., 1986), and Head Start (Chapter 8), which has demonstrated that children (and families) benefit from exposure to high-quality preschool environments; 2) a growing embrace of a developmental frame for understanding children's education in which relatively greater importance is placed on experiences in the early years and that has provided the conceptual support for preventive intervention programs; 3) concerns over disconcerting levels of failure, often for African American children or children from poverty backgrounds, the response to which has been an effort to provide enriching experiences throughout school, but particularly in the early grades; and 4) political pressures that have provided support for funding prekindergarten programs. For example, Head Start and its expansion were supported even during the Bush administration. President Clinton supported an expanded educational agenda and promotion of high-quality child care and budget surpluses at the state and national level, creating a political climate that makes expansion of prekindergarten programs possible and acceptable. Expansion of prekindergarten public school programs is likely to continue into the foreseeable future.

What are the consequences of the expansion of public school programs for younger children? How does the reality of elementary schools that serve 3- to 4-year-olds change the way the transition to school is viewed? These are questions that are fundamental to assumptions about the transition to school and that are foreshadowed by the previous chapters.

As the "transition to school" comes to refer to an event for 3- or 4-year-olds, three domains of activity appear to be most clearly affected: 1) policies regarding age of entry and registration/screening mechanisms, 2) curriculum and classroom practices, and 3) community and family participation in transition processes and practices.

Policies Regarding Age of Entry and Registration/Screening Mechanisms

The most obvious way in which public prekindergarten programs affect the transition to school process is by moving the age of entry to earlier in life. Transition will occur for younger children. Thus, all the issues raised in previous chapters, regarding topics such as readiness and its assessment (Chapter 3), equity and stratification processes related to school entry (Chapter 2), teacher qualifications (Chapters 4 & 12), and parent expectations (Chapter 6), all of which affect the mechanisms by which children enter school, will now be salient for 4-year-olds and their families.

Consider for a moment the issue of age of entry. Note that for the 5-year-old who entered school at age 4, school entry will have occurred 20% earlier in his or her life. How will this affect decisions that parents make to send or to not send their child to the universal prekindergarten program? Will academic "redshirting," a concern of kindergarten educators who must meet the needs of redshirted 6-year-olds and just-turned 5-year-olds (Chapter 5), emerge at the prekindergarten level? One year is a long time to a 3-, 4-, or 5-year-old. Individual differences among children, always a challenge for any kindergarten teacher, are likely to be exacerbated even further if the class is filled with 15 4-year-olds.

What will be the criteria for parents' decisions to send or not to send their child to universal prekindergarten? Similarly, what will the criteria be for schools' decisions to enroll or not enroll children if they operate programs that are not universal access programs? How will eligibility or readiness for a program be determined or assessed? Meisels (Chapter 3) points out the dangers related to different answers to these thorny issues. Certainly, if readiness of 5-year-olds, as Meisels notes, is strongly determined by context, then it can be surmised that this will be even more the case for 4-year-olds. Assessments will need to be far more sensitive to the contexts in which the child has been reared and might be placed and will need to incorporate methods for assessment of interactions with adults (parents and teachers) as well as performance variables that reflect the child's use of contextual resources. Social processes will need to be prominently featured. This raises challenges for researchers and educators to develop a new generation of assessment procedures that reflect the realities of development at age 4.

One of the reasons for the development of the first generation of prekindergarten programs was to counteract inequity in educational opportunity and stratification of educational outcomes (Chapters 2 & 8). Serving mostly children in poverty, these programs operated either under the auspices of Head Start or were locally run and administered programs that served as research sites or as pilot programs. In fact, it was the documented benefits of such programs that gave rise, as noted previously, to the acknowledged importance of preschool programs to ensure children start school ready to learn.

But, if prekindergarten programs are offered universally, to all children, can they serve as effective counterweights to inequity? Or will they merely replicate class and ethnic differences found to start as early as kindergarten? Similarly, will programs offered by "poor" schools be of as high a quality as those offered by "rich" schools (see Chapter 2)? Policies related to school funding and resource inequity, and the consequent differences in program quality, are all likely to be reproduced in these new programs for 4-year-olds unless some mechanism for unlinking funding from the local base is attempted.

Finally, issues of staffing also challenge the widespread implementation of prekindergarten programs. On the one hand, if such programs are offered as part of the public school system, then teachers of 3- or 4-year-olds can be compensated at a level considerably higher, with more benefits of job security, than they could as teachers in a preschool or day care center. This could result in early childhood teachers with higher levels of education, a factor that has been linked with higher-quality programs (Howes, 1997; NICHD Early Child Care Research Network, 1996). On the other hand, many people with experience and expertise working with 3- and 4-year-olds are not certified teachers, and such jobs may not be open to them. If public schools end up staffing these classrooms with teachers from the higher grades, however, concerns about quality and appropriateness of the experiences they might offer young children must be raised.

Curriculum and Classroom Practices

The new American elementary school may be responsible for educating 3- to 8-year-olds. The presence of public school programs for 4-year-olds raises a whole set of issues related to curriculum and programming at the classroom (and school) level.

Graue (Chapter 5) and Bowman (Chapter 10) raise a host of issues related to classroom practices in kindergarten and the early grades that affect the nature and quality of a child's transition to school. Prominent among these is how classrooms will be organized and the nature and form of instruction in those classrooms. For the most part, prekindergarten programs, as currently operated, function independently from the rest of the grades. Children attend the 4-year-old program for 9 months then go to any of a range of classroom organizations, such as regular kindergarten (full or half day) or K–1 programs. If prekindergarten programs proliferate as part of the public school offering, will they be fully integrated into the educational opportunities available? What permutations of age- or grade-based grouping will emerge? Similarly, practices such as looping, in which teachers remain with a child or group of children for more than 1 year, are increasingly popular with young children. Will programs for 4-year-olds be included in looping arrangements so that a teacher might have a child for the 4-, 5-, and 6-year age range?

Curricular issues are also of concern as prekindergarten programs expand. Most operate using a modification of any of several early childhood curricula. These programs differ substantially from the skill-focused programs emphasized in most elementary school classrooms. Will the presence of a new early childhood emphasis in the public schools make kindergarten more like second, third, and fourth grade with an emphasis on skill building, or will such programs bring early childhood perspectives into the mainstream of public school education for children younger than age 8, as many advocates believe should occur?

Ensuring smooth progress through the prekindergarten to third-grade curriculum sequences will require not only careful attention to the actual skills and competencies that are defined as goals and objectives at different age/grade points but also to the means and processes by which these skills will be taught (Bredekamp & Copple, 1997; see also Chapter 5). Unfortunately, there is little agreement on these matters; thus, the likelihood of fully integrated prekindergarten and elementary programs remains an elusive goal at best. It will be necessary for educators to join in discussions of how best to resolve these disagreements if the goal of smooth transition is to be realized.

Community and Family Participation

One of the many ways that early childhood programs can be distinguished from elementary programs is in terms of family and community involvement in program delivery. The Head Start model is perhaps the clearest example of early childhood prekindergarten programs in which families and communities play an integral role in program definition, content, and operation. This model has been adopted and adapted in various forms by most prekindergarten programs such that the program has the goal of not only facilitating the development of children's competencies but also of enhancing family competencies. This is in contrast to elementary school programs in which goals for the family are rarely articulated and program-based professionals dedicated to working with the family are increasingly infrequent.

As Christenson (Chapter 6) and Melton, Limber, and Teague (Chapter 7) discuss, integration of the family into educational programs is both difficult and sensible. The developmental model underlying early childhood programming explicitly embraces the notion that development is better supported when key players find ways to integrate their efforts. Successful efforts to reform and improve schools, particularly elementary schools, are often marked by the integration of parents and family members as well as community members on school governing and policy boards. In many localities, communities have taken the lead in school reform, wrestling control of schools from professional educators. Although these are extreme indicators of community participation and involvement in schools, they reflect the need to create pathways for community participation over the long haul.

Yet data clearly indicate that the nature of community and parent involvement is different, even in kindergarten, in contrast to preschools (Rimm-Kaufman & Pianta, 1998). In kindergarten, parents are more likely to be involved in formal conference-like situations as opposed to school visits, they are less likely to receive family support in contacts with the school, and contacts are more likely to be initiated by the school and are more likely to convey negative information about the child. A national survey of kindergarten teachers' practices related to the transition of children to school showed that personal contacts with families (calls or visits before or after the start of school) were the least likely form of practice related to facilitating the transition of the child to elementary school (Pianta, Cox, Taylor, & Early, in press). By all indications, this pattern of diminishing personal or supportive contact increases as the child moves through the elementary grades (National Education Goals Panel, 1997; see also Chapter 6). Teachers and parents become increasingly distant from one another. It is not surprising that parental participation, in the form of constructive home–school partnerships, is also one of the national educational goals (National Education Goals Panel, 1997).

From the perspective of the developmental systems model, these features of family–school connections in elementary school portray a relationship between home and school that is not likely to be resourceful or functional when required to solve problems or support the child (Chapter 6). Elementary schools can benefit from the early childhood experience in communicating and building relationships with communities and parents. Contact with parents is emphasized in early childhood professional training and accreditation and does not receive similar attention in corresponding elementary school professional development or accreditation.

As programs for prekindergarten children expand in number, their influence on elementary education is also likely to expand. Although this phenomenon creates challenges in terms of issues related to eligibility, equity, assessment, and curriculum, it also creates opportunities to address some of the serious shortcomings related to the current processes by which most children enter school. Expanded early childhood programs, as they reach critical mass and gain a voice in public school education, hold potential for enhancing the ways public schools forge and sustain relationships with families and the broader community and for forcing discussions and interactions among professionals.

ACCOUNTABILITY

What are children supposed to learn in kindergarten (or prekindergarten)? Is this an important question? Can parents or educators answer this question any better than Robert Fulghum? How specifically should this question be answered—at the level of "increased self-confidence in literacy" or when a child "recognizes three phonemes in *cat*"? Recognizing the legitimacy of these questions opens the discussion on accountability.

At almost no other time in the history of American education has there been such pressure on schools to produce high-quality performance in students and to increase the current quality of performance. Accountability and the movement toward standards are simply extensions of this larger pressure. Increased accountability in American education has at least two major implications for the transition to school. These include the benefits and costs of articulating specific objectives for children's performance in the early grades and proliferation of systems for assessing children's progress in these objectives.

As Meisels (Chapter 3) and Graue (Chapter 5) note, there is increasing pressure on early childhood and elementary educators to state the competencies that children are expected to achieve as a result of participation in their programs. Revision of the National Association for the Education of Young Children (NAEYC) statements on developmentally appropriate practice (Bredekamp & Copple, 1997) discusses the need for early childhood programs to move in this direction. This is in contrast to the earlier version (Bredekamp, 1987) that was often interpreted as simply discouraging statements of expectations for children's performance. This change reflects that the early childhood community has recognized the need for accountability; interestingly, many early childhood programs are actually intervention programs and have the stated intention of improving the likelihood of children's success in school. Thus, it is likely that the next several years will see an emphasis on articulating the body of knowledge and skills that children are expected to possess and perform as a consequence of attending kindergarten.

Interestingly, one of the identifiable ways in which articulating performance expectations can enhance the transition process is in communication between contexts—home and school or preschool and school—both before and after the child enters kindergarten. One of the complaints lodged by many parents, as reported in the parent involvement literature, is a lack of specific knowledge about expectations for performance in school (Chapter 6). Similarly, there is little evidence of contact between preschools and kindergartens that attempts to align the goals and curriculum of these environments (Pianta et al., in press). The downside of this failure to communicate expectations is that it becomes hard for the "sending" unit in the transition process to know what the goals of its activities should be in relation to the "receiving" unit. As Wolery (Chapter 9) so clearly states, a fundamental aspect of ensuring a smooth transition into school is aligning the sending and receiving contexts' perceptions of the child and communicating the ways in which activities in the one setting relate to those in the other. Such processes are likely to be helped by efforts of kindergartens to state specific goals and expectations for performance and to communicate this information to constituents in the community.

Yet, there are dangers or challenges posed by the accountability movement, particularly in relation to how student performance and progress can be assessed and how the results of assessment will be used (Chapter 3). The Goal 1 Early Childhood Assessment Resource Group (Shepard, Kagan, & Wurtz, 1998) submitted a report on early childhood that responded in large part to the accountability movement, attempting to reconcile the principles and procedures of accountability in education with corresponding principles and procedures that reflect the needs of young children.

Six general principles are described in this report and have implications for how future efforts at accountability can be integrated into smooth and supportive transition plans and procedures. These principles emphasize that assessment should bring benefits to children in terms of improved program quality or access to service, that it should serve a specific purpose, be technically and psychometrically adequate, and should involve parents as informants and consumers (Shepard et al., 1998).

Meisels (Chapter 3) warns of some of the consequences of not clearly understanding issues related to how constructs such as readiness, for example, are defined and assessed. Some of these consequences include the use of unreliable or invalid tests for the purpose of making high-stakes decisions about student placement or eligibility, the use of standardized group-administered tests to understand student progress and make instructional decisions or comparisons, or the failure to adequately understand the role and function of different contextual parameters in students' performance. All too often children get excluded from certain programs because of test performance or are given a label such as "disabled" based only on difficulty performing some skill out of context. The consequences of such actions should be cause for educators to proceed with great caution in the use of accountability assessments in young children. As Meisels (Chapter 3), Graue (Chapter 5), and Wolery (Chapter 9) note, although it is in the interest of ensuring a smooth transition to school (and across grades or programs in school) to communicate accurately and efficiently about student performance, reliance on tests rather than systematic observation of performance in context is not appropriate practice.

Finally, it should be noted that the trend toward accountability holds dangers for the transition to kindergarten per se. Parents and educators can often be obsessed with questions of whether a child is "ready" for kindergarten, whether a particular classroom is a good "match" for the child, or whether the child is "eligible" for a specialized program. To the extent that a locality offers programs that differ in terms of the ways they focus on children's needs, some means of sorting children into these programs—at the point of transition to school—will be a prominent feature of the transition process. Thus the transition to school can be quite formalized, perhaps with a strong focus on screening and placement assessments, or can use a period of extended observation in classroom settings to make these decisions. In either case, the transition process can become skewed toward sorting children, perhaps at the expense of welcoming and building relationships with them and their families.

Accountability will be here for many years. It has become a value in American education. Yet, the chapters in this book remind the reader that the transition to school holds other meanings and can be affected by other values. These could include the importance of building relationships among home and community and school, recognizing the somewhat inconsistent nature of young children's performance, or the importance of supports from teachers and parents to produce a best performance. In considering how the accountability movement affects the transition to school, it will be necessary to examine how implementation of accountability can embody values that enhance the experience of children and families.

CONCLUSION

The education of young children is receiving an unprecedented level of attention in the United States and, for good or bad, will be a focus of educational reform as the twenty-first century begins. Understanding and influencing the transition from home to school, from child care to school, and from early childhood to elementary programs will likely be a focus of a great deal of attention in the policy, research, and practice communities. Moreover, the faces of America's children, as they enter school in the year 2000, will not be the faces that are seen 10 years from now, particularly in terms of color and ethnic origin. These cultural, linguistic, and racial transformations of American society will often be first felt, at the population level, when children enter school. As the transition to school for the nation's young children and families is planned, attention to the diversity of the society and the lack of diversity among the education community must be a high priority. The chapters in this book provide a range of conceptual tools for tackling these tasks, and they hopefully lay the foundation for the work to be done.

REFERENCES

Bornstein, M.H. (1989). Sensitive periods in development: Structural characteristics and causal interpretations. *Psychological Bulletin, 105,* 179–197.

Bredekamp, S. (1987). *Developmentally appropriate practices in early childhood programs serving children from birth through age 8.* Washington, DC: National Association for the Education of Young Children.

Bredekamp, S., & Copple, C. (1997). *Developmentally appropriate practice in early childhood programs* (Rev. ed.). Washington, DC: National Association for the Education of Young Children.

Bronfenbrenner, U. (1979). *The ecology of human development: Experiments by nature and design.* Cambridge, MA: Harvard University Press.

Bronfenbrenner, U., & Morris, P.A. (1998). The ecology of developmental processes. In W. Damon & R.M. Lerner (Eds.), *Handbook of child psychology: Vol. 1. Theoretical models of human development* (5th ed., pp. 993–1029) New York: John Wiley & Sons.

Brooks-Gunn, J., Duncan, G.J., & Maritato, N. (1997). Poor families, poor outcomes: The well-being of children and youth. In G.J. Duncan & J. Brooks-Gunn (Eds.), *Consequences of growing up poor* (pp. 1–17) New York: Russell Sage Foundation.

Ford, D.H., & Lerner, R.M. (1992). *Developmental systems theory: An integrative approach.* Thousand Oaks, CA: Sage Publications.

Goldenberg, C. (1996). Latin American immigration and U.S. Schools. *Social Policy Report: Society for Research in Child Development, X*(1), 1–31.

Greenspan, S.I. (1989). *Development of the ego.* Madison, CT: International Universities Press.

Hernandez, D.J. (1993). *America's children.* New York: Russell Sage Foundation.

Howes, C. (1997). Children's experiences in center-based child care as a function of caregiver background and adult:child ratio. *Merrill-Palmer Quarterly, 43,* 404–425.

Lazar, I., Darlington, R., Murray, H., Royce, J., & Snipper, A. (1982). Lasting effects of early education: A report for the Consortium for Longitudinal Studies. *Monographs of the Society for Research in Child Development, 47*(2–3, Serial No. 194).

National Education Goals Panel. (1995). *National Education Goals report executive summary: Improving Education Through Family-School-community Partnerships.* Washington, DC: Author.

National Education Goals Panel. (1997). *The National Education Goals report: Building a nation of learners.* Washington, DC: Author.

National Institute of Child Health and Human Development (NICHD) Early Child Care Research Network. (1996). Characteristics of infant child care: Factors contributing to positive caregiving. *Early Childhood Research Quarterly, 11,* 296–306.

National Institute of Child Health and Human Development (NICHD) Early Child Care Research Network. (1997). Poverty and patterns of child care. In G.J. Duncan & J. Brooks-Gunn (Eds.), *Consequences of growing up poor* (pp. 100–131) New York: Russell Sage Foundation.

Pianta, R.C. (1998). *A national perspective on entry to school: The National Center for Early Development and Learning's Transition Practices Survey.* Symposium presented at the American Educational Research Association annual meeting, San Diego, April 14.

Pianta, R.C., Cox, M.J., Early, D., & Taylor, L. (in press). Kindergarten teachers' practices related to the transition to school: Results of a national survey. *The Elementary School Journal.*

Pianta, R.C., & McCoy, S. (1997). The first day of school: The predictive utility of an early school screening program. *Journal of Applied Developmental Psychology, 18,* 1–22.

Pianta, R.C., Steinberg, M., & Rollins, K. (1995). The first two years of school: Teacher child relationships and deflections in children's classroom adjustment. *Development and Psychopathology, 7,* 197–312.

Pianta, R.C., & Walsh, D.J. (1996). *High risk children in schools: Creating sustaining relationships.* New York: Routledge.

Ramey, C.T., & Campbell, F.A. (1991). Poverty, early childhood education, and academic competence: The Abecedarian experiment. In A.C. Huston (Ed.), *Children in poverty: Child development and public policy* (pp. 190–221). New York: Cambridge University Press.

Resnick, L.B. (1994). Situated rationalism: Biological and social preparation for learning. In L. Hirschfield & S. Gelman (Eds.), *Mapping the mind: Domain specificity in cognition and culture* (pp. 1–20) Washington, DC: American Psychological Association.

Richters, J.E., & Martinez, P.E. (1993). Violent communities, family choices, and children's chances. *Development and Psychopathology, 5,* 609–627.

Rimm-Kaufman, S.E., & Pianta, R.C. (1998). *Differences in family involvement between kindergarten and preschool.* Poster presented at Head Start's fourth national research conference, Washington, DC July 24.

Rogoff, B. (1990). *Apprenticeship in thinking: Cognitive development in social context.* New York: Oxford University Press.

Sameroff, A.J. (1983). Developmental systems: Contexts and evolution. In W. Kessen (Ed.), *Handbook of child psychology: Vol. 2. History, theory, and methods* (pp. 237–294). New York: John Wiley & Sons.

Schweinhart, L.J., Weikart, D.P., & Larner, M.B. (1986). Consequences of three preschool curriculum models through age 15. *Early Childhood Quarterly, 1,* 15–45.

Shepard, L., Kagan, S.L., & Wurtz, E. (1998). *Principles and recommendations for early childhood assessments.* Washington, DC: U.S. Department of Education.

Shepard, P.H., & Smith, M.L. (1989). *Flunking grades: Research and policies on retention.* New York: Falmer Press.

Skinner, D., Bryant, D., Coffman, J., & Campbell, F. (1998). Creating risk and promise: Children's and teachers' co-constructions in the cultural world of kindergarten. *The Elementary School Journal, 98,* 297–310.

Smeeding, T., & Rainwater, L. (1995). Cross-national trends in income, poverty, and dependence: The evidence for young adults in the eighties. In K. McFate (Ed.), *Poverty, inequality, and the future of social policy.* New York: Russell Sage Foundation.

Sroufe, L.A. (1989). Relationships, self, and individual adaptation. In A.J. Sameroff & R.N. Emde (Eds.), *Relationship disturbances in early childhood: A developmental approach* (pp. 70–96). New York: Basic Books.

Index

Page numbers followed by *f* indicate figures; those followed by *t* indicate tables.